CHURCH DOGMATICS

KARL BARTH

EDITORS
G. W. BROMILEY
T. F. TORRANCE

THE DOCTRINE
OF CREATION

CHURCH DOGMATICS

KARL BARTH

VOLUME III

THE DOCTRINE
OF CREATION

PART 3

TRANSLATORS
G. W. BROMILEY
R. J. EHRLICH

EDITORS
G. W. BROMILEY
T. F. TORRANCE

T & T CLARK INTERNATIONAL
A Continuum imprint
LONDON • NEW YORK

T&T CLARK INTERNATIONAL
A Continuum imprint

The Tower Building   15 East 26th Street
11 York Road   New York 10010
London SE1 7NX, UK   USA

www.tandtclark.com

First edition copyright © T&T Clark Ltd, 1960
First paperback edition copyright © T&T Clark International, 2004

Authorised English translation of *Die Kirchliche Dogmatik III:
Die Lehre von der Schöpfung 3*
copyright © Evangelischer Verlag A.G., Zollikon–Zürich, 1950

ISBN 0 567 09033 7 (hardback)
0 567 05099 8 (paperback)

British Library Cataloguing-in-Publication Data
A catalogue record for this book is available from the British Library

Printed and bound in the United States by the Data Reproductions Corporation

EDITORS' PREFACE

In the first part-volume of his massive doctrine of creation (III, 1), Barth emphasised the relation between creation and the covenant. In the second (III, 2) he turned to man as the accessible creature in whom, in the light of Jesus Christ, the relationship between Creator and creature may be discerned. Now in the third (III, 3), he studies the providence of God as the continuation of this relationship in terms of preservation and direction. As in creation an *analogia relationis* between Creator and creature is erected by God's free grace, so in providence there is an *analogia operationis* between the activity of God and genuinely contingent and spontaneous creaturely activity. Like creation, providence is thus to be understood on the presupposition of the election of grace fulfilled in Jesus Christ and the covenant of grace concretely actualised in salvation history.

This means that belief in providence cannot be linked to a world-view. It is explicit faith derived from the knowledge of Jesus Christ. From this knowledge it draws its thought-forms to relate the vast and complex range of creaturely experience to the divine action. Providence is the faithfulness to the creature of Him who has joined Himself to it. It is His continuing affirmation of it as the Lord of its history. As God co-exists with the creature, it may exist in dependence on Him, secure under His fatherly lordship as vindicated and finally to be manifested in the actualisation of His mercy in Jesus Christ.

If earlier there was no ontology of heaven and earth, so now providence is not presented as a metaphysic. It is the history of creation as seen in the light of the history of the covenant. All history is thus related to salvation history. This is not by reason of an *analogia entis*. It is by God's free choice. If there is implied a correspondence of the two histories, this consists only in reflections and images, and may be perceived only as world history is mirrored in salvation history. In other words, the conception of providence, of God with His creatures, derives strictly from the reconciliation and revelation accomplished in Jesus Christ as Emmanuel, God with us. In providence we do not stare into the empty framework of an idea; we look into a face and consider a history.

Providence, however, confronts us with the great problem and threat of what Barth calls *Das Nichtige*, i.e., evil considered as the terrible, uncanny reality which God has rejected and which He has

overcome in the desperate agony of the cross. In terms of this understanding, Barth cannot accept views of evil which find its causality
either in God or the creature. Yet it is a formidable reality, as may
be perceived, not from self-analysis, but from the divine attack upon
it. In the light of God's victorious rejection of it, we see something
of its strange existence and appreciate the gravity of its threat. This
section should command attention for the particularly powerful and
detailed discussions of the thought of such men as Julius Mueller,
Leibniz, Schleiermacher, and Heidegger and Sartre in relation to this
theme.

Since God is the Maker of heaven as well as earth, a final section
is devoted to the kingdom of heaven, the angels as God's ambassadors,
and their demonic opponents. Because of the interrelation of heaven
and earth, God's providential ordering is also heavenly and implies
the presence, co-operation and revelation of the heavenly sphere.
The interest of the section centres in Barth's famous doctrine of angels,
which strikingly reveals the similarity and dissimilarity between
Barth and Thomas Aquinas the mediæval *doctor angelicus*. For
Barth the doctrine has no independent meaning in abstraction
from Christology. Angels are thus expounded, not in terms of their
nature, but in terms of their service as God's messengers on the boundary between heaven and earth. In this service part of their significance
is to bear witness to the fact that the relationship between world
history and covenant history may be known only by the revelation of
God. ·

Due to unavoidable changes in the original programme, the translation is all by one hand except for § 50. We owe a particular debt to
the Rev. Dr. R. J. Ehrlich for courageously undertaking this difficult
section at relatively short notice. We are also indebted again to the
Rev. Prof. J. K. S. Reid as Assistant-Editor for his many acute
corrections, criticisms and suggestions at the proof stage. Finally, the
invaluable co-operation of the printers calls for notice, and readers
may be interested to know that they are already at work on the last
two part-volumes (III, 4 and IV, 3) thus far available in the German
original.

EDINBURGH, *Ascension Day* 1960.

PREFACE

AFTER two years a further part-volume of the *Doctrine of Creation* is now to hand, and this should be followed after a rather shorter interval by a final chapter on the ethics to be deduced in this context. In relation to the expansiveness with which I now express myself on this theme, I may at least recall with some satisfaction the time when I was charged with having far too little to say about the first article of the creed.

The three great themes of this part-volume—the fatherly providence of God, His kingdom on the left hand, and the ministry of angels—do not fall quite so readily under the one title " The Creator and His Creature " as the sub-divisions of the earlier volumes. But the stricter formal systematisation which attracted the admiration of some and the mistrust of others was not of vital concern to me. If I had and have any such concern, it is to hold fast at all costs and at every point to the christological thread, i.e., to what I have recently been accused of under the label and catchword " Christomonism." It is my one concern to cling to this in these spheres too. And my question to those who are dissatisfied is whether with a good conscience and cheerful heart Christian theology can do anything but seriously and finally remember " Christ alone " at each and every point. And I am rather concerned to find that, in spite of Church, Pope, Mary, sacrament and other impedimenta, some Roman Catholic friends seem to understand me remarkably well, whereas that not very pretty slogan emanated from the mouths or pens of prominent (and not " Liberal ") Evangelicals.

It is inevitable that many, impelled perhaps by curiosity, will turn first to the section on angels. If only their perusal is full and scrupulous, and they do not break out too quickly into exclamations at the too much or too little which they think they find there, I have no complaints. But if there are any who begin right at the end, namely, with the demons, they should be told that I regard them as lacking in seriousness. Those who do not reject the problem of angelology altogether, which I do not advise, will bear in mind that it has not been resolutely and explicitly treated for a long time, that a good deal of hampering rubbish has accumulated in this field in both ancient and more modern times, and that it was and is, therefore, very difficult even to pose correctly the correct questions. It is my sincere hope that others will come and do much better without diverging into the

xi

old blind alleys or blocking up the exit into more open country which is here indicated.

In the doctrine of providence, which I desire should be regarded as the real substance of this volume, I have found it possible to keep far more closely to the scheme of the older orthodox dogmatics (*conservatio, concursus, gubernatio*) than I anticipated. The radical correction which I have also undertaken will not be overlooked. And I hope that the leaven of the scribes and Pharisees has not had too great an influence, and that I have thus been able to state the matter itself in all its actuality.

In the central section on nothingness our concern is with the problems which in the older doctrine of providence are usually treated in direct connexion with the positive exposition (*De providentia Dei circa malum*). So far as possible I have tried not to mention God and the devil together, and therefore I have given the matter this special treatment, with accompanying discussions of Schleiermacher, Martin Heidegger, Sartre etc. The doctrine of sin properly speaking will obviously have to be developed separately in a later volume. What is offered is the basic material essential to an understanding of brief and summary remarks about demons at the close of the treatise on angels. I love angels, but have no taste for demons, not out of any desire for demythologisation but because they are not worth it. It is thus of set purpose that I have spoken of them as I have. For the same reason even in this sinister context my human opponents have again escaped in spite of my warning in the Preface to the last volume ; and it may be that they have now escaped finally, though they must be careful. It is thus in the discussion of nothingness that there should be sought a serious treatment of the serious problem which is in view in all demonology.

It is a particular pleasure to me that the *Church Dogmatics* is now again available in Germany, where it was first conceived and published, and that it is being carefully read by many individuals, as I learn from several moving letters. With the new forces officially active and recognised in ecclesiastical and theological circles there, I can have little to do, and it is little wonder that for the majority—quite irrespective of any real concerns—I have become almost a legendary instead of an unpopular figure, linked with a good deal of talk about Law and Gospel, East and West, Lutheranism and Calvinism, Infant Baptism and Congregationalism, Bismarck and Frederick the Great. As I see it, Evangelical Germany will sooner or later have to see another dividing and regrouping directed no less against Bultmann than Communism ; and it may be—but who can say ?—that the *Church Dogmatics* will have some part to play in this respect. At any rate, if it is read with understanding it will not contribute either in Germany or elsewhere to the formation of a " Neo-Orthodoxy."

I should not like to conclude this Preface without expressly drawing the attention of readers of these seven volumes to what they and I owe to the twenty years of work quietly accomplished at my side by Charlotte von Kirschbaum. She has devoted no less of her life and powers to the growth of this work than I have myself. Without her co-operation it could not have been advanced from day to day, and I should hardly dare contemplate the future which may yet remain to me. I know what it really means to have a helper.

Particularly good work has been done by Herr Dieter Schellong in the correction of the proofs and preparation of the indexes.

BASEL, *Whitsuntide* 1950.

CONTENTS

xv

CHAPTER XI

THE CREATOR AND HIS CREATURE

CHAPTER XI

THE CREATOR AND HIS CREATURE

§ 48

THE DOCTRINE OF PROVIDENCE, ITS BASIS AND FORM

The doctrine of providence deals with the history of created being as such, in the sense that in every respect and in its whole span this proceeds under the fatherly care of God the Creator, whose will is done and is to be seen in His election of grace, and therefore in the history of the covenant between Himself and man, and therefore in Jesus Christ.

1. THE CONCEPT OF DIVINE PROVIDENCE

We have dealt with the work of creation as such in the first part of the doctrine of creation, and with man as the creature of God in the second. In this third part we now compare and contrast the Creator and the creature. We thus take up the doctrine of what is called providence, *de providentia Dei*. Medieval scholasticism treated it as part of the doctrine of the being of God. Post-Reformation dogmatics brought it into very close relation with the doctrine of creation. We follow the latter tradition, and our first question is how far it is correct and meaningful to take this course.

By " providence " is meant the superior dealings of the Creator with His creation, the wisdom, omnipotence and goodness with which He maintains and governs in time this distinct reality according to the counsel of His own will.

The word " providence " requires clarification. It is derived—and this derivation is materially important—from Genesis 22¹⁴, ⁸—the passage in which Abram called the spot where he had been prevented from offering up Isaac, and where God's path and man's had so unexpectedly crossed, Jehovah-Jireh, in remembrance of Isaac's question concerning the lack of a burnt offering and his own answer : *Elohim jireh*, or, according to the Vulgate : *Deus providebit*. This text gives us exegetical reasons for avoiding the view that providence means only foreknowledge. It is no *nuda et otiosa rerum praescientia et cognitio, sed actuosa et efficax rerum omnium* (Bucanus, *Instit. theol.*, 1605, 14, 2). In this passage " to see " really means " to see about." It is an active and selective predetermining, preparing and procuring of a lamb to be offered instead of Isaac. God " sees to " this burnt offering for Abraham. A modern term like the German *Vorsehung* needs to be expressly filled out in relation to the unity of

3

the divine knowing, willing and acting. In earlier German *providentia* was more strongly and accurately translated as *Fürsehung* (e.g., in *Qu.* 28 and 29 of the *Heidelberg Catechism*). For the world, for men and for the Church God sees to that which in their earthly lot is necessary and good and therefore planned and designed for them according to His wisdom and resolve. And as He does so, He cares for them, and therefore sees to the fulfilling of His own purpose for them and to His glory in face of them. The proposal of the Saxon theologian S. F. N. Morus (1789) to use *procuratio* instead of *providentia* showed a correct appreciation. The " for " does, of course, include the fact that the eternal God does basically see " before " His temporal creatures what they at best can only see afterwards, as in verse 13 of this passage Abraham saw the ram. In view of this active meaning of the word, it may be asked why *praedestinatio* should not be preferred to *providentia*. There was a certain tendency to do this in the older Reformed theology : *utroque nomine idem significatur* (A. Heidanus, *Corp. Theol. chr.*, 1686, I, p. 347). But the difference in content between predestination, election, the covenant and its history on the one hand and providence, i.e., the preservation and overruling of the creatures as such on the other, should not be obliterated, even linguistically. Predestination is more than a special example of the general divine government of the world. It is not a *quaedam pars providentiae* (Thomas Aquinas, *S. theol.*, I, *qu.* 23, 1c). Nor can we accept the statements of Zwingli : *Est autem providentia, praedestinationis veluti parens . . . Nascitur praedestinatio . . . ex providentia, imo est ipsa providentia (De vera et falsa religione, Sch. u. Sch.,* III, p. 282 f.). Predestination is rather the presupposition, and its fulfilment in history the constitutive centre, of God's overruling, and the basis and goal of its realisation. In predestination we certainly have to do with the creature under God's lordship, but with the creature, i.e., man, as the object of the original, central and personal intention of God, with man as the partner in the covenant of grace made by God in and with creation. In providence, on the contrary, we have to do with the creature as such and in general ; with God's active relation to the reality created by and therefore distinct from Himself. For this reason it is better not to use *destinare* but *videre* or *curare*, both of which stress the reality of the distance between the Creator and His creation, and emphasise the reality of the latter. The only thing is that if we keep the word *providere* we must remember that this is the divine seeing, and therefore we must not interpret it except as filled out in that dynamic and active sense. It has been simply defined in this purified and fuller sense as ἡ ἐκ θεοῦ εἰς τὰ ὄντα γενομένη ἐπιμέλεια (John Damascene, *Ekdos.*, 2, 29), or God's *cura rerum creatorum* (Quenstedt, *Theol. did. pol.*, 1685, I, 13, *sect.* 1, *th.* 5) ; and more fully as *actualis et temporalis omnium et singularum rerum, quae sunt et fiunt iuxta decretum Dei aeternum immutabile et liberrimum conservatio, directio et deductio ad finem ab ipso determinatum sapientissime et justissime facta ad ipsius gloriam (Syn. pur. Theol. Leiden,* 1624, *Disp.*, 11, 3), or as *aeterna et omnipotens illa Dei vis seu voluntas, quae juxta aeternum decretum de rebus in tempore futuris se exerit, ut illa, quae apud Deum constituta sunt, ita existere faciat, sicut Deus voluit et porro conservet, quamdiu decrevit, et gubernet, dirigat et ordinet in fines a se constitutos ad suam gloriam* (A. Heidanus, *l.c.*, p. 348).

Our first task is to see why we cannot follow the example of the Scholastics and treat the subject denoted by this word, like predestination, in the context of the doctrine of God. On this point it is to be observed that in predestination it is a matter primarily and properly of the eternal election of the Son of God to be the Head of His community and of all creatures. It is a matter of the divine resolve and action, of the eternal decree, which does not presuppose the act of creation and the existence of creatures, but is itself their presupposition. And it is a matter of the eternal decree without which God would not be God, i.e., the God who reveals Himself to the Christian Church in the witness of Holy Scripture, and is known and attested by it. He is either the gracious God of this eternal choice, or He is not this God, the true God, at all. Providence, however, belongs to the execution of this decree. It is eternal, divine providence to the extent that it is grounded in this decree. But it presupposes the work of creation as done and the existence of the creature as given. It is God's knowing, willing and acting in His relation as Creator to His creature as such. We cannot, of course, develop the doctrine of God's being and perfections, or the doctrine of predestination, without referring constantly to this relationship, because God's being and the decree of His election of grace are revealed to us only in this relationship. But we cannot import this relationship into the being of God as though the creature too were eternally in God. The root of the doctrine of predestination is to be found in the being of God. But the doctrine of providence has no corresponding root of which this may be said. On the presupposition of the finished work of creation and the given existence of the creature we can certainly say that as Creator God would be untrue to Himself in His relationship with His creature without the knowing, willing and acting described in the doctrine of providence. But He would be no less God even if the work of creation had never been done, if there were no creatures, and if the whole doctrine of providence were therefore irrelevant. Hence there can be no place for this doctrine in that of the being of God.

This is the objection which we have to bring against the presentation of Peter Lombard and Bonaventura among the Scholastics. Bringing together the being and perfections of God and His providence, they obscure the fact that the being of God does not intrinsically and necessarily include God's knowing, willing and acting in relationship to His creature. They obscure this the more because, like Thomas, they treat the election of grace, the mark of the being of the biblical and true God, as only a particular form of this general providence. Thomas Aquinas was obviously trying to avoid obscuring this when in the context of the doctrine of God he dealt only with what was later called the doctrine of providence in the narrower sense (*S. theol.*, I, *qu.* 22), i.e., a doctrine of the *ratio ordinandorum* eternally to be found in God, returning at a much later point (*qu.* 103 f.), in direct conjunction with the doctrine of creation, to the corresponding real knowledge, will and action of God, the *gubernatio rerum in communi*. This division of the problem is still to be found in a modern Roman Catholic dogmatics such as that of F. Diekamp. But it has been tacitly dropped in the works of J. M. Scheeben, J. Pohle and B. Bartmann. It is not really of any avail. For even an eternal *ratio ordinandorum* cannot be described without this entailing a description of the relationship of the Creator to a creature (even if only future), and the consequent integration of this creature in the being of God. Even Thomas could not avoid this either at the first point or the second. This *ratio ordinandorum* could belong to the being of God Himself only if it not merely did not compete but was radically identical with the election of grace in Jesus Christ, the election of grace being understood as this *ratio*, the root of the doctrine of providence. That this is the case is what has actually to be said of this relationship. But for this very reason there can be no place in the doctrine of the divine being for a doctrine of providence above or even alongside that of the election of grace. Like the doctrine of creation, and together with it, that of providence describes an outer and not an inner work of God. Like the doctrine of creation, and together with it, it rests on the doctrine of the *opus Dei internum* which as such, while it is an *opus ad extra* as decree, belongs to the being of God and is identical with it, i.e., on the doctrine of God's eternal election of grace.

But we have also to show positively how far it is actually connected with the doctrine of creation. And first it is only proper that we should see and maintain the difference between the two concepts. The work of creation, the positing of the reality distinct from God, its summoning forth from nothing to appropriate creaturely being, is a once-for-all act, not repeated or repeatable, beginning in and with time and ending in it. That the creature is, presupposes this finished act in all the temporal developments, extensions and relationships of this being, in all the individual forms of the creaturely world and in all the historical manifestations and modifications of its existence. It also presupposes a further action of God, namely, His activity in providence. But it does not presuppose further acts of creation. As distinct from creation, providence is God's knowledge, will and action in His relation to the creature already made by Him and not to be made again. Providence guarantees and confirms the work of creation. And no creature could be if it did not please God continually to confirm and guarantee and thus to maintain it. This does not mean, however, that He continually creates it afresh. It is presupposed that the work of creation is done, and done perfectly, and therefore concluded. What follows this unique act is first and decisively the history of the covenant which is the meaning, basis and goal of this act. It is the execution of the eternal decree of God's eternal election of grace. This is the occurrence which can be called a new creation in Gal. 6[15] and 2 Corinthians 5[17]. But this new creation belongs to the order of the reconciliation with God of a world in need of reconciliation. It is not a repetition of the first creation. It transcends it by a distinct and radical alteration and even transformation of the creature in which its existence as such is presupposed but not re-established. A second thing which follows that unique act, however, is the rule of divine providence which accompanies, surrounds and sustains the history of the covenant, the fulfilment of divine predestination, as what we may and must call a second history strictly related to the first and determined by it. Its necessity rests on the fact that the creaturely partner in the covenant of grace is not merely this but also a mere creature needing creaturely life, and therefore its Creator, and therefore that the Creator should manifest Himself as such, as its Lord, Preserver and Governor. If the covenant is the internal basis of creation (Gen.

2), creation is the external basis of the covenant (Gen. 1). From the second of these statements, and therefore from Genesis 1, we can see the necessity of this second history accompanying, surrounding and sustaining the first, and therefore the necessity and meaning of divine providence. The history of the covenant which follows creation also needs an external basis. Its external basis is the sway of divine providence. This does not repeat or continue creation. It corresponds to it in the continued life and history of the creature, proving the faithfulness which its Creator wills to maintain and does maintain in relation to it. Why? Because at its head, in man, the creature is the partner in His covenant, elected by His grace in Jesus Christ. Because it continually needs Him as Creator, and His action (in correspondence to the act of creation) as a confirmation of the external basis of the covenant. Because He is resolved and able and ready to meet this need.

The most important biblical representation of the relationship but also the difference between creation on the one side and the covenant and providence on the other is the account of the seventh day of creation which concludes the first creation saga (Gen. 2^{1-3}, cf. *C.D.*, III, 1, pp. 213–228). " Thus," we read, i.e., with the fact that on this day God rested from all His work, " the heavens and the earth were finished." The fact that God rested means that He did not continue His work of creation. He was content with the creation of the world and man. He had planned and had now accomplished this and not another work, completing and concluding it with the creation of man. The Creator-God of the Bible is not a world-principle developing in an infinite series of productions. His freedom is demonstrated in the fact that His creative activity has a limit appointed by Himself, and His love in the fact that He is content with His creature as a definite and limited object, and has addressed Himself only but totally to it as such. To this extent the seventh day implies a break between the work of creation and all the divine work which follows—a break which we must not forget when we consider the relationship between Creator and creature. It is tempting to think that creation and providence (especially from the standpoint that the former entails the preservation of the creature) are necessarily identical *realiter, respectu Dei*, providence being only a *continuata rerum creatio* (A. Heidanus, 1 c, p. 348). *Utraque enim dicit eandem Dei voluntatem seu iussionem, per quam res existunt et esse perseverant; atque eundem habet terminum nempe ipsum esse rerum* (F. Burmann, *Syn. Theol.*, 1671, I, 43, 12). *Est enim respectu Dei eadem actio creatio et providentia, cum Deus per unicam simplicissimam voluntatem omnia operetur, ut existant, in existentia permanent et operentur* (J. Braun, *Doctrina foederum*, 1692, I, 2, 12, 4, quoted from Heppe, *Dog. d. ev. ref. Kirche*, ed. 1935, p. 204). But this view was not so important in the older Reformed theology as Heppe maintains. Calvin did not know it, and even in the presentations of later writers it does not play any very striking, let alone a dominant role. Systematised and posited absolutely, it could only be harmful to Christian perception in this matter. It would force us to choose between not understanding creation as genuine *creatio* (*ex nihilo*) in view of providence, and regarding providence as a series of pure creative acts in view of creation. It is true enough that creation and providence, like all the works of God, are one in their divine origin. But in God there is multiplicity and fulness as well as unity, and these are not *realiter* mutually exclusive antitheses, just as God's eternity does not exclude but includes time. Hence we do not violate the dignity of God, but properly regard it, if without denying their unity in the divine will we accept the real difference between creation and providence as seriously demanded by Gen. 2¹⁻⁸. In creation we have to do with the establishment, and in providence with the guaranteeing and determination, of the history of creaturely existence by the will and act of God. If the one God wills and does both, we must not say that He wills and does the same thing in both cases. We must not interpret providence as *continuata creatio*, but as a *continuatio creationis*. The very passage in Gen. 2¹⁻³ which demands a break impressively reveals this continuity and real connexion. That God rested on the seventh day, and therefore in the time created by Him, like a workman on holiday when his work is done, means that in His pure deity—and this is the crown of His work of creation and the sign of the continuation of this work on very different lines—He wholly identifies Himself with the world and man, willing to be fully immanent even in His transcendence. He has made this final day and act of the history of creation an element in His own life-act. He willed to co-exist as Creator with His creature. He has given Himself to be one with him in all the majesty of His freedom and love. And this final day in the history of creation, on which God did not make anything new, but in resting did the greater thing of giving Himself to be one with the creature in all His majesty—this seventh and last day was the first of the finished creature, and above all the first in the life of the man created on the sixth day. With this day there thus begins within the history of creation the history of the covenant, the fulfilment of the eternal election, and in connexion with this, and determined by it, this second history, the history of the general encounter and co-existence of God the Creator with the reality created by Him, the sway of divine providence.

Creation and providence are not identical. In creation it is a matter of the establishment, the incomparable beginning of the relationship between Creator and creature ; in providence of its continuation and history in a series of different but comparable moments. In creation we see particularly the difference of the nature, position and function of the Creator on the one side and the creature on the other ; in providence their reciprocal relationship, the address of the Creator to the existence of His creature on the one side, and the participation of the creature in the existence of its Creator on the other. The act of creation takes place in a specific first time ; the time of providence is the whole of the rest of time right up to its end. Creation has no external basis apart from the free will and resolve of God, and no internal apart from the mystery of the election of grace in the divine being itself ; providence has its basis not only in God's unconditioned freedom and decision and the mystery of His election of grace, but also externally in the presupposed being of the creature and internally in its neediness in relation to the Creator.

Yet we cannot speak of the difference between these two works of God without also drawing attention to their relationship. Those who sought to equate them were right to the extent that in both we have to do with the same sphere of divine action and Christian knowledge. In both, as distinct from the doctrine of God on the one side and that of reconciliation on the other, we have to do with the relationship between Creator and creature as such. In both we have to do with the unconditional lordship of the will and Word of the

Creator over the creature—a lordship which in both cases has its meaning in the divine election and covenant as its final secret and basis. If we cannot identify them, we cannot separate them. We cannot think of the one without the other. And the obvious reason for this is that the one does not occur without the other.

It would be a weak and poverty-stricken concept of providence which did not rest on the presupposition that the One who sees and cares for the creature is also its Creator, so that it is not to Him an alien other but His own work and most original possession for which He knows that He is directly responsible and which stands unconditionally at His disposal.

Credibile non esset curari a Deo res humanas, nisi esset mundi opifex (Calvin, *Instit.*, I, 16, 1). The *curare* envisaged in a serious concept of providence is a radical one in the strict sense appropriate to it. It embraces its object, namely, the continuation and history of human reality, and indeed all the reality distinct from God, in every respect and throughout its whole range. If this concept is to be credible, the One who provides and cares must be the One in whom this reality has its absolute origin. It cannot be self-grounded. It must be creature. And it cannot be the creature of another. It cannot be the product of a third and alien principle. It must be the creature of the One who is its *curator*. We have not yet said with what right and necessity we have to reckon with a strict concept of providence and therefore this serious and radical *curare*. But if this is the case, we can accept the dictum of Calvin that it belongs to the concept of providence to be preceded and accompanied by that of God's creation, and to receive its meaning from it. The power of the *Deus providebit* is that of the *Deus creavit*.

In Christian dogmatics, however, the primary emphasis has always and rightly been laid upon the opposite truth that He would obviously not be the Creator who, having willed and made the creature, left it to its own devices, and did not act towards and with it, or ceased to do so, in the sense of the concept of providence, as its Preserver and Ruler. The theological concept of Creator and creating, of creation and creature, must be kept in view. God the Creator must not be equated with a mere manufacturer, or His work with a manufactured article. The man who makes something, however noble, talented or powerful he may be, can easily leave what he makes to itself, and the more easily the more perfect it is. But the Creator cannot do this in relation to His creature. Between Creator and creature in the sense of biblical theology there is a connexion which makes it impossible for the Creator to leave His work to itself, and makes immediately necessary the reality and knowledge of a second action of the Creator following the first, i.e., His action in the sense of the concept of providence. In no sense is God a creature in Himself. He has in Himself absolutely nothing of the nature of a creature. He does not need a creature to be perfect in Himself. Alongside and apart from Him there can be nothing like Him with its origin, meaning and purpose in itself. Yet on these strict conditions of His own being this God posits Himself as Creator, and apart from and alongside Himself He posits the creature, a reality distinct from Himself. This God who confronts His creature with such transcendence obviously stands, in respect of its continuation and history, in a relationship which could only be contingent and possibly alien to a supreme being or demiurge. The majestic freedom in which the relationship of Creator and creature is grounded is the guarantee of its preservation. The eternity of God is the pledge that He will give it time so long as He wills. The conclusion is compelling when we add that this Creator is the God to whose being there belongs that eternal election of grace, that *decretum internum ad extra* which characterises the concept of God in biblical theology, on the basis of which the covenant of the Creator with His creature is the meaning of its creation, and in virtue of which the creature has attained its reality and entered its existence with the promise of the faithfulness of God, and may thus look forward to continued existence.

" Thou hast granted me life and favour, and thy visitation hath preserved my spirit " (Job 10¹²). Calvin was thus right to begin his exposition of the doctrine of providence (*Instit.*, I, 16, 1) with the assertion that Christian thinking on the Creator is distinguished from profane by the fact that to it the presence of the divine *virtus* is no less evident in the continuance of the world than its origin, as opposed to the cold and lifeless notion of a *momentaneus creator, qui semel duntaxat opus suum absolverit. Nisi ad providentiam eius usque transimus, nondum rite capimus, quid hoc valeat, Deum esse creatorem : utcunque et mente comprehendere et lingua fateri videamur . . . nec quisquam serio credit, fabricatum esse mundum a Deo, quin sibi persuadeat operum suorum curam habere.* Similarly, J. Gerhard opened his *Locus de Providentia* (*Loci theol.*, 1610 f., VI, 1) with the delimitation : *Creator omnium Deus non discessit ab opificio a se condito, sed omnipotentia sua illud adhuc hodie conservat et sapientia sua omnia in eo regit ac moderatur.* And he adduced as his first text Jn. 5¹⁷ : " My Father worketh hitherto, and I work " ; then Ac. 17²⁴ᶠ· : " God that made the world and all things therein, seeing that he is Lord of heaven and earth . . . giveth to all life, and breath, and all things " ; then Ps. 121²ᶠ· : " My help cometh from the Lord, which made heaven and earth. He will not suffer thy foot to be moved : he that keepeth thee will not slumber. Behold, he that keepeth Israel shall neither slumber nor sleep." Other sayings quoted by many in this connexion are Heb. 1³ : " Upholding all things by the word of his power," and Col. 1¹⁶ᶠ· : " For by him were all things created . . . and he is before all things, and by him all things consist," and (like Jn. 5¹⁷) both are more important for the inner establishment of this matter than was perceived in the older Protestant theology.

This theology was primarily directed against Epicurus and his school, the " swine of the herd of Epicurus " as they were called in the clear and amiable language of the time. Epicureanism, like Stoicism, was a form of antique philosophy which had been brought back into discussion by the Renaissance. The positive point at issue could be particularly well made in this antithesis because, while the Epicurean system allowed the existence of gods, its denial of a divine πρόνοια governing the world involved at once and quite logically a denial of creation. According to Epicurus and his followers, the world, or rather the plurality of worlds, is a free play and interplay of atoms existing from all eternity, with no need of a superior Creator or Ruler even in the form of a fate or destiny, as was strongly emphasised in opposition to the Stoics. In the spaces between the different worlds gods do exist. Formed of the finest atoms, they are like men, but with a supreme excellence and distinction, and therefore to be worshipped. But it belongs to their perfection that they are ceaselessly happy in and amongst themselves. They are free of all strivings and obligations (ἀλειτούργητοι), and therefore quite unconcerned about the rest of the world, and especially the world of men. It would be beneath their dignity to be otherwise, and the innumerable contingencies of the world-process, and especially the evils which are so inconsistent with their nature, prove that they have no part in the affairs of the world and man whether by way of creation or control. From this consistently " liberal " view we can indeed see clearly that where there is no Creator, where there are only gods of this calibre, there is no Lord, Governor and Provider, and *ex opposito* that the real Creator, the God to whose being in majesty there belongs also His *decretum internum ad extra*, is as such necessarily the Lord and Governor and Provider as well.

The more perspicacious of the older Protestant polemicists like A. Heidanus (*l. c.*, p. 350 f.) thought it right to mark off themselves no less from the theology and cosmology of Aristotle. For him the world is eternal and there can thus be no question of a creation. What then is his deity, his prime mover which is itself unmoved, his immaterial form, his actuality unburdened with potentiality, his reason which thinks itself (and therefore the best) ? Does this πρῶτον κινοῦν move otherwise than as the principle and exemplary model of all other movement ? Does it move otherwise than as the good and goal which has no other goal beyond itself, towards which everything else strives in virtue of the attraction which everything loved (and this unconditionally as the perfect and the imperfectly loved) exercises on that which loves, on which therefore everything depends and towards which everything must move ? Does it even move, asks Heidanus, as a captain moves his ship, a conductor his choir or a field-marshal his troops ? Is this prime mover of all things more and other than the law, the eternal *prius*, of their movement ? That in which alone the Aristotelian world-principle would resemble the God of the Christian doctrine of providence is obviously the freedom of will and movement, the sovereignty and above all the inner self-determination of a God who confronts the world as its Creator and can thus approach its movement independently and determine it from without. But since the Aristotelian mover of all things is not their Creator, it is necessarily too exalted (or from the standpoint of the Christian doctrine of providence too poverty-stricken) to be capable of this movement in relation to the reality distinct from it. The Aristotelian cosmos has a kind of god ordering it, unlike the Epicurean. But since this god is not the Creator of his cosmos, since he is not above but in it (thus finally resembling the Epicurean gods), the Aristotelian cosmos is also in fact one which is abandoned by God. The older Protestant theology was right to treat Aristotle as an adversary in this respect, and we can only wish that it had freed itself more basically and radically and generally from the spirit of this picture of god and the world, and the argumentations dictated by it.

More difficult was the discussion with those who held the view that there was indeed a creation and a divine Creator, but who like the Epicureans, although for different reasons, could not agree that this Creator had any further interest in the world which He had made. This is the view which since the 18th century has been known as Deism. According to Augustine's polemical representation (*De Gen. ad Lit.*, 4, 12), God is supposed to have acted like an architect who once he has erected and finished a house leaves it for good, and is no longer needed—the less so, the better his work. To be sure, God is more than an architect, and His creature rather different from a house which is of no further interest to Him. Yet in terms of this picture it might not unreasonably be asked why this should not be a true picture of the relationship between Creator and creature. Thomas Aquinas (*S. theol.*, I, qu. 104, art. 1, vid. 2) saw the force of the argument that it belongs to the perfection of a divine Creator and His work that it should be made in such a way that it no longer needs Him but can continue in motion *sua operatione cessante.* For the mechanically minded 18th century a clock assembled, wound and started once and for all was the perfect work, and God was thus compared to a great clock-maker whose work exalts its maker by no longer needing him. But even the finest clock can obviously run down, and so an ingenious thinker formulated the argument as follows (according to D. F. Strauss, *Chr. Glaubenslehre,* 1841, Vol. II, p. 354 f.) : " The praise which would be accorded the human inventor of a *perpetuum mobile* is won by God only if in creation He has given the world the ability to maintain itself in motion."

The argument falls to the ground for three reasons. First, it overlooks the fact that a creature independent of the Creator and maintaining itself in life and movement would no longer be His creature but a second God. It thus ascribes to God the absurdity that He can and must cease to be the one and only God. Second, it overlooks the fact that it not only belongs to the nature of the creature, but constitutes its true honour, not merely occasionally but continuously to need and receive the assistance of God in its existence. Third, it overlooks the fact that the existence of even the most perfect creature is not an end in itself, but stands under a determination in relation to its Creator whose meaning is established and conditioned by the further dealings of the Creator towards and with it. In other words, the deistic argument is void because it equates the relation between Creator and creature with that between a manufacturer and his work, and decisively because it does not take into account the fact that in this relation as understood in biblical theology we have to do with the external presupposition of the covenant, which for its part is the fulfilment of the divine election of grace which is as such a denial of God's lack of concern for being outside Himself. The God with whom we have to do at this point cannot be compared with an architect, a clock-maker or even the awaited inventor of a *perpetuum mobile.* His praise consists in the fact that He acts very differently from the way in which a human workman either does or could : *non discessit ab opificio a se condito.* And so the praise of His creation according to the insight of biblical theology consists in the fact that it is not present as an eternally self-subsistent and self-moved cosmic nexus, whether this is understood with Aristotle as an order ruled by supreme reason or with Epicurus as a disorder comfortably ignored by the happy gods.

The simple meaning of the doctrine of providence may thus be summed up in the statement that in the act of creation God the Creator as such has associated Himself with His creature as such as the Lord of its history, and is faithful to it as such. God the Creator co-exists with His creature, and so His creature exists under the presupposition, and its implied conditions, of the co-existence of its Creator. God does this as His free will normative in its creation, and His wisdom, goodness and power therein displayed, remain the same. He does it as He is always to the creature the One He was when it did not exist and came into being, as He continually acts as such towards and with the creature which He has called to life, as He sovereignly exercises His lordship over His work and possession in new acts and revelations of His free will, wisdom, goodness and power, and therefore as He causes the history of the creature to be the history of His own glory. He does it as—far from leaving the creature to itself and its own law or freedom, its dissatisfaction or self-satisfaction—He causes it to share in His own glory, namely, by the fact that it may serve Him in His immediate presence and under His immediate guardianship and direction, thus fulfilling its own meaning and purpose, having its own honour and existing to its own joy. Hence whatever may take place in the history of the creature, and however this may appear from the standpoint of its own law and freedom, it never can nor will escape the lordship of its Creator. Whatever occurs, whatever it does and whatever happens to it, will take place not only in the sphere and on the ground of the lordship of God, not only under a kind of oversight and final disposal of God, and not only generally in His direct presence, but concretely, in virtue of His directly effective will to preserve, under His direct and superior co-operation and according to His immediate direction. In this history, therefore, we need not expect turns and events which have nothing to do with His lordship and are not directly in some sense acts of His lordship. This Lord is never absent, passive, non-responsible or impotent, but always present, active, responsible and omnipotent. He is never dead, but always living ; never sleeping, but always awake ; never uninterested, but always concerned ; never merely waiting in any respect, but even where He seems to wait, even where He permits, always holding the initiative. In this consists His co-existence with the creature. This is the range of the fact that in the act of making it He has associated Himself with the creature. He co-exists with it actively, in an action which never ceases and does not leave any loopholes. And so the creature co-exists with Him as the reality distinct from Him, and in its own appropriate law and freedom, as He precedes it at every turn in His freedom of action and with His work—He its Creator, who as such must no less necessarily precede it than it must follow Him as His creature, and be directly upheld by Him in its own existence, and stand under His direct and superior co-ordination, and be directly ruled by Him. Again, it is the majestic freedom of the Creator in face of His creature which is as such the guarantee of the faithfulness and constancy with which He is over and with it.

The simple lines of J. J. Schütz are thus an exact statement of this general truth :

" That which the Lord our God did make,
He surely will sustain ;
O'er all the way that it may take,
His grace will always reign."

It is obvious that the deistic view of a Creator who has no further interest in the creature when He has made it is here abandoned. The notion of a mere divine *providere* can only be dropped as one which is basically atheistic. *Providentiam vocamus, non qua Deus a coelo otiosus speculetur quae in mundo fiunt sed qua mundum a se conditum gubernat : ut non unius tantum momenti sit opifex sed perpetuus moderator. Sic providentia, quam Deo tribuimus, non minus ad manus quam ad oculos pertinet* (Calvin, *De aet. Dei praed.*, 1552, *C.R.*, 8, 347). Zwingli made the point as follows (*De providentia*, I). It would be in conflict with the concept of supreme truth. and presuppose obscurity in God, if anything that happens were concealed from Him, so that He allowed it to take place blindly. It would be in conflict with the concept of the supreme power of God if He willed good for His creature, but could not procure respect for His will or guide and help things. And it would be in conflict with the concept of His goodness if He could do this but for some reason, e.g., disgust or boredom at His work, would not do so. On all these assumptions God would not be God but a kind of demon of very doubtful qualities. But God is the highest Good, and He is the Father, the Son and the Holy Ghost, and as such the fulness of power, goodness and wisdom, and all in inseparable unity. Thus He cannot act like that demon, but acts as the sovereign and living Lord of His creature.

2. THE CHRISTIAN BELIEF IN PROVIDENCE

Belief in God's providence is the practical recognition that things are as we have said. It is the joy of the confidence and the willingness of the obedience grounded in this reality and its perception. In the belief in providence the creature understands the Creator as the One who has associated Himself with it in faithfulness and constancy as this sovereign and living Lord, to precede, accompany and follow it, preserving, co-operating and overruling, in all that it does and all that happens to it. And in the belief in providence the creature understands itself as what it is in relation to its Creator, namely, as upheld, determined and governed in its whole existence in the world by the fact that the Creator precedes it every step of the way in living sovereignty, so that it has only to follow. And in the belief in providence this does not have the character of idle speculation, just as God's providence is not the idle onlooking of a divine spectator, but takes practical shape in the fact that the creature which enjoys this recognition may always and in every respect place itself under the guidance of its Creator, recognise its higher right, and give it its gratitude and praise.

Along these lines, the particular belief in God's providence, or the one Christian faith in this particular form, became a favourite theme, as is well known, in Christian instruction, edification and not least hymnology in the 17th and 18th centuries. Paul Gerhardt was able to give it classical and unforgettably pregnant expression. The hymns of confidence and consolation in this period, or rather that which stood behind them, the trust which was wrestled for and the joy which was attained thereby, are elements in Christian faith without which this cannot exist, and to return to which, and simply to live in them, many later and supposedly more profound or more extensively occupied periods, including our own, would be only too glad. In the sense of the Gospel there can be no doubt that to believe always means with childlike directness to accept the providence of God, to rejoice in it, and to follow its governance. And it is no accident that the Reformation with its rediscovery of the all-sufficiency of the person and work of Jesus Christ, and the true divine sonship in Him of the sinful man who may cling to the grace of God and this alone, self-evidently carried with it in all its great representatives, Calvin no less than Zwingli and Zwingli no less than Luther, a kind of re-birth of the Christian belief in providence. One witness among the many which could be adduced may be quoted *in extenso*, namely, *Questions* 26–28 of the *Heidelberg Catechism*, in which, amongst other things, the connexion between creation and providence, and between these two on the one side and grace and the covenant on the other, is finely stated, and which are most instructive in respect of the other points still to be made in this introduction.

Question 26 : What dost thou believe when thou sayest : " I believe in God the Father Almighty, Maker of heaven and earth ? "

Answer : That the eternal Father of our Lord Jesus Christ, who made out of nothing heaven and earth and all that therein is, and sustains and rules the same by His eternal counsel and providence, is my God and Father for the sake of His Son Christ, so that I may trust in Him, not doubting that He will care for my every need of body and soul, and turn to good all the evil that He may send me in this vale of woe, seeing that He can do this as an almighty God, and will do so as a faithful Father.

Question 27 : What dost thou understand by the providence of God ?

Answer : The almighty and present power of God by which He still upholds and therefore rules as with His hand heaven and earth and every creature, so that leaves and grass, rain and drought, fruitful and unfruitful years, food and drink, health and sickness, riches and poverty and all other things do not come by accident but from His fatherly hand.

Question 28 : What fruit doth it yield to know the creation and providence of God ?

Answer : That we should be patient in adversity and thankful in prosperity, and that for the future we should have confidence in our faithful God and Father that no creature will separate us from His love, because all creatures are in His hand, and none can stir or move without His will.

In the light of this statement several sharp delimitations are indispensable.

1. The Christian belief in providence is faith in the strict sense of the term, and this means first that it is a hearing and receiving of the Word of God. The truth that God rules, and that the history of existent creation in its given time is also a history of His glory, is no less inaccessible and inconceivable, no less hard for man to grasp, than the truth of the origin of creation in the will and power of the Creator. In regard to the former there is as little to discover, comprehend and maintain, as little to conceive and postulate, as little room for pious or impious, practical or theoretical ventures, as there is in the latter. In both we find ourselves in the sphere of the confession which is possible only as the confession of faith or not at all. It is quickly said, and apparently easy to understand, that the history of created being takes place in every respect and in its whole range under the lordship of God. But we have only to consider one little portion of this history of created being even in outline, let alone in its concrete differentiations and details, and honesty forces us to ask whether these are not empty words. We start back from what we say, for it obviously goes far beyond what we know from our own experience and conviction, and what we can see and know and say responsibly falls far short of what is said with this confession. Indeed, it is better not to say it if in and in spite of this hesitation we do not have to say it as we confess our faith. Sincerely ? Yes, if this sincerity consists in the fact that we are directed to say it by the Word of God, but not if it rests only on our own experiences and convictions. And we have

only to ask how far, i.e., how little what we say with this confession squares with a corresponding heartfelt trust and obedience, to be honestly arrested afresh by the question whether it is not a cheap and unimpressive saying because we have never really answered it with our lives, and never will. If in spite of this more serious hesitation we do not have to say it as we confess our faith ; if we do not know that we can say it only to our own shame, it is better not to say it. In this matter, too, Christian faith begins where the sincerity of our own experiences and convictions reaches its limit with faith, where the measure of our corresponding trust and obedience obviously does not suffice, where we must completely abandon any self-confidence. It begins where we can cling only to the Word of God, where we may cling to this Word, but may do so with the indisputable certainty which is legitimate and obligatory and even self-evident when a man looks away from himself to God, when he has to do with His gift, when he makes use of the possibility which is created by the free work of the Holy Spirit within him, within his despondent heart, his foolish and fickle thoughts, his sinful life. In this faith man must say what a Christian has to say concerning the providence of God. If it is a confession of this faith, it is *eo ipso* a solid confession, because *eo ipso* one which has reference to this objective content and derives from the revelation of this objective content.

The notion against which we have to delimit ourselves at this point is that which regards the Christian belief in providence as an opinion, postulate or hypothesis concerning God, the world, man and other things, an attempt at interpretation, exposition and explanation based upon all kinds of impressions and needs, carried through in the form of a systematic construction, and ventured as if it were a pious outlook which has a good deal in its favour and may be adopted if we ourselves are pious. We can formulate and adopt opinions, postulates and hypotheses of this type, and sometimes abandon them again. But it is important to remember that even in the form of belief in providence Christian faith is grounded on the Word of God, and can draw its life from this alone. On this basis alone can we be sure, and on this basis we must, that it is not a non-obligatory and ultimately insecure view, and that the lordship of God over the history of created being is not therefore a problem, but an objective fact which is far more certain than anything else we think we know about this history or even ourselves. We can and must understand that the knowledge of this lordship of God can be compared only to the category of axiomatic knowledge, and that even in relation to this category it forms a class apart. If the Christian belief in this lordship were a view which ultimately had behind it only the thinking, feeling, choosing and judging human subject, both it and its confession would always be unstable. But it is not such a view. It consists in a realisation of the possibility which God gives to man. It is the freedom which God

Himself has given to man for God. And as such it cannot vacillate. The matter itself, God's lordship over the history of creaturely being, has spoken in the Word of God as in His revelation to man, and it no longer permits him even hypothetically to think as though it were not present and this history took place under no lordship at all, or that of another. Man has not elected himself, but is elected, to believe in the lordship of God. He has thus no option but to believe in it, and to confess this faith. In this sense the statement concerning providence is a statement of faith. We shall have to take pains to understand and assert it as such in all its details. We shall have to avoid the temptation of slipping back from the level of faith to the level where there can be only interpretations, opinions, postulates and hypotheses which it would be difficult to establish dogmatically.

We have already recalled with admiration the belief in providence reflected in the edificatory literature and hymnology of the 17th and 18th centuries. Its witness is still impressive as given by P. Gerhardt because in him there may still be seen clearly the Reformation connexion between " Commit thou all thy griefs and ways " and the Christmas hymn " All my heart this night rejoices." But even in him are we not astounded at the extent to which the Christian subject dominates the presentation with a depiction of his own experiences and convictions of faith ? What if this tendency becomes more pronounced ? What if it is forgotten that belief in providence is possible only on the basis of the living Word of God, and can be confessed only in the form of an answer to its address ? What if the one who believes and confesses begins to take himself more seriously and to ascribe more power to his own view of the course of events under the sway of providence ? What if hesitation at the inadequacy of what we see and know in relation to what has to be believed and confessed, and at the feebleness of our faith and obedience in relation to what this reality believed and confessed must mean in our lives, quietly disappears ? What if it is no longer seen that we can believe in providence only on the basis of a Nevertheless which does not spring from our own pious hearts but is forced upon us from without, i.e., that we can only *believe* in it in the strict sense ? What if it gradually becomes easier and more obvious to believe in providence than in God's triunity, or the deity of Christ, or His reconciling work ? What if it is no longer grasped that the former belief is identical with the latter or it is nothing ? What if the former belief is preferred to the latter, and found secure by comparison ? What if it is found an excellent thing that at least in respect of belief in providence we are on the same ground as tolerable heretics and enlightened pagans ? What if for the sake of simplicity we finally place ourselves on the ground of this obviously general and natural religion, and regard belief in providence as in the last resort only one of the most important ingredients in this natural religion which in the last resort is alone normative and indispensable, trying to maintain, exercise and understand the belief only in this sense ? This is the great apostasy which actually took place in the 17th and 18th centuries and afterwards, i.e., from an orthodoxy which lost its inward context, by way of a Pietism which exalted the Christian subject to be the measure of all things, to the Rationalism which will listen only to the human subject as such and the expression of his own opinions, postulates and hypotheses. It is no cause for surprise that in this way the belief in providence necessarily becomes pale, indistinct, shy, hesitant and impotent. What man can think in this matter has neither colour nor contour, power, constancy nor force. The confession of belief in providence, for all that it is so unassuming as in the *Heidelberg Catechism*, is genuinely alive and happy and impregnable when it refers to the fact that God's lordship over the creature has spoken for itself in His Word, and has seized man, or rather freed him for it, in spite of all his own thinking and feeling and knowing, and all the inadequacy of his own trust and obedience. Only in these circumstances is this the case, and not when it is a so-called world-view, even a Christian world-view. For a world-view is an opinion, postulate and hypothesis even when it pretends to be Christian.

According to A. Ritschl (*Unterricht in d. chr. Rel.*, 1875, § 60) it is the glory of faith in the fatherly providence of God that it is the Christian view of things in a nut-shell. He formulated this view as follows : " In this faith we assess our momentary position in relation to the world according to our knowledge of the love of God and the resultant superiority of every child of God above the world as this is divinely led to its goal, i.e., our salvation." Every word and connexion in this statement shows that in it we really have to do with a world-view. It is palpable that it is fashioned with reference to the naturalistic and historicist positivism which dominated the cultured world in Ritschl's age. There is thus no place for the " eternal Father of our Lord Jesus Christ " as the Creator of heaven and earth in *Qu.* 26 of the *Heidelberg Catechism*, or for the almighty and present power of God sustaining and ruling heaven and earth in *Qu.* 27. Nor can there be any place for the quiet but forceful answer to *Qu.* 28 : " What fruit doth it yield to know the creation and providence of God ? " All that is left is a judgment of the Christian subject, or strictly not even this, but an assertion of the way in which the Christian subject actually assesses his momentary position in relation to the world in the confession of his belief in providence. According to this assertion the self-consciousness of this subject is so astonishing that what we learn concerning the believing man in the three questions of the *Heidelberg Catechism* seems feeble by comparison. Knowing the love of God, and deducing its own position from it, it finds itself above the world. It is in possession of lordship over it, as Ritschl customarily says. And the goal to which God leads the world is its own salvation as a Christian subject. It is obvious why there is so much dubious self-consciousness in this statement. If the objective matter to which the Christian believer in providence is suppressed or no longer heard ; if it has become so much irrelevant metaphysics, as Ritschl believed, then obviously there remains only the believer's confession of himself. And the assurance that as a child of God he is above the world—a world which is divinely ordered in his favour—cannot really have been given with sufficient confidence. Everything now depends on himself. Hence he cannot rate himself too highly. The belief in providence can have no other certainty but this dubious self-assurance. It is weak because it is a world-view which as such can have only this certainty. For even if the believer's confession of himself—and this has still to be proved—is genuine and meaningful ; even if it is at least subjectively honest, it is always marked by the property that it can go as it comes and disappear as it arises. We must take good care, therefore, not to be guilty of aberration in this direction.

2. The Christian belief in providence is also faith in the strict sense to the extent that, with reference to its object, it is simply and directly faith in God Himself, in God as the Lord of His creation watching, willing and working above and in world-occurrence. The consolation and impulse of this faith is that it points man to God in respect of the whole history of created being including his own. The man who lives by his faith may know that in everything which may happen to him he has to do with God. And beyond his own personal situation and history, as a near or distant witness and participant in all world-occurrence in all its dimensions, he may realise and count on it that

God Himself not only has a hand in it all, but is in the seat of sovereign rule, so that no other will can be done than His. Whatever the distance, the heights or depths, they are all bounded by the horizon that God exists as and where His creatures exist, and that His existence as such controls theirs. God's disposing is the kernel by which faith in His providence is nourished, to which it always strives and must continually return. Much may vary in the sphere of the divine disposing. In it there is a place for prosperity and adversity, victory and defeat, peril and protection, life and death, angels and demons, even human sin and human liberation. God is Lord in all these things. He is so in very different ways. But properly and in the last resort exclusively it is He who is always Lord. And this reference to Him is the meaning and power of the belief in providence. In face of all the variations of world occurrence the trust and obedience of this belief always have Him in view as Helper, Commander, Judge and King. They look always to His mercy, holiness, faithfulness and omnipotence. Belief in providence depends on God and God alone : on God as the One who works all in all ; but only on Him and on the fact that He is Lord of all.

It does not depend, therefore, on creatures and the different determinations proper to them in the world of His control, whether in detail, so that this or that good and fine and beautiful or in some way illuminating creaturely being is its true object, or as a whole, so that even though we say God we really mean creation and its life and their goodness or beauty or some other distinction. God is not creation. Neither in detail nor as a whole is He a determination of creation. To be sure, in its various determinations creation is, in the fine phrase of Luther, the mask of God, namely, to the extent that its history is also the history of the glory of its Creator. But it is only His mask and never His face, so that in it and its determinations in detail or as a whole we never have to do with God Himself. For as the history of God's glory takes place in, with and under that of creation, it is a hidden history, which is neither felt, seen, known, nor dialectically perceived by man, but can only be believed on the basis of this Word of God. We do not now speak of the divine manifestations, particularly that which fulfilled all others as the incarnation of the Word, the becoming creature of the Creator. In divine manifestation it is a matter of the establishment of faith in which the glory of God breaks through its concealment and man finds himself in direct confrontation with God. Even here the acting subject and therefore the basis of faith is God Himself and not His creaturely appearance in itself and as such. Even as the person of Jesus Christ it is the eternal Son of the Father, and only in unity with Him the man in whom this glory is revealed. Our present reference is to faith in God's more general presence and lordship in world-occurrence. Of this it falls to be said that it is real, and takes place in the world, but is concealed in world-occurrence as such, and therefore cannot be perceived or read off from this. Its revelation is not world-occurrence itself, but the Word of God, Jesus Christ. On the basis of this Word, in the freedom created by it, it may be believed, but prior to the consummation of the time of the world it can never be seen. Hence the object of the belief in providence can only be God Himself, as God Himself in His revelation in Jesus Christ is its only basis. The object of this belief cannot, then, be a creature, or any of its variable and varied determinations, instead of God. How could this belief stand if God were to it only what this or that glorious or apparently glorious creature is, or if He were only the Lord of the good and beautiful, of light and love and life, in the cosmic process, in a process which obviously stands so largely and we might often think totally under opposite determinations ? If He is not the Lord in the latter, He is not in the former, and this is not the Christian belief. The Christian belief is not directed to any creature, or any modification or aspect of the creature, but to the Creator who is the Lord of His creature in all its modifications and aspects.

But this means—and here we come to the decisive point in this delimitation—that no human conception of the cosmic process can replace God as the object of the belief in providence. Man makes such conceptions. It is inevitable that he should do so, for otherwise he would not be capable of any practical orientation and decision. It is difficult to see how to forbid this. It belongs to his very life as man to do it. Every man has some conception at least of his own life and that of his nearest fellow ; a picture of his own or someone else's life-work as it has so far developed and will do so, or should or should not do so, according to his insight, understanding and judgment. His particular notion of those different determinations of creaturely being, of good and evil, right and wrong, weal and woe etc., will naturally play an important part in this. Such pictures may have a wider reference. They may be pictures of the life-process of a society, e.g., the Church, or a particular form of the Church, or a nation, or group of nations, or the whole of human history. Some standards, moral or amoral, technical, cultural, political or economic, will dominate the one who forms them, leading him to assert progress or decline, formation, reformation or deformation, and determining both his assessment of the past and his expectations, yearnings and fears for the future. And such pictures, always on the same assumptions on the part of the one who forms them, may have an even wider reference. They may embrace the whole of being known to man, perhaps as a kind of history of evolution, perhaps more modestly as an analysis and description of the eternal movement of all being and its laws and contingencies, possibly including or defiantly or gaily excluding the good God, who at bottom, subject to what the one who forms them thinks concerning Him, might well be able to call some place his own within this total picture. There is no objection to man making these small and great conceptions of the course of things. Indeed, there is much to be said for it. It is itself quite definitely part of the world-process, and therefore of the history of creaturely or at any rate human being, that there should always be such conceptions, which whether small or great can never be conceived as mere pictures of history, but raise the claim, and can always make it good in some depth and breadth, to shape and actually make history. Our present point is that no such conception can replace God as the object of the belief in providence. No such picture can come in question as a picture of God. The belief in providence does not rule out such conceptions. It can allow them their specific place and right as necessary expressions and media of human life. In certain circumstances it can take them very seriously. It can sometimes, transitorily and with a particular application, see its object in the similitude of such pictures. But it will realise that even in them, in the strict sense of the concept, it has to do only with the masks of God, or more accurately with the masks through which man—not without the divine appointment, will and permission— can see these masks of God, and behind which he usually hides himself from God and his fellows (under the name and pretext of an " ism "). The belief in providence embraces these conceptions, but it also limits them. It reckons with the truth which they contain. It also reckons with the distinctive dynamic with which they do not merely reflect but shape history. But it remains free in face of them. It does not rest on any of them. ´ It cannot do this. For it is faith in God and His dominion and judgment to which all history, even that of the spirit, even that of human conceptions of human history, is wholly subject. It cannot, then, become belief in a human system of history invented by man, even when this system is the one to which the believer himself would give the preference and his heartiest approval. When a man believes, he will understand and apply even his own system, his own more or less distinct picture of history, only as a working hypothesis, and thus maintain the humility, the humour and the freedom to modify or abandon it as occasion may demand. He will treat it as an instrument which he has fashioned or taken over from others, which he uses so long as it can be used, but which he may see himself compelled and authorised to alter or to set aside and replace by another. He may give it much *fides humana*, but he will not give it any *fides divina*. He will be seriously convinced of its relative truth and goodness, but he will not believe in them. He will believe in God's providence, and not in his own as documented in his system. In all that follows we must beware of any aberration in this respect.

What we have to avoid is the equation of the belief in providence and its confession with a philosophy of history.

To see clearly at this point, we must refer back to our first contention that the belief in providence is not an opinion, postulate, hypothesis or world-view of the believing subject, but his freedom born of the Word of God. It is as God Himself tells man that He is the Lord of history, and man hears and accepts this from God Himself, that he believes in the providence of God. He thus believes in God. To be sure, he also reads in the book of history, whether of his own life or of the narrower or wider historical contexts in which it is lived. He makes some sense of what he reads and thinks he understands there. He forms his own opinion of it. On the basis of this opinion he sees himself forced to certain postulates. He thus works with certain hypotheses. And therefore independently, or stimulated and taught by others, he fashions with some degree of comprehension and accuracy a kind of philosophy of history. Why should he not do this? Again, and rightly again, he hazards the supposition that the rule of God's providence corresponds in some degree to his philosophy of history. But he will not think that he can really read the rule of God's providence from the book (or his own little booklet) of history. He will listen to the Word of God, and not to the inner voice which suggests that he should regard this or that historical picture as perhaps the most accurate. For in the providence of God he does not have to do with a picture but with the reality of history. And in the belief in providence he does not have to do with a tenable or probable knowledge, but with the true knowledge of this reality. If he believes in the providence of God, he does not believe in himself. He does not rely on or appeal to his own eyes which he uses to read the book of history, nor the inner voice which seems to suggest the best interpretation of what he reads, but the ears which God has given him to hear His Word. He believes in God, and therefore in the voice of truth, and therefore in the revelation and reality of history. He believes in the divine providence itself, not in an assertion or estimation, however well-founded, of what he thinks is perhaps its previous course, or present *kairos*, or future purpose, in short its plan.

But this entails a further step. As man believes in God, even in the form of his belief in providence he can believe only in God, and only God. This object cannot be confused with any other. As no philosophy of history can be the basis of the belief in providence, none can be its object. This faith believes that God is the Lord who rules over and in all things, not that history is the unfolding of a specific process, the execution of a specific schema, the development of a specific programme. Sometimes with all seriousness we can regard it as probable that all or many things have previously come to pass in a particular interconnexion which we think we see, that they now stand in a particular crisis, and that they will develop in a particular direction. But no matter how firmly we are convinced of this, we cannot believe in it, nor live by it, nor find comfort in it. We may receive from it our penultimate, but not our ultimate and proper directives. We cannot believe, as Lessing did, in an education of the human race, played out in history, to a moral and religious rationality to be attained in time or eternity. Nor can we believe, as Hegel did, in a self-development of the absolute spirit to be realised in history and more or less attained in 1830. Nor can we believe, as Karl Marx did, in a purpose of history worked out in the clash and counter-clash of the economic classes culminating in the victory and liberation of the economically oppressed. Nor can we believe, as did Treitschke and his contemporaries, in the conflict of nations which reached its most important phase with the rise of a united Germany. Nor can we believe, as did Spengler, in history as the evolution and conflict, the rise and fall, of different cultures. Nor can we believe, as did J. Burckhardt, in history as the mounting and tragic crisis of humanity, and therefore in the pathology of world history. We can think we see many of these things. We can be very seriously determined in practice by some such view. But while we may quietly or enthusiastically accept these constructs, and count on their validity, we cannot believe in them. We cannot think that to see them is to see God. The identification of the leading principles of such pictures with the God of the Old and New Testaments has never been possible. On the contrary, their inventors and champions have usually been wise enough to refrain from claiming such things for them, preferring to deny this God either directly or indirectly, and to give their principles another name (or no name at all) in accordance with their character. The fact is that we cannot believe in these principles. Unfortunately we can offer them false worship as what the Bible would call alien and false gods. But we cannot really impose them upon ourselves or others. We can absolutise them. But they can never be more than relative absolutes. We cannot really rest on them. They are not capable of any genuine faithfulness or reliable direction. They have their own dynamic. But they can reign only in part and for a time (whether a thousand years or only twelve). And at bottom they can do so only in appearance. In their place and time they, too, are naturally objects of the divine providence. But they can be confused with this providence only if we have very poor sight. We may add by way of warning that all that we have said applies fully to Christian or supposedly Christian views of history constructed with the aid of the Bible, like those championed by Gottfried Arnold or J. A. Bengel.

And now we must take a third step. In faith in God's providence man will certainly consider history with very open, attentive and participating eyes. How could it be otherwise ? He exists in it, and as he does so—how else ?—he has to live out and exercise his faith in the ruling God, and to show his little trust and obedience. The history of created being in its great and little consequences and connexions is the sphere over and in which there takes place the mighty and penetrating sway of this ruling God. It is in it that there is fulfilled secretly but very really the history of His glory. And so the belief in God's providence undoubtedly consists in the fact that man is freed to see this rule of God in world-occurrence, this secret history of His glory. This does not mean that faith becomes sight. It will know how to separate itself from a supposed and arrogant and certainly deceptive sight. Yet this does not mean that it is blind. It would not be faith if it were not knowledge in this respect, relative, provisional and modest knowledge in need of correction, yet true and thankful and courageous knowledge. When a man believes in God's providence, he does not know only *in abstracto* and generally that God is over all things and all things are in His hand, but he continually sees something of the work of this hand, and may continually see God's will and purpose in very definite events, relationships, connexions and changes in the history of created being. He notes in this history disposings and directions, hints and signs, set limits and opened possibilities, threats and judgments, gracious preservations and assistances. He knows how to distinguish between great and small, truth and appearance, promise and threat. He knows how to distinguish between necessary waiting and pressing on, speech and silence, action and passion, warfare and peace. He perceives always the call of the hour, and acts accordingly. He is free for this intercourse with the divine providence.

But it is not a philosophy of history which gives him this freedom. Perhaps he has such a philosophy. Perhaps he is constructing one. And we repeat that there is no reason why he should not do so. But even at best such a philosophy cannot free him for this thankful and courageous recognition of the sway of providence. On the contrary, if he were under the delusion that in it he possessed the key to this knowledge, he could only be hampered. For it would then be a serious matter that it is only his own idea and invention or that of some other man, and that as such it may serve as a non-obligatory guide, but cannot give knowledge of the ways of God. If it fills and dominates his vision, it thus blinds him to God and makes him unfit for that intercourse with His providence.

No, " thy word is a lamp unto my feet, and a light unto my path " (Ps. 119[105]). Our attempts to orientate ourselves in the dark, in the great movement of the masks of God which we call history, are necessary, right and good. But when it is a matter of receiving and having light in this darkness—and faith in God's providence does receive and have light in the darkness—we are forced back upon the Word of God, and this alone is to be received. To believe is to believe only in God and only God, we have maintained. But to believe in God in this twofold sense means concretely to believe in the Word of God and to believe the Word of God. This is the light which when and as we see it shines over history and causes us to see at various points in its course the sway of the Creator, disclosing the masks of God as such. It is not the case, then, that the man who believes in providence may easily or by means of any art read the book of history and see there the ways of providence. It is the case, however, that the Word of God in which he believes, and which he believes, can as such cause him to see something of God's rule, not His universal plan or total view, but God Himself at work at various points, and always and in every respect enough to give the man's faith in Him the character of a knowledge in which he may genuinely and rightly live by his faith. It is thus the case that when and as a man accepts the Word of God he does not have to interpret the cosmic process of himself, or according to the patterns given him by others, on the basis of his own assertions and judgments of right, value or taste, but that even while he does this he may also hear the infallible voice of his Lord, and cleave to it.

In faith in God's providence what is needed is the relationship to history of which we have an exemplary form in the Old Testament prophets. What makes them prophets is not that they can rightly perceive and publicly appraise past and present and future history, but that the hand of the Lord seizes them (cf. Is. 8[11]), that He says something to them which in relation to the thoughts of their contemporaries and even their own is always new and strange and unexpected and even unwanted, a " burden " laid upon them (Hab. 1[1]), a fire kindled and burning in them (Jer. 20[9]), even a superabounding joy filling them (Jer. 15[16]). It is not that they had or acquired a particular insight into the things which happened, but that these things, far from happening by chance or according to an immanent law which man could and should divine, were done by the Lord God, who does nothing " but he revealeth his secret to his servants the prophets " (Amos 3[7]). Hence it is not from history or their own view of history but into history, apart from and even against their own view, that a very definite light is given to the prophets in the form of concretely directed and fashioned perceptions which are not only clear to themselves, but have to be shown by them to others, in individual assertions, in agreements and repudiations, in threats and promises, in particular decisions, and also in more or less connected and far-ranging historical pictures. Basically and structurally this prophetic relationship to history is also that of the belief in providence. It consists in the fact that the man who is apprehended and freed by the Word of God is not without light and therefore always sees light in the obscurity of world occurrence.

It is to be noted again that this is not the light in which all things are open to God. It is not the revelation and contemplation of *the* mystery, *the* history. But it is light, and as much light as God thinks necessary and salutary for the believer in his time and place, and will therefore give him.

It is to be noted further that in the knowledge of God's providence by faith there can never be any question of speculation or theory. The seeing of the ways of God can never be an end in itself. It can never be a matter of aesthetic contemplation. It is always a matter of the practical insights necessary and salutary for man at specific points. What man can receive through the Word of God in this respect is knowledge for life. It is daily bread, manna from heaven, which must be gathered and eaten but not kept. We cannot boast of having it, or become complacent. If it is not to be given in vain, we can only live with it, stretching out our hands for a further gift that we may always have it afresh.

It is to be noted further that in this knowledge even a practical principle is not given to man in the sense of a constant programme. The continuity and consistency of this knowledge rest with God who will give it to man by His Word. It arises for man only as he listens openly and attentively to what God will say to him in His Word, not as he reduces what is already said to inflexible rules. The relationship of the Old Testament prophets to the history of their time never took the form of a programme. Hence a vitally self-renewing knowledge of faith in this matter, as its object is the faithfulness and constancy of God, can never be rigid, or clearly enough distinguished from an obstinate clinging to insights already won, a sterile repetition of a position already adopted. That history necessarily repeats itself, and that pictures once seen must be regarded as necessary to-day, is the very last thing to be expected by the man who believes in the providence of God. Hence he will not allow even a sound view of the historical process to become a strait-jacket. Indeed, he will not allow even the best view, even and especially when he believes that at the time he did not adopt it out of human caprice but in obedience to the Word of God. It will not be his concern—and in this respect the different attitudes of Luther to such problems of his age as the Turkish War, the Peasants' War and the Jewish question are formally at least important models—to try to give his view and attitude a particular character or aspect by the rigid insistence upon a certain line. He will not be ashamed if it can be shown that he once thought or spoke otherwise. The man who believes in the providence of God is distinguished from the man who does not, but rests instead upon his own prudence, by the fact that he is not too proud to be a continual learner. If he is under the instruction of the Word of God he need have no fear that his way will not finally have and show far more line and character than the ways of those who so wish to be true to themselves that they cannot really be true to God.

It is to be noted further that it belongs to this knowledge of God's providence by faith that although it refers to the infallible Word of God it is a human and, as such, a fallible knowledge. Not everything which the serious believer seriously listening to the Word of God regards as such is in fact a divine disposing and directing in history, a hint and sign of providence. He might have misunderstood what God has really said to him. We surely have such a misunderstanding when Eusebius of Caesarea, the father of Church history, saw in the emperor Constantine a second Moses, and in his kingdom a kind of definitive revelation of the kingdom of God. That he did not take this from the Word of God but his own judgment may be seen from the fact that he could make nothing of the Apocalypse, which would surely have warned him in this respect, but wanted to see it demoted from the true Canon. A similar misunderstanding arose when the great J. A. Bengel, who was much too cocksure in his understanding of the Apocalypse, thought that he could fix on 1836 as the date of the defeat of the beast from the abyss. For the rest, Bengel had so clear a vision of his time and the then future that in spite of this blunder—or accepting the fact that there could be this admixture of error—we may adduce him as an outstanding example of the fact that, even though an only too human misunderstanding of the Word of God may disturb in detail the knowledge of God's providence by faith, it cannot prevent it in general (and therefore also in detail). We have to remember that there are fruitful as well as unfruitful misunderstandings of the Word of God. If the believer's understanding is false in one respect, it is perhaps so much the better in others. And in any case it is better to misunderstand the Word of God than not to understand it at all. We may well say that not only is it no *pudendum*, but it belongs to the very best in the Old Testament, to the character of Holy Scripture as human witness to the revelation of God, that in the history of its prophecy there should obviously be some clear historical errors and prophecies either unfulfilled or fulfilled in a very different sense from that of the prophets. The lesson to be drawn for the doctrine of providence from this side of the matter can consist only in the affirmation that since man is so capable of error in relation to God it must not rest on any of its achievements. It must be free to withdraw in all its detailed insights. It must be continually ready to receive new and better instruction, and to that extent to censure itself. In short, it must be willing as a movement of knowledge to take part in the great movement of reality which is its theme, the co-existence of the Creator with His creature in which the Creator constantly increases and the creature decreases, in which the Creator always precedes and the creature can only follow. Only, but always, as it takes part in this movement is it the faith for which man is given freedom in this matter.

It is to be noted finally that in the upshot the knowledge peculiar to the belief in providence can consist in its decisive content only in the knowledge of God Himself. It is a matter of God in His quality as the Lord of all lords and King of all kings, of His world government, and therefore of the concrete knowledge related to the course of great and small world-occurrence and filled out and shaped accordingly. It is not a matter of a dead knowledge of God's lordship over all things, to which there might correspond a blindness for the details. It is a matter of the living seeing of the living Lord in the details of history. Hence it is not a theoretical seeing but a practical, not a programmatic but a free, not an infallible but one which stands in need of correction. The unconditioned and constant element in this seeing will not consist, therefore, in something that man sees in the course of the world as such, but in what he sees in the course of the world of God Himself as its Lord and Ruler. The Word of God continually places the history of creaturely being in its light in order that God Himself, who speaks to man, may be the better known by him. God Himself is what is necessary and wholesome for man. God Himself is the goal and measure of human action in the world. God Himself is the free One in face of whom man cannot entrench himself in any programme. God Himself is the true One who speaks infallibly even when man is deceived as to what He has really said. That God Himself is known as Lord is the decisive difference between the belief in providence and every philosophy of history as stated in this second delimitation.

3. We now come to the third and most important delimitation. In its substance the Christian belief in providence is Christian faith, i.e., faith in Christ. The Word of God which it believes, in which it believes and which sets it in the light in which it may see the lordship of God in the history of creaturely being, is the one Word of God beside which there is no other—the Word which became flesh and is called Jesus Christ. And the history of creaturely being is—secretly but really—the history of the glory of God in the fact that it does not merely run alongside the history of Jesus Christ and therefore the history of the covenant of grace between God and man, but has its meaning in this, is conditioned and determined by it, serves it, and in its reflected light (and shadow) is the place, the sphere, the atmosphere and medium of its occurrence and revelation.

Hence the belief in providence is not a kind of forecourt, or common foundation, on which the belief of the Christian Church may meet with other conceptions of the relationship of what is called " God " with what is called " world." The lordship of God over world occurrence which is its theme is not a general form which might have a very different content. It is not a genus comprehending not only the lordship of the Father of Jesus Christ, the God of the election and covenant of grace, but also the sway of any other deities freely selected by religion or philosophy. In virtue of its relation to what God has done once for all in Jesus Christ, it is a happening *sui generis*.

In most religious and philosophical systems there is some conception of a relationship between a higher and lower principle, an absolute, infinite, unconditioned or heavenly being and an earthly, spirit and matter, nature and reason, and of the superiority and even dominion in this relationship of the first and higher element over the second. There are, of course, exceptions. We remember the Epicureans. We can also think of older and more recent forms of scepticism and agnosticism. And we reserve the right to ask whether in many (and perhaps strictly all) the so-called polytheistic religions the relationship between the two principles is not one of ambivalence, with no radical superiority of the one over the other. What is really meant by higher and lower ? There can even be different opinions, though there ought not to be, as to the priority of the absolute over the relative, spirit over matter, reason over nature. But the relationship between Creator and creature with which we have to do in the Christian belief in providence stands outside this debate. The question whether there is in this relationship a Lord, and who this Lord is, is settled before it is asked. This alone shows us that the belief does not belong to the same category as religious and philosophical systems.

If we confine ourselves to the systems in which there seems to be a certain clarity in this respect, all kinds of pantheism drop away, because the superiority and dominion of one principle over the other as presupposed in them is from the very outset without centre or form. To be sure, there is a lordship. There is a regnant power which permeates and determines all things and is described as that of Godhead. But we cannot distinguish and decide who or what is this regnant Godhead on the one side and the world controlled by it on the other. There is no confrontation. The controlling element and the controlled are identical, or so fully interfused that neither can take on a definite shape or character or have a distinct history, and there can certainly be no question of a history between the two. The Christian belief in providence has also to do with a relationship in which the controlling element confronts the other with penetrative and determinative superiority. But this superiority, the omnipotence of God, has a formed and distinctive centre in which the controlling element has its own life in face of the controlled, and the controlled, the creature, has also its own life, so that the two stand in genuine confrontation and the relationship between them can and must be a history. From this standpoint the difference of view cuts so deep that we cannot possibly bring the pantheistic unity of Godhead and world and the object of the Christian belief in providence under a single denominator.

But the sharp contrast between the Christian belief and what might be compared with it in polytheistic and pantheistic systems begins at a much earlier point. Even the elements and principles whose relationship is envisaged in these systems are not what the Christian belief means by Creator and creature. They are rather antitheses within what the Christian belief would call creature. The absolute, infinite, unconditioned, and even heaven, spirit and nature are not the Creator, the ruling God, with whom we have to do in the belief in providence, but more or less clearly the one and higher side of the creaturely world, confronted in the form of another and lower side by the relative, finite and conditioned, by the earth, matter, nature. Both of them, including the first and higher principle, are determinations of what the belief in providence does not regard as God, but the reality distinct from God and controlled by Him. It is thus no wonder that there is that ambivalence of the two principles in polytheistic systems, and that it is open to discussion whether the one or the other or both or neither is really in control. Nor is it any wonder that in pantheistic systems there can be no question of any distinction and confrontation, of any encounter and history between them. The Christian belief is not involved in this debate as to priority, and it understands the relationship of the two principles as encounter and history, because its controlling principle, i.e., God as the Creator of heaven and earth, is above this antithesis, which for it is simply played out within what is for it the controlled principle. In virtue of this very different conception of the principles in question it cannot be compared with any of these views.

But it is only in appearance that it can be compared with views which seem to take quite seriously the concept of God as the Creator and Lord who is superior to the whole world and therefore to these antitheses within it. We refer to the semi-biblical religion of post-Christian Judaism and the paganised form of this religion, Islam. Here we have a Ruler of the world and His lordship over it. Here we have the will and work of a God with known physical and moral attributes, and a history between Him and His creation. Here, at least in Judaism, we have a history of salvation as the meaning and centre of universal history. But it is a history of salvation which has not reached its goal and strives towards it in endless approximation. And the fact that Judaism refuses to know anything of a history of salvation which has reached its goal means that it cannot penetrate beyond the knowledge of a supreme being furnished with those attributes, and beyond the confession of His omnicausality. Its God and Ruler of the world has necessarily a strangely obscure and hidden character. The devout Jew is never wholly clear as to His love or wrath, His grace or judgment. And His obscure character is projected into His government of the world, which the devout Jew follows, but only with anxious and hypercritical concern to justify it, and not with the childlike confidence of the clear presupposition that He the Lord will always be in the right. Where it is not known that God has already done the right in a fulfilled history of salvation, it is impossible to attain to this presupposition in respect of His rule of the world. And in Islam this obscurity of God and His rule has been made a principle and therefore a caricature. That God rules, and the creature is wholly subject to Him, and can only serve Him in the dust to win a supreme creaturely felicity, is all that now remains of the unfulfilled Jewish thought of God and the belief in His rule. Is it any wonder that in both ancient and modern times there have been so many ways which have led back to pantheism and even polytheism, and at the end of which the idea of a history between God and man is inevitably lost ?

The Christian belief in providence is given its content and form, and therefore its distinction from other views apparently similar, by the fact that the lordship of God over the world which is its object is not just any lordship, but the fatherly lordship of God. And this " fatherly " does not mean only " kind " and " friendly " and " loving." It means all this, yet not abstractly, but on a specific basis. Similar attributes of the supreme ruler or principle of the world are to be found elsewhere, but only in a way which is non-obligatory, contingent and problematical. In the language of the Christian belief in providence, " fatherly " means first of all, quite apart from any such predicates and as their solid foundation, that the God who sits in government is " the eternal Father of our Lord Jesus Christ." The Christian belief does not gaze into the void, into obscurity, into a far distance, height or depth, when it knows and confesses God as the Lord of the history of created being. It really knows this God, and therefore His rule. Under our second point we have established that it knows Him as it receives His Word. But His Word is not empty. It is not the reference to a supreme being which is supposed to have certain qualities. It is He Himself. But it is He Himself in a way in which He can be accepted by man. It is His person as a human person, His Word in the flesh, His eternal Son born in time as the Son of Mary, and crucified and raised for us. This " God with us " and " God for us " is God in eternity, the Son. And no other, but this God, is also " God over us," the eternal Father of this eternal Son. In the belief in providence it is a matter of " God over us," of God the Creator in His majesty, transcendence and lordship over His creature. But God the Creator is one God. The One who is for us as the Son is over us as the Father. As God has elected to be for us in His Son, He has elected Himself our Father and us His children. We are not in strange hands, nor are we strangers, when He is over us as our Creator and we are under Him as His children. We are His children for the sake of His Son and with Him (in whom He is so really for us that He becomes one with us). And it is as such that we are creatures in His fatherly hand. This fatherly hand is the divine power which rules the world. We can know no divine power over us, nor is there any such power, which is not this fatherly hand. As and because it is this fatherly hand, it is kind and friendly and loving. It has these qualities as the grace with which the same God who elected Himself our Father in His Son is also over us as our Creator. He is over us in a way which corresponds to this election of grace, to this eternal " for us " in His Son. Even as our Creator He is not alien or ungracious, but gracious. He is gracious as a Father to His children. And in this connexion we have to remember that the truth of this relationship is not to be found in what might take place between a human father and his children, but in what has taken place from all eternity, and then in time, between God the Father and the Son. He is our heavenly Father, in a way which surpasses all that we can see or think. We are thus warned in advance that we cannot make what we think we know as fatherly or any other kindness, friendliness and love the measure and criterion of His. It is a matter of the eternal fatherly fidelity which we can only try to see and grasp where it is revealed to us. " He that hath seen me hath seen the Father " (Jn. 14⁹). It is here that the Christian belief in providence sees the Father, and therefore God over us, and therefore the Lord of the world-process. It is here that the will which rules the history of created being is not concealed. It looks to the history of the covenant which is fulfilled in the mission, in the person and work of the incarnate Son, of the " God for us." And through and beyond this it looks to the divine election of grace. And it thus sees the Father, the " God over us," as it sees the Son. As it sees Him it hears the Word of God, and as it hears the Word of God it receives the light on God's rule in the world beside which there is no other. The light which it receives and by which it lives will thus consist always in the fact that it may there perceive not only the will of an unknown Lord, not only the lines of an order and consistence, not only the stages of a process, but the demonstration of the Lord who is our Father for the sake of His Son, of the Lord of the covenant of grace, of the God of the eternal election of grace. In very general terms this is the specific and incomparable element in the Christian belief in providence.

For this reason, we cannot equate God with a principle whose superiority and lordship over all other principles must first be discussed. This may be true of spirit as compared with matter, of reason as compared with nature, etc., but it cannot be true when " God for us," the Son, has spoken, and in this " God for us " revealed " God over us," the Father. On this basis we cannot equate God any longer with a principle which in its unity with its opposite is formless and incapable of history. This may and must happen to the Godhead of pantheism, but it cannot do so to the " Father of Jesus Christ," for His rule is essentially encounter and history with the distinct reality of the creature to which He is gracious and with which He is not therefore identical. And on this basis we certainly cannot equate God with any of the principles which are themselves only elements of the reality created by God. For if God is the God of the covenant and election of grace, this decides His being in a freedom which can only be that of the Creator as compared with that of the creature. This God is in a freedom which cannot be proper to any principle. And as the God of the Christian belief is seen in the fulfilment of the covenant between Himself and man as this has taken place in Jesus Christ ; as His will is not therefore an obscure and concealed but a clear and revealed will, it is obvious that He is also different from the God of Judaism and Islam.

All these differences may now be accepted as already elucidated, and this means that we are not only not obliged but forbidden to use a non-Christian concept of God, i.e., a concept which does not rest on a christological basis.

But we have to take note of the astonishing fact that the older Protestant theology was guilty of an almost total failure even to ask concerning the Christian meaning and character of the doctrine of providence, let alone to assert it. Even in Calvin (*Instit.*, I, 16–18) we seek in vain for a single pointer in this direction. It would be excellent if we could accept the assurance of W. Niesel (*Die Theologie Calvins*, 1938, p. 66 f., E.T., 1956, p. 71 f.) that Calvin understands the doctrine of providence wholly on the basis of the revelation of God in Jesus Christ, and in it " praises the power and goodness of the triune God who has drawn near to us in Jesus Christ." But unfortunately I have not found this assertion supported in the very slightest by the passages which Niesel quotes. That Calvin did occasionally think along these lines is shown by the preface to his commentary on Genesis. He there explains that Christ is the image in which God has shown us not merely His heart, namely, His love addressed to us in Him, but also His hand and feet, namely, His external works in the sphere of creation. And he there warns us that if we do not keep strictly to Christ we can only be betrayed into the wildest hallucinations in respect of these external works of God (cf. *C.D.*, III, 1, p. 31). We find a similar gleam of light in the statement (*De aet. Dei praed.*, 1552, *C.R.*, 8, 349) : *ecclesia propria est Dei officina, in qua suam providentiam exercet et praecipuum eiusdem providentiae theatrum.* But surely this thought should have been worked out in *Instit.*, I, 16–18, if it was as important as Niesel says. Such ideas did not control his own exposition, nor were they developed in the age which followed. We recall *Qu.* 26–28 of the *Heidelberg Catechism* with their repeated underlining of the decisive concept of the fatherliness of God and their express christological explanation of this concept. And what important consequences it would have had if the dogmaticians had taken seriously what is written under *Qu.* 50 (with references to Eph. 1[20f.], Col. 1[18] and Mt. 28[18]), namely that Christ has gone up to heaven to show Himself there as the Head of the Christian Church " by whom the Father rules all things " ! But to the best of my knowledge these are isolated texts in the 16th and 17th centuries. The orthodox Lutheran and Reformed teachers are rather at one in teaching the divine lordship over all occurrence both as a whole and in detail without attempting to say what is the meaning and purpose of this lordship. They understand it as the act of a superior and absolutely omniscient, omnipotent and omnioperative being whose nature and work do of course display such moral qualities as wisdom, righteousness and goodness, etc. But this is all. According to the agreed doctrine of orthodoxy, this empty shell is the object of the Christian belief in providence. It does not seem to have occurred in whole generations of Protestant theologians to ask what this lordship has to do with Jesus Christ, and the knowledge and confession of this lordship, and readiness to subject oneself to it, with faith in the Gospel of Jesus Christ. How does man really come to trust in this lordship ? Strangely enough, the question is not raised even by Johann Cocceius and his disciples, who in their concern for a biblical system make the covenant and its history the basic concept in theology. The formula that this ruling activity of God takes place *ad ipsius gloriam* is sometimes met with in Reformed and Lutherans, but when we ask what is meant by the glory and glorification of God we receive the mere shell of an answer (cf. A. Calov, *Syst.*, III, 1659, p. 1142) : *Omnia enim operatur, ut cuncta ipsi respondeant humiliter et voluntati eius obediant, vel id praestent, ad quod facta sunt et quae iubentur a factore suo.* What does this imply but the absolute exercise of the absolute will of an absolute power in an absolutely subjected sphere of power ? The meaning, goal and purpose of this action are one with the action itself. In other words, it is its own end. The *gloria* of God consists in the fact that He is so powerful in relation to the creature ; that He asserts Himself so thoroughly. And the question what this controlling God actually wills of His creature can be left open. To be sure, there were many who for the sake of fulness said that the God whose lordship is in question is naturally the triune God : *Deus Pater, Filius et Spiritus Sanctus*. But no one thought of deducing any consequences from the Christian definition of this subject in the description of its lordship. Even in the establishment of the knowledge of God's providence there was no thought of looking in the direction of the triune God, but the usual procedure was that of F. Turrettini (*Instit. Theol. el.*, 1679, VI, 1, 3 f.), who simply argued as follows. To deny providence is to deny God Himself. It is thus a *primarium caput fidei et religionis*. The voice of nature and the *consensus populorum* confirm its reality. Seneca and Cicero (and according to Turrettini even Aristotle) taught it. It results from the being of God as all-knowing, all-powerful and all-good. But it also results from the being of the creature as wholly dependent on its Creator and in need of His support. It results from the marvellous harmony and order of all things, which would be unthinkable without a supreme Director ; from the existence and fulfilment of so many prophecies ; from the fact of the preservation and renewal of the benefit of political orders ; from the occurrence of extraordinary favours and judgments including human conscience. To be sure, A. Calov (*ib.*, p. 1132) in a corresponding list maintains under 8 that God's providence may be perceived *e miranda ecclesiae et fidelium conservatione*. But under 9 he then says that it may be known *e conscientiae dictamine*, and under 10 *ex interno testimonio animae*. He obviously had no inkling that there might be a very special relationship between the government of the world and the Church, or that the Church might occupy in this matter the central position which Calvin once sought to ascribe to it. And confidently and self-evidently the *testimonium scripturae sacrae* was normally adduced in this list, usually at the beginning and often with the explanation that it is impossible to cite all the relevant passages :

tot enim fere sunt, quod sunt scripturae paginae, quando nihil frequentius, nihil clarius in verbo Dei inculcatur (F. Turrettini, *ib.*, 1, 5), or even more strongly : *Tota scriptura nihil aliud est, quam pellucidum speculum, e quo, quocunque te vertas, promicat pervigil ille oculus providae directionis* (D. Hollaz, *Ex Theol. acroam.*, 1707, I, 6, 5). But what it means, and how it is connected with the theme of the Bible, that it is in fact so strong a witness to God's providence, is never discussed. Allusion is simply made to John 5[17], Acts 17[24f.] and some of the more impressive Psalms and chapters of Job, these being set alongside the witness of reason and the *saniores Gentiles*, and nothing materially new or decisive being seen in them. The total impression is that there was a naive belief that in this matter there could be agreement with all schools (except in detail, and apart from the Epicureans, Deists and Atheists). There was no perception of the fact that a concept of God was used, and a corresponding concept of providence developed, which in its essential features could be filled out in a way very far from Christian. There was no concern as to the possible consequences— the invasion of secularism so unsuspectingly prepared by adopting in the basic understanding of the relationship between God and the world the ground of a *theologia naturalis* and even *naturalissima*. There was no attempt to ask whether the Keeper of Israel who neither slumbers nor sleeps (Ps. 121) is really identical with this directly visible all-wise, all-powerful and all-good being and his omni-causality, or whether what is said in the Sermon on the Mount about the need-lessness of anxiety and the Father who causes His rain to fall on the just and the unjust really amounts to no more than what Seneca and Cicero could say in other words.

Unfortunately the connexion between the belief in providence and belief in Christ had not been worked out and demonstrated theologically by the Re-formers themselves. Only occasionally and from afar, if at all, had they seen the problem of natural theology and the necessity of a radical application to all theology of their recognition of the free grace of God in Christ. In their case, to be sure, we almost always feel and detect, even though it is so seldom palpable theologically, that when they speak of the world dominion of God they are in fact speaking with Christian content and on the basis of the Gospel, not abstractly in terms of a neutral God of Jews, Turks, pagans and Christians. And this is what gives warmth and force to the matter in P. Gerhardt. But if in him there is an unmistakeable movement away from the Word of God to the experience of the Christian subject, this was to some extent a reaction against the dominant and self-evident abstraction with which the orthodoxy of his day followed another self-evident rut in these matters. This was the rut of a general theism which, apart from the mention of the *Deus triunus*, occasional quotations from the Bible and references to Church history, lacked any distinctive Christian content, being primarily concerned to distinguish itself from atheism, and limiting its consideration of the Gospel to the establishment and development of Christology and resultant doctrines. As if this were the real way to treat that *primarium caput fidei et religionis* !

The truth is that in this matter the older, strict and true Protestant orthodoxy was blatantly " liberal " in its life and thinking long before there was an " en-lightened " orthodoxy, or orthodox Enlightenment, or what is still called Liberal-ism and simply consists in liberation from the constraint of faith in Christ as the one Word of God not only in matters of providence but because at this point at every point, preference being given to a resolute attachment to the views which Jews, Turks, pagans and finally Christians can have in common concerning the existence and lordship of a supreme being. It was the older orthodoxy which made possible the question whether this was not everywhere legitimate and even necessary, and suggested only too plainly the answer to those who were inclined in this direction. At this point at least the references to the Trinity, the Church and passages of Scripture had no inner necessity for the orthodox. But if they were dispensable here, why not in other respects, and finally everywhere ? The whole movement which followed was inevitable, and the subjectivism of the Pietists could not arrest but only further this necessary development. It also followed that this syncretistic belief in God and providence with no specifically biblical and Christian substance inevitably proved to be inadequate even in face of the Lisbon earthquake, let alone the external and internal catastrophies of the 19th and 20th centuries. The hour had to come, and has now come, when belief in history and its immanent demons could replace faith in God's providence, and the word " providence " could become a favourite one on the lips of Adolf Hitler. It was the older, genuine orthodoxy which first open the sluices to this flood. In face of this supposedly generally apprehensible doctrine of providence the Epicureans, Atheists and finally Nihilists have always been secretly and openly the stronger.

The result of this historical survey cannot be that we should dismiss as worthless what the older Protestant theology attempted and achieved in this sphere. It is fortunately the case in theology—and the true Christian belief in providence allows and requires us to count on this fact—that even from very dangerous presuppositions (*hominum confusione Dei providentia*) ¿interesting, instructive and illuminating consequences can and usually do follow. For all the strange duality of their vision in this matter, the older orthodox were seriously trying to be Christians (as were many who went much further than they did). We cannot deny this from any superior seat of better knowledge. And if not, we cannot refuse to learn from them what can be learned in spite of their dangerous presupposition. Yet the fact remains that a better knowledge of providence is needed than that which they can give us. The Christian belief in God's providence is Christian and not general, and what Christian theology has to win and teach in this matter must be a Christian and not a general perception, not an extract from what Jews, Turks, pagans and Christians may believe in concert. The God of whose lordship we speak in this matter is the Father of Jesus Christ who as such is our Father. He is not another god, and must not be confused with another, with any of the principles on the basis of which attempts have been made to describe and explain the co-existence of a freely invented higher being with an opposed and subordinate principle quite apart from the Word of God in Jesus Christ. There is no place here for vague notions of higher and lower. If the doctrine of providence is a *primarium caput fidei*—and the older orthodoxy was right in this—it is hard to see how there can be in it any question or application of a different ontics and noetics from that which obtains in the case of sin or reconciliation, of justification or baptism. The upshot of this historical review is that in respect of the paths taken by the older orthodoxy in detail we must always note carefully whether the dangerous presupposition proves fatal or not, i.e., whether we can follow their suggestions because they are usable when taken up on a different basis, or whether they will lead us astray and must therefore be ignored.

3. THE CHRISTIAN DOCTRINE OF PROVIDENCE

Our only remaining task in this introduction is briefly to describe what is meant by a doctrine of providence which is Christian, i.e., which corresponds to Christian faith and is therefore resolutely worked out from a Christian standpoint and with Christian material.

It is quite plain what God wills as the Lord of the being created by Him, and as the Lord of its history, namely, what is the meaning and purpose, the goal and therefore the glory of His lordly action.

It is not plain, however, because we have lifted the veil of this history and discovered its secret. It is not plain because we have perceived, planned or determined it of ourselves. It is plain because God Himself has revealed it to us in His Word. And He has revealed it in the simple way in which He has revealed Himself—and we must take this seriously—as the triune God who as the Father is over us and as the Son for us, and both in the unity in which as the Holy Spirit He creates our life as a life under Him and again for Him. He has revealed Himself as the One who in essence is free, sovereign and omnipotent grace. He is this so certainly as He is the triune God who, even before the creature was, addressed Himself in His eternal counsel to us men and created us in order that the fulfilment of this counsel should be the covenant between Himself and us. This is the eternal glory of God revealed in His Word. This, revealed again in His Word, is His glory as Creator. And this, revealed yet again in His Word, is His glory as Lord of the history of His creature. What God wills as He works " all in all " (1 Cor. 12⁶), and what He therefore works, is that His free grace should be radiant, and take form, and conquer and rule in the creaturely world. He wills and works what He has revealed as His will and work in Jesus Christ, His Son ; what is revealed in Jesus Christ as His eternal will as the Father and also His eternal and life-giving will as the Holy Spirit. He wills and works this alone, with no reservations or secret suspicions that He might perhaps be doing something very different, willing and working a plan and purpose distinct from and quite independent of His glory, of His free and omnipotent grace. And He wills and works this wholly, in accordance with His sovereign will and almighty power to do it, so that there is no cause for anxiety lest something great or small should drop out of His will and work, or be able to disrupt it. If faith in providence is Christian faith, and therefore faith in Jesus Christ as the Word of God and therefore the self-revelation of God, there is for it no obscurity concerning the nature and will and work of the Lord of history, no ambiguity concerning His character and purpose, and no doubt as to His ability to see to His own glory in this history. This is the starting-point from which we must set out and to which we must continually return in this matter if we are not to go astray.

It is strange that the older theology never thought of deducing from the much quoted John 5¹⁷ that in the question as to the meaning and goal of the ἐργάζεσθαι of God the Father we should look simply, directly and fully at the ἐργάζεσθαι of the Son which is equated with it. It is strange that Colossians 1¹⁷ (τὰ πάντα ἐν αὐτῷ συνέστηκεν) was constantly adduced and yet the lesson was never learned from it that all things not only have their existence (v. 16) but also their consistence, their order and continued existence, their σύστημα (v. 17), in the Son of whom it is said in v. 14 that we have in Him our redemption, the forgiveness of sins, and in v. 15 that He is " the image of the invisible God, the firstborn of every creature." Quenstedt rightly observed concerning this passage : *totum*

Systema mundi dissolveretur, nisi per potentiam conservatricem Christi sustentaretur (*Theol. did. pol.*, 1685, I, 13) ; but he did not draw the deduction from this insight. It is strange that there was not a more fruitful recollection of Hebrews 1³, where the Son of God is again indisputably described as " upholding all things by the word of his power," and immediately afterwards as the One who " when he had by himself purged our sins, sat down on the right hand of the Majesty on high." It is particularly puzzling in this case because in the second article of the creed this is given its full New Testament sweep and the *qui sedet ad dexteram Dei Patris omnipotentis* is fully accepted. This meant, and still means, that He sits at the place from which heaven and earth are ruled and all power has its origin and centre, not as a passive spectator, but as the epitome of the wisdom, will and power of the Father, and with the Father as the source of the πνεῦμα ζωοποιοῦν without whom no creature can live and move. Yes, the Son of God, born of the Virgin Mary, crucified under Pontius Pilate, dead, buried and raised again, is seated at this point. Had it not been noted in Ps. 118¹⁶ that the right hand of the Lord " is exalted and doeth valiantly," or in Ps. 139¹⁰ that it holds man, or in Ps. 73²³ that man for his part holds it, or in Ps. 18³⁵ that it upholds, or in Ps. 44³ that it brings Israel into its own land, or in Ps. 48¹⁰ that it is " full of righteousness " ? What could have been more obvious, one might have thought, than to equate this ruling right hand of God with the One who according to the witness of the New Testament has His place at this right hand ? Why did not Calvin and others work out that insight that the hands and feet of God, like His heart, are revealed in Christ and Him alone ? And why did not this perception break through when it was read and sung in the best known of Luther's hymns ?

> " Ask ye who is this same ?
> Christ Jesus is His Name,
> The Lord Sabaoth's Son ;
> He, and no other one,
> Shall conquer in the battle."

How could the subject of the universal lordship at issue in the doctrine of providence be left so indistinct, as if it were not known " who is this same " ? How could it be left neutral, and necessarily subject to a different interpretation, as if it were another god than the One confessed in the second article of the creed, or as if side by side with the world dominion exercised by this right hand of God we had to reckon with another divine rule on the left hand which is perhaps to be regarded as the true sway of the Creator over and with His creature ? All the astonishment which is legitimate at this point may be summed up in the question why it was not seen that, in the passage in Genesis 22¹⁻¹⁹ from which the *Deus providebit* was usually taken, the God who so wonderfully foresees and provides is not a mere supreme being but the God who, in this happening in which Abraham was to spare his son, acted as the Lord of the covenant in the fulfilment of which He Himself was finally not to spare His own Son. It was with a view to this goal of the history of the covenant of grace that Abraham was promised and given his successor Isaac, that he had then (as a prophecy of the One who was to come) to separate and bring him as an offering to God, but that he had not to die but live as a type of the One who was to come and give life through His real death, a substitute being found for him in the form of the ram. This divine *providere* belonged to this concrete context of the history of salvation. In view of this, ought not supreme importance to have been attached to the qualification of the presupposed concept of the subject ?

If we take seriously the starting-point and concept of the subject given by the Word of God as His self-revelation, in its centre and substance we must have the following decisive understanding of the history played out under this lordship. It is the execution of the election of grace resolved and fulfilled by God from all eternity. It is thus the history of the covenant between God and man. It is the history in which God establishes His fellowship with man, and prepares and accomplishes its completion in His own self-giving to human nature and existence, to conduct it to its manifestation at the expiration of the last time. As the creation of all the reality distinct from God took place on the basis of this purposed covenant and with a view to its execution, so the meaning of the continued existence of the creature, and therefore the purpose of its history, is that this covenant will and work of God begun in creation should have its course and reach its goal. There is no other meaning or purpose in history. For there is no other God, and in the will of this God there is no other purpose but the election of grace resolved and fulfilled by Him from all eternity. In the distinct reality created by Him, and even in the freedom of this action of the creature, all things always serve this purpose of its continued existence. They take place as they have a part in the history of this covenant. They take place for the sake of this history. They constitute an occurrence distinct from the activity of God. But they have no significance or value apart from God's covenant will and work or in independence of them. They do not have their purpose and goal in themselves or apart from the purpose and goal to which the covenant work of God hastens. They can only hasten with it in the one direction. As they come from God, from His election of grace and creation, they can go only where they are ordained to go by the very fact of their existence, serving this will and work of God, participating in it, executing what God has resolved in His free and omnipotent grace.

We should certainly not forget or erase the fact that the history of the covenant, and therefore the history which is the meaning of all creaturely occurrence, is within the totality of this creaturely occurrence a particular history selected for this purpose and determined and directed accordingly. It is an astonishingly thin line in a confusion of apparently much more powerful and conspicuous lines which seem to be independent and mutually contradictory, and especially to run quite contrary to the one narrow line of the history of the covenant. That world history in its totality is the history in which God executes His will of grace must thus be taken to mean that in its totality it belongs to this special history ; that its lines can have no other starting-point or goal than the one divine will of grace ; that they must converge on this one thin line and finally run in its direction. This is the theme of the doctrine of providence. It has to do with the history of the covenant, with the one thin line as such. Or rather, it has to do with it only to the extent that it for its part is undoubtedly one among the many other lines of general world-occurrence, and that these many other lines of general world-occurrence have their ontic and noetic basis in the fact that the God from whom they come and to whom they return pursues on this one line the special work which the creature must serve on these other lines. The doctrine of providence must not level down the special history of the covenant, grace and salvation ; it must not reduce it to the common denominator of a doctrine of general world occurrence. In so doing it would lose sight of the starting-point and therefore of its concept of the subject. And then it would no longer be speaking of the world dominion of God revealed in His Word. This God is the Father of Jesus Christ, the God of Abraham, Isaac and Jacob, the God of the prophets and apostles, the God who pursues His special work on this special line of world-occurrence. The doctrine of providence presupposes that this special history is exalted above all other history. It can and will understand all other occurrence only in its relation to this special occurrence, namely, as an occurrence under the lordship of the One who there pursues the work in which His will for the whole is revealed and operative. This is what gives it its proper theme.

It has to do with the history of the creature as such. The man to whom God has addressed His eternal grace, and with whom He deals in His eternal grace on the special line of this special history, is also quite simply His creature, and indeed His creature within a creaturely cosmos, under heaven and on earth. And as the history of the covenant, grace and salvation takes place ; as Abraham and his descendants are called by God to be His people ; as God in His Son Himself becomes a man of this people, to be as such very God and very man for all men ; as the community comforted by the Holy Ghost proclaims the name of its Lord and awaits His manifestation ; as all this takes place, there is simply enacted the history of the creature as such, the psycho-physical history of man in time, and the history of the near and distant cosmos around him, the whole titanic continuation of creaturely existence as such—a history of apparently quite a different type, of what seems in part to be a more modest and in part a more expansive content, the incommensurable drama of the coming and going, the rising and falling of what is outside God. And the special occurrence in Israel, in Jesus Christ and in His community is not merely embedded in this general occurrence, but so inextricably woven into it that what takes place particularly in the one all bears the character of the other, and can and must be understood from the standpoint of this general occurrence, as a part of the history of the creature. Abraham, and his descendants, and the prophets and apostles, and even Christians as men called and awakened to the consciousness, thankfulness, obligation and mission of covenant-partnership with God, are all men in the cosmos and participants in its history. For this reason their faith must be faith in providence, faith in the God who even as their Creator, as the Lord of this general occurrence, is the same as the One whom they may know by His summoning Word, or conversely faith in the fact that the God who has called them by His Word is also their Creator and the Lord of this general history. The doctrine of providence relates to the fact that Christian faith is faith in the relationship thereby posited between the one occurrence and the other. It tells us how far information is given us on this inner relationship by the Word of God.

To the extent that it does not deal with the history of the covenant as such, but with the history of the creature ordered in relation to it, it has its own theme. It is not obvious that the history of the creature takes place under the lordship of God in such a way that it is ordered in relation to the history of the covenant. This is open to question. If it is true, it is a matter of special knowledge, of a special content of the Word of God. But it might well be otherwise. There might be two histories of the same divine origin and under the same divine control, running parallel as two independent and unrelated sequences. The covenant is not creation, but its internal basis. And creation is not the covenant, but its external basis. It is not self-evident, but has to be seen particularly, that the covenant in virtue of its external basis and creation in virtue of its internal are also connected in their history, and in this too stand in a positive relationship to each other.

That there is a participation of man in the covenant, that there is a grace addressed and a salvation ascribed to him, might be related to his creaturely being only in the sense that the same God wills this who posited this being from the first as that of a creature under His protection and provision as Creator. Even then there might not be a positive relationship between his existence as a partner in the covenant, a recipient of God's grace and participant in His salvation, and his being as a creature of God. It might be established only at the end of the two histories and by way of a new creation. On the way from the beginning to the goal, in the course of his special history as the covenant-partner of God, man would then be able only to cling to the fact that the Lord of the covenant is also His Creator, and is therefore in some way the Lord and Guarantor of his creaturely being. But he could not count on the fact that his participation in God's covenant, grace and salvation definitely has and has had a direct significance even for his being as God's creature.

On the other side, the possibility might be formulated as follows. That man is God's creature, and has a history as such, might be related to his participation in God's covenant, salvation and grace to the extent that the God who has addressed this to him has also granted it to him to be his creature, and as such to have and fulfil his course under His protection and providence. It might be that this creaturely course of his under God's lordship has materially and properly nothing whatever to do with his history under the direction of the same God as the Lord of the covenant of grace. A true and proper connexion between his creatureliness and his determination as God's covenant-partner might arise only on the basis of a new creation. On the way between his creation and this goal, man as a creature would be able to cling only to the identity of God and therefore the parallelism of his own being as a creature with his history in covenant with God, but not to a positive significance of his creaturely history for the other.

We have to make at this point a decision of great importance and far-reaching consequence.

If the matter were as assumed, and as unfortunately taught both explicitly and implicitly, then a passage like 1 Peter 5⁶ : " Humble yourselves therefore under the mighty hand of God, that he may exalt you in due time : casting all your care upon him ; for he careth for you," would have to be expounded as follows. Now that you must suffer persecution, you find yourselves as God's creatures under an absolutely superior and obviously grievous order and power. It is the order and power of God, the hand of your Creator, who is the " Lord of history." To be sure, you are Christians, but you have no option but to humble yourselves under the hand which so painfully overrules your creaturely existence, acknowledging that its sway is just, even though so strange and incomprehensible, because it is that of God. In another respect, in respect of the salvation addressed to you in Jesus Christ, God is not unknown to you. But in this respect, in relation to the present form of your creaturely existence, in relation to your being in world history, you must blindly trust that what He does is right. You may do so in view of the fact that the One before whom you can only humble yourselves now can and will exalt you in another hour of His own choosing. Therefore let your care in respect of creaturely existence be His. You can do this because you know Him well in that other respect, as the Lord of the covenant of grace. Indeed, it is because you know Him well in that other respect that you may trust Him blindly in this respect, although you do not know Him in this respect, as the One who rules over your creaturely existence, your external history, your living and dying.

A passage like Matthew 6²⁶ᶠ· (about the birds which neither sow nor reap and yet are fed, and the lilies which neither toil nor spin and yet are more gloriously arrayed than Solomon) would then have to be regarded as a picture from this other order, the order of creaturely being and history ; and the Christian could gather from it that even in this order to which he also belongs there is a divine lordship, protection and providence to which he may confidently commit himself in respect of food and clothing.

It will be seen that the expositions possible on the assumption of two parallel sequences are neither bad nor unhelpful. But on this presupposition how can we interpret Ephesians 1¹¹, where we are told that Christians are made heirs, being predestinated according to the prior decision (the πρόθεσις) " of him who worketh all things after the counsel of his own will " ? And what about Romans 8²⁸ : " We know that all things work together (συνεργεῖ) for good to them that love God, to them who are called according to his prior decision " (κατὰ πρόθεσιν) ? If this is true, our whole assumption is obviously called in question. We have not to reckon with a parallelism of the two sequences, but a positive connexion between them. The particular decision of God concerning His elect and His government of all things, their love for God and their existence in the totality of things, are obviously not to be regarded apart but in conjunction, in material co-ordination. But if the One who has foreordained them heirs works all things, and if all things work together for good to those who love God, Christians can accept the occurrence of their creaturely history, certainly in faith alone, yet not in a blind faith, but in a faith which is objectively grounded, in a seeing faith, in the faith that there is here not merely a factual but a materially positive and inner connexion, so that even in their creaturely being they are wholly in the kingdom of Christ and not another kingdom.

It may thus be asked whether the foregoing exposition of 1 Peter 5[6f.] exhausts the meaning of the passage. If the mighty hand of God humbles Christians in respect of their creaturely existence, and if they really accept this humiliation in the hope of future exaltation, this is because this mighty hand is none other than the right hand of God where Christ is seated, and therefore in what comes upon them in some sense from without, as is constantly emphasised in the First Epistle of Peter, they are simply led by the divinely willed fashioning of their earthly life to the discipleship and fellowship of the suffering and dying Lord Jesus Christ. And if they may now cast all their care upon Him and know for certain that it is lifted from them and is no longer theirs, if in their sufferings they may live by that hope of future exaltation, this means that in their creaturely existence they may participate in the freedom and even the glory of the covenant-partnership with God given them in Christ. " Beloved, think it not strange concerning the fiery trial which is to try you, as though some strange thing happened unto you : but rejoice, inasmuch as ye are partakers of Christ's sufferings ; that when his glory shall be revealed, ye may be glad also with exceeding joy " (1 Pet. 4[12f.]). There are certainly two standpoints from which the being of man and God's dealings with him may be seen and understood. But it is not the case that these confront and continually contradict one another. The case is rather that the standpoint of creation history is lit up by that of salvation history. Is it not a fact that only on this assumption does the apostolic admonition amount to more than general edification in the sense of Stoicism and receive the stamp of distinctive and incontrovertible Christian truth and necessity ?

It may be asked again whether we really have in Matthew 6[26f.] no more than a picture of the divine order of creation held out to the disciples. Is this only a parable from which they may gather that like the birds and lilies they need not be anxious about their external preservation ? That they need not be anxious is surely made clear to them in the fact that with the reference to the birds and lilies they are told that as the disciples of Jesus—much more than these—they live in the world of the heavenly Father who not merely as the Creator of all things, not merely as He has power over them and is responsible for their preservation as such, but as their heavenly Father knows that they need food and clothing and sees to it that they need not be anxious. Hence v. 33 : " But seek ye first the kingdom of God and his righteousness ; and all these things shall be added unto you." In " all these things," in their creaturely existence, their history, their needs and reversals, in this whole sphere of divine lordship, there is no question of a history taking place independently of the kingdom of God and their seeking it. The point is that in what takes place in the one we have a προστίθεσθαι to what takes place in the other. That there really is this προστίθεσθαι or συνεργεῖν (Rom. 8[28]), that the history of creaturely being is really ordered in relation to the history of the covenant, is the true theme of the Christian doctrine of providence as opposed to the assumption which we took as the starting-point of this excursus.

There is thus—and this is the not very obvious, but from the Christian centre true and clear point to be stated and developed in the doctrine of providence—a positive, material and inner connexion between the two series. The faithfulness of God, which is its supreme and proper theme, is indivisible. It is not first the faithfulness of the One who called Abraham, fulfilled the promise given to him and will finally manifest it in its fulfilment, and then again the faithfulness of the Creator who will not abandon His creature, but give it His support and continually direct its history. But the faithfulness of God is that He gives support and direction to the history of His creature in the fact that in this history He calls Abraham, and rules His people, and gives Himself in His Son, and will finally manifest Himself in this One as the Lord of the whole. The faithfulness of God is that He co-ordinates creaturely occurrence under His lordship with the occurrence of the covenant, grace and salvation, that He subordinates the former to the latter and makes it serve it, that He integrates it with the coming of His kingdom in which the whole of the reality distinct from Himself has its meaning and historical substance, that He causes it to co-operate in this happening.

The question arises whether in the whole witness of the Old and New Testaments to God's work and revelation any other meaning is given to creaturely being as such and its history than that of an integration and co-operation of this kind. Every page speaks, of course, of heaven and earth, natural and historical events, great and small historical contexts, peoples, kings and nations, rain and sunshine, health and sickness, wealth and poverty, joy and suffering, life and death. That man as the partner of God is also quite simply man in the cosmos, and the concrete meaning of this for him, are everywhere displayed and taken seriously, i.e., brought into relationship to God as the Lord of all. But this is never done in such a way that an independent significance and role are ascribed to him, or to God's rule over him. It is never done in such a way that a neutral and general world dominion of God becomes the theme of the biblical presentation, or even emerges from it. It is never done in such a way that we may suspect that in the history of creation as such we have to do with a sphere in which God is active according to a plan and law peculiar to it. On the contrary, the great and little things in this continually visible sphere are all taken seriously in the fact that they are seen and described as this integration and co-operation. They may and must all serve, not merely God in general and indefinitely, but God concretely willing and working in the history of the covenant and salvation. They all have their seriousness, their glory or shame, light or darkness, greatness or littleness, in the fact that they stand in this relationship. How can man in the cosmos, in his creatureliness and among other creatures, be at home or otherwise in creaturely history? How can he be justified or unjustified, blessed or cursed? How can he be exalted or abased as a creature, rewarded or punished, great or little? This is possible and necessary in the fact that here on earth under heaven, in natural and universal history with all the implications which it has for man at every stage and in every direction of its occurrence, God's covenant, grace and salvation are in action and His kingdom comes. As the Bible sees it, the occurrence of creaturely existence as such follows and corresponds to this occurrence. It receives from this occurrence its meaning and character. And as it stands in this relationship, it comes to man and for good or evil becomes his destiny. A free and secular creaturely occurrence, standing in a neutral relation to this other, is quite inconceivable in the context of biblical thought and perception.

But our primary emphasis must now be upon the fact that this accompaniment of the history of the covenant of grace by that of creaturely being, this co-ordination, integration and co-operation of the latter, is the work of God. It is this no less than creation, and the establishment of the covenant in and with creation, and the history of the covenant. If in its continued existence the creature may serve the will of God in His covenant, grace and salvation, it does this in the individuality and particularity given it with its creation by God, in the freedom and activity corresponding to its particular nature. The creatures of the earth thus live their own lives. Man, too, lives his own life in accordance with the particular spirit which is the basis of human nature. All creation is made to exist in this relationship according to its own manner and freedom. But the fact that it actually does this is first and last the direct work of God. For neither generally nor in detail has God created a machine which works at once in harmony with His will and therefore with the history of the covenant of grace. To the relative freedom and autonomy in which the creature has begun and continues to exist in face of Him, there corresponds the perfect sovereignty in which God is present in its whole history and in which He Himself co-ordinates and brings it into a positive relationship with the history of the covenant of grace. As He is free in His dealings with the patriarchs and Moses, with judges, kings and prophets, and finally in His incarnate Son, and as He is gracious and omnipotent in His freedom, so He is in the dealings with and to and through and in creation with which He accompanies this history at every step. The perfection of creation is not the power with which the latter sets and maintains itself in motion in this sense. The power in which it does this is the perfection of God, and concretely the perfection of His free and omnipotent grace, and even more concretely the perfection of the kingdom of Jesus Christ. Creation has its own perfection. We are told that God considered what He had made, " and behold, it was very good." But the goodness and even perfection of creation consists in the fact that God has made it serviceable for the rule of His free and omnipotent grace, for the exercise of the lordship of Jesus Christ. But this serviceability would be futile and concealed if there were no such rule and lordship, if it were not the living good-pleasure of God actually to use it. In other hands than His it cannot render the service for which it was ordained. There is needed the Master who has fashioned this instrument if its goodness and perfection are to be effective and revealed. This meets all the complaints of the creature against its supposed imperfection, which can be raised only by those who cannot control or see it in its perfection because it is not for them to use it. It also takes from creation all boasting or self-glory, because its glory can consist only in the fact that God has made and found it useful for Himself, and especially in the fact that He will and does use it in the service of the " kingdom of his dear Son " (Col. 1[13]). It is not glorious in itself ; it can become so only in the right hand of the living God. That He uses it in the service of this kingdom ; that

He co-ordinates and integrates it with His work in this kingdom ; that He causes it to co-operate in the history of this kingdom, this is the rule of His providence. In so doing God acts with a sovereignty which has its self-evident limit in His own being, in the unity and steadfastness of His will, in His own glory and mercy, in the immutability of His purpose. Accordingly it has its limit also in the nature of creation, in the goodness and perfection given it, in its serviceability to Him. But in what this consists is known only by God Himself as its Creator and Lord. We can perceive it, and therefore the limit of the sovereignty of God which it sets, only when we perceive the use which God wills to make and does make of it. The extent of this use is the extent of its nature, goodness and perfection, and the extent of His sovereignty over it. Since we do not know the totality of His rule, it is not for us to fix the limit of His sovereignty. It certainly cannot have its limit in what we know of it, or of creation.

From this character of providence as an actual and sovereign work of God there follows the fact that in its sway we have always to do with God Himself. We certainly have to do with Him in His relationship with His creatures, His presence in their presence, His working in their works, His freedom in their freedom. To that extent we have certainly to do with the creatures too, with their history, self-expressions, nature and perversion, immanent harmony and contradictions, riddles and revelations, indeed with the great drama of being and its impelling and imposing autonomous significance. We have already seen that on the thin line of the history of the covenant we have also to do with a part of the general history of the creature. If there were no revelation there ; if it were not objectively real and subjectively true that God Himself is present, we might well think that this is only an act in that great drama of being. But what if on this thin line revelation takes place and awakens faith, because here God is present and active in the creaturely world in such a way that He makes Himself known and is actually known in the course of creaturely occurrence ? A decision is then made not only for this particular history but for all the general sphere of creaturely occurrence, even for the innumerable and extended spheres in which God is concealed. This is that He is the Lord of this whole occurrence. But this means that the impression of an autonomous significance of this whole drama is broken and called in question. We can accord it only a relative autonomous significance. For it is finally clear, and generally and fundamentally so, that in creaturely occurrence we have to do not only with this as such, but properly and decisively with the doing of the will of God. The faith awakened at the one point by the revelation of God, being faith in God the Lord, is necessarily faith in His lordship even at points where there is no such revelation, where to all appearances we have to do only with creaturely occurrence, where the orders and contingencies of nature, the works of caprice and the cleverness or folly, the goodness or badness of men seem to be the only reality. Nevertheless, God Himself is He who is freely and graciously and mightily present and active at these points too as the One who is prior to all creaturely occurrence, supreme over it and at work in it.

This Nevertheless is the problem of the belief in providence and the doctrine of providence. It can only be a Nevertheless. What man sees is simply the multiplicity and confusion of the lines of creaturely occurrence, which in itself and as such—for creation is not God—cannot be identified with the doing of the will of God, with the work of His freedom, grace and power. There can be no question of a transparency proper to this occurrence as such, or of an inherent ability of man to see through it. What man sees is simply creation in all the regularity and contingency of its own movement and development. If he did not begin with faith in God's providence, he might try to intepret this movement and development in different ways. But he certainly could not maintain and confess that God is the Lord who is prior to this occurrence, supreme over it and at work in it. The belief in providence maintains and confesses this with its Nevertheless. It has itself the character of a " foreseeing." In faith in God's particular revelation man sees God before he sees the general history of creation. And it is for this reason that as he sees the latter he sees God as the One who in concealment but supreme reality is before and over and in it as the Lord. Hence his Nevertheless is not blind. It is grounded in a supremely illuminating Therefore. And the man who ventures this Nevertheless, because he may so venture, is not ignoring reality. He does not imagine another reality. He does not think he sees through reality. On the contrary, he sees it as it is just because he encounters it with his Nevertheless, not believing in its apparently autonomous significance, but in the significance given it by the fact that in all its developments it stands under the lordship of God. He confronts world reality in all sobriety in the fact that he knows that in all its developments he has to do with God Himself, with His co-ordinating and integrating of creaturely occurrence with the history of His covenant, with the doing of His gracious and saving will, with His providing that all things must work together for good to them that love Him, and in all these things with God Himself, with the work of His right hand.

Is there a legitimate answer to the question of the concrete significance of this actual and sovereign work of God, and therefore of this co-ordinating and integrating of creaturely history with the history of His covenant of grace, to the question of the concrete significance of the co-operation of creation for good, and therefore in the doing of His gracious and saving will, as effected by God's disposing ? If the answer is to be legitimate, it must be given at least with great caution. It cannot in any circumstances maintain that in the history of the covenant of grace the creature can be a sovereign subject side by side with God. The fellowship of the creature with God actualised in the person of man is of course the goal of the covenant of grace, and again in the person of man it is God's partner in this covenant. But the creature does not establish, maintain or rule this covenant. Its history is the history of the divine acts and achievements, not those of the creature. In it, it is a matter of God's grace, and not of its own capacities and merits ; of the salvation which God ascribes to and secures for it, and not of a salvation which it can attain of itself. If there is a co-ordination and integration of its history, of the history of the totality, to this particular history, and a consequent co-operation of the creature in this history, there can be no question of the created world either as a whole or in detail sharing with God in the establishing, maintaining and ruling of the covenant, in the dispensing of grace and in the sending out of salvation. There can be as little and even less question of this than of its sharing with Him in its own creation. Grace would not be grace if it were not free, but were conditioned by a reciprocal achievement on the part of the one to whom it is addressed. Nor would it be an eternal and true salvation if the creature for whom it is destined co-operated independently in its accomplishment and mediation. In the covenant of grace it is a matter of the reconciliation of the world with God, of the redemption of man, of the hushing of the sighing of all creation, of the revelation of the glory of God. What takes place in the covenant of grace does so wholly *for* man and not—even in part—*through* man. A *creatura mediatrix gratiarum* or even *corredemptrix* is a self-contradiction. One alone can be the subject of *gratia* and *redemptio* and none other beside and with Him— namely, God Himself.

But something else has to be taken into account, and this is the theme of the Christian belief in providence. It is no accident that we cannot properly define it, but only indicate it in descriptions which are not really adequate in detail. While God alone is the ruling, determining and conditioning Subject in the history of the covenant of grace, He is undoubtedly not alone in this history, but has a partner in man, and to that extent in the cosmos. Again, as the history of the covenant is enacted, the creature is undoubtedly present as the subject of a separate history, nor is it present in vain as a passive spectator or mere object, but meaningfully. From the very outset the covenant had its external basis in creation. Similarly, the history of the covenant continually has its external basis in the existence and history of the creature. And it is a matter of the establishment and preservation of this external basis of the history of the covenant in the sway of the divine providence. How are we rightly to portray this " external basis " within the accepted limits of what is legitimate, not saying either too much on the one side or too little on the other ?

If in the first instance we simply ask concerning the function in which the creature is this external basis of the history of the covenant, there primarily suggests itself the concept of service on which we have already touched. A servant is certainly present at the work of his lord, and has a meaningful part in it. The lord himself is exclusively the subject of this work and responsible for its planning, undertaking and fulfilling. At every point it must be his own work if it is to be good. But he must have time, space and opportunity for this work of his which none can lift from him and in which none can help him. And to create this according to his own direction and order he needs a servant wholly familiar with his work and engaged in it, yet restrained, avoiding any material interference and absolutely selfless. This servant, wholly involved in the work of his lord, but strictly from outside, and yet meaningfully involved in his particular function and indispensable in his own time and place, is the being and work of the creature in the relationship to God's action in the execution of His gracious counsel. But the metaphor is inadequate. For no human servant is at the same time the creature of his lord. Again, the value and glory of a human servant consist in deploying within his limits as much of his own initiative as possible in his participation in the work of his lord. Again, a human servant might ultimately serve another lord than the one he does. And finally, a wholly selfless purpose is too much to ask of the work of even the most loyal servant. The service of the history of creaturely being in relation to God's action in the history of the covenant of grace is to be understood, in contrast to this inadequate comparison, as a pure service in which the servant can have in view no purpose or advantage of his own, and cannot possibly transfer his service to another.

We shall now attempt a different comparison. The service of the creature is that of an instrument. We have said already that God uses it. An instrument is also present, and indeed meaningfully and indispensably, when it is used for a particular purpose. There can be no question of it being a subject. It knows nothing of the purpose for which it is used. And it cannot make the slightest use of itself. It is nothing if it is not picked up and used by the one who knows his purpose and the use of the instrument. But in these circumstances it is indispensable. And this is how things stand with the creature and its history. This metaphor speaks more clearly than the first of the freedom of God in relation to His creature. But it is no less obviously inadequate. The freedom of God in His dealings with the creature is very different from that of a human master in relation to his tool. For the latter is not also the creator of his tool, and the adaptation of the latter to the designed use can never be more than limited. The comparison is inadequate again because the creature is in God's hand not only with the passivity of an instrument but also with its own activity.

As God co-ordinates and integrates the history of the creature with that of His covenant of grace, so that it may co-operate in this history, the creature is not only a means but also an object of the divine action. As God works through creation, He works on it and for it. He makes of it what is in conformity with His good-pleasure. He shapes it according to His gracious will. From this standpoint it is tempting to describe it as the material of His action, as in the well-known comparison of the potter and the clay in Jeremiah 18[1f.]. This comparison gives a general indication of the majesty of God and the insignificance of the creature. But it, too, fails to bring out the specific majesty of God which consists in the fact that He has not found but created the creature, and the specific insignificance of the creature, which is not alien matter in the hand of the living God but His own living possession.

Thus in answer to the question concerning the concrete purpose of created existence, or its co-ordination and integration with the history of the covenant of grace and co-operation in this history, we cannot give any true definition, but only some inadequate comparisons. In describing it as service, we have already said that it provides time, space and opportunity for the divine will and action in the covenant of grace.

In this connexion we may well recall the first creation story, in which creation is described almost as the building of a house or temple, man being finally introduced as the true inhabitant. It is also to be noted that the distinctive relationship between the work of the sixth day and the seventh as the day of God's rest points at once to the fact that the relationship of man with God or God with man which is the basis of the covenant in the midst of creation, is the goal for which the whole building is constructed, and that it is for the history of this covenant that time, space and opportunity are created with creation as such. Calvin perhaps had this in view when he described the totality of the cosmos and cosmic occurrence as the *theatrum gloriae Dei*.

There is one indispensable presupposition of the covenant of grace and the kingdom of Christ and its history even outside the free and gracious will of God. It consists in the fact that God is not alone but with the creature, so that the latter has existence and continued existence alongside and outside Him. In order that God may work for and to and in it, it must be there in its distinct reality. But to its being, and therefore to God's dealings with it, there also belongs the fact that it has time, space and opportunity both to exist and to do so for God's glory. The psycho-physical life of man, and therefore the God who addresses Himself to this man in His grace, needs this. It must all be co-ordinated and integrated with the work of His grace and co-operate in it. It cannot in any degree help to effect this work.

It cannot be its subject. It is genuinely an external and not an internal basis of this work, whether as *causa prima* or *causa secunda*. But it is indeed the external basis of this work. It is its *conditio sine qua non*. This work of God, which is not an *opus ad intra* like the inner acts of the trinitarian God but most definitely an *opus ad extra*, needs outside (*extra Deum*) a theatre on which it can be enacted and unfolded. The created cosmos including man, or man within the created cosmos, is this theatre of the great acts of God in grace and salvation. With a view to this he is God's servant, instrument and material. But the theatre obviously cannot be the subject of the work enacted on it. It can only make it externally possible. This is done by the history of the creature as such. As it fulfils this purpose, it is indispensable. And the fact that it really serves this purpose is the meaning and problem of the doctrine of providence. This tells us that provision has been and is continually made for this theatre of the history of the covenant of grace, for time, space and opportunity for the divine work of grace and salvation. It tells us that this provision is made by God Himself. It speaks of the specific and as it were supplementary divine work of this provision. There will be time, space and opportunity for the history of the covenant of grace, for faith, knowledge, repentance, love and hope, until this history reaches its divinely appointed end. In great and little things alike all this will be continually furnished by the sustaining and overruling sway of God as the Lord of heaven and earth. This is the divine co-ordination and integration of cosmic history with the history of salvation. It is seen by the Christian faith in providence as follows. Even as God's creatures, and within the world of other creatures, caught up in the great drama of being, we are not in an empty or alien place. It is not God's fault if we do not feel at home in our creatureliness and in this creaturely world. This is a notion which can obtrude only if we suspend as it were our faith in God's providence and do not take seriously our membership of the kingdom of Christ. If we take this seriously, our eyes are open to the fact that the created world including our own existence fulfils that purpose and constitutes that *theatrum gloriae Dei*. It and we are present in order that God may have time, space and opportunity to pursue in the history of the covenant of grace the work which is the goal of His creative will and to hasten towards which He has made it His own most proper cause with the interposition of Himself in Jesus Christ. We are in the house of our Father, in a world ordered according to His fatherly purpose, as we are in the created cosmos, under heaven and on earth, and ourselves cosmic creatures. It cannot help us, or deliver us, or reconcile us with God, that we are at home in this sense. Our salvation and future glory do not have their source here. Yet it is not a matter of indifference, nor can we perceive it without joy and gratitude. The fact that we are given by God Himself the *conditio sine qua non*, the time, space and opportunity without which we could not have a share in the kingdom of Christ, is co-ordinated and integrated with the divine work of grace and salvation. We certainly cannot and must not say that even the picture of the theatre and home is wholly adequate. It lacks the things which are plainly brought out concerning God's working through the creature by the pictures of the servant and instrument, and concerning the creature as the object of God's working by that of the material. But in the sense indicated it does at least indicate the way in which the teleology of the divine work is to be described.

But the question as to the concrete meaning of that co-ordination. integration and co-operation can be carried a step further, and may finally be put as follows. What recognisable character is proper to creaturely occurrence in relation to what it has to accompany under God's providence ? What does it mean for an understanding of creaturely occurrence that it takes place in this co-ordination under the divine rule ? We venture to answer, as we may well do in the light of 1 Corinthians 13^{12}, that creaturely occurrence acquires in this co-ordination the character of a mirror. The distinction and inter-connexion of the two historical sequences are both brought out in this comparison. The original, God's primary working, is the divinely ruled history of the covenant. The mirror has nothing to add to this. In it the history of the creature as such cannot play any role. The mirror can confront it only as a reflector. It cannot repeat it, or imitate its occurrence. It can only reflect it. And as it does so it reverses it, the right being shown as the left and *vice versa*. Yet the fact remains that it gives us a correspondence and likeness. The creature does not exist for nothing in this co-ordination. It does not have for nothing the same Lord in both cases. Its history under His lordship as Creator is indeed a different one from that of the covenant instituted and fulfilled by the same Lord. But its twofold history is comparable as creature is comparable with creature (for even the history of the covenant takes place in the creaturely sphere). Jesus Christ as very God and very man, the basis and fulfilment of the history of the covenant, is certainly not to be found again in general creaturely occurrence. This cannot then be more than a mirror and likeness. And everything thus takes place differently for all the similarities. Yet there are similarities. The contrast and connexion of heaven and earth, of the inconceivable and conceivable world, is not the same as that of God and man in Jesus Christ ; but it is similar. The confrontation and fellowship of man and woman in marriage is not the same as that of Christ and His community ; but it is similar. The antitheses of above and below, of light and dark, of beautiful and ugly, of becoming and perishing, of joy and sadness, which are obviously to be found in creaturely occurrence, are certainly not the same as the true antithesis of grace and sin, deliverance and destruction, life and death, in the history of the covenant ; but they are at least similar. In the same way there is something of good and bad, right and wrong, spirit and the opposite, if not in cosmic history as a whole, at least in the history of man. How strange it is that there is still a people Israel, and that this people is so brightly spotlighted in our own day ! Nor is there lacking the phenomenon of gods and their worship, of sacrifices, prayers and the like, of religious history. We must be careful not to identify the reflection with the original, the history of the creature with the true history of salvation. For reasons which have nothing to do with its creatureliness, the former is one long history of the very opposite of salvation, as emerges even more clearly in religious history, and in what is known as " Israel " in world history. But we cannot overlook or deny the fact that creaturely history is still similar in every respect to the history of salvation, as a reflection resembles the original. Creaturely history is not for nothing the theatre of the great acts of God, the Father's house. In virtue of its origin and in its whole structure its occurrence is calculated to reflect and illustrate and echo these acts of God. And this is what actually happens.

" The heavens declare the glory of God ; and the firmament sheweth his handywork. Day unto day uttereth speech, and night unto night sheweth knowledge. There is no speech nor language ; their voice is not heard. Yet their line is gone out through all the earth, and their words to the end of the world " (Ps. 19$^{1f.}$). What can be known of God is manifest (φανερόν) among men because God " hath shewed it unto them " (ἐφανέρωσεν). His invisible being, namely, His eternal power and Godhead from the creation of the world, may well be understood as seen in His works (νοούμενα καθορᾶται, Rom. 1$^{19f.}$). But is this image really seen, this reflection recognised, this likeness understood ? Are there the necessary seeing eyes to see it ? The original must obviously be known to make this possible. But to know the original we need faith in God's Word and revelation to have a part in the history of the covenant, and then genuinely in creaturely history. If we are children of the Father, we certainly recognise His house in more and more likenesses. But we shall certainly not be guilty of the confusion of thinking that the house of the Father, what can be only a similitude, is the matter itself. We shall always see the likenesses as such. We shall always hear the echo as such. We shall therefore be at home even in creaturely occurrence. Is it not the case that the biblical view of cosmic occurrence, of natural and universal history, is one which, as opposed to every kind of dualism, is open and relaxed, and in the best sense attentive and grateful ? It can and must be this, for its presupposition is that creaturely occurrence has its meaning and substance and centre solely but genuinely in the history of the covenant. The Bible regards creaturely occurrence as the circumference of this centre. It sees it set in the light in view of this centre. This light is not extinguished by the fact that what takes place outside the history of salvation is a history of the very opposite. This light is still light even when it becomes so deceptive in the perverted eyes of men, even when it causes so much of that confusion, even when it usually summons them to so much natural theology (in complete misunderstanding of the truth which is to be joyfully but soberly recognised at this point).

In great and little things alike world-occurrence is a reflection and likeness. We can and must say, of course, that this description, too, is not without its faults. It has something static about it. It gives rise to the impression that creaturely occurrence is an object which can simply be speculatively contemplated, whereas it, no less than the history of the covenant, is really an occurrence which comes upon man as such, and claims him totally, and leaves him no place for mere contemplation or idle experience. A mirror is indeed a futile implement which can be dispensed with if necessary. And when creaturely occurrence is called a mirror it may easily be forgotten that in it there take place service, work and action. Speculative thinkers are warned that they can find no entrance here ; that this is only one aspect of the problem ; that this aspect cannot be absolutised as such but can have significance only in respect of the character of creaturely occurrence in its relation to the divine activity of grace and salvation. And those who perhaps fear the rightly suspect *analogia entis* are reminded of the earlier descriptions in which it is quite clear that there can self-evidently be no question of anything but the *analogia fidei sive revelationis* even in this description of creaturely occurrence as a mirror and likeness.

As we sum up, we must try to be more precise. For not only this final venture but the whole discussion of the concrete meaning of the divine co-ordination and integration of creaturely history with that of the covenant of grace, or of the divinely occasioned co-operation of the creature in this matter, stands in need of more precise statement. We have spoken of the function of creaturely occurrence, and described it as that of a servant or instrument. We have spoken of its *telos*, and described it by calling the created world a theatre. We have spoken of its character, and finally described it as a mirror and likeness. These statements constitute a legitimate answer to the question of the meaning and purpose of this occurrence, and a permissible description of it as the external basis of the history of the covenant, so long as they are all taken together, the fragmentary nature of each of them being perceived and therefore none of them understood or asserted as though it were absolute. Each is merely an imperfect indication of what is here to be described, namely, the divine rule operative in creaturely occurrence. We are not to think, therefore, that what is to be described is really indicated or introduced in any one of these descriptions.

This condition, on which alone all that we have said here is valid, must finally be given an even stricter formulation. What we have said is legitimate only if we realise that it cannot be said of creaturely occurrence in itself and as such, but only of creaturely occurrence as it takes place under the sway of God's sovereign and actual providence. It cannot be said of qualities and determinations inherent to it, but only of qualities and determinations ascribed and imparted to it by God's action in the power of His omnipotent mercy. Creation in itself and as such never has the power, capacity or competence on the basis of the election of grace to be the servant and instrument of the God who acts in the covenant of grace and kingdom of Jesus Christ, to be the theatre of His action and therefore to afford it time, space and opportunity, to be for His children their Father's house and as such a mirror and likeness of His fatherly action. It has no power for this. How could it have ? It was not with God when His counsel of grace took shape concerning it. It can know and fulfil the will of God only to the extent that in this counsel decision is made concerning its existence as such. But as creation it has no knowledge of the ways which God will take with it as it exists, and no control of the part which He will allot it. It can neither take, give nor keep the function, purpose and character in which God will and does use it in His dealings with it. We cannot say, therefore, that in itself and as such it possesses and has these qualities and determinations. It possesses and has them only as it receives them, as they are given it by God. We thus say too much if in the sense of an ontological definition we try to say that creation *is* God's servant and instrument, the theatre, mirror and likeness of His gracious and saving action. At this point any " is " can strictly relate only to moments in God's universal rule in which creation may become a servant and instrument, a theatre, mirror and likeness, by God's sovereign and actual will. It is all this as He takes it into His omnipotent and merciful hand in the execution of His plan, giving it these qualities and determinations. It is it in the event of the divinely accomplished co-ordination and integration, in the event of the co-operation for good, to which it is called, authorised and capacitated by Him. That it is created good and even very good by Him means only that it is prepared by Him to be grasped in this way. He has not prepared the creature in vain or for anything else. But as He speaks and commands, it is so (Ps. 33[9]). And it is so in the manner and form, in the function, with the *telos* and character, which it is to have ineluctably and with supreme objectivity, and therefore not merely in the sense of a human opinion, but with God's own truth. We must not abstract from this divine Speaker and Commander if we are to give a legitimate answer to this question of the concrete sense of creaturely occurrence. We must think always of God's living hand which continually lends creaturely occurrence this concrete sense. As the creature cannot anticipate its creation, or give itself existence and essence, so it cannot anticipate God's providence or its use in God's living hand, as though it already were what it must be in this use, or already had what it must have in it. It can only be ready for God, or more exactly for God's action in the covenant of grace and kingdom of Christ. It can only wait for His omnipotent mercy, acquiring its function, *telos* and character, and becoming God's servant and action, the theatre of His action and mirror and likeness of His glory, in the event of His rule and dominion.

We must see clearly that this rule of God's providence over and in creation does not give up or break off, and has and leaves no gaps. It is not the case, then, that sometimes the creature does not acquire these qualities and determinations. The hand of God never rests. And it will never withdraw. Everything is always involved in its power and therefore in that receiving and becoming. For the faithfulness of God never ceases in the kingdom of His grace. There is no moment, place or situation in which His creature escapes Him or becomes indifferent, in which He has no further use for His creature or some part of it, or in which He forgets it. But we must be clear that it is God's faithfulness alone if creation in its totality is in fact always involved in this receiving and becoming, and may thus have this function, *telos* and character, and be this servant and instrument, this theatre, mirror and likeness. God does not owe it His love. He is under no obligation to co-ordinate and integrate it with His work in this way, and enable it to co-operate in His action. It has no glory of its own in this. It can only participate in His glory and glorify Him. What help would it be to have existence and essence by God's creation, and therefore to be made ready for His use, if He did not continually take it to Himself, and lend it this dignity and significance, and cause it to participate in His work, and give it the appropriate glory ? What would it be without this active good-pleasure of its Creator ? It can only receive, and receive grace for grace, and receive of His fulness (Jn. 1^{16}).

This is the insight without which there could be no legitimate answer to the question of the concrete sense of creaturely occurrence under God's providence, and of its participation in the doing of God's gracious and saving will. We shall conclude by mentioning some of the important deductions to be drawn from this insight.

1. We began this final discussion with the assertion that there can be no question of an independent co-operation of creation in the establishment, direction and fulfilment of the history of the covenant of grace, of a participation of creation in the procuring, attainment and mediation of the love of God which comes to it in this covenant. We made this assertion without giving any reason for it in this particular context. We can now give this specific reason. It takes the form of a conclusion *a minori ad maius*. There is no question of an independence of creation in its co-ordination and integration with the divine work of grace, or in respect of its determination as a servant and instrument, a theatre, mirror and likeness of the kingdom of grace. The free love of God alone can give it this function, *telos* and character, and not its own goodness. But if this is so in this sphere, how much more is it the case when it is a matter of the preservation, reconciliation and redemption of the creature fallen into sin and hopelessly threatened in consequence! Since it has no glory, merit or claim of its own on the one side, since God has no obligations towards

it, since it is referred exclusively to the active good-pleasure of its Creator in this whole sphere, how could it possible add anything to God's work on the other with its own capacity and action ?   How could it possibly be *creatura corredemptrix* ?

2. Creaturely occurrence is the external basis of the history of the covenant.   How far this is the case we have tried to show in our consideration of its concrete meaning.   But after our last and more precise statement, we cannot overemphasise the fact that it is this external basis, and has therefore constitutive significance even for the occurrence of the history of the covenant, to the extent that it is enacted under God's providence, and this significance is not withdrawn from it, but continually given it by God.   It thus has it, but only as it may receive it.   Not even momentarily, therefore, can we think away God's free faithfulness towards it if we are to see this significance, and see it in its capacity as the external basis of the history of the covenant.   God Himself and God alone continually sees to this external basis of the history of the covenant.   He Himself and He alone makes creaturely occurrence His servant and instrument, the theatre, mirror and likeness of His action.   It thus follows that we can recognise it as such only in faith in God and His free faithfulness. Hence there follows the simple but pregnant fact that in this respect we walk by faith and not by sight.   We can never have this recognition if we look past the internal basis of the history of the covenant, namely, the divine election of grace revealed in Jesus Christ.   This recognition can thus take place only in the act of hearing the Word of God, in the act of adoring His inconceivable goodness, in the act of gratitude and the corresponding willingness and readiness to do the will of God.   It can be achieved only in the light and power of the Holy Ghost and by the man whom the Father draws to the Son and the Son to the Father.   In relation to this recognition we do not find ourselves in a forecourt but in the very centre of the sanctuary. As the kingdom of Jesus Christ is revealed to men in Jesus Christ, so too is the sway of divine providence, the determination of creaturely occurrence, its function, *telos* and character.   It is always a matter of recognition from within outwards, from the cross and resurrection of Jesus Christ to all other occurrence, from God's grace to the world of its addressees and recipients.   The freedom of the divine providence by which all things are upheld and sustained and meaningful and right can be known only in the freedom of faith which has its origin where God Himself does the work for the sake of which He has created all things, and where He is revealed in this work.

3. This way can be traversed only in this direction.   Not even subsequently can this sequence be reversed.   We are confronted by the necessary impotence of all systems which radically or practically, primarily or subsequently, abstract from God's work of grace and the kingdom of Jesus Christ.   In making this abstraction, they forfeit

their inward and outward vision. They lack that which alone could justify their vaunting claims. Even without the freedom of faith, as those who are closed to the revelation of God, we could investigate in all kinds of ways the meaning of creaturely occurrence. But on what principle of exposition could we give an answer? If we do not know of a Creator, we do not know that in world-occurrence we have to do with a creaturely and therefore relative occurrence taking place in a definite connexion and definitely ruled in this connexion. We shall therefore posit absolutely one of its aspects, even perhaps that of its insolubility. But how then can we avoid ascribing to it an autonomous significance supposedly found in this aspect? How can we escape the unending debate whether this significance of the external world is to be found more in its historical aspects or more in its natural, more in its law-abiding or more in its contingent, more in its spiritual or more in its material, or in what combination of all of them? How can we justify ourselves in ascribing this particular significance to world-occurrence? World-occurrence as such does not speak unequivocally. If we hear it say this or that, how can we justify ourselves except on the basis of a significance with which we ourselves have already encountered it? From world-occurrence as such there are obviously only arbitrary and highly debatable ways to a world principle whose superiority, power and credibility can even remotely be compared with the world rule of God. And in that centre from which man in the freedom of faith and under the constraint of the Word of God can continually see afresh the ever new and living work of His hand, he stands quite alone, renouncing his own cleverness and responsibility, his own decision for this or that possibility, his own opinion. What is a world-view if it does not consist in the contemplation of a world rule, and therefore of a reality which is superior to the world and all its contemplation and interpretation, and can effectively order and co-ordinate world-occurrence? But how can there be the contemplation of a world rule if there can be no question of that of a world Ruler?

4. We have said that this sequence, and this way of considering it, cannot subsequently be reversed but must always be from within outwards. But this means that there can be a contemplation of the divine world-rule, and therefore of world-occurrence under this rule, and therefore a Christian view of things, only in the movement of faith itself from within outwards, and in the concrete realisation of its perception. We have said that this perception or recognition is possible only in the light and power of the Holy Ghost, in the freedom of faith in which the freedom of the divine providence is manifested. But on both sides this means that there cannot be a closed and static Christian system. What might be given this name can only be the insight of many or few individuals grounded in a concrete perception of God's work of grace and then expressed as such in an equally

concrete perception of God's action in the creaturely sphere. This insight can never take the more solid form of a more permanent view, of theoretical notions of what constitutes God's work in the creaturely sphere, of definitive assertions concerning the extent to which creaturely occurrence is God's servant, instrument, theatre, mirror and likeness. For the freedom of faith in which alone this insight is possible must always be given to man afresh as the gracious gift of the Holy Spirit. And when it is given afresh, it must always be a new freedom. The establishment of a fixed Christian view, of a lasting picture of the relationship between Creator and creature, would necessarily mean that in taking to-day the insight given him to-day man hardens himself against receiving a new and better one to-morrow. Having thought and spoken as a believer to-day, he would no longer do so to-morrow, but place himself on the same level as the unhappy inventors and champions of non-Christian systems. For what distinguishes him from them but the freedom of faith ? What will distinguish him from them if he renounces the freedom of faith to-morrow ? The knowledge received in enlightening and empowering by the Holy Ghost will never be closed but always open. Yet it is the objective side which is really decisive. As we have seen, we do not have to perceive immanent qualities and determinations of creaturely occurrence, but divine actions by which it is continually given afresh its function, *telos* and character. In the freedom of faith man follows the way and movement of the divine providence which is free in a very different sense. What God has done to-day, and revealed to man as His action, He will do again to-morrow, but He will perhaps do it quite differently, and reveal it to man in a very different form. That to-morrow as to-day He will give creaturely occurrence its function, *telos* and character is the faithfulness of God on which we can and should count, the constant element for which the believer will look even in respect of to-morrow. But what he cannot say is how God will do it. His world-view as his understanding of creaturely occurrence and the divine providence reigning in and over it will always be that which corresponds to the present measure of his faith and knowledge, to the insight given him by God to-day. It will certainly be a modest insight. Probably it will not usually concern itself with larger or total issues. It will be content to be a clear perception of individual points and questions making possible practical decisions for the next stretches of the way. It will probably consist less in the maintaining of principles and leading tendencies than in the discovery of a small series of promising standpoints. It will probably display many reservations and gaps. In this form it is less likely to acquire a form which will compel the believer sooner or later to become entangled in blatant self-contradictions. It will not become so easily the basis of a programme or party, or an object of debate. It will be an instrument to promote understanding with as many others as possible. But within these limits it will always be sure of itself and fruitful. If the matter is understood within these limits, we may well say that as the believer has faith in God's providence in world-occurrence he may live with a partial world-view which is provisional and modest but also binding. He will not, of course, believe in this partial world-view. But as he believes only in God the Lord, he will have enough light to make some such partial view of world-occurrence—the part which meets his own requirements —indispensable. And he will be the more glad of it the more he is prepared to be continually led from this point. Man has always many new things to see even when he ostensibly made a serious beginning long ago, and has thus acquired no little genuine skill, in having open eyes for the ways of God in creaturely occurrence.

GOD THE FATHER AS LORD OF HIS CREATURE

God fulfils His fatherly lordship over His creature by preserving, accompanying and ruling the whole course of its earthly existence. He does this as His mercy is revealed and active in the creaturely sphere in Jesus Christ, and the lordship of His Son is thus manifested to it.

1. THE DIVINE PRESERVING

Our present task is to unfold and clarify what takes place when God accomplishes what we define as His providential ordering and therefore His fatherly lordship over the creature.

We shall begin at once with the first affirmation that God fulfils His fatherly lordship over the creature by preserving it, that is, by upholding and sustaining its individual existence—the existence which He gave to it as the Creator and which is different from His own existence—and by giving to this existence its continuity. He does this—and on the basis laid down in § 48 we must give precedence to this statement—in His fatherly wisdom and power, as the Lord of the creature who is also the Lord of the covenant of grace. The power in which He sustains the creature is the mercy with which in His Son Jesus Christ He is revealed and active within creation and in creaturely form. And the purpose in which He sustains creation is the revelation of the lordship of His Son, for whose sake He has given to each creature its individual being. Therefore it is this specific power and purpose which makes divinely necessary and operative the preservation of the creature as such. The creature has to be preserved, and is in fact preserved, because this particular will of God has to be done, and is in fact done, both in heaven and on earth, because Jesus Christ is at the right hand of the Father and is our Advocate. It is He who represents our right to existence and the necessity of our existence, and of the existence of the whole creaturely world. It is He who is the divine basis of the preservation and continuance of that existence. For its preservation is for His sake. It is the outflowing, the presupposition and the consequence of the grace which God gave to the creature in His Son, and it takes place in order that in the creaturely world God may be glorified in and through His Son. It can be, and indeed it must be, because He is. This is what makes the preservation of the creature a divinely meaningful and a divinely effective work. Its wisdom and power consist in the fact that it has its basis in Jesus Christ the only beloved Son of God, and therefore in God Himself. It takes place as and because God the Father is (in His Son) for the creature. For that reason and in that sense it is the work of His fatherly lordship and therefore the work of real, genuine, authentic and true lordship, a work which in its holy mercy is quite different from the self-seeking care of the owner for the preservation of his possession, and in its holy freedom quite different from the logical necessity with which a given B is maintained by a given A, a given effect by a given cause. It is the love of God which preserves the creature. This preserving is not, therefore, by chance. It is purposeful at the deepest possible level. It is not menaced by any external circumstances. It is a perfect act of lordship. Whatever we may say by way of definition and description, it must always be measured by the fact that we are dealing with this act of fatherly lordship, and therefore with an act of the eternal God.

We may aptly take as our starting point the Pauline ἐξ αὐτοῦ τὰ πάντα (Rom. 11³⁶), which not only looks back to the act of creation but in so doing envisages the whole continuance of the universe as it derives from God, upon the basis of His effective preservation. Yet we must not interpret the phrase according to the sense which it originally bore in the non-Christian source from which Paul perhaps adapted it, but according to the sense in which Paul himself— baptising as it were an originally non-Christian expression—takes and uses it in this particular context, that is, in the thought of the mystery of the existence and history and future of Israel in relation to those who had hitherto been τὰ ἔθνη. According to the similar passage in I Corinthians 8⁶ the αὐτός from whom all things have their being is the εἷς θεὸς ὁ πατήρ; and it is the same in the famous and relevant saying in the speech at Athens : ἐν αὐτῷ γὰρ ζῶμεν καὶ κινούμεθα καὶ ἐσμέν, a saying which is clearly of non-Christian derivation, but which, in relation to all the θεῖον native to a world still hostile to Jesus Christ and needing the service of men's hands, either Paul or the author of Acts now uses in order to indicate the perfect rule of God over all creatures as fulfilled in the sending and raising again of Jesus Christ, and also the dependence of all creatures upon Him as the Sustainer of all things. In Hebrews 1³, where the reference is to the One who upholds all things by the Word of His power, it cannot be denied that it is the Son of God who does this. The God of whom it is said in Isaiah 40²⁶ that He " bringeth out the hosts of heaven by number : he calleth them all by names by the greatness of his might, for that he is strong in power ; not one faileth "—that God is the God of Israel, a God who is basically different from all other gods or idols. And undoubtedly it is the same God of whom David so truly says in 1 Chronicles 29¹¹ᶠ· : " For all that is in the heaven and in the earth is thine ; thine is the kingdom, O Lord, and thou art exalted as head above all. Both riches and honour come of thee, and thou reignest over all ; and in thine hand is power and might ; and in thine hand it is to make great, and to give strength unto all." And more precisely in Nehemiah 9⁶ᶠ· : " Thou preservest them all ; and the host of heaven worshippeth thee. Thou art the Lord the God, who didst choose Abram, and broughtest him forth out of Ur of the Chaldees, and gavest him the name of Abraham." And we must not forget Psalm 104²⁷ᶠ· : " These wait all upon thee ; that thou mayest give them their meat in due season. That thou givest them they gather : thou openest thy hand, they are filled with good. Thou hidest thy face, they are troubled ; thou takest away their breath, they die, and return to their dust. Thou sendest forth thy spirit, they are created : and thou renewest the face of the earth." And similarly in Psalm 36[6f.] : " Thou preservest man and beast. How excellent is thy loving-kindness, O God, therefore the children of men put their trust under the shadow of thy wings." And more precisely again in Psalm 73[23] : " Nevertheless I am continually with thee : thou hast holden me by my right hand. Thou shalt guide me with thy counsel, and afterwards receive me to glory." It is clear that these are not merely general thoughts concerning the dependence of the creature on the Creator and the care of the Creator for the creature—although they certainly are that, and have to be taken into account in the present context—but they are the concrete reflections of the great saving fact of the incredible and unmerited preservation of the people Israel, by which it is at once apparent and revealed who it is that maintains the existence of the creature as such, the creature Israel in its fields and its vineyards, and also with what goodness He does so. If we were to overlook the concrete reference of the Old as well as the New Testament passages to the history of salvation—to the extent that this is possible in the case of some of them—we should rob them of their general meaning and relevance. It is only in appearance that they say something which can be and is in fact said in other spheres of religious history. They have their true significance and substance from the biblical context, whose explicit witness makes it unnecessary to look further afield in the case of almost all the passages here adduced.

By treating of God's providence primarily in terms of His divine preserving of the creature we are following the order of the older dogmatics. But on the basis already laid down we have already given to it a point which it does not have in the older dogmatics, for we differentiate between the God who sustains the creature and a mere supreme being, identifying that sustaining God with the God of the biblical revelation. It is significant that we should begin with the important recognition that the one God the Father is the One to whom all things owe and will always owe not merely their continuance but even the fact that they are there at all. The fact that God is for the creature, that in His own creaturely existence He becomes the pledge and guarantee of its creaturely existence, is the presupposition of the fact that He is also with and above the creature, and of all that as the Lord of the covenant of grace He wills to be towards it in the work and revelation of Jesus Christ. The recognition that of His free and unmerited goodness, and therefore with the highest degree of certainty, God and God alone guarantees the existence of the creature, its being and nature and the whole expression of its life—this belongs indeed to the very beginning of the doctrine of the divine providence.

The traditional concept of *conservatio* contains the right idea. It speaks of preservation in being, of the maintaining of that which is, against the threat of dissolution. The *Leidener Synopsis* (1624, *Disp.* 11, 12) uses the expression *permansio*, by which it obviously means the abiding faithfulness of God towards the creature. Another expression occasionally used is *manutenentia*, which has all the richness of late Latin and yet is clear in content. With respect to the commonly used *conservatio* A. Heidan (*Corp. Theol. chr.*, 1686, p. 359) observes that it is not altogether a happy choice because it carries with it the idea of co-operation and therefore of a twofold *servatio*, whereas neither first nor last can there ever be any question of another *servator* side by side with God. But perhaps a more relevant question is whether the word *con-servatio* should not be construed and taken with all seriousness in the sense that in the *servare* which is here envisaged we may well have to do with a *servare* which is subordinate to another and true *servare*, that is, with the external and additional grace of the preservation of the creature which necessarily corresponds to the internal and genuine grace of redemption in Jesus Christ. In the 17th century no one thought of this explanation of the *cum*, but in so far as we have to explain it we can obviously do so only along these lines.

1. We will now consider in what sense we have to understand the statement that God preserves the creature. At first sight the answer seems to be quite simple. He arranges that it has its reality not only outside and beside Him in a moment which corresponds to His eternity (only to be snuffed out again), but also in a temporal sequence, so that it can have it again and again, thus enjoying a continuing existence. If God maintains the creature, then it is clear that there is no creaturely moment corresponding to His eternity. According to the first biblical record, did not the fashioning of the creature take place with the creation of time, and therefore within time? But the statement that God preserves the creature means much more than that He gave it time. When He created it, He might well have given it time in order not to preserve it indefinitely, but to set an early end to its being with the time which He created with it. But if He really sustains it, this means that He gives it more time, that He confirms it in its being in time. In the same way that He willed and gave it to the creature to become and to be, so He wills and gives it to the creature to be again and again, to continue to be. This is how he preserves it. And He preserves it as is fitting that He the Creator should preserve it, and that the creature should be preserved by Him. He preserves it eternally. He does not allow His creation to perish. He keeps faith with the creature. And yet He does not preserve it illimitably, but within the limits which correspond to its creaturely existence. The fact that He preserves is not exclusive but inclusive. Not merely creaturely individuals but the creaturely species and forms are all limited, as is indeed the creaturely world in its totality. Everything has its own time, and no more than that time. And the appointment of such a time shows that its being, and all created being as such, is a limited being. To no creature does it belong to be endless, omnipresent or enduring. The preservation which God grants to the creature is the preservation of its limited being. In its totality this preservation relates to a space which is limited, and in its eternity to a time which is limited. It will be understood that it is not for this reason partial, transitory or imperfect. Indeed, for this very reason it is a complete and final and perfect preservation. For what could be more perfect than that God should give to the creature—to individuals, and species and forms, and the whole creaturely world—that which is proper to it, that to each one He should give that which is proper, that is, that which it is able to

have of being, and of space and time for that being, according to
its existence as posited by the wisdom and power of God, and that
which it ought to have of being and space and time according to the
righteousness and mercy of God ? It is in this way and this way
alone that in the biblical sense the divine preserving is a divine work
and the preservation of the creature a divine favour.

For the creature to have its part in that history in which God
displays His grace, and finally in the kingdom of Jesus Christ, it
must continue to be there, and therefore it must be preserved. It
must have a continuing existence in space and time ; not of course
an unlimited but a limited existence. Creaturely history can take
place only amongst and on behalf of a plurality of many subjects
which exist side by side with and in succession to each other. A
creature which had an infinite existence would as such be excluded
from the history of the covenant of grace which is the meaning of all
creaturely occurrence. A preservation which consisted in extending
the being of creation to infinity would certainly not be the work of
God, who as the Preserver of the creature is also the Lord of the
covenant of grace and of the history of the covenant. And it would
certainly not be a benefit on the part of God. It is with a definite
limitation that the Creator who is also the Lord of the covenant
must preserve the creature, and it is with a definite limitation that the
creature must be preserved by the Creator. And if it is asked whether
a preservation which relates to a finite creature and is therefore
itself finite can be a genuine and serious and full preservation, the
answer is that its fulness is seen in the connexion in which it takes
place. And this connexion is as follows. It is an eternal and divine,
but also an external and additional preservation of being, which is
complementary to that internal and proper preservation which is by
participation in the kingdom of Jesus Christ, in whom there is given
to the creature—to the individual, the species and forms, and the
whole of creation—even within the limits of time and space the most
genuine and serious and full preservation, namely, that which is
ordained and promised in fellowship with the perfect and eternal
being of God.

It is surprising that in their doctrine *De conservatione* the older dogmaticians
did not feel more strongly the difficulty which lies in the fact that the divine
preservation of the creature obviously has a limit even in relation to creation
as a whole, let alone the individual or the forms or species ; that everything as it
now is will some day only have been. The problem was of course touched on
occasionally and in part. *Creaturam . . . libere conservat, quamdiu ipsi placet. . .
individua conservat in esse semper, dum sunt, non ad semper sive ut semper sint,*
writes Quenstedt (*Theol. did. pol.*, 1685, I, 13, sect. 1, *th.* 14). And perhaps
P. van Mastricht (*Theor. pract. Theol.* 1698, III, 10, 8 f.) had in mind the eschatological problem of the end of the world when he defined the *conservatio* as the
action *qua persistere Deus res omnes facit, quamdiu sibi videtur,* or negatively as
Dei voluntas, qua res ad illud usque tempus et non ulterius existat. But we are

not told to what extent this limitation of the *conservatio* may not signify an imperfection of the divine act, a limitation and therefore a denial of the faithfulness of the Creator to the creature. They could portray quite impressively the mighty divine *sustentare* of all things, but is it an act of the eternal and perfect God or is it not ? And if it is, how can it have an end ? Thomas Aquinas was occupied by this problem and the explanation which he gave is rather tortuous (*S. th.* I, *qu.* 104, *art.* 4, *ad.* 2). There derives from one and the same sustaining God a *contrarium agens* which prevents many although not all creatures (he is probably thinking of the immortal soul) from participating in the power of the divine preservation granted to them, and therefore from being preserved eternally. Although everything (both individually and collectively) has its time and some day will only have been, the sustaining love itself has no such limits and is therefore unceasing. As we have tried to show, this fact is reflected in the presupposition that the being of all things as preserved by God is correlated to the history of the divine covenant of grace. To recall *Conf. Aug.* VIII in this connexion : *Item docent, quod una sancta ecclesia perpetuo mansura sit,* is to see that there is no problem in the limitation of created being as such. And according to the *Heidelberg Catechism, Qu.* 54, in and with the knowledge " that out of the whole human race, from the beginning to the end of the world, the Son of God, by His Spirit and Word, gathers, defends and preserves for Himself unto everlasting life, a chosen communion in the unity of the true faith," we can have the direct and comforting assurance that " I am, and forever shall remain, a living member of the same."

Hence we may see that there is no contradiction between the death and end and passing of the individual and of creation as a whole, and its eternal preservation by God. For in its relationship to Jesus Christ, in its participation in the continuing history of His people from the beginning of the world to the end, each in its limited time and space can receive and enjoy its own perfectly satisfying participation in eternal life in fellowship with God. It does not have anything more than a finite preservation. Only in that finite preservation can it participate in the history of Jesus Christ and His people, and therefore in eternal life. But the older dogmatics could not deduce this line of thought from its presuppositions, and therefore it was unable to meet or even face the difficulty which confronted it at this point. Hence its praise of the faithfulness and constancy of God as the Preserver of all things, however sincerely meant, could not but fail to ring entirely true.

2. We enquire further concerning the order of the divine preserving of all things, and after full consideration we must reply that it takes place wholly and utterly as a free act of God, but in such a way that creation itself is the means by which it is preserved in being : the human body by the soul which directs it ; the human soul by the body which serves it ; the race as a whole and all the species of beasts and plants by natural propagation ; the individual by his human and cosmic environment ; and every creaturely thing by its environment and according to the particular order of that environment. God Himself sustains the creature, but He sustains it in the context in which He has created it and ordains that it should exist. That God preserves the creature means properly speaking that He preserves this context of its being and that He preserves it in this context. At this point we are confronted by an important formal distinction between the activity of God in His providence, and His activity as Creator on the one hand and as Lord of the covenant of grace on the

other. In creation God acts directly, i.e., without the intervention of other things, for other things could enter in only as the product of His creative activity and not as the co-efficient of it—not even as a pure means. And the creative work of God has this in common with His work of grace—that when God calls Abraham, when He elects Israel, when He leads Israel through the Red Sea, when He awakens the prophets, when He causes Jesus Christ to be born of the Virgin and to die for the salvation of the world and to rise again from the dead to reveal that salvation, when in the whole course of these happenings He heaps up miracle on miracle, when He sanctifies water in baptism and bread and wine in the Lord's Supper, when He gathers and protects and sustains His Church, when the Holy Spirit calls a man by the Gospel, and sanctifies him and preserves him in a true faith, all these things take place within the created order with the very same immediacy as the act of creation itself, and creation is now as fully the object of His activity as it was then its product. But when it is a matter of the preservation of creation as such, when it is a matter of that which succeeds creation but precedes redemption, there is need of a free but obviously not of a direct or immediate activity on the part of God. In order to continue in being subsequent to creation and with a view to redemption, all that the creature needs is the preservation of the context of its being and its own preservation within that context, a context which was created by God in order that the individual might have its permanence and stability and continuity within the whole, and the whole within the individual, according to the will and ordination of God.

But again, if we are to see how necessary this matter is, we have to consider the significance acquired by creaturely existence within the divine covenant of grace. For there is more to be said than that within this covenant the creature can be only the object of the divine activity, nor is this the positive side of the matter. For in so far as the creature is the object of the divine activity and the recipient of the grace of God, it becomes *ipso facto*, not the means of this grace, for grace works directly or not at all, but its witness and herald and proclaimer. Thus even in the utter humility of its spiritual existence it acquires an active function within the history of the covenant. It has a mission to fulfil, or a commission to execute, a mission or commission to its fellow-creatures. Abraham becomes the father of Isaac and Jacob and therefore the forefather of Jesus Christ. Israel becomes a light of the Gentiles. The prophets are not prophets to themselves but to their people. Jesus Christ had to become man to represent as man all other men. The biblical miracles, and later baptism and the Lord's Supper, are signs of the work and revelation of God. The Church is either a missionary Church or it is no church at all. And Christians are either the messengers of God (with or without words) to both Jew and Gentile or else they are not Christians at all. Within the very covenant of grace in which, as in creation, we have to do wholly and utterly with the direct initiative and activity of God to the creature, there at once arises, and again wholly and utterly, a relationship of creature and fellow-creature, and creatures themselves are marked and singled out for the service of God towards other creatures. It is a purely spiritual relationship in which God Himself acts directly, and the creature can only point other creatures to that divine work and testify concerning it, but cannot in any way advance or mediate that work. And yet there can be no doubt that the relationship which we discern here is also a creaturely relationship. Even the covenant of grace both consists and is spiritually renewed and sustained in a creaturely nexus of this kind. God acts directly in the great complex of the covenant history as it takes place in the creaturely world, beginning in Israel and continuing in the Church. He does not act by means of creation, but He certainly does not act apart from it. He acts towards it and within it. And the spiritual relationship of the creature in the covenant of grace is the dominant pattern or type of what God does when He preserves creation as such in being. God maintains its existence in a way which is not parallel but corresponds to the significance which it acquires in this covenant. He does this by maintaining the context of the being created by Him, and by maintaining all being created by Him within this context. The context, and itself within this context, is the means to the preservation of the creature. In the covenant of grace the creature is not the means but only the witness and sign, the liturgical assistant as it were to God, who is the only effective Minister. But when it is a question of its preservation here, with a view to what it is to become in the sphere of grace, here in the midst between creation and redemption the creature is a means both for God on the one hand and for itself on the other—always presupposing, of course, that God the Creator wills to use it as such. Its actual preservation is no less the free act of God because in this case He acts indirectly and not directly. Hence it is not really the creature which sustains the creature. It is not the context of the whole which guarantees the continuance of the individual, nor is it the individual which guarantees the continuity of the whole. And there can be no question of the creature being able even vicariously to do in its own strength that which God wills it to do. It is God alone who does everything according to His own free good-pleasure. But He does it by maintaining this relationship and therefore by maintaining the creature, by means of the creature. If we note the correlation between His work here and His work within the covenant of grace we shall be kept from the error of regarding either the creature or its nexus as the sustaining principle of creation. As we consider His work within the covenant we shall be constantly aware of the fact that His indirect work here in the nexus of being is no less His free decision than is His direct work there in that other and spiritual nexus. And even here in the nexus of being we shall not see anyone else at work save God Himself, not to mention the fact that we shall always distinguish sharply between the nexus of being which is the means and the One who uses this means.

When we say this, we are in some degree following Thomas Aquinas (*S. th.*, I, *qu.* 104, *art.* 2) in his treatment of the question : *Utrum Deus immediate omnem creaturam conservet ?* His answer is as follows : No, He does not preserve creation directly, but *Deus conservat res quasdam in esse mediantibus aliquibus causis.* The crucial objection which he has to meet is that if God is *immediate creator omnium* then of necessity He is *immediate* the *conservator* of all things. And his answer is as follows : *Deus immediate omnia creavit : sed in ipsa rerum creatione ordinem in rebus instituit, ut quaedam ab aliis dependerent, per quas secundario conservarentur in esse, praesupposita tamen principali conservatione, quae est ab ipso (ad 1).* It will be seen that Thomas did not intend this *conservatio secundum ordinem* to apply to the whole of created reality, but only to a part, the other part being obviously reserved as the object of a *conservatio immediata.* In the context it is not definitely stated, but it is also not excluded, that by the part to which he was not referring (according to our reading) he meant that which belongs to the particular activity of the saving grace of God. At all events it was merely the caprice of a temporally conditioned natural philosophy which led Petrus van Mastricht (*loc. cit.*) to take a different path, specifying something very different, *quaedam immaterialia* (the heavens, the *materia prima*, the elements), as the object of a direct divine preservation in contradistinction to the rest of creation.

It was R. A. Lipsius (*Lehrb. d. ev. prot. Dogm.*[2], 1879, p. 394 f.) who on the other side pressed the concept of *conservatio mediata* to the absurd length of identifying the sustaining activity of God with the uniformity which rules in all things, and conversely of regarding the uniformity which we cannot yet perceive in its totality as the constant expression of the divine will of preservation. This is only typical of the total sacrifice which the Liberal theology of the 19th century felt that it must make to the spirit of the age—in the case of Lipsius perhaps to his Jena colleague Ernst Haeckel. But in making it he allowed two evident errors to creep in : 1. that we understand the nexus of being of all created things (what Thomas described as the *ordo* by which one thing is dependent on another) quite one-sidedly and therefore falsely if we understand it only from the standpoint of the uniform interconnexion of all being and events, for, as the (in this respect) far wiser older theology almost universally maintained, it has also the aspect of contingence in which all things must be considered according to their freedom ; and 2. that even if we do understand the creaturely nexus of being more comprehensively, its identification with the divine preservation involves a bland surrender of the concepts God and creation. For the identification of the divine preservation with the creaturely nexus means a flat denial of the fact that this nexus is not grounded upon or maintained by itself, but has over it an independent Lord and Sustainer. And it is a poor expedient when all that the religious understanding can do is to interpret as an act of divine preservation that which otherwise would have to be regarded merely as the foundation and preservation of the world by itself. To make a more cautious distinction and to interpret the ἐξ αὐτοῦ primarily as a sign of lordship above the τὰ πάντα, we do not need to overlook and deny the significance and power of the nexus which God created, of the *ordo* which has to be understood not only as a uniform process but also as a free movement, nor do we need to overlook and deny the constant, relative and immanent preservation of the creature by the creature. Augustine saw his way clearly at this point : *Sunt qui arbitrentur tantummodo mundum ipsum factum a Deo, cetera iam fieri ab ipso mundo sicut ille ordinavit et iussit, Deum ipsum autem nihil operari. Contra quos profertur illa sententia Domini : Pater meus usque modo operatur* (Joh. 5¹⁷) . . . *sic ergo credamus, vel, si possumus etiam intelligamus, usque nunc operari Deum, ut, si conditis ad eo rebus operatio eius subtrahatur, intercidant.* He says this, and yet he does not fail to see that to all things, to angels and stars and winds and seas and the animal world and human history, God has lent the specific form on whose basis they have their own specific movement (*De Gen. ad lit.* 5,20). He says this, and yet his view of the relation of God to the creature is as follows : *Implet Deus coelum et terram praesente potentia, non absente natura. Sic itaque administrat omnia, quae creavit, ut etiam ea proprios exercere et agere motus sinat.* And J. Gerhard (who was also of Jena) reasons as follows : Nothing is more natural to man than to move of himself, *et tamen in Deo movemur* (Acts 17²⁸). Nothing is more natural for the sun than to rise day after day, and yet it is God who causes it to rise (Mt. 5⁴⁵). And this is how we have to understand Matthew 4⁴ (" Man doth not live by bread alone ") : Even bread has no power to nourish in the sense that it could do so apart from the Word of God by which it was created and has its power to nourish, but in order to exercise this property it needs the continual influence (*influxus*) of the creative and sustaining Word of God. Similarly neither herbs and prepared medicines nor the physician who administers them can of themselves and as such heal a man, but only the hand of God present within them (*Loci*, 1610, VI, 6).

In short, even in the indirectness in which it is undoubtedly fulfilled, the preservation of the creature must still be regarded as an action of God as He freely disposes of the whole mediation of the creature, an action which is not conditioned by this mediation but on the contrary conditions it. In practice the older theology held fast to this truth, and when it referred to the " hand " or " Word " of God in this context, and quoted the text John 5¹⁷, it came very near to giving to this decisive insight a certainty which, if it had been present and active at a later date, would have made quite impossible any defection along the lines of R. A. Lipsius. In the light of the fatherly sovereignty of God in the kingdom of Jesus Christ, in which the meaning of creaturely existence is manifested in its office as a witness to fellow-creatures of the grace of God, the identification of this existence with God the Father, and of the sustaining power of this existence with the sustaining power of God, is basically excluded. But if we cease to look to this sovereignty, ignoring the correlation between the means of being and the spiritual nexus of creation, we may refrain from this identification, as did the older theology both unanimously and resolutely, but it is not basically excluded. In these circumstances the prohibition of the identification of the preserving of the Creator with that of the creature has no compelling force. It does not have the force of a conclusion *a maiori ad minus*. And it is to this weakness of the " orthodox " position that we have here to draw attention in spite of our respect for all the faithfulness which it displayed in practice.

3. It has been rightly said that the *modus* of the divine preservation is inconceivable. It is inconceivable because we can understand it only as an act of the free goodness of God. God does not owe it to the creature to preserve it, to give to it continuance, and to give to its continuance time. He did not owe it to the creature to create it. When He did create it, He might well have caused it to exist only in that moment and then not to exist any longer. His perfect will— and it would still have to be regarded as good—might well have been fulfilled towards the creature in that way. That He willed it otherwise, that He has willed to preserve the creature thus far, and that He

obviously wills to preserve it further, is an overflowing of His free love and therefore of His incomprehensibility. But since this overflowing does actually take place, we have to reckon with the fact that the preservation of the creature is in accordance with His good-pleasure and therefore with His holy being, for in God there is no caprice. God is, and is good, in such a way, and His goodness is inconceivable in the fact, that He wills to preserve the creature, to fulfil His will towards it in its permanence and continuity. And for this reason when we are face to face with the work of God there is always room for surprise and wonder and praise and thanksgiving. The election which God already made and executed when He created the creature was not a transitory, let alone a capricious election. It was God's eternal election, and it is confirmed to be such in the work of His eternal preservation of the creature. And this confirmation—at which we can never sufficiently marvel—is the modus of His preservation. God does not cease but continues to be to the creature the One who eternally elects, and who upon the basis of this election has already created it.

We cannot say that He continues to create it. That is unnecessary, for it has already been created, and created well. If He were to create it afresh with every moment of time, as has been suggested, this would not merely presuppose an imperfection in the original creation but it would also involve in some measure its continual dissolution and complete renewal, so that its continuing existence would consist in a permanent fluctuation between life and death and life, between being and non-being and being.

This view can have its attractions, for not only do we find something like it in the mystical teaching of all ages and countries, but also (it may be) in the thought expressed by Goethe in the poem entitled " One and All " (1821) :

> " And to create anew that which is created,
> That it might not arm itself to immobility,
> This is the task of unending, living activity.
> And that which was not will now become
> Clear sun and coloured earth ;
> But it can never rest.
> It must arise in creative action,
> First forming and then transforming itself ;
> Only in appearance can it ever stand.
> The eternal moves forward in all things,
> For everything must dissolve into nothingness,
> If it is to continue in being."

In the poem entitled " Testament " (1828) Goethe with the wisdom of old age did of course place alongside this teaching a relative—but very relative !— *sed contra* :

> " No being can dissolve into nothingness !
> The eternal moves forward in all things,
> Consider yourself blessed in being ! "

Being is eternal : for laws
Protect the living treasures
By which the cosmos is adorned."

There can be no question that in these two poems, as a close analysis would show, he is not really contradicting himself, but, as is quite possible within his total conception of things, he is simply saying the same thing in two different ways. It was certainly not intentional when, in contradistinction to the corresponding line of the one poem, in the first line of the other he made a statement which is patent of a Christian interpretation. And the contention that in both poems he consciously foreshadowed poetically the law of the conservation of energy as discovered in the latter half of the 19th century (cf. E. v. d. Hellen, *Jub.-Ausg.* 2, 352) definitely overlooks what was for Goethe both that which preserves and also that which is preserved.

The understanding of divine preservation as a series of acts of creation, and the consequent notion of a divine constant in the flux of the being and non-being of creation, cannot possibly be right, for in such an idea the very thing upon which everything turns at this point in the Christian doctrine of preservation, the identity of the creature in its continuity, is wrapped in an unrecognisable obscurity if not completely destroyed. This is true even though it is a question of its continuity outwith identity, and not its non-continuity.

The " continuance in change " of which Goethe speaks was stated by him under this title in an older poem (c. 1800) which treats of the passing and transitoriness of all phenomena :

" Let the beginning and the end
Come together in one !
Let thyself flow past
More swiftly than circumstances !
Give thanks that the Muses' favour
Promises thee the immortal :
The content in thy bosom,
And the form in thy spirit."

And similarly in the original words of the poem of 1817 entitled " Daemon " (according to his own commentary Goethe means by this the necessary, finite and unchangeable individuality of the person) :

" As on the day which lent thee to the world,
The sun stood still at the greeting of the planets,
Thou didst at once and constantly increase,
According to the law by which thou didst begin,
So must thou be, thou canst not escape thyself,
Thus did the Sibyls and the prophets speak,
And neither time nor force can ever mar
The form already stamped in its living growth."

And similarly in the famous protest against Albrecht von Haller's distinction between the kernel and husk in nature :

" Nature has neither kernel,
Nor husk,
It is all things all at once.
Consider yourself first of all,
Whether you are kernel or husk ! "—

taken together with the closing words of Goethe's " Ultimatum "

> " Is not the kernel of the nature
> Of men in the heart ? "

The decisive verse in the superficially contradictory " Testament " of 1828 is in complete agreement :

> " Enjoy in measure fulness and blessing ;
> Reason is always present
> When life rejoices in life,
> For the past is constant,
> The future lives in advance—
> The instant is eternity."

Bernhard Groethuysen (cf. *Evang. Theologie*, 1948, p. 256) has given us a fine and pertinent restatement of Goethe's position. Man must not try to transcend himself if he is to be truly himself. What then ? " I will constantly rediscover myself. I will be myself. There is only one life, the life of Goethe. There is nothing outside, everything is within. And everywhere you encounter yourself. You never escape yourself. You never escape your own life." There is no question of not being to-day the man I was yesterday. " I am to-day what I was yesterday and will be to-morrow. Looking back, I see myself, and I converse with the man I was. Are not he and I and the countless others which I once was all united in the same life ? It was the life of childhood, and the life of old age, but both reach out to one another. The old man has not destroyed the child. Look, it plays there still." Is it a terrible thought that there is no continuance, only change ? On the contrary, " If I remained as I am, how could I be myself ? Should I be alive at all if nothing changed either within or without ? " This abiding element may in some sort be equated with the root of the soul which according to the teaching of the mystics is timelessly constant in its union with God even in the flux of phenomena. And in the last analysis may it not be that this view leads us to that of the moment in which the world created by God might have existed and not existed had God so willed ? Supposing God only dreamed the creature ? Or supposing a creature like God only dreamed its fellow-creatures—dreamed them in Goethe's sense, in what was for that god-like creature the most glorious and fruitful and constructive way ? The company into which we are betrayed when we accept a *creatio continuata* is no recommendation. Its charms must therefore be resisted. We must pay heed to the somewhat isolated objection which G. Thomasius (*Christi Person und Werk*, I, 1886, p. 146) once made to the application of this concept, that it destroys the limit laid down by Genesis 2² and Hebrews 4⁴, and that consistently carried through it threatens to change into a mere appearance both the context of the creature and also the whole process of its existence. And it is a matter for surprise that a man like J. Coccejus (*S. theol.*, 1662, 28, 12 f.) did not perceive this, but like many others espoused the concept with some enthusiasm.

Leaving this view, we understand the *modus* of the divine preservation of the creature to be simply that God willed to be faithful to the eternal election of the creature which He made prior to creation and in which He ascribed to it its being and content and existence, and that even when the work of creation was finished He was faithful and will always be faithful to it. In relation to the creature He does not cease to acknowledge His obligation to that eternal election and to the act of creation grounded upon it. He does not repent of having associated with Himself the created cosmos, or of having associated Himself with that cosmos, of having made Himself co-existent with it, and to that extent (that is, in that context) of having made Himself cosmic and human, as we read in the story of His Sabbath rest. He does not repent of having surrendered Himself to this attachment to the creature. The fact that He does not repent, that He wills to be and to remain to the creature that which in its creation He became and was, is His overflowing goodness in the preservation of the creature. We must reiterate that it is His free and unmerited goodness. Its basis is revealed only in the election of grace from which the election of the creature and therefore its preservation derives; and how should it not be revealed, in all its inconceivability, in that election, in Jesus Christ? It is therefore the majesty of God which is active in this His goodness. This is what makes His preserving effective. This is the guarantee that He who wills to preserve us can accomplish that which He wills, as an almighty God. And the almightiness of God is neither obscure nor capricious. There is no other majesty but that of His goodness. This is what makes His preserving reliable. It is the guarantee that He who alone can preserve us will in fact preserve us, as a trustworthy Father. If we describe the preservation of the creature as a divine act, a divine work which is done to it, a divine power which is given to it, we must be quite clear that by this we mean simply that God continues to be to the creature this God, the God who on the basis of the election of grace elects it to its own specific being and existence. It is preserved in virtue of the fact that He is this God. In the fact that He is this God the act or work of preservation takes place.

Augustine spoke boldly but quite accurately of the *stabilis motus* of this preservation (*De Gen. ad lit.* 5,20). Anselm of Canterbury (*Monol.*, 13) described it as a *servatrix praesentia*. And Thomas Aquinas expanded as follows : *conservatio rerum a Deo non est per aliquam novam actionem, sed per continuationem actionis qua dat esse ; quae quidem actio est sine motu et tempore* (*S. theol.*, I, qu. 104, *ad* 4).

On this living and trustworthy basis in God Himself, it is decided, and continually decided, that the creature may have permanence and continuity. Without this living and trustworthy basis in God Himself, without the continuity in which God continually abides by His election, by His free but overflowing goodness, and finally, without the election of His grace which is the basis of His goodness, the creature could not and would not continue. But the living and trustworthy basis in God continues, and therefore the creature continues. Because of God it cannot not continue ; it cannot perish.

Thomas Aquinas (*S. th.*, I, qu. 104, *art* 3–4) advanced the following consideration in relation to this aspect of the problem. The question is rightly put : *Utrum Deus possit aliquid in nihilum redigere ?* And we must answer in the affirmative : God had the power to do this. The preservation of the creature is just as much a matter of the free good-pleasure of God as its creation. Only if the existence and therefore the creation of the world were necessary for God (which they are not) could we answer the question in the negative. We cannot even appeal to the goodness of God, as though God were under some constraint either to or by that goodness to preserve the creature. For if the goodness of God is the basis of all things, it is so, not *ex necessitate naturae*, as though God had need of the created order, but *per liberam voluntatem*. Hence the goodness of God could be withdrawn from the created order without in any way ceasing to be perfect goodness. The matter is quite different if we ask : *Utrum aliquid in nihilum redigatur ?* Put in this way, the question must be answered most definitely in the negative. God does in fact preserve all things, although he had the power not to do so. We see what Goethe might have meant (but did not) with his saying : " No being can dissolve into nothingness ! " when Thomas explains briefly (*simpliciter*) : *Quod nihil omnino in nihilum redigetur.* And we must take note when after various other arguments we come to his final statement : *Redigere aliquid in nihilum non pertinet ad gratiae manifestationem, cum magis per hoc divina potentia et bonitas ostendatur, quod res in esse conservat* : which seems to suggest that the undeniable freedom which God has not to preserve the creature but to allow it to perish is not compromised by the revelation of the freedom which He has actualised as the freedom of His grace. As demonstrated in practice, His power and might are better attested in the fact that He does maintain things in being. In this context, this is the only occasion that Thomas mentions the point, and he makes striking use of it. It is perhaps of a piece with these presuppositions that he is so sure of the matter. He was far more sure of it than was F. Burmann after him (*Syn. Theol.*, 1678, 1, 43, 17), who only believed that perhaps there could not be any *annihilatio* of anything that is—on the ground that God did not create any creature in vain—which is something that Burmann could not really know.

If we do not keep before us the living and trustworthy basis in God Himself, then either we cannot assert at all that His preservation of the creature is directly and eternally effective, that no being can perish, or else we can do so only in the form of a hazy surmise. It is the God who abides by His election of the creature, whose goodness overflows because it is in fact grounded in His election of grace, it is this God who sees to it that no creature can dissolve into nothingness. If the assertion is to be solidly grounded, it must relate to this God and it must be grounded in the work and revelation of this God. Related to any other god, or to a supreme being, it can never be made with certainty. And this means that to be made with certainty it must be a deduction from the primary assertion that for the sake of His Son God has elected the creature from all eternity, that in His Son he loves it eternally and that for the sake of His Son He will not allow it to perish. It must be an assertion grounded in the knowledge of the Father in the Son. Only in this form is it necessary or compelling. But in this form it is necessary and compelling. If the purpose of God in creation is the covenant of grace, then necessarily God gives to the creature an unshakeable continuity. We may go further and say that necessarily it cannot not have that continuity for the sake of God. And the necessary reminder that God is free to deprive it of that continuity then becomes an indispensable elucidation of the fact that His election of grace is an election of *grace*, His covenant of grace a covenant of *grace*, and that therefore any rights or claims which the creature might advance on the ground of its preservation are quite without foundation, are indeed completely excluded, as is the idea of an inward compulsion to which God in subjected in virtue of His Godhead, so that He has to preserve the creature. But taken seriously this reminder does not involve in any way a weakening or compromising but rather a constant deepening of the knowledge that, because the almighty God and trustworthy Father interceded for it with His own eternal being, the creature of God is indeed eternally hidden and kept and preserved in the whole temporal span of His eternal being. We have only to keep before us the living and trust-worthy basis of this knowledge in God himself, the *manifestatio gratiae*, Jesus Christ, and we can have complete certainty in the matter. Without this ontic basis everything would, of course, be quite different. And without the noetic presupposition we should be dealing with something quite different—or at any rate what we have said could not be said with any certainty or on any very adequate basis.

It is true that the affirmation with which we began, that the *modus* of the divine preservation is inconceivable, derives from F. Burmann (*h.c.* I, 43, 13), but again he establishes it somewhat inadequately : *cum operationes entis infiniti a natura finita plene percipi non possunt.* This is not the Christian basis and therefore it is not the effective basis which we have to lay. It is not as *ens infinitum* but in His grace that God is inconceivable, and He is so not to *natura finita* but to the man who glorifies His grace. That is why the fact of man's preservation, and of the preservation of the whole creaturely world, is inconceivable. But to man and to that world grace brings with it the unexpected and undeserved and unmerited fact of the free movement of the free God. It brings with it that which can be recognised as fatherly goodness but cannot be apprehended as such, i.e., that which cannot be deduced from anything higher, but simply accepted with thankfulness as a fact.

4. We must now take expressly into account the fact that the creature for its part stands in need of preservation by God and therefore of His free goodness. Its creation rested upon the free resolve of God ; it was God's free act. The creature was not from all eternity like God. There was a time when it was not. And God was not under any obligation to cause it to come into existence and to be. He created it " out of nothing," that is, by distinguishing that which He willed from that which He did not will, and by giving it existence on the basis of that distinction. To that divine distinction it owes the fact that it is. And to the same distinction it owes the fact that it can continue to be. By preserving the distinction God preserves the creature. It is a matter of its preservation, and we must now apply ourselves to the development of the concept *conservatio* and say that it is a matter of its being maintained against overthrow by that which is not. That which is not is that which God as Creator did not elect or will, that which as Creator He passed over, that which according to the account in Genesis 1² He set behind him as chaos, not giving it existence or being. That which is not is that

which is actual only in the negativity allotted to it by the divine decision, only in its exclusion from creation, only, if we may put it thus, at the left hand of God. But in this way it is truly actual and relevant and even active after its own particular fashion. At this point we touch on a whole complex of problems which we shall have to face more specifically in the next section of this chapter. It is a question of the reality which we can adequately describe only by defining it as the possibility which God in His eternal decree rejected and therefore did not and does not will, which has and can have its actuality only under the almighty No of God, but does have and is actuality in that sense. To this sphere there belongs the devil, the father of lies. To this sphere, too, there belongs the world of demons, and sin and evil and death—not death as a natural limitation but eternal death, the enemy and annihilator of life. The power of God extends even over this sphere, for apart from His creative act it certainly would never have had or been this negative actuality. And from all eternity judgment has been pronounced and executed upon it by God. But creation in itself and as such does not have this power over it and cannot pronounce or execute judgment upon it. Creation in itself and as such is menaced by it, menaced by the chaos which to some extent borders it, couching at the door. It was not creation itself which distinguished itself from chaos. Nor can creation itself maintain this distinction. It cannot, therefore, guard itself against chaos. It ought not to do so. It is appointed to live, not by itself, but by the grace of God, and to triumph by that grace over all its enemies and over all the enemies of that grace. It stands always— we are still speaking of creation in itself and as such—in unavoidable and mortal peril of falling a victim to those enemies, of being swallowed up by them, of itself becoming chaos. It is not God. It is the reality which is distinct from God, elected, willed and actualised by Him, but differentiated from Him, and therefore not participating in His sovereignty or in the freedom of His election and decision. And as such, if God did not will to save and keep it, it might well, indeed it must, be overwhelmed by chaos and fall into nothingness.

Necessarily, then, it rests in what Genesis 1³⁻⁹ describes as division, that is, the marking off and confirmation of light from darkness, of the waters above from the waters below, of the dry land from the sea, in a word, of the cosmos from chaos. Because the creature rests in this division, it is God who preserves it. Indeed, this passage might well be described as the biblical *locus classicus* for the doctrine with which we are now occupied. But the story of the flood (Gen. 6–8) and the plagues of Egypt (Ex. 7–11) and many other biblical contexts show that it is not at all self-evident that the creature should be preserved from the danger which threatens it. It would indeed be given up to it without a struggle if God were to turn away His face from it. For good or evil it is referred to the fact that God does not do so.

The older theology undoubtedly tried to make this point with all possible force. Augustine, for example, rightly (*De Gen. ad lit.* 4,12) thought that we must explain the ἐν αὐτῷ ἐσμέν of Acts 17²⁸ as signifying that we are in Him, not as though we were partakers of His essence, nor as though (according to John 5²⁶) we had life in ourselves, but *cum aliud sumus quam ipse, non ob aliud in illo sumus, nisi quia id operatur et hoc est opus eius, quo continet omnia.* Similarly Thomas (*loc. cit., art.* I c), in generalising an image applied by Augustine (*loc. cit.,* 8,12) to the justification and sanctification of man, finely amplified it as follows. The whole of creation is related to the preservation of God as is the atmosphere to the sun which illumines it. The sun illumines it in virtue of its essence. The atmosphere becomes bright because it partakes, not of the nature of the sun, but of its illumining. If the illumining were to cease, it would become dark. In the same way God alone is *ens per essentiam suam* ; the creature is only *ens participativum.* It can have continuity only as God gives it. There is a corresponding note in the Reformed theology of the 17th century. If the creature could maintain itself even for a single moment, this would mean that it is *a se* as God is, that it is eternal as God is, and therefore that it is a second God. But conversely, the fact that it is not this means that it cannot continue a single moment without God. Without God it would crumble away, just as a building whose main supports are removed must inevitably collapse. It needs the mighty hand of God to be able to continue (F. Burmann *loc. cit.,* 43, 8–10, 14). *Creaturae omnes, cum ex nihilo sint adeoque de nihilo participent . . . indigae virtutis alienae quocunque momento existunt* (H. Heidegger, *Corp. theol.,* 1700, quoted in Heppe², p. 208). And this *aliena virtus* can only be that of God *quinetiam tanta ad rem conservandam quanta ad creandam virtus requiritur* (Abr. Heidan, *Corp. theol. chr.,* 1686, I, p. 361).

All this is correctly perceived and logically inter-related, but are we left entirely free from the impression of a certain facility in this form of argumenta- tion ? And is it not of a piece that the very concept which ought to indicate that which menaces the creature and from which the creature can be preserved only by God, the concept of *nihil* as opposed to *essentia* and *esse,* is here under- stood and pressed only in a metaphysical and not a theological sense ? By definition a relative being cannot continue without an absolute being—and notwithstanding the reservation in respect of the divine freedom it may be that by definition an absolute being guarantees the continuance of a relative. But it has still to be asked whether the reference is really to God's preserving as we have it in Gen. 1². Does the creature's whole need consist in the fact that it is only *ens participativum* and therefore *participans de nihilo* and therefore depend- ent upon the *sustentare* of the *ens per essentiam suam* to which it owed its own *essentia* and *esse* ? We must not be unjust to Augustine and Thomas and our own older orthodox dogmaticians. In their expositions there is a certain agita- tion at this point which would hardly be commensurate with the problem as they almost forcefully mastered it, if by the *nihil* they had not instinctively at least envisaged something other than mere non-being in its formal antithesis to being. But they never consciously raised the question of that something other, the true *nihil,* as it arises in this connexion. Certainly they never made any pronouncements concerning it.

Of all the older theologians known to me it occurred to only one, Anselm of Canterbury, to describe the preserving activity or being of God not only as *conservare, sustentare, communicare, influere esse* and the like, but also at times (*Monol.,* 13 and 65, *De casu diab.,* 1) quite simply as *servare,* thus picturing it as a deliverance and indicating a preservation of the creature which has to be con- sidered seriously from the theological standpoint. And Anselm then proceded (*De casu diab.,* 1) to connect the fall of the devil, who according to him as to the older theology in general was originally an angel, with an exclusion from this divine *servare* which God did not owe to any of His creatures.

Why is it that the being of the creature is menaced by nothingness, menaced in such a way that it needs the divine preservation and sustaining and indeed deliverance if it is not to fall victim to it and perish ? Obviously it is menaced by something far more serious than mere non-being as opposed to being, although it is of course menaced by non-being too. But what makes non-being a menace, an enemy which is superior to created being, a threatened destroyer, is obviously not its mere character as non-being, but the fact that it is not elected and willed by God the Creator but rather rejected and excluded. It is that to which God said No when He said Yes to the creature. And that is chaos according to the biblical term and concept.

We have to do here with a concept which was lacking in the normative philosophy of the older Christian theologians. It was lacking because the outlook to which it corresponds was also lacking. And that outlook was lacking first and foremost because our present understanding of preservation and deliverance was necessarily unknown. If the older theology had filled out its admittedly not inapplicable concept of *nihil* from this understanding instead of taking it over in the purely formal sense from the normative philosophy of the time, it would have attained at this point to the more significant and serious conclusions which were certainly within its reach but to which it did not in fact attain.

What God has eternally denied, what is not willed by Him, constitutes that which is not, that which is empty, which is necessarily nothing. But in all its singularity the non-existent which is characterised as such by God, the shadow which flees before God, possesses everywhere in the Bible its own ponderable reality. God knows this nothing as the opponent of the creature, as that which may and can seduce and destroy the creature. God knows that under the dominion of this nothing the creature must perish. It is always present—as it were on the frontier of the cosmos to which He has given being. It continually calls this cosmos in question. It has mounted an offensive against it. If only for a moment God were to turn away His face from the creature, the offensive would break loose with deadly power. In its relation to God chaos is always an absolutely subordinate factor, but it is always absolutely superior in its relation to the creature.

The tremendous danger, the most serious peril, which the non-existent involves for the creature may be seen already in the fact that the non-existent is so utterly opposed, that it is so completely hostile, that it is such an absolute denial of the essence and existence of the creature. It is the very fact that it stands on the frontier of the creature, that it is on the frontier and yet itself not a creature, which makes it so strange to it. And it is in virtue of this fact that it appears to be similar to and even like God, perhaps a second god. And yet it is still nothing. But again, its strangeness and its appearance of god-likeness are not without serious foundation. For in its absolute opposition and hostility to the creature, in its very non-creatureliness, in the nothingness in which it borders on the creature and is to some extent its neighbour, it is not present by its own caprice, by a chance which is above both God and the creature and makes fools of them both, and therefore without God, but in a sense by means of God. Without God—in this case without His wrath and rejection and judgment—even nothing could not be present or of any power or consequence. It is present and of power and consequence because of the wrath of God. When in creation God pronounced His wise and omnipotent Yes He also pronounced His wise and omnipotent No. That is His wrath and rejection and judgment. He marked off the positive reality of the creature from that which He did not elect and will and therefore did not create. And to that which He denied He allotted the being of non-being, the existence of that which does not exist. God created light, approved it, divided it from darkness, and called it day, but the darkness He called night (Gen. 1^{3-5}). In the power—that is, the negative power— of this divine creating, approving, dividing and calling, there enters in with the creature that which in all these things is marked off from it, and it enters in with menacing power, the power of the denial of that which God has affirmed, as the non-being which does not exist, as that which is not created, as that which is so absolutely opposed and hostile to the creature, as that which is not, chaos. It is not an adversary to God, but only the shadow of His work which both arises and is at once dispelled by His wrath. But to the creature it is an adversary for which the creature as such is no match. To God it is no problem. But it is the radical problem which faces the creature. In face of God it has no power, but it has supreme power in face of the creature. As that which God has denied it has the tendency and power to negate the creature of God. It has the attractive force of a whirlpool—we are reminded of the power of a single minus placed before a bracket, which cannot be offset by any plus within the bracket—in whose eddyings the creature in itself and as such can only sink and perish. To set up of itself any effective opposition, to offer any real resistance, the creature would have to repeat the divine act of creating, approving, dividing and calling to which it owes its being and its distinctness from this sinister neighbour. It would need to maintain that distinctness and therefore that being. But the creature is not God, and therefore it is in no position to do this. And that which is denied and itself denies confronts it as something infinite. God elected and willed one thing. Therefore that which He did not elect and will, the non-existent, comprises the infinite range of all the possibilities which He passed over and with good reason did not actualise, the abyss in which the one thing which He did create must inevitably sink, the ocean by whose waves it must inevitably be overwhelmed, if He who created it did not also preserve and sustain it. If we could not count upon that, if there were no divine preserving and sustaining, then it would be the holy will of God first to utter a mighty Yes to a reality distinct from Himself, and then immediately to withdraw it by an even more mighty No, thus causing the light to perish as He caused it to arise. We should then have to understand creation, not as the work of a will which is finally gracious even in its wrath, but as that of a will which is finally wrathful even in its grace, of a will in which God conceived and executed the idea of a non-divine or creaturely reality only immediately to withdraw it, thus remaining completely alone—for the non-existent has no autonomy over against Him—in the activity of His inner life as He was from all eternity, and just as glorious in His isolation. There are some conceptions of God, and there have been even within the sphere of Christianity, which approximate to this understanding. But the creature lives by and is dependent upon the fact that in practice this understanding is false, that the holy will of God was not and is not and will not ever be a will of wrath, that although His Yes to creaturely reality is accompanied by a No, He still causes it to be and to continue to be a Yes, not giving to that which He has denied the power to carry through the denial of that which He has affirmed. This is one point at which our conception of the creature's need of preservation by God must be quite different from that of the older theology. The non-existent is a more dangerous factor, its menacing of the creature is greater, and the creature's need of the divine support and preservation is more penetrating, than the older theology could ever reveal, confined as it was by the outlook and language of its metaphysical basis.

But now we must draw attention to another aspect of the matter which unfortunately the older theology did not present either forcefully or feebly, but completely overlooked. Our starting-point must be the proposition that the assurance that God does preserve the creature in spite and in the midst of this great and immeasurable danger is not at all a self-evident one, but one which requires a serious basis if it is to be convincing and credible. For why should the idea of a creation of wrath be a false one ? We might put it in this way. God did at first will to preserve the creature even after creation, and He has done so for quite a time. But now He has had enough of us. Where formerly He exercised patience He now allows free rein to His wrath. He repents of having made the creature. He abandons it to the chaos towards which it always strove in spite of His patience. The creature is now threatened again by an *annihilatio* beyond which God will be alone again and glorious in Himself. The question must surely have presented itself in many periods and situations in the past, and it surely calls for further consideration at the present juncture, whether there are any specific reasons why this should not be the case.

And the only valid answer is that it is not so because according to the work and revelation of God in Jesus Christ it is not at all the will of God to abandon the creature in its proximity to the non-existent, in its conflict with chaos ; to withdraw to the secure height of His own remoteness from contradiction, and then (in consideration perhaps of its greater or lesser merit) to grant or not to grant it His assistance, preserving or not preserving it in its need. On the contrary, from all eternity—that is, in the eternal counsel of His grace as it is effective and revealed in Jesus Christ—His merciful will was to take up the cause of the creature against the non-existent, not from the safe height of a supreme world-governor, but in the closest possible proximity, with the greatest possible directness, i.e., Himself to become a creature. He placed Himself within the contradiction. He drew to Himself and bore away the whole enmity and problem and power of the non-existent. He tasted and suffered the whole onslaught of sin, the devil, death and hell, and in so doing He broke it, blunting its weapons and depriving it of all claim against the creature or superiority over it. He allowed Himself to be denied in order to remove the denial, thus completing the work of wrath but also the work of grace, uttering a complete No but also a complete Yes, and giving to the creature its freedom. This is the eternal will of God fulfilled and accomplished once and for all in time in Jesus Christ. And in the light of this will and work we have to regard the question of the *conservatio* of the creature as one which has already been decided. It does not stand in the obscurity of a hidden will of God which may be fulfilled in one way or may be fulfilled in another. It stands in the light of a will which has already been accomplished and revealed, of a *servatio* which has already been fulfilled. In this light the understanding of creation as a creation of the wrath of God can only disperse like a wisp of smoke, however seriously it may be presented. Certainly there is no other way of meeting the question whether it may not be so. But in this way it is completely met, for God does preserve the creature.

And in the light of this truth we can understand why and to what end He does so. The creature exists as the mercy of God operative in Jesus Christ is effective towards it, and in order that the glory of the beloved Son of God may be manifest in it. And this is why God preserves it. He does so because His representing of the creature is the beginning and centre and end of its existence. He does so because it has been promised and given to it to come to terms not with the non-existent, not with chaos, not with its own denial, but with God's gracious intercession for it. He does so because its destiny is to participate in this work of salvation. And for this participation it must be able to be ; it must have permanence and continuity. It must be preserved by God. God wills to be revealed and active in the created order. He wills to be glorified and honoured in this order because He frees it, because He deprives the non-existent of its power over it, because He prepares for this order freedom, the divine freedom which He Himself enjoys over that contradiction. God wills in this order a history, a history in which the share of freedom which it has already acquired—and for whom is it won if not for it ?—will be attested and proclaimed and seized and apprehended : the share in His denial of the non-existent ; the share in the sentence which He has pronounced upon it from all eternity ; the share in the judgment which in His counsel He has executed upon chaos from all eternity ; and above all, and positively, the share in His own eternal life, a life which is quite unthreatened because it is self-grounded and self-renewing. It is because God wills this history for this reason that He willed the creation and that He wills also the preservation of the creature. Because *servatio*, therefore *creatio* and therefore *conservatio*. For this history to take place the creature must have space and time and permanence. Because God wills the history He creates and gives it these things, and thus preserves the creature. At this point we can speak quite confidently of a necessary consequence and let go the restriction in favour of the divine freedom. The God who made use of His freedom to win for us salvation and liberation in Jesus Christ also wills and creates our preservation in the same freedom and for the same purpose of liberation. The *caveat* that had He so willed He might have acted otherwise is not only meaningless but most suspicious, for those who enter it may well have begun to turn their thoughts to another god than the One who in the work of Jesus Christ has revealed His whole heart and all the goodness of His Godhead.

And it is in the light of this fact that we can now give a serious theological answer to the question of the creature's need of pre-servation by God. This need has a more urgent and indeed a more profound basis than the older theology would ever allow. It does not consist in the first instance in the powerlessness of the creature in face of the non-existent. It cannot then be described or understood in the first instance only as a weakness, privation, or imperfection of the creature. It has its root in the foreordination of the creature to participation in the divine covenant of grace. Because it has to be present in the divine work of deliverance and liberation, it can therefore be present—present as a creature—in all the immeasurable perils in which it cannot preserve or sustain itself. In the light of this fore-ordination it is not simply a limitation or humiliation to be present only in this way, and therefore in need. If its destiny is to live of and by the grace of God, and if the fulfilment of this destiny is the unfolding and revealing of the honour and dignity and glory which it attains thereby, then what it attains, what is foreordained for it, is already reflected in its existence and the limitation and need of this existence. The fact that it is to partake of the *servatio* is proclaimed already in the fact that it needs the *conservatio* of its existence, that it needs it so utterly and with so complete a reference to the help and activity of God. For what else does this mean but that even here, in respect of its very existence, it is referred to the grace of God ?

Its very need carries within it the promise : the promise of the honour and dignity and glory still to be unfolded and revealed ; the promise of its life in grace ; the promise of the work of salvation in which God takes up its cause against that which is not, and carries it to a successful issue. But if this is the case, then to be present as only the creature can be present, in the divine preservation, in total need, is strength as well as weakness, riches as well as privation, perfection as well as imperfection, the highest exaltation as well as shame and need, is something which not only has to be but ought to be.

And now we come to the last and decisive reason why this is so. Our need of the divine preservation has to be so utter and complete because existence in this need is the creaturely existence which corresponds to our participation in the divine covenant of grace. In the fulfilment of this covenant God our Creator first gave up Himself to that need. He did not redeem us from outside, from a safe distance, but from inside, by taking our place, by entering into our resistance to that all-powerful negation of our being, by coming into the very midst of our actual subjection and impotence in face of that negation. This is how the covenant of grace was fulfilled. This is how our cause against nothingness and chaos was maintained in Jesus Christ and carried through to victory. It is the first and chief greatness of the divine triumph, the honour and dignity and glory of God, that He Himself fought and suffered and conquered, not in the heights but in the depths where we are, in the midst of the immeasurable perils in which the creature exists, thus being able really to act on behalf of the creature, and actually doing so. The work of grace in which it is the purpose of our existence to participate took place when the Creator Himself became a creature in His Son, not counting it loss to expose Himself fully to the immeasurable perils of creaturely existence or to allow Himself to be totally denied or to become wholly dependent upon free and undeserved and unmerited grace. In this way He did for the creature that which the creature itself cannot do. He repeated that creating, approving, dividing and calling, thus achieving for the creature its impossible self-assertion and self-distinction in face of the power of chaos, in face of the denying of that which is eternally denied. If the creature exists only in these perils and therefore in this need, it exists at the very place where in Jesus Christ God Himself has existed and triumphed. In this respect, too, we have to reckon seriously with the situation. It is not a matter of caprice or chance. It is not something which has to be accepted and endured as an evil fate. It is the situation in which God Himself made, established and fulfilled His covenant with the creature ; in which He vindicated His honour as the Creator by confronting and annihilating that which is not. The creature is not the Creator, nor can it do what the Creator can do. But in Jesus Christ the situation of the creature was also that of the Creator, and this means that it was a hallowed situation, sanctified and pregnant with promise. At the point where we are powerless, He put forth His power on our behalf. At the point where we are defeated, deliverance was already effected. There is, therefore, no further reason to be ashamed of our situation, nor to bewail it, nor to complain against God for putting us in this and not in some other situation. By making the situation His own He ennobled it and made it a promise, justifying His creative Yes and No. Hence it is no empty assertion when we say that the future honour and dignity and glory of the creature is reflected in its need. In fact its need means that the creature discovers itself as such at the very place where in Jesus Christ God Himself entered in to save it. This very place has all the brightness of His presence. Therefore there can never be any question of the creature not taking its need seriously. There can never be any question concerning its immeasurable peril, its powerlessness, its being referred to God alone for preservation. There can never be any question of its secretly regarding itself as its own preserver. It is more than doubtful whether it could be kept from such a belief merely because by definition it cannot advance or make good that claim. But it is completely kept from it by the fact that at the very place where it might advance that claim its true Preserver has acted in person, accomplishing its salvation and at the same time assuring its preservation. And in so doing He has not so much destroyed that claim, the concealed or open titanism of the creature ; He has simply rendered it superfluous. If it is saved, it is also preserved, and the anxiety or pride in which it might preserve itself is deprived of its object. And if it is saved there, its preservation is assured at the very place where the anxiety and pride could arise in which it might argue that it has to preserve itself. It is saved, and therefore it is assured of preservation even in its total need. And if this is the case, it cannot lack either the courage or the humility to admit its total need. Proof of its need is given in the very fact that it is assured of preservation. This is the second way in which the assertions of the older theology have to be deepened and enlarged.

The connexion between *servare* and *conservare*, between saving grace in Jesus Christ and the gracious preservation of creaturely being by God the Father, emerges most clearly in the New Testament and especially the Pauline passages in which the verbs τηρεῖν, φρουρεῖν, φυλάσσειν, βεβαιοῦν, and στηρίζειν are used to describe a specific activity of God or Christ in relation to Christians. An interesting side-light is also thrown upon our theme by the fact that of these five *conservare* concepts at least φυλάσσειν, στηρίζειν, and above all τηρεῖν are also used to describe a corresponding activity on the part of Christians, and therefore in the context of exhortations to them. We are reminded of what was said concerning the divine preservation of the creature by means of the creature itself. But the application of these concepts to the activity of God seems to be the more characteristic, and in the New Testament φρουρεῖν and βεβαιοῦν are used to describe this activity alone. This preserving, maintaining, guarding, assuring and strengthening is something which Christians have need of. According to some passages they already have these things. Thus in Jn 17¹² : " I kept them (ἐτήρουν) in thy name, and have kept them (ἐφύλαξα), and none of them is lost." Again, in 1 Peter 1⁵ Christians are defined as those who are kept by faith (φρουρούμενοι), and in Jude 1 the readers are described as τετηρήμενοι κλητοί. In 1 Jn 5¹⁸ we have the present : " The begetting of God keepeth him (τηρεῖ), and that wicked one toucheth him not." More generally this divine activity is either proffered to them or requested on their behalf. Thus side by side with Jn 17¹² we find : " Holy Father, keep (τήρησον) through thine own name (Jn 17¹¹)," and : " I pray thee . . . that thou shouldest keep them (τηρήσῃς) from the evil (Jn 17¹⁵)." Again, the words which are put in the mouth of Jesus himself in Rev. 3¹⁰ are in the form of a promise : " I will keep thee (τηρήσω) in the hour of temptation." An event, salvation in the death of Jesus Christ, is something which lies behind those to whom the words are said, but in its final and general revelation it is still before them. It is on the basis of this event that preservation is promised to them, and therefore the preservation corresponds to the basis. The assurance is given by Paul that God will keep (φρουρήσει) the hearts and minds of Christians through Jesus Christ (Phil. 4⁷). He prays for the stablishing (τὸ στηρίξαι) of their hearts that they may be unblameable in holiness (1 Thess. 3¹³). He desires that as they have received Christ Jesus the Lord they may walk in him, stablished (βεβαιούμενοι) in the faith (Col. 2⁷). He is confident that Christ will give them this confirmation (βεβαιώσει) unto the end (1 Cor. 1⁸). He exalts Christ as the faithful One who will stablish and keep them (στηρίξει καὶ φυλάξει) from evil (2 Thess. 3³). Conversely, he calls God the One who stablishes (βεβαιῶν) both himself and them in Christ (2 Cor. 1²¹). " The very God of peace sanctify you wholly . . . and may your whole spirit and soul and body be preserved (τηρηθείη) blameless (ὁλόκληρον). Faithful is he that hath called you, who also will do it " (1 Thess. 5²³). It is striking in how many of these passages this preservation is related to the final hope which still awaits Christians of their future deliverance with the return of Jesus Christ. This makes it plain that our concern is with the permanence or continuity of human, or better of Christian, existence—a matter which has become all the more pressing now that the last time has begun. The question is that of a specifically Christian existence, of the preservation of Christians in the name of God and in faith against temptation and the evil one. We are told this unequivocally in 2 Tim. 1¹². Paul is persuaded that Christ " is able to keep that which I have committed unto him (τὴν παραθήκην μοῦ φυλάξαι) against that day." But according to the New Testament view Christian existence implies a human and creaturely existence. When in the days of the Flood (2 Pet. 2⁵) God saved (ἐφύλαξεν) Noah and seven others the reference is not merely to the office of Noah as a preacher of righteousness but to Noah himself in his creaturely existence as the bearer of this office. According to these passages the hearts and spirits and souls and bodies of Christians are all to be preserved (" whole " in 1 Thess. 5²³) in Christ and in faith against the evil one. And this means that during the time allotted to them, and to the very goal and end of that time, their hearts etc., and they themselves, are literally preserved. In and with that which is committed to them their existence is preserved. In and with their spiritual life, in virtue of its origin and with a view to its destiny, their life is preserved in itself and as such. In so far as they live for Christ in faith, this παραθήκη of Paul is not as it were clothed upon them like a foreign body. And on the other hand the fact that they live in time and in the cosmos cannot be abstracted from the higher and more decisive fact that they are in Christ and that they stand in faith. And the temptation or evil one frequently alluded to in these passages attacks and menaces not merely their Christian existence but in and with it—we are reminded of Paul's description of the thorn in the flesh in 2 Cor. 12⁷—existence itself. Therefore if there is a preservation of Christian existence, the preservation of existence generally is fulfilled in and with it. Something of this implication appears in the saying : " Now our Lord Jesus Christ himself, and God, even our Father . . . stablish (στηρίξαι) you in every good word and work " (2 Thess. 2¹⁷). As long and in so far as they can exist as Christians in virtue of this divine preserving, maintaining, guarding, assuring and strengthening, they are generally preserved and maintained and guarded and assured and strengthened. It is from this standpoint that we should consider the absolute freedom, the complete absence of worry or anxiety, which was displayed by the men of the New Testament in face of all the problems of existence, whether spiritual or natural, psychological or physical. This freedom was not so hostile to the world and to life as it has often been represented (simply because the synecdoche, the implication of the creaturely in the Christian, the connexion between *servare* and *conservare*, has not, or has not sufficiently, been taken into account). The very fact that the question of the *conservare* of an existence based upon the *servare* can arise at all in the living form in which we find it in these passages ought surely to have drawn attention to the further fact that the New Testament regarded the Christian as such, apart from the new birth, as a being existing in time and in the cosmos, and therefore in need, and also assured, of the divine preservation. And conversely, we may learn from this fact in what legitimate sense and with what reference we can speak at all of the divine preservation of a creature which lives in time and in the cosmos, referring back the divine *conservare* to the divine *servare* which is known by Christians and to that extent forms the basis of Christian existence.

And now we must add rather generally that all the Old Testament statements concerning Yahweh as the confidence and protection, the rock and fortress and refuge, both of Israel and also of the Israelite, have to be understood in the light of this relationship between *servatio* and *conservatio*. As life itself shows, neither in prosperity nor in adversity is there any comfort or security either for the people or the individual except in the election, in the covenant, in the history of the covenant with its concrete experiences, and finally and decisively in Yahweh Himself as He who acts as Lord of the covenant. In the Old Testament Yahweh as the Founder and Preserver of the covenant, the faithfulness of His activity in the history of the covenant, the covenant itself as a spiritual reality (to use the language of the New Testament) is the one foundation upon which and by which Israel and the Israelite live according to their creaturely existence, and for the sake of which they are able to be in time and in the cosmos. This is the real basis of their preservation in being. And conversely, the meaning of their being is revealed in the works of grace and judgment performed by Yahweh as Lord of the covenant. Only with that reference back can their being be accepted and understood and valued, and truly magnified and extolled, as a divine benefit and favour.

We may conclude that as God preserves the creature, it may continue in being. Man may continue to be man. Individuals may continue as such. Natural and historical groupings may continue. Humanity itself may continue as the sum of the temporal and spatial totality of human creation on earth and under heaven and in relation to the whole conceivable and inconceivable cosmos. And finally, the known and unknown creatures of this cosmos may continue, following their own path in relation to man and in that autonomy over against him which to us is enshrouded in mystery. Not only did all these things become actual by the creative Word of God. They may continue to be actual because already that creative Word means Jesus Christ and therefore covenant and grace and mercy and goodness. They may continue to be because God willed to fulfil and has already fulfilled this Word by Himself becoming a creature in his Son, by giving up Himself for the creature and its salvation, by Himself accomplishing this salvation. Because the creature is saved by Him, because it partakes of this salvation by Him, the creature is sustained and preserved by Him. It may continue to be because the Word of God is true and actual, because the grace of God is not merely an optional addition to its creaturely existence but the solid basis and wholly effective condition of this existence.

That the creature may continue to be in virtue of the divine preservation does not mean that either as an individual or in its totality it is a creature without any limits. It may continue to be as a creature within its limits. It may have its place in space, and its span in time. It may begin at one point and end at another. It may come, and stay, and go. It may comprehend the earth but not heaven. It may be free here, but bound there ; open at this point, but closed at that. It may understand one thing, but not another ; be capable of one thing, but not another ; accomplish one thing but not another. That it may be in this way, within its limits, is not at all an imperfection, an evil necessity, an obscure fate. Were we in a position to compare and comprehend all the possibilities of all creatures, and the possibilities of the individual with those of the totality, we should be astonished at the magnificent breadth of these limits. And certainly it is not a curse but a blessing that there are these limits to humanity and creation, and that in some cases they are notoriously narrow limits, of which the brevity of human life is only a single if rather drastic example. The creature must not exist like the unhappy centre of a circle which has no periphery. It must exist in a genuine circle, its individual environment. It must not exist everywhere, but in a specific place. It must not exist endlessly, but in its own time. It must not comprehend or understand or be capable of or accomplish everything. It has freedom to experience and accomplish that which is proper to it, to do that which it can do, and to be satisfied. It is in this freedom that it is preserved by God. It is in this freedom that it comes directly from God and moves towards Him. It is in this freedom that it is ready to fulfil its destiny, i.e., by the grace of God to live by the grace of God. The fact that it is here and now, that it exists in one way and not another, is its opportunity; the one opportunity which does not recur ; an opportunity which corresponds to the oneness of God and the uniqueness of the work of liberation which He accomplished in Jesus Christ. It is its own particular opportunity, the opportunity which is given specifically to it, the opportunity which is so definitely rich and pregnant with promise. As this opportunity is given to it, the creature is preserved by God for the kingdom of God. Having this opportunity, it is the object of the goodness of God. And by

accepting it, by making a right use of it, it magnifies the Creator :
" I will sing unto the Lord as long as I live : I will sing praise to my
God while I have my being " (Ps. 104³³ ; 146²). And why not within
these limits ? Why not rightly within these limits ? The creature
will only stumble at a supposed imperfection or obscure fate when it
magnifies God in its own strength, when it does not admit or accept
these limits, when it loses itself in generalities or grasps concretely at
another opportunity which is not its own. But where there is nothing
to seek it will not find, and it cannot know that it is preserved by God.
Of all creatures only man seems to have this impossible possibility
of repudiating his preservation by God as a preservation within
appointed limits. But he cannot alter the fact that like all creatures
he is in fact preserved in this way, and rightly so, and to his own
salvation.

That the creature may continue to be in virtue of the divine
preservation means that it may itself be actual within its limits :
actual, and therefore not a mere appearance engendered by some
heavenly or hellish power ; itself actual, and therefore not an emanation
from the being of God and certainly not from non-being. God
preserves the creature in the reality which is distinct from His own.
It is relative to and dependent upon His reality, but in its relativity
and dependence autonomous towards it, existing because it owes its
existence to Him, as a subject with which He can have dealings and
which can have dealings with Him. In this way it is adequate to its
determination for existence in the divine covenant of grace. As it
did not proceed out of chaos, but was marked off from chaos by God
the Creator, so according to the will and on the basis of the saving
act of God its Saviour it cannot and should not and must not be
overwhelmed by chaos and perish. And as it did not proceed from
God's own being, but was freely created by God, so it cannot return
to God, nor can it or should it in any way forfeit or surrender its
autonomy in face of Him. God is to be all in all (1 Cor. 15²⁸), but
this does not really mean that the " all " will no longer be, that God
will be alone again. It means rather that in the final revelation
of His ways He will be seen by the creature to have attained His
ultimate goal in all things with the creature, the creature not ceasing
to be distinct from Himself. In all its forms pantheism is a conception which does violence and injustice not only to God but also
to the creature. The creature itself may be actual within its limits.
For this it is indebted to the divine preservation. And we saw that
this preservation is direct in the sense that God gives it to the creature
to preserve itself within the context in which it exists. The fine
saying in Proverbs 8³¹, which tells us of the wisdom of God which was
daily His delight and rejoiced before Him, rejoicing in the habitable
parts of the earth, and having its delights with the sons of men, is far
truer in its mythological form than much that has been said in

apparent exaltation of the sole efficacy of God but really in disparagement of the creature and therefore of its Creator. That the creature may not only be, but may continue to be what it is, running its course within the limits marked off for it ; that God does not begrudge it this, or deprive it of it ; that there is a delighting or sport in which first the Creator and then the creature has a part : this is the grand free mystery of the divine preservation. Not merely the creaturely worlds of the sidereal kingdom, and amongst them the tiny planet which is the vast dwelling-place of man, may tread the path appointed for them, but also the small and the very smallest things which are around and far below us. And so " man goeth forth unto his work and to his labour until the evening " (Ps. 104[23]) ; to which it belongs that he can use his senses and understanding to perceive that two and two make four, and to write poetry, and to think, and to make music, and to eat and drink, and to be filled with joy and often with sorrow, and to love and sometimes to hate, and to be young and to grow old, and all within his own experience and activity, affirming it not as half a man but as a whole man, with head uplifted, and the heart free and the conscience at rest : " O Lord, how manifold are thy works " (Ps. 104[24]). It is only the heathen gods who envy man. The true God, who is unconditionally the Lord, allows him to be the thing for which He created him. He is far too highly exalted either to take it amiss or to prevent it. Does not the divine wisdom have its true delight in the children of men ? This is a bold assertion, and one which calls for closer analysis and more profound meditation. But there can be no doubt that with an autonomous reality God does give to man, and not only to man but in different ways to all His creatures, the freedom of individual action. There can be no doubt that as the One who is the Giver of this gift He is the One who preserves them.

That the creature may continue to be in virtue of the divine preservation means finally that—itself actual and active within its limits—it may continue before Him eternally. We have already seen what is meant by the phrase " within its limits." It does not only mean a limitation to its own particular place. It means also a limitation of its possibilities and capacities, of its development and operation. Above all, it means a limitation of its existence in itself and as such. There are myriads of creatures which have been, and only have been. There are myriads more which are and continue to be, but which one day will only have been. And the time will come when the created world as a whole will only have been. In the final act of salvation history, i.e., in the revelation of Jesus Christ as the Foundation and Deliverer and Head of the whole of creation, the history of creation will also reach its goal and end. It will not need to progress any further, it will have fulfilled its purpose. Everything that happened in the course of that history will then take place together as a recapitulation of all individual events. It will be made definitive as the temporal end of the creature beyond which it cannot exist any more. Its life will then be over, its movement and development completed, its notes sounded, its colours revealed, its thinking thought, its words said, its deeds done, its contacts and relationships with other creatures and their mutual interaction closed, the possibilities granted to it exploited and exhausted. And in all this it will somehow have a part in that which Jesus Christ has been and done as its Foundation and Deliverer and Head. It will not need any continuance of temporal existence. And since the creature itself will not be there, time which is the form of its existence will not be there. Yet this does not mean that its preservation by God is terminated. It is a preservation within appointed limits; the preservation of its being in its limited place, with its limited possibilities, and in its limited temporal duration. But inasmuch as it is a divine activity and attitude, the *motus stabilis* of the divine being; inasmuch as the faithfulness of God is an eternal faithfulness, this preservation is an eternal preservation. It does not end with the ending of the existence of the creature, just as it did not begin with that existence and is not limited by its limitations. In the eternal counsel of God it was applied and assured to the creature before creation itself. Similarly it is still applied and assured to it even when the creature has completed its appointed course, even when it does not exist any longer. It lays hold of the creature as it were in and with its limitations; even in and with the limitations of its temporal duration. This is how God willed and created the creature. This is how He preserves it in time as in all its other limitations. And this limited creature—limited in time, but only in time—He loved and preserved from destruction by Himself becoming man in His Son, by constituting Himself in the Son its Foundation and Deliverer and Head. He took to Himself that transitory speck of dust in order that in that restricted and mean and insignificant setting He might give to the covenant of grace its history. And He gave to that transitory speck temporal duration as the setting of that history. Its limitations do not involve its destruction because God preserves it in those limitations. How could the limitations of temporal duration involve its destruction, as though God could not or would not preserve it even in that limitation, or as though God did not guarantee eternal preservation by Himself becoming a creature, by Himself entering that limitation?

Eternal preservation does not mean a continuation of the existence of the creature. To what end and for what purpose could it continue to be when already it has had and fulfilled its course, when in that course it has already accomplished its purpose and in the revelation of Jesus Christ attained its end, when the cover under which it had real life and activity in temporal duration has been removed, when the fire of judgment without which it cannot depart at this uncovering of its existence has already passed over it ? What need has it of more time and duration, of more reality and activity, when in the limits marked off for it God has already given to it all things, namely, Himself, in the person of His Son, when its end was to be manifested as the recipient of that gift ?

The eternal preservation of the creature of God means negatively that its destruction is excluded no less by its beginning in the creation of God than by its end in the revelation of Jesus Christ, and therefore by its very limitations. It was not in vain that God gave to it time and duration, and in time and duration reality and activity. He gave them to it as to the transitory speck of dust which it is, but He gave them in reality and not in appearance. And that which was no appearance He will not allow to become appearance even when it is over. If it did become appearance, this would mean that the non-existent had triumphed over the creature of God, that by giving such power to the non-existent God had finally revoked His own work, and that He had finally retracted that Yes and given Himself to isolation. But the love of God for the creature was far too costly, in Jesus Christ God gave to the creature far too high a dignity, and God bound Himself to the creature far too seriously and unreservedly, for Him to be able to repent and to desire to be in isolation and apart from the creature. By means of that which He did on behalf of the creature when He Himself became creature, He has in fact broken the power of the non-existent against the creature, destroying it and removing the threat of it. Where, then, is the power which can force the creature to become appearance and not reality ? It can only be the power of God Himself. But God—the God who acted and revealed Himself in Jesus Christ—will not make exercise of His power to that end.

The eternal preservation of the creature means positively—and this is the final point—that it can continue eternally before Him. God is the One who was, and is, and is to come. With Him the past is future, and both past and future are present. There was nothing that He could not perceive and know of all that began to be, and was, and was preserved by Him. Nothing could escape Him, or perish. Everything was open and present to Him : everything in its own time and within its own limits ; but everything open and present to Him. Similarly, everything that is, as well as everything that was, is open and present to Him, within its own limits. And everything that will be, as well as everything that was and is, will be open and present to Him, within its own limits. And one day—to speak in temporal terms—when the totality of everything that was and is and will be will only have been, then in the totality of its temporal duration it will still be open and present to Him, and therefore preserved : eternally preserved ; revealed in all its greatness and littleness ; judged

according to its rightness or wrongness, its value or lack of value ;
but revealed in its participation in the love which He Himself has
directed towards it. Therefore nothing will escape Him : no aspect
of the great game of creation ; no moment of human life ; no thinking
thought ; no word spoken ; no secret or insignificant enterprise or
deed or omission with all its interaction and effects ; no suffering or
joy ; no sincerity or lie ; no secret event in heaven or too well-known
event on earth ; no ray of sunlight ; no note which has ever sounded ;
no colour which has ever been revealed, possibly in the darkness of
oceanic depths where the eye of man has never perceived it ; no
wing-beat of the day-fly in far-flung epochs of geological time.
Everything will be present to Him exactly as it was or is or will be,
in all its reality, in the whole temporal course of its activity, in its
strength or weakness, in its majesty or meanness. He will not allow
anything to perish, but will hold it in the hollow of His hand as He
has always done, and does, and will do. He will not be alone in
eternity, but with the creature. He will allow it to partake of His
own eternal life. And in this way the creature will continue to be,
in its limitation, even in its limited temporal duration. And how
could it not be when it is open and present to Him even at its end,
even as that which has only been ? This is how it will persist. In
all the unrest of its being in time it will be enfolded by the rest of God,
and in Him it will itself be at rest, just as even now in all its unrest
it is hidden and can be at rest in the rest of God. This is the
eternal preservation of God. It is not a second preservation side by
side with or at the back of the temporal. It is the secret of the
temporal. It is a secret of the temporal which is already present in
the fulness of truth, which is already in force. And yet it has still to
be present in the fulness of truth ; it has still to come into force ;
it has still to be revealed in all its clarity. As we read in Psalm 136
(repeated twenty-six times) : " For his mercy endureth for ever."

2. THE DIVINE ACCOMPANYING

The proposition that God preserves the creature describes only
one aspect of His fatherly lordship. We shall now describe a second
aspect with the proposition that He accompanies the creature. This
concept refers to the lordship of God in relation to the free and
autonomous activity of the creature. Already in order fully to
describe the divine preserving of the creature we had to take into
account the fact that its preservation as actuality necessarily includes
its preservation in activity. As God gives to it duration, it persists.
Going through a series of changes and movements it is what it can
be according to its own nature and potentialities. Its being is its

activity. It is the object of the *operatio* of God in creation and preservation, and as such it is caught up in an *operatio* of its own : in the limited efficacy which God has created and maintained for it ; in its own finite activity which is different from the activity of God, just as its actuality is different from the actuality of God.

But in this autonomy of the creature in its own activity we see in a new light the activity of God in providence, in the exercise of His fatherly lordship over the creature. Quite obviously the concept of preservation is not of itself adequate to describe this lordship. The fact that the divine lordship extends beyond the creation of the creature means also and primarily that He maintains it in its own actuality, that He gives it space and opportunity for its own work, for its own being in action, for its own autonomous activity. How could He really preserve it if He grudged it that, if either He did not concede it at all, or conceded it only in appearance ? But again, He would not be acting as the true Lord if He gave it in the same way as a father might hand over to his son an interest-bearing property to be used and applied according to his own good-pleasure, if He let it go its own way in its autonomous activity, if He left it entirely to its own devices. The fatherly providence of God involves far more than that God preserves the creature and gives it its own autonomous activity. He does do this, of course. As the older dogmatics put it, this is the " first act " of the divine providence. We have never to lose sight of this act for a single moment. We have not to say anything which might compromise it, or cross it, or destroy its force. But this can only be the first thing. And now we have to describe a second with the proposition that God accompanies the creature.

At this point I am following the formulation of J. Cocceius : *nutus voluntatis in Deo . . . comitatur operationem creaturae* (*S. theol.*, 1662, 28, 25). The concept is a very general one and for that reason most hazardous. It might suggest a being who acts with weakness, or indifference, or indeed passively, or with only a partial interest, side by side with another. But if we remember and consider that the subject is God, *nutus voluntatis in Deo*, we shall easily avoid any false notions suggested by the predicate " accompanies." And Cocceius was careful to safeguard himself at once in this direction. When the subject and object are both taken seriously, the predicate being understood in the light of the subject and the subject interpreted in the sense of the predicate, then the general proposition that God accompanies has the advantage that it does at least suggest with an initial exactness, and under the three crucial headings, that which we have now to consider as the second aspect of the divine providence.

God accompanies the creature, and therefore (1) He certainly does not preserve it merely to abandon it to its own activity once He has set in motion. Every moment of its activity and existence the creature has need of a momentary preservation. And the fact that God does preserve the creature means already that He goes with it.

And He does so not merely as the One who preserves it but in all His activity as the living and holy and mericiful God, in an activity which is not exhausted by His preservation of the creature, in all the richness of His divine being, in all the definitiveness of His will and counsel towards the creature in its own activity. Thus the activity of the creature takes place in its co-existence with God, in the presence of God, His *praesentia actuosa*. It is therefore accompanied and surrounded by God's own activity. Let us at once lift the matter above the level of a merely formal consideration. Alongside the act of the creature there is always the act of the divine wisdom and omnipotence. The history of the covenant of grace accompanies the act of the creature from first to last. When by divine preservation the first creature came to exist in activity, God had already acted, offering His grace, making His mercy in Jesus Christ operative and effective to the creature, revealing the majesty of His beloved Son. Where or when could the creature accomplish or perform even the slightest act without this also taking place, without God being with it in this act of lordship ? It is in view of the enactment of His own gracious will that God preserves it. But there is more to it than that. For when the creature is at work and active on the basis of its pre-servation, the gracious will of God is executed in that which borders upon it, in its environment, in the nexus of being in which it has its duration. Whatever that may or may not mean, it is not alone on the way, but as it goes it is accompanied by God, by the God who is this Lord. It is accompanied by the divine wisdom and omnipotence in their specific form as fatherliness. It is accompanied by its Lord in the attitude and purpose towards it which are characterised by His fatherly will. Its own activity stands under the controlling sign of the activity of this companion. Since God is God, He is the one who inevitably and inescapably accompanies the creature, no matter what may be the attitude which the creature adopts towards Him.

God accompanies the creature. This means (2) that He affirms and approves and recognises and respects the autonomous actuality and therefore the autonomous activity of the creature as such. He does not play the part of a tyrant towards it. He no more wills to act alone than as the Creator He willed to be alone or as the Sustainer of the creature He affirms that He does not will to continue alone. Alongside Him there is a place for the creature. Alongside His activity there is a place for that of the creature. We even dare and indeed have to make the dangerous assertion that He co-operates with the creature, meaning that as He Himself works He allows the creature to work. Just as He Himself is active in His freedom, the creature can also be active in its freedom. God Himself can guarantee this to the creature. It is His creature. And even the freedom in which it can work is His gift. And since He Himself accompanies it as the Lord in the use which it makes of that freedom, it is provided that His own freedom will not only not be hampered but will actually prevail by it. The concept " accompany " is a particularly good one because it includes the freedom which God has granted and allowed to the creature. God Himself is not alone on the way. But at this point the decisive consideration must be the material one that the God who accompanies the creature is the Lord of the covenant of grace. If God had willed to act alone, or by means of non-autonomous agents or instruments, there would have been no need to institute a covenant, and the fulfilment of His will in creation need not have taken the form of a covenant-history. Again, grace would no longer be grace if its exercise consisted only in the elimination or suppression as an autonomous subject of the one to whom it was extended. The gracious God acts not only *towards* the creature but also—however we explain it in detail—*with* the creature. His lordship is not despotism. If it were, could it ever have attained its goal by God Himself becoming a creature in His Son, and in that way by His free act of obedience and suffering effecting the liberation of the creature ? If over against Him the act of the creature were autonomous only in appearance, the Lord of the covenant of grace would not be God the Creator, the true and living God. It is not in the might of an autocrat but in the power of fatherly majesty that God Himself, the living God, accompanies the creature, doing all things, and yet not doing them without the creature, but working with the creature.

God accompanies the creature. This means of course (3) that He goes with it as the Lord. God is not any kind of companion. Nor is it a matter for jesting that He goes with the creature and co-operates with it. God is the Creator and Sustainer of the creature. It is not of itself that it can exist and work side by side with Him ; it is always the work of God and the gift of God. The creature does not belong and is not subject to Him like a puppet or a tool or dead matter— that would certainly not be the lordship of the living God—but in the autonomy in which it was created, in the activity which God made possible for it and permitted to it. And this is how God really overrules the creature, in a way which is congruous to and worthy of Him. God rules in and over a world of freedom. And this is how He rules genuinely and unconditionally. This is how He rules with the absoluteness which is possible only for the Creator ruling over the creature. This is how it is provided that His will is done on earth as it is in heaven, that nothing may or can take place as the action of the creature which is not in a very definite sense His own action. No compulsion is exercised towards the creature. No necessity is worked out in relation to it. It is better not to speak at all, or to do so only infrequently, of the dependence of the creature—although sometimes the expression is perhaps unavoidable—because the word " dependence " almost necessarily suggests a mechanical relationship. But the free God is always a step in advance of the free creature. The free creature does go of itself, but it can and does only go the same way as the free God. It goes its own way, but in fact it always finds itself in a very definite sense on God's way. And if we are to understand, then at this third and decisive point we must again think of the form in which God is almighty, genuinely and supremely almighty, in Jesus Christ and in the covenant of grace. And what is it that is done here ? What is it that we experience here of God's dealings with the creature ? Manifestly this, that He loves the creature, that He genuinely recognises and affirms it for what it is in itself and what it does by itself, that He does not annihilate it but for the first time reveals its true nature. But He loves the creature—and here already we have the actualisation of His majesty towards it—quite freely and without any question at all of merit or achievement on its part. And He loves it—and here we see the culmination of His majesty—in such a way that He gives himself to it. He loves it in accepting solidarity with it. Has it anything which He did not give it ? Is there anything which it did not derive from Him ? Can it or does it do anything which He does not do with it, which is anything more than a magnifying of His inconceivable goodness and the presence of His grace ? And how can the divine lordship be more complete than that ? How can it be more secure and exclusive than that ?—even although and by the very fact that here can be no question of compulsion, or of a mere dependence of the creature on God ; even although and by the very fact that all that happens between God and man takes place quite freely, in the freedom of the spirit. Our experience of God's dealings with the creature at the point where He opens His heart as the Creator and reveals His will and plan, and therefore Himself, and the creature too in its relationship with Him, is that He Himself is the true and genuine Lord and King and Law-giver and the sole Ruler of the creature by His own Holy Spirit, who does not strike down but raises up, who does not bind but looses, who does not kill but makes alive. The preceding of the Creator and following of the creature would be inconceivable, and the lordship and obedience could and would indeed be constantly questioned, were it not that at this point—where their claim and power are highest—they are seen in action : the fatherly lordship of the Creator ; the childlike obedience of the creature ; and the Spirit in whom both take place together. At this point there is actualised in its original form the fact that the activity of the creature along the way on which God accompanies it and it can accompany God is simply a confirming of the divine activity. At this point, where we do not see any law but only grace, the fact of God's accompanying can and must be understood as the law of the whole divine co-existence with the creature, as the law of the activity of the divine providence.

In order to describe this divine accompanying the older dogmatics coined the concept of *concursus*.

What particular moment in the concept of the divine providence they had in mind may best be seen if we take note of the passages of Scripture to which reference was customarily made. Especially we must recall the second application of the statement in Rom. 11³⁶: δι' αὐτοῦ τὰ πάντα. Surely P. van Mastricht (*Theor. Pract. Theol.*, 1698, III, 10, 1) was basically correct in his exegesis of this expression when he believed that the διά did not define God as the *causa instrumentalis* but indicated the *ipsa operatio* of Father, Son and Holy Spirit as it takes place in the work of providence. Reference was also made to Ac. 17²⁷: "Though he be not far from every one of us"; to 1 Cor. 12⁶, where God is described as ἐνεργῶν τὰ πάντα ἐν πᾶσιν; to Phil. 2¹³, where it is stated expressly of God that He is ὁ ἐνεργῶν ἐν ὑμῖν καὶ τὸ θέλειν καὶ τὸ ἐνεργεῖν ὑπὲρ τῆς εὐδοκίας; to Mt. 10²⁹, where the disciples are told that without the will of the Father not a single sparrow can fall to the ground; to Ps. 127¹: "Except the Lord build the house, they labour in vain that build it: except the Lord keep the city, the watchman waketh but in vain"; to the particularly impressive saying in Is. 26¹²: "Thou also hast wrought all our works in us"; to Jer. 10²³: "O Lord, I know that the way of man is not in himself: it is not in man that walketh to direct his steps"; to the words of Joseph in Gen. 45⁸: "So now it was not you that sent me hither, but God: and he hath made me a father to Pharaoh, and lord of all his house"; to Prov. 16³³: "The lot is cast into the lap; but the whole disposing thereof is of the lord"; to Prov. 21¹: "The king's heart is in the hand of the Lord, as the rivers of water: he turneth it whithersoever he will" (on which Abr. Heidan commented: *Quid magis independens quam cor regis? At illud ita est in manu Dei, ut rivi aquarum, Corp. Theol.*, 1686 1, p. 363); to 1 Sam. 10²⁶: "And there went with him a band of men, whose hearts God had touched" (on which Heidan says: *Quomodo adduxit? Nunquid corporalibus vinculis alligavit? Intus egit, corda tenuit, corda movit, eosque voluntatibus eorum, quas ipse in illis operatus est, duxit*); to Prov. 16¹: "The preparedness of the heart in man, and the answer of the tongue, is from the Lord"; to Prov. 16⁹: "A man's heart deviseth his way, but the Lord directeth his steps"; to Prov. 19²¹: "There are many devices in a man's heart; nevertheless the counsel of the Lord, that shall stand." Summary reference was also made to the great theodicy at the end of the book of Job, in which Chapter 38 adduces all the works of nature, Chapter 39 more specifically the remarkable life-stories of the wild goat, the wild ass, the wild ox, the horse, the hawk and the eagle, and Chapters 40 and 41 those of the rhinoceros and the crocodile—in these cases heightened and depicted with mythical splendour—all of them as direct testimonies to that same overruling of God which is none the less real because it is concealed from man.

The problem raised by these passages is indeed a genuine one, and that is why we have addressed ourselves to it in this sub-section. And the fact that in more than one of the passages express mention is made of the way trodden by both God and man and of their mutual relationship upon that way is a confirmation that generally at least we were on the right track when we selected the concept of accompanying. It is in accordance with the biblical view if we understand the action of God as Lord of the creature as a living relation to the action in which the creature—in whom it is accompanied, differentiated and overruled by that of God—is also involved. For the *concursus* doctrine of the older dogmatics, and therefore for us too, the problem is to present this relation clearly in all the individuality in which it is revealed in Scripture. And so far as this is possible at all, the problem is also to mark it off from all the misleading conceptions which might creep in at this point. We might well conceive of the antithesis as the antithesis between an intrinsically unmoved and passive God and a moved order of creation. Or we might conceive of it as the antithesis between a living, active and working God and an order of creation which is moved by Him from without, and therefore passively and without any activity on its own account. Again, we might conceive of a divine action which consists in the invention, establishing and initiating of a *perpetuum mobile* which would have its own limit on the limit of creaturely action, which would make creaturely action possible, and then hand over the control to it, leaving it to run its own course. And finally we might conceive of an identity between the divine and creaturely action, of the undifferentiated existence of a God-world, which in all its elements and movements might be interpreted equally well as divine or not divine, with a constant amphibole of concepts. The older theologians were right when from the scriptural passages they at least made the deduction that according to the Christian knowledge of the Old and New Testament attestation of the divine work and revelation all these possibilities have to be negated. And it was in an attempt to do justice to the problem of a co-existence and anti-thesis of the divine and creaturely action which should correspond with the testimony of Scripture that they worked out their doctrine of the *concursus*.

At this point it is as well to correct a false representation which appears amongst other places in R. A. Lipsius (*op. cit.*, p. 397 f.) and the *Lehrbuch der. ev. Dogmatik* of Nitzsch-Stephan (1912, p. 421). According to this account the doctrine of the *concursus* was peculiar to Lutheran dogmatics, the Reformed school holding to the view that God alone is active, and regarding the creature merely as his tool, thus excluding all idea of co-operation apart from an in-significant application amongst some of the younger representatives of the tradition. But even with the Lutherans the question of the *concursus* as a third problem between that of the *conservatio* on the one hand and that of the *gubernatio* on the other was raised as an independent issue only by Quenstedt, Hollaz and Baier, and under the heading *De providentia* J. Gerhard treated only *De con-servatione* and *De gubernatione*. It is remarkable that even A. Calov kept to the same outward form, dealing with the *concursus* only in relation to two questions of detail. On the other hand, it was not only the Lutherans who in this matter took up what was a problem and formulation of the Scholastics, and especially Thomas Aquinas. Nor is it the case that only a few of the younger Reformed dogmaticians adopted the Lutheran approach to the question. For already in J. Wolleb (*Comp. chr. Theol.*, 1626, I, 6, *can.* 5) we find the decisive affirmation whose wording recalls a famous dictum of Thomas : *Providentia Dei causas secundas non tollit, sed ponit*, and Wolleb also speaks expressly (*can.* 9) of the *praecursus, concursus et succursus divinae virtutis*. Again, in the *Leidener Synopsis* (1624, *Disp.* 11, 11) it is stated expressly not only of acts of the human will but of the factual contingent action of all created things that the *operatio* of the divine providence not only does not destroy but rather confirms them in their autonomy : *Non corrumpit naturam sed perficit; non tollit sed tuetur*. And again in the same context (11, 13) we find the extremely clear and comprehensive definition of the *concursus* : God so co-operates with His creatures *ut actione sua immediate in actionem creaturae influat, et una et eadem actio a prima et secunda causa dicatur proficisci, quatenus unum opus seu ἀποτέλεσμα hinc existit*. And in all the later Reformed dogmaticians the closest attention and the greatest possible care is given to this issue : certainly not less than in the case of their Lutheran contemporaries. The palpable error may perhaps be traced back to Alexander Schweizer's *Glaubenslehre der ev.-ref. Kirche*, from which the 19th century rather rashly assumed that it could give instruction in the older Reformed theology. In this work (Vol. I, 1844, p. 320) we read the following : " The Reformed view does not recognise any effective potencies side by side with or outside or independent of God. Hence *praecursus, concursus* and *succursus* are all properly excluded." For such a conclusion Schweizer could appeal only to some of the more extreme utterances of Zwingli, and it is not shown to be re-presentative of even one, let alone *the* Reformed standpoint. Indeed, it is no more than an element in his own quite modern systematisation, and one which we can only reject as a denial of the divine preservation of the creature. For what sort of a creature would that be which was divinely preserved and therefore existed without any real potency of its own ? Surely there are no grounds for ever believing the legend that this was a normative tenet of Reformed theology. As *particula veri* of the legend there is only the fact that in the development of the doctrine of the *concursus* the Lutherans had a special interest in the second point mentioned in our introduction, the relative autonomy of creaturely activity, in the light of which they interpreted the concept of the divine *concursus* more along the lines of a *succursus*, whereas the interest of the Reformed school was rather in the point raised by us under the third heading, the absolute priority of the divine over the human activity, an interest which decidedly led them to interpret the *concursus* more along the lines of a *praecursus*. In putting the emphasis where they did the Reformed theologians had the advantage that all the biblical passages commonly alleged have the same emphasis, speaking of the *maior Dei gloria*. This is a fact which we must bear in mind. But what the Reformed thinkers wanted to emphasis, in stricter accordance with Holy Scripture, can only be brought out when the *minor gloria creaturae* asserted by the Lutherans is also taken into account, as implicitly affirmed in the same Scriptures —we have only to think of Job 38–41. Certainly there can be no question of any antithesis between the two, and we cannot see that we are in any way compelled to choose between them.

It is clear that according to the sharpness or carelessness with which the two parties expressed themselves distinctions and contradictions could easily arise, and even a split in confessional theology. And it is understandable enough that this is what actually did take place. But what is more important is to establish the fact that on both sides the problem was at any rate perceived and therefore tackled. Whether or not they succeeded in their efforts to deal with it, whether or not they were able to bring out effectively this difficult union of opposites, we cannot deny that in their own way the Lutheran dogmaticians did try to establish the absolute majesty and primacy of God no less than the Reformed, nor can we deny that in their own way the Reformed dogmaticians did aim to set forth the autonomy of creaturely activity no less definitely than the Lutheran. As always in the difference between Lutheran and Reformed it is a question of academic antitheses. In many cases these antitheses are of such a kind that to-day we can pass them by as out-moded. But in many others —and this is one of them—they are of a kind still to call for decision. It is not a matter of indifference whether in the last analysis the *gloria Dei* is more important to us than the *gloria creaturae*, or *vice versa*. But what we have here is a shade of emphasis within the same confession and not an irreconcilable contra-diction. Therefore here, too, the antithesis is only academic.

There is, however, a fundamental question which we have to ask and answer in respect of the achievements of both wings of the older Evangelical theology.

F. Turrettini (*Instit. Theol.*, 1679, VI, 5, 1) commenced his exposition of this doctrine with the profound sigh : *Quaestio de concursu Dei est ex difficillimis, quae in theologia occurrunt.* Certainly it is not at all easy to give either to oneself or to others a reasoned account of the fact or extent of the divine co-operation with the creature. Already we have seen that within Protestantism itself two not irreconcileable but at any rate quite different interests were asserted. Again, both Lutheran and Reformed theologians had to mark off themselves from the Romanists on the one side. One clumsy movement, especially in the development of the Lutheran emphasis, might have had the most serious consequences in the form of a fresh outbreak of synergism in the doctrine of grace. And in this connexion it had also to be considered that there were two wings in the Romanist theology of the time : the Thomists, who in Romanism sought after their own fashion to represent the *maior gloria Dei* so dear to the Reformed branch of Protestantism, with the result that the Thomists could be appealed to quite freely as *testes veritatis* ; and the Jesuits, for whom as for the Lutherans the *minor gloria creaturae* was the main point of interest. And on the other side the

Lutheran and Reformed theologians had to make common cause against the monism and determinism of modern philosophy as determined partly by the Renaissance and partly by the exact natural sciences then in process of development. And behind that philosophy as a relative limit there might well be discerned the more dangerous monism and fatalism of Islam, which at that time practical politics brought forcibly to the notice of Christendom. And if the Lutherans had leanings towards the Romanist side, the Reformed had undoubtedly a similar tendency in this direction. But since, as we have seen, the Lutherans and the Reformed represented the same cause in spite of all the differences between them they had to be on guard no less on the one side than on the other.

Face to face with the difficulty both schools, the Reformed no less than the Lutheran, made a formal borrowing at this point from a philosophy and theology which had been re-discovered and re-asserted at the end of the 16th and the beginning of the 17th centuries—the philosophy of Aristotle and the theology of Aquinas. The borrowing consisted in the adoption and introduction of a specific terminology to describe the two partners whose activities are understood and represented in the doctrine of the *concursus* in terms of a co-operation, the activity of God on the one side and that of the creature on the other. The concept which was adopted and introduced was that of " cause." For it was by developing the dialectic of this concept that they both effected the differentation of themselves on the one side and the other, and also decided the difference which already existed at this point within the Evangelical faith itself. This, then, is the controlling concept for the form assumed by Evangelical dogmatics in this and in all kindred topics.

As the starting-point for our consideration of the problem we will take the comprehensive formulation of the doctrine of the *concursus* given by H. Heidegger (quoted from Heppe[2], p. 200) : *Concursus s. cooperatio est operatio illa Dei, qua is cum causis secundis utpote ab eo sicut in esse ita etiam in operari dependentibus immediate ita cooperatur, ut et ad operandum illas excitet s. promoveat et una cum iisdem modo primae causae conveniente et naturae causarum secundarum accomodato operatur.*

Now we cannot deny that even from the standpoint of the subject itself the concept *causa* could and necessarily did both advance and commend itself. It was indeed the whole problem of *causa* which had formed the topic for discussion even in the 16th century, and this not only in the doctrine of providence of Zwingli and Calvin but also in Luther's *De servo arbitrio*.

It is ostensibly a question of the relation between the divine activity and the creaturely. But activity means *causare*. Activity is movement or action which has as its aim or object a specific effect. To act means to bring about an effect. The subject of such *causare* is a *causa*, in English, a " cause," something without which another and second thing either would not be at all, or would not be at this particular point or in this particular way. A *causa* is something by which another thing is directly posited, or conditioned, or perhaps only partly conditioned, that is, by which it is to some extent and in some sense redirected and therefore altered. Now if we are speaking of the activity, and therefore the *causare*, of God and the creature, then wittingly and willingly or not, we are describing and thinking of both of them in terms of *causa*. And at once we have to begin our manipulation of the dialectic of the concept, and it was in this process that the older dogmaticians found inspiration and guidance in Aristotle and Thomas. For quite obviously God is a *causa* in one sense, and the creature in quite another.

The peculiarity of God as a *causa* consists primarily and supremely in the fact that since He is the source of all *causae*, the basis and starting-point of the whole causal series, there is no *causa* which is either before or above him, but He is his own *causa* : *causa sui*. But it also consists in the fact that since everything which is distinct from him is caused by Him, is His effect, all *causae* outside Him and their *causare* are not merely partly but absolutely conditioned by Him —indeed they are not merely conditioned but in the first instance posited by Him, seeing that they are created. All other *causae* can only affirm and attest Him as the one *causa*. All other *causare* can only affirm and attest His *causare* as the true and genuine *causare*. As the *causa pure causans* He is the *causa causarum*. It was in this sense that He was known to the older theology as the *causa prima*, the *causa princeps*, the controlling cause which governs all other *causae* and their *causare*.

The creature is also *causa*. But the peculiarity of the creature as *causa* consists primarily in the fact that as *causa* it is posited absolutely by God. Without God it would not be at all, and it would not be *causa*. Its *causare* can only be a participation in the divine *causare*, from which it is materially distinguished by the fact that it can consist only in a conditioning or partial conditioning but never in a positing. But again, its peculiarity consists in the fact that not only does it condition other things but it is itself conditioned or partly conditioned by other divine operations and therefore by other *causae*. Not only does it work under God but it also works in connexion with a creaturely series of causes in which it is itself something which is effected by other creatures. As *causa causans* it is therefore *causa causata* in this twofold sense. And that is why it is called *causa secunda*, a *causa* of the second order, of the order to which the whole reality of heaven and earth which is distinct from God belongs, or *causa particularis*, one cause amongst many others, and as such a cause which has only a limited share in the full force of the concept *causa*.

This was the conceptual basis on which the older Evangelical dogmatics understood the *concursus Dei* within the overruling of providence. As *causa prima*, or *princeps*, God co-operates with the operation of *causae secundae*, or *particulares*. The divine *causare* takes place in and with their *causare*. And this means that their operations are also His operations, and in view of the difference in dignity between the two orders they are first and decisively His operations. Now if the problem defined by us as that of the accompanying of the creature by the Creator, of the activity of the creature by that of the Creator, is seen to be a genuine problem in the light of Holy Scripture, there would appear to be no fault in the introduction of this terminology. Every terminology is a possible source of error. From this truth not even terminologies based upon the vocabulary of the Bible are absolutely exempt. The term *causa* does not derive from the Bible, but this does not mean that its introduction into the language of theology is a mistake. The term may well be useful in the developing and applying of the message of the Bible. It could be a particularly useful weapon in the controversies in which the theologians of the 17th century were involved. And it has to be shown—if it can be shown—how the use of some such concept can be avoided if we are to deal radically with the question of the activity of God and that of the creature in their relationship the one to the other. When we talk at all of the divine working, do we not necessarily say *causare* in that primary sense ? Do we not necessarily speak of the original working which is not merely a conditioning but a positing ? And again, when we speak of the working of the creature of God, do we not necessarily say *causare* in the secondary sense ? Do we not speak of the derived and dependent working which is posited and caused by God, and also caused and partially caused by another working which is itself caused ? It is indisputable that to talk in this way can lead to error, for the terminology is not so unequivocal that it cannot become the instrument of false theological conceptions or asseverations. But whether or not it does lead to error depends upon the use to which it is put. It depends upon whether the dynamic and teleology of its use are determined by and continue to be determined by the fact that when it is introduced into theology its task is to help to an understanding and exposition of the message of the Bible, or whether its use gives rise to a dynamic and exposition which are foreign to the message of the Bible and under the pressure of which there emerge theological conceptions and asseverations which are foreign and even completely antithetical to that message. But the fact that the terminology is pressed into service does not of itself mean that error necessarily arises.

Historically, then, it is not at all the case that in the older Evangelical theology positive error derived merely from the introduction of the term *causa*. If we consider the conceptions and asseverations of the older Lutheran and Reformed dogmaticians, we shall find on both sides dangerous approximations to the forbidden frontiers. In the Lutherans we shall often catch notes which have a remarkably Romanist and even Jesuit sound, and in the Reformed we shall catch notes which have a remarkably Stoic, or contemporary monistic, or even slightly Turkish sound. But on neither side is this due to the fact that they made use of the term *causa*. It is due rather to the fact that quite apart from the application of this concept they did not always show the same sureness of touch in this matter as they tried to build up the form and content of their doctrine upon the message of the Bible. Apart from such vacillations we have to allow that the doctrine which they expounded is as a whole formally correct and even serviceable and normative. The experiment in Aristotle and Thomas did not in fact turn out quite so badly as a careful observer might at first have expected. And we have also to allow that by the remarkable *concursus* which they not merely discussed but without realising it attained, they were able to shed a light which without this *concursus* (of the Bible and Aristotle !) they might not have been able to do. Apart from any other considerations, it is utterly monstrous that E. Troeltsch (*Glaubenslehre*, 1925, p. 254) should have had the audacity, without any good reason, to dismiss as " completely worthless " the efforts made by the older theology in this matter.

Two points have constantly to be borne in mind. Formally, the orthodox presentation is correct even in and in spite of and indeed by means of the new terminology introduced at that time. But materially, the same cannot be said concerning it. For it missed completely the relationship between creation and the covenant of grace. In its whole doctrine of providence it spoke abstractly not only of the general control of God over and with the creature, but of the control of a general and in some sense neutral and featureless God, an Absolute. It spoke abstractly of a neutral and featureless creature. It separated between world history and salvation history. And the result was that when the dogmaticians came to speak of the *causare* of the *causa prima* and the *causae secundae*, neither in the one case nor in the other had it any specifically Christian content. There is indeed a form of co-operation as they described it, and the older theologians gave a fine and correct and instructive picture of that form. But it lacked the content without whose express indication even the form which is finely and correctly and instructively pictured may well be the form of a content which is completely different. It lacked the Christian content without whose express indication that well-developed abstraction may well be informed by a dynamic and teleology which have nothing whatever to do with the exposition of the message of the Bible. And this brings us to the second point. In the older orthodoxy, the doctrine of *concursus* in the form determined by the term *causa* lacked any definite safeguards against the mischief which might result simply because it was expressed in that form. The enemies which it was its business to repel, the enemy of synergism on the one hand and monism on the other, of the Papacy on the one hand and the Turk on the other, could also make use of exactly the same form. They could not be repelled merely by the use of that form. When the Evangelicals were seen to be looking to Thomas, it might easily have been a cause of triumph and a source of hope not only in Rome itself but also in countless other states which openly or secretly were seeking a uniform doctrine. The antithesis and conjunction of *causa prima* and *causae secundae*, wherever the emphasis was laid, might easily have been interpreted as the conjunction in antithesis of systems which had nothing whatever to do with the message of the Bible but were rather opposed to it. This mischief never did result in the older Evangelical theology. But this theology was not so proof against it that it could not result later, and even make a strange appeal to this theology. And seeing that it did result later, we must regret that it was not prevented in time.

We have to ask, therefore, on what conditions the concept can legitimately be applied to this doctrine.

We may begin by mentioning certain preliminary conditions, and we shall then show that the fulfilment of all of them is dependent upon the fulfilment of one decisive condition with which we shall deal in conclusion.

1. If it is to be applied legitimately, the term *causa* must not be regarded as the equivalent of that of a cause which is effective automatically. If we had no choice but to think of *causa* or cause as the term is applied in modern science, or rather natural philosophy, with all its talk about causality, causal nexus, causal law, causal necessity and the like, then clearly it is a concept which we could not apply either to God or to the creature of God, but could only reject. That was how A. Ritschl understood the term, and in consequence he conceded that the whole doctrine of the *concursus* has to be dismissed, as though it stood or fell with this particular understanding of cause. As he saw it, the idea of God cannot be squared with the scientific explanation of nature, and therefore we should be doing violence to God if " under the concept cause we compared Him with natural causes which can be understood by observation " (*Unterr. in d. chr. Rel.*, 1875, § 15). We cannot charge either Thomas or our own orthodox dogmaticians with being guilty of any such comparison. The *causa prima* as they envisaged it cannot easily be identified with a natural cause which can be understood by observation. They did not even explain their *causae secundae* altogether within the limits of the modern idea of necessity. According to their understanding of the creature, even within the uniform course of events peculiar to the *ordo naturae* there was still a secure place for natural contingency and the freedom of the human will, for miracle and the suspension of law, quite outside that *ordo*. Even within creaturely history there was still a secure place for the history of the covenant and the Church. These were genuine conceptions of *causae* and *causare* which were not overlaid by the concept of automatically effective causes. Naturally the divine and human operations do have a mechanical component to the extent that in their mutual relation they have the element of necessity. In this respect there are some equivocal statements on the Reformed side, especially in Zwingli and Calvin, and occasionally in the 17th century. But the element of necessity is not to be explained by a foreign concept of mechanical. The mechanical aspect of the relation must be viewed and understood in its peculiar distinctness from what is usually understood by the term mechanical. All that is needed at this point is to perceive and affirm in principle the freedom which the older theology did enjoy and exercise in practice in their concept both of God and also of the creature. But to do this it is necessary to have a basis which we do not find in the older writers.

2. If the term *causa* is to be applied legitimately, care must be taken lest the idea should creep in that in God and the creature we have to do with two " things." The German word for cause, *Ur-sache*, might easily suggest this. A " thing " or " object " (*Sache*) is something which in part at least is perceptible and accessible to man. If we have to do with a " thing " then this means that even if only defectively we believe that we are capable of examining, recognising, analysing and defining, in short of " realising " it, and in some degree we know how to control it. But neither God nor the creature is a *causa* in this sense. When we turn to Thomas and our own orthodox fathers we have to ask seriously whether on their definition God and the creature as primary and secondary *causa* could not easily become something very like " things." For at this point we are

confronted by the mortal danger which faces all theology. All theology is a meditation about God and the creature. But since it meditates and speaks *about* them they are always in danger of becoming things. The human thinker and speaker is in constant danger of forgetting the inconceivable mystery of their existence and being, their presence and operation, and of imagining that he can think and speak about them directly, as though both they themselves and also their relationship to each other were somehow below him. Now when the Aristotelian dialectic of the causal concept was applied to the operations of God and the creature, did it not to some extent involve thinking and speaking about them in that way ? The causal concept, like the concept of being, is certainly an invitation to error at this point. And if the concept is used, this invitation must be resisted at all costs. Rather remarkably, a true theological realism consists primarily in a constant awareness of the fact that neither God nor the creature is a " thing," that on the contrary, to those who really want to think and speak about them, to theologians—if they are not to thresh empty straw—they must always be *self*-revealed. If the purest and strictest orthodoxy once relaxes this awareness, then immediately it becomes a dead orthodoxy. And that is what we must not allow to happen at this point. But a particular basis will be needed if our awareness is to be awakened and kept awake in this matter. Our forefathers knew the basis, but they did not make any use of it. Hence it is hardly surprising that there are good reasons for thinking that they did not have the awareness in sufficient measure.

3. If the term *causa* is to be applied legitimately, it must be clearly understood that it is not a master-concept to which both God and the creature are subject, nor is it a common denominator to which they may both be reduced. *Causa* is not a genus, of which the divine and creaturely *causa* can then be described as species. When we speak about the being of God and that of the creature, we are not dealing with two species of the one genus being. When we speak about the divine nature and the human nature of Christ, we are not dealing with two species of the one genus nature. And so, too, in this case. To put it rather differently, it must be clearly understood that when the word *causa* is applied to God on the one side and the creature on the other, the concept does not describe the activity but the active subjects, and it does not signify subjects which are not merely not alike, or not similar, but subjects which in their absolute antithesis cannot even be compared.

It is true, of course, that although there is no identity of the divine and creaturely operation or *causare*, there is a similarity, a correspondence, a comparableness, an analogy. In theology we can and should speak about similarity and therefore analogy when we find likeness and unlikeness between two quantities : a certain likeness which is compromised by a great unlikeness ; or a certain unlikeness which is always relativised and qualified by a certain existent likeness. The great unlikeness of the work of God in face of that of the creature consists in the fact that as the work of the Creator in the preservation and over-ruling of the creature the work of God takes the form of an absolute positing, a form which can never be proper to the work of the creature. But at the same time the divine work in relation to the creature also has the form of a conditioning, determining and altering of that which already exists. And inasmuch as the conditioning of another also belongs to creaturely activity, there is a certain similarity between the divine and the creaturely work. In view of this likeness and unlikeness, unlikeness and likeness, we can and should speak of a similarity, a comparableness, and therefore an analogy between the divine activity and the human. We have to speak of an *analogia operationis*, just as elsewhere we can speak of an *analogia relationis*.

But the concept *causa* does not merely describe activities, but acting subjects. And between the two subjects as such there is neither likeness nor similarity, but utter unlikeness. We cannot deduce from the fact that both subjects are *causa* the further fact that they both fall under the one master-concept *causa* ; that they may both be reduced to that one common denominator ; that they are both species belonging to the one genus. On the contrary, they cannot even be compared.

Indeed, it would be a mistake to try to compare them simply because they are both *causa*. In the same way it would be a mistake to argue as follows. The Creator exists and has being no less than the creature. Therefore although the being of the Creator and that of the creature are unlike, in some respects they are like and therefore similar. There is therefore an *analogia entis* between God and the creature. To that extent there is a master-concept, a common denominator, a genus (being) which comprises both God and the creature. And it would be a really serious mistake if we were to adopt this argument. Jesus Christ has a divine nature and a human. Therefore, although the two natures are unlike, they are also alike and similar. There is therefore an *analogia naturae* between God and man. And to that extent we can speak of a master-concept, a common denominator, a genus (nature) which comprises both God and man. This is the type of mistake which we have to avoid at this point. This is the deduction which we have to recognise as false and therefore illegitimate.

The divine and creaturely subjects are not like or similar, but unlike. They are unlike because their basis and constitution as subjects are quite different and therefore absolutely unlike, that is, there is not even the slightest similarity between them. The divine *causa*, as distinct from the creaturely, is self-grounded, self-positing, self-conditioning and self-causing. It causes itself—and it is the Christian knowledge of God which gives us the decisive word on the matter—in the triune life which God enjoys as Father, Son and Holy Spirit and in which He has His divine basis from eternity to eternity. This is how God is a subject. And this is how He is a *causa*. And for this reason there is not a single point at which the creaturely subject can be like Him. For the creaturely *causa* is not grounded in itself but absolutely from outside and therefore not at all within itself. It owes the fact that it is a *causa*, and is capable of *causare*, not to itself but first of all to God, who created it and as the Creator still posits and conditions it, and then to the other *causae* of its own order, without whose conditioning or partial conditioning it would not exist. This is how the creature is a subject. And this is how it is a *causa*. What likeness is there then between the creature and the Creator who in His unity and triunity posits Himself without any outside assistance at all ?

It is quite indispensable to a true doctrine of the divine accompanying that the absolute unlikeness of the two *causae causantes* should be brought into sharp relief, with the consequent rejection of any idea of an *analogia causae*. For otherwise there can never be any certainty that we are speaking of two distinct subjects, God and the creature, when we deal with that twofold *causare* which is our present subject. In respect of other essences we can easily take two quantities and range them under a single master-concept, a common denominator or a genus, thus comparing them the one with the other. But we cannot do this with God and the creature. If we tried to do so, the twofold activity whose relationship we should be discussing would not be the activity of these two subjects.

To return to the doctrine of the *concursus* as it is presented in the older Evangelical dogmatics, it is from this standpoint that we have to judge whether and to what extent the characterisation of the two causes as *prima*, or *princeps*, and *secunda*, or *particularis*, can really do justice to the absolute unlikeness of the two *causae causantes*. It is clear that in the philosophy of Aristotle and the theology of Thomas, from which they took the characterisation, this absolute unlikeness was not safeguarded. Indeed, it is more likely that in these two cases, in which the analogy of being was also envisaged, no such unlikeness between God and the creature was even intended by the characterisation, but at the back of it there was the idea of an *analogia causae* which would involve a complete denial of the unlikeness of the two subjects. But if this was so, then necessarily they would come under a single master-concept, they would form part of a single genus, they would be reducible to a single common denominator. And we could only conclude that we are not really dealing with God and the creature and their mutual co-operation. Now it cannot be denied that we should be far happier if the older dogmaticians had clarified this aspect of the matter when they adopted and introduced that particular terminology. They might have done so quite successfully if in view of the unsatisfactory usage of the sources they had dropped altogether the predicates *prima* or *princeps*, and *secunda* or *particularis*, and spoken simply of *causa divina* or *creatrix* and *causa non divina* or *creata*, in the same way as they spoke of *natura divina* and *natura humana* in their Christology. This material instead of purely formal description would have expressed the unlikeness of the two subjects and safeguarded their peculiarity as God on the one hand and creature on the other. They could also have made the clarification successfully if they had taken over the predicates but radically reinterpreted them in a way quite different from the sources : *prima* or *princeps* with express reference to the doctrine of the Trinity and in the sense of *divina* or *creatrix* ; and *secunda* or *particularis* just as expressly as *non divina* or *creata*. But since the older theologians did not make the clarification either the one way or the other, it is an open question whether with the terminology they did not also take over the uncertainty who or what is really intended by the two causes, and whether they are really speaking about God and the creature. We for our part cannot dispense with the clarification. Without this safeguard, without a clear perception of the absolute unlikeness of the two *causae* in question, we cannot accept as legitimate an application of the causal concept in the present context. But once again we must add that we still need the particular basis which we do not find in the older theologians if we really want to attain absolute clarity on the point.

4. The third condition is the most important so far mentioned, and if it is fulfilled the fourth will also be fulfilled. We do not need to speak of it, therefore, except very briefly. When the causal concept is introduced, it should not be with either the intention or the consequence that theology should be turned into philosophy at this point, projecting a kind of total scheme of things. If it is clear (1) that in its application both to God and the creature the concept *causa* must be kept quite free from the encumbrance of mechanical ideas, (2) that it ought not to have the result of making God and the creature two " things," two known and controllable quantities, and (3), and above all, that it must not be interpreted in such a way that the incomparableness of God and the creature is compromised, then from the negative standpoint at any rate the autonomy of the theological thesis here propounded should be quite secure in face of a philosophical conception which apparently approximates to it. But even this negative safeguard was lacking in the older theology. And it is noticeable that the Scripture proofs certainly adduced in this theology do not have any real bearing upon the statement of the problem. They remain in the background behind the discussion proper, and there is an almost grotesque attempt to make it clear that in virtue of these proofs the being who is later discussed as *causa princeps* is necessarily the God of Job and Paul, and that all the Old and New Testament statements about man as he goes his own way and therefore God's way (not to speak of Behemoth and Leviathan) can quite comfortably be included in the concept of *causae particulares*, thus completely losing their original form. It is true that in the δι᾿ αὐτοῦ (Rom. 11[36]) P. van Mastricht perceived the *operatio* of the triune God, that is, the God of the biblical revelation, but this interesting exegesis was peculiar to himself and was not followed by any of the others. Yet it is absolutely essential that there should be this safeguard against defection into purely philosophical thinking. For when theology is guilty of

such a defection it is wilfully entangling its tenets in the contradictions and uncertainties of problems which are alien to it, it runs the risk of speaking about
what are really two quite different quantities when it uses the titles God and the
creature, and the encumbrance with another and alien task necessarily means
that its own work suffers. And this is something which we cannot allow to happen
at this point.

5. But this safeguard, and all the negative safeguards so far mentioned, can
be recognised as necessary and therefore valid only if we set against them the
positive pre-condition which must be fulfilled in this matter. As the doctrine
of the *concursus*, and indeed the whole doctrine of providence, is expounded,
there must be a clear connexion between the first article of the creed and the
second. If the causal concept is to be applied legitimately, its content and interpretation must be determined by the fact that what it describes is the operation
of the Father of Jesus Christ in relation to that of the creature. Basically, the
doctrine of the *concursus* must be as follows. God, the only true God, so loved
the world in His election of grace that in fulfilment of the covenant of grace
instituted at the creation He willed to become a creature, and did in fact become
a creature, in order to be its Saviour. And this same God accepts the creature
even apart from the history of the covenant and its fulfilment. He takes it
to Himself as such and in general in such sort that He co-operates with it, preceding, accompanying and following all its being and activity, so that all the activity
of the creature is primarily and simultaneously and subsequently His own
activity, and therefore a part of the actualisation of His own will revealed and
triumphant in Jesus Christ.

Who and what is this *causa prima* which confronts us here as the solemn
companion of the *causae secundae* ? Certainly we cannot speak yet of the God
who became flesh in Jesus Christ, identifying Himself in this way with a *causa
secunda* and effecting eternal salvation. But we can speak of the God who in
the execution of His election of grace and the fulfilment of His covenant of grace
willed and effected this inconceivable benefit, of the God who was already the
Father of mercy and the God of all comfort (2 Cor. 1³), of the God who thereby
accomplished this eternal deliverance. In the very purpose and intention and
in the execution of the will thereby revealed and effected, He was already the
Creator of the creature, and He is also its Sustainer, and the One who co-operates
with it in its own work—always and everywhere. As *causa prima* He precedes
and accompanies and follows the *causae secundae*. Therefore His *causare* consists,
and consists only, in the fact that He bends their activity to the execution of His
own will which is His will of grace, subordinating their operations to the specific
operation which constitutes the history of the covenant of grace. In all things
and in all their particular operations this is the first and final achievement. And
it is because of this that His *causare* is almighty and all-powerful, the true and
original *causare* above which there is no other. It is because of this that the One
who is *causans* at this point is the *causa causarum*, the *causa sui*, the *causa
princeps*, in relation to which all other causes can be only *causae particulares*.
He is *causa* in the sense specified and qualified by the power of His grace. And
it is in this form and for this reason that He is *causa prima*.

And who and what is the *causa secunda* which confronts us here as that which
is sovereignly accompanied by the *causa prima* ? Certainly it is not yet the new
creation which is taken up into unity with the Creator in Jesus Christ. Certainly
it is not yet the creation which as the Church and people of Jesus Christ, in the
knowledge and faith of Him and in His discipleship, already has a part in the
eternal deliverance which was accomplished by Him. But already it is the
creation which in some degree approximates to this new creation, which by its
very existence is posited and sanctified with it under the promise, which already
is ordained to be the object and recipient of the divine mercy. There is no
creature which does not owe its existence as such and as *causa*, which does not

owe its opportunities and operations, to the Creator and Sustainer whose will was from all eternity the election of His grace, and whose will is already accomplished in the deliverance which was effected in Jesus Christ. As *causa secunda* it is accompanied by the *causa prima* and preceded and followed by it. Therefore its own *causare* can take place only under the determination and limitation appointed by it. Its own operations can have a place only as they are subordinated to the divine operations which constitute the history of the covenant of grace. They can therefore be only the indirect divine operations of grace. Seeing that all things with their own particular activity must serve the activity of grace, their activity is a subordinate one even in its autonomy. The operation of *causae particulares* is under the direction of the *causa princeps*. They have to be thought of as *causae secundae* in the true sense i.e., *secundae* not in relation to some higher power, but to the grace of God and the almighty operation of that grace.

This is the positive condition under which the introduction of the causal concept into the doctrine of the *concursus* may be regarded as theologically possible and incontestable. If this condition is fulfilled the proofs from Scripture adduced by the older dogmaticians lose the air of fortuitousness which clings to them in their writings. We see the biblical centre which makes the matter a genuine problem of theology. Interpreted in the light of this centre the causal concept is certainly not exposed to the dangers against which we have been considering a defence. And in the light of this interpretation of the causal concept the defence itself is meaningful, compelling and effective.

In these circumstances the concept *causa* has (1) on both sides a content in virtue of which it certainly embraces natural events and the uniformity of their processes, and yet cannot be identified with the narrow concept of a mechanical natural cause which effects and is effected automatically. For what can there be in common between Jesus Christ and a despot ? What can there be in common between the fulfilment of His gracious will in heaven and on earth, the strictness with which His activity of grace precedes, accompanies and follows the activity of the creature, and an absolute compulsion ? What can there be in common between the activity of the creature under the conditioning and within the limitation of this governance, and an automatic process ?

The concept *causa* has also (2) a content in virtue of which it certainly cannot be identified either on the one side or the other with a " thing." If the *causa prima* is the mercy of God, and the *causa secunda* is its object and recipient, then it follows that neither the one nor the other can ever be controlled by the one who meditates or speaks concerning them. For what is there here that we can " realise " ? We stand before the mystery of grace both on the one side and on the other. It is clear that the *causa prima* can be known only in prayer, and the *causa secunda* in gratitude, or else not at all. No thinker or speaker can ever be above these things, but only under them. If in a dead orthodoxy he is over something, then *ipso facto* it is not either the *causa prima* or the *causa secunda* in this sense.

The concept *causa* has (3) a content in virtue of which the two things signified by it cannot possibly be compared. If we keep before us the archetype of divine-human co-operation, the co-operation of the holy God and sinful man in the covenant of grace ; if we have regard to the antithesis which in Jesus Christ became an antithesis in unity, we shall refrain from drawing any parallels or comparisons, we shall be delivered from the evil desire to find a master-concept, a common denominator, a genus, a synthesis, in which God and the creature can be brought together, and we shall be kept from the pleasure of finding analogies between the two subjects. In fact the two subjects are together and they work together, but this fact can be understood only as the gracious mystery of an encounter in which that which is quite inconceivable and unexpected and undeserved has actually come to pass.

And self-evidently, the causal concept has (4) no content in virtue of which it ceases to be part of the Christian confession and theological knowledge and becomes part of a philosophical scheme of things. For when the two subjects are so very different, but so closely inter-related, clearly it is only by revelation and in faith that the *causa princeps* and the *causa particularis* can be known both in and for themselves and in the *concursus* of their two-fold *causare*.

These, then, are the five conditions under which we can approve the use of the causal concept which was so significant in the *concursus* teaching of the older dogmatics. The fulfilling of the first four of these conditions depends upon the fulfilling of the fifth. And of the fifth the older dogmatics unfortunately did not make any mention. No wonder, then, that they were not secure even in respect of the first four. It is true that the experiment with Aristotle and Thomas did not turn out so badly as it might have done. But this merely goes to show that even the history of doctrine *hominum confusione Dei providentia regitur*. It is, therefore, a living example of that which we are here concerned to maintain. But this fact does not absolve us from the task of developing the interpretation of the causal concept in which alone the form of the proposition as we have made it cannot be disputed.

We now turn to the material side of the question and our answer to it. But first we make the methodological observation that even here we have to do only with the operation of God. It is the question of His operation from the standpoint of a co-operation with that of the creature, but it is still a question of His operation, of His accompanying of the creature even in its own operation. And this means that we cannot consider propositions concerning the creature as such, but only concerning God the Creator in His relationship with the creature.

When God works, His operation is almighty in relation to that of the creature. It is an operation which is absolutely above the power of the creature. The majesty in which He accompanies the activity of the creature and co-operates with it is quite unconditional both in general and in particular. And the majesty of the operation of God consists in the fact that it is the operation of His eternal love. We describe it very badly if we simply ascribe to it formally a much greater potency than that of the creature. It is the relation of purely creaturely potencies that we have to measure and understand quantitatively, not that of the divine potency to the creaturely. And we also describe it very badly if we count its potency relative to the creature as part of the general relationship of infinity to one. We could not describe even the relation of heaven and earth in that way. And in any case it would give us only an immanent contrast without touching the real antithesis between God and the creature, and their mutual inter-connexion. The divine potency, and therefore the divine working in relation to that of the creature, is above that of the creature because God is eternal love. The love of God is primary. The creature can only be loved by God, and then at best love Him in return. The love of God is essential. As Father, Son and Holy Ghost, God is love in and of Himself, and in the overflowing of this love He loves the creature. But the creature can only accept this love, and be content to try to respond to it. The love of God is eternal. God loves even as the Creator of time. But at best the creature can love God, and does love Him, only in the time allotted to it. And all this means distance in the relation between God and the creature—and not only distance, but the pre-eminence of God over it, the relation of his absolute power to the lowly power of the creature. Hence the almightiness in which God accompanies and co-operates with the creature consists in this absolute distinction of the two potencies. And the difference in the potencies at work carries with it an irreversibility in the order of precedence and dignity of the divine and human activities. It is hardly possible to see any necessary irreversibility in the order of precedence of the greater and the less, or infinity and one. The greater needs the less, and infinity one, no less than the reverse. But the order of precedence of the eternal love of God and the creature as the object of this love is absolutely irreversible, for God does not need the creature, but the creature has absolute need of God.

This means that we can never look too high when we think of the Father of Jesus Christ who accompanies the creature as *causa prima*. The power of natural phenomena, or historical forces, or even ideas, may have something shatteringly great about it. And so too, in the proper context, can that which we mean by natural necessity. And so too can that which in many languages and forms has been described as destiny, fate, *ananke*, or *kismet*. But we do not look high enough if we expect to find the greatness of God in the greatness of experiences and perceptions and concepts of this sort. There is no irreversibility in the relation of these high quantities to the other quantities ostensibly ranged so utterly beneath them. We cannot question their superiority. Not in any form or to any degree can we defy or oppose their pre-eminence. But we can at least explain their superiority as a relative superiority. It is a superiority which is not grounded in a qualitative distinction. God alone is genuinely and ultimately and absolutely superior in relation to all the reality which is distinct from Himself. God alone is unequivocally *causa prima*, and He is so because He is eternal love, and His activity is eternally to love. This is why His activity is greater than all these other activities, of which the same cannot be said. This is why He Himself is holy as contrasted with all the beings with whom He co-operates. This is why He is to be feared by all those whose ways and works He accompanies. He is the Lord of all lords and the King of all kings. He is the One who dwells in a light which is inaccessible to all those who go and work with Him. Can there be any question which they have more reason to fear as they themselves are active according to the measure of their creaturely being—the depth of the abyss of nothingness which is always ready to engulf them and to frustrate all their striving on the one hand, or the height of God on the other, of the God who upholds them, and without whose upholding they would immediately be lost, and the futility of their striving would immediately be confirmed ? It is because God is love, and no creature can continue for a moment if it refuses this love, that God is the only One who is really to be feared.

We have not made any secret of the way in which we know that the divine activity accompanies that of the creature with so great a superiority. We have understood this supremacy as the supremacy of God's eternal love. We have not deduced it from any human conception of God. We have sought it rather in the holiness which is at the heart of all divine activity. We have listened to the Word of grace in which God has Himself revealed Himself in Jesus Christ. We have learned and perceived who and what God is, and how He works, according to His own Word. It is there in that Word that we have seen the height from which He works. It is there that we have seen the irreversibility in the order of precedence of His own activity and all other activity. It is there that we have seen the qualitative distinction of His power as contrasted with all other powers, and its absolute superiority over them. It is there that we have seen Him as eternal love. And what we have received there, we possess with a decisive and final certainty. That is why we cannot treat of the perception and understanding of the superiority of the divine work in the same way as we can of a human opinion, or as indeed we must of even the most serious of human suggestions. In other words, we are not in any position to treat of this perception and understanding as though they were open to discussion. Naturally, our own comprehension and exposition and formulation of them are always open to discussion. By its very nature the matter is one which demands constantly a better formulation. But as it does so, it remains outside and above the sphere in which it can itself be called in question. It is a matter which questions us. Our relation to it can consist only in our rendering an account *to* it rather than *of* it.

It is because it is eternal love that the power of the divine operation is superior to all other powers, and the knowledge of it is not open to discussion. But if this is the case, then in relation to all other operations or activities we must think of the divine activity as first and foremost a free activity—free in the sense that it is a work which God does not owe either to Himself or to the creature. God does not will to work without the creature but with it. And He holds to this and does it. He does it with an inward necessity. And this involves an unbreakable order in the work of the creature, for in that the creature exists God exists with it in the supremacy of His own work. Because God wills to preserve it in its reality, and because this reality is change, God accompanies it in this change. This law of the creaturely world, that God is present and active in all that occurs within it, is more fixed than any natural law or mathematical axiom. But the necessity with which God does hold to this and do it is the necessity of His love. And love is free or it is not love. Therefore when God accompanies the creature He gives Himself. In so doing He is not the prisoner either of Himself or of the creature. He still acts according to His good-pleasure. When the love of God overflows in the creating, the preserving, and now the accompanying of the creature, this means that it is revealed in its freedom. And it is in this freedom that it is necessary to God.

It is excellent to see how in H. Heidegger a knowledge which is Christian in origin and character—although it is not of course recognised to be such— can still break through the limitations of Aristotelian conceptuality in which a freedom of this kind cannot be ascribed to God : *Causae primae convenit, ut ad extra independenter et libere operetur. Proin concursus est libera Dei operatio, quam adhibere vel non adhibere possit.* By His own eternal decree (and only so) God has bound himself actually to fulfil this *operatio*, constituting His co-operation with the creature a *firma et adamantina lex* (quoted from Heppe[2], p. 210). Even as He gives Himself to this relationship to the creature, God is still its Lord.

For this reason the presence and co-operation of God cannot be thought of as a predicate or exponent of creaturely occurrence. The proposition that God is immanent in this occurrence is a true one in the sense that in face of it He does make this and not another use of His freedom, that He gives Himself to it as a Companion, that in His supremacy—the supremacy of His love—He on His side co-operates with all creaturely activity. It is true in so far as it speaks of the fidelity with which God is true to His own resolve and therefore to the creature. But since this first proposition is true only in this very precise sense, the further proposition that all occurrence is immanent in God is necessarily false. When we speak of God in nature, or God in history, we cannot mean that in some degree it belongs to nature and history, as one of their properties, that God should be at work in them. They have no claim upon God for that. They on their side have no power to co-operate with God. It can only turn out that they do so in fact to the extent that God takes the initiative towards them, He Himself co-operating with them and giving them on their side the opportunity—beyond any capacity of their own—to co-operate with Him. By the grace of God the events of nature and history are authorised and qualified to co-operate with him. In itself and as such their activity is their own. It is limited as they are limited, and it cannot go outside those limits. And when God with His activity associates Himself with them, this does not mean that nature and history become God. Even when the events of nature and history are in every respect the work of God, the same is not true of nature and history as such. It is rather that God Himself accompanies those events, co-operating in them, introducing them and revealing them as His own work. Hence it follows that the work of God in the working of the creature, and His revelation in the revealing of the creature, can never be ascribed to the creature, but only and always to God

Himself. That which works is His co-operating love. That which speaks is His co-operating Word. And for that working and speaking the creature on its side has no capacity. It is not, then, the creature which works in God's working, but God Himself who works on and in His own working. God alone is and remains eternal love. The creature can only be loved by Him, or at the very best love Him in return. The freedom of God cannot be violated. An awareness of the supremacy of God over all the power of the creature, of the qualitative distinction between divine and creaturely potency, of the irreversibility of the order of precedence in divine and creaturely activity, must be brought into play and relentlessly kept in play at this juncture.

It is quite impossible to build upon the doctrine of the *concursus*, the perception that God accompanies all creaturely occurrence, a scheme of things in which the world as such is also divine, nature as such is the nature-God, history as such is the history of God, and man as such is the God-man. Such a view can only be a magical one. The godhead or divinity to which it refers can only be a plurality of demons, or a single arch-demon. This is a possible point of entry for all the dangerous heresies which have first endangered the knowledge of the divine providence and then Christian knowledge as a whole. In one connexion or another we are given the (within its limits) quite legitimate impression of the power of creaturely activity. It may be the activity of nature, perhaps an isolated phenomenon or a great natural process. It may be the activity of men as they are caught up and swept forward in a specific movement. It may be the activity of the human spirit in one or other of its different forms. We are so mastered and carried away by the impression that we think it impossible to conceive of anything more majestic or significant, more solemn or overpowering : *quo majus cogitari non potest !* And we think it necessary to attribute this *causare* to a *causa* of a similar character, to a first and final subject, personal perhaps or impersonal, but in either case incomparable. We think that we are driven back to an A and O. We participate in the revelation which it brings, subjecting ourselves to its dominion, and receiving from it comfort and direction. And this—we deduce quite logically—is the power in all events. It is this which is before and after and above and with all things and all events. It is this with and by and to which man must live. It is this which he must love and praise—this goodness, it may be this utility, perhaps this beauty, perhaps quite simply this greatness, this force, this extreme and potency of creaturely occurrence. And it is to this that the trembling finger points, and the eye is rooted and turns, and the ear bends and the whole heart strains—this demon or arch-demon by which man has been overpowered and to which he has made surrender : " They changed the truth of God into a lie, and worshipped and served the creature rather than the Creator " (Rom. 1[25]). That is what may happen when the perception of the almightiness of God as contrasted with all the power of the creature is not so safeguarded that it cannot possibly be disputed. Secretly or openly, a powerful creaturely *causa* is exalted to the divine dignity and function, and under this one sign and at this one crucial point the doctrine of the providence of God becomes the doctrine of the divinity of the cosmos. And it is not impossible that this type of secularised doctrine of providence may for a time be accompanied by what is in the narrower sense a religious doctrine of salvation and redemption, in which on one or another view or interpretation there may even be a place for Jesus Christ. The first half of the 19th century had its Schiller and Goethe, its Fichte and Schelling and Hegel, but taken as a whole it was not immediately or in any exclusive sense hostile either to the Church or to Christianity. And when the building of the National-Socialist temple first began, it was commonly believed that at least in the forecourt there would be a Christian, a German-Christian chapel, and that in that chapel there would be a place and a use for the Bible, and for Jesus and Paul and Luther. But this type of alliance does not usually last long. A decision is required, for we cannot really serve two masters. On the one hand, the Christian chapel, assuming that it does not disappear altogether, will quickly become the cult-centre of the god who is really believed to be the world-ruler. On the other, it will come to be seen, or it will be remembered, that Jesus Christ will not allow Himself to be relegated to the place of a redeemer side by side with whom there may be a world-ruler of quite a different stamp, whether ideal or aesthetic or technical or political. Jesus Christ Himself occupies the position of World-ruler, and side by side with Him there is no room for another—and as this is seen or remembered there will grow up a centre of resistance even within that chapel. But quite apart from this Christian decision, and quite apart from the fact that Christians may or may not resist, such heresies and the demons which achieve power by means of them usually have their day, and then when their course is run their dominion passes. In our own age we have lived to see the temple-building of a newly resuscitated slavery. Its façade is radical Marxism. It seems in this case that a Christian chapel has been provisionally omitted. It would be to the honour of the Gospel if it could remain so. But what is certain is that this error, too, will have its day, and then go the same way as it came. It is only unfortunate that in spite of all our previous experiences the hydra-heads continue to spring up, and one error seems so rapidly to be dissolved by another which is apparently contrary to it, and yet no less deadly. For example, the idolising of the spirit in the first half of the 19th century was followed by that of matter in the second, and both by the strange absolutising of human existence in the first half of the 20th. The only thorough and comprehensive and radical safeguard is in the Christian decision. If the supremacy of the activity of God is not secured first, the creaturely forces are too strong for such impressions not to be made and such errors not to arise. But the supremacy of the activity of God is secured only when the irreversibility of its relationship to all other forces is secured, and this is secured where its qualitative distinction from those forces is secured, and this in turn is secured only when it is secured that it is the power of eternal love. But it is only in the knowledge of the work and revelation of God in Jesus Christ that all this can be perceived to be secure, and perceived in such a way that categorical decisions can and must be taken in the light of it—decisions which will give us a thoroughgoing and comprehensive and radical safeguard against all the quidproquos possible or conceivable at this point.

A first thing which we have to say concerning the freedom of God is that God applies His activity only on the basis of His own good-pleasure. The *concursus*, or divine operation in relation to the creature, is an act of sovereignty the honour of which is God's honour. There can be no question either of transferring this honour to the creature or of sharing it between God and the creature.

But now we must go on to say that it is God's own will which is done in this act of sovereignty. And this will is not limited by the " givenness " or determination of the creature, nor is it conditioned by any act of the creature. On the contrary, it is the will which conditions these acts. The concept of *concursus* is itself irreversible. God " concurs " with the creature, but the creature does not " concur " with God. That is, the activity of the creature does not impose any conditions upon the activity of God. As against that, the " concurrence " of God with the creature, being His own and absolutely supreme, means that the activity of God conditions absolutely the activity of the creature. As God co-operates with the activity of the creature, His own activity precedes, accompanies and follows that activity, and nothing can be done except the will of God.

It is here that we see clearly how necessary it is to explain the doctrine of divine providence from the biblical and Christian standpoint, that is, to consider the rule of God over and with the creature in the light of His rule in the covenant of grace, and of His work and revelation in Jesus Christ.

Let us suppose for a moment that we found it quite impossible to perceive or understand from this biblical centre that which we have already said generally concerning the sovereignty of the will and work of God in relation to the creature. In that case " God " would be a purely formal concept, denoting a supreme being endowed with absolute, unconditioned and irresistible power ; the " will of God " would be a purely formal concept denoting the unconditioned and incontrovertible purpose of this supreme being ; and the " work of God " would denote the unconditioned and irresistible execution of this purpose over against and in and on the activity of the creature. It is obvious in what an impasse we should then find ourselves. We could think of God's rule over and with and in the creature only as that of a sovereign caprice, in the hands of which the creature would appear to act, but in fact would only be acted upon, and this in pursuance of a purpose which is utterly obscure. The demand for belief in God would then be a demand for the recognition and willing acceptance by man of the unconditioned work of the unconditioned will of this unconditionally supreme being, and his willing submission to it without any real perception of what it is that he must approve, or of the extent to which there can be any question of a real willingness on his part. And what will our reaction be when we find ourselves in such a position ?

It may be that we will cease to reflect upon the goodness or nongoodness of the lordship imposed upon us, or our own willingness or unwillingness in face of it, and simply decide upon submission to superior force, or resignation. But if we do this, how far are we really obedient to God ? That is, how far is this a genuine faith, involving a perception of the will of God and a real submission to it ? Is not this what the Stoics are taught to do in face of an all-powerful destiny, or the Moslems in face of the inscrutable will of Allah ? How can a consciously blind decision of this character be a genuine decision of the Christian obedience of faith ?

But who knows, may it not be that we will take up the opposite attitude of complaint, protest and rejection in face of this dominion imposed upon us ? We will perhaps describe this dominion as the dominion of caprice, and the God who rules with this absolute sovereignty a tyrant. And in this opposition we will either despair or conclude that we are absolved from all further responsibility and justified in frivolity. And we will argue that God is responsible either for our despair or our frivolity. We will not presume to deny His supreme and unconditioned and irresistible disposing, but openly or secretly we will hate and despise it. And it will not be long before we refuse to this all-dominating force the name of God, rejecting a God who is the author of the inescapable process of events, and speaking instead of destiny or nature or the like. And under this title we will finally conclude with this force a separate peace of exhaustion, thus returning to the first path. Clearly, this second possibility has nothing whatever to do with the Christian obedience of faith.

But is it really any wonder that we vacillate between those two possibilities when we learn of the will and work of God only in this formal way ? Where there is only this formal instruction, is not the demand for belief in Almighty God too great ? Does not this kind of instruction almost necessarily drive us to one or other of those forms of unbelief ? But there is still a third possibility. It may be that we will simply deny that the divine will is so sovereign in execution, or its operation so unconditioned and irresistible, as has so far been assumed. May it not be after all that the concept *concursus* is in some degree reversible ? May it not be that there is as it were a conditioning and determining and to that extent a limiting of the activity of God by the activity of the creature ? May it not be that although God did in fact know of this activity from all eternity, so that in this sense at least it is still under His dominion, yet this divine foreknowledge is not an omnipotent operation, but a proportionate liberty is granted to the activity of the creature, and the work of God is fulfilled with a regard to that of the creature which means in effect an accommodation to it ? Obviously, this line of retreat is open. It has been taken with innumerable variations. And we have to admit that in that impasse, if we are not to give way to resignation or to go over to complaint and protest, if we are not to fall victim to either despair or frivolity, the path is attractive and readily accessible. It removes the unbearable tension of the assertion that God is all in all. The demand for belief in God becomes a possible one because in effect it resolves itself into the twofold invitation, to believe in the divine will and work as it is limited by the creature, and to believe in a creaturely will and work which limit the Creator. This demand is obviously supportable, for after all, what is there to believe ? At a pinch, such a relationship could be imagined quite apart from God. But even in that form, does it really give us God when it offers us a supreme being whose will is not sovereignly executed in all the activity of the creature, whose eternal knowledge is not his will and work but only the knowledge of a helpless or disinterested spectator, whose activity is " concurred " in and conditioned by that of the creature ? And does it really give us the creature of God when it offers us a creature which can " concur " in the activity of God, conditioning and influencing this activity and forcing its accommodation to its own creaturely activity ? And if we subject ourselves to the will of God on this presupposition, is it really the Christian obedience of faith ? Is it subjection at all ? Is it obedience ? And what has it to do with faith ? Is it not another form of unbelief, and perhaps the worst form of all, seeing that it removes this serious demand ? But to be fair we must admit that if the first two possibilities fall to the ground because of their manifest impiety, what is there but this third possibility with its secret impiety—always assuming, of course, that we have only that formal knowledge of God and of the will and work of God.

It is here that from the historical standpoint we come to what might be called the tragedy of the Reformed doctrine of providence and more particularly of the divine *concursus*.

The great advantage of this doctrine is that it did venture, and even carried to its logical conclusion, the proposition which alone corresponds to the true relation between God and the creature : that it is absolutely the will of God alone which is executed in all creaturely activity and creaturely occurrence. It did genuinely think of the *concursus divinus* as irreversible. It did not take into account any possible concurring of the creature in the will and work of God. It conceived of this will and work as unconditioned and unlimited and irresistible. It accepted and emphasised the demand implicit in this confession. We can see this in Calvin (*Instit.* I, 16–18) no less logically if not so provocatively as in Zwingli's *De providentia*, and in the Reformed orthodox theologians of the 16th and 17th centuries no less logically than in Calvin. Indeed, the concepts and terminology taken over from Scholasticism were applied by them in such a way as to push this aspect of the matter to its logical conclusion. We must be quite clear in our minds that it is this conception which stands at the back of *Questions* 26-28 of the *Heidelberg Catechism*, and that we cannot expound the *Catechism* literally if this conception is denied.

If only the Christian sense of it, as it appears in the *Heidelberg Catechism*, had been more clearly perceived, or better, more radically developed ! But this was not the case either with Zwingli or Calvin, or the later Reformed dogmaticians. They ventured the proposition and carried it to its logical conclusion, and for this we must applaud them when we consider the way in which it has been weakened and watered down in the later history of the doctrine right up to the present time. But they ventured it—and this we can and must describe as their tragic fault—only on the same presupposition of purely formal concepts of God and His will and work as that of their opponents. Naturally, they maintained and protested that the will and work of God is holy and just and good. But they could never explain or say how it is that those qualities can be ascribed to it, or how far men can reasonably and justifiably be demanded to believe in the God who works all in all, or to what extent submission to the will and work of God is the obedience of faith necessarily required of the Christian. They were in fact pointing us to the dark when they spoke about the decree of God fulfilled in creaturely events. In their general discussion of the relation between God and the creature they could not and would not take into account the content of this decree. They pointed to the supremacy of God which excludes any possible conditioning by the creature, but they could not characterise this supremacy.

The result was that in practice at any rate they could not exclude the possibility of an interpretation of the Christian obedience of faith in terms of a Stoic or Islamic resignation. And a further result was that in practice they did not cease to foment the murmuring of the clay against the potter (Rom. 9$^{20f.}$), the revolt against a capricious sovereign rule, and the despair or frivolity which is the inevitable consequence of this revolt. But the chief result was that those who held back from the first two possibilities were provoked to take the line of retreat—a retreat to the mediaeval synergism which the Reformation had victoriously left behind with its doctrine of grace and justification, and which the Reformed divines were seeking to overthrow in this very matter. The Romanist propaganda of the Counter-Reformation must have taken malicious pleasure in what appeared from a distance to be the quite absurd picture of a Calvinistic God who rendered illusory any individual activity on the part of the creature. So this was the evil consequence of the mistake which the Reformers had first committed in the sphere of grace and justification! And at this point there rang out the challenge—which the fathers of the Council of Trent thought that they had heard, but now in respect of the whole field of theology—to put forward more prudently than with the later Scotists, with a proportionate regard for the contest of Augustine with Pelagius, and a clever mobilising of the new Humanistic interest, but all the more consciously and determinedly and tenaciously, the solution according to which the sole dominion of God has its own conditioning in the work of the creature, and must not transgress this limit. In the same way Lutheranism—which after the death of Luther had quickly abandoned the *De servo arbitrio* and committed itself to the mediating theology of the older Melanchthon—necessarily took serious offence at the over-logical Reformed doctrine of God and providence, some Lutherans even going so far as to accuse and convict all Calvinists of apostasy to Islam, and protesting that they themselves had more fellowship with Rome than with a Geneva which maintained such a doctrine of the *concursus divinus*. Again, even within Calvinism itself it was inevitable that there should be many reactions towards synergism under Renaissance influences. The most famous of these was the movement of Jacob Arminius and his friends, which was defeated only with great effort and at great cost at the Synod of Dort. The final upshot was that the school of Saumur at the end of the 17th century, and the later orthodoxy of the Enlightenment, relapsed into a fairly crude semi-Pelagianism of a pietist-rationalist type.

We may bewail the many-sided declension from the older Reformed conception, but we cannot overlook the fact that, in so far as it meant a demand for faith which, constituted as it then was, it could not possibly meet, it was itself the cause of this declension. The concept was a correct one, but from the very outset it lacked the foundation which would have made it credible, distinguishing it from a questionable philosophoumenon. It is no less true, of course, that the synergistic constructions opposed to it by the Romanists, Lutherans, Arminians, and later the Moderns, could not be distinguished from a mere philosophoumenon, but all of them lay sick in the same ward, playing with the same empty concepts without any reference to the biblical centre. But although their conception was correct in itself, the Reformed fathers were in no better case than the others. On the contrary, their opponents had the advantage that in their statements they did seem to take more account of the demands of ordinary reason and practical piety than did the sinister heralds of an even more sinister deity. For this was what the Reformed divines appeared to be. Indeed, this is what they were—shockingly enough—and all because of their inability to apply fruitfully to this field the proper centre of all Reformed knowledge, the doctrine of grace and justification. It is certainly no accident that, notwithstanding the zeal with which it was defended throughout the 17th century, the doctrine which they did not fruitfully apply quietly became so much dead capital, so that when a great inventory was made at the beginning of the 18th century, it was inevitably discovered that for a long time it had only been valueless paper with no possible purchasing power in the age which was then dawning.

And it was little consolation that against all the expectations of the Reformed Church there arose a great theologian, of a stature approaching that of Zwingli and Calvin, namely, F. E. D. Schleiermacher, who apparently, but unfortunately only apparently, exalted against all forms of synergism the great conception of the sole dominion of God and the absolute dependence of the creature. For what Schleiermacher discovered was as little influenced by the Reformation doctrine of grace and justification (which he never understood) as was the doctrine of providence held by Zwingli, Calvin and their Reformed successors, who had certainly understood it, but did not know how to apply it. What Schleiermacher discovered was a kind of compromise, a philosophical doctrine of the sole supremacy of God which rested upon the dialectic of nature and spirit, and within which there was of course a specific and indeed a central place for the religious possibility as such. Hence the historical religions could be rated very highly, and especially the religion founded by Jesus of Nazareth. And in the same way Schleiermacher could speak quite cleverly of the self-evident nature of the Evangelical Church in its Reformed dress. But in no sense did he succeed better than the older Reformed divines in giving a sounder or deeper basis to the Reformed conception of the *concursus divinus*, or in rendering the conception more credible, although it is one with which he must have had some sympathy as an expression of the absolute dependence of the finite on the infinite, of the individual on the totality. On the contrary, we have to admit that the way in which he championed the conception exposed it to all the suspicions which have surrounded it from the very outset, even to that of Spinozism, or more generally of a pantheistic-naturalistic monism. The result was that it was pushed more and more into the shadows, and this time seriously, in the eyes of all right-thinking men. In this respect Reformed theology reaped what it had sown as early as the 16th century with its failure to think out the basis of its doctrine of providence from a serious Christian standpoint.

To understand the *concursus divinus*, the divine accompanying of creaturely activity, in a Christian sense as the sovereign act in which the will of God is unconditionally and irresistibly fulfilled in the activity of the creature, we have not to begin with empty concepts but with concepts which are already filled out with Christian meaning.

When we say " God " we have to understand the One who as Father, Son, and Holy Ghost is eternal love, and has life in Himself ; the One who as such is the self-existent One, the Almighty high above all creatures, the *causa causarum*.

When we say " the will of God " we have to understand His fatherly good-will, His decree of grace in Jesus Christ, the mercy in which from all eternity He undertook to save the creature, and to give it eternal life in the fellowship with Himself ; the will which as such is His kingly will, disposing unconditionally and irresistibly of the existence and activity of the creature.

And when we say " the work of God " we have to understand His execution in history of the covenant of grace upon the basis of the decree of grace, with its fulfilment in the sacrifice of His Son and its confirmation in the work of the Holy Spirit awakening to faith and obedience : the work which as such is His work of power in the whole created sphere, above and in and before and with and after all creaturely activity ; the work in virtue of which all creaturely activity is completely under His control and subject to Him.   And in all these things what is needed is a radical re-thinking of the whole matter.   First we have to drop the ordinary but harmful conception of cause, operation and effect.   Then, when we know who God is and what He wills and how He works, we have to take it up again, but giving to it a new force and application in which we do not look back to what are at root godless notions of causality.

If we will take this course, we can avoid the impasse into which we are inevitably led by those empty concepts.   We can also avoid the extremely unpleasant choice between the three false possibilities by which we are otherwise inescapably confronted.   If this is the meaning of the sovereign and almighty rule of God, if it has this aspect, the only aspect which is really commensurate with it, then it cannot be described as obscure or capricious, nor can the creaturely activity which occurs under the divine lordship be thought of merely as an effect.   The overruling love of the triune God is light and not darkness. And although the rule of this love confronts the creature as supreme in fact, and externally inscrutable in detail, in itself, and known to be the rule of God, it is still light and not darkness.   Again, the world-rule of the fatherly good-will of God, if it is known to be such, does not bear any relationship to caprice.   And since its activity is the activity of grace, its almightiness does not in any sense destroy the free activity of the creature.   On the contrary, we have to think of the majesty and absoluteness and irresistibility of the divine activity as the confirmation and continually renewed basis of the singularity of the creature to whom God is gracious, and of its worth, and independent activity.   It is only empty concepts of God and His will and work which will give rise to perverted notions of this type.   They are excluded by concepts which are filled out with a Christian meaning.   And if we take this seriously, then it means that the demand for faith in God, and in the dominion of God, is also meaningful.   We can learn in the Word of God who and what this invisible and inconceivable God is who rules over all things, and what it is that this God wills and does.   And with all the inscrutability of the form of creaturely occurrence, we can take this knowledge to our hearts.   And as believers in the Word of God and witnesses to the work of the Spirit we certainly lose any desire to discuss whether in face of the unconditional supremacy of God there can be such a thing as a human willingness to believe.   We are now in a position to say to all the errors to which we are inevitably led in that impasse : No, No, and again No.   No, for in the decision of faith we are worlds removed from the apathetic surrender to the inevitable, which may work out either for joy or sorrow, but is always fatal, because it is fatalistic.   We are worlds removed from such a surrender, because at the crucial point of decision we are not blind, but see.   And No, for we cannot for a single moment continue to repudiate the almighty lordship of God, and certainly we cannot allow ourselves to slip into despair or frivolity. For what sense is there either in a weak capitulation or in the futile defiance of despair or frivolity when it is the fatherly good-will of God which is the power over all things. And No again, for least of all can we take that line of retreat ; least of all will it occur to us to make of the God who is all in all a God who is only much in much, regarding His sovereignty and omnipotence as limited, His activity as conditioned, concurred in or partly conditioned by the creature, and therefore the divine *concursus* as reversible. If we hold fast to God's decree of grace in Jesus Christ, and to His activity of grace in the history of the covenant, we can never dream of setting the creature over against God as a kind of second party to the contract, knowing as we do that the creature has no freedom but that which is grounded on the unconditioned and irresistible freedom and supremacy of God, having no power to concur but only to corroborate and understand and glorify. If we take absolutely seriously the meaning and character of the divine lordship, we are in a position to take with equal seriousness recognition of it as such.

The activity of God precedes, *praecurrit*, that of the creature. As we vindicate and follow the older Reformed theology we must take this proposition first.

What concerns us is the activity of the merciful God. It is the Father of Jesus Christ whose almighty will and work precede all other will and work—His eternal love. God precedes with His own will and work all other will and work because His decree of grace in Jesus Christ has already preceded the creation of all things and therefore the being and activity of the creature. He precedes it in the same way as His eternity—not any eternity but the eternity of His love, His eternal being as Father, Son and Holy Ghost—precedes all time and all being in time. Always and everywhere when the creature works, God is there as the One who has already loved it, who has already undertaken to save and glorify it, who in this sense and to this end has already worked even before the creature itself began to work, even before the conditions, and pre-conditions, and pre-pre-conditions of its working were laid down. " My Father worketh hitherto, and I work " (Jn. 5^{17}). God created the conditions and pre-conditions and pre-pre-conditions of all creaturely working. God gave them to the creature. All the preliminaries of creaturely activity were the effect of God's activity, of His friendly activity in the sense and to the end revealed and active in Jesus Christ, and in the history of the covenant of grace, of His activity as it was determined and controlled by His saving will. From the very first the purpose of God was to save and glorify the creature. All the works which are causes of this or that creaturely activity are the works of His mercy. Already in the sphere from which this or that creature comes to do this or that work He is the sovereign Lord of the creature, not limited by any contradiction or opposition, but sovereign in the definite sense. And it is from this sphere that God accompanies the creature and controls its activity.

Concursus Dei praevius est, quo . . . causa secundam . . . ad agendum praedeterminat adeoque creaturae actum non tempore sed ordine, dignitate, et praecellentia praecedit (H. Heidegger quoted from Heppe[2], p. 210). We accept this formulation generally, although understanding by *ordo, dignitas* and *praecellentia* the fatherly wisdom of God. But we must not overlook the extent to which the *concursus Dei* must precede the *actio* of the *causa secunda* even in time as well : certainly not in time only ; but in time as well to the extent that the creaturely conditions normative for the operation of the *causa secunda* are also in time, and even in their temporality are the effects of His eternal divine activity. *Aeternitate et tempore, ordine namque dignitate et praecellentia gratiae praecedit*—this is how Heidegger's statement ought to run. And the correction is important because it means that the predetermining activity of God cannot be given a Kantian sense as the *a priori* of reason as opposed to an empirical event. On this view the opposition and connexion between divine and creaturely activity would be immanent within the world. Our understanding is a safeguard against any such transformation. It is quite impossible to demand that the work of the Father of Jesus Christ should be expounded as an *a priori* of reason. But any such view is precluded by the fact that the eternally preceding activity of God does not exclude but includes a temporal preceding.

What concerns us is a preceding activity and not merely a preceding knowledge of the merciful God. It is not merely that God foresees a certain work of the creature in virtue of His eternal knowledge of all things, and then awaits the accomplishment of it, leaving the creature the choice between this or that possibility of action, and then in its execution granting the indispensable assistance of His own almighty operation.

At this point the older Lutherans attempted artifices of which we can say only that they are equally suspect and unnecessary. According to their account the *concursus divinus* in a sense only begins with the creaturely action. *Non antecedit sed fit cum actio ipsa producitur : concurrit, coagit, cooperatur.* That the creature chooses this or that movement is its own doing, not God's. What is of God in it is simply the *vis operandi* in the execution of the movement chosen (A. Calov, *Syst. theol.*, 1655 f., III, *art.* 6, 2, *qu.* 1). In opposing the Calvinist view of the *concursus*, and therefore the predetermination of creaturely activity, the intention was to avoid fatalism, and especially the dreaded conclusion : *Deus auctor et mali.* But it was done at the price of making God a strangely passive spectator and assistant of the creature, excluding the divine activity at the decisive point where the creaturely activity is itself decision—a truly fateful secularisation of creaturely freedom for which the honour paid to the divine activity in wider spheres was no adequate compensation. And in any case we cannot escape fatalism and the *Deus auctor et mali* simply by denying the *praedeterminatio* but accepting the *praevisio*, ascribing the will to the creature, but the execution of it to God. In theology as elsewhere it is an ill-advised policy to try to avoid much-dreaded dangers by half-measures.

The foreknowledge of God is a movement of His omnipotence. It has therefore to be distinguished in concept although not separated in fact from the totality of His preceding will and work. What God knows He wills, and what He wills He does. Not only does He know all in all but He also works all in all, and He does so as the eternal God. If we are clear in our minds that what concerns us is the knowledge and the will and the work of the Father of Jesus Christ, this proposition is not a dangerous one, let alone one which we need to suppress, but a necessary and indisputable one. The activity of God cannot, then, be split into two distinct parts : on the one hand His restraint and inactivity in face of the creaturely freedom of decision ; and on the other His giving to the creature the physical capacity to carry out the decision reached by it. On the contrary, the one God effects both the will and its accomplishment, the decision and its execution. Again, if we are only clear in our minds with whose and what kind of activity to do, we need have no anxieties with regard to the affirmation. In the Christian doctrine of providence the dreaded conclusion that on this view God can and must be thought of as the author of evil can be avoided by other means than by the partial— and this means the total—repudiation of its decisive content, i.e., that the sceptre and dominion are in the hands of God.

When we think of the *concursus divinus* as the divine foreordination (*praedeterminatio*) of creaturely activity, this means that the divine activity has to be differentiated from all other forms of ordination or determination which may underlie creaturely activity, and that in its difference from such forms it has to be given precedence over them. Undoubtedly we can and must consider all specific creaturely actions in their conditioned and conditioning relationship with other actions, and ultimately with the totality of creaturely activity. No creature appears to act except as it is surrounded and impelled and conditioned, in a word accompanied, by the total activity of all creatures. And this total activity, too, appears to accompany it in such a way that it also precedes it. To that extent there seems to be some similarity between this total activity and the work of God. It is a conjecture which necessarily gives rise to reverence and awe by its utter vastness and incomprehensibility that whenever I move my little finger I am perhaps determined by all the activity which has taken place up to the moment of my doing so, and that of all the creatures and their movements which have been, not one could fail which was necessary to lead up to that movement. Yet it is still the case that the totality of creaturely activity which accompanies and precedes my movement, and the determination of that action, however rigorous it may be, is not at all the same as the divine foreordination. The sceptre is not in the hands of even the totality of created things in heaven and on earth. It is in the hands of the One who is before creation. And no matter how comprehensive the activity of creation may be, it is not the same as His activity. And it is not the same as His because its determinative power is wholly and utterly at the disposal of His power, of the divine foreordination. Just as human nature does not become the divine even in their union in Jesus Christ, so creaturely activity does not become the divine simply because God conjoins the divine with it. Even the total creaturely activity of heaven and earth is not the true and proper preceding of individual creaturely actions. As compared with the true and proper preceding of God and the work of God, the totality of creaturely activity takes place on a level of its own, and that a lower level. And the inter-relationship on this level is reversible. The individual activity no less than the totality of creaturely activity is wholly and utterly at the disposal of the divine foreordination. We can think of the individual activity as the final link in a causal series, and therefore as conditioned by the totality of preceding activity. But if the series is regarded as final, we can also think of the totality of activity as pre-conditioned by the final link, and therefore determined by that individual activity in which it attains its end and goal. Supposing that everything that happened did so only that it might culminate in that movement of my finger ? And might not that be an elevating thought too ? But the relation between the divine and creaturely activity cannot be reversed as the relation between the individual activity and the totality of creaturely activity can be reversed. And this is what distinguishes the divine activity from the totality of creaturely activity, no matter how highly we may rate the totality in relation to the individual, or how greatly superior it may actually be.

If the individual activity does take place under a creaturely ordination, i.e., on the presupposition of the totality of all previous creaturely occurrence, the totality of activity which determines the individual is not an autonomous causal nexus but one which is itself accompanied and dominated and controlled by the divine activity. It is not absolute but relative. It does not subsist of itself but its ordering and cohesion are the work of God. It is not closed but open. Not merely in its creation and beginning, but at every point in its history it is open to the divine activity which does not rend and destroy it but continually gives it the form which it has to have according to the divine good-pleasure. Hence it has no autonomous or absolute power over individual creaturely occurrence, but only the limited and qualified power which is given to it by the superior power of the pre-ceding divine activity. Similarly it has no native wisdom of its own. There is no cosmic reason, no world-soul, by whose principles or intuitions the activity of the creature has its ordination. It has wisdom and reason only in the sense and to the extent that the preceding operation of God enables it to be a witness to the divine wisdom and reason. Our next task will be to consider two different conceptions of the causal nexus which precedes the activity of the individual creature, and in the light of these we will make our own meaning more precise.

Materially, we can conceive of this nexus as the sum-total of all moving forces in the cosmos. If we do, the total force may be thought of as infinite or finite, inexhaustible or at some point exhaustible, according to the individual metaphysical standpoint, and quite irrespective of what the nature of this force is supposed to be. But we do not have to accept responsibility either for this conception or for the detailed way in which it is worked out, for it has no positive significance either in the Bible or in theology. Let us grant, then, that before and in all individual creaturely activity there does operate the active force of creaturely being as a whole and in general, and that the activity of the individual creature has to be understood as a participation in this total force. But if we grant this, then the divine activity which is the foreordination of all creaturely activity cannot possibly be equated with the activity of this total force. The idea of such a force may be useful as a comprehensive concept to describe the life which is given to the creaturely world by God and which indwells it as His gift. But we must remember that even this total force is still the gift of God. It is not the giver. Its operation is not the divine operation. It operates independently only as God allows it to do so, and where and how He wills to co-operate with it. It is not the case that the creature participates in the power of God and is preceded by the overruling divine activity, in virtue of the participation of its own activity in this total force. On the contrary, it is in virtue of its participation in the power of God, and its preceding by the over-ruling divine activity which co-operates with it, that its individual activity participates in the total force of the creaturely order. For the activity of God is not exhausted by its preserving of this total force for the creaturely world as such, confirming it in its possession and making possible the exercise of it. Naturally, it does do this. But this does not mean that it then as it were withdraws, to be vicariously represented by the activity of this total force, and only indirectly to precede and overrule individual creaturely activity. It does, of course, do this. But it also overrules and ordains this activity directly. It is true that the total force is preserved and confirmed by the divine working, and its operation made possible by it. But this does not constitute it an autonomous subject which mediates as such between the activity of God and that of the individual creature. Rather, it is itself an instrument in the hands of God. Both in individual activity and in relation to the activity of the individual creature it operates conformably to the divine foreordination of that individual activity.

But it is not necessary or legitimate to deduce any specific event finally or properly or seriously from a cosmic force of this kind. To do this is heathenism, even if the total force is differentiated from God ; even if it is in some sort regarded as the delegate of God ; even if provision is made to bring this event into a direct relationship with the activity of God as well. As is now known, there is no heathenism which does not make provision for a chief or supreme God superior to all the gods who in practice are honoured and worshipped and served. But obviously the interesting and the finally and properly and seriously significant relationship is necessarily the practical one to the delegate of God and not the theoretical one to God Himself. What determines the outlook, the imagination, the conscience, the heart, and ultimately the decisions or non-decisions of the human onlooker is not the conception of God, but that of the *élan vital* in all things, that of the inbreathing and outbreathing *universum*, that of the total nexus of nature or history, or perhaps a concrete conception like that of the influences of sidereal events upon those of this world, or of a real or fancied power of spirit or spirits, or of certain physical or psychical or social structures. And in such circumstances is it not inevitable that God should become an " old Lord," to whom regard must occasionally be had, but who is not normally considered because all genuine and practical consideration is claimed by the contemplation of the principles of power which in any case operate between God and individual occurrence? And this is heathenism and nonsense precisely because the operation of this cosmic power, however we may conceive the power or its operation, cannot possibly take place except under the foreordination of the divine operation, being released and directed and formed and aimed according to the good-pleasure of God, and not enjoying in any sense the plenary powers of a divine delegate. Therefore those who contemplate and participate in the individual event have to do only indirectly with the total force of creation, but directly and therefore practically and vitally with a consideration, not of this force, but of God Himself. Hence the imagination and conscience and heart and ultimately the decisions are in fact claimed by this consideration, and they cannot be claimed by any other conception except subsequently and under the control of this prior consideration of God.

There is a precise and accurate statement of the matter in H. Heidegger : *Cooperatio illa Dei immediata est, non quod solus nulla adhibita causa secunda operetur, sed quia inter actionem Dei et inter effectum non intercedit efficacia creaturae, quae propius attingat effectum quam Deus. Non enim Deus creaturae duntaxat facultatem et virtutem agendi ita tribuit et conservat, ut creatura interim proxime et immediate, Deus mediante sola virtute, quam creaturae dedit et conservat, actionem edat aut effectum producat—sed ob rationem illam dependentiae creaturae omnem actionem et effectum creaturae immediate attingit.* δι' αὐτοῦ τὰ πάντα (Rom. 11[36]) means : *omnia immediata et proxima eius ut primae causae virtute facta* (quoted from Heppe[2], p. 210).

But formally, we can also think of the creaturely nexus which precedes individual creaturely occurrence as the sum and substance of the norms to which all creaturely occurrence is subject according to the judgment of human experience and the capacity of human thought. Once again, theology cannot accept responsibility for this conception or its individual features. But hypothetically—and even Christians will not cease to do it—we can reckon with the fact that there are such things as the so-called unbreakable and unbroken external physical laws, i.e., laws which in human experience are so regular as not to admit of any exception, and also the intellectual laws which conform to them, mathematically comprehended perhaps in a higher logicality to form a system of objective laws of being and motion in which room may well be found for a kind of moral law of nature as the norm of historical occurrence. In biblical thinking this idea plays absolutely no part at all, and in this it may be compared with the

conception of a total force. But does this mean that there is any
reason not to reckon with it as a hypothesis? We can still accept
norms of this kind, and perhaps a sum and substance of all these norms.
We can still presuppose and expect that every individual occurrence
will take place within the framework of these norms and therefore as
a process predetermined by law. It may still be the case that

> " According to great, eternal,
> Brazen laws,
> We must all
> Fulfil the circle
> Of our destiny." (Goethe 1783)

But even conceding that that is the case. we still cannot equate
the practical validity and actuality of those laws with the divine
activity which foreordains creaturely occurrence. We can perhaps
make this clearer in the following way.

Let us begin with the absolutely maximal assumption possible
with a view to such an equation, that to the exclusion of all doubt or
exception we have a knowledge not only of individual laws but of *the*
law of all creaturely occurrence, the law which embraces the whole
creaturely nexus and comprehends every event within that nexus ;
and that we have a knowledge of this law with the same certainty as
we have the knowledge of God by the Word of God, and with such
clarity that we know what it is that we say when we maintain that
this law involves the foreordination of this or that individual creaturely
activity. Now assuming that that is the case, we have to ask what
is the exact significance of the term " foreordained." Obviously it
means that the individual activity, supposing it takes place at all,
must always do so within the limits of the order and form imposed
by this law. But even on this maximal assumption it would not be
a foreordination whether or not this activity should take place at all,
and if so, where and when. An effective law is a valid law, and no
more ; valid, that is to say, in respect of the order and form of a
particular event. No law, not even that which is absolutely valid
and therefore absolutely effective in that sense, has as such the power
to cause even the most trivial of creaturely events actually to take
place. Even a law which embraces and comprehends all creaturely
occurrence cannot do that. Even the existence of such a law, if we
were in any position to appeal to it, could only reveal itself in the form
of a prior decision concerning the order and form of an actual event.
Even on this maximal assumption we should have to look elsewhere
for provision that the event should actually take place—granting that
when it did, it did so in the order and form foreseen by this law.
Therefore even on this maximal assumption the concept of a law of
this kind presupposes that the nexus formed and to be formed, ordered

and to be ordered in accordance with it, is effected and actual from some other source. The reality of such a law foreordains only in respect of the order and form of creaturely activity, but the object of the divine activity is creaturely activity in itself and as such. Therefore even on this maximal assumption the two cannot be equated.

The antithesis between the divine activity and what is denoted by the concept law is all the sharper when we take our original presupposition and relate it more closely to the actual facts of the case. For then we shall make the far more modest assumption that to the exclusion of all doubts and exceptions we have a knowledge not of *the* law of all creaturely occurrence, but of certain laws which are normative for particular fields of creaturely occurrence, and that we have a knowledge of them with such clarity that we can responsibly maintain that the foreordination of this or that individual activity consists in the actuality of these particular laws. But if we reckon only with certain laws or a few such laws—and obviously we shall be nearer the truth if we do—then this means that even the given foreordination of the order and form of a specific event is restricted to the particular spheres of creaturely occurrence for which these laws are normative, while around these spheres there is a large area where they are not normative and where they cannot predetermine even the order and form of occurrence. Thus the concept of divine operation is further distinguished from that of this kind of law by the fact that no such limitation is imposed upon the divine operation in its sphere, but it embraces and comprehends, not merely a particular creaturely nexus, but every nexus, and all creaturely activity as a single nexus. Naturally, with this more modest concept of law the first antithesis still stands in all its rigour. However valid or effective a law may be in its own sphere, it cannot foreordain more than the order and form of an event which is already presupposed in that sphere, and certainly it cannot foreordain the event itself.

But we still have formulated the maximal and more modest conceptions of law far too favourably for the sake of a comparison or even an equation with the activity of God. For we have supposed that either the one all-comprehensive law or the individual laws of creaturely activity can be known with an absolute certainty which excludes all doubts and exceptions, and with such clarity that we can responsibly describe the law or laws as in their own sphere at least the formal foreordination of a particular event. But in fact we are going much too far if we seriously suppose that there is any such knowledge. What we know as the law or laws of creaturely activity are noetic assertions for whose ontic content we have no guarantee which can justify us in raising them to such a height or ascribing to them the same qualities as the divine activity. At very best they are assertions which necessarily impress themselves upon us on the basis of the scrupulously tested fulness of our experience or in a conscientious realisation of the possibilities of our thought. It is we ourselves who discover and guarantee them. They are great and brazen laws in virtue of the exactness, the completeness, the logical consequence of our human knowledge by which they are discovered and guaranteed; in virtue of the high measure of noetic clarity and certainty which we think it permissible and obligatory to ascribe to them, and of the high degree of reliability which we impute to them. Seeing that they are great and brazen in this sense there is no reason not to regard them as practically valid and therefore effective in all occurrence. But there is also no reason to pass them off as " eternal " or to compare or equate them with the law or laws of God. There is no reason to do it even in the restricted sense which is the only possible sense—as though they were the foreordination of at least the order and form of all actual occurrence in their own sphere. No law is known to us with the certainty with which God is known to us by His Word, or with such clarity that even in relation to its own sphere we can responsibly pass it off as at least the formal foreordination of all actual occurrence within that sphere. No high measure of noetic certainty or clarity can give to laws known to us, i.e., discovered and guaranteed by us, the character of ontic laws, the character in virtue of which we necessarily perceive in them the laws of God, and therefore in effect the real foreordination of creaturely occurrence at any rate from the formal standpoint.

But the laws known to us are obvious attempts within the framework of our own experience of creaturely occurrence, and the possibilities and necessities of our own thought, to establish and attest the fact that there are such ontic laws, and a foreordained order and form of all creaturely occurrence. The laws known to us are well-grounded hypotheses on the basis of which we can go forward prepared in some measure for further experience and thought and equipped for further reliable knowledge, with the certain expectation that all further events which confront us will at any rate take place within this or that order or form. Concerning the actuality of the laws known to us we will already think rather more modestly because we will be aware that they cannot in any case originate or effect the event itself and as such, that even presupposing their validity they must still be referred to the fact that the event takes place at all only on the basis of a completely different operation. And we will also leave the laws known to us open to the revision of content and formulation which may become necessary as a result of our encounter and their confrontation with new and actual occurrence. These laws are as it were arrows pointing in the direction of real order and form, i.e., of the order and form which are objectively immanent in and proper to actual occurrence itself. But for this reason they can never become absolute dogmas, nor assume the character of ontic law, and therefore of a foreordination even of the order and form of any given event. We take account of the laws to which the causal nexus of creaturely existence is subject in respect of its order and form. We believe that we can perceive and describe and define at least some of these laws. And to this extent we acknowledge and proclaim—not from the standpoint of the Creator, but from that of the creature—that there is a necessary order and form in the nexus by which all individual existence is conditioned. It is not chance which rules but constancy, not caprice but faithfulness. All occurrence, inasmuch as it takes place at all, takes place within the framework of a definite rule.

But we will acknowledge this the more seriously and proclaim it the more effectively, the more scrupulously we cease trying to equate even one of the laws known to us, even the law which we perceive with what we imagine to be the greatest clarity and certainty, with the order and form or constancy and faithfulness which rule in that causal nexus, with the rule to which all occurrence within it is subject. Only as we cease doing that do we give evidence that in the laws perceived and described and formulated by us we are aiming at real law ; at the ordering and forming which takes place in the occurrence itself and not simply in our experience and thinking, which is not merely an ordering and forming but also an effecting and calling forth of the actual occurrence itself. It is remarkable enough that the less we believe that the laws known to us have anything at all to do with the real foreordination of creaturely occurrence, the more they really have to do with it, the more clearly they testify by their own particular, that is, noetic, clarity and certainty that there are indeed valid laws, that in the causal nexus in which each individual activity has its place and by which it is conditioned there does rule a unitary and—we can now legitimately use the description of Goethe and say—an " eternal " law, which no occurrence can escape, in accordance with which we must all fulfil the circle of our destiny, and not merely must but can, for this law is not simply one of order and form, but as such it is also *the* law, the positing of existence, life, activity itself. It is the foreordination of God.

The divine foreordination is not subject to the limitations to which our concepts of law are subject. It does not relate merely to order and form. Nor does it relate only to specific spheres. Nor has it only a noetic character. Freely and correctly understood and handled, our own limited concepts of law can be to us witnesses of the divine foreordination. They still attest it involuntarily even when they are not freely and correctly understood and handled. But there can be no question of interpreting the divine foreordination in terms of our concepts of law, as though the divine foreordination of creaturely occurrence were only what on the basis of those concepts we thought we could expect in view of the order and form of the occurrence. There can be no question of thinking that the foreordination of God, and therefore His working and forming and ordering, are limited by what we can perceive and describe and define as the order and form and rule of creaturely occurrence.

Hence it follows that we cannot interpose an autonomously controlling subject between God and the individual creaturely event under the name of any law known to us. It also follows that we cannot hypostasise the concept of law, as though in our dealings with it we really had to do with the ruling representative and vice-gerent of God. It is also not the case that we are only indirectly before God, but directly before all kinds of operative laws of nature, spirit and life. The very reverse is the case. We have to do directly with God, and only indirectly with the laws, so far as they are known to us. It is God Himself, in fact, who is the law of all occurrence. What we see to be law can only remind us of this law, and therefore of Him. Foreordaining all creaturely activity by His will and work, He also orders and forms that activity. This forming and ordering is unbroken and unbreakable. It is the very essence of constancy and continuity. But even this forming and ordering is not identical with the laws known to us, but with the free disposing and directing of His own good-pleasure. Naturally there can be no question of His contravening or overturning any real or ontic law of creaturely occurrence. This would mean that He was not at unity with Himself in His will and work. But we must allow that He can ruthlessly ignore the laws known to us, that is, our own perception of the ontic laws of creaturely occurrence. Even then God does not act as a god of disorder, but as the God of His own order, who precedes creaturely occurrence even in the fact that He is not bound by our human concepts of order, however great may be the noetic clarity and certainty which we believe them to possess. Of course, it cannot be that He precedes creaturely occurrence in such a way that there is no possibility of a subsequent understanding of His action in the sphere and orbit of the concepts of order which we know. It cannot be that we are able to understand His foreordaining work only as a work *supra et contra naturam*. And yet it could be so. There is no reason for irritation if our concepts of order prove inadequate to an understanding of God's order and form. There is no reason for surprise when—especially in the attestation of covenant-history, and the more so as we approach the centre of this history—mention is made of miracles, and the impossibility of a purely " historical " consideration, i.e., of one constructed upon our concepts of order, is revealed. The more definitely the coming of the Son of God is announced in the Old Testament, and the more directly His revelation is attested in the New, the more natural it appears to unprejudiced reason that mention has to be made of events which can be understood only as an activity *supra et contra naturam*, as an ordering and forming which is beyond the stage of development so far reached by our concepts. And the final revelation of the Son of God at the end of all times will be an event of the same kind. The creation of heaven and earth at the beginning of all times was an event of this kind. We must be quite clear in our minds that what is revealed in these events is not a *miraculous* exception but the *rule* of divine activity, the free good-will of God Himself, i.e., the law at which we are aiming with our concept of law. And we must also be quite clear in our minds that with all our concepts of law we can never do more than aim at this law.

To sum up, the divine foreordination of creaturely occurrence always and everywhere takes place before and above all the other foreordinations and determinations which may fall to be considered side by side with or apart from it. It is not conditioned or limited by the self-determination of the creature. Nor is it supplanted or replaced by those predeterminations of creaturely occurrence which seem to derive from the idea of an effective total force, or effective laws of the cosmos. It includes all such determinations. It does not destroy but relativises them. It is the only true foreordination or predestination. It is the only one which works directly. It is the only one which works unconditionally and irresistibly.

If we hold fast to our starting-point it becomes meaningful to say that what we speak of is the activity of the merciful God, who to His own glory and the salvation of the creature has turned to the creature in eternal love. *Per se* the foreordaining activity of this God is not a constraining or humiliating or weakening of the creature. Such a postulate is possible only in relation to the activity of a God who is omnipotence, a supreme cause, and no more. But of this God we cannot merely postulate the very opposite, but can definitely expect and confess it. The God who Himself became a creature in Jesus Christ, the God who places the creature so absolutely at His own disposal only that He may place Himself absolutely at the disposal of the creature—this God is not exalted in the suppression of the creature. He does not find His triumph in the creature's lack of freedom or power as compared with His own unconditional and irresistible lordship. He does not work alone when He works all in all. In His kingdom there are no co-gerents, representatives or vice-gerents. The least thing no less than the greatest derives directly from Himself. But the least thing no less than the greatest has its own sphere of action. And all things can attain their own rights, and exist in freedom. And what better provision could be made for this freedom than that the freedom of God—of *this* God—is unconditional and irresistible in relation to it, that it is radically denied every other freedom but the one genuine freedom which God gives it in His grace? In Him, and not somewhere near Him, we live and move and have our being—and not on the basis of our self-determination, or of the determination of a field of force within which, or a system of norms under which, we may happen to find ourselves. The only free God, who is the Father of Jesus Christ, is the Creator and basis of all freedom worthy of the name. But how absurd and sinister, how unworthy of the name, would be a freedom consisting in the fact that the creature is wholly or in part independent of this God, that it has to look to a field of force or a system of norms instead of to Him !

If we hold fast to our starting-point, however, it is clear that this knowledge of the unconditional and irresistible nature of the divine lordship is not only meaningful but necessary. As long as the concept *causa prima* is not filled out in a Christian manner, we can think in many different ways, according to the inclination and ability of the predominant theological metaphysician, concerning the relationship between the *causa prima* and the autonomy of the *causae secundae*, and between these and the intermediate concepts of cosmic force and cosmic law. We can understand predetermination either rigidly or loosely, either directly or indirectly, as Calvinists, or Catholics, or Lutherans, or Arminians. And the matter can never be decided. A decision is possible, and in one definite direction, only when we know and remember that it is the Father of Jesus Christ who is the Lord over all things, and keep continually before us the majesty and omnipotence and the constancy and faithfulness of this Lord. For this God does not let go the creature ; He does not allow it to fall, not for a single moment or in any respect. This God does not allow Himself to be mocked or trifled with. This God has taken into His own hands the relationship between Himself and the creature, and He has no time for representatives or vice-gerents. This God is directly present to the creature always and in all places by the Holy Spirit. This God cannot stand towards the creature in the broken relationship envisaged in Calvinist and Catholic and Lutheran and Arminian teaching. The operation of this God is as sovereign as Calvinist teaching describes it. In the strictest sense it is predestinating. If only the older Calvinist teaching had made it clear that what concerns us is the predestinating activity of this God ! Unless this is made clear we cannot confidently prefer that teaching. But once it is made clear, we can do so without hesitation.

We can now turn to the second essential proposition, a proposition which is central by its very nature and which has given its name to the whole doctrine in the older dogmatics, namely, that the divine activity accompanies that of the creature : *concurrit*.

The difference between the *concurrit* and the *praecurrit* which we have just considered is self-evidently only a difference of concept and not of content. What we speak of is the activity of Him who was and is and is to come, who precedes and accompanies and follows all actual concurrence. But the fulness of the divine activity must be revealed in the light of its relationship with creaturely activity. We are not dealing with another or second activity of God side by side with His predetermining activity. There is one indivisible operation. And the conclusions which we have reached when considering its aspect as foreordination are still valid and need only to be reconsidered and reaffirmed under a different aspect. For the predestinating activity of God itself takes on the character of an accompanying of the creature —an accompanying in the first and most evident sense that it goes hand in hand with it. As the creature works in time, the eternal God works simultaneously in all the supremacy and sovereignty of His working. The *concursus divinus* is a *concursus simultaneus*.

In the light of what has gone before, the first thing that we have to say on this point is that it is God who effects creaturely occurrence, that is, He is the living basis of its occurrence as such, and the living basis of its order and form. Both the fact that it happens and the way in which it happens derive from Him ; they are decreed and brought to pass by Him. The divine foreordination now comes into force. He could not lose the creature, nor could it escape Him, for the sovereign almighty God, which was and is, is the living God now at very moment of the occurrence of the individual event, not as an idea which hovers over it, nor as a bored spectator, but as the One who acts as Lord, as the One who is true to His own will and sets it in action. The creature does not have any kind of companion. God is with it. And the Emmanuel, whose point and meaning are of course revealed only in the history of the covenant of grace, can never be taken too seriously in the understanding of the general rule of the divine providence. The fact that God is with us, even with us creatures as such, means that He is so as the sovereign and almighty Lord. It means that His activity determines our activity even to its most intimate depths, even to its most direct origins. It means that always and in all circumstances our activity is under His decision. It means that He rules over us as He foreordained before us : and all with the certainty that He does not take any repose or rest, that He does not pause or cease, that there are no lacunae in the fulfilment of the decree of salvation and grace without which heaven and earth would not be, and in the execution of which they were created ; all with the same certainty as that all things and events must serve the one final purpose.

The conclusion to be drawn from this first insight is that we have to understand the activity of God and that of the creature as a single action. And already we have indicated the limits of the concept " accompanying." If God the Lord accompanies the creature, this certainly does not mean—with a single exception—that the Creator becomes a creature, let alone the reverse—for even in the case of the exception we cannot say that the creature became the Creator. If God the Lord accompanies the creature, what it does mean is that He is so present in the activity of the creature, and present with such sovereignty and almighty power, that His own action takes place in and with and over the activity of the creature. It is He Himself who does what Moses and David do. It is He, Yahweh, who thunders out of Sion when the prophet speaks. It is He who judges when the Assyrians capture Samaria and the Babylonians Jerusalem. It is He who speaks to the Church when Paul composes his Epistles. And according to the testimony of both Old and New Testament Scriptures there is no difference here between salvation history and world history in general. It is He who does what heaven and earth and the sun and rain and lightning and thunder do. In the rule of God we do not have to do first with a creaturely action and then—somewhere above or behind, but quite distinct from it, like a hidden meaning and content—with an operation of God Himself. To describe the *concursus divinus* we cannot use the mathematical picture of two parallel lines. But creaturely events take place as God Himself acts. As He Himself enters the creaturely sphere—and He does not cease to do this, but does it in the slightest movement of a leaf in the wind—His will is accomplished directly and His decisions are made and fulfilled in all creaturely occurrence both great and small. He would not be God at all if He were not the living God, if there were a single point where He was absent or inactive, or only partly active, or restricted in His action. The earth is His and all that therein is (and the heavens as well), and this is something which continues to be true in the directest possible way.

In this sense, and with an appeal to Is. 26[12], the doctrine of the *concursus* was already held by Thomas Aquinas: *Sic intelligendum est Deum operari in rebus, quod tamen ipsae res propriam habent operationem* (*S. theol.*, I, qu. 105, art. 5 c). In relation to it he asked and answered the following questions: Does not this involve an unnecessary duplication? Would not the activity of God be sufficient alone? Is not that of the creature superfluous (*vid.* 1). To these he replied: The activity of God is indeed sufficient as *primum agens*, but this does not make superfluous the activity of *agentia secunda* as such (*ad.* 1). Again, can the same activity be carried out by two agents at the same time (*vid.* 2)? To this he replied: It would be impossible if the two agents belonged to the same order, but not when the one *primum agens* and the other *secundum agens est* (*ad.* 2). The conclusiveness of both answers clearly depends upon whether the distinction between the *primum* and *secundum agens* is of such a kind that the two subjects cannot be compared, but belong to two different, two totally different orders, and confront each other in a necessary relation of superiority and subordination. It is only then that the activity of the former can accompany that of the latter. It is only then that there is a legitimate place for the latter side by side with the former. But are there two subjects which stand in this relation, and between which this kind of *concursus* is possible? Thomas defined his *primum agens* and *agentia secunda* as though there were. But is definition enough? It would obviously have been better to refer to the relation between Creator and creature revealed in the Word of God, the relation between the Creator who is gracious and the creature which receives His grace. It is here that we see both the incomparableness and the interconnexion. It is here that the *concursus*, the simultaneous activity of God and the creature, is not merely possible but necessary. But this was not the path chosen by Thomas, and that is why his arguments are not redeemed from an ultimate lack of certainty.

In relation to the identity of the divine and creaturely action, A. Quenstedt (*Theol. did. pol.*, 1685, I, 13, sect. 2, qu. 3, ekth. 13) expressed himself in the following unimpeachable terms: *Non est reipsa alia actio influxus Dei, alia operatio creaturae, sed una et indivisibilis actio, utrumque respiciens et ab utroque pendens, a Deo ut causa universali, a creatura ut causa particulari.* And it is quite refreshing when he goes on to compare the relationship in this action with that of writing, which is done wholly by the hand and wholly by the pen, and not partly by the one and partly by the other.   If we overlook the defects which cling to this as to all illustrations, the comparison necessarily teaches us that as in the one action of writing the hand guides and the pen is guided, so the divine activity overrules in its conjunction with the creaturely, and on the part of the creaturely there can only be submission.   It was far from the intention of a Lutheran like Quenstedt to make this point, yet strangely enough this is how he expounds the parable : *Ita concursus Dei non est prior actione creaturae propria prioritate causalitatis, cum in re sit omnino eadem actio, adeoque totum effectum producit Deus sicut et causa secunda, quod fit per actionem Dei exteriorem, quae intime in actione creaturae includitur, immo una eademque est cum illa.*   In the comparison of the hand and the pen what interested Quenstedt was the unity and not the obvious difference in unity of the action of the two agents.   What interested him was the fact that the hand and the pen work together, and not the irreversible peculiarity of the way in which they co-operate in the one action. There is a real danger at this point.   An interest in the legitimate assertion that the *concursus Dei* and creaturely activity have to be understood as a single action can very well take the form of a mere emphasising of the fact that God accompanies creaturely occurrence with such sovereign power that the occurrence as such is quite simply and directly the execution of His will and therefore identical with His own action.   This could easily be said in a straightforward exposition of the parable.   But Quenstedt's interest—and it is not easy to see the theological justification for it—is directed to the *una eademque actio* as such. God and the creature (unlike the hand and the pen) apparently share equally in this action without any *prioritas causalitatis* on the side of God.   Hence we can describe it only as an external action of God which is secretly enclosed or included in that of the creature.   The danger here is the danger of reversibility ; the possibility of understanding the *divine concursus* with the creature as also a creaturely *concursus* with God.   But this kind of reversibility is absolutely forbidden if we are not to fall into wild speculation about God and the world. We must always be clear who is and who is not the Lord in this nexus and therefore in this one action.   It is God who has called forth this action of the creature, and in and with this action He Himself is at work in sovereign power.   And inasmuch as He is at work in and with it, He determines the action.   However strong our emphasis upon the unity of the action, to affirm the reverse would be patent blasphemy.   For this reason we cannot deny the *prioritas causalitatis.* Strictly speaking, the one-ness of the action (like the one-ness of the two natures in Jesus Christ) can be maintained and perceived and understood only in the light of the operation of the divine subject.   We cannot, therefore, deduce from it abstract propositions about an action of the creature which takes place in conjunction with the action of God and encloses the divine action within it. We cannot gather from it the abstract theory of a secret operation of God within the general occurrence of nature and history.   Otherwise we shall suddenly find ourselves—and this was the danger in the Lutheran understanding of the *concursus,* a danger which had threatened already in Lutheran Christology and Lutheran eucharistic teaching—in the midst of the Hegelian dialectic, in which there can be all kinds of reversals between the higher and the lower, *prius* and *posterius,* God and the creature.   In considering the one-ness of the action we have always to give the glory to God and not in the same way to the creature. But this is what Quenstedt's exposition denies.   And since Lutheran theology was working with a concept of God which did not safeguard it against this type of reversal, that is what makes it highly suspect.

But the time has now come when we must consider what we mean when in this matter of God's operation, and therefore in the exercise of His sovereignty and omnipotence, His pre-eminence over the activity of the creature, we speak about the fulfilment of His will in creaturely occurrence. How does God call forth the activity of the creature? How does He control it? How is it that He is so completely the master of it, and so disposes concerning it, that we can say that it is the fulfilment of His will and therefore His own activity?

The reminder and warning which J. Cocceius (*S. Theol.*, 1662, 28, 22) inserted at this juncture must not pass unheeded : that the How ? of the relation between God and the creature escapes our understanding no less than the How ? of creation. This is something which is known only to God, for He alone knows His own power and resources. Job 28[20f.] may be recalled in this connexion : " Whence then cometh wisdom, and where is the place of understanding ? Seeing it is hid from the eyes of all living, and kept close from the fowls of the air. Destruction and death say, We have heard the fame thereof with our ears. God understandeth the way thereof, and he knoweth the place thereof." What more can we say except to repeat the words of Eccles. 3[11] : " God hath made everything beautiful in his time," and satisfy ourselves with Ps. 139[1] that God knows all our thoughts and ways, in which we have to confess that we have no conception of the divine doing and knowing, and no concepts to describe them. But Cocceius himself then continues that we have a duty to declare all that is open and manifest in this matter, to the glory of God.

To the glory of God, we have at any rate to declare as open and manifest the fact that in the operation of God as a co-operation with that of the creature we have to do with the mystery of grace in the confrontation and encounter of two subjects who cannot be compared and do not fall under any one master-concept. And that means that from the standpoint of the creature what takes place in the divine operation is always inconceivable, unexpected and unmerited. It is not merely that the divine Subject is quite unlike the creaturely, but also that the divine operation is itself quite unlike the creaturely, being not simply a conditioning and determining of what already exists but a pure and free and absolute positing and therefore a conditioning and determining in a way which is impossible for creaturely activity. Hence the divine work is not merely done after a higher and superior fashion, but within a completely different order. And the fact that there is still a connexion between them, a positive and indeed an intimate and direct connexion ; the fact that the divine activity is fulfilled in and with and over the creaturely, and that the creaturely is itself the fulfilment of the divine will—this is the high truth and the high mystery of grace which we have now to bear in mind.

And if we do bear it in mind there is no room for those conceptions of God's operation which are no more than the ascribing to it of a higher potency as compared with the lower potency of that of the creature. It is not merely that God works with a higher or absolute force on beings whose force is less, so that they have no option but to yield and submit to the pressure of His power and accommodate themselves to it. For that is how stronger creatures work on other and weaker creatures. But the work of God on the creature is far more than comparatively a stronger or superlatively the strongest work.

Again, there is no place for conceptions in which the divine operation is related to the creaturely in the way that an actual is to a potential, as for example, a motor to the mechanism associated with it, which has the power to propel but in practice can do so only when it is caused to do so by the action of the motor. For creatures can act in this way on other creatures which are capable of action but do not act. But the work of God on the creature is far more than an action which stirs up the creature itself to action.

Finally there is no place for conceptions in which the operation of God produces that of the creature in the way that a first and general action gives rise to a series of actions and thus brings about a united activity, like a locomotive setting in motion the carriage immediately next to it, and by means of this carriage all the carriages and therefore the whole train. For creatures can also act upon each other in this way. But the work of God on the creature is far more than the first of a series of actions which sets in motion the whole series, and in and with it each individual action.

It now becomes clear how essential it was, when we considered the introduction of the causal concept into the discussion, to safeguard ourselves against all mechanical interpretations of the divine *causare*. In all the conceptions mentioned the divine operation is obviously thought of as mechanical. But to that extent we remain only in the sphere of the creaturely. We conceive, but what we conceive is not the divine operation, for whose peculiar nature there is no parallel in the creaturely sphere.

But of course we shall fall into the opposite error if we try to represent the divine operation in terms of the imparting of a quality or quantity of the divine essence or operation to the creature and its activity, as a kind of infusion of divine love or divine power or divine life into the essence of the creature. The difference in order between the working of God in, with and over the creature, and the working of the creature under God's lordship, cannot be envisaged as one which has been resolved or removed. It is still in force even when God stoops down to the creature and the creature is raised up to this close proximity with Himself. It is the secret of grace that God does this, and the creature experiences it. But it is also the secret of grace that even when He does it He alone is God, that He alone has and retains the divine essence, that the essence of the creature is not affected or altered. By His unconditioned and irresistible lordship He does not subtract anything from the creature or add anything to it, but He allows it to be just what it is in its creaturely essence. Even in the union of the divine activity and creaturely occurrence there remains a genuine antithesis which is not obscured or resolved either by admixture or transference, either by divine influence or infusion. There is still a genuine encounter, and therefore a genuine meeting, of two beings which are quite different in type and order.

Our older divines were careful to safeguard themselves quite definitely at this point : the *concursus* is not a *virtus Dei in creaturas transiens* (B. Pictet, quoted from Heppe², p. 209). But they used the (in this context) ambiguous expression *influxus* far too readily and freely not to give occasion for this kind of error. In this respect caution must also be exercised in relation to the intrinsically attractive power-terminology of the 18th century, in which especially the South German theology deriving from J. A. Bengel and developed mainly by F. C. Oetinger and later J. T. Beck (but we must also mention the Bremen divine G. Mencken) came to speak about the reality, substantiality and dynamic of the activity of God in creaturely activity. But from this it is only a step and we are suspiciously close to gnostic and gnosticising doctrines of emanations and infusions. Again, it is only a step and we are involved in dangerous affinities to the Roman Catholic conception of the impartation of grace. This theology was not formed only from the Bible, as it claimed. It was also drawing on a contemporary theosophical movement which is characteristic of the whole period 1750–1850 but has not even the remotest connexions with the Bible. On quite different grounds did not J. G. Herder and Franz Baader and finally Schelling make use of a very similar terminology to leap over all the barriers which stand between God and the creature ? To speak strongly on this point, we have not to speak too strongly. We must not weaken the reality, substantiality and dynamic of the activity of God in, with and over that of the creature by removing the barrier of creaturehood and ascribing to the creature properties and capacities which can belong as such only to the Creator. It is not by way of a higher naturalism (which can so easily revert to a lower) that we shall do justice to the mystery of this divine activity, and with it to the participation in the divine activity allotted to the creature.

Having safeguarded ourselves on both sides, we are now in a position to go forward to something more positive. But before doing so, let us draw yet a third line of demarcation. Like the divine essence, the divine activity is single, united and therefore unitary, but it is also manifold, and therefore not uniform, monotonous and undifferentiated. It does not owe its manifoldness to that of the creature while in itself it is without form or colour, a formal act of power lacking any specific character or content, like a sunbeam, perhaps, which shines in all its colours only in the rain, or perhaps like the heat of a single radiator which melts or dries up or kindles according to the character of the objects reached, or it may be like a master-key which will open a hundred locks. The divine activity is indeed one and the same in all things, but it is not one and the same in the sense of eternal recurrence, or as the only constant pole in the flux of phenomena. It is not something which is enriched ; it is something which is already rich in and of itself. The divine *concursus* is not simply as manifold as the *causae secundae*. From the very first and prior to the existence of these *causae*, it is more manifold than they are. It is the operation of the Creator of all things, who knows not only the things themselves but all the potentialities intended for them, who is also free to give them new potentialities, i.e., those hitherto concealed both from the things themselves and from those who observe them. It is the operation of One whose power over the creature is so complete because it is differentiated, because it can find and re-determine each one according to its particular nature, because it can use it in its particular place, because in controlling it, it gives to each one that which is proper to it, that which God Himself has ordained should be proper to it. God is not a pedant. He is not like a schoolmaster who gives the same lesson to the whole class, or an officer who moves his whole squadron in the same direction, or a bureaucrat who once an outlook or principle is embedded in his own little head rules his whole department in accordance with it. But, if the term may be allowed, God is a genuine aristocrat who can achieve a highly personal rule without any fear for His own authority or for the unity of His plan. The events in which He co-operates with His creatures, and His and their activity are a single occurrence, are not therefore so many " cases " in the one rule, but individual events which have their own importance and have to be considered in and for themselves, but which He Himself holds together as a single whole in the one objective form and structure : He Himself who in the very fulness of His individual works is always the same in being and purpose.

We must not be led astray at this point by a false conception of the simplicity of the divine essence. This simplicity has not to be explained as the simplicity of the absolute as compared with the relative, or of the general as compared with the particular, or of the digit 1 as compared with its multiplications and divisions, or of the concept as compared with its perception. It is the simplicity of the God who is eternally rich in His threefold being : " May God in His eternal riches always give us in our lives a cheerful heart and noble serenity." It is simplicity as opposed to divisibility and separability, as opposed to inward disloyalty and inconstancy, as opposed to all forms of self-contradiction. But it is the simplicity of the One who in Himself as Father, Son, and Holy Ghost is love, who in Himself does not merely exist but co-exists, who in Himself has space and dimension, who in Himself has life (Jn. 5²⁶). It is the simplicity of the One who in His own being is not nowhere but everywhere, not never but always ; of the One who is therefore omnipresent before and above and after all space, and eternal before and above and after all time : who at one and the same time is distant and near, yesterday, to-day and to-morrow. It is this God, who is not poor in Himself but rich, who works together with the creature. He does not do it uniformly or monotonously or without differentiation, for He is not uniform or monotonous or undifferentiated in Himself. If He were to do it in this way He would be doing violence to His own nature ; He would not be God.

In the light of this fact we can understand the unconditioned and irresistible nature of the divine activity. All the theologoumena in which these characteristics are imprisoned and exposed to dispute, as though the creature were playing its own game over against God, have as their presupposition one or other of these false conceptions of the simplicity of God, the idolatrous notion of a god who in himself is uniform, monotonous and undifferentiated, who is not really living, omnipresent and eternal. The result is that the operation of God can be understood only as a neutral operation which encounters something alien and therefore limited in the manifoldness of creaturely activity, which in becoming manifold necessarily adjusts and orientates itself according to creatures and their activity, which in determining and conditioning them is itself determined and conditioned by them, and is not therefore an omnipotent operation. The god of all synergistic systems is always the absolute, the general, the digit 1, the concept. And it is clear that the operation of this god and that of the creature (the relative, the particular, the multiplied or divided part, the perception) have necessarily to be thought of as reciprocal. But this god is not God. Between this god and the creature all kinds of reversals are possible, and the devious dialectical mind of man has constantly made them. This in itself is proof enough that when we conceive of this god our thought is still moving in the creaturely sphere and any notions we have of the divine operation are radically false. As against that the God who is eternally rich in Himself is not imprisoned in His own simplicity, but the differentiated nature of the world created by Him derives from Himself even as the one. He cannot encounter any limits in the creaturely sphere which can and must compel Him to conform, differentiating, and adjusting and orientating Himself according to the activity of the creature, and therefore allowing Himself to be determined and conditioned by it. He is absolutely sovereign in relation to all the different possibilities of the creature, for there is not one of them which was not preceded by His own long before the creature ever laid hold of its own possibilities, long before it ever existed or was free to lay hold of any possibilities. This can be done only in the sphere of the divine freedom. And this means that the reign of God is indeed unconditioned and irresistible.

We can now proceed to answer positively the question of the How ? of the divine operation.

From all that has been said it might appear that the conditions which such an answer must fulfil are almost insuperably difficult. The positive answer must not describe the relation between God and the creature in terms of the relation between creature and creature. It must be quite free from mechanistic influences. Again, it must not compromise the character of the relation between God and the creature as a genuine encounter. It must avoid any idea of emanations of infusions of the divine essence. Again, it must not overlook the richness of the being of God or the manifold nature of His work. It must not be an answer merely in terms of a principle. From first to last it must do justice to the inconceivability of the being and work of God. It must speak quite definitely of the divine mystery. But it certainly cannot take the form merely of an *ignoramus*, for is not the question thrust upon us by the very fact that the divine work is continuously in the world as event, demanding to be known and recognised ? The difficulty with which we are faced appears to be an insuperable one, and it would be so, and would remain so, if we had to consider whether we could give an answer, and if so what, merely within the framework of a general philosophy of God and the world. For then we should have no option but to fall back, on very poor grounds and certainly with a very bad conscience, on one of the conceptions which we have definitely excluded. Otherwise we could only admit that a positive answer is impossible. And when we weigh up the different possibilities of this or that general philosophy, everything points to the fact that the best of them simply omit or reject or ignore the whole problem. But then we have to ask again whether the matter can rest at that, and at once there is the lurking danger of a relapse into one or other of the conceptions already excluded.

Unless I am mistaken, in the older Evangelical theology this problem of the How ? was first formulated, and the answer at any rate indicated, by Cocceius and his disciples, that is, at the time when the necessity of a biblical basis even for theological method was again being considered. Previously, and for some time after in circles where the necessity was not recognised, the various divines had always acted as though they knew exactly what they were talking about when they referred to the divine *causare, operari, efficere* etc. This could only mean that they were leaving the question open, with the result that they were all the more defenceless against the temptation to make a casual and unregulated use of the various quite unsuitable conceptions, speaking of the operation of God in mechanical or emanationist terms, or in complete forgetfulness of the richness of the divine being, and always in constant violation of the divine mystery, with all the unfortunate consequences which were bound to result, and did in fact result, on every hand.

In theology we must always be suspicious when questions are left open and problems evaded, for in practice it means that they are linked with certain necessary answers which because they are casual and unregulated may well be completely false. It is in those situations where we can proceed only by surreptitiously leaving questions unanswered that we easily find ourselves in deep waters in our theological thinking and utterance. And to a large extent that is what happened to the older Evangelical theology on this particular issue.

Within the framework of a general philosophy, whatever it may be, the one factor upon which everything depends is the unknown one of this operation of God in and with the creature as it actually takes place, continually becoming event, and demanding to be known and recognised. To know this factor it is not enough merely to be an eye- or ear-witness of the general occurrence of nature or history. It is not enough merely to contemplate this occurrence and then for some reason to decide that we have to describe and understand it as the operation of God, of a being who is endowed with supreme power and wisdom and certain other maximal qualities. For even if, when we do this, we bring this occurrence under the highest concept accessible, without too much serious exertion, to the mind of man, this does not mean at all that we have known them and recognised them as the work of God. This is possible only when the true God, the Creator and Lord above all the creaturely world, who foreordains and sovereignly determines its activity even in His conjunction with it, and who is not accessible to human conceptuality, when this God makes Himself known, and in so doing is known and recognised by man. The true God and His activity can never be perceived within the framework of a general philosophy. Otherwise it would not be a general philosophy. It would not be looking first of all to cosmic occurrence in general, and then bringing what it sees and hears there under a highest concept as its presuppositions allow. It would have to look first at the true God and His activity—in a specific occurrence. And in the light of this it would then consider cosmic occurrence in general, understanding it in its conjunction with the divine operation. But since it does not do this, since it cannot do it without destroying itself, without abandoning its claim to be a general philosophy, the operation of God as it actually takes place can never be to it a known but only an unknown factor. Always supposing that its nature allows, it believes, it presupposes, i.e., it has decided to conjecture, and it now maintains, that its own conceptual image is the true God, and therefore that the cosmic occurrence in whose light it has evolved this image is His operation. But how does it know that? Where and how does it perceive it? How can it recognise it? And how can even the problem of the How? of this operation arise in any serious sense, let alone the possibility of a serious and worthy answer? Theoretically it may have the wisdom, if not to see, at least to suspect the brokenness of all the broken answers which crowd in upon us, and therefore to refrain from returning any such answer. But what alternative remains except to evade the problem, thus admitting that it does not really know what it is talking about when it speaks about the operation of God. But when for some reason it still tries to do so, without knowing what it is that it is doing, is it not necessarily reduced to foolishness? Can it possibly avoid in practice a casual and unregulated harking back to one or other of those broken answers? Can it possibly avoid a form of extremely hazardous borrowing?

But Christian theology can and must differ from a general philosophy of God and the world in the fact that to Christian theology the factor upon which everything depends, the activity of God which becomes event, is not an unknown but a known factor, and known in such a way that it demands a knowledge and an acknowledgment of the How? If Christian theology sticks to its own last, not launching out into problems for whose origin it cannot accept responsibility, it will concern itself with seeing and hearing the work of the true God which precedes any consideration of cosmic occurrence as such. It has to do with the God who foreordains all cosmic occurrence, who joins Himself to it only that He may determine it with full sovereignty, who is not accessible to any human conceptuality, but who has made Himself known, and in so doing can now be known and recognised. As its very name suggests, Christian theology has to do with Jesus Christ, with the history of the covenant of grace as it leads up to Him and has its source in Him, and therefore with the almighty operation of God governing all cosmic occurrence as it is revealed at this point. It does not first consider the creature and its activity in general, then work out a concept of the supreme being, then confer upon this being the name of God, and then conclude that there may perhaps be an activity of God in and above the activity of the creature. On the contrary, it first knows the activity of God in a particular cosmic action in which God has made Himself known. It perceives that the One who acts at this point and in this way is the supreme being. And in the light of that perception it sees that this God is at work in and over the activity of creation as a whole. It does not rest upon conjecture but upon knowledge. It is not an assertion but a confession of the divine operation. It knows about this operation. And that means that the problem of the How ? is raised for it in such a way that its reaction cannot possibly be one of omission or evasion. It is raised in such a way that it not merely suspects but necessarily perceives the brokenness of those broken answers. It is raised in such a way that those broken answers are excluded once and for all, and cannot play any further part in the discussion. The problem of the How ? of the divine operation is raised in such a way that it is confronted with the answer to this problem as it is given in the event of the divine operation itself. Its one necessary concern must be to find the description which can do justice in our thought and utterance to what we see and hear of the divine operation.

And now we can and must give the simple positive answer that the operation of God is His utterance to all creatures of the Word of God which has all the force and wisdom and goodness of His Holy Spirit. Or, to put it in another way, the operation of God is His moving of all creatures by the force and wisdom and goodness which are His Holy Spirit, the Spirit of His Word. The divine operation is, therefore, a fatherly operation.

This is the answer already given to us when by the revelation of God we are summoned and empowered to believe in Him, and in believing in Him to know His operation, in the actuality of His operation in the covenant of grace, in and through Jesus Christ. This is how God works in the specific event which forms the centre and meaning and goal of all creaturely occurrence : objectively, proceeding from God by His Word ; and subjectively, moving towards man by His Holy Spirit. For everything which happens there, no matter how great or small, does so in the relation of claim and response, of speaking and hearing, of command and obedience, which both objectively and subjectively God Himself has instituted and ordained and in which He Himself is in both cases the One who acts, in the one case as Word and in the other as Spirit. Every time that God shows forth His power to the men of His choosing, and through them to others, every time, then, that He acts, He does so in the following way : His Word goes forth to these men, to be received by them in the power of His Spirit ; His Spirit is given to these men, to receive His Word of power.

The question facing us is simply this : Are we to understand the general activity of God in and over the creature in the light of this true centre and meaning and aim of all creaturely occurrence, or are we required or authorised in respect of this general operation either to seek some other concept, or perhaps to claim that we cannot know anything at all about the *modus* of the divine activity ? To this question we must give the simple answer that we are free only to accept the first alternative, that the second is neither required nor authorised because, if it is God Himself who teaches us always and everywhere about Himself, there is no point at which we can break free from that instruction and seek a different answer from that which He Himself has given, or fail to recognise that answer as all-comprehensive and final. For the God who in Jesus Christ is active by His Word and Spirit reveals Himself as the One beside whom there is no other being or operation. And He Himself is the One who is and works only in the one way, who works always and everywhere as there revealed, and who does so even when He does not encounter us directly as in the history of the covenant of grace, in Jesus Christ, but is rather concealed and hidden. As we believe in Him and confess Him at this point, so we believe in Him and confess Him at all points—as the One who is always active in and with and over His creatures by His Word and Spirit. The fact that this is true always and everywhere allows and indeed compels us to think of all His activity as fatherly. It if were not true, or if we would have it to be true only in some other way, we should have to ask ourselves whether to speak about the fatherly providence of God is not mere sentimentality without any basis in fact. The fact that the Lord of the world is our Father stands or falls with the fact that even in the world His activity is the activity of His Word and Spirit.

Unless I am mistaken, it is the merit of the school of Cocceius to have introduced the concept *iussio* into the discussion of the *concursus*. So F. Burmann : *Actio (Dei) hic concipienda est, qualis in creatione et conservatione, nimirum iussio aeterna, unica et simplicissima voluntatis Dei (Syn. Theol.*, 1678, I, 43, 25). Indeed, it was already clear from the plain text of Gen. 1, quite apart from the particular activity of God in the covenant of grace, that God created heaven and earth by His Word. Why then should we suddenly arrive at a different conclusion, or at no conclusion at all, in respect of His activity in, with and over the creature ? The language of the Bible, and especially of the Old Testament, necessarily gives us pause. What is the biblical understanding of this How ?, of the technics of the divine sovereignty over the creature ? Is it not obvious that in the Old Testament the creature—especially individual man, but also universal history and its events, and finally all natural occurrence—is set in train by a divine address, word, call, command or order ? The Word of God and creaturely occurrence seem to form an indissoluble unity. Everything that happens can be traced back to a Word of God. Therefore " the Lord God will do nothing, but he revealeth his secret unto his servants the prophets " (Am. 3[7]). And conversely : " The word that I shall speak shall come to pass. . . . I will say the word, and will perform it, saith the Lord God " (Ez. 12[25], cf. 37[14]). " I the Lord have brought down the high tree, have exalted the low tree, and have made the dry tree to flourish. I the Lord have spoken it and have done it " (Ex. 17[24]). He called his Son, the people of Israel, out of Egypt (Hos. 11[1]). He calls the kingdoms of the north to the siege of Jerusalem (Jer. 1[15]). And again, " he saith to Jerusalem, Thou shalt be inhabited ; and to the cities of Judah, Ye shall be built, and to the deep, Be dry " (Is. 44[26f.]). He calls Cyrus, the bird of prey from the north (Is. 46[11], 48[15]). He appoints him His shepherd (Is. 44[28]). And He also commanded Shimei to curse David (2 Sam. 16[10]). He calls the generations one after another (Is. 41[4]). When He turns man to destruction He says, " Come again, ye children of men " (Ps. 90³). He speaks, and it means the pulling down and building up of whole peoples (Jer. 18⁷ᶠ·). He calls for a sword upon all the inhabitants of the earth (Jer. 25²⁹). But He also summons the heaven and the earth to action (Ps. 50¹⁻⁶). He brings out the host of heaven by number, calls them all by names, (Is. 40²⁶.) He commands the snow and the rain (Job 37⁶), the gad-fly (Ps. 105³¹) and the great fish of the prophet (Jon. 2¹¹). He calls for the corn (Ez. 36²⁹). He sends out His Word, and the ice melts (Ps. 147¹⁸). And when the grass withers and the flower fades, it is because His Spirit blows upon it (Is. 40⁷). This is how God works by His Word. And it is to be regretted that while the disciples of Cocceius saw this quite clearly they merely indicated the thesis and did not maintain it more strongly.

Nor is it the fatherliness alone but also the divinity of this operation which depends upon the fact that it is an operation in the Word and therefore by the Spirit, in the Spirit and therefore by the Word. If we perceive this and say it, then we stand within the Christian and Trinitarian conception of God, and we are on firm ground. To have a good conscience, we can only be silent in relation to the operation of a supreme being, as of all dumb idols, for we really know nothing about it. But we do justice to the operation of the one true God when we describe it as Word and Spirit, because when we do so we again pronounce the holy name of God ; because as we are invited and enabled to speak by God Himself, we speak concerning Himself, His active person. The mystery of His operation is also safeguarded when we think of it as Word and Spirit. For it is only in the divine inscrutability that it can be revealed to us how in His covenant of grace God calls, illumines, justifies and sanctifies man by His Word and Spirit, and it is in this inscrutability that we believe and recognise the whole activity of God as the activity of the Word and Spirit of God. And if this is so, it is also meaningful to speak about the eternity, omnipresence and omnipotence of the divine operation, for as predicates of this Subject the concepts lose the emptiness and coldness which inevitably characterise them as the predicates merely of a supreme being. They acquire life and light. The Word of God is omnipotent, and His Holy Spirit is eternal and omnipresent. Again, on this presupposition we can gladly and unhesitatingly ascribe to the divine work the honour which is due to it. It is an unconditioned and irresistible work. And the flight into synergism becomes unnecessary, for if the supremacy of this work is the supremacy of the Word and Spirit it does not prejudice the autonomy, the freedom, the responsibility, the individual being and life and activity of the creature, or the genuineness of its own activity, but confirms and indeed establishes them. The One who rules by His Word and Spirit recognises the creature which He rules as a true other, just as He Himself as a Ruler of this type remains a true Other. He takes His creature seriously ; He respects it by acting towards it so incomparably as a Ruler of this type, and in so doing He Himself continues to be respected.

We can therefore conclude our exposition of the *concursus simul-*

taneus, the sovereign and overruling accompanying of the creature by the divine operation, with the proposition that even under this divine lordship the rights and honour and dignity and freedom of the creature are not suppressed and extinguished but vindicated and revealed.

From the standpoint of historical theology we come here to the specific concern of the Lutheran (and in Roman Catholic theology the Jesuit) doctrine of providence. But to do justice to it, it is quite unnecessary to make the movement which under Jesuit inspiration the Lutherans themselves made : the dissolving of the divine *praedeterminatio* into a mere *praevisio*.

Now it is true that the *concursus simultaneus* takes place on the presupposition of the divine predetermination of creaturely activity and therefore of the unconditioned and irresistible lordship of the divine activity over the creaturely. But this does not mean that only God is really active. The idea that God alone effects all things to the exclusion of all *virtus creata* had already been rejected by Thomas Aquinas (*S. Theol.*, I, qu. 105, *art.* 5 c) on the very good ground that it would mean that the Creator had not given to the creature any *virtus agendi* at all—which would be contrary to His own *virtus agentis* as Creator. Therefore the Lutherans were certainly quite right to emphasise the fact that the divine activity in *concursus* with that of the creature cannot mean an abrogation of that of the creature or of its manifold individuality. So Quenstedt (*Theol. did. pol.*, 1685, I, 13, *sect.* 2, *ekth.* 12) : *Neque enim immutat Deus naturas agentium aut eorum agendi rationem et ordinem, sed agentia naturalia sinit agere naturaliter, libera libere.* But our suspicions are naturally aroused when he continues with a quotation from the Spanish Jesuit Francis Tolet (*sex pontificum concionator*, as he admiringly calls him) : *Concurrit Deus cum causis secundis iuxta ipsarum naturam, cum liberis libere, cum necessariis necessario, cum debilibus debiliter, cum fortibus fortiter, pro sua suavissima dispositione universali operando.* And our suspicions are confirmed when Quenstedt himself explains : *Concurrit Deus cum causis secundis iuxta uniuscuiusque indigentiam et exigentiam h. e. quando, quoties et quomodo causa illa concursum illum postulat pro conditione naturae suae. . . . Naturis rerum agentium sese accomodat et cum illis . . . concurrit descendendo ad singula iuxta uniuscuiusque capacitatem et indigentiam.* Well may we ask what the author of the *De servo arbitrio* would have had to say about a Lutheranism of this kind. And we can also ask quite pertinently what would become of the rights and dignity of the creature if the lordship of the Creator in and with and over its activity consisted only in meeting and satisfying the particular needs and requirements of the creature (almost as though on request !).

The older Reformed divines, while they avoided this more Jesuitical than Evangelical over-emphasis, unanimously accepted the proposition formulated by J. Wolleb : *providentia Dei causas secundas non tollit sed ponit.* We find exactly the same view in the definition given by the *Leiden Synopsis* : *pro ratione naturae uniuscuiusque ad agendum movet et applicat creaturis concursum suum.* The Calvinists did not question the particularity of the activity of each creature, the contingency of natural occurrence, or even the freedom of the human will. Certainly they never doubted the spontaneity of human action, as they are frequently accused of doing. If Calvin himself (*Instit.*, I, 16, 2) occasionally described the function of at any rate unconscious creatures as that of instruments which are merely used, the later divines expressly corrected the thought, stating with much greater precision that we are not to believe *causas secundas simpliciter et in se mera Dei instrumenta esse, adeoque passive non etiam active se habere, quasi Deus cum causis secundis agat sicut artifex cum instrumentis suis, quae non aliter agunt, quam quatenus a principali agenti moventur. . . . Causae secundae proprie et insita virtute operantur.* God does work *effective* in and with them, as *causa prima* and the Lord of their power to act, but He does not work *subjective, inclusive* or *exclusive*, passing over their activity as though the power which He had given them were an empty power (H. Heidegger, quoted from Heppe[2], p. 210). The point at issue between the Lutheran and Reformed divines was not whether but how to state the autonomy and particularity of creaturely activity in its difference from the relationship with the divine. What separated the Reformed from the Lutherans was that they would not concede any *libertas voluntatis in creatura, quae non sit ex participatione libertatis summae increatae, quae sit causa prima propria atque intima omnis creatae libertatis omniumque liberarum actionum (Leiden Synopsis,* 1624, *Disp.* 11, 10). It was because they did not wish their position to be compromised by the *suavissima dispositio universalis* of Jesuit invention that they rightly resisted the Lutherans on the point. But it is much more important to assert that they agreed with them both in a definite repudiation of the idea of the sole efficacy of God and in a positive concern to safeguard the freedom of creaturely activity. The ethical indifference and quietism which would have resulted had things been otherwise were never characteristics of the older Calvinism in its historical form. But we may ask : What was the historical result of that strange " disposition " by which God is not strictly speaking the Lord but only the omnipotent Supporter and Helper of creaturely activity ? Was it not the peculiarly Lutheran conception of the autonomy of all events, and the corresponding tendency to a secular ethics whose application God could ultimately assist only with a pious blessing, but certainly not as the Lord ? This much at least is certain, that a pre-deterministic understanding of the *concursus simultaneus* obviously gave to Calvinism all the greater cause to reckon seriously with creaturely occurrence as a whole, and especially with human spontaneity and activity—in direct responsibility, of course, to the commandment of God Himself.

The unconditioned and irresistible lordship of God means not only that the freedom of creaturely activity is neither jeopardised nor suppressed, but rather that it is confirmed in all its particularity and variety.

Tantum abest, ut operatio divinae providentiae destruat libertatem voluntatis creatae, ut haec absque illa prorsus consistere nequeat (Leid. Syn., 1624, *Disp.* 11 11).*

The basic condition for a perception and understanding of this proposition is not intellectual but spiritual, that of overcoming and removing the fear-complex which suggests that God is a kind of stranger or alien or even enemy to the creature ; that it is the better for the freedom and claim and honour and dignity of the creature the more it can call its own a sphere marked off from God and guaranteed against Him, and the worse for it if this sphere is restricted, and worst of all if it is completely taken away ; that it may be and necessarily is a legitimate interest to defend the claim of the creature in face of an unjustified and dangerous claim on the part of God. To put it in the older terminology, the *causa secunda* is not secure unless it can play the role of *causa prima* in a secret corner of its own. But let us suppose for a moment that there is absolutely no foundation at all for this complex. God is the Father—not the father of a father-complex but the Father of Jesus Christ and therefore our beloved Father. It is thus the better for the creature the more fully it stands under the lordship of God, and the worse for it the more that reservations and restrictions are placed upon this lordship. The rights of the creature are most radically known and acknowledged—indeed they are only really known and acknowledged—when the rights of God over against it are fully and unreservedly acknowledged. It is good for the *causa secunda* simply to be a *causa secunda* and no more. But if this is the case, then how simple it is not merely to ask the question but to answer it. And is it not a remarkable testimony to the hardness of the human heart and the unrepentant nature of man that even Christendom, and even the specialists of Christendom, the strange breed which we call theologians, and the Evangelicals as well as the Catholics amongst these theologians, have been so little free from this complex that they have always thought it necessary to see and make new difficulties in the matter? What is the value of all our thought and talk about Christ and His resurrection, about grace, about the glory of our regeneration and the new creation, about the majesty of the Word of God, about the Church as a divine institution, about the causative and cognitive power of the sacraments, if in face of the simple demand to acknowledge God as the One who does all in all we are suddenly gripped by anxiety, as though perhaps we were ascribing too much to God and too little to the creature, as though perhaps we were encroaching too far on the particularity and autonomy of creaturely activity and especially on human freedom and responsibility? As if there could be any sense in sheltering from such a demand under the safe cover of a crude or subtle synergism! What sorry lip-servants we are! And there is a reason for it. For in the very depths of the Church, in the very depths of the Christian conscience and Christian theology, our fear of God is in fact far stronger than the love with which we are able to love God. This phenomenon makes it devastatingly plain that if in the proper place theology and Christian preaching has to speak about sin and demons and chaos generally, it would do well not to study the subject remotely but in its own conduct, in the characteristic fear of God and fear for the creature in which we Christians barricade ourselves against the truth which we confess with our lips, with the result that we can see that truth only over a barricade—there is a real *circulus vitiosus* in the matter—and therefore confess it only with our lips and without any genuine conviction. If our Christian perception and confession does not free us to love God more than we fear Him, then it is obvious that we shall necessarily fear Him more than we love Him. At root, this is the only relevant form of human sin. And this is the one and only reason why it is so hard to grasp that the freedom of creaturely activity is confirmed by the unconditioned and irresistible lordship of God. And a reason of this kind cannot be disputed away by theological arguments. If we fear God and fear for ourselves, then we do fear. And since we all of us have the habit of fear of God, this habit will not go out of us except by prayer and fasting. All that we can say is that when and to the extent that it does really go out, the theological arguments which follow will acquire force and validity.

The God who is the true God and on the seat of power is the One who reveals Himself to Abraham and Moses, who speaks to and through the prophets, who has made Himself the God of the people Israel and the Lord of its history, who has become man in Jesus Christ and the Head of a congregation of men, who is active in all these ways with sovereign power, unconditionally and irresistibly, and yet with mercy and forbearance, who has dealings with men after the manner of a man. Man himself in his doing and non-doing, in his thinking and acting, in his greatness and insignificance, in his own nature and its limitations, was and is the object and end of God's work. But as man he also was and is the means, or instrument, or organ of this work. The history of the divine covenant and glory and salvation is also the history of man—not merely of human passion, but of every conceivable form of human action. If we consider the prophets and apostles, who can mark off the boundary where the freedom of God ceases and the freedom of the creature begins ? Is there any humanity more free or autonomous or proud than that of the men after God's own heart who according to their own confession experienced the divine activity towards them without any will or response at all on their own part ? Is it not the case that such men—not to speak of Jesus Christ their pattern—were activated by this experience in a way which we cannot explain by any other liberation than that which brought them so absolutely under the lordship of God ? And this is the God who rules the world, who rules unconditionally and irresistibly in all occurrence. It is He who is at work in all the great or small things which can happen to man, dealing with him not as a stock or stone but as a man, as a being who can know and will, as a free being, with an appeal to his responsibility, He Himself being the One who makes him responsible. And it is He who is at work in all other happenings, allowing the creature to act according to its own nature and limits, which are of course known only to Him, and given by Him. The very fact that this God rules as Creator means that in their own way, and at their own time and place, all things are allowed to be, and live, and work, and occupy their own sphere, and exercise their own effect upon their environment, and fulfil the circle of their own destiny. That He is the Master in all things does not alter the fact that each is allowed to develop in its own activity. On the contrary, the rule and disposition of God consists in the very fact that each may and can do that. And whenever and wherever it does so, it has to thank the divine rule and disposition for it. It could never do it at all unless from first to last it was allowed to do so by the divine rule and disposition. Far from being a threat to its freedom, this is the very reason why at its own time and place, in its own existence and form of existence, it can reveal its highest possible spontaneity, i.e., magnify the Lord who has made it what it is and permits it to work as such.

Once it is established who the God is to whom we refer in this matter, then we have to say, secondly, that just as the activity of God over against that of the creature (which He makes His own in virtue of His mastery over it) remains His own, so too it is provided that the activity of the creature over against that of God remains the creature's own. It would be a twofold misunderstanding of the grace of God to try to suppose that the overruling will of God involves a kind of absorption and assimilation of creaturely activity into the divine, and therefore a disintegration and destruction of the creaturely in favour of the divine. To do this would be to forget that the activity of God is the activity of His continually free grace, an activity from above downwards, a condescension in which God is beyond comparison, in which He does not cease to be the true God, in which there cannot then be any question of the suppression of the variety, and therefore of the autonomy and particularity, of creaturely activity in face of His own. And it would also be to forget that, since the activity of God is indeed an activity of His grace, it does not aim at the destruction and suppression of the creature but its affirmation, deliverance and glorification. The contemplation of the true God preserves us from all theories of emanation and infusion. It is our safeguard against pantheism and monism. And it also our assurance against the fear that little and ultimately nothing will be left for the nature and activity and freedom and responsibility of the creature. For it is not only that not nothing and not too little is left, but that everything is left. And why say : It is left, as though the creature were subjected to a kind of assault in face of which it has to console itself more or less with the fact that this or that is left to it ? The very fact that there is still a gap between the activity of God and that of the creature— it is overcome by God's lordship below as well as above, but being overcome only by God it is still there—means that what is proper to the creature, to the being below, to that which is distinct from God, is not removed from it but assigned and granted to it. Just as God Himself is respected by reason of His unconditioned and irresistible activity, the activity of His grace, so He respects as such the creature to whom He is gracious. That creature cannot ask for itself anything better than to be ruled absolutely by the divine activity of grace. If this activity were to cease or pause, if God were to reveal to the creature a sphere in which it would be something other than the object of His grace, then there would be every reason to fear for its freedom and rights and honour and dignity. And if anyone thinks it necessary to diminish the sovereignty of the activity of God or to set a limit to His omnipotence, let him consider well what he is doing. For if that is the direction in which his thoughts and utterances run, then he is contending for the greatest possible evil that could ever befall the creature as such.

And now thirdly, and finally, we must recall all that we have already said concerning the *modus* of the divine operation. To emphasise again the decisive point, it is an activity of the God who is eternally rich, and it is His activity by His Word and Spirit. And in saying this we are simply describing two different aspects of one and the same thing. The eternal riches of God are the riches of His trinitarian life as Father, Son, and Holy Spirit. And for this reason His operation by Word and Spirit is the demonstration of a life which is eternally rich. From both angles we arrive at the same result. If God works by His Word and Spirit there is no reason whatever why the activity of the creature should be destroyed or suppressed by His omnipotent operation. On the contrary, it is necessarily the case that the omnipotent operation of God not merely leaves the activity of the creature free, but continually makes it free. Where the Word and Spirit are at work unconditionally and irresistibly, the effect of their operation is not bondage but freedom. We could almost put it in this way, that the bondage which results from the operation of the Word and Spirit is itself true freedom. What room is there for anxiety in face of the omnipotence of the Word and the omnipotence of the Spirit ? How can we ever think of reservations of this omnipotence ? What kind of concept of freedom would that be which had the result of an attempted safeguarding of the creature against the threat of this bondage ? But again, if God works as the One who is eternally rich in Himself, there is no reason to be afraid that the variety of creaturely activity will as it were be ironed out by His activity, and that we ourselves will have to guarantee with the wisdom of a *suavissima dispositio* that everything in our little cosmos can maintain its own place and individuality : as though the plenitude of all the possibilities either given or about to be given, i.e., still to be revealed, were not already contained in the omnipotent divine operation in itself and as such ; as though the variety of the creature and its activity were not guaranteed continually by the activity of God, beside whose riches all the variety of our cosmos is the veriest poverty. Surely it betrays an appalling ignorance of the Word and Spirit of God, and therefore of the true and triune God, or it betrays perhaps a forgetfulness of all that we ever knew, if we are afraid of this God and afraid for the creature at this point.

These, then, are the theological arguments which we have to put forward. But I repeat that we stand here at a place where the theological arguments can have force and validity only as the habit, the bad Christian habit, of a fear-complex in face of God is in process of expulsion. In adhering so decidedly to the older doctrine of the Reformed Church and theology in our own conclusions in this matter, we have dared to count upon the fact that even yet this bad habit can be—

not reformed, but expelled. It is a risk to count upon that expulsion. But unless we take the risk, it is difficult to see how we can say anything meaningful about this subject.

We conclude the sub-section as a whole with the third proposition that the activity of God follows that of the creature, *succurrit* (*sc. ad effectum*). What we have to say on this point really merges into the theme which must be developed in the next sub-section on the divine directing of creaturely being (*De gubernatione*). We can, therefore, be brief.

Again it is our first duty to assert that we make this third distinction only to help the conceptual development, that is, to make it plain that the one operation of God in relation to that of the creature has this dimension as well, that it covers the whole range of creaturely activity. In its totality, the conception of God accompanying the creature on its own path includes not merely His preceding and accompanying it as the Lord, but also His following it, again as the Lord. And this " following " as well as the " preceding " must be related to the eternal being of God as well as to his temporal action. God is eternal. It is as the eternal God that He acts in time. And this means that He acts not merely before the work of the creature as this work occurs within the limits of its own time, not merely contemporaneously with it, but also after this work is concluded, and therefore after the time allotted to it has come to an end. God was, and was at work, even when the creature had not commenced its work. God is, and is at work, in the accomplishment of this work. God will be, and will still be at work in relation to this work, when the creature and its work have already attained their goal.

The goal of all activity is an effect, that is, an alteration in the active subject, and to some extent of its environment, which is either purposed in the particular action, or at any rate produced, or brought about, or in some way caused by it. Now if we were dealing only with the activity of the creature we should have to say that once the creaturely subject—admittedly under the influence of many earlier actions of its own and also of many actions of other creaturely subjects which preceded its own activity—has performed this or that action, once the change produced by its action is complete, a fact has been established, a fact which may be changed again by the future activity of the same subject or of others, but which is still a fact, which has been caused and is therefore present as an effect in a way which corresponds exactly with the desire, capacity, and actual execution of the particular subject. What it has done it has done, what has happened has happened, in the form and compass and with the meaning and range foreseen by the particular subject, and according to its conscious or unconscious purposes and possibilities, and to the extent of its actual execution. " What I have written I have written." As we make our beds, so we must lie on them. What a man sows, that he must reap.

What comes to pass, is—is in a way which corresponds with that by whom or which it came to be, and with how it came to be. No matter what may happen in the future, this change has already been made, and is irrevocable and unalterable. The decision reached has produced a situation whose factuality, and nature, and limits, cannot be disturbed. The effect is there, just as it was bound to be as a result of the activity of the particular creaturely subject.

This is how we should have to conceive of the end of creaturely activity, and therefore of the situation obtaining at this end, if we had to do only with the activity of the creature, and did not have to reckon first and last with the activity of God accompanying the activity of the creature. But God accompanies the activity of the creature as its Creator and Lord. And this means that even the effects of this activity, even the changes brought about by it, are still subject to His disposing and control. There is no withdrawal on the part of God. God does not retire when the creature has attained its end and goal, when the effect was there as it is meant to be and could be and actually was according to that activity. God's arm remains outstretched even when that of the creature has been allowed to fall. God outruns the creature, and His activity follows the activity of the creature, in the sense that He acts as the Lord even of the effects of creaturely activity. The end of the temporal act is like its beginning. The act could only begin with God, and it can only end with God. And in the one case as in the other " with God " means in the service of His omnipotent operation.

Therefore the forward as well as backward context of the activity of each creature is not merely that of its relation to similar activities which either were before or will be after it, and under the effects of which its own operation takes place, and upon which it exercises a reciprocal effect. Certainly it does stand in this context, but it does so only with God. For it was the omnipotent operation of God that the preceding of other creatures and the effects of that preceding helped to bring about here and now the particular activity of the particular creature. And it will again be the omnipotent operation of God that the particular activity produced helps to bring about the later activity of other creatures. From the very first the individual activity of the creature—and the same is true of the preceding activity of other creatures—stands under the dominion of God. But for the moment we are stressing the other side of the matter—that the effect produced by it stands under the same dominion. The activity can end only as it began. It can attain its goal only in the source to which it owes its will, capacity, and execution.

But if this is the case, then the effect produced by the particular creature, the change which it effects either in its own circumstances or in those of its creaturely environment, is not its own. The moment it is produced, the effect which I produce is no longer mine. I did produce it, and the fact of it is irrevocable, for I did not produce it apart from God, but with God, and under the lordship of His *praecursus* and *concursus*. But just because the effect is brought into being under the divine lordship, it does not belong to the creature to appoint or fix the form and compass or the meaning and range of this effect, no matter how ineluctably the effect follows from the most personal being or activity of the creature. Nor does it belong to those other creatures who experience that effect to appoint or fix its character, no matter how deeply they are affected by it or how thoroughly they make it their own.

The word which I utter now is absolutely my own. And having uttered it, I have really uttered it. I have given rise to a specific fact which cannot be recalled. But for all that, I cannot hasten after my word, and arrange that as my word it will be received and understood and repeated in the way that I myself intended. It remains the word which I uttered, but as a word which has been uttered it acquires its own history quite independently of anything that I contributed to it. I have no further power over the fact to which I gave rise. And again, when someone has heard my word, he has really heard it. But it is not in his own power to give that word the content and meaning and power in which it will become to him a relevant and enlightening and convincing word. Just as I cannot hasten after it, he cannot hasten towards it. It is the word which he has heard, but as such it has its own history independently of him. It is for him a fact, but it is a fact over which he has no power.

In its independence of the creaturely subject, and of all similar subjects, the effect produced by the creature has its own history. The change brought about in the creaturely sphere when it becomes an event has its own freedom. This history and this freedom are the freedom of God and of the rule of God. God Himself decided concerning my word even before I uttered it. He decides concerning it at the very moment when I utter it. And He will decide concerning it, what it is and what it means, after I have uttered it. He decides concerning my word as an actual effect, a divine effect which undoubtedly is my effect as well, an effect which has become a fact for my creaturely environment, my hearers. He decides concerning the form and compass and meaning and range of this fact, concerning the content and meaning and power of the word which I have spoken as a creature and my fellow-creatures have received as such. This is the assistance, the help, the succour which God causes to be given to creaturely activity. It was not in vain that He preceded it with the decision of His will. It is not in vain that He accompanies it as Lord and Ruler. And now He follows this activity where the operation of the creature itself cannot go, to the result of its activity which is beyond the reach of the creature. It is He who arranges its effect. As an event, as something which is beyond the reach of the creature, the effect of the creature is in the hands of God. It is under the judgment of God. It is quite literally at the disposal of God. It is wholly subordinated to the context of His wider purpose. It is, therefore, in good hands.

It is this positive aspect which we have to emphasise. The fact that as effect everything is merely what it can be and is for the creature and similar creatures in virtue of the active creaturely subject is only a provisional aspect of occurrence. And it is only a provisional aspect that in relation to its own effects the creature cannot do more than adopt an attitude of resignation, simply stating that they are this or that, that they have this or that character, and that they came about in this or that way. Just as its activity derived from a higher source than its own planning and determining, and took place under a higher lordship and ordaining than its own nature and requirements, so its effects are in higher hands than its own, which at the end and goal of its activity could hardly prevent it from falling. What actually happened is something which God decided and ordained. And since it is God who does it, there is no place for resignation when we consider the effects of the creature, but only for confidence and assurance and hope. For the fact that God does it means that for every effect produced by the creature, whatever it may be, there is in the final and best sense of the word a meaningful and good and right application, that not one of these effects is lost, and that no activity of the creature is in vain. It is these effects of the activity of all the creatures of God as willed, produced, assessed and co-ordinated by God which together, in the forward and backward context, constitute the expression of His rule and government of the world. In their obvious independence of any creaturely contribution, in the definitive character which appears to be peculiar to them, these effects all serve the divine overlordship. Their true independence and definitiveness are not proper to them in their relation to the active subjects and their environment, but in the plan and in the process of fulfilling the will of God. Seeing that they belong to this order—and how can it be otherwise when the activity which produced them also belongs to this order?—it is the freedom of God which we have to respect and to love and to honour within them. That it has to be loved and honoured results from the fact that He who is Lord and Master in this respect, too, is not a God who is unknown to us, but the God who is our Father in Jesus Christ, the eternal Father of all His creatures.

3. THE DIVINE RULING

We come now to the third aspect of the fatherly lordship of God over all His creatures, and one that is decisive for the whole doctrine of the divine providence. The fact of His overruling as such is the fact that in the majesty of His mercy He continually preserves us in being and continually accompanies us with His presence. But this fact itself is one which calls for explanation. The power of God over all things is not a blind power. He does not rule merely for the sake of ruling. He rules as a Father. His ruling is the ruling of His definite and conscious will. Behind it there is meaning and purpose, plan and intention. God has an aim for the creature when He preserves and accompanies it. His preservation and accompanying are as such a guiding, a leading, a ruling, an active determining of the being and activity of all the reality which is distinct from Himself. He directs it to the thing which in accordance with His good-pleasure and resolve, and on the basis of its creation, it has to do and to be in the course of its history in time ; to the *telos* which has to be attained in this history. It is He Himself who has set for it this *telos*, and it is He who as Ruler guides it towards this *telos*.

De *gubernatione* was the title under which the older theology arranged this third discussion within the general framework of the doctrine of providence. And in their definitions of the concept they referred to an *ordinare, moderari, derigere, perducere (in fines et in finem)* which embraces all created beings, all their powers, and all their ventures and achievements, their whole existence both in totality and as individuals.

Their main concern—and it must also be ours—was to develop an insight already expressed in the Old Testament when Yahweh is described as King. In the later books of the Old Testament He is " the king of the whole earth " (Ps. 47[8]) ; " the king of all peoples " (Jer. 10[7], Ps. 47[9] and cf. Rev. 15[3]) ; " the king of heaven " (Dan. 4[34]). He is " king over the whole world " (Ps. 47[3]) and also " king over all the gods "—that is why He can be called in the New Testament " the great king " (Mt. 5[35]), " the blessed and only δυνάστης, the king of kings and lord of lords " (1 Tim. 6[15]), " the king of the ages " (1 Tim. 1[17]). But in itself the concept of the kingship of God is older than its universal form. And did it first arise only under the so-called monarchy ? For if so, how could the institution of a human king over Israel (1 Sam. 8[7], 10[19], 12[19]) be described so sharply as a wrong against God which at best He could only tolerate ? Already in Ex. 15[18], at the end of the Song of the Red Sea, we read : " The Lord is king for ever and ever " ; and in Num. 23[21], in the second song of Balaam : " He hath not beheld iniquity in Jacob, neither hath he seen perverseness in Israel : the Lord his God is with him, and the shout of a king is among them " ; and again in Deut. 33[4f.], in the blessing of Moses : " His inheritance is the congregation of Jacob, and he was king in Jeshurun." What the older form of the concept signified is that only Yahweh, and Yahweh in all His peculiar love and power and readiness to help, is the King of Israel, a King who at best cannot be more than represented by a human king, and even then not without danger. And when in Is. 43[15] Yahweh calls Himself " your Holy One, the creator of Israel, your King," we see that the older understanding did not completely disappear even in the later and universalist. The God who is high above all peoples is also the God of Israel who is great in Sion (Ps. 99[2]). And it is as Judge of the whole world that Yahweh is King in Mount Sion and Jerusalem (Is. 24[23]). The verse in the call of Isaiah has sometimes been described as the earliest example of the fuller understanding (Is. 6[5]). It contains the distinctive name of God : The King, the Lord of Hosts, which is later taken up by Jeremiah (46[18], 48[15], 51[57]) and Zechariah (14[16]). This title perhaps indicates the way in which the later and universalist extension arose. For clearly the later universalism was an extension of which the idea was capable and which it required even before it was actually made. The concept is a dynamic one, in keeping with the historical nature of the Old Testament concept of God, and this is proved by the fact that in some sense it swings between two poles, the one at which the enthronement of Yahweh is thought of as still to come, or in the process of coming, or only just come, and the other at which His kingly rule seems to have been long established, and already in full sway. It is this Old Testament idea of the divine kingship which challenges and directs us to expound the divine ruling.

But in the New Testament the Old Testament idea assumed a far more radical form from which we cannot abstract in the present context. For in the New Testament we find that the idea of the divine kingship was united with another idea which is certainly present in the Old Testament, but independently and without any attempt at reconciliation. This is the idea of the Saviour-King who is awaited at the end of the age, the Son of Man, the Messiah of the House of David ; and He, too, is a figure who to some extent moves from a particularist Israelitish significance to a world-historical and universalist. It is under the concept βασιλεία (cf. the article by K. L. Schmidt in G. Kittel, I, p. 579 f.) that the union is effected in the New Testament. The word βασιλεία (τῶν οὐρανῶν, τοῦ θεοῦ, τοῦ πατρός, τοῦ Χριστοῦ) denotes at one and the same time both the dignity and power, the majestic actuality of the divine being and essence and action, which is absolutely supreme over all men and all human ordinances and indeed the whole cosmic structure and process, which breaks through and reveals itself from above, as absolute miracle—and also the concrete, once-for-all actuality of the Son of Man and Son of David, the Messiah and Saviour of the world, *Christus ipse* (Marcion) manifested as αὐτοβασιλεία (Origen). But the New Testament concept of God, actualised now in the accomplished incarnation and epiphany of the Word, is also historically dynamic, and for the first time truly so. At this point too, then, we meet with the same tension as we find in the Old Testament conception of kingship. The βασιλεία is here, and yet it is not here ; it is revealed, yet also hidden ; it is present, but always future; it is at hand, indeed in the very midst, yet it is constantly expected, being still, and this time seriously, the object of the petition : Thy kingdom come. In the task before us we must always bear in mind this New Testament development of the conception of the divine kingship.

But in this respect, in spite of all its fidelity to the Bible, the older theology deviated widely from the concept of God as found in the Old and New Testaments, and it paid the inevitable penalty in the striking insipidity of its exposition. According to the Christian sense of the concept *gubernatio* the God who rules is not merely a supreme *gubernator*, a *gouverneur* who accidentally finds himself in the place of authority and is respected because of this authority. He is βασιλεύς and His lordship is βασιλεία. And this means that His position and function and authority and claims and decrees and measures are not merely sovereign, but in their sovereignty they are also right. They are grounded not only in His person, but in the office which is inseparable from His person. They are determined not only by His will, but by the regal content of His will. In the true sense He is the King of the people elected and called by Him, and for their sake He is the King of the universe elected and created by Him. He has associated Himself with this people and cosmos, even accepting likeness and solidarity with it. He has entered into this relationship with a purpose. And it is in this purpose, or as the older divines had it, on the basis of this *propositum*, that He rules. It is this purpose which makes His sovereignty right, which characterises Him as the One whose office it is to be sovereign, which constitutes the very definite content of His will. For this is no casual purpose, but the purpose of His heart, which corresponds exactly to His being as Father, Son and Holy Ghost, and is therefore the source of all rightness and worth and reality. In this purpose He enjoys and exercises supreme power. And where He does so—and there is nowhere where He does not—this purpose is the meaning of that power. That power is royal power. God does not merely control. He rules, rules as a King rules, rules as He alone, the true King, rules and can rule. And it is because He rules in history, because in Jesus Christ, in the divine-human αὐτοβασιλεία, He rules in history, and therefore in time, and therefore in the movement from yesterday to to-morrow, that according to the remarkable testimony of the Old and New Testaments His rule or government is always a completed fact from which we derive and which can be known to us, and yet also an imminent event towards which we are only moving and which is still concealed from us.

This is the first lesson that we have to learn at this point from the biblical conception of God the King and of His kingdom.

When we make the simple but meaningful and momentous statement that God rules, we must understand it primarily to mean that God alone rules. He alone as Creator has the right and power and freedom and wisdom necessary to rule. It is a question of ruling over the reality which is distinct from Him and yet posited by Him, posited by Him and yet distinct from Him. It is a question of ruling over His own creature, and therefore over His possession in the highest sense of the term. And as such, this ruling can be only His work. No one else has any legitimate claim to rule His creature. To no one else is it so closely bound that it has to obey him. No one else perceives and understands and knows it in such a way as to be able to rule over it in any meaningful sense. The rule of another would be an alien rule : usurped, incompetent, weak ; the bungling of an amateur. Open or secret opposition to any such rule would be possible, imminent, and probably successful. Certainly it would be legitimate and necessary. And even if the rule succeeded, the final upshot of it would be anarchy and destruction. No one can represent God in this task : no other god, for God is the only God, and there is none beside Him, and even if there were, no matter who or what it might be, not being the Creator, it would not be eligible or competent for this task, or in any way adapted to it ; and no creature, for there is no creature, not even the highest of all, which is qualified to take up this office and function in relation to its fellow-creatures ; and not the sum total of created reality, for it would not be created reality if it did not need to be ruled, or if it could satisfy this need itself. God Himself is irreplaceably and unexchangeably the Subject of this rule. There are, of course, in and under His rule celestial and terrestrial powers and agents and officers which exercise a limited and provisional rule. But there are no autonomous powers, no powers independent of Him, no powers which are not in some way instituted or authorised by Him and controlled by Him. There is no collateral rule side by side with His, and no counter-rule opposed to it. He alone can rule, and ought to rule, and wills to rule ; and He alone does so.

We may now take up the third obvious application of the words in Rom. 11³⁶ : *Eἰς αὐτόν τὰ πάντα. Eἰς αὐτόν* because ἐξ αὐτοῦ, because δι' αὐτοῦ, because

He alone is the Lord who preserves all things and accompanies all things. But *εἰς αὐτόν* means (P. Van Mastricht) *ad finem suum*. The goal towards which everything moves in its own history is the goal which God alone has fixed and appointed for it. During the course of this history lesser and provisional goals are sought and attained. But there are no autonomous or definitive collateral goals which can be finally sought and attained side by side with or apart from the goal which God Himself has appointed. If there were such goals, they could only be the counter-dominion which had at some time and in some way been set up and established. But the kingdom of God is the only true kingdom. In the attainment of its own collateral ends such a counter-dominion could exist only in the form of a revolt against that only reality—an outstanding revolt, it may be, but at bottom, foredoomed to failure. Any revolt against that reality is as such foredoomed to collapse and failure. And this means that the goal of such a revolt can never be an autonomous, definitive, absolute goal side by side with the divine rule. There cannot be an *εἰς αὐτούς* or *εἰς αὐτά* side by side with the *εἰς αὐτόν*. There is no real collateral or counter-government which can limit or compromise the rule of God. We shall have to give separate consideration to the problem of chaos, which is the problem of sin, evil, the devil and demons in their relationship to the divine providence. In this sphere it does seem, of course, as though something like an autonomous collateral government, or counter-government, is at work, limiting and compromising the sole rule of God. But we must already oppose any such idea. Whatever we may have to say concerning this peculiar sphere in its peculiar relationship to the created universe and the government of this universe by God the Creator, one thing we definitely cannot say is that the rule of God meets with competition in this sphere. No matter how seriously we have to take this particular factor, we cannot in any circumstances ascribe to it the dignity of a second creator and ruler of the universe. We do not take it seriously by conceding more to it than the peculiar being of a potent appearance. We can say at once, then, that even the potent existence and reality of this particular factor does not in any way alter the fact that God alone rules. And it certainly does not mean that there are or can be other ends for the cosmos which God has created side by side with those which God has ordained for it. We can properly consider that hostile appearance only when we have first made this decision, this conscious prejudgment in face of it. Those who cannot make such a prejudgment in face of chaos as such have already become its victims, as is seen in the fact that in this respect they necessarily limit and deny the divine providence. But if it is denied at one point —and a point so decisive—the providence of God is no longer His providence. We can only confess and maintain this providence when we take as our starting-point the quite definite and conscious prejudgment that God alone rules. And this means an end of chaos and all its sinister powers.

But the phrase " God alone," although at first sight it might appear to be a rather formal definition, provides us at once with a first and general filling out of the content of the idea of God's ruling. For literally, the fact that God alone rules includes the further fact that He Himself is the only goal which He has appointed for the creature and towards which He directs it. Proceeding from God and accompanied by God, the creature must also return to God. It must ; for this is its greatness and dignity and hope. The movement towards God is the meaning of its history. Basically there is nothing greater or richer or finer that we can say concerning its goal, and therefore concerning the goal and intention, the plan and purpose of the divine government, than that God Himself is the goal. For the exclusiveness

with which God Himself leads all things to this goal has its justification
and glory in the fact that the goal is no more and no less than Himself :
Himself as the One who confirms and unfolds and expresses and reveals
His wisdom and goodness towards the creature ; but Himself in all
these things. For all the things which might presumably be called the
goal side by side with or apart from Him, all the benefits which He
assigns to the creature and which are therefore the end of His government, are simply an expression of Himself in the form of His own
attitude and movement towards His possession. He Himself is the
benefit of all the benefits which He has intended for the creature, and
which He makes, therefore, the end of His overruling of creaturely
history. It is not, therefore, because He is jealous of competitors—
for how can He be jealous when there are no competitors ?—but
because of His loving zeal for the creature that He retains to Himself
the control of all things and will not and cannot share it with another.
There is no other who could have his glory as world-ruler by himself
being at the same time and as such the true and supreme and only
benefit which can give meaning to world-history. The glory of God is
the salvation and glorification of the creature. That is how and why
God is the true and great King, and His kingdom an unlimited and
unconditioned kingdom.

In this respect we may well describe as the most gifted definition of the
gubernatio that of J. Cocceius (*S. theol.*, 1662, 28, 38). He will not allow that the
divine operation has any other goal but God Himself, and he explains it quite
simply as the *actio Dei, in qua sapientiam suam in suis operibus demonstrat, sive
manifestet misericordiam et clementiam, sive iudicium, sive dominium et potestatem.*
Others such as Calov and Quenstedt—and in substance they were right—
referred to the glory of God on the one hand and the salvation of man on the
other : *ad universi huius bonum*, Quenstedt added. More nicely, the goal of
God's overruling will might within this basic definition be identified as the will
to reveal His wisdom, i.e., to declare and make manifest the true and original
and eternal meaning of His own life, or, to put it in another way, to declare and
make manifest His own being in a Word—and that *in suis operibus*, in the works
of creation, which in some sense form, therefore, the consonants and vowels
of this Word and thus serve the revelation of Himself. It is only with this
purpose, for the sake of this self-revelation, that He rules the creature. And in
this way He acts both as a King—to His own glory—and also as a Father, to the
supreme good of creation and the salvation of man. The fact that He reveals
His wisdom, and therefore Himself, includes all other benefits.

We can now understand rather better what might be called the
absolute majesty of the divine rule. Because He rules alone, and
because He Himself is the goal to which He directs creaturely history,
He is uplifted both above the necessity which rules and is revealed
in this history, and also above its real and obvious contingency,
above the continuities and discontinuities, above the various unifor-
mities and the various freedoms of world-occurrence : and not merely
above the necessity which is known to us, but also above the necessity

which is concealed from us or only suspected by us ; not merely above
the contingency which is known to us, but also above that which is
concealed from us or only suspected by us. It belongs to the divine
ruling of creaturely occurrence that it can be known or conjectured
only under this twofold and antithetical aspect : that every generalisation is challenged by the individual factor which will not harmonise
with or allow itself to be negated by the general ; and that every
individual factor is challenged by the great generalisations which
compromise its individuality. It belongs to the world-rule of God
that this is the case, and this is one of the most cogent reasons why
we can believe in this rule but cannot see it. What we can see is only
necessity and contingence, continuity and discontinuity, law and
freedom, which exist side by side with each other and in opposition to
each other. That is why God laughs at all our attempts to see His rule
with the eye of our human reason, let alone at our efforts to take the
throne and play the part of world-ruler ourselves. This divine laughter
rings out over the folly of all our crude or refined human imperialisms,
and they will inevitably come to grief on this laughter. One day it
will be granted to us to see what now we cannot see—that beyond the
antithesis God is the true King and World-ruler, the Lord of all things
and everything, the Lord of the general and also of the particular.
But we ourselves are not beyond the antithesis. Only God is that, and
He always was and always will be. God controls it. God uses it. God
avails Himself of it. Perhaps we may risk the illustration that the
general and the particular, or however else we describe the antithesis,
are as it were the two basic sounds by which God wills to manifest
His wisdom, to declare His Word and therefore Himself, in the works
of creation. Not only does He rule over the antithesis. He also rules
in it and by it. For it is in and by the antithesis, in the distinction
and relatedness, the contradiction and co-existence of the general and
the particular, of necessity and freedom—it is in and by all this that
there arises creaturely history in time as opposed to a timeless existing.
But in and by this antithesis there also arises the ruling of God from
His own divine place, from the throne established over this antithesis.

God Himself is not one of the necessities which the cosmic process
reveals. Nor is He the sum and substance of them. God's rule is
not as it were identical with the logic with which natural events are
seen to occur according to the norm of what we call natural laws,
although no doubt it is present in and by this logic. Nor is it in the
least identical with the logic with which we think of ourselves as
morally bound by certain laws, and perhaps by the one all-inclusive,
or at any rate formalised law of custom or habit, although obviously it
does take this form. Nor is it identical with the logic of world-historical,
political or economic developments and relationships, although there
certainly are such things, and God's overruling is certainly present in
and by them. A clear perception of necessity in world-occurrence does

not mean that God has to be explained or approached as though He were so tied to this necessity that He is virtually its prisoner. God rules in and by this necessity, but He also goes His own way through it. He is also Father and King in the contingency and discontinuities and above all the freedom of world-occurrence. This way of God cannot be calculated or foreseen. There will constantly be new surprises even for the wise. God is always doing something new and disclosing something new. He is the God of miracles.

But it is also not the case that God is found only in the extra-ordinary, in the exceptional, in the unexpected climaxes and nadirs of world-occurrence. The rule of God is not at all identical with a series of events which can be explained only as contingent, individual, unique and thus discontinuous. The marvels of natural phenomena, the inscrutabilities of physico-psychic individuality, the border-line cases of moral conduct and action, the freedom which defies all expectation or prevision in the wider or narrower coherences of history—all these are obviously the work of His rule. And naturally, whatever our view of things may be, we must admit that He can perform true and genuine miracles. But a clear perception of the fact that creaturely history has this aspect and the rule of God this undoubted character, a clear refusal to rationalise or civilise or domesticate the divine control, must not lead us to think of God as subject to a higher power on this side too, as though He were merely the God of the exception, the incident, the individual case ; as though He were merely the God of a magical conception of things, the archetype and ideal of every form of ir-rationalism and surrealism, of daemonic striving and bohemianism. No : God honours law as well as freedom. He loves the law-abiding bourgeois as well as the nomad. And it would be an inversion, a new form of spiritual Philistinism, if we were to wish it otherwise. Those who for the sake of their own spirits preferred a God of disorder to a God of peace were not true prophets (1 Cor. 14[32f.]). Even in the form of the divine activity represented by the prophet He is still a God of peace and not of disorder. And so the victories of common sense, with their rules and inevitabilities and generalisations, are also a part of the revelation of His wisdom, and therefore of Himself. To this revelation there belongs the wonderful revelation which is particularly dear to His Holy Spirit that two and two make four and not five. To this revelation there belongs supreme law, and therefore the necessary application of sound common sense. In short, if God rules in and by freedom, He goes His own way through it, and He rules no less in the necessities and continuities, in the static nature of creaturely occurrence. We cannot identify with the divine dynamic, or substitute for it, that which we ourselves think to be dynamic as opposed to static.

If we are to understand the true character of the divine rule— and if we have already apprehended that He alone rules, and that He Himself is the only meaning and purpose of this rule—then everything turns upon the fact that we must not make deductions from His transcendence over both these aspects of world-occurrence. A deviation either to the right hand or to the left will inevitably lead to the worship of a god which has nothing whatever to do with the true God who is Father and King, that is to say, of an idol.

We must compliment the older Evangelical dogmaticians on the fact that they saw this problem, and tried to steer a middle course between this Scylla and Charybdis. Their doctrine of *gubernatio* was aimed specifically against the two ancient systems of Stoicism on the one hand and Epicureanism on the other, both of which had come to life again as a result of the Renaissance. On the one hand they opposed the Stoic doctrine of fate, and on the other the Epicurean doctrine of chance. It is of a piece with the varying interests of the Reformed and Lutheran schools that the Lutherans broke the more expressly and sharply with the doctrine of fate, and the Reformed with that of chance. But basically the same two enemies were engaged quite decisively on both fronts. There is, therefore, no real point in concerning ourselves with the foreshortenings of perspective with which the Lutherans and Reformed viewed each other, leading the Lutherans to accuse and ridicule the Reformed as Stoics and the Reformed to accuse and ridicule the Lutherans as Epicureans.

But it is instructive to note how the older Calvinists did preserve the doctrine of *fatum* on what was ostensibly, and often actually, their weaker side, in their opposition to a belief in destiny. Even at a first glance it is still suspicious that this school did not *a limine* and absolutely repudiate the concept *fatum*. But they could rightly appeal to Augustine. In *De civ. Dei*, V, 1, 8, 9, Augustine said that in order not to foster false ideas he preferred not to use the word *fatum* to describe the *connexio seriesque causarum* which is ruled by the divine will and power and in which everything occurs. But he also agreed that the use of the word should not be prohibited. *Fatum* derives from *fari*, and its original meaning is simply *dictum*. We may recall Ps. 62[2f.] in this connexion : *Semel locutus est Deus. . . .* This *semel locutus* is the legitimate sense of the concept *fatum*. It means : *Immobiliter h. e. incommutabiliter est locutus, sicut novit incommutabiliter omnia quae futura sunt et quae ipsae facturus est.* On the ground of this opinion of the father, and in his sense, many of the older Reformed divines were confident, in spite of Lutheran suspicion, that they could rightly speak of a *fatum Christianum*. Burmann (*Syn. Theol.*, 1671, I, 44, 29) defined it as the *rerum et causarum a divino decreto dependens ordo et series*. He definitely opposed it to the *fatum mathematicum*, astrological predestination ; the *fatum naturale seu physicum*, the compulsion of sublunary natural causal sequences ; and the *fatum Stoicum*, the depriving of creatures and of God Himself of any contingency or freedom by an all-controlling necessity. H. Heidegger (Heppe[2], p. 206 f.) draws a particularly clear and distinct line of demarcation between the Christian view of the divine world governance and the inadmissible sense of the concept *fatum*. He makes five points. 1. The divine governance, which is an eternal and free resolve, is located in God Himself, but fate in the inadmissible sense always resides in things, in the series of causes and effects. 2. The divine world-governance is the action of God as *agens liberrimum* ; therefore far from constraining, things and their order can only follow it. It is therefore unconditionally free to dispose of them *vel praeter, vel supra, vel contra naturam*. But fate in the wrong sense confines God to the prison-house of the Parces, not allowing Him to act at all outside the *ordo causarum*. 3. Faith in the divine governance distinguishes between the eternal (divine) and the temporal (immanent) necessity of world-occurrence, but belief in fate confounds the two. 4. Within the framework of the divine governance and in the light of a perception of it there is a place both for contingency in general and for a freedom of the human will in particular, but fate and the belief in it involve a mechanisation and destruction of the two. 5. The world-governance of God extends even to the sphere of sin, yet not in such a way as to make God the author of it. But the rule of fate inevitably means that sin is one of the necessities posited by God side by side with others. We have to admit that this Calvinistic demarcation against Stoicism was as clear and exhaustive as possible, and it certainly did not give occasion for any justifiable objections on the other side.

Similarly it is instructive to note how the Lutherans for their part opposed the Epicurean doctrine of chance. If we wished to be malicious it would be possible, in view of their particular doctrine of the divine *concursus*, to rank them with the Epicureans just as they ranked Calvinists with the Stoics. But in reality they represented the absolute directing of all occurrence by the providence of God just as emphatically as in the light of their particular understanding of providence the Calvinists maintained both natural contingency and human freedom. For instance, when A. Calov (*Syst.*, III, 1659, 6^1, *qu.* 1) discusses the question *Utrum mundus casu vel fortuna, in vero providentia divina regatur ?*, he replies that we can speak of luck or chance only *respectu nostri*, and in consideration of *causae secundae*, but not *respectu Dei*. In other words, we can speak of them only relatively and not absolutely. For providence we can never substitute chance, or the goddess *fortuna*, which can be represented only as blind, inconsequent, capricious and oscillating, the benefactress of the undeserving. The Epicureans say that it would disrupt the blessedness of the gods and be a weariness to them if they had to concern themselves with the governance of the world. But for God (and here Calov opposes the Epicurean and Neo-Platonist philosophy of Ammonius, Plotinus—and Augustine) the work of world-governance does not carry with it any distaste, or burden, or weariness. The essence of God is always the same, whether He works or not. *Novit ipse quiescens agere et agens quiescere* (Augustine, *De civ. Dei*, XII, 17). The Epicureans say that to rule the universe and its excesses would in some sense defile God. But does not the sun shine on filth without itself being defiled ? How much less can God be defiled ! They then point to the obvious imperfections and anomalies which are found in the world-process. But in respect of these we have to say with Augustine (*De Gen. ad lit. imperf.*, 7) that as there are pauses in a song or musical composition, as there are shades in a picture, so contrasts belong to the perfect beauty of the cosmic whole. And often is it not because of our own limited nature that we do not see how the things which we regard as ἄτακτα καὶ ἀνόμαλα are really, *si providentiam Dei spectes*, ἀνάλογα καὶ εὔτακτα ? Does not the wisdom and goodness and power of God—and here the Lutheran is dangerously near to the Calvinistic heresy !—consist in the fact that God is able to bring forth good out of evil ? It is alleged in favour of a doctrine of chance that in the actual course of events things often turn out badly for the good and well for the evil. But according to Scripture God does well to the good when by means of hard experiences He summons them to a knowledge of their sin, to trust in Himself, and to prayer, thus proving their faith, whereas in His longsuffering He either calls the wicked to repentance or in the words of Jer. 12^3 keeps them as fatted beasts for the day of slaughter. The final objection is this : Can the existence of evil be brought into line with the world-governance of God ? Does it not rather point to the existence of something very like chance ? To this Calov replies that for the sake of its freedom God did not make it absolutely impossible for the *creatura intellectualis* to sin. His governance, therefore, can take the form of *permissio*. And once again we have to remember that, as the story of Joseph shows, even sin can be made to result in the salvation of men. Of the Lutheran, too, we have to admit that within his limits he did vigorously maintain his position on what was for him a very dangerous front.

We have not seen either party on its stronger side. The Reformed were naturally at their strongest when they had to defend their position against the doctrine of chance, the Lutherans against the doctrine of fate. But by listening to what they had to say on what was proportionately the weaker side, we have been able to grasp the main point at issue. For both sides saw that it was a question of the transcendence of God over every immanent necessity or contingency, generalisation or particularisation—and therefore over fate and chance. And what both parties knew that they had to avoid at all costs was a compromising of the divine world-governance by identifying it with a cosmic principle either on the one side or the other.

It must be granted that on neither side do the arguments lead us to the necessary end : not because most of what is said, and perhaps all of it, is not quite true in itself ; but because neither side saw on what basis and therefore with what specific emphasis it had to be said. The proof of all proofs, the height from which the argument really proceeds, is never revealed. And the result is that there remains an impression of flatness, and even of uncertainty. Have the arguments really proved what they set out to prove ? However, it is still a fact that our Evangelical Fathers did see and tackle the real problem at this point, and it is our present concern to draw attention to this fact.

We have now contended that God alone rules, that He Himself is the goal of His ruling, and that He rules in transcendence over the cosmic antithesis of freedom and necessity. We must now turn to the concept of divine ruling itself. Having clarified the presuppositions we can take as our starting-point the statement that God rules creaturely occurrence by ordering it. In this context the concept order does not have the passive sense of the permanent structure of a thing, its qualities and circumstances, but the active sense of a continuing operation by which an occurrence in time takes place in accordance with a definite plan, and is determined and formed and directed through constantly changing situations and stages. In this sense rule means order. The rule of God is the operation of God over and with the temporal history of that reality which is distinct from God ; the operation by which He arranges the course of that history, maintains and executes His own will within it, and directs it wholly and utterly in accordance with that will. The rule of God is the order of God in this active sense, His ordering of all temporal occurrence.

In this connexion the older, especially the Reformed, dogmaticians liked to use the concept of the eternal divine *propositum*. We have not to think of this one-sidedly as signifying a fixed divine plan which precedes the creation of the world and therefore all temporal occurrence, finding its subsequent fulfilment in this occurrence. Not one-sidedly : for certainly we must say that everything which occurs in the temporal course of that history is ordered and determined and overruled by God. P. van Mastricht (*Theor. pract. Theol.*, 1699, III, 10, 12) is quite right when he speaks of an already existing *ordo rectus, immobilis, et indissolubilis*, which no creature can escape. But this does not mean that in all His activity God is not in the fullest sense Himself. It does not mean that He is not the living God. It does not mean that He ceases to will, to decide, to plan, and therefore constantly to order. The plan of God is, and consists, and is divine, in the fact that He actually carries it out, that by His power His decision continually becomes an event. This is its essence and content. The divine activity in time is identical with His willing, so that the divine willing is not somewhere behind this activity but has to be perceived and adored within it, and the activity cannot be a later fulfilment of His willing, nor can it be understood as such. It is in the temporal activity of ordering that the divine order is realised, and it is because God causes it to be realised in time that it is eternal. And since in the order willed and executed by Him it is a matter of an eternal *propositum*, this *propositum* has the nature and force of a self-realising *proponendum*, so that we can never represent God as the prisoner of His own design, but He enters in and is known as the absolutely free Lord in the execution of His own design. M. F. Wendelin's definition of the *gubernatio* (*Chr. Theol.*, 1634, 1, 6, 11) is therefore illuminating. It is the *ordinatio, qua Deus* . . . *omnia in ordinem redigit, fines certos et bonas constituendo et media ad fines disponendo et disposita regendo.* The definition is illuminating because in the concept *ordo* it quite rightly reveals the presupposed decision and plan of God as such, but at once connects it with that of the *ordinatio*, the living divine *constituere, disponere, regere*, thus giving it its full dignity and power. It cannot be otherwise if we are not to make temporal history completely empty, removing the living God, fundamentally denying His actual and sovereign and therefore free activity, and making a dead idol of the eternal *propositum*. We have here an exact parallel to what we said earlier about the unity of the divine *praecursus* and *concursus*.

If God orders world-occurrence, then this includes at once the general fact that He controls creaturely activity. This does not mean that He suspends it as such, substituting for it His own activity. That would not be to order it, but to suspend and destroy it. It would result in the undoing, or at any rate the ignoring of His creation. God has created and He preserves the creature, and in so doing He gives to it a sphere in which to work. And the work of the creature is the object of His divine ordering. The fact that He controls it means that He is the Lord of the creature even while it has its own activity. He controls its independent activity as such. He uses it for His own ends. And in so doing He does not encroach too much upon it. He does not do violence to the character and dignity which it has as the reality which is distinct from Him. On the contrary, as the reality posited and existing by Him, this reality is different and autonomous, and it is therefore maintained by Him and given a sphere in which to work. Its character and dignity, its individuality as a creature, are safeguarded in the mere fact that He confirms His relation to it and its relation to Him. He could not pay it any higher honour, nor treat it more seriously, than by acknowledging in face of His own lordship as Creator the fact that He makes the activity of the creature the means of His own activity, that He gives to the creature a part in His own operation. This is the depth of His mercy. This is the greatness of the glory which He intends for it and lavishes upon it. We can and must accept the fact, without demur or resentment, that God does actually control creaturely activity. This activity is always the individual and free activity of the creature. The fact that according to its own nature and its place in the context of the existence of fellow-creatures the creature works under law and necessity is a separate issue. Its activity is still free, contingent and autonomous. But God controls the activity in its freedom no less than its necessity. The control of God is transcendent.

Between the sovereignty of God and the freedom of the creature there is no contradiction. The freedom of its activity does not exclude but includes the fact that it is controlled by God. It is God who limited it by law and necessity and it is God who created it free. And it is also God who in preserving it gave to it a sphere in which to exercise its freedom. And it is also God who in accompanying it through time is the Lord of the use which it is able to make of its freedom. It does use this freedom. It is active at every moment. But in every moment it uses this freedom on the basis of the particular divine permission to do so. It works always within the framework and the limits of this permission. There can be no question of a compulsion laid upon it. But also there can be no question of an activity apart from this divine permission. In this permission the creaturely freedom encounters the divine freedom from which it derives and in which it finds its natural and self-understood limit. And this limit is at the very place where its creaturely conditioning by law and necessity also has its limit. Freedom apart from this limit would not be creaturely freedom but the freedom of a second god. To claim this kind of freedom would be sin and death for the creature. Hence we have to think of the activity of the creature as an activity which is limited by the permission constantly given to it by God, being directed by a series of permissive acts and therefore controlled by God. If it is not to sin, and in so far as it does not do so, in so far as it does not cease to affirm its own nature even when it does, the creature does not do anything but that which God wills, i.e., it does not do anything but that which God causes it to do even in its freedom by constantly giving to it this permission.

It is even more evident that this is the case, and that it cannot be otherwise, when we remember that all creaturely activity aims at a certain effect. This aiming at an effect is as such a matter of the free striving and willing of the creature, directed of course by God even in its freedom. It is in this striving and willing that the creature is active. But its activity as such is not effecting, and its striving and willing is not attaining and achieving. The end attained and the goal achieved and the bringing about of the effect desired—all these lie quite beyond the striving and willing and working of the creature. It may be that the effect does come and crown the endeavour. But it may be that it does not, or that if it does it has a different form and bearing from that which corresponds with its striving and willing and working. Whether the effect comes, and if so how it comes, is a completely new factor in relation to the activity. This is true whether we consider it from the standpoint of necessity or from that of freedom. And if it is God who controls creaturely occurrence and not fate or chance, then we have to say quite baldly that the decisive moment, the very meaning of creaturely activity, its effect, and the goal or end in which it culminates, are all the gift and dispensation of God. The activity can exist at all only on the basis of the divine preservation of the creature. It is constantly formed and directed by the permission given to it by God. And in the same way it is God who decides where and how it will actually culminate, what will be its upshot, as the saying goes. And this is true both when the culmination and effect correspond more or less to the creaturely activity and also when either by its non-existence or its different form and bearing it is a complete surprise in relation to it. In every case the result of the creature's activity is something new, something from God. This is not altered in the least by the fact that it is the result of the creature's activity, and that there is therefore a connexion between the activity and the effect, between the freedom of the acting creature and the ends actually attained by it. At the end of its working the creature itself will always be the same as at the beginning. It will, therefore, be confronted by its own effect. It will reap what it has sown. It will answer for what it has said and done. But what this is, what harvest comes up from the seed, what happens as the goal of its striving and willing and the result of its working, whether it is non-existent or existent, whether it is what was striven after and willed or something quite different, whether it is good or bad, salvation or perdition—this is not the creature's concern. It is decided, decreed and directed by God. Both in general and in particular God Himself fixes for the creature its goals, that is, the goals that it will actually attain. In one way or another it will ultimately realise the divine decree.

This, then, is the divine order of world-occurrence ; the controlling of creaturely activity in its execution and also in its results. Since this control is universal, and embraces and concerns all creaturely activity and its effects, it is actually an ordering of everything that happens. If fate were the controller of occurrence it could not and would not guarantee this order ; nor certainly would chance. If these are forces at all, they are blind and meaningless, and simply control. But while all ordering is undoubtedly a controlling, not all controlling is necessarily an ordering. God controls, but in so doing He orders. Hence we see that in so far as God determines all creaturely activity and its effects, it is settled that the individual actions which go to make up world history are at least co-ordinated actions, co-ordinated, that is, by His all-embracing ordination.

But if we are to understand the divine rule as the ordering of world-occurrence, we shall have to go much deeper than this. In determining creaturely activity and its effects, God directs it to a common goal, that is, Himself. But this does not mean that particular creatures and individuals and natural and historical groupings and relationships are prevented by Him from existing in their particularity and for particular ends. Nor does it mean that the particularity of their activity and effects, and the endless variety of happenings which go to make up world history as a whole, will later be ironed out and destroyed in favour of an all-comprehensive and unified plan. The Ruler of world history is also the Creator who has given this particularity to the various creatures and creaturely groupings. And in preserving them, He gives them room for their particular activity. It is this particular activity which He directs by His constantly renewed permission. There are also particular effects which He sets as individual goals that they are allowed to attain. He Himself as the Lord is so rich that by His lordship He does not need to do violence to any creature in its particularity—He is far too free not to be able to accept and joyfully to affirm it in its particularity—and yet at the same time He can direct all creatures to the one goal, and subordinate all other goals to this one. He has a unified plan which is in the process of execution, and there is no creature which this plan does not embrace, and which does not in its own place and its own way help forward this plan. But in its own place and its own way. This unified plan has nothing whatever to do with a levelling down and flattening out of individuals and individual groupings. On the contrary, God's *propositum* and *proponendum* relates to individual and their individual features as such, and it is realised in their purely individual aims. God can affirm these aims. To each of them He gives its own glory, its lasting worth, its definite value. And He does so by allowing them to serve this common aim, and therefore Himself. In so doing, He does not take anything from the creature. He gives everything to it, just as He does not take anything from it but gives everything to it by directing its free activity and furthering its individual aims. For what would creatures be without this common aim, without the subordination of their individual aims to this one, without this orientation towards God ? What would they be in all the particularity of their activity and its effects ? God preserves them from the wretchedness of a pointless existence in and for themselves, from the mutual contradiction and opposition from which they could not keep themselves, from which in the last resort they obviously could not be kept by the dominion of fate or chance. The totality of world-occurrence, and within it all individual happenings, and all individual creatures as the subjects of these happenings, are preserved by Him from the descent into chaos into which they would at once slide if He were to abandon these creatures and their activity and effects to mere individualism, if together with their many aims as given and posited by Him He did not also direct them to a single goal. In so doing He answers the question : Why does He will to control all creaturely activity and its effects, and to what extent is this control really an ordering ? The answer is that God controls all things because in and with and by and for all things He wills and actually accomplishes one thing—His own glory as Creator, and in it the justification, deliverance, salvation, and ultimately the glorification of the creature as it realises its particular existence as a means of glorifying the Creator. He gives it this office by subordinating its particular ends to this common end, by allowing it even in the particularity of its activity and effects to have a place in the fulfilment of His own plan.

At this point a further consideration arises. If God directs the individual to Himself as the common goal, this does not mean only that He preserves it from individualism or from the opposition of other individuals. Nor does it mean only that He preserves the totality from chaos. It must also have the positive meaning that a subordination of all creatures to God, the ordination which is thereby effected is also a co-ordination of the creatures one with another, i.e., the creation of a mutual relationship between the individual creatures and creaturely groupings. If they are not abandoned to individualism in their activities and effects towards God, neither can they be in their relationships one with another. We must again emphasise that the fact of this relationship does not encroach upon the individual meaning and right of even the most lowly of creatures. God harmonises and co-ordinates the creatures one with another, but this does not mean that the individual creature has no meaning nor right to exist except as a non-autonomous atom, a mere cog in a machine, a functionary in a collective action, and ultimately and supremely in the one collective action of world-occurrence as a whole. The rule and dispensation and authority of God refer to the individual creature as such. And if we ask what is the practical significance of this direct relation of God to each individual creature, the answer is that, as it shares with its fellow-creatures a common aim, so in its activity and in the effects of this activity it is brought into an active, and passive, and on both sides a positive relationship with them, a relationship of giving and receiving. Not merely in its relation to God, but also in its relation to its environment, it is not isolated and left to its own devices, it is not referred back to itself or responsible to itself. In directly accepting it, in dealing with it directly as the Lord, in making use of it, God incorporates it into the history of creation as a whole. He assigns it a place and status in this history. He gives it continuity and protection and light both from right and left, from near and far, from above and below. He allots it specific functions in which it has to serve Him, i.e., to serve its fellow-creatures, mediating to them continuity and protection and light. This is how the creature can exist by and to its fellow-creatures. It belongs to the glory of God and its own salvation that it can exist in this way. It could not experience the justification and deliverance of its existence in particularity by subordination to God if it did not also know this co-ordination. And it could not resist the latter without resisting the former, without forfeiting its particular meaning and right, and the individual worth of its activity and effects. But as no creature can truly or fully withstand this subordination to God, no creature can truly or fully withstand this co-ordination with its fellow-creatures. That which occurs as an individual action also occurs with this horizontal relationship from and to others. And this co-ordination of creatures is God's ruling. It cannot be understood of itself, and it is not fulfilled of itself. Like the attaining of the effects of individual creaturely actions, it has continually to take place. It is quite certain that neither fate nor chance can guarantee that this will happen. It is God Himself who does it. It is He who arranges that His creatures can praise Him together, and therefore truly as individuals. It is He who arranges this *nexus rerum et actionum*, and therefore creation itself, both in its individual parts and also in its totality, and in either case for His own glory. And in doing this, He rules and orders all world-occurrence.

Before we turn to the true substance and centre of the doctrine of the divine world-governance, certain distinctions and elucidations must be made which are forced upon us by a study of the history of the doctrine.

We have referred to the subordination of all creaturely occurrence to the one goal posited by God, which is itself God, and also to the mutual co-ordination of its individual moments and actions as thereby conditioned. Now it is clear that both these concepts involve a thoroughgoing relativisation of all creaturely occurrence. If God gives it His own end and ends, then this means that the occurrence has a significance outside itself. It is not moving in circles, but moving towards a destiny which is posited and given from without, whose fulfilment it can only await as it makes this movement. In the most literal sense creaturely occurrence is only preparatory, i.e., it is engaged in a process. The creature itself cannot decide either why it moves or whither it moves. This decision belongs to God who rules the creature. It is His action which determines the world-process in its true and definitive form. This is in a sense the vertical relativisation of creaturely occurrence. God co-ordinates the various events and the various activities and effects of individual creaturely subjects. He allots to each one its own place and time and function in relation to all the rest. And this means that we can speak of the significance of any one thing only in the light of its connexion with all other things. The individual thing is as it were a word or sentence within a context. It is indispensable to this context. But only within this context does it say what is really intended. Only within this context can it be read and understood rightly. And this is in a sense the horizontal relativisation of creaturely occurrence.

But we must be more precise. The twofold relativisation of creaturely occurrence has reference to its relationship to the rule of God. It is God who arranges for each creature its end and ends. Thus He subordinates all creatures to Himself. And under Himself He co-ordinates all the ends, and therefore all the activities and effects of all creatures into a totality. To this extent all creaturely occurrence and all creatures are relegated to a position of lowliness and dependence and relativity. This means that in themselves they are nothing, and that of themselves they can neither mean anything nor do anything. God is the " yonder-side " of all creaturely being and activity from which alone the light and life and power of creaturely occurrence can derive. In relation to God the creature is lowly and dependent and relative. But this position of lowliness and dependence and relativity in relation to God does not involve a degradation or depreciation or humiliation of the creature. To be lowly before God is its exaltation. If it is nothing without Him it is everything by Him : everything, that is, that He its Creator and Lord has determined and ascribed and allotted to it ; everything that He will continue to be for it, and to execute with and by it. And since this is the optimum of light and life and power, making possible its own value and dignity, it is really everything. If we are to understand the divine world-governance rightly, there is one idea that we can never resist too strongly, one notion that we can never reject too sharply. The fact that God causes His will and His will alone to be done in all things, does not mean that the ruling God is an oppressor who grudges it to the creature even to exist at all, let alone to have its own value and dignity over against him. It is the glory of the creature to be lowly in relation to God. For when it is relative to Him, it participates with all its activities and effects in His absoluteness. To be able to serve Him alone with all its activities and in all its joint-effects, to be in His hands and under His control only as a means, an instrument, the clay of the potter—this is its direct and original glory. It is exalted in this necessity ; it is rich in this poverty ; it can go forward on the basis of this humiliation. To exist in any other way but in this relativity towards God would mean misery and shame and ruin and death for the creature. Its full and perfect salvation consists in this subordination to Him, and in this subordination in the co-ordination with its fellow-creatures which is ordained by Him. That this is the case, and the reason why it is the case, will become clearer when we turn expressly to the substance and centre of the divine world-governance.

We must not obscure the positive sense of the relativity of all creaturely occurrence by ignoring the fact that God and God alone is the One in relation to whom the relativity exists. It is from a misunderstanding of the second and horizontal form of this relativity, of the co-ordination of all creaturely occurrence in the divine world-governance, that danger may threaten. We could substitute for the divine work of this co-ordination the very human idea of a cosmic relationship which curves in upon itself. We could substitute for the King and Father who co-ordinates the individual to the whole the abstract idea of the whole itself, the idea of the universe as co-ordinated by God. We could substitute for the dependence of the individual creature and its activity upon God the idea of its dependence upon this *universum*. The first and vertical dependence of the creature in its direct relationship to God could in a sense merge and disappear into the second and horizontal. Its subordination to God could be forgotten in favour of its co-ordination with the creature. Everything depends upon this not happening ; upon our understanding the second and horizontal dependence in its connexion with and as a consequence of the first, as a second factor which has its basis in the subordination.

For if the misunderstanding does arise, the individual creature with its action can never be more than a part or organ or function of the whole. It can never be more than an integrating moment, a point of transition, in the existence and history of this whole. It can have its own right and glory and determination only from this whole, only in the course of this history and process, only as a contribution to its development. Its activity and effects, therefore, are only stages in this higher creaturely history. Its task is to serve this history in its own place. Its distinction is to be able to do this in its own way and at its own time and place. Its destiny is to be a particle and function of this whole. And now let us consider whether we could just as easily recast our earlier statements and say that it is the glory of the creature to be lowly in relation to this universal whole ; whether the positive sense of the dependence of the creature could be maintained if it were referred only to its co-ordination with other creatures, its being in relation to that whole. Obviously this would be the case only if the whole were itself God, and its life and development were the life and activity of God, granting and guaranteeing a certain honour and freedom to individual creatures and their actions in spite of its superiority to them. But no concept of a creaturely whole, not even that of a whole co-ordinated by God, can ever take the place of God Himself. Even if we think ourselves capable of forming such a conception, it will not lead us by a long way to the knowledge of the God who is the Creator, and therefore the Lord, and therefore the King and Father of the creature. For any creature, to be lowly in relation to this universal whole could mean only to be absolutely less than this whole. For the individual creature, to be subordinated to this whole, and therefore to be lowly and dependent and relative in relation to it, could mean only degradation, depreciation and humiliation. To be ruled by this whole, to be subject to it, to exist and work only because of it and in the service of its aims and ends at this or that time and place and in this or that way, could mean only the suppression of the individual creature. Why ? Because the whole itself is only a creature. To be sure, it is the sum and substance of creation and its activity, and it is therefore an all-powerful creature. But it is still a creature, with no claim to rule either itself or its individual moments or particles, to determine either itself or individual creatures, to be beneficent towards these creatures, or to give them value and honour. The totality of creaturely being and occurrence has need that someone should do this to it. The totality of creaturely being is in no position to do it either to itself or to its individual constituents and their movements. No matter how comprehensively or deeply we understand the life-process of creaturely being, it does not have within itself or by itself the power to do this. It may well be powerful, and power in its own sphere can be achieved only at the expense of the individual moments and stages of its course and development. In the context of this totality individual things can only be small and not great, dependent and not exalted, poor and not rich. And the totality cannot give to them that which it does not itself possess, but of which it has absolute need. We cannot, then, attempt an equation of this kind. Schleiermacher was not the first to undertake this false switching of the doctrine. We can find it here and there in the older Protestant theology. It passes almost unnoticed, and yet the danger is clear. Let me quote as an example *Syn. pur. Theol.*, Leiden, 1624, where we read in *Disp.* 11, 18 f. that it does not belong to the providence of God that each individual thing *ad finem particularem sibi convenientem dirigatur*, but only that it should attain *absolute* the goal *qui toti operi congruit* ; just as when we burn wood in the house, we do not do something which corresponds to the particular purpose of the existence of wood, but something which corresponds to the purpose of the house in general. The divine world-governance has to be compared to the *providentia* with which the father rules his house and the king his country. The *bonum commune* is more important to it than the *bonum singulare*, so that he has to pay more heed to the well-being of the community than to that of the individual. When we consider the objects of the divine *gubernatio* there is a difference between those *quibus Deus providet propter seipsas*, and those *quibus providet propter aliud* ; just as in a house there are the things about which we are concerned for what they are in themselves (e.g., the family and the family property), and things like tools and vessels which are important only *ad horum utilitatem*. In the universe as a whole there are some things which belong *essentialiter* to its perfection and therefore must not be destroyed, and others which can and necessarily do perish and therefore last only as long as they have to do in the interests of the first group. This is a type of argument which is very enlightening and most dangerous in its amiable brutality. It is most dangerous because its brutality is far more noticeable than its amiability. And the reason for this is that between the free governing will of God subordinating and co-ordinating all things and individual creatures and their existence there is interposed quite independently an all-embracing third factor, the house or state, the *totum opus*, the *universum*, the *communitas*, in the interests of which and in relation to which the individual is reduced to a mere means, and in the light of which one thing may be and act *propter seipsum* and the other only *propter aliud*, the one being permanent and the other transitory. It may easily be seen that a divine world-government of this type will inevitably result in the unequivocal abasement of the individual creature or at any rate the majority of individual creatures. This matter is of the greatest practical importance. At the end of the thread which begins here there lies in the ethical sphere the political or economic totalitarianism which has caused us so much anxiety to-day both in its Western and also in its Eastern forms. To avoid this result we must not start along the road which leads to it. The forces at work in this conception of the divine rule are the motives and logic and law of an immanent hierarchy of power and value. The articulated whole is greater and more important than its component parts. Its life is greater and more important than that of the parts. And if this is the case, then amongst the parts themselves there arises the further distinction between those which are more important and necessary for the whole and those which are less. The former can and perhaps will rise up and assert themselves, achieving honour and attaining their own particular ends in so far as they are advantageous to the whole. But the latter can only sink into obscurity, rendering their service to the whole at the proper time, but disappearing like the Moor when they have fulfilled their obligation. It is obvious that countless beings are in this second case, existing only to be sacrificed at the last for the life and progress of the whole and the favoured few. It is all very well for those who for the sake of the whole belong to that earlier class, continuing as its heads and bearers and representatives to the glory of the whole. But it is impossible to equate this much too primitive ordering of the world and society with the divine world-governance.

For if the kingdom of this King means order, if it is, therefore, a kingdom of righteousness, then this means that His plan and will, His co-ordinating of all the activities and effects of all His creatures, does not encroach too much upon any one of them, not one being simply used and then dropped and trampled underfoot. If the ruling of God consists first and foremost in His subordinating of all things to Himself, this means that without prejudice to their mutual relations He deals with each one in a direct and immediate encounter and relationship with Himself. There is not one of them which His rule does not abase, but there is also not one of them which being abased by Him is not exalted. There is not one of them which His rule does not co-ordinate and fuse with others into a single whole, but there is also not one of them which is made only to suffer by this relationship, which is not comforted and gladdened by it, seeing that God Himself created it. For this is what distinguishes the totality which is raised up and sustained and maintained by the divine governance from the unholy hierarchy of a universal collective whole. It is the totality of the freedom and right of each individual. It is the totality in which each individual has to the full its own honour. It is the totality which has its own honour in the fact that no person or thing which it comprehends and orders has simply to do its bit and then to be sacrificed. It is the totality in which each individual moves towards and is certain of its own goal even as it serves the common goal. In this whole there is nothing which at its own time and place and according to its own function is simply instrument, material, cannon-fodder, in the fulfilment of this or that development, or the establishment of this or that *bonum commune* ; which in practice, then, is merely a means to further the ends of certain favoured creatures, a ruling class within this whole. But as each individual with its own being and activity is co-ordinated with all other individuals under God and according to the will and plan of God (and certainly not without this subordination and co-ordination), by this very fact it has its own independent significance and validity, its own independent value and dignity, being granted that which is good, which is indeed the very best, for it, attaining its own individual ends, and in this way the common end of all individuals. It is in loving and ruling each individual creature that God loves and rules them all. He loves and rules them, therefore, in their inter-dependence, their mutual association. But on this account He does not love and rule them any the less but to the highest degree possible in their particularity and singularity.

We have to admit that at this point the older Lutherans had relatively a better insight and happier touch than the older Calvinists. They were not so anxious to interpret the individual activity under the divine in terms of the concept *instrumentum* (or more commonly, with Thomas Aquinas, *medium*). It was and is legitimate to use these concepts so long as it is clear that it is God Himself who directly and immediately holds these *instrumenta* or *media*, which means that their own honour is not merely safeguarded, but constantly ascribed and accorded to them. But the concepts necessarily involved danger once the direct relationship to the lordship of God was obscured, once the notion of a universal whole was interposed between God and the creaturely individual, once the creaturely individual could and indeed had to be understood as a mere instrument and means in the service of this third factor, the universal whole. We have to admit that what the *Syn. pur. Theol.* says on the point does tend at least to obscurity in this respect.

On the other hand, it was of value that the older Lutherans (e.g., Calov, *Syst.*, III, 1659, 6, 1, *qu.* 2, and Quenstedt, *Theol. did. pol.*, 1685, I, 13 *sect.* 2, *qu.* 1) laid particular stress upon the thesis that the divine world-governance extends to all things and to each individual thing, and therefore *ad singularia et vilissima quaeque*. They were again wrestling with Democritus and Epicurus, but also with Aristotle and a text ascribed to the Latin father Jerome ; with the view that some things and events are too small, too insignificant, too unimportant, indeed too futile, for us to be able to suppose that the Godhead will in any way be interested in them. *Minima non curat praetor.* Will God really concern himself with the growth of caterpillars in the grass sprouting in the province of Saxony in any given year ? Or with the thread hanging from the beggar's coat ? Indeed, He does, they quite rightly answered, with a reference to Augustine (*S. 6 in Matth.*) : *Videte, quia minima non contemnit Deus ; nam, si contemneret, non crearet ;* and of course to all the texts in which we are told that God clothes the grass of the field (Mt. 6[30]), that He feeds the ravens (Ps. 147[9]), that He does not allow one sparrow to fall to the ground without His will (Mt. 10[29]), that He numbers even the hairs of our heads (Mt. 10[30]), that He keeps all our bones (Ps. 34[20]), that He knows our downsitting and uprising (Ps. 139[2]). The saying in 1 Corinthians 9[9] did cause a little difficulty, for expounding Deuteronomy 25[4] (" Thou shalt not muzzle the mouth of the ox that treadeth out the corn ") Paul asks : " Doth God take care for oxen ? Or saith he it altogether for our sakes ? " But it was rightly perceived from Psalm 36[6] that God does take care for the ox (" O Lord, thou preservest man and beast "), and the saying of Paul was rightly explained within the whole context of the Old Testament as a prophecy of the events and the ordering of events attested in the New. What was meant is that although God takes care for the ox with one kind of care, and in some sense a " typical " care, with the other and true care He is concerned for the preachers of the Gospel with whose sustenance the apostle is incidentally dealing in the context of 1 Corinthians 9. The final reply to the objection was a counter-question : What does great or small mean to God ? Both small and great, both what appears to us to be mean and what appears to us to be important and outstanding, are alike the work of God and His possession, and therefore worthy to be ruled by His wisdom and to be used in some sense in the fulfilment of His purposes.

It is clear that the older Reformed divines could not and indeed did not differ from this view. But if we take these texts and the whole insight seriously, our thinking cannot be along the lines to which some of the Reformed seemed to approximate rather too closely. Nothing, however small or insignificant, can be understood simply as a means to fulfil the purpose of a greater whole, and therefore of other better-placed creatures. Quite irrespective of its being in relation with the whole, indeed quite irrespective of this relation, we have to ascribe to each creature its own immediacy towards God and therefore its autonomous validity and worth. The command in Mt. 18[10] not to despise one of these little ones thus takes on the character of a basic principle which apart from its direct meaning in the Gospel can be applied indiscriminately and consistently to creation as a whole. Even amongst the older Lutherans we do not find the resultant repudiation of the contrary opinion in the form in which it is required, so that although their answer to the question did in fact provide a useful stimulus to further thinking, they did not provide any proper safeguard against the false ideas which threatened at this point.

But it is now time not so much to leave or abandon the formal consideration of the divine ruling which has so far engaged us as to complete it by turning to the material content of what we have just said. What we have said demands completion in this way. When God rules all creaturely occurrence as King and Father, what does this really mean ? What is it that actually happens ? What do we mean when we confess God as Lord over all things, when we confess God alone, God in Himself, God in His transcendence over all immanent contradictions, God as the One who subordinates all things to Himself, and therefore co-ordinates them one with another, God as the One who is and does these things in the same immediacy both to the whole and also to the individual ? How do we arrive at the point where we can confess the reality and unity and exclusiveness and totality of such a ruling, and God Himself as such a Ruler ? Where are we to turn to find the assurance that what we have said is actually the case ? And finally, what does it mean for us to fulfil this knowledge ? What is it that the Christian community says both to its own members and to all other men when, in and with its message, and as an integral part of the truth which it proclaims, it has to tell them that God is the Father who exercises His lordship in this way over and with all creation, that in this way He is the Almighty, the Creator of heaven and earth ? The Christian community confesses this truth as something which is well-founded and not unfounded. It is a truth which could not be perceived or confessed at all unless its foundation were known. And in dogmatics generally, and therefore in the present context, it can be affirmed as something which is well-founded and not unfounded. And all that we have said so far has been said in the light of the fact that it has this solid foundation. It is this which has guided us in all that we have said, both in general and also in detail, pushing us forward in one definite direction, and keeping us on the right lines. It is this which has enabled us to grasp the very idea of the divine ruling, to think it through with a tolerable order and consistency, and to express it, so far as we can say this of any idea. But so far we have not examined the solid foundation which we have had constantly in view. So far we have not expressly related the idea to the reality which distinguishes it from a mere idea, and it may be an empty one. No order or consistency can distinguish it from a merely empty idea. It is distinguished in this way only as its relationship to this foundation, to the reality envisaged in it, is expressly revealed. It is only as the community sets in this relationship its confession of the Father, the Almighty, the Creator of heaven and earth, only as each individual member of the community sets in this relationship his perceiving and confessing of this God, only as dogmatics sets in this relationship its thinking about Him, that the thinking and perceiving and confessing become an activity filled with real meaning.

The weakness of the older orthodox theology was that in all its doctrine of the divine providence, and of the creation and man, and earlier of God and the election of grace, it believed that it could dispense with this relationship either entirely or almost entirely. It thought and spoke about the divine ruling as about an idea. With all its divergence from individual philosophical systems, its development of the concept was far too like the philosophical development of a concept. In spite of the testimonies from Scripture, it was content with what was basically a quite formal and abstract consideration of the subject. It did not make it at all clear to what it ought really to be looking as a Christian theology, and more often than not it did not even look there, but somewhere else. This was the root of all its uncertainties and deviations, of all the dangers to which it more or less openly exposed itself as it proceeded, and above all of the insipidity or colourlessness of all its thinking to which we drew attention at the outset. The One who is described as King in Holy Scripture is acknowledged to be such, but He does not act as such. At any rate, it is not at all clear that He controls dogmatic thinking concerning Himself. At many points He seems in fact not to control it. What does control it, and what is passed off as the authority which controls the whole universe, seems rather to be the concept of a supreme being furnished with supreme power in relation to all other beings. And the credibility of what is ostensibly said about the rule of God seems to depend upon the existence of this being. With regard to this, we may say : 1. that the existence of such a supreme being is itself highly doubtful, and therefore the credibility of a doctrine of God's rule based upon it can only be very conditional ; and 2. that such a doctrine of God's rule cannot be a Christian doctrine because the God of Christian teaching is certainly not identical with that supreme being. If we are still under the shadow thrown by this twofold difficulty, it is high time that we moved away from it.

The Father, the Almighty, the Creator of heaven and earth, about whose lordship over all things we have been speaking, is the King of Israel. There in one normative biblical concept we have the solid foundation of all that we have said, the foundation which we have now to unfold, and to which we have now to relate all that we have said. The King of Israel is the King of the world. It is His will that is done in the ruling of all creaturely occurrence. It is He who is the Lord over it. It is He who is transcendent over all contradictions. It is He who subordinates all things to Himself, and co-ordinates them one with another. It is to Him that we must look if we are to have assurance that everything really is as we have described it. And a knowledge of this matter means a knowledge of Him which presupposes and includes and involves everything that is necessary for a knowledge of Him. The fact that it concerns Him, the King of Israel, is what distinguishes all that we have so far thought and said about the divine ruling from a merely empty idea, or from the uncertain and in any case unchristian idea of the power and activity of a supreme being. If it concerns the King of Israel, we are on solid ground and under sure leadership. The King of Israel is the God who rules all things.

At its simplest, this is the definition with which we have to fill out our hitherto formal consideration. And again, we can elucidate the definition most clearly and simply by saying that the God of Israel, and therefore the God who rules all things, is the Subject whose speaking and acting is the source and also the object and content of the witness of the Old and New Testaments. To put it in another way : The King of Israel is the One who according to the witness of the Old and New Testaments spoke the " I am," and in speaking it actualised it for seeing eyes and hearing ears by acts of power within the created cosmos and human history. The concrete name " the King of Israel " covers both the Old Testament and New Testament forms of the spoken and actualised " I am " in which we have to do with the Subject of the divine world-governance.

It may be noted that with this definition and its elucidation the idea of the divine world-governance, whatever may be our attitude towards it, does at least cease to be a mere idea and is related to a reality. The form of the idea acquires concrete substance. The colourless idea takes on colour. And this takes place when it is seen that in the idea of the divine world-governance the Subject God bears this concrete name. To apprehend and affirm the idea we have to think of definite periods in human history as this name leads us. And we have to think of definite places—the land of Canaan, Egypt, the wilderness of Sinai, Canaan again, the land on the two sides of Jordan, Jerusalem, Samaria, the towns and villages of Judaea and Galilee, the various places beyond in Syria, Asia Minor and Greece, and finally Rome. We have to think of definite events and series of events which according to the witness of the Old and New Testaments actually took place at these periods and in these places, relating them always to the spoken and actualised " I am." And then necessarily we have to think of the concrete Scripture which bears witness to these events, the text of the Old and New Testaments. And if we cannot apprehend and affirm the idea of the divine world-governance, then quite concretely this means that we stand in a negative relationship to these events which took place at definite periods and in definite places, to this reality, and to this concrete Scripture. Belief or unbelief in the divine world-governance, whether we do or do not apprehend and confess it, is no longer a matter of the right or wrong development of the idea, but of the right or wrong relationship to this reality to which the idea has reference, and therefore to these definite events as according to the equally definite witness of the Old and New Testament Scriptures they took place at definite periods and in definite places. For the Subject who speaks and actualises the " I am " in these events, the King of Israel, is the God who rules the world.

Thomas Aquinas (*S. theol.*, I, qu. 103, *art.* 2) postulates and in his own fashion tries to prove that the Subject that rules the world and directs it to Himself as the one supreme end and goal is necessarily *aliquid extra mundum*, a *bonum* or *principium extrinsecum a toto universo*. We can and must accept this postulate. For if the Subject that rules the world is not recognisable and actually recognised as something distinct from the world, how can it really be a Subject that rules the world and posits itself as the goal of all world-occurrence, and how can it be recognisable or recognised as such ? But we may question whether this quite justifiable postulate ought to be filled out by the particular concept of God which Thomas presupposes and uses in his own demonstration. For this concept of God, the concept of a being in Himself, quite independent of all other being and to that extent absolutely superior to it, is indeed an attempt to point away beyond the world. But the reality of this supramundane being cannot be reached by an attempt of this kind. For the only reality that we can point to in this concept is that of the world as it attempts to transcend itself, so that even in such an attempt it is still the world and not this *principium extrinsecum* which might as such be the Ruler of the world and recognisable and recognised as such. We thus have a concept of God which demands proof of the existence of God. If it is to be recognisable and recognised as a being which is different from the world and therefore qualified to be its Ruler, something more is needed and something more must be perceived than the attempt of the world to transcend itself in this concept. What is needed is that the being itself should transcend the limit and self-knowledge of the world, and thereby demonstrate itself. For the idea of the world-governance of such a being can only have substance, the power postulated by Thomas, if by its own initiative and activity and revelation it actualises and makes perceptible the reality of its supramundane being over against the world, thereby demonstrating itself in the midst of the world. This supramundane being can make itself present in the world only by free grace. And it is the source and object and content of the biblical witness that this did actually occur. Of course, this witness does not refer us to the so-called natural proofs of God's existence in which Thomas found support at this critical point. It witnesses to the very intramundane and temporal and spatial " I am " as the work and revelation of grace in which the *principium extrinsecum*, which can as such be the World-ruler, has actually demonstrated itself to be such ; intramundane and temporal and spatial as opposed to the concept of God as an extramundane reality.

This is why in the biblical witness the divine world-governance is related to the King of Israel. From a philosophical standpoint the naivety with which it does this is highly objectionable. But it is in this naivety that its real strength lies. For it does not find any difficulty in the counter-question whether this supramundane being who as such can rule the world really exists. No second postulate is needed to fill out the first. No resort to natural proofs is needed to fill out the second postulate, and by means of the second the first. The outfilling is itself the starting-point. The basis is the intramundane self-demonstration of the extramundane God and World-ruler. And dogmatics has to take over this naivety and strength in its own thinking and utterance. There is no alternative if it is to be Christian thinking and utterance. If we are really to have a World-ruler, one who is capable of world-dominion as a *principium extrinsecum*, we have to relate the matter to the King of Israel.

In the Old Testament form of the spoken and actualised " I am," the King of Israel is the Lord who made a covenant with the twelve tribes of Israel, thus making them one people and His own people. " I am the Lord thy God, which brought thee up out of the land of Egypt, the house of bondage " (Ex. 20^2). In this event He is the One who initiates the history of this people, and in all that follows He is the One who directs and fulfils it. He does this in such a way that He separates it from other peoples and keeps it as a people to serve Him. To that end He gives it His Word as commandment and promise and warning. But in return, from the very outset and in the whole course of its history, He experiences at the hands of this people only a lack of recognition, confusion with the idol-gods of the nations, ingratitude, disobedience, unfaithfulness and backsliding. The One who elected Israel has to be and is content continually to be rejected by Israel ; to be its despised and rejected King. And by that very fact Israel is itself delivered up, putting itself in the sphere of the legitimate wrath of its King. Hence its history is simply a series of the predicted and inevitable judgments of this King. But he is still its King. The unfaithfulness of Israel calls down upon it the judgment of its King, but it cannot alter His faithfulness. He is still faithful and gracious to Israel, confirming his election and calling, even when He chides and judges Israel. He does not cease to separate and keep and sanctify and bless this people. Nor does His Word cease. His prophets rise up continually and pronounce it. And there is always a remnant which, even in its solidarity with the people in sin and judgment, perceives that the King reigns, remembering that He has done so in the past and confident that He will do so in the future ; which pays heed to His Word and recognises in the adversity of the people the judgment of its King ; which humbly acknowledges His judgment to be just and even in judgment recognises His grace, and therefore outside and alongside His judgment the continuance of His favour ; which on this account can still rejoice even in its isolation, praising the King on behalf of the whole people ; which sets its hope upon Him and has therefore a living hope. This is the kingly rule of God according to the Old Testament witness : a history which is clear in itself, yet very obscure ; a history which is a whole in itself, yet obviously incomplete ; a history of the presence of God at its most actual, in a form which apparently cannot be surpassed in directness, and yet a history only of the expectation, implicit here and explicit there, of a future towards which it is only moving.

And in the New Testament form of the spoken and actualised " I am, " the King of Israel is the same Lord of the same covenant : except that now he illuminates the obscurity which dominated the history of covenant in its Old Testament form, removing the incompleteness of it and fulfilling the expectation ; except that now, in utter discontinuity with all that Israel has been and accomplished, He Himself in free grace directs to its goal the covenant which He had instituted and faithfully maintained and which Israel had constantly broken. " I am—the way, the truth, and the light " (Jn. 14⁶). Now the King Himself comes, and He comes from Nazareth in Galilee, from the place where the Old Testament obscurity was most pronounced and backsliding and the divine judgment most evident. Hence the sayings : " Can any good thing come out of Nazareth ? " (Jn. 1⁴⁶) ; " Shall Christ come out of Galilee ? " (Jn. 7⁴¹) ; " Search and look : for out of Galilee cometh no prophet " (Jn. 7⁵²). And yet from that very place there has come a good thing, *the* good thing ; there has come a Prophet, *the* Prophet of whom all the other prophets were the forerunners—even though he was born at Bethlehem, as the son of David and heir of David's throne. From this place there has at last come the Israelite who does that at which the whole history of Israel aimed, repaying faithfulness with faithfulness to the King and Lord of the covenant. And late as it is, and only in the one man, is not this the true being and achievement of Israel ? Indeed it is, and to the extent that there lies in this One Israel's justification in the day of judgment. But Israel will reject this last and true Prophet from the company of His loyal predecessors —reject Him more consciously and drastically than any of the others. It will remain only too true to the attitude in which it always despised and rejected its King. " Jesus of Nazareth, the King of the Jews " (Jn. 19¹⁹), will be the pagan irony to which Israel will deliver up the One in whom it is justified. And by this attitude Israel will prove that its justification is in no sense its own work, but only His kingly mercy, the remission of sins, the fulfilment of its yearning with the answering of the prayers of the remnant, not the acknowledgement of what is finally revealed to be its own righteousness. No : in the person of the one loyal and righteous man, the one true Israelite—and this is the new feature in the New Testament witness—King Yahweh Himself has come into the midst of His people on behalf of His people, to turn this people to Himself, to confirm in His own person its election and calling, to vindicate His kingly honour. Hence the confession : " Rabbi, thou art the Son of God ; thou art the King of Israel " (Jn. 1⁴⁹). He is the King whose faithfulness to Israel has triumphed in the fact that He Himself has become flesh in the one Israelite. He is the King who in the person of the one Israelite has Himself achieved the faithfulness which His people owed Him. He is the King who judged the people in the crucifixion of the One who is His Son, but in so doing, Himself fulfilled the Law and justified His people. This is the King of Israel according to the witness of the New Testament, and this justification of Israel by Him is His kingly rule. And now the New Testament community, whose foundation is a part of the object of this witness, is the community of this King of Israel ; the people which consists of those who have seen His glory in the new and absolutely clear and full and definitive form of the one Israelite, and who have found in Him both their own salvation and the salvation of the whole world. It is this community which from amongst Jews and Gentiles He has called to faith in Himself by His own Word and Spirit, which in its weakness has put itself in the position to rely only upon His grace, and to praise His grace in its life and by its witness, both with and without words. This New Testament community is the new Israel : Israel, because those who are gathered within it live by the justification which has come to Israel in this One ; the new Israel, because even if they are Jews they cannot do this on the basis of their birth and circumcision as Jews, but only on the basis of the fact that the King of the Jews has Himself come on His people's behalf and called them, only because in this coming on His people's behalf He has come on behalf of the whole world. This is why the people and possession of the King is the community not of the Jews only but also of the Gentiles ; the catholic, the ecumenical, the universal Church ; a community which is destined to be a shining light to the whole cosmos, knowing what the world does not know, and looking forward to the culminating revelation of the King and therefore to the end of all His ways.

This is the " I am " spoken and actualised in world history according to the witness of the Old and New Testaments. Concerning the mutual relationship of the two forms we can say only this. In the Old Testament it is primarily the question of an all-powerful Word which has been declared. The King reveals and proclaims His election and will and love and command. He does, of course, confirm these things by what He does in the history of His people. But the characteristic relationship of His people to Him seems to be decisively fixed by the " Hear, O Israel," and the specific servants of God in the midst of Israel are the prophets who mediate His kingly calling and Word. As against that, in the New Testament it is predominantly the question of an all-powerful act which has come to pass. The King Himself has come ; He has brought a sacrifice for His people, and in this way He has demonstrated Himself to be the Victor. In so doing He does, of course, speak and teach and command. But the beholding of His glory seems now to be the decisive thing in the relationship of His people to Him, and His specific servants are now the apostles who carry the news that He has appeared, who tell what has occurred, and does occur, and has yet to occur. Thus in the Old and New Testaments, and in the movement from the one to the other, we see the King of Israel treading always the one path. In His movement from the one to the other He has in a sense His own history, but in both He is obviously one and the same, so that in both His Word and act belong together. In both the ascendancy which marks Him as a King is the ascendancy of His free grace. How free it is, is shown in the Old Testament by all that makes it so obscure and incomplete, so much a witness only to expectation, with the shattering demonstration of the contrast between the faithfulness of the King and the unfaithfulness of His people. How much it is grace is shown in the New Testament by all that in contrast to the Old makes it so obviously a witness to fulfilment, with its comforting demonstration of the way in which the faithfulness of the King has itself overcome the unfaithfulness of

His people. But in both it is both free and also grace, just as in both it is both Word and act. And in both it is supreme and royal. According to Old and New Testaments alike the " I am " is an act of government.

But the phrase " an act of government " is far too weak and casual and relative to describe that which all the biblical witnesses saw and to which prophets and apostles, and to some extent as both, they all tried to bear witness. The great " I am " as a royal Word and act, as the irruption of the supremacy of free grace to which they testified, is far more to them than an individual act of government beside which, and independent of and perhaps superior to which, there might be other acts of government by other subjects, or beside which we might have to see and expect other acts of government by the same Subject, but this time of a completely different and perhaps totally antithetical character. No : in the act which those witnesses heard and saw, with its definite character of free grace, there takes place the one rule of the one Subject, to which all other in some sense ruling subjects and their power and rule are absolutely subordinate, which is indeed normative for all other rule by the one Subject. All actual rule in this world can be only the rule of this one Subject, and therefore a rule which has the one form and purpose peculiar to this Subject. The fact that the Old and New Testament witnesses were wholly and absolutely claimed by what they heard and saw of the King of Israel who met them in this Word and act of His is sufficiently clear of itself. But we must look further, and we see that for these witnesses other kings, if there are such, cannot possibly be the rivals of this One, for the throne at whose steps they stand is uniquely exalted. And again, they quite definitely do not reckon with the possibility that this King might display a different character, or that different acts of government might proceed from this throne. In His encounter with them, He and His rule claim them totally because He alone is in a position to do so, and because in this encounter He allows them to see Him as the One who will be the same at all times and in all circumstances. The King of Israel attested in the Old and New Testaments is a King who is absolutely superior as compared with all other kings, and absolutely consistent in Himself. For the biblical witnesses that which is peculiar to His kingdom, the supremacy of His free grace, which the Old and New Testaments attest as the meaning of these particular events, is something which undoubtedly stands behind and above all things, behind and above world-occurrence in general. There is no other who in fact rules as the King of Israel rules, and outside this particular history the King of Israel does not rule differently or with a different purpose than He does within it.

This is the insight which must be the filling out and substance of the Christian doctrine of the divine *gubernatio*. And we are again faced with a basic insight without which a Christian doctrine of providence as opposed to a mere scheme of things would not even be possible, and in the light of which we have already considered the sustaining and accompanying activity and will of God in and with and over world-occurrence. The rule of God as opposed to the control and outworking of a natural or spiritual cosmic principle is characterised by the fact that it is here in the particular events attested in the Old and New Testaments, in the " I am " spoken and actualised by the King of Israel, in the covenant of free grace instituted and executed, promised and fulfilled by Him, that it has the centre which controls and is normative for everything else. The power which rules the world is the power which is active and manifest here as the power of this King. There is no other power equal to this power. And as His power it is never different in any way from this power. To understand the divine governance we have to observe a twofold rule.

1. We have to look at world events in general outwards from the particular events attested in the Bible, from God's activity in the covenant of grace which He instituted and executed in Israel and in the community of Jesus Christ. The particular events do not take place only for themselves, but as the inner basis of all creaturely occurrence. They take place as the fulfilment of the meaning of this occurrence, as its preservation and deliverance and glorification and manifestation—an anticipation of what the totality of heaven and earth, and what man on earth and under heaven, is one day to be according to the will of God. These particular events are not a final end, but an original and pattern of the general events. They are not an end in themselves, but a ministry in and to the whole of God's creation. Already in the Old Testament the King of Israel is secretly the King of all the nations and of the whole earth. In the New Testament His coming on behalf of His own people means that He is active and manifest as the Lord of a community of Jews and Gentiles, as the Light of the world. Therefore when we have to do with the particular history of the covenant and salvation as it took place to and in and of Jesus Christ, we cannot make it into a private history. For if we did, we should be denying the fact that in this history, if we hold to the biblical testimony concerning it, we are dealing with the one act of rule which as such embraces and determines all other events over and above its own fulfilment, which even in its particularity is the centre of a circumference, of all creaturely occurrence both in heaven and on earth. We cannot deny this ; we cannot try to think abstractly of the events described in the Bible, of the supremacy of free grace as it is there spoken and actualised, without completely misunderstanding, or worse still denying the majesty and sovereignty, the "I am," of the King of Israel, as it was perceived and clearly enough extolled by the biblical witnesses

2. We have to look back from the world events of nature and history, both far and near, both above and below, to the particular

events which are attested in the Bible, to the history of the covenant of grace from the promise which initiated it to its final fulfilment. The general events do not happen for their own sake. They do not form a self-contained and self-motivated whole as contrasted with the particular events. There is no such thing as secular history in the serious sense of the word. What we have tried to describe as such abstractly, the history of created reality as such, occurs concretely only as an outward platform for the fulfilment of the particular events. The general events have their meaning in the particular. It is only as the particular events take place that they are preserved and delivered and secretly filled with glory, and move towards the revelation of this glory. In the particular events the divine will and plan for them is anticipated. They are not, therefore, a final end, an end in themselves; they serve rather as the copy and reflection of the particular events. In the Old Testament the nations have a place only as instruments of the will of God for Israel, and in expectation of their appointed salvation as it is to be proclaimed in Jerusalem. The earth and all that is in it is important only because in its totality it belongs to the Lord who comes from Zion. And in the New Testament the Gentiles who have come into the community have no glory of their own (Rom. 11^{17}), but are only engrafted branches which are borne by the root Israel (not the reverse). And the earnest expectation of all creatures waits for the manifestation of the sons of God (Rom. 8^{19}). For the very same reason that we are not allowed to make the history of the covenant a private history, we are also forbidden to make universal history private over against it. If we did, we should have to reckon with other and rival kings, or with an inner instability of the King of Israel. Again, and from a different angle, we should be denying the public nature and claim of what did occur, and does and will occur, in the history of the covenant and salvation to and from and in Jesus Christ—in the greatest particularity, to be sure, yet not apart from but at the very centre of creaturely occurrence. We should be failing to recognise that in all creaturely occurrence—however far it may seem to be from the " I am " of the Bible—we have to do with the circumference of this centre. We should be forcefully wrenching away that circumference from the supremacy of free grace which rules it from this centre. Again, we should be betraying the most central content of the prophetic and apostolic message. We should be acting as if the King of Israel had not spoken or acted, as if an act of government had indeed taken place, but not *the* act. And that is something which we cannot allow from this standpoint either.

We can now define our position in relation to two conceptual distinctions constantly met with in the older theological doctrine of the *gubernatio*. On the one hand, a distinction is made between a *providentia generalis* and a *providentia specialis*, and on the other between a *providentia ordinaria* and a *providentia extraordinaria*. By *providentia generalis* is meant the divine government of the whole world-order as such, and by *providentia specialis* the government of the Church and the faithful and men generally. By *providentia ordinaria* is meant the divine government as it occurs within the framework of what we can recognise as the laws which underlie the cosmic events of nature and history, and by *providentia extraordinaria* the divine government in so far as it takes the form of miracles.

From a different standpoint, these distinctions might be applied to the two spheres of which we have just been speaking—the activity of God on the one hand in the history of the covenant and salvation, and on the other in history generally. But the order in which the concepts are brought up makes it clear that there is something wrong. For if we are on the right track in relation to the divine world-government, that is, if we are on the track indicated to us by the Bible, we shall have to reverse the order, i.e., to move from a consideration of the *providentia specialis* or *extraordinaria*, i.e., salvation history, to that of the *providentia generalis* or *ordinaria*, i.e., world-occurrence in general ; and then back again from the latter to the former. In fact, the general with its recognisable laws has been treated as if it were the norm, and the particular (this particular) as if it were only a single application, or from a different angle, a single infringement of the norm. We can explain this procedure only on the presupposition that the subject of the whole activity was thought of in terms of a speculative supreme being and not of the God of Holy Scripture. In this connexion we may add that simply to bring the two spheres under the one concept *providentia*, to reduce them to single common denominator, is a confusing levelling down of the problems involved. Certainly the concept " providence " can be used in a wider sense, and we can then say that the divine government of this particular sphere, the divine control of the history of salvation, is also an act of divine providence. But it is certainly something more and something quite other than a particular instance of general and orderly world-governance corresponding to the norm, or even an isolated case contradicting it. The whole concrete difference between these particular visitations and the general as it dominates all Scripture is that in the one case we are dealing with the centre, in the other with the circumference ; in the one with the controlling original, in the other with the subservient copy ; in the one with the particular as it is normative for the general, in the other with the general as it stands under the law of the particular. And this difference is a vital insight which is obscured when the two spheres are brought equally under the one master-concept *providentia*. But further, if we restrict this sphere of the particular only to the Church, or to men generally, or, from another angle, to miracles, then we are obviously missing the decisive thing, the history of the covenant and salvation, to which even the divine miracles belong as representative of its particularity, and in the light and context of which the history of the Church, and the life of the individual Christian, and in connexion with the Church and Christianity the life of all men in world history generally acquires a central importance. But it is not the Church or Christianity or humanity which constitutes this centre, this primary and particular sphere upon which the significance of the second and general sphere is grounded. It is not miracles, not the miracles of the Bible or any other miracles. It is the activity of God to and in and of Jesus Christ, the activity of the King of Israel as the object of the biblical witness. Therefore we have to make several important reservations with regard to the traditional distinctions. And if we do make them, we shall depart widely from the sense in which the distinctions were introduced into the older theology. But if we are not prepared to make them, it would be better to abandon the distinctions altogether.

We maintain, then, that the King of Israel is the King of the world and the Subject of the *gubernatio*. The fact that God rules means that there rules the supremacy of the free grace which according to the witness of the Old and New Testaments irrupted into the world in the promise and fulfilment, the institution and execution of this covenant, in the Word and act of this King, as he went His own way. This same is God: "Christ Jesus is his name, The Lord Sabaoth's Son; He, and no other one, Shall conquer in the battle." There we have the clearest expression of the Christian faith in the divine world-governance. And the Christian idea of the matter is not an empty idea, or an idea which can be filled out in a variety of ways. When we think of the divine governance we are not thinking of an empty form, of a general and overriding order and teleology in all occurrence. We are not looking either up above or down below. We are simply looking at the Old and New Testaments; at the One whom Scripture calls God; at the events which Scripture attests in their relationships the one to the other; at the incursion of the supremacy of free grace which Scripture records; at the Subject who is active in this incursion; at His inconceivable but manifest act of election; at the faithfulness which He demonstrates and maintains; and, at the very heart of these events, at Jesus Christ on the cross; at the One who was not crucified alone, but two thieves with Him, the one on the right hand and the other on the left (Mt. 27[38]); at the One who accepted solidarity with all thieves both Jew and Gentile; at the One who is King over them all and on behalf of them all. It is from this point, and in this sense, and according to this purpose as it is active and revealed in these events, that the world is ruled, heaven and earth and all that therein is. This is the Christian belief in the divine world-governance. The history of salvation attested in the Bible cannot be considered or understood simply in and for itself. It is related to world history as a whole. It is the centre and key to all events. But again, world history cannot be considered or understood simply in and for itself. It is related to the history of salvation. It is the circumference around that centre, the lock to which that key belongs and is necessary. And in view of this relationship we must give up trying to develop the idea of a general kingship of God, and turn to his kingship in the Old and New Testaments, in the light of which we can again consider and understand His kingship in general. Without this substance and form the doctrine of the divine world-governance might, and necessarily would, be erroneous, or remain an empty scholasticism.

Why is it that God rules alone? Why is it that He alone has the right and the power and the wisdom to rule, when the rule of others can lead only to oppression and confusion? Why is it that God is so indispensable as the Subject of this rule? Why is it that there cannot be any collateral or counter-government? Our answer is that it is because He is the One who in His freedom is gracious, and in His grace free; He alone is the One who can elect, and who can confirm His election by giving Himself; He alone is the faithful One who cannot be wearied or thwarted by any unfaithfulness. He alone is the fountain

of mercy, the eternal Father of the eternal Son. Similarly, He alone
is the source of the Holy Spirit, the only One who has true power.
He alone is capable of a transcendent Word and a transcendent act.
In all this He is absolutely unique. In all this He is high above all
idols and dominions and powers. And in all this, and in this way,
He is God as the King of Israel. It is as the King of Israel that He
is the only Ruler of the world, and can be known as such.

Why is it, and in what sense, that God makes and posits Himself
the goal of all creaturely occurrence ? Why is it that it is the blessing of
all blessings, and the true glory of the creature, to promote His glory ?
Why is it that the guiding and direction of all things and events to
Himself can be understood only as an act of the supreme and divine
self-seeking ? Our answer it that it is because He Himself, the Son of
the Father and the Father of the Son, is love, and in His Son, as
Creator, Reconciler and Redeemer, He is love to another, to the
creature which needs His love, which can live only by His love, which
may and must live by this love. The glory of God is in His being as the
One who loves eternally. The greatness of His glory is in the fact that
His love is actualised. And it is actualised in the fact that He does
not abandon the creature to itself ; that He does not direct it to other
ends, but to Himself as the one end ; that He wills that He Himself
should be its end and blessing. And it is as the King of Israel that
He is God in virtue of that love. It is as the King of Israel that He
is and may be known as the One who in asserting Himself, in gaining
the victory, in triumphing, gives Himself ; who is therefore active
and revealed in this way as the great and radical Benefactor.

Why is it that there belongs to Him that transcendence over the
universal antinomies of necessity and contingence, of law and freedom ?
Why is it that He rules not only over these antinomies but also in and
through them ? Why is it that He is not fate and not chance, and yet
both—the One who implacably orders all things, and the One who
freely disposes in all things ? Our answer is that He is over these
antinomies, and in His own way in them, because in Himself He is
both valid law, and also in favour of the highest individuality and the
richest concrete life ; because in His own most proper reality, which
is above law—which is a reality self-conditioned and free in itself—
He has willed to turn to the creature and to speak and act towards it
(and finally to speak and act as Himself one creature with others) ;
because in this reality He has in fact spoken and acted towards it.
It is in the almightiness of His mercy and in the mercy of His almightiness that He is above and in these antinomies. And it is as the King
of Israel that He acts and manifests Himself in this way, that He is
both unity and life, that He is almighty and merciful in an unfathomable and incomparable, a truly incomprehensible and yet manifested
divine union of the two, in the union in which He overlooks and controls and is thus superior to all the tensions which these antinomies

necessarily mean for the creature and creaturely thinking, in which the antinomies can only serve him. We can never be deceived or go astray in the matter if we look at what the King of Israel actually says and does.

And why is it the case that God orders creaturely events, that from all eternity and yet also at every moment He is Himself both the Planner and the plan, the *ordinator* and the *ordo* ? The answer is that in the supremacy of His free grace, in His zeal for His own glory and therefore in His love for the creature, in His transcendence over and in the contradictions of the world, He has pursued a definite course, executing His eternal will in a temporal history, moving from promise to fulfilment, from Word to act, from grace to judgment, and back to a new and inconceivably greater grace, and yet through it all remaining exactly the same. The One who speaks and acts in the greatest freedom is inexorably caught up in the execution of His own project, and the One who executes His own project is the One who continues the most free Lord of His own will. It is thus, then, that God orders, i.e., that the King of Israel is seen to order : always according to an eternal necessity, and yet always with a surprise ; always with freshness ; always on the basis of incalculable presuppositions ; always with the most unexpected results ; but really ordering ; really planning from stage to stage ; manifestly proceeding according to a plan which since it is this plan could not be more strictly determined or appointed. Do we really understand this ? All that we can do is to perceive the fact of it as a fact, and to understand that the King of Israel is both the Planner and the plan, the Orderer and the order of His own Word and act. We cannot for a moment doubt the fact that He is, and if He is the God who rules the world we cannot for a moment doubt that His rule is an ordering.

What is the nature of the relationship between the rule of God and the operations of His creatures ? It is true that He directs them all to one goal and subordinates them all to His own operation. It is also true that He does not suppress them in their distinctiveness over against His own operation, but affirms and honours them. We have already stated the fact, and as far as possible explained it. But on what basis can we properly state and explain it ? Is there not an intolerable contradiction at this point ? Are we not faced again by a question which is wearisome because of its age and yet still a burning issue—the question of the relationship between the freedom of God and our freedom, between the freedom of God and that of the creature ? With all its wearisomeness the question will flare up again and again as long as hazy notions prevail concerning who or what we mean by God, as long as we answer the question in another way than the Christian. But where God is at work in the supremacy of His free grace, where the King of Israel is active with His Word and act to and by His people as opposed to the world at large, there we really see the two in a single relationship, not in a unity of tension, but in a relationship which is inwardly calm and clear and positive. Manifestly God wills and determines and effects all things in this relationship, so that all creaturely activity and effects have to strive wholly and unceasingly towards Him, adjusting themselves to His plans and purposes and executing His commands : Israel itself and the nations ; the good and the evil ; the sun and its heat and the sea with its waves ; the stars of heaven and the grasshopper in the fields. Where is the creature which ever does anything different or differently from that which the will of God has ordained for it ? And yet it is still the case that all creaturely activity has its own meaning and determination ; that Israel itself and all other peoples live out their own individual history ; that all men, the obedient no less than the disobedient, think and speak and act according to the manifest desire of their hearts ; that the desert is dreary and the night dark ; that the sea roars and honey is sweet ; that bread sustains and wine makes glad the heart of man ; that everything is and acts as it does. It has to be noted that, although miracles are ultimately unexpected and inexplicable as series of creaturely actions and effects directly initiated by God Himself, they do not involve any setting aside of such actions and effects. In the particular occurrence whose Subject is the King of Israel, God is of course absolutely the Almighty. But we cannot overlook the fact that men—and not only men—are also there over against Him, with their own particularity and activity, with their own being and action. And they are there not merely like chessmen—let alone like chessmen already out of the game—but all of them, from Moses and Paul to Judas Iscariot, from the cedar of Lebanon to the hyssop that grows on the wall, are there with their own individual being and the individual activity which corresponds to that being. And self-evidently everything depends on men and other creatures, on their individual actions and effects. It is with them that almighty God is concerned in His own almighty work. This is the case even in the history of salvation. It does not offer any solution at all to the technical problem raised. If we read the Bible with a desire to find any such solution, we shall find that it has nothing to say. But it offers us something far greater and far better, the fact of a relationship between the Creator and His creatures, between His freedom and their freedom, which is still clear and positive in spite of the existence of this problem. If we look at this factual relationship, and therefore at the rule of the God of Israel, we see that it is actually true that in the world-goverance of God everything has to be and is absolutely under God, and yet everything attains in freedom to its own validity and honour.

But is it true that in subordinating everything to the one end the divine rule involves the co-ordinating into a single whole of all the activities and effects of individual creatures, the establishment of a horizontal relationship and order ? Is it true that in spite of this co-ordination there is no question of a suppression or conjuring away of the creature, of the individual creature in its existence as such, but rather of its exalting and glorification ? We have already stated the fact and made some attempt to explain it. But unless we give a clear and Christian account of who and what we mean by God in this con-nexion, there must always be doubt whether these things are not really incompatible. When we turn, however, to the history of the covenant and salvation as attested in the Bible, we have to do with a totality of creaturely being and activity co-ordinated by God in face of which no such doubt can ever arise. The people of Israel with whom the Yahweh of the Old Testament entered into covenant, and the com-munity of the New Testament which has Jesus Christ as its Head (in relationship to this King, and ruled by Him), are no chance conglomera-tions of individuals, but wholes, and indeed in the strict sense a single whole, with a common guilt in virtue of their solidarity in obligation and responsibility, but also with a common justification and sancti-fication. This fact has often been misunderstood both in theory and in practice, but exegetically there is not the slightest doubt about it. On the one hand, we have the election and calling of the people (the twelve tribes, and their individual families, and the members of these families in all their generations, but all of them bound together like a single man). On the other hand, we have the one Holy Spirit of the one Lord as the bond of peace which embraces the whole community, so that they are not like many men, but only one. And in both cases the meaning and result are the same. The supremacy of free grace has created in this history a historical cosmos, a living but perfect unity, a body. But we must beware of trying to follow through this thought to its logical end. " This body " is not a collective whole in which the totality is everything and the individual nothing. How sadly we should misunderstand this body if we did not perceive that in both the good and the evil the whole has only the form of particular individuals, and that individuals are always this whole before God. Where can we see the people more clearly in its common sin and need and with its common promise than in Deutero–Isaiah ? And where are the people surprisingly addressed as such in words which in every page, and rightly so, have been received and accepted and passed on as the most powerful of all words in the individual and personal cure of souls ? Who ever addressed the community of Christ so consistently as a unity, a body, as Paul did ? And yet who but the same Paul saw this body so fully represented in his own apostolic but highly individual person ? It is true, of course, that the history of the covenant and salvation as it occurred under the rule of the King of Israel, and with this history the Bible, does not offer us any solution to the technical problem which arises, any formula which will reveal to us how the individual and the community can properly co-exist. But it offers us far more. It shows us the fact. They are together, and together in such a way that there is no need to safeguard the individual against the community or the community against the individual, to defend righteousness against freedom or freedom against righteousness. If we cling to the actual fact as it is attested in the Bible, if we think in the light of this fact because in it we see the one true God at work, we shall see that in the divine world-governance it is actually the case that all things are co-ordinated, that in this very fact each individual receives its own kingdom, and that in this fact again all things are co-ordinated.

At all points, then, to fill out the idea of the divine world-governance along biblical and Christian lines is to make it concrete, to actualise and verify it. If we think of it as filled out in this way we are not considering the empty framework of a mere concept of God, but a form, a face, a history. We are as it were caught up and forced to tread a definite path. We are not concerned with an empty idea, but with something real. And this means that our thoughts can no longer roam about freely. We are taken out of the sphere of vacillating opinions, and at all these different points we are led to the definite conclusions indicated.

But this is not all. For it is only when we can presuppose this filling out along biblical and Christian lines that the idea of the divine world-governance becomes a practical idea : an idea which illuminates both individual life and the life-process generally ; an idea which gives direction ; a significant idea. If it is really the King of Israel, the Lord of the covenant ; if it is really God in Jesus Christ, who is the Subject of this governance, then even the concept of the world-occurrence to which it relates signifies something much more than a mere mass of things and events, which in spite of all its variety lacks finally either contour or direction. World-occurrence is no longer the endless wave-beat of a sea which has neither shore, colour, nor form, but is everywhere the same, flowing out of itself and flowing back into itself. It is no longer the basically uninteresting and even boring *universum* of monads all of which in principle have the same status and form, a *universum* to which our thinking merely adds the basically uninteresting and even boring truth that both in its totality and in each of those monads which have the same status and form, it is directed only by God the chief Monad.

It is to be noted that if God Himself has no form nor face nor history, if in the name God we can only look at the empty framework of a concept of the original being and activity of a chief Monad, then the truth that God rules the world is at bottom a dispensable and superfluous luxury. We have to represent world-occurrence as in some sense a self-ordered unity. And to this unity and order we give the name of the divine governance. If the concept God is an empty one, it may well give greater solemnity to what we say, or to our feelings as we say it, but in practice it will not make the slightest difference to the significance or lack of significance of the unity and order. For all practical purposes they would have no significance at all, and even if our apprehension of them were correct, it would still be unimportant. A thought is not important because it is a correct thought. In any case, a unity and order which embrace the whole world uniformly can only be a theoretical idea, whether the unity and order are immanent in the world or imposed by God. If the idea is to have any practical significance, i.e., a significance which determines the existence of the man who conceives it, it must acquire this significance elsewhere. It will probably have to be added by the man himself as he adopts a practical attitude towards that immanent or transcendent unity and order, and his own peril. Any importance that it has will be due to himself and to the measure of importance that he attaches to it.

But if the King of Israel is God, and therefore the King of all occurrence, the idea of the divine world-governance is not only clearly differentiated from that of a unity and order immanent in the world, but as such, as a distinctive idea of the divine world-governance, it has a practical and not merely a theoretical significance. It is not only correct ; it is also important in itself. It is not an idea that we can only think, and then have to give to it a practical significance ; it is an idea that is practically significant in itself. It determines human existence. It is an idea by which we can immediately live, and, if we really think it, must live. World-occurrence under the rule of the King of Israel is more than a mass of events which may perhaps be self-directing or may even be directly and uniformly ordered by God but is still lacking in either contour or direction. If the King of Israel rules, then of course this means that each thing and everything takes place in a uniform order as He directs it. But it means more. It means that all occurrence has a definite form. There is direction in the all-embracing unity. And this means that there is a first and a last, an above and a below, a foreground and a background. It means that the unity and order involve a definite disposition and economy. And while it is the same King who rules all things on the basis of this economy, things cannot be both above and below, both great and small, both first and last, at one and the same time. On the basis of this economy there is a continual differentiation within that occurrence. There is an advance and a corresponding withdrawal. There is an illuminating and also an obscuring. There is authority and also subordination. On the basis of this economy occurrence acquires the character of a motivated history. It is still the case that in the kingdom of this King there is a purpose behind every individual thing as such, that nothing at all is lost, or exists and acts merely for the sake of something else. Indeed, it is on the very basis of this formative disposition and economy that with all its particularity the individual thing can exist and act in immediacy towards God. But the individual thing receives its particular dignity and value on the basis of a formative economy which assigns to all things a place and time and function. And this means that the true image of the cosmos which this King rules, and of the unity and order which He gives to world-occurrence, is not the image of a sea but of a river which has its source and course and estuary. It is certainly not that of a globe, on whose surface and in whose interior any one point may in principle be exchanged for any other, since all of them have exactly the same function in their own place, and the only difference between them is that they happen to be this or that point and not another. An image of this kind would be basically uninteresting and even boring, whether accompanied or not by the corresponding concept of God as an empty framework. It is an image to which the form and significance of any kind of life—we will not ask what—would have to be added and read in theoretically by the existential decisions of man himself. But the true image of the cosmos which is ruled by this King is undoubtedly that of a natural structure, a living plant perhaps, or some other organism, in which the various parts, root, stem, branches, leaves, buds and fruit are all mutually ordered, in which the presence of all the others demands that each one should have its own place and function, in which they all have a different place and function and are therefore different the one from the other. Or else it is the image of a human work of art, a building for example, in which the plan and purpose and meaning of the whole, to which all the parts must conform, is revealed in both the individual significance and also the indestructible variety of the parts.

In 1 Cor. 12¹⁴⁻²⁶ Paul uses a well-known image to describe the relationship between the community and its individual members as they are endowed with various gifts of the Spirit. Trait for trait, the image is normative for a description —not of the concept of an empty framework—but of the cosmos which is ruled by the living God, the King of Israel. We must allow Paul to speak for himself : "For the body is not one member, but many. If the foot shall say, Because I am not the hand, I am not of the body ; it is not therefore not of the body. If the whole body were an eye, where were the hearing ? If the whole were hearing, where were the smelling ? But now hath God set the members (ἔθετο τὰ μέλη) each one of them in the body, even as it pleased him. And if they were all one member, where were the body ? But now they are many members, but one body. And the eye cannot say to the hand, I have no need of thee : or again the head to the feet, I have no need of you. Nay, much rather, those members of the body which seem to be feeble are necessary : and those parts of the body, which we think to be less honourable, upon these we bestow more abundant honour ; and our uncomely parts have more abundant comeliness ; whereas our comely parts have no need : but God tempered (συνεκέρασεν) the body together, giving more abundant honour to that part which lacked ; that there should be no schism in the body ; but that the members should have the same care one for another. And whether one member suffereth, all the members suffer with it ; or one member is honoured, all the members rejoice with it."

But if this image, and not that of the sea or globe, is normative for our understanding of the cosmos which God rules and of universal occurrence as He directs it, this means that we can never think this thought without a Word being addressed to us. We cannot linger before the picture of the God of Israel ruling the cosmos as we would before the picture of the universe directed by an indefinite authority which might just as well be God as anything else. We cannot merely consider it, having to discover for ourselves any unity and order which it may have, and to work out for ourselves the practical bearing of that unity and order. For if the idea of the divine world-governance is concretely filled out as we have suggested, then at once we are caught up in the divine economy and disposition. We at once begin to have dealings with this King, with the Lord of this history, with the will of this Lord and King, with the supremacy of this free grace. We at once find ourselves in a concrete relationship with this concrete act of government as the act which is decisive for all events and therefore for our own life and existence and activity. In advance of all our own opinions and attitudes we see ourselves questioned and invited and called. And we know that with all that we are to be and to do we will always give either an affirmative or a negative answer. For good or evil we have to answer individually to this Lord of the world who is our Lord. We are not at one of those neutral points on a globe which in principle are identical and interchangeable. In virtue of the formative economy and disposition of the One who rules the world, we have our own definite time and place and function. Whether it be far or near, above or below, in the foreground or the background, whether we accept it with a good grace or a bad grace, it is at any rate different ; it is the function which is assigned to us ; and we are in a definite relationship to what is specifically willed with us and through us by the One who is Lord of the world both in general and in particular. There is no room for the uninteresting and even boring idea of a unity and order which arise in the process of events either with or without God. The idea of the divine world-governance is no longer a theoretical and speculative idea. It is a practical (" existential ") idea. We cannot think about the relationship between the Creator who rules and the creaturely world which is ruled by Him without thinking about ourselves, without thinking about ourselves as a definite factor within that economy and disposition, i.e., within the history of that relationship. The very fact that we think the thought means that we have begun to put it into effect in our own particular sphere. If we think the thought, we cannot alter the fact that, if the King of Israel is the Lord of the world, He is also our Lord, and therefore He is thinking of us and laying claim upon us. We cannot think the thought without understanding the Word of God and being caught up in the work of God ; without seeing in the election and calling of Israel our own election and calling ; without seeing in the unfaithfulness of Israel our own unfaithfulness ; without seeing in the faithfulness of God His unmerited faithfulness to us ; without seeing in Jesus Christ the Saviour who came down and was manifested and died and rose again for us ; without seeing in free grace the reality to whose service we are pledged and by whose glorifying we can live—we who are called here and now, and have cause for gratitude, being indebted for our very selves. The very fact that we fill out the idea in a biblical and Christian way means that the divine world-governance necessarily becomes an event in our own lives and that we have to recognise and affirm it as such. Even as we think the thought we ourselves are the creature which is ruled by that ruling Creator, and we recognise and accept ourselves as such. If the King of Israel really is for us the Lord of the world, and therefore the Subject with whom we have to do when we think this thought, then necessarily the thought is for us concrete and actual and true in all its parts, and more than that, it acquires this immediate practical significance.

As we have tried to understand the divine world-governance as the rule of the King of Israel, we have frequently referred to it as a formative economy and disposition. By this we mean only that all world-occurrence receives from this ruling Subject its goal, thus acquiring a unified line and direction, and also that this Subject gives it a context, the interconnexion of individual events, the significance of their sequence, of the way in which they mutually cause and condition and limit and overlap each other, of the way in which they follow and accompany and are mutually related to each other. And it is by means of this context that the King gives form and character to world-occurrence. That is why we cannot possibly compare world-occurrence as it takes place under the divine rule with an amorphous and self-diffusing mass, but only with an organism or building.

What this context is, is revealed to us in the history of the covenant and salvation to which the Bible bears testimony. It is grounded in the free election of grace. It has its beginning here in the form of the particular and sacred work of God in the creation of the world. It continues with the reconciliation of the world to God as it was foretold in the history of Israel and accomplished in Jesus Christ. And when the interim period of the proclamation of this work is over, it will culminate in the perfecting or redemption which consists in the general revelation of the creative and reconciling act of God. It is in this that we find true economy and disposition. It is here that creaturely occurrence acquires line and direction, and meaningful sequence and context, and therefore form and character, by the rule of God. It is in the name of Jesus Christ that this economy is comprehended. This name, which is present at both the beginning and the end, is the centre which reveals the economy. It is in this name that it really consists. But at every point in this particular and sacred work, at the beginning and middle and end, we find that its concern is with the world. It is the world which God created in His grace. It is the world which He loved and reconciled in His Son. It is the world which He will finally perfect in Christ. And the opening event in this particular sacred history is the calling into being of a special people, a holy community, whose existence is not an end in itself, but something which has to testify and proclaim to the world the Word of the King to it and the work of the King for it. And this means that the context, the economy, the disposition is not only revealed in the history of the covenant and redemption whose centre is Jesus Christ. In a hidden form it is also present and active in world-occurrence generally. The two spheres are distinguished only by the fact that in the one case it is hidden and in the other it is revealed. From this particular, sacred history we see that even world-occurrence generally had its beginning by the grace of God the Creator, that it was decisively altered and conditioned by the love which appeared in Jesus Christ and was authenticated by His death and resurrection,- and that it moves towards its own perfection and therefore to the end of the age in the still future revelation of Jesus Christ. The existence of this particular, sacred history means that we can no longer think of world-occurrence generally as a raging sea of events which has neither form nor direction. World-occurrence is something formed, and it is formed indeed according to the sense revealed in this history. Its unity and order are identical with the unity and order which were manifestly achieved in this history. Its Lord is identical with the One who is called the Lord in this history, and therefore with the King of Israel.

But of course this does not mean that the lordship and economy can be directly seen and demonstrated in world-occurrence as such. The history of the covenant and salvation in which the King of Israel rules, in which His plan and will and acts take place and are revealed, does not cease to be a particular history, a history which is not continued or repeated outside its own sphere. It is from this history and this history alone that we learn that world-occurrence generally stands under the same lordship and has the same relationship, because the King of Israel is its King too. If we will accept it from this source, we will progressively confirm that it is actually so. We shall not discover that it is so, but confirm it. Instructed by this history, accepting what it reveals, we can have a prior assurance of the presence of this context, of the existence of this line and direction in world-occurrence generally. On this basis we can count upon the fact that all occurrence really has form and character, that there is purpose and unity and order in all things. And we can do so according to the same sense and in virtue of the same formative economy and disposition as were revealed and active in Jesus Christ. From the very outset, then, we can acknowledge only Him as the Lord of all occurrence, as the One who is decisively at work behind and within its relationships and movements, behind and within the sequence of its events. With a certainty which is absolute we can count upon the fact, and only upon the fact, that even where there is no trace of a particular or sacred history everything does move from the gracious creation of God, by way of the reconciliation accomplished in Jesus Christ, to the final revelation. And how could it be otherwise ? For the conclusions already reached from the knowledge of Scripture and of the revelation to which it bears witness cannot be a general conclusion. With all boldness we shall venture to apply this conclusion concretely to all kinds of relationships and developments in world-occurrence generally. And in all of them we shall find that it is concretely confirmed. But the power or force of our knowledge will always be that of the revelation which is fulfilled in the particular and sacred history. It will always be that of the presupposition with which we approach and view world-occurrence in the light of this revelation. The measure of the certainty of our knowledge will be determined by the extent to which it really derives and is illuminated and directed by this revelation. Only in the light of it can we accept the conclusion as self-evident, or venture with such boldness and joy and certainty to reckon even in world-occurrence generally upon the sole lordship of the One who directs the creature from grace to grace. And the very consolation and help and support and counsel which, as the answer to this venture, we again and again receive in the midst of world-occurrence in the form of surprises, or it may be quiet perceptions and insights, the discovery of definite traces of this context—all these can be true only as we already have elsewhere, in His own direct revelation in that particular and sacred history, a knowledge of the King of Israel who creates this context. For if we did not know Him already in this revelation, how could we ever perceive Him in world-occurrence as a whole ?

For the way in which He creates the context in world-occurrence does not reveal Him to us, but conceals Him from us. In world-occurrence He can be revealed to us only in the light of the particular occurrence. It is true that the divine governance does give rise to an economy and disposition in world-occurrence generally. And it is true that this economy and disposition are identical with the economy and disposition of the saving events of biblical history which culminate in Jesus Christ and derive from Him. But it is not at all the case that this economy and disposition can be understood directly from world-occurrence itself, as though this occurrence were a second Bible. It is not at all the case that we have this economy and disposition before us in the form of a handy system of world-goverance, or of certain easily recognisable features in such a system. In world-occurrence it is a question only of the hiddenness of God and of the ruling power of God. We can and must expect the removal of this hiddenness by the revelation which He has already given to us, but we cannot achieve it ourselves. Even the history of the covenant and salvation is not yet complete. It will be complete only when we can see the full reach of the grace of God and of His love for all creation in the revelation of what He has already done for it as Creator, in the reconciliation effected in Jesus Christ, and therefore in the revelation of this context. But from that which the history of the covenant and salvation has already revealed and demonstrated we have seen and learned that the King of Israel, Jesus Christ, is Lord of all. Like all other created things, however, we have not yet seen and learned the way in which He is Lord of all, the extent to which this economy and disposition are executed and revealed in world-occurrence generally. The plan of God and this context are concealed from us even when we venture to acknowledge Him as Lord. Even in the perceptions and insights which are from time to time vouchsafed to us, they are not so clearly revealed to us that in the light of them, in the light of our own ventures or of the understanding which is given us, we can enter fully into the thought of the divine world-goverance. We are always referred back to the one and only Bible, or to its content, this one particular and sacred history. And we must and can content ourselves with this. For to come to know the Lord of all occurrence ; to have the revelation of His free grace as the secret of the cosmos which is ruled by Him ; to be absolutely certain that there is no such thing as secular history, i.e., history apart from or opposed to this economy ; to have the courage and joy and certainty of the knowledge that there is one, this One, who occupies the seat of power ; to risk again and again the venture of that confirmation ; to give ourselves the consolation and help and support and comfort that are so necessary to us ; in a word, to have our eyes opened, and to be able occasionally to see at any rate the traces of this rule—for all this it is enough if we have the one Bible with its witness to the history of the covenant and salvation, and there is no need to supplement it by looking for a system, or the features of a system, which underlies the context of world-occurrence. Indeed, it is much more likely that if we do discover such a system, we shall merely check and disturb and hinder if not completely mislead ourselves, in the true and serious application of what has been discovered already without any assistance that we can give. It belongs to a right understanding of the divine world-governance that we should be content with the form in which it is revealed to us here and now, i.e., with its biblical form. It belongs to a right understanding of it that we should be aware of the fact that in its other and complete, because direct form, it is here and now concealed from us.

But we shall fall short of completeness if we do not throw one definite light even on our assertion of the provisional hiddenness of the divine world-governance, and therefore of the formative economy and disposition of world-occurrence as such. There is in this occurrence no second revelation of the divine world-governance, no second Bible. The first is quite sufficient, and it has to suffice us. But as we consider it we cannot deny that within world-occurrence as such there are certain constant elements which do indeed belong to it ; which in themselves and as such do not constitute a further revelation, or a continuation or repetition of the one revelation ; from the existence of which we can no more deduce the How ? of the divine rule than we can from that of any other elements in world-occurrence ; but which have all the same a special character and function in this regard. By their special nature they stand in a special relationship to the history of the covenant and salvation, and therefore to that one revelation of the divine world-governance. We can and indeed have to say concerning them that their existence and activity and the effects which they produce are as it were a permanent riddle in relation to history as a whole, and that in the last analysis they can be explained only when we can consider them from the one distinctive place. In some sense they point to the fact that world-occurrence is bordered by this one distinctive place. To this extent they are signs and witnesses that world-occurrence is really ruled from this place, i.e., by the One who at this distinctive place is called God. Of course, it belongs to the very nature of these elements that their character as signs and witnesses to this fact can easily be overlooked. As signs and witnesses they will inevitably be overlooked if they are not considered from this one place. They will be seen only as elements like others. The riddle of world-occurrence will be so much greater. But why should there not be these mysteries like so many others ? Why should they not be ignored like so many others ? Even if they can be explained only from the one distinctive place, this does not mean that there is a general compulsion to acknowledge that all occurrence is bordered by this place, or that the One who is called God there, the King of Israel, is the Ruler of the world. The existence of these special elements does not even give us an indirect systematic indication of the divine world-governance, the critical material for a systematic apologetic or a philosophy of life and history. But at the same time it does belong to the nature of these elements that we can consider them as signs and witnesses to this God. They have no advantage in other respects. In their creatureliness, and with their activity and its effects, they are no dearer to God than other creatures. But they do in fact stand nearer than all other creatures to this centre of all creaturely occurrence, this centre of the history of the covenant and salvation which is enacted at the heart of the whole. And when we see their particular proximity and affinity to this central event (and we certainly cannot see it except from the event itself), we also see that away from this centre, in the midst of world-occurrence generally, they do not prove to us, but they do testify and confirm and demonstrate, from where and by whom that occurrence is ruled. They do not tell us how it is ruled. They affirm that the Ruler and His work are here and now concealed. When we ask concerning His economy and disposition they refer us back to the one source of all true knowledge in the matter, and they also refer us forward to the promised consummation. But as signs and witnesses they do affirm that the One who rules is the Lord of the history and the covenant to which the Bible bears testimony—the King of Israel. And they do not affirm it as it may occasionally be affirmed by other elements in world-occurrence, or to the extent that there may be similar perceptions and insights—if not with a final, at any rate with an all but final certainty—in the experience of all men. They affirm it according to their special character as constant elements in world-occurrence, as universal and objective historical contexts of this kind. Of these signs, too, it may be said that only those who have eyes to see will see them, only those who have ears to hear will hear them. And yet they can be heard and seen at all times and in all places. They do not penetrate the hiddenness of God as it is penetrated in the history of the covenant and salvation. But within world-occurrence, in the sphere where God is hidden, they are standing, permanent, objective reminders that the penetration did take place at this point, that it will take place again and again from this point, that the economy and disposition of world-occurrence can be seen at this point. We shall not do justice to the problem unless we consider these special elements in all their different forms. I shall mention the most important of them, in each case adding what seems to be most necessary by way of comment and explanation.

1. The history of Holy Scripture. We are thinking now of its origin and transmission, and its exegesis and influence in the course of history generally. Certainly we cannot say that from this standpoint it sheds any compelling, universal, direct or necessary light upon its content, i.e., the occurrence of that particular and sacred history, and therefore the King of Israel as the Lord of world-occurrence. For there is no doubt that these aspects can be considered and explained as simply the result of a particular epoch in the religious development of mankind, or even as the result of certain peculiar superstitions and delusions, or it may be of the most serious and profound experiences and insights of the human race, according to the standpoint of the individual observer. And this certainly does not mean that they can be regarded as the result of a demonstration of the world-governance of the One concerning whom this Scripture speaks. We cannot say more than that the history of Holy Scripture can also be considered quite differently from this standpoint. But this we can say. We can take up the position which man necessarily occupies according to the content of this Scripture. And then we can receive and accept its witness, and the Old and New Testament message of the Word and work of God to which it bears testimony. It can then be the case that as we encounter this witness we encounter God Himself and His gracious and compelling existence, and that we are claimed and liberated and captivated by it. It can then be the case that in consequence we are men in whose lives the governance of this God—far

from being the governance of a particular god in his own sphere, or the power of a particular idea—has actually shown itself to be the governance of the world. Clearly, the history of Holy Scripture can be considered from quite a different angle on this presupposition, and we may think that on this presupposition it has to be considered from this quite different angle.

We can see this already in relation to its origin. If we accept the witness of Holy Scripture, then implicitly we accept the fact that, quite irrespective of the way in which they were humanly and historically conditioned, its authors were objectively true, reliable and trustworthy witnesses. It is not merely that we recognise their opinions to be good and pious, or appreciate their part and significance in religious history. We perceive rather that it pleased God the King of Israel, to whom the power of their witness is pledged as to the Lord, to raise up these true witnesses by His Word and work. In this fact, at the very beginning of the history of Scripture, and at the heart of world-occurrence, even while the fact itself is a moment in occurrence generally, what we see is not merely a moment in occurrence generally, and in religious occurrence in particular, but a trace of the governance of God as the one and only true God, a trace of this God as the Lord of all world-occurrence.

And this is what we also see in the continuation of this history, the rise, completion and transmission of the Canon of the Old and New Testaments. Certainly it is not a history which is apart from the developments and complications which affect all human history. Certainly it is not a history which is preserved inwardly from the follies and errors and oddities of all human history. It is a history which is not accidental but necessary in its whole course and sequence. It is true history, not a perverted history. It is a history whose necessity and truth have constantly to be recognised, understood, tested, and actualised. And as such it is a history which can be interpreted in many different ways at different times. But however it is considered and interpreted, it is a history whose meaning persists and maintains itself. It is a history which gives rise to constant questioning, but which constantly puts more important questions on its own account. From this angle again, what we see is not a trace of creaturely occurrence but of the plan and will which rule this occurrence—the plan and will of the One whose Word and work are the subject of the Scripture whose peculiarity is so much emphasised.

And this is also what we can and must see in the history of exegesis which begins already with the history of the text and Canon and necessarily returns again and again to this history. Here, too, we are not outside the sphere of world-occurrence generally, but inside it. Here, too, we see the powerful and far-reaching effect of the various languages and racial characteristics, the politics, economics, philosophy, scholarship, artistic sense, faith, heresy and superstition of the different ages, the individual talents of the various individual readers and exegetes. And here, too, we must give sober consideration to all these factors : how it was all a help or a hindrance ; how it was that such singular honour came to be paid to the Old and New Testaments, and what they had to put up with ; to what extent men faithfully reproduced the teaching of Scripture, and to what extent they wilfully read their own teaching into it ; how again and again Scripture was continually discovered and forgotten, esteemed and despised ; how at all times it was continually understood and misunderstood. Should our estimate of this history be an optimistic or a pessimistic one ? If our attitude to the content of the texts which we are considering is the attitude of that original freedom and constraint, there can be no doubt at least that we shall always see in that history a history of their own self-exegesis. And this means that we shall never look upon the prophets and apostles as merely objects for the study and assessment of later readers ; they will always be living, acting, speaking subjects on their own account. The fact that they have spoken once does not mean that they have now ceased to speak. On the contrary, they take up and deliver the Word afresh in every age and to every people, at every cultural level and to every individual. And they do it in such a way that what they have to say is far more acute and relevant than what may be said or thought about them. What are all the commentaries and other expositions of the Bible but a strong or feeble echo of their voice ? If we are in that direct relationship to the Bible, then in the last and decisive analysis we shall not consider the history of biblical exegesis in the light of what took place outwardly. On the contrary, we shall consider the history of its outward experiences in the light of its own continually renewed and for that reason always surprising action, as a history of its self-declaration and self-explanation in the midst of that general occurrence to which it belongs and within which it constitutes its own life-centre and origin in virtue of its affinity with the divine Word and work to which it testifies. It was not merely a rhetorical flourish when at the time of the Reformation Scripture was gladly described and magnified as *dux* and *magistra*, or even as *regina*. The fact is—and it does not make the slightest difference whether it is recognised or not—that in all ages Scripture has been the subject of its own history, the guiding, teaching, ruling subject, not under men but over men, over all the men who in so many ways, and with such continual oddities and contradictions, have applied themselves to its exposition. And for this reason its history is in this respect too—those who have eyes to see, let them see —a trace of the ruling God whom it declares. It has a concealed but not a completely hidden part in His kingly rule.

And finally, we have to consider the history of its influence or effects. At this point we touch upon the second of the special historical elements about which we shall have to speak in a moment. What happened to that witness ? What is happening to it now ? What does it actually accomplish in the world in which it is spoken and transmitted and continually expounded ? In this respect, too, we have to consider it in the sequence of all the other factors of world-occurrence and their effects. Let us take as an illustration the well-known theory that what we call Western Christendom is a hybrid product deriving from biblical Christianity on the one hand and Graeco-Roman antiquity on the other. But how many other causes do we have to mention side by side with the Bible, some of them oriental and some occidental, some of them spiritual and some very strongly material ? If we have not already done so, we shall have to accustom ourselves to thinking of the historical effect of the biblical witness as one effect among many others. And when we do this, we cannot be too serious in reckoning with the fact that what we have to do with here—we need only think of what we call Western Christendom—is a historical effect which is very much diluted and distorted, and which in addition is always restricted in power, and constantly threatened with extinction. In a genuinely historical investigation it can even be asked whether one day this force will not be exhausted and lost like so many others. But what is this force, the influence of the Bible in world history ? If we consider it in the light of the influence which we know as an event in our own lives, then we know it as a wonderful election and calling which we cannot explain merely as a possibility of our own. To our own astonishment we find that we are added to the people, the Church, the community of the King of Israel. We find this particular influence of the biblical witness in the quite extraordinary existence of this community and its commission in the world. And in face of this influence we can only be amazed, first that we are not excluded from it, that we can be aware of it in our own lives, and then that we are not alone in this experience, but can publicly share it with so many others both past and present, both far and near. It claims our whole attention to take this influence seriously, and gratefully to do justice to it. And this means that we have neither the time nor the energy for general historical considerations. We have a prior claim and commission within and in face of all other occurrence. And we shall not experience any surprise at the way in which the influence of the biblical witness is necessarily diluted and distorted and threatened as seen against world-occurrence generally. This fact will not cause us any anxiety or despair. We shall be well enough aware of it from the way in which this influence is diluted and distorted and threatened in our own lives as members of the people of God both individually and corporately. Far from despairing, we shall be ashamed, and do penance, and pray, and work, not only for ourselves, but for the whole people of God. And we shall remember that it would be something far more strange if this high and solemn thing were something triumphant in the midst of world-occurrence, if it were an enormous and undiluted and unequivocal success, if it were something popular. We know that all the influence of the biblical witness can itself have only the form of a witness, the witness of most inadequate creatures. By our commission and its execution we shall not cease to aim at what the Church either is accomplishing or could accomplish by means of it. And there can be no mistake as to the influence which—with all the ambiguity and weakness of that which results from it—the biblical witness does actually have, and always has had, and always will have— in the fact that new witnesses are called out and new confessing communities are assembled by this witness. In the vast ocean of other influences we shall be aware of the fact that at all times and in all places this calling out and assembling has taken place and still does take place. And we shall not look at this influence merely as one among many. We shall not weigh and evaluate it optimistically or pessimistically in relation to the others. In this influence, in the power of the prophetic and apostolic witness at all times and in all places to call out and assemble, we shall again find traces of the One with whom that witness has to do, of the One who is manifestly present as King not only in this influence, but everywhere and always.

2. The history of the Church. We have necessarily had to touch already on this second sign and witness within world-occurrence. The Church is a result. It is a result of Holy Scripture. It is built upon the foundation of the apostles and prophets. To that extent it belongs to the history of Scripture. But it obviously has its own history in that there takes place within it the transmission and exegesis and effective operation of Scripture both amongst and also by means of others outside the circle of the first witnesses. Called out and assembled by those first witnesses, others enter upon the scene. We now live in the last time to which they pointed in their message, i.e., the time of the expectation of the final and definitive and universal revelation in the return of Jesus Christ of the reconciliation of the world which God has already accomplished in Him. This last time is the time of the Church. The Church is the communion of saints, i.e., the fellowship of those who by the self-revelation of the King of Israel to which Scripture bears testimony are personally called : called out of the world ; called into the community ; called to faith in the kingdom of God and to the proclamation of this kingdom. Church history is the history of this fellowship within world history generally. And it is one of those special elements in world-occurrence which point to the divine world-governance.

We make contact at this point with the older doctrine of *providentia specialis* as it appears particularly in the preservation, direction and confirmation of the Christian Church. The special protection and preservation of the church is referred to, for instance, in *Questions* 51 and 54, and most impressively in *Question* 123, of the *Heidelberg Catechism*, where in the commentary on the second petition we have the words : " Preserve and increase thy Church ; destroy the works of the devil, every power that exalteth itself against Thee, and all wicked devices formed against Thy holy Word, until the full coming of Thy kingdom, wherein Thou shalt be all in all." And a passage from F. Burmann's *Syn. Theol.*, 1671 (I, 44, 88) will show in what form the Dutch theology of the 17th century believed that it could discern and estimate the controlling of divine providence in this special sphere : " The Church has no cause to be ashamed of its lot right up to our own days. It is still illuminated by the light of the Gospel. Liberated from its Babylonian captivity, it can breathe freely amongst pious kings and magistrates. Tested in conflicts, it has not been destroyed, and the conflicts have merely revealed the truth the more clearly. Never has the Gospel triumphed more gloriously over error than in our own epoch. The heat of persecution has been tempered, and by the grace of God many enemies of the Church have been converted. And almost everywhere God maintains civil order, providing that peace should always follow strife. He also adds his blessing in the economic sphere, so that the generation and instruction of a holy posterity is assured. Similarly, there are both higher and primary schools in which those things are taught which pertain to God and are beneficial to the race. And even to-day God raises up prophets from our sons and Nazarites from our young men. Therefore, although the Church still sighs in many places by reason of its heavy adversity, we have every cause to render our thanks to God for so great benefits." We shall have to pursue the matter rather more deeply than this, even if in the last analysis we come to the same conclusion.

We think of the remarkable claim with which the Church exists. We think of its capacity for resistance and renewal. Again, it is not as if the Church were in a position either to proclaim directly or to prove to the general satisfaction its own status as the communion of saints and thus the lordship of God in world-occurrence which it believes and proclaims. It is true that its time, the last time, exemplifies the presence and lordship of the King of Israel. The fact that He sits on the throne is the revelation with whose particular form this time begins and to whose universal form it moves. But even the last time is still time. It is a perishing but an even more powerful old aeon. It is the time when the glory of God does not yet fulfil all things, when the rule of God is over all world-occurrence and yet concealed by it, when we walk by faith and not by sight. Even the Church belongs to this time and is under its conditions. It is not a continuation or repetition of the biblical revelation. It is not a breaking-through the order and disorder, the progression and the pauses and retrogressions of world-occurrence generally. It is nowhere unequivocally distinguished from this occurrence. It can be perceived—and will be perceived only—as one phenomenon among many others. Its history allows of this even more than that of the Bible. And this is true even of the greatest periods and purest forms and most promising movements and developments and achievements in the history of the Church. Perhaps it is too summary a judgment to describe this history as " a medley of error and violence." But basically we cannot dispute either this or similar verdicts, unless we are in a position to look at it from a different angle. " As secular history, Church history (F. Overbeck) is at all events a very tempting programme and one that seduces by reason of its consistent honesty." We can only say that there is no compelling reason why the consideration of Church history in its solidarity with world history generally should be regarded as the only possible way of considering it. Like the history of the Bible, it can also be considered in the light of the presupposition that the observer and critic himself is not outside the Church but inside it ; that he is one of those who are called, called out and from and into ; that he is one of those who on the strength of the biblical witness can and must believe and proclaim the lordship of the King of Israel ; that he is, therefore, one of those who are both liberated and bound. And in the light of this fact it may be that he really begins to know what Church history is about, and what it has been about from the very first. It may be that he really begins to know with whom and with what we are confronted in this sphere, and will be continually confronted in the ever-changing constellations of history. He can really begin to experience joy and terror at the greatness of that which takes place in the events and relationships, the movements and pauses of Church history, i.e., the Word and work of God constantly seeking new realisation from generation to generation. To some extent he can begin to know the great decisive characters of this history, not from outside but from inside, in the knowledge of his own solidarity with them. He may, therefore, find himself in the situation in which he has to think of the historical sphere of this community of faith and proclamation not merely as one among many others, not merely in its entanglement in the problematical character of all similar spheres, but in and for itself, as a special and strangely isolated sphere. And in this isolation he will have to see a trace of the divine world-governance, of the same divine world-governance under which he finds himself in his own existence, and of which he is therefore a personal witness. And if we consider it from this always possible standpoint, we have to say something rather more about Church history than that it is merely a part of secular history.

And first we have to consider a remarkable claim of which the Church, if it is the true Church, is always and necessarily aware when it thinks of the significance of its own history in the midst of occurrence generally. For if we ourselves belong to the company of those who are both liberated and bound, then we know that it is the character of our time to be the last time. As the recipients and bearers of the good news of the resurrection of Jesus Christ we are awaiting the return of Jesus Christ. And this means that we cannot think of the time between these two events as infinite, or empty, waiting to be filled in one way or another. It is a time which is limited, which is marked off for a definite filling, which shares a very definite meaning and purpose. And we know that this filling consists in the believing of the Gospel and its world-wide proclamation. It consists, then, in something which is the work and gift and task of the Church. Hence we know that all other events, however great and important they may be, however glorious or terrible they may be, are still co-ordinated with, and subordinated to, this one purpose of the time. And this means that we know what is the really urgent and necessary thing in all possible circumstances. We see the utter insignificance of Church history in the midst of the other events of our so-called era. But we also understand the claim which has always been advanced by the Church for the importance of its history. We are not ashamed of this claim, nor do we reject it. In theory, and above all in practice, we have to confess that Church history does actually have priority over all other history, that with all its insignificance and folly and confusion in history generally, it is still the central and decisive history to which all the rest is as it were only the background or accompaniment. We shall be most careful in our concrete applications of this insight, because we know that it can be maintained only with the demonstration of the Spirit and of power. But we cannot give up our insight that our time as it is still given to us is the time of the Church. And in its fulfilment we are faced by Church history as a continuous trace of the One in whose name the Church offers its most modest and equivocal service, which is still the highest service of all.

Furthermore, we have to consider the capacity for outward and above all inward resistance which the Church has continually shown in the course of its history. The fact that it is in time, and in history generally, the fact that it is indeed one element in history generally, means that in all the expressions of its life, at every stage and in every form of its history, it has to wrestle with the overwhelmingly oppressive and powerful strangeness and even hostility of all other elements in that history. It has always had to believe in the world what the world does not and cannot believe. It has always had to proclaim to the world what the world does not want and is not able to receive. That this is the true situation of the Church no one is more fully aware than the one who is called to the Church, who is himself one of those who are both liberated and bound. He knows the overwhelming opposition of the world to his Lord, as the Old Testament bears dramatic witness to it in the relationship between Israel and Yahweh. He knows it in the most intimate way from his own Israelitish heart and mind and will and life. But in the most intimate way he also knows the more powerful resistance which is already offered to all the turmoil and strangeness and hostility of world-occurrence. He knows the almighty faithfulness of the King of Israel. And it is the wonderful operation of this faithfulness which he obviously sees in action in the Church. He does not see there indomitable character, or inerrant ideas, or infallible courts or institutions. What he does see is all the power of the assault of that strange and hostile element, and in face of it all the human pusillanimity and compliance and helplessness and weakness which have always appeared in a more unfavourable light in the Church than in any other sphere. He sees that continually real dangers were not recognised as soon as they should have been, and others feared when they might coolly have been ignored. He sees that clever and pious folk who were apparently sound and living members of the Church have gradually or suddenly gone to pieces and become a target for contempt and scoffing. He sees that with the passage of time lights which had once been bright have become dim and eventually been extinguished. He sees so much apparently undeserved and inexplicable and meaningless suffering on the part of the community and its members, so much unjust and yet triumphant persecution, so much crude or refined repression, so much sacrifice and destruction. But understanding only too well his own outer and inner involvement as a member of this Church, he not only sees all this, but he also understands it. And this means that he will not be too greatly shocked at it, or too full of criticism and complaint. For he also sees that in and through it all the Church has continually resisted, that it has continually been snatched from its anxieties and preserved at the last from a complete submergence in its temptations, that suddenly or after a period its wounds have been healed, that its Babylonian captivities have ended, that its enemies and persecutors have one day vanished from the scene, that it has continually been raised up from the dead to newness of life. He sees in its history something persistent and persisting—a continuity. Certainly he does not deduce it from the insights and capacities and piety and good-will of the men who take part in this history. Nor does he deduce it from the soundness of the majority of Christians, or from particularly Christlike personalities, or from the dogmas and institutions of Christianity, or from the Christian cultus. He sees the equivocal nature of all these things, and yet he sees also this something persistent and persisting in them. This is why he cannot fail to give thanks for all these things, for the life of the Church, for the faith of the people of God, for what is given to him by individual leaders and teachers, for the constant power to enlighten possessed by the dogmas and institutions of Christianity and the Christian cultus. In spite of inevitable criticism, his thinking about them will be basically positive. For he knows that even in their weakness and proneness to evil they could and can be the instruments of this resistance and signs of this persistence ; just as he himself as a bound and liberated member of the Church, irrespective and in spite of his own merits, and quite inexplicably in the light of his own weakness, can also resist in his own thoughts and decisions, in his own heart as a believer. That which persists, that which resists, is simply the power of the divine call. Or primarily, it is simply the power of the living Word of the prophets and apostles. At every other point in this matter we can and must set a question-mark. But the divine call, the living Word of Scripture, does persist and resist ; it does actually win through in the Church. The divine call is the Church's enabling : the power of resistance which in spite of all its outer and inner wretchedness it has continually displayed in its history ; the power to remain what it is ; the power to believe again and to take up again its task of proclamation in spite of its defeats and declensions and difficulties. If we are to see our way clearly at this point, we must see this divine Nevertheless. And if we do see it, we shall see in Church history the trace of that supremacy of free grace. We shall see that it is supremacy even in the midst of world-occurrence. And we shall also see the King of Israel, and therefore Jesus Christ, as the One who is Lord of all.

Furthermore, we have to consider the power of renewal which the Church has continually and no less clearly manifested in the course of its history. In relation to other elements in world history, the Church often appears either to be age-old—the curious remnant of a magical epoch, or of some other age which has long since disappeared—or else relentlessly to be growing old. It is indeed old, and there is nothing to be ashamed of in that fact. For the fathers boasted that in the true sense its existence began even in Paradise. But the point is that this Church which to its glory or shame we have to call old has continually displayed its capacity in some astonishing fashion to become new—far more new than all the novelties of secular history. Again, of course, we know this renewing in the most intimate way, as an event in our own lives. For if in our encounter with the Word of God we have really begun to live as members of the Church, then we know something of the goodness which is new every morning ; we know something of the way in which the inward man is renewed day by day ; and, knowing this, we know something of the secret of this renewal of the Church. We cannot deduce it from inherited human factors, although in this case, too, we have to reckon with them, and reckon with them observantly and thankfully. If we were to look only to these factors, the total picture would be only of a confirmed old age, or a relentless ageing of the Church, just as humanly speaking the total picture of the life of the individual Christian can only be of his growing old. But we can also think of the work of God's Word in the Church, remembering that the Church is the place where His honour dwells. We can think, for example, that the prophets and apostles are always in its midst as living subjects speaking something new. Then we shall see that it does not merely persist and resist, but that it is in fact made new. Then we shall see that Church history is not merely one of restorations but also of reformations. We shall know the Church not merely as *perpetua mansura*, but also as *perpetua reformanda*. We shall see that if it has any power its *manere* is always a *reformari*, that its triumphant *manere* consists in its *reformari*. And then perhaps we shall ask whether the processes of deformation, the distortions and disturbances which are caused in the Church by human error and ill-will, must not be regarded as necessary reactions against what have come to be dominant over-emphases, or as beneficial challenges to a new and better faithfulness. The fathers were perhaps right when along these lines they tried to find a positive meaning even in the existence of heresies and schisms. Certainly, if we are members of the Church participating for ourselves in its daily renewal we learn to be amazed at the economy which rules in its history, not merely modulating and correcting but constantly reviving, so that it seems to be ordained that a secularised Christianity should always be followed by the counter-thrust of a vigorously eschatological, a narrow and restricted by that of an open and free, an old-fashioned by that of a modern, an intellectualised by that of a practical, a naive by that of an instructed, an indolent by that of an active, an over-busy by that of a contemplative, a clerical by that of a lay, and a too popular by that of a healthily authoritarian. These have all been actual renewals. They have not been accomplished without new errors and apostasy, but from the standpoint of the basis of the Church they still have to be recognised as necessary renewals, in which the Church as a whole has come to life again, in which we can on the whole, therefore, recognise a guiding of the Church, a guiding which does not ever desire its death, but always its life. And if we do not fail to see this, we shall not fail to see a trace of the divine world-governance in the Church which is also a trace of the divine world-governance as such.

3. The history of the Jews. It may well be said that of all the phenomena so far mentioned this is the most astonishing and provocative. At this point we are almost tempted to speak, not of an indication of the world-governance of God, the God of the Bible, but of an actual demonstration of it, as the physician of Frederick the Great did to the king. But we shall not do this. For it is not impossible to consider the history of the Jews, like that of the Bible, without coming to the conclusion that the world has a ruling King, and that Jesus of Nazareth is this King. This is something which can be proved only by its own self-demonstration. But even as an indication not only of the matter itself but of its self-demonstration, the history of the Jews has a very special cogency. It is easier to turn away unenlightened from the history of the Bible and that of the Church than from this history. And it is harder with this history than with the others to be content with a view which does not accept the theological insight and explanation. Yet even at this point we cannot actually see any more than we can at the others. All that we can do is to begin to think along rather unusual lines.

With the fall of Samaria in 722 and the disappearance of the ten Northern tribes from biblical and secular history, in practice the Jews, or the two Southern tribes, became Israel, and Israel became the Jewish people. From that point onwards the content of the Old Testament is the particular and provisional history of this people with God, or rather of God with this people. The question is one of a provisional history. It is one of the tortuous history of a much threatened people, which is still this people, and as such has this history. The judgment overhanging it had not yet been fully executed. Even the temple which the Babylonians destroyed in 586 was built again in 520 under Zerubbabel. The people went into exile, but they returned again to take up their own life in their own country. The second violation of the temple by Antiochus Epiphanes in 168 was followed in 165 by a second restoration. To this period according to the usual reckoning there belong the last and most recent portions of the canonical Old Testament. In the first century the Canon was fixed and closed in its present form, and the temple was destroyed a third time, and a third time— and now more gloriously than ever—it was re-established. It was in this form that Jesus Himself saw it, and it was at the end of this development, which was no longer a development, that He who was Himself a Jew visited His people : this people which was still Israel and yet only representative of Israel ; this people which still had the consciousness of its divine election and of the divine covenant established with it, but which strictly speaking had the consciousness only of their written documentation. For what had really happened after 722, or before ? And what was going to happen ? Who were these Jews, and what was to become of them ? It seems that even amongst the surrounding nations there had already been a good deal of speculation on this point. (Cf. for what follows, Kurt Emmerich, *Die Juden*, 1939.)

After the death of Jesus there was a significant interval of some forty years—a kind of final period of grace, a last opportunity for repentance. Then the real history of the Jews began with what was to be the final destruction of Jerusalem and the temple by Titus. On this point there is no doubt at all in the witness of the New Testament. The definitive destruction of the old form of Israel was the negative side of the death of Jesus as a saving event, the shadow thrown by that event in the wider sphere of world history generally. The connexion between the two is a whole subject in itself. What is quite indisputable is that after this double event there is on the one hand no continuation of the history of the covenant as a history of God and this one people to the exclusion of all others, and on the other a particular history of the Jews within world history generally, a history which is no longer provisional but has all the marks of being final. The die is now cast. From now on the Jews will be that which they became in the year 70. And what is that ? What have they been during these last 1900 years ? What are they still to-day ? This is the problem with which we are now faced.

We may begin with the simplest and most impressive factor. The die is cast, but this did not mean that they disappeared like the ten tribes. It did not mean that they were destroyed as their then enemies intended. They outlived the Roman Empire to which they were then subject, just as they have notoriously outlived other empires since. They are still there. This is in itself a highly astonishing fact. We have to remember how small they were. We have to remember how unfavourable the conditions were for their continued existence. We have to remember what had become of the powerful nations which had once been their enemies, the one-time Assyrians, Babylonians,

Persians and Syrians, not to speak of the lesser peoples which had once been their neighbours and oppressors. They had all long since lost their identity. We no longer know any of them as they once were. But in spite of the destruction and persecution and above all the assimilation and interconnexion and intermingling with other nations the Jews are still there, and permanently there. And how active and prominent they are !—an isolated element in history ; a leaven which maintains itself and in its own way succeeds amongst other elements ; not often loved or even assisted or protected from outside by the others, but quite the reverse ; usually despised for some obscure reason, and kept apart, and even persecuted and oppressed by every possible spiritual and physical weapon, and frequently exterminated in part ; yet always and everywhere surviving ; again and again demonstrating its continued existence by the fact of it ; again and again winning for itself an involuntary respect. The only thing that has been missing is something that we have seen in our own days— the Jews (or at any rate many of the Jews) actually living again in Palestine, claiming and setting up and establishing a new state of Israel, and this quite irrespective of the conflict between East and West which threatens the stability of the rest of the world and its culture. In the shortest possible time it has produced the most striking results, culturally, diplomatically, and against all expectation militarily. It seems to have behind it—and we could not say this of all states—an enthusiastic and self-sacrificing youth. Not from any point of view can we ignore or make light of the existence of this state. And in it all its representatives have displayed in an astonishing way the very qualities which distinguished the Jews as far back as the time of Jeremiah, and again in that of Judas Maccabaeus, and the defenders of Jerusalem against Titus, and Bar-Cochbar, and similar figures from their distant past. There they are again, there they are still—the remarkable, representative remnant of Israel. It ought not to be so. In the year 70, in that destruction of Jerusalem which corresponded in so sinister a way to the death of Jesus, it was clearly not intended that it should be so. Jews as Jews were not meant to have any continued existence. They were not meant to have any perceptible existence. But they always have had, and they still have to-day ; and to-day genuinely so, and directly after what was apparently the worst disaster in all their history, completely eclipsing all previous disasters. There they are, actual witness to Old Testament history, actual members of the race to which Jesus Himself belonged and without which there would never have been a New Testament or a Christian Church. There they are, the " librarians of the Church," as Augustine called them, because the Old Testament without which even the Church cannot live is ultimately the book of their books, and originally their sacred Canon. There they are, not as antique-dealers, but as a constantly self-renewed actualisation and demonstration of the man who in virtue of these books was God's partner in the covenant upon whose fulfilment the Church is founded. For if we hear of man before God either in the Old Testament or in the greater part of the New it is this man, Jewish man, who is meant. And if any of us wish to identify ourselves with man before God in the biblical sense, we have to identify ourselves with this Jewish man. Both inside and outside, outside and inside the Church, this Jewish man as such is incalculably present, forcing us to take note of him in world history. And seeing there is this Jewish representation, are not the ten lost tribes there as well? Is not all Israel always present unrecognised? When the name of the new state jumped so surprisingly from the language of the Bible and the Church, the language of Canaan, right into the modern newspaper, did it not express a solid fact and not merely a presumption?

We speak of the Jews, and yet in the strict sense we' cannot say with any certainty who and what we really mean by the term. Even if we accept the equivocal expression, it is impossible to prove conclusively that the Jews form a single race. If the Jews do belong to a race, it is to the Semites to which their former enemies also belonged, and to which the most bitter of their modern enemies belong. And from the biological standpoint it is impossible to point to any specifically Jewish characteristics within the generally Semitic. The physical traits which were once regarded as specifically Jewish are all characteristic of the Semites as a whole, and not only of the Semites, for the same features can be found just as clearly amongst Mediterranean peoples with quite a different origin, and even within the so-called Aryan peoples. The idea of a specifically Jewish blood is pure imagination.

Again, there is no particular speech which marks off the Jews as Jews. In those branches of Judaism which have held fast to the religion of Moses Hebrew has been preserved as a cultic language, or as the language of theological scholarship. And in certain well-defined areas of Jewish life degenerate forms of Hebrew have been preserved as the common speech. And to-day in connexion with Zionism and its fulfilment in Palestine there are Hebrew newspapers and the beginnings of a Hebrew literature. But this does not mean that the overwhelming majority of Jews have thought and spoken in Hebrew throughout the centuries, or that they do so to-day. In the modern state of Israel, Hebrew has again attained to a place of honour, or rather it has been artificially given a place of honour, but even there its obvious character is that of an Esperanto introduced for the purpose of mutual understanding between people who speak so many different languages. It is merely a confirmation that the Jews as such have no mother-tongue.

Again, we cannot speak of a specifically Jewish culture. What the Jews have always achieved in this sphere has been by way of an outstanding and peculiar contribution to the formation and more particularly to the development and purification—and often to what for other reasons, and not through any fault of theirs, turned out to be the dissolution—of the culture of other peoples. So far they have never produced a specifically Jewish culture in the sense in which we can speak of specifically German and French and Italian and English cultures. They have never given a recognisably Jewish character to culture generally, as the Americans are doing to-day, and as the Swiss did formerly. It has yet to be seen whether or not something of this kind will happen in Palestine. But it has not happened so far.

Again, for a long time now the Jews have obviously not been marked by a common religion. There is the Jewish Synagogue, but for many years the Synagogue has not been identical with the Jewish people or representative of it. And who can say whether even the Synagogue, so far as participation in the life of it does characterise some Jewish circles, does really continue along the orthodox lines of the older post-exilic Judaism, and not according to one of the many Liberal re-interpretations of the Law, as actually happened at the time of the assimilation, when it more or less consciously adopted the modern philosophy of the *Goyim*?—not to speak of the fact that Jews can be pantheists or atheists or sceptics or even good or bad Christians without ceasing to be Jews. With all their veneration for the Jewish past, the authorities and people of the state of Israel—and with good reason—do not seem even to have thought of regarding any religion, whether Mosaic or otherwise, as constitutive for its inauguration.

Finally, even the concept of the history of the Jews as we ourselves have made use of it is a most ambiguous one. Since the year 70 there have been many different and disconnected histories of the Jews, that of the Polish Jews, the Spanish Jews, the Portugese Jews, or the German Jews. There has, of course, been the history of the Jewish Synagogue and its various ramifications, the history of its scriptural exegesis, its worship, and its piety. There have been the histories of countless Jewish groups and individuals. There have been the histories of Jewish movements and undertakings, as, for example, modern Zionism. But there has never been a connected history of the Jews as a single community, a history which itself has helped to form this community. In the individual histories there has been much that was common to all of them, but at no point did the common element produce that which is essential to the history of a people—a common movement from the past to the future. Even that which is taking place in Palestine is provisionally only the work of a comparatively small proportion of Jewry as a whole. It is still an open question whether the overwhelming majority of the others will want to participate in it. And even if they do, it is still a question whether they will be able to do so, considering their numbers in relation to the particular spatial, climatic and economic factors.

Since the same peculiar circumstances obtain in relation to a common physique, language, culture, religion and history, there is every justification for what is admittedly a perverse question : Are the Jews really a people at all ? Certainly the question is not at all an impossible one. In respect of all these criteria there is need of clarification when we speak of the Jewish people. And no such clarification is possible. The Jews are really and perceptibly there, and in face of this fact we cannot easily deny that they are a people. But when we say this, we have to realise that strictly speaking we do not know what we are saying. As the history of this people was determined in the year 70, it seems to consist in the fact that the people then took up its existence again, and yet ceased to be a people in the usual sense of the term, and has never been one since. It necessarily continues to exist in this unique way, as a people which in the usual sense of the word is not a people. It necessarily has history which strictly speaking is non-historical ; the history of a guest and alien and stranger and exception amongst the nations, with the eternal Jew, perhaps, as its legendary pattern.

What we have seen, then, is the mysterious persistence of the Jews, and their even more mysterious existence in world history. Surely the providential significance of their history must be immediately apparent to everybody. And yet we have to say that even here there is no question of a " must." It is possible either to overlook or to deny this significance. In the light of what we have seen the possibility is a singular one, but it is still a real possibility. The historical facts can carry a very different message without any detailed differences in the way in which they are seen and assessed. It is obvious that the Jewish question as a whole does not have to everyone the same acuteness as we have found in it. Even the fact of the continued existence of the Jews to which we first referred does not have to be regarded as quite so astonishing as we pictured it. And the question who and what are the Jews can be put in a far less penetrating and emphatic way than we have put it. The perplexity in which we find ourselves cannot be denied, but at any rate it can be concealed, perhaps with the help of different pretexts at one or other of the points that we have touched on. Certainly it is possible to dispute our own conclusion that the Jews have to be understood as a people which is not a people. And this conclusion is in fact disputed : not only by the champions of what is in principle a relativist view of history, to whom *a priori* the existence of any such paradox is necessarily uncongenial ; but also by those who are passionately involved in the question, by the Jews themselves, who will certainly protest against having to exist in the last resort only as the strange shadow of a people among other real peoples ; and also by anti-Semites and philo-Semites, who if our view were correct would have to admit that they were fighting either for or against a shadow, and who are certainly not prepared to make an admission of this kind. As against the view of Jewish history which we have developed, those who regard it from these different standpoints can conclude only that it is not at all perplexing, and that the people is not at all shadowy, as we have suggested, but that in their own way the Jews are a normal phenemonon in world history generally, and that it is wrong to ascribe to them any special or providential significance as compared with other peoples. And none of them is at a loss for restrictive or attenuating explanations of the historical facts to which we have alluded.

It will be as well to accept this possibility at once. But we do not propose to make use of it ourselves. In face of a historicism which is in principle relativist, in face of the Jews themselves, in face of anti-Semites and philo-Semites, we maintain that when we deal with the phenomenon of the history of the Jews we are dealing with a problem *sui generis*. We maintain that within world history generally the Jews are a people in the distinctive way which in the last resort we can describe only as negative. We maintain that it is only as a people of this kind that they have a history. But we have to admit that when we say this we are considering and assessing them from a standpoint which it is not within the powers of everyone to adopt. Certainly we cannot speak of any necessity to consider the matter from this standpoint. It is a question here, and categorically so, either of knowing or not knowing. It is a question of the inseparably inter-related message of the Old and New Testaments. It is a question of the divine electing and calling of this people as it culminated and was fulfilled in Jesus Christ as the King of Israel. It is a question of the faithfulness of Yahweh in face of the unfaithfulness of this people. It is a question of the supremacy of His free grace towards this people as it was revealed and actualised in that One. It is a question of the saving event of His death and its meaning for this people. It is a question of that event in whose shadow the history of the Jews began in the year 70. To those who know all this, the history of this people and its continance and being in the midst of other peoples will always be a miracle and a riddle. They cannot think of this people merely as one people among others. They are amazed that it does exist, but they are no less amazed that it exists in this way, as a people which is not a people, and has no true history. And they see in this special history a trace of the divine world-governance, and they see that the world-governor is the One whom the Bible calls God, the Lord who is called Yahweh in the Old Testament and Jesus of Nazareth in the New. But again, those who do not know this, and perhaps will not know it, can only reject this view, thus leaving it an open question whether the history of the Jews should not be regarded as the normal history of a normal people incorporated as such in world history as a whole, either after the manner of historical relativism, or according to the proud self-understanding of the Jews themselves, or the interpretation of their opponents or sympathisers. And from one or other of these standpoints they will deny that in the history of the Jews we are confronted with a particular manifestation or trace of the divine providence in the Christian sense of the word. We freely allow that we ourselves made use of the first and not the second possibility when we regarded and represented the history of the Jews as something inexplicable, as a great question-mark. We claim indeed that that history is explicable, but only in its inexplicability, only as a question-mark interposed into world history. And we make this claim because and to the extent that we are able to view the matter from the standpoint of the Christian message. For it is only as we ourselves know this message, only as we know it in such a way that we are committed by it, that we are forced to start our thinking at this point and at no other, and can and will see the history of the Jews as we have here represented it. Seen from this point, the history of the Jews does necessarily take the form of an *aporia*, a riddle, as we have represented it. Seen from this point, it does so necessarily ; although necessarily, as we have granted, only as seen from this point.

The Jews, the remnant of Israel, did not disappear from world history in the year 70. As a submerging minority amongst other peoples, they alone of all the great and small nations which once surrounded them continued an inexplicably and unprecedently active and visible life, a life which they are still energetically continuing to-day. It was in that year indeed that they really entered world history for the first time. And from the standpoint of the Christian message the reason for this is that God's decree in His election of this people and covenanting with it is an eternal and unshakeable decree. The people was an unfaithful people. From the very first it willed to be a people like others, to have a king and a history like others. But this could not alter the faithfulness of God, and it has not altered it right up to the present time. It was not altered even by the provisional judgments and finally the definitive judgment which in the year 70 ended its existence in identity, or at any rate similarity, without her peoples. How could it be altered by the judgment in which God finally ratified His grace towards this unworthy partner by Himself taking its place, the judgment of Golgotha ? Far from turning aside from His people, far from allowing it to fall, in the One who died for His people and for all men God not merely turned towards it but accepted solidarity with it. His appointment and constitution of Israel as the bearer of light and salvation to all nations are actualised in the death and revealed in the resurrection of the One who is the remnant of the Jewish remnant of Israel, and who definitely died and rose again on behalf of this remnant, indeed of Israel as a whole. What it involves to be the unfaithful and disobedient Israel, and the unfaithful and disobedient remnant, of this faithful and gracious King, is worked out and manifested in the judgments which continued all through the earlier history of Israel and finally culminated in the events of the year

70. Progressively, and at last completely, these judgments and this final judgment whittle away that which Israel and the Jews had allowed to become a snare to them—their identity, or at any rate their similarity with other peoples. Those who according to the word of the prophet had willed to be " Not my people " now became " Not a people." They can be a people now only as the people of God, only on the basis of His election and grace and long-suffering. At the very moment when salvation comes, and comes of the Jews, Jerusalem and the temple fall—the Jerusalem and temple of the Jews who even in that saving event remain only too true to themselves in their unfaithfulness. But their election and the covenant which God made with them do not fall with the fall of this external glory. How could they fall when they were actually confirmed both by the act of salvation and also by the act of destruction ? And since the election and the covenant still stand—not removed but fulfilled in Jesus Christ—the Jews also stand in world history. This is the secret of their continued existence, which seen against the message of the Old Testament is not in a sense a historical riddle, nor an accidental miracle, but the declared mystery of God, the mystery of His faithfulness and grace, of the constancy of His will and decree. It is not to their race or language or culture, and least of all to their Mosaic religion, but to the faithfulness and grace of God, that they and the world owe the fact that they are still there : the descendants of those who murmured in the wilderness and set up the golden calf ; the people who did not hearken to their prophets and later adorned their sepulchres ; the people who finally rejected their Messiah and delivered Him up to the Gentiles ; and yet the people to whom God had sworn and has kept an unchanging faithfulness ; the people to whom He never denied His witnesses and succour ; the people whose history He fulfilled by Himself becoming one of them, and as an Israelite, a Jew, maintaining the covenant which they broke and ratifying the promise ; the people from whom this Israelite, this Jew, came forth, to be the Saviour of the world. It is because they are this people that the Jews are still there with their own particular history within world history generally : a people which is no people, and as such is *the* people, the people of God ; a people which has no history, and as such, with all the problems which it raises in world history, has the only truly human history, the history of man with God. It is because the Jews are this people that it is true of them right up to our own day : " He that toucheth you toucheth the apple of my eye " (Zech. 2⁸). But no man can touch the apple of His eye. Therefore the Jews can be despised and hated and oppressed and persecuted and even assimilated, but they cannot really be touched ; they cannot be exterminated ; they cannot be destroyed. They are the only people that necessarily continues to exist, with the same certainty as that God is God, and that what He has willed and said and done according to the message of the Bible is not a whim or a

jest, but eternally in earnest, and the theme of creaturely occurrence in all ages. The history of the Jews is the embodiment of this theme of all world history. Hence derives not merely the explicability but the necessity of the proofs of existence which they have continually displayed, the power of which has manifestly not decreased but increased with the passage of the centuries, and which are still being displayed to-day with a likeness to the situations attested in the Old Testament which is almost uncanny. And the historicists and the Jews themselves and their opponents and sympathisers must ask themselves whether in the last analysis it is not futile to try to explain it all from any other standpoint. But if we do see and explain it from this standpoint, with all its necessity, then we perceive that what confronts us is the trace of the divine world-governance in all creaturely occurrence, a trace in which we recognise at once who it is that exercises the divine control.

But from this standpoint, and in the light of the biblical message, we can also understand the enigmatical being of the Jews in world history, and in all its enigmatical character. Who and what is the Jew ? We can now answer that the Jew is the man who belongs to this elected people. Because this election is still valid, he is therefore a man who continues right up to the present time. He is a man who always participates in it. But we have to add that he is a man who belongs to the people which from the very first has shown itself to be unworthy of the election ; which has always supposed that it ought to have elected its own king rather than be elected by Him ; which again and again has looked upon its election as a favour shown towards it in virtue of its own electing ; which for this reason could easily and readily elect other kings, perhaps at bottom preferring another king ; which for this reason rejected its King when He appeared amongst it, ratifying His grace but also quite definitely endorsing His claim to lordship. The Jew, therefore, belongs to the elected people, but he also belongs to the people which is unfaithful to its election. It is for the sake of the election that this people, and the Jew himself, persists and lives, but it is also for the sake of its unfaithfulness that it persists and lives, that the Jews exist as they actually do exist, that they are not a people, that this is the form in which they have traversed world history since the year 70. It is not in vain that they are a people ordained as bearers of light and salvation to all nations. It is not in vain that they are the holy remnant of Israel. It is not in vain that they are the human servant of God. It is not in vain that they are the people of the Jew Jesus of Nazareth who died on Golgotha laden with their sin and the sin of the whole world. It is not in vain that they are represented by this One. What man is in the light of the divine election and calling, how he is an object of the free grace of God, what is his relation to it and in what capacity he is judged by it—it is this whole shadow of the history of the covenant and salvation and its fulfilment which the Jews embody and reveal. Let it be understood :

not in spite of their election, but because of it, on the basis of it. It costs something to be the chosen people, and the Jews are paying the price. Everything has to fall away that makes a man great and glorious in himself, all the pride of his own religion and culture and language and race. Living only by the grace of God, he is not allowed anything of his own by which to justify or adorn himself, or to vindicate himself and make his way in world history as a whole. All that he can do is simply to be there. He cannot be overlooked, or banished, or destroyed —for the grace of God holds and upholds him—but he is not allowed the glory which counts in world history generally. He is everywhere the minority. He is everywhere the guest and stranger. He is always the one who has no home, no city, no temple. How can he have, when the judgment of God is necessarily active and revealed in him together with the grace of God ? Abraham was a stranger in the land of promise. Moses was a stranger to his own people. So were the prophets. The foxes have holes, and the birds of the air have nests, but the Son of Man hath not where to lay His head. The elect of God, whose very existence proclaims light and salvation to the world, but in whom the judgment of all flesh is also active and revealed, will always and necessarily be strangers in the world, with no home of their own. In this sense, too, the Jews are the elect of God.

And obviously the Jews are not merely strangers, but in their strangeness they have always been looked upon with disfavour. They have been unloved and despised and hated. Why especially the Jews ? What is the reason for anti-Semitism, directed only against these particular Semites ? How can we explain the strange disease from which every non-Jew seems to suffer in one form or another, the disease which can affect whole masses of people and break out so terribly, as it did in the Middle Ages and even more so in our own days, and can then be suppressed and forgotten, only to break out again like the plague ? What is it that we have against the Jews ? We cannot explain it merely by the few not very pleasant traits which we customarily attribute to them. All peoples have their unpleasant characteristics. Why is it that, although we are indignant at the unpleasant characteristics of other peoples and yet pardon them, we can never pardon those of the Jews ? Why do all peoples react against the characteristics of this particular people as though they were something unusual ? Is it not as though the enigmatic nature of the whole being of the Jews in some way affects other peoples at this point, so that an enigmatic attitude is forced upon them ? It is pure illusion to suppose that on account of their characteristics the Jews are objectively worse, or harder to tolerate, than other peoples ; that quite deservedly they give rise to a greater aversion than other peoples. And this means that we cannot understand anti-Semitism merely as a disease. It cannot be denied, however, that in fact the human race does suffer from this disease, and it must also be asserted that with all the available rational and moral arguments we cannot overcome the disease. It is explicable (i.e., meaningful, as the meaningless thing which it is), only if as strangers, even as a people which is no people amongst other peoples, the Jews are still the elect of God, whose humanity shows up in a different and special and more penetrating light than that of other men, even though they themselves are neither better nor worse than other men. What is it that we see in the Jews ? What is it that incites us against them ? What is it that fills us with horror ? What is it that can lead us to those most shameful and damnable outbreaks ? If we are going to explain it theologically, and therefore radically prevent it, two things have to be said.

It is a source of annoyance to us—whether consciously or not makes no difference, for whether we are aware of it or not this is the one thing that really annoys us about the Jews—that in the Jews and their habit of life we have held out before us, and we recognise only too clearly, our own. The Jew as a Jew is neither better nor worse than other men. But in the Jew we have revealed and shown to us in a mirror who and what we all are, and how bad we all are. Even in this respect the Jew pays for the fact that he is the elect of God. The mercy of God to all man has been manifested in him, in this people. The Word and work of God in which salvation appeared to the whole world were actualised in the history of this people. God Himself was made flesh of our flesh in a member of this people. Hence it is revealed in this people what man is, man in his relationship with God, man before the judgment seat of God, sinful man : the man who resists and opposes the grace of God ; the man who counts it too mean a thing to live only by the grace of God ; the man who wants another king instead of this King ; the man who does not want to be elected by God, but wants to elect God, and secretly wants to be his own god ; the man who wants to preserve and help and save himself by his own efforts, taking to himself all the glory. And is this only the Jewish man ? Not by a long way. This is every man, without exception. But what every man is before God, as the object of His mercy, is revealed in the Jewish man (as elect man) in a way in which it is not revealed in any other. How finely it is suppressed and concealed in the former neighbours and enemies of Israel, the Amalekites, Philistines, Moabites, etc., the Egyptians and Assyrians and Babylonians, and later the Greeks and Romans ! How finely it is still suppressed and concealed in the British and French and Germans, and above all the Swiss. How easily, with our usual one-sided anger and hatred, we can ascribe to one another the characteristics and failings which are common to us all ! How easily, after our momentary quarrels, we can again understand and acknowledge and approve one another, and even find one another interesting and likeable ! Why ? Because the evil in man—the true evil in his relationship with God and therefore with his fellow-men—is not at all revealed in the habits and bad habits of

these other peoples. It is undoubtedly there. But who is to tell ?
Who is to recognise the primal revolt of man against God and his own
nature ? Who cannot cloak over this revolt ? And who can see through
the cloak in the case of these other peoples ? Who can see right through
to what they really are—enemies of grace, and as such necessarily
enemies of one another ? Who can see right through to man himself as
the enemy of the human race ? If we are to know this, we must first
know that there is such a thing as enmity against the grace of God,
and therefore against man ; that there is such a thing as sin. And if
we are to know this, we must first know ourselves. But the nations and
the individual members of the nations do not know themselves ; they
do not know what sin is. They can fight with one another and they can
treat with one another. They can make war and they can make peace.
There can never be real enmity between them. There can never be
anything like anti-Semitism. There can never be that original and
unconquerable aversion which they all have to the Jew. Why to the
Jew ? Because that which is suppressed in them is not suppressed in
the Jew ; that which is concealed in them is not concealed in the Jew.
The Jew is the man from whom the cloak has been torn off. The
Jew stands before us as that which radically we all are. In the Jew
there is revealed the primal revolt, the unbelief, the disobedience, in
which we are all engaged. In this sense the Jew is the most human of
all men. And that is why he is not pleasing to us. That is why we
want him away. That is why we want to remove this alien element
from our midst. It is the very fact that we know him only too well
which makes his strangeness repulsive. That is why we are so critical
of the Jews. That is why we make them out to be worse than they
really are. That is why we invent the absurd notion of a Jewish race,
which we invest with every conceivable unpleasant characteristic.
That is why we ascribe to the Jews as such every possible crime. Our
annoyance is not really with the Jew himself. It is with the Jew only
because and to the extent that the Jew is a mirror in which we immediately recognise ourselves, in which all the nations recognise themselves
as they are before the judgment-seat of God. That is what we can
never forgive the Jew. That is why we think we have to heap hatred
and contempt upon the stranger. And obviously it is because they
are this mirror that the Jews are there. The divine providence has
arranged it that the Jews should still be there, and continue to be
there, and no anti-Semitism, however refined or crude, can ever alter
the fact. Because they are the elect people of God they have to be
there openly and visibly. And because their election is a pattern of
the election of all peoples, of the whole of the human race, this mirror
cannot be taken away and must not be taken away. All men have to
look in this mirror and see themselves as they really are, and confess
that their cloaks are only cloaks, and that in reality they too are
manifestly the enemies of God. It is obvious that it needs more than

the existence of the Jews actually to reveal this fact to men and to the nations. It needs the Gospel and faith in the Gospel ; it needs their ingathering into the community of Jesus Christ, if men are to read and understand the sign and testimony which is given them in the existence of the Jews, and are actually to be convinced that they too are the enemies of God, enemies to whom He has turned in the supremacy of His grace and not according to their own merits or deservings. Otherwise it is natural that the existence of the Jews should merely prove to be an annoyance, a source of irritation. But the objective meaning of the irritation and annoyance, the objective truth of the sign and testimony which has here been given to man, is not in any way dependent upon whether they perceive and understand it as such. It is still the case that the sign and testimony is given to them with this meaning and this truth. And the fact that it is given is proved by the non-Jews themselves when they are so annoyed and irritated and estranged and offended, when they cannot let the matter rest. It is clear that they know well enough that something unpleasant is being said to them at this point. They cannot deny the existence of the point. They cannot deny that they are in danger of hearing this unpleasant thing even though they have not already heard it. They must always return to the point, like a criminal to the scene of his crime. Their anti-Semitism betrays them, even though they may not know what it is that they are trying to do, or actually doing, when they are so obstinately anti-Semitic. In face of this trace of the divine world-governance, they do the most perverse thing conceivable, but in so doing they make it only too clear that they have come across this trace and cannot evade it. This is the first thing that we have to say from the theological standpoint.

The second is this. It is a source of irritation to us—and again it makes no odds whether we are conscious of it or not—that in the actual existence of the Jews, in their strange being as a people which is not a people, we are positively confronted with the fact of God's electing grace, with the fact of His mercy as the sole and mighty basis of human existence. And by our irritation we confirm that we do not really like this fact. It annoys and irritates us that the Jew is undoubtedly there as he has been there for 1900 years. It annoys and irritates us that he obviously can be there, even in and in spite of the unfavourable historical situation in which he is placed, even though he is not marked by any of the things which normally make possible the existence of a people as a people, even though he is not protected by the qualities which normally differentiate other peoples the one from the other, constituting them individual peoples and giving them a right of domicile, a claim to a place in world history. Even when it had a certain similarity with other peoples, how pushed about this people was !— first into Palestine, then down into Egypt, then into the wilderness, back again into Palestine, and so on right up to its great and final dispersion among all the nations. And what an existence it has since had in all the different groups and individual members of these groups !—an existence which defies all outward and inward probability. But it still does exist, and it can still be perceived. Is it really possible to exist as the Jews have existed ? Well, this is what they have done, and in doing it they are obviously a mirror, a mirror of the election of the divine grace and mercy on whose basis they were clearly able to do it. And not on any other basis !—that is what annoys and irritates us so much from this standpoint. In their persistence the Jews are absolutely exceptional, and they obviously surpass us. We ourselves have to exist in the normal way, and we are content and even proud to have an assured place and an assured path. But we see only too clearly that placed in the same unfavourable conditions we could never have achieved a similar persistence. There are plenty of examples to prove it. It took only a century for the Frenchmen who emigrated to Prussia to become Prussians, and in some cases ultra-Prussians ; and when the Swiss settle in America they immediately become Americans. Now the Jew himself can become a German, or a Swiss, or an American, but in so doing he never ceases to be a Jew, either in his own consciousness or consequently in that of others. In this respect the Jews can do something which we cannot do. And this fact irritates us, and the more so because we cannot explain why they can do it. In existing in so strangely relative and unrooted and uncertain a fashion, and yet doing it with such unparalleled persistence, they remind us painfully of the relativity of our own existence. Both phenomena are comprehensible from the standpoint of the divine election. If they are the elect people, and if they continue to exist by the divine grace and mercy, it is quite comprehensible that they should exist without any other root or security. And it is also comprehensible that they are able to do it with this persistence, that they are obviously preserved in a way which cannot be said of other peoples. The one phenomenon is explained by the utter freedom and unmeritedness of the divine mercy, by the glory which God wills to lay up to Himself. The other is explained by the force and omnipotence of His grace. But supposing that their existence is not an end in itself, a final end ? Supposing that as the elect people in the midst of others they are the mirror of the election of all peoples, of the whole race ? What a close and unwelcome reality we see in this one people ! For in this one people we perceive that if the divine election is a fact, and if it is the secret of human existence, the basis upon which all peoples and all individuals live, then what remains to us of all our assurances, of all that we imagine we can think and boast of as our own ? Are these qualities of ours of any more lasting worth ? Do we not exist far more dangerously than we either know or will admit ? In this respect, too, is it not the case that the existence of the Jew reveals something which is otherwise concealed ?—that no one, neither people nor individual, really has a home in world history, that no one is finally secure, that we are all pushed about, that we are all eternal strangers, since it is only in God that we are finally at home and secure. To us, the *beati possidentes*, the history of the Jews seems to convey something of this sort. And it is hardly surprising that we do not like either the message or those who deliver it. One of the reasons why we become anti-Semites is because of the anxiety aroused in us by this elect people and its fate. That is why we have a compelling desire that the mirror should be removed. And supposing we add the second fact, the uncanny persistence of Jewry in its very character as not a people ? Supposing we realise that these Jews, stripped of all the things with which we think we can console ourselves, can still do that which we have been proved in practice incapable of doing, still remaining what they are even in destruction and dispersion, even in their long-continued exile through the centuries ? Supposing these Jews have achieved in practice the very thing which other peoples devote so much energy to achieving, and at the last achieve only paritally and imperfectly, i.e., the practical demonstration of genuine national identity and independence ? How irritating—and the more so the more we are feverishly concerned about our own nationality—to have to see nationality attained in the history of this people almost playfully, without any effort and against all expectation ! Is it anything but sheer envy that has always enlisted the frightful support of nationalism against these Jews, this impotent not a people ? What is it that we see in this mirror of the election of the Jewish people ? Why is it that we are so unwilling even to be told that it is the elect people ? Why is it that we ransack Christianity for proofs that it is no longer so. But obviously, if it is so, if this people which is not a people is the people of God, if in all its world-historical weakness it is still the true people, a nation without equal, then what becomes of the rest of us ? And what a frantic sin is all other nationalism ! From the existence of this people we have to learn that the elect of God is not a German or a Swiss or a Frenchman, but this Jew. We have to learn that in order to be elect ourselves, for good or evil we must either be Jews or belong to this Jew. And who among us is really willing either to learn this or to admit it ? Yet it is a fact, and perhaps the wild fury of the anti-Semite is more perspicacious at this point than the gentle humanitarianism of those who are not patently guilty of the sin. For in the existence of the Jew we stumble upon the fact that the divine election is a particular election, that we ourselves have been completely overlooked in the particularity of this divine election. What the history of the Jews tells us is that the divine election is the election of another. Our election can be only in and with this other. If the grace and mercy and long-suffering of God are to be to us, if we are to remain, to persist, to be preserved, we cannot possibly avoid this other, for the goodness of God can be to us only as it is first to him, and to us only in and

C.D.—III.–III.—8

through him. And who is this other? The Jew? So we believe and suspect, and we hate and oppose the Jew as the rival who has eclipsed us and to whom we are unwilling to concede this superiority. But really it is the one Jew Jesus Christ who is looking out upon us from the desolation and persistence of the existence of the Jews. He is this Other who is for us. He is the one Elect as the new Head of the whole human race. It is true, of course, that He actually looks at us face to face only when we first encounter Him in the Gospel, in faith, in His community. It is true that only indirectly does His face meet us in the history of the Jews, agitating us in all this Jewish question. It is true that He Himself and His Word and Spirit are necessary if we are to perceive and understand this sign and testimony and not grossly to misunderstand it. But the sign and testimony is there—we have only to understand aright our own irritation at the Jews and we shall perceive it at once—and it is a sign which speaks of the election, which speaks of divine grace, which speaks of the One who was Himself a Jew, and outside whom there is salvation in none other, but in whom there is fulness of salvation for all men of all nations. The sign and testimony of the history of the Jews is waiting for open eyes and unstopped ears. But it has been set up in the midst of world history, as a manifestation of the kingdom of this One, and therefore of the One who is the Lord of all world history.

4. The limitation of human life. We now make what is apparently a quite illegitimate leap. For what is the connexion, and how can we conjoin into a single series the history of Scripture, the history of the Church, the history of the Jews—and then suddenly, the limitation of human life? The first three are all concrete historical sequences with a definite content, and in virtue of their distinctive character all three stand in a clearly recognisable relationship to the history of the covenant and grace. But in the latter we have a general and formal condition of human life of which we can immediately add that it is a condition of all life. All life has to be lived as limited life. How, then, can we be dealing with a further sign and testimony to the fact that all world-occurrence is occurrence controlled by God, by the God of the Bible, by the King of Israel? Are we not deviating from the centre from which our thinking must start and to which it must return? Are we not leaving sacred history for the great and dark and always equivocal sphere of creaturely occurrence in general, which needs the light that may perhaps fall on it from sacred history, but which has no light of its own in virtue of which it can take its place with the elements already mentioned and tell us something about this sacred history, and about the One who is the active Subject in this history, and as such the ruling Subject in all occurrence?

By way of introduction to this pressing question, we will say this. Let us assume that at this point, in this arrangement which is no doubt very general and formal and embraces not only man but all life, in the fact, then, that all men have to live within a definite limit, we really have to with a sign and testimony of the divine world-governance, the governance of the holy and gracious God of the Bible, the King of Israel. Let us suppose that this arrangement is in fact one of the characteristic or significant elements in world-occurrence, one of the traces which it is always and necessarily rewarding to contemplate as traces of the divine Lord of the world. If we make this assumption, then this trace has one specific advantage over all the others so far mentioned. For it can be contemplated directly. We have always to be made aware, and to be aware, of the fact that there is a history of Scripture and a history of the Church and a history of the Jews. They are indeed objective facts. Even if they do not enable us to give any specific proof, we can always describe them as such and to some extent discover them to be such. But we have to describe and discover them specifically. Even as facts they can in themselves remain concealed from countless numbers of men, simply because they do not lie within their orbit of vision, and perhaps never come within their orbit of vision. And they are never present to any of us so continuously and naturally and self-evidently that they can always speak to us. But if we have one of these signs and testimonies in human life itself, in its limitation and conditioning as the passage of a definite space of time from the beginning to the end, in its prolongation from the one to the other, then we are dealing with a fact which—whether we think of it or not—is at any rate constantly present to all of us, because it directly concerns the basic determination of our own existence. Even if I have never heard of Scripture or the Church or the Jews, or even if I have heard of them only as a concept which makes very little impact upon me, or even if they have not been present or spoken to me for some time past, it is still the case that I myself am a sign and testimony of the divine world-governance, and I myself am always present to myself : I myself, who am somewhere on the way between the beginning and the end, and conditioned by both ; I myself, who once was not, and one day will be no longer ; I myself, with my own individual life characterised by its individual limitation ; I myself as the object of this disposing. And the fact of my limitation does not affect me any the less definitely and movingly, any the less decisively and personally, because I know that it extends not merely to me but to all men, and indeed to all living creatures. That I am a particular form of this general truth only makes it more relevant to me ; it certainly does not make it irrelevant. That the truth is a general one does not alter the fact that, in so far as it is particular to me, it affects me and is undoubtedly present to me.

For example, in the well-known syllogism : All men must die ; Caius is a man ; Therefore Caius must die, the first proposition does not make the last untrue or irrelevant, but merely emphasises the truth and relevance which quite apart from the syllogism it still has for Caius himself.

If in itself and as such the limitation of human life is one of these distinctive elements in world-occurrence—distinctive as an indication of the divine world-governance—then this means that in fact, and irrespective of whether he considers the fact or not, each individual man as such is a sign and testimony in this respect. His own individual life—the fact which is to him only too close and perceptible, the element in world-occurrence which he knows most intimately—is as such a sign and testimony which will speak to him in this respect even if he has never heard of Scripture or the Church or the Jews, even if he is unable to appraise their significance, even if in their significance they are not actually present to his consciousness. Always and in all circumstances we are conscious of ourselves. And therefore if the limitation of human life does belong to this series, its unmistakeable advantage as a sign and testimony to the divine world-governance is that it is always before us in a way which cannot be said of the others.

It is not my own inspiration to introduce the theme at this point, but I am simply following the curious and specific doctrine which the older theologians regularly introduced into their discussion of divine providence—the doctrine of the *terminus vitae*, i.e., the temporal goal and end of life as God has foreordained it for each individual with all its outer and inner circumstances. Many of the older theologians (as, for instance, D. Hollaz, *Ex. theol. acroam.*, 1707, I, 6, *qu.* 8) expanded it into a doctrine of the divinely ordered *ingressus, progressus et egressus*, and therefore of the divine conditioning of human life generally. But the accent was always upon the *egressus*, and therefore upon the frontier of life which is still before us. In all that they said on the point we can sense the atmosphere of an age to which the thought of death was on the one hand more familiar and self-evident, but on the other more pressing and serious ; an age which in this respect showed itself to be far wiser than many. They had continually before them the saying in Ps. 139[16], which tells us about the eye of God which sees all our days, and the book in which they are all written ; or in Ps. 31[15] : " My times (destiny) are in thy hand " ; or in Job 14[5], which tells us that " his days are determined, and the number of his months are with thee, thou has appointed his bounds that he cannot pass." It is surprising that they did not think of other Old Testament passages, as for example Genesis 9[5f.], in which murder is forbidden because the blood, that is, the life of man as created in the image of God, belongs to God and must therefore be sacred to man, seeing that it is not his affair but God's to desire and will and encompass the end of a man. But at least they did face with a proper awe this fact of the limitation of human life, and in the single, concrete application and form of this general disposing, the death of the individual at his appointed hour, they saw a particular overruling of the divine providence, and one which called for particular notice and honour. The conflict between the Reformed and Lutheran groups came to the surface on this issue. The former spoke of a *terminus immobilis et fixus cum omnibus suis circumstantiis* which God had appointed for each individual life, and in which it was naturally arranged that in the divine decree everything would be seen and foreordained which in his freedom man himself might contribute to the shortening or lengthening of his days (cf. F. Burmann *Syn. theol.*, 1671, I, 44, 8 f.). As against this, the Lutherans could allow only an absolute foreknowledge on the part of God, but they regarded His will and decree as partly conditioned by the course of nature which God had ordained, by the free conduct of man, good or bad, rational or irrational, and also by prayer, by which the *terminus* already proclaimed and appointed for man can be deferred, as is shown by the story of

Hezekiah in Isaiah 38[1f.] (cf. D. Hollaz, *loc. cit.*). But the really remarkable feature is that they were all at one in regarding this appointment of a *terminus* as a particularly important mark of the overruling of providence. It is this hint which we are following. But as we do so, we shall try to evaluate more precisely than they did the specific content of the thought which was in their minds.

The proposition that God sets a term to the life of man, so that it begins at one moment only to end at another, is one which belongs to the sphere of theological anthropology, i.e., to the nature of man as God created it and saw that it was good (cf. *C.D.*, III, 2 § 47). We shall not labour this point in our present context. Our concern now is with the fact that this natural limitation, as it is willed by the Creator who is also Lord of the creature's history, takes on the form of actual events in the individual life, first at the beginning of this life, and then at the end, i.e., that we were all born, and shall all die. For the moment we shall leave aside all evaluation of the two events, for example, whether it is good to be born and bad to die, or perhaps the reverse. We shall simply claim that taken together the two events do constitute the outline of the disposing or limitation of the life of all of us. Our life is like the small mediaeval town whose main street and side streets and back streets all stemmed out from the one gate and led back again to the other, the whole city being surrounded by a moat which on both sides formed a connecting link between the two gates and the towers above them. All of us are on the one way from birth to death. We live within the limits imposed by this fact. Whatever happens in our life between birth and death is only an open or secret variation upon the one theme which is imposed upon us by this basic disposing. Some of the variations are apparently, and it may be actually, decisive, and some are less important. Some are determined by our own individuality and some by our environment. But our coming and going, our rising and falling, our increasing and decreasing, our establishing and fulfilling, are all of them imposed by this basic disposing. The question which we have now to answer is that of the significance of the fact that this twofold limitation is the basic disposing of our human life.

And first we have to assert that the past event, our birth, and the future event, our death, are not in the least like permanent towers, just as a city with its permanent buildings and thoroughfares is a poor image of what actually takes place between birth and death. There is a moment when a man begins to be, and there is another when he ceases to be—and who can know with certainty when either moment will be ? In both these moments there takes place something absolutely unpredictable, something entirely new, something that was never there before. The new factor may be the Here which is given to us once and for all in our birth, or it may be the Yonder which meets us irresistibly in our death, but in either case there is a change. And what are all the changes and novelties which take place between as compared with these first and last events ? Measured by these events, are not all the other events in our lives conditioned by the fact that they take place between these two ? either as a development subsequent to birth, or as a decay preparatory to death ; and all of them probably both a development and a decay, a decay and a development ; all of them both repetitions of the new fact of our birth and anticipations of the new fact of our death. These two events condition and characterise all that lies between them. They are in sequence with all other events, but as the first and last in the sequence they are unique and incomparable. And what is it that makes them so ? Obviously the fact that in the life of the individual they reflect the two great acts of God at the beginning and end of all things, the creation and the consummation. Obviously the fact that in them the individual participates in the mystery of the origin and goal of all creation, its limitation by God, its derivation from God, and its movement to God. And it is because man is the one creature who is called by God to receive the revelation of this mystery and to be aware of this derivation from God and movement to God, and in this knowledge to be responsible to God, that the disposing and limitation of his life, his birth and death, are " events " in a unique and emphatic sense of the term.

We claim further that in both these events, if in a reverse direction, there is a sharp conflict between the spontaneity of life, in which we know and understand and fulfil ourselves as the free subject of all our knowing and willing and doing and suffering, and the lordship by which sovereign disposition is made concerning us. The first event is primarily an act of that lordship. Before any question of spontaneity arises, without my being consulted, without my being able to do anything about it, it simply happens to me that I am as it were liberated for individual life, for being as an I. And the last is also an act of this lordship, for when I have made some use of the freedom given to me—perhaps made use of it to destruction as in the paradoxical case of the suicide—it is irrevocably taken from me, and again there can be no question of spontaneity. This is how I actually live. This is how I am actually enclosed both behind and before as though by unavoidable brackets : first called to the sphere of spontaneity, and then called away from it ; first kindled as a self-illuminating light, and then extinguished. It is I who live, but both in my birth and in my death it is made clear that to live is something which I myself cannot take, or give, or maintain ; something which is ordained and given to me. It is I who live, but in so doing I do not belong to myself ; I am indebted to the power which ordained that I should live within the limits laid down not by myself but by that power. It does not make any difference whether we call the ordination permission or command ; as permission it is command, and as command permission. And it certainly does not make the slightest difference whether we find it acceptable or otherwise. Obviously it is not for us to interpret it in either the one way or the other. Either way it is an ordination, an act of lordship, which encloses our whole life and to which we owe its spontaneity. That there are divine decrees—and whatever its nature, a divine decree is one that is necessarily made and executed—is something which is revealed in our lives by the fact that they are disposed and limited. In the knowledge of our life and death, and therefore of the lordship which disposes concerning us, we know in fact—even though we do not know what we know—the decree of God which affects us, yes, us personally : the decree which we cannot escape ; the decree in whose omnipotence we are safe ; the decree by which we are held.

We continue that it is these two events which give to human life its character of once-for-allness. In all the other events of which this life is made up and by which it is characterised, this character is to say the least equivocal. We have here the only thing which a man possesses absolutely alone, in the greatest possible disproportion and isolation as against that which is possessed by all other men and all other creatures. All other things he possesses only as in some degree he participates in a disposing and order which are either general or determine the life of his particular environment. In all other things he is engaged in various kinds of continuations and repetitions and variations of his own existence. In all other things there is a general or particular uniformity in his life. But in the two events which happen only once even in his individual existence, his birth and his death, he is utterly himself, absolutely original, and absolutely alone. The individuality and originality which may characterise other events in his life are only relative, being conditioned by the fact that he proceeds from the absolutely original event of his birth, and returns to the absolutely original event of his death. But these two events, his birth and his death, he does have entirely to himself, even outwardly, even in relation to his general and particular environment. In neither of them was he represented, or could be represented, by another. They take place only once. And in the once-for-allness which is established by them he exists not merely for himself but for all other creatures within the context of world-occurrence generally. It is these events which define for man his particular place and function ; the function in which, in spite of the well-known saying, he is in fact irreplaceable, indispensable, and non-interchangeable. His function may be extremely unimportant. His coming and going and all that lies between may outwardly be very ordinary. But the greater or lesser importance of his coming and going, and the attention which he claims, hardly matter as compared with the fact that he actually is, that in the midst of all other men and all other creatures he has his own personal life, he who never was before, and will never come again. He is not merely *a* man ; he is this particular man. And who is to say what he really is or is not for others, and in the context of world-occurrence as a whole ?

All that is certain is that this whole would not be the whole without the once-for-allness in which, isolated from all others and yet associated with them by these two movements at the beginning and end of his life, he is this particular man. The eternal singleness of God Himself is reflected in the small creaturely once-for-allness of this life of his which has a single beginning and a single end. And who is to say that it really is so small? Who is to say whether the singleness of God is not reflected quite differently, and far more clearly and significantly, in this creaturely once-for-allness than appears either from his importance or the attention which he claims? The only certain point is that this singleness of God is reflected there in a way which is itself peculiar and once and for all. The only certain point is that in the once-for-allness of his birth and death, and in virtue of the disposing and limitation of his life—whether he is aware of it or not—he himself, this particular man, does have to do only with God, who is also primarily and originally for Himself, isolated and unique, in the fact that He alone is worthy of confidence, that He alone can lay claim to obedience, that He alone persists where everything in human life with its desire for greatness and importance and indispensability can never be anything more than a continuation or repetition or variation of the divine claim and the divine promise.

We continue that it is these two events which always make human life into a history. The brackets by which we are enclosed and held are not the same. The acts of lordship under which we stand and which determine the once-for-allness of our existence are not the same. The one is a giving, the other a taking. The one is a calling to, the other a calling away. The one is an establishing, the other a completing. And the order of the two events is irreversible. The path from the one to the other can be traversed only in one direction. The life of man has a definite upward thrust from birth and a definite downward drag to death. Neither physiologically nor psychologically is it possible to separate the two forces. From first to last their operation seems to constitute only the one movement. And there is no reason to regard the one (most likely the upward) as positive and the other (most likely the downward) as negative. In all respects our life is the co-operation of these two forces. Without being asked either to separate or evaluate them, we undoubtedly live at a stage in the movement which is determined by them. And in so far as I am caught up in this movement from my beginning to my end, my life becomes my history—we might almost say my drama—in which I am neither the author nor the producer, but the principal actor. I did not place myself in this movement, nor do I maintain myself in it. But I myself am in this movement. Between my birth and my death the freedom is given to me to be myself in this movement, in this ascent and descent. To be in this freedom is to live. Therefore my life consists in the possibilities offered by this movement. They will all have something of the character of ascent, and they will all have something of the character of descent. At one and the same time I will always be coming and going, receiving and wanting, called and called away, summoned and discharged, working or resting, waking or sleeping. But in the contrariety set up by my beginning and end I am continually choosing and deciding, now grasping and making use of this possibility, now of that, now being caught up in the movement away from birth, now in that towards death. For a large part of our life, of course, we are simply and necessarily asleep, and therefore we have constantly to decide simply to sleep again. Even this fact shows very clearly that in our life's drama the choice of the second possibility is in its own time and place just as inevitable as that of the first. But like a real drama, this drama has its time. A history without an end would not be a history. The lordship under which we live, and the once-for-allness which it gives to our life, have provided that it should be a real history with both a beginning and an end. In a single moment, the beginning of the movement means the beginning of my wrestling with the possibilities which it offers, and in a single moment its ending means the ending of this wrestling. My birth and my death characterise it as a true history, in which something inter-connected takes place, which in its totality acquires and assumes the character of a definite decision. It is a question this time of over-riding decision how I fulfil my role, i.e., along what lines, with what consistency or inconsistency, according to what law or with what disregard of law, I continually choose between ascent and descent, receiving and wanting, doing and resting, waking and sleeping ; what form it will all have when it is finished ; who and what I myself will become and will have been in the whole course of my wrestling. This is the crucial question at every stage in my life's history, which is consti-tuted a totality by this disposing and limitation. Even from this standpoint I am always dealing with God in this limitation of my life. For the overriding decision in my life-history—who and what I really am as I am caught up between birth and death—is obviously not my own decision, but is controlled by the One who, limiting me as He did, is so vastly superior to me, and, limiting me in this way, causes my life to be so once-for-all before Him. This One is the King of my life's history. And since my life is constituted by my birth and death, and moves in terms of that ascent and descent, and is peculiar to me in my wrestling with the two, the question of its overriding decision is that of the reflection or promulgation of the divine sentence under which I stand. I live. I am caught up in that wrestling. And whether I realise it or not, this means that I am delivered up to His hands, to His severity and His mercy. It is as He decides that it will come to pass. If I can hope at all, I can hope only in Him.

And now finally it is in virtue of these two events that we are witnesses of world-occurrence generally. In virtue of these two events, that is, in the limits fixed by them, in the freedom given within them, and on the basis of the peculiar possibilities offered by them, all world-occurrence in heaven and earth takes place for us. Here and now, in the history which is our wrestling with this two-fold movement, all world-occurrence has its effect upon us, and actively and passively, in action and in contemplation, both moving and also moved, we participate in it. Knowing ourselves, we know heaven and earth. Proving ourselves in the tiny place which is seriously allotted to us and the short hour which is seriously accorded us, we prove creation as such and as a whole. We are not merely the pawn in a secondary theatre of action, but the responsible person on the spot at the very heart of things, the one who decides what creation is to become. For what do we know of creation except as we know ourselves between birth and death, ourselves in our once-for-allness, and therefore all the thousand and one open or secret relations and connexions, similarities and identities to some or many or all other creatures in which we are what we are ? And how can we know ourselves without knowing what it is that binds us to these others, without therefore knowing them ? We live, i.e., we have experience of ourselves, i.e., we wrestle with that upward and downward pull, and as we do so, in the course of our lives we encounter these others and have experience of them too. Our eyes may be open or blinkered, our ideas clear or hazy, our actions decided or undecided, but they are all there for each one of us, and we wrestle with them, and experience their influence upon us, and exercise our own influence upon them. In the history of our life there takes place *in nuce*, but very truly, all history. And far from cutting us off or isolating us, the limitation means that we are laid open to the whole ; that our existence is given solidarity with that of heaven and earth ; that we are given a stake in the law and the promises, in the peril and the preservation, of all creaturely reality ; that we participate in its life and are responsible for its nature and continuance. And if in virtue of those two events we are the witnesses of all world-occurrence, and all occurrence is under the dominion of that Lord who is the Creator of all things, then this means that in virtue of these two events we too, and—*hic Rhodus, hic salta*—we especially, are confronted by this Lord at every step on the way from the one event to the other. For we are certainly not outside the existence of heaven and earth, nor can we escape it. So, too, we are not outside and we cannot escape the lordship of the One who created heaven and earth. And the divine will and decree concerning the whole reality posited by and distinct from Him is His divine will and decree in respect of each individual man, the will and decree which will be fulfilled in the life of each individual.

To sum up, the commonplace fact of the limitation of human life has from every standpoint the same high significance. It testifies— and since we ourselves live the life which is bounded by these two events, we too testify—not merely to a higher being, but to God ; not merely to a divine nature, but to the activity of God ; to a God who does a new work in which He is the almighty Lord, in which He is unique, in which He is the Judge of men and as such the Ruler of all things. In our movement from birth to death we are the sign and testimony to ourselves of this Lord of life and death, of the lordship of this God. And who is this God ? We must not forget to concede that as we can easily miss the history of Scripture or the Church or the Jews, so we may easily miss this history of our own life in its most significant limitation, the *terminus vitae*. We may easily be insensible to the question raised by it and blind therefore to the corresponding answer. We may perceive neither God Himself nor the activity of God which characterises His Godhead. We may see only the common-place fact that we come and go. It may be all in vain that we are a sign and testimony to ourselves. But it is certainly not in vain when we already know the God whose activity we do in fact denote and attest by living this limited life. It is necessary already to have heard His Word if we are not to miss the fact which confronts us, if we are actually to understand ourselves, if we are actually to understand this basic determination of the history of human life, if we are actually to understand the most ephemeral of all things. Once again, if it is a question of the knowledge of God, it is a question of recognition. And that we do recognise Him presupposes that He has given it to us to know Him in His Word. By calling the limitation of human life a trace of the divine world-governance, we dare to presuppose that God has given it to us to know Him in His Word, so that we are now able to make this recognition. And if we can do this, then the question, Who is the God who is the Lord of life and death ? cannot remain unanswered, or receive varied answers. The bit of world-occurrence which is identical with our own life obviously speaks with a special and continuous power and a quite exceptional intimacy about the One who is the active Subject of sacred history, the history of grace and the covenant, and as such the ruling Subject of all occurrence ; about His new work, His lordship, His singleness, His judgment and His mercy to all His creatures. In the limitation of our life we recognise the faithfulness in which He has pledged Himself to the unfaithful, the supremacy of His grace, the severity and goodness of the King of Israel. In the bracket which encloses us behind and before we recognise the hand of His in which we are held, and in which we are both secure and free because it is the hand which preserves all creatures. Neces-sarily we have not to miss this hand. We can recognise it with thank-fulness. We can know and experience the great freedom which is given to man in his limitation by these two events. And for this knowledge and experience is it not enough that in this limitation we are put in exactly the same place as that of the Son of God when He went the short and narrow way from the cradle to the cross ? Yet in this limitation He rose again from the dead, and in the same limited being He will return in glory. As the man who is limited as we are He now reigns at the right hand of the Father. Living in this limitation, we are like him. That is why the limitation declares to us a great freedom. Certainly it cannot mean more than declaration. But it can mean declaration, and it does mean it if we have heard the Word of God. That is why we esteem it the closest visible trace of the One who is the King of Israel, and as such the King of the cosmos.

But in the witness to this King in world-occurrence generally there is one constant element which is more important than any of those so far mentioned. We have seen how the fourth element is quite distinct from the first three. But the one to which we now refer is distinct from all the others. It does not stand in any possible sequence with them. It can only be opposed to them. And we can do it only allusively, in the form of a preliminary introduction of a whole context which we have not so far touched on but which has its own special place in the framework of the Christian doctrine of the Creator and creation, and will therefore require a more specific enquiry and statement (in § 50). It is simply a question of the existence and function of the beings which with a surprising frequency in Holy Scripture, and consistently in the traditional language of Christianity, are referred to as angels. This is not the place at which to do more than introduce the problem in so far as it is significant for the present discussion, *non ut diceretur, sed ne taceretur* ; for it is a fact that in this respect, as a sign and testimony of the lordship of the King of Israel in world-occurrence, the existence and function of angels, if rightly understood, not merely surpasses but includes all other elements. Angels are the sign and testimony κατ᾽ ἐξοχήν, *par excellence*, the sign and testimony which stands behind and above all others. That is why, if we were to list the others but omit this, our list would not merely be incomplete but unsatisfying, for the power of all the others—apart from the self-attestation of God—depends upon the power of this sign and testimony. It is therefore indispensable that we should give a preliminary indication of the way in which we shall fill the gap.

All too easily we forget that God created not only earth, but also heaven. With the cosmos which we can comprehend and approach and at bottom control, He created the higher cosmos which we cannot comprehend or approach or control. All too easily we forget that heaven is the higher cosmos because, although it is created, it constitutes that side of created reality which is much more closely related to God, and to that extent nearer and in a closer affinity to Him. And all too easily we forget that world-occurrence does not cease with the earthly events which we can understand as natural history or the history of man, which we experience directly because like ourselves they too are earthly, but that with the earthly events there is also a heavenly occurrence which we do not understand in the least, and which as such is directly related to the earthly events both in its original and essential affinity to the determinative lordship of God and also in its absolute difference from them. All too easily we forget that, just as earth and man upon it are under heaven, so earthly occurrence takes place under the powerful determination of heaven. What is the source of this heavenly occurrence ? The aim of God, the object of His election and activity, is upon earth and not in heaven. It is an earthly history, the history of the covenant and salvation, which begins with the creation of the universe and constitutes the central part of its history. It is the lower cosmos, this world of ours, which is the scene of the magnifying of God's mercy for the greater magnifying of His glory. For this reason the Son of God does not become a heavenly creature, but He becomes flesh, man, an earthly creature. In the history of the covenant and salvation, and in all the divine world-governance, it is a matter of the will of God being done on earth as it is done in heaven, always, and without any particular forethought, as befits the character of heaven. God has no independent goals and ends in heaven. There did not need to be any specific heavenly occurrence merely for the sake of heaven. This occurrence arises only as in the divine relationship to earth, heaven, the higher cosmos, is the throne or dwelling-place from which God sets out to establish on earth His own order and glory, and therefore that of earth as well. According to the stricter biblical interpretation it is by this invasion of God for the deliverance and government of man and His world, our lower cosmos, that heaven is set in motion, and a heavenly occurrence arises which precedes the earthly. God arises in power to come to us, to come to the place where we are, to speak to us, to act amongst us and with us, to interest Himself in us and in our needy world, the lower cosmos, both as King and as Lord. But since He is still God, and heaven is still His throne, it is inevitable that heaven and all the higher cosmos, both in its incomprehensibility but also in its affinity with Him, should follow the movement which He Himself makes, imitating and accompanying it, adoring and extolling His will and Word and work amongst us in the lower cosmos, standing by and supporting His activity, His forceful striding down from above to below. Where God Himself is, heaven is also there to serve Him, as a sign and testimony. That is why (in Matthew at any rate) the kingdom which comes to us is called the kingdom of heaven. In coming to us, it rends heaven apart. It sets it in motion. It changes its structure. And in coming to us, it brings heaven with it. It brings the higher world down to the lower. It is the kingdom in which the kingship of God means that the forces of what is in principle the unseen and heavenly world assume form and enter the earthly world and become active in it and real factors in its occurrence. In their being and function they cannot for a single moment or in any one respect be separated from the Word and work of God, or be autonomous over against the will of God. They are truly active and glorious to the extent that they fulfil His will. Naturally they have to be distinct from God, but like the totality of heaven and earth they are only the creatures of God, and they are real factors only to the extent that they are absolutely under His lordship. But they also have to be distinct from all earthly factors. Within the earthly they are heavenly factors with all the high incomprehensibility of heaven, participating in that proximity and affinity to God which finally distinguishes the higher cosmos from the lower.

Speaking in a preliminary and provisional way, these factors are angels, i.e., heavenly messengers ordained to service, or heavenly servants ordained as messengers, in the plurality corresponding to the fact that heaven develops its apparently rigid unity into flexible richness in virtue of the concrete will and work of God (both in itself and to the world). But they are the heavenly world as it is set in motion by God and with God. That is why they do not belong to a doctrine of the creature, and are never even considered in the biblical story of creation. They do not exist at all as man does, not simply because they are heavenly, but primarily because as heavenly beings they are distinct and special creatures, acquiring and enjoying their being and function only in and with this invasion and Word and work of God. They belong essentially to the Word and work of God, to the covenant and saving activity and rule of God in the creaturely world, to Jesus Christ, the Prophet, Priest and King. They are still creatures, but as heavenly beings, as beings which belong to the Word and work of God, they stand side by side with man and all other creatures, and also above them.

And it is in respect of these two characteristics that they are the primary sign and testimony of the world-governance of the King of Israel—which is our concern in the present context. Therefore of all that has to be said concerning them we shall select only that which is immediately apparent in the Scriptures of the Old and New Testament. Obviously their being and function is everywhere presupposed, but they actually appear, and are described as active, only when it is a matter of declaring the Word and work of God Himself as fulfilled in speech or action. They are as it were the luminous border of this Word and work, marking it off from world-occurrence generally. This is how they appear, for example, on the margin of the events of Advent and Christmas, or of the Easter incidents during the forty days, or of the prospective *parousia*. On this margin, or as they themselves form this margin, they are watchers, calling and speaking and singing, and when the time comes sounding the trumpet to awaken all those who are asleep or half-asleep. But they are all this as the sign and testimony of the One who is the Lord and Master of all things and over all things. And they are the primary witness because they belong to this higher cosmos, and belonging to it, in their being and function they take precedence over the lower, over all the prophets and apostles, over the whole Church, over the Jews, over ourselves and our witness to ourselves. The other signs and testimonies are there only because they are there first. Therefore we cannot really compare any of the divine constants in world-occurrence with this constant, this chorus of angels in heaven which accompanies the Lord on his way.

It is true, of course, that we can miss the angels. We can deny them altogether. We can dismiss them as superfluous, or absurd and comic. We can protest with frowning brow and clenched fist that, although we might admit that there is a God, it is going too far to allow that there are angels as well. They must be questioned or completely ignored. There are, therefore, even Christian and theological systems in which there is no place for angels. We have to be careful that they are not the very systems in which there is no place for the other constants either. For if we do not know anything of the primary sign and testimony, how can we know anything of the secondary ? If we cannot or will not accept angels, how can we accept what is told us by the history of Scripture, or the history of the Church, or the history of the Jews, or our own life's history ? And since it depends upon our acceptance of these secondary signs and testimonies whether or not our own system includes within it the living God, we have to ask ourselves whether a system in which there is no place for angels, and therefore for the primary sign and testimony, will not at bottom be a godless one. Where God is, there the angels of God are. Where there are no angels, there is no God. And whatever our system may be, it is comforting and good that the world and its occurrence should not be without God and the angels of God, that our lower cosmos should not be without the encounter and contact with the higher cosmos set in motion by the Word and work of God. The worse for us if we are not aware of it ! For if this is the case, it is a fairly sure symptom that we have not heard the Word of God and that we are not aware of the work of God. Just as the Word and work of God wait to be heard and received by us, so the heavenly cosmos and the angels wait to be perceived and considered by us. And in the meantime they offer us their services even though we are not aware of the fact, or do not remember it, for there can be no doubt that the Word of God is true, and His work proceeds, even though we are not, or even before we are, thankful for it. That side by side with and high above all other sign and testimony, these primary and supreme signs and testimonies to the divine world-governance do in fact stand in their office, and wait on their office, is the preliminary fact concerning angels of which we have to take cognisance in the present context.

4. THE CHRISTIAN UNDER THE UNIVERSAL LORDSHIP OF GOD THE FATHER

We have now given an outline of what we are required to believe by the Word of God concerning the great objective reality of the activity and rule of God the Father as Lord of the creature, concerning His divine preserving and accompanying and ruling of the creature, and the basis and meaning of its history. But our sketch would be incomplete if in conclusion we did not expressly consider the creaturely subject which participates in the divine lordship, not merely from without, as a creature which is preserved and accompanied and ruled by Him like all other creatures, but in some sense from within, as a creature which not only experiences this rule in practice but perceives and acknowledges and affirms and approves it, which is in fact thankful for it and wills to cleave and conform to it. So far we have tacitly presupposed the existence of such a subject, and all our propositions and their elucidation are based upon this presupposition. In our final discussion, when we listed and described the constant traces of the divine world-governance in all creaturely occurrence, it was particularly clear, and we had constantly to draw attention to the fact, that although these traces can be seen they can easily be missed. It is only a certain kind of subject which can see them. The precondition was particularly clear at this point, but in reality the same precondition governs all theological propositions, including the doctrine of providence as a whole. But who is the subject, and what is his specific nature and attitude, to whom the *conservatio, concursus* and *gubernatio* as we have described them are not empty concepts, but who has actual knowledge of them ? We cannot avoid trying to give a right answer to this question, not merely in order to reveal in conclusion what is the basis of our knowledge of this whole matter, but because a right answer to this question is calculated to put the whole matter in a light which is absolutely indispensable if it is to be perceived aright.

The doctrine of providence—at any rate as we have understood and presented it—is with all its elements an integral part of the Christian confession. Therefore the subject to which we were referring is the living member of the Christian community, the Christian. We will not at this point try to explain how this subject is constituted, and how far there can be and is a Christian community, and a Christian as its member. What concerns us now is that the Christian alone is the creaturely subject which can join in a confession of the divine providence because it knows this providence, because it participates in the divine world-governance in this special and inward way. What concerns us now is the Christian as the point from which all that we have said in the matter can be understood as actual reality. We are enquiring into the specific being and attitude in which the *conservatio, concursus* and *gubernatio* are just as visible to the Christian in the developed form of the divine operation as are happenings on the street to a man looking out of a window. We are asking how it is that this self-evident manifestness of the divine lordship is both possible and actual in the Christian community.

We can best begin by making the simple assertion that even the Christian is only a creaturely subject, and that in solidarity with all other men and creatures he stands therefore wholly and utterly under the universal lordship of God : with the same disadvantage that this means for every man or every fly, that he cannot be his own lord ; but also with the same advantage, that he does not need to be anxious concerning his own preservation or way or end. The Christian, too, is upheld by God without being able to do anything towards it or about it. He, too, has in God an almighty Companion who embraces his whole being, whose activity sovereignly precedes and accompanies and follows his own activity. He, too, can only let himself be ruled. What, then, distinguishes him from the others ? In the first instance, only the fact that with all its consequences he accepts and affirms the fact that he is only a creaturely subject like the others, that in this respect there is nothing to distinguish him from them. Of all creatures the Christian is the one which not merely is a creature, but actually says Yes to being a creature. Innumerable creatures do not seem to be even asked to make this affirmation. Man is asked. But man as such is neither able nor willing to make it. From the very first man as such has continual illusions about himself. He wants always to be more than a creature. He does not want merely to be under the universal lordship of God. But the Christian makes the affirmation that is demanded of man. This is his distinction. It is the distinction of renouncing all claim to distinction. He makes the common confession of what all creatures really are, sometimes without even being asked, sometimes in defiance of their own wrong answers. The Christian, therefore, is the true creature. All the virtue and activity, all the joy and worth of the Christian must begin with this simple fact, and must finally lead back to it. It is important to assert this at the very outset. The glory of the particular relation and attitude of the Christian to the universal lordship of God consists in the fact that it does not give occasion for any glorying in self. It begins and ends with the laying aside of all claim to self-glory. The height of the Christian in this matter is always the depth—and it is no height at all, but a very real depth—of the reality with which he can and may and must and will stand towards the fact that as a creature he is in no sense superior to other men, or to the dust under his feet, but can exist only under the universal lordship of God. Whatever advantage he may have over other men—and he really has a very big advantage— he has it only under the continually present and actual presupposition that as a creature he has no advantage at all.

How is it that the Christian of all men attains to the reality of acknowledging this fact ? Our answer can be the very simple one that he sees what the others do not see. The world-process in which he participates in solidarity with all other creatures might just as easily be a vain thrusting and tumult without either master or purpose. This is how many see it. But the Christian sees in it a universal lordship. The lordship might just as easily be that of natural law, or fate, or chance, or even the devil. This is how many see it. But the Christian sees in it the universal lordship of God, of the God who is the Father, who is the Father to him, his Father. He sees the constitutive and organising centre of the process. What makes him a Christian is that he sees Jesus Christ, the Son of God, in the humiliation but also in the exaltation of His humanity, and himself united with Him, belonging to Him, his life delivered by Him, but also placed at His disposal. And seeing Him, he sees the legislative, executive and judicial authority over and in all things. He sees it as the authority of God. He sees it as the authority of the Father. He sees himself subjected to this authority as the one who is united with and belongs to the Son. Only the Christian sees this centre of the world-process. Only the Christian sees at this centre, as the One who has all power in heaven and on earth, the Son of God, and through Him God the Father, and on the circumference himself as a child of the Father for the sake of the Son. The whole Christian community is simply a gathering together by the Word which tells us this and explains and reveals it to us ; a gathering together of those whose eyes are opened to the fact of it. Only the Christian is a member of this community, i.e., one who is gathered together with others by this Word, one whose eyes are opened to this fact. There are some creatures which do not need to have eyes for it because even without seeing it they are carried along by the power of this order and are secure in its peace. There are other creatures which have eyes for it but they will not and cannot open them. But the Christian has open eyes. That is why he has the reality freely and joyfully to confess his creatureliness and his consequent subjection to the universal rule of God without reserve and without claim. What he sees at that centre and on that circumference is not something which frightens him, something which he has to reject. God the Father as the ruling Creator is obviously not an oppressor, and Christ as a subject creature is obviously not oppressed. There is nothing here which need frighten him. There is nothing here which need cause him to flee or rebel. To be wholly and unreservedly under the universal lordship of God, to be wholly and unreservedly a creaturely subject, is not in any sense a constraint, a misfortune, an outrage or a humiliation for the man who as a Christian can see actualised in Jesus Christ both the lordship of God and also the subordination of the creature. For him all attempts to evade this fact are purposeless, and the illusion by which it is obscured or avoided is superfluous. If the relation between the Creator and the creature is the relation which he can see in Jesus Christ, then existence in this relation is the existence which is to be truly desired, an existence in the highest possible freedom and felicity. To have to confess this is not an obscure law, but a friendly permission and invitation. It is not unwillingly but spontaneously, not grudgingly but gladly, that the Christian will affirm and lay hold of this relation and his own existence in it. Hence the reality does not cost him anything. He does not have to force it. He does not have to struggle to attain to it. It comes to him in the same way as what he sees comes to him. And this means that he does not screw himself up to a height when he is a real creature. It also means that there does not arise any claim or merit on his part just because he confesses so unreservedly what other creatures and other men cannot and will not confess. The fact that he does so is not a kind of triumph for his individual honesty. Other people are just as honest, perhaps more so. He is simply made real by what he sees. And as such he is simply availing himself of a permission and invitation. He is going through an open door, but one which he himself has not opened, into a banqueting hall. And there he willingly takes his place under the table, in the company of publicans, in the company of beasts and plants and stones, accepting solidarity with them, being present simply as they are, as a creature of God. It is the fact that he sees, and that which he is able to see as the centre and the circumference, the Creator and the creature, which constitute the permission and invitation and open door to his peculiar reality.

To summarise provisionally, we may say that in virtue of what he (and only he) can see, the Christian is the one who has a true knowledge in this matter of the providence and universal lordship of God. This providence and lordship affect him as they do all other creatures, but he participates in them differently from all other creatures. He participates in them from within. Of all creatures he is the one who while he simply experiences the providence and lordship of God also consents to it, having a kind of " understanding "—if we may put it in this way —with the overruling God and Creator.

In practice, of course, he is faced every day afresh with the riddles of the world-process, with the precipices and plains, the blinding lights and obscurities, of the general creaturely occurrence to which his own life's history also belongs. Of course he can only keep on asking : Whence ? and Whither ? and Why ? and Wherefore ? Of course he has no master-key to all the mysteries of the great process of existence as they crowd in upon him every moment in a new form, to all the mysteries of his own existence as a constituent existence in the historical process of all created reality. On the contrary, he will be the one man who knows that there is no value in any of the master-keys which man has thought to discover and possess. He is the one man who will always be the most surprised, the most affected, the most apprehensive and the most joyful in the face of events. He will not be like an ant which has forseen everything in advance, but like a child in a forest, or on Christmas Eve ; one who is always rightly astonished by events, by the encounters and experiences which over-take him, and the cares and duties laid upon him. He is the one who is constantly forced to begin afresh, wrestling with the possibilities which open out to him and the impossibilities which oppose him. If we may put it in this way, life in the world, with all its joys and sorrows and contemplation and activity, will always be for him a really inter-esting matter, or, to use a bolder expression, it will be an adventure, for which he for his part has ultimately and basically no qualifications of his own.

And all this is not because he does not know what it is all about, but just because he does know. All this is because he has an " under-standing " with the source from which everything derives, from which directly or indirectly everything happens to him ; the " understanding " of the creature with its Creator, which is, for him, that of the child with its father. One thing at least he does not need to puzzle about. About this one thing he has no need to enquire, to be always on the look-out for new answers, new solutions. For he has learned once and for all who is this source, and what basically he can expect from it, and what will always actually come from it. But how the decision is reached, and in what form everything will come as it proceeds from this source, he is as tense and curious as a child, always open and surprised in face of what comes. Yet whatever comes, and in whatever form it comes, he will see that it comes from this one source. However, strange it may seem, however irksome in the form in which it comes, he will approve it as coming from this source. He will always be, not perhaps able, but at least willing and ready to perceive the positive—and in the light of its source the most definitely positive—meaning and content of what comes. He will always be willing and ready —again a daring expression—to co-operate with it instead of adopt-ing an attitude of supercilious and dissatisfied criticism and opposi-tion, or, if it were possible, retiring sulkily into a corner as a sceptical spectator. He will always allow everything to concern him directly, and, with all the dialectic of his experiences and attitudes, he will ultimately and basically allow everything to concern him positively. Ultimately and basically he will always be thankful, and in the light of this thankfulness he will look forward to what has still to come. He will always know both what was intended and what is intended. He will always be the child having dealings with its father. This is the knowledge of the Christian in matters of the divine lordship. There is nothing arrogant about it. It remains within the bounds of the reality in which the Christian can know himself—know himself as a creature under the lordship of God like all other creatures. It is in a sense only the reverse side of this reality. Naturally the confession of the providence and universal lordship of God is not the same as the expression and product of this Christian knowledge. It is rather an answer to the Word of God. It can be understood only as an echo of the call of this Word, not as a human or even a Christian achievement or acquirement. But obviously, where the Word of God is really heard, this Christian knowledge will also arise as a historical determination of the existence of the hearer. Obviously, too, the confession of the providence and universal lordship of God will inevitably be cold and formal in the heart and on the lips of anyone who misses this Christian knowledge, who does not know what it means for him personally when he speaks of the divine preserving, accompanying and ruling, to whom the matter arises only in a distant and alien height and not in his own sphere, not in the form of a historical determination of his own existence. In relation to everything that went before, the question of the Christian subject is a kind of controlling question : Understandest thou what thou readest ? Have you reached the point where both in your heart and on your lips the doctrine of the divine providence is not the type of speculation in which you are interested only as a more or less clever spectator, but where you are affected and laid hold of by the object of the doctrine itself, where you have therefore appre-hended and understood it from within ?

This Christian knowledge has nothing whatever to do with mere speculation. Nor have we to think of it as a kind of insight or per-ception which has been miraculously implanted in or imparted to the Christian as the one who sees, and which has now passed into his possession. It is nothing at all if it is not an exercised science or craft. Certainly it is given to him, not as a supernatural quality, but as a capacity which is actual only as it is used, which is not in any sense magical, but absolutely free and natural in its exercise. And it is, of course, the highest knowledge, but because it is the highest, it is a knowledge which claims not only his eye and intellect, but the whole man. Its reference is to a relationship, to the relationship effected between the operation of God the Creator and the totality of creaturely occurrence as overruled by Him. It is, therefore, an attitude, but a dynamic attitude, in which the Christian, being totally claimed, participates in the operation of God and creaturely occurrence : con-templating to be sure, but active as well ; perceiving, but also working ; and both in such a way that it is quite impossible to separate the one from the other, because proceeding from the one he is always leaping along the way to the other. It is all perceiving and understanding and knowing. But, as we had to add at once, it is all affirming and approving ; it is all a willingness and readiness to co-operate ; it is all thankfulness. If the divine providence and lordship are reflected in the Christian as in pure glass, if the Christian knows them in such a way that this " speculation " takes place, then this obviously means that the occurrence which proceeds from God and embraces heaven and earth is repeated in the narrow sphere of his own creaturely existence, of his own thoughts and will and deed, of his own life. The providence and universal lordship of God are not merely true to him, but in this repetition they are actual. How they are actual to him it will now be our task to indicate and explain.

They are actual to him in faith, in obedience, and in prayer. These are the three forms of this dynamic and totally Christian attitude. We shall find all of them more or less impressed on all expressions of this Christian attitude, and we shall recognise them fully and clearly. And we can test our own attitude by the simple but sure standard whether it seeks to express itself in these three forms; whether any one of them is lacking ; whether it is straining to express itself equally and fully in all three. If it does, but only if it does, it is the Christian attitude. And if it is the Christian attitude, none of the three must be omitted or stunted, none must obscure or absorb the others, none must try to replace or crowd out the others. If only one of the three is completely missing, our attitude is not a Christian one. Even though the other two may be intact, or perhaps strongly developed, it is still definitely not a Christian one except in appearance. And we must note that in faith, as in obedience and prayer, it is not a matter either of pure theory or of pure practice, but always of the step or leap from the one to the other, from seeing to doing, from knowing to acting. When the Christian believes and obeys and prays, all doubt or debate concerning the precedence of the one over the other is transcended. To dispute concerning the more contemplative or active nature of Christianity, or the respective merits of waiting and hasting, of grace and freedom, of comfort and exhortation, or however else we may express the antithesis—all this is superfluous. In none of its three forms does the Christian attitude know anything of such abstract antitheses. Antitheses of this kind are always relics of a wrongly speculative approach to the divine providence and lordship. As they are truly considered in the dynamic and total form possible only in the Christian life, and as they are repeated in this subjective sphere, the divine providence and lordship render all such antitheses superfluous. From first to last the truly Christian attitude is a knowing of God in His own Word, and this means that from first to last it is a doing according to the rule of this Word. This applies to faith no less than to obedience and prayer. Therefore we cannot possibly understand the three forms as three parts of the Christian attitude which limit and complete each other, so that the Christian first believes, then has to obey, and finally must pray ; or first believes, then has to pray and finally must obey ; or first obeys, and then has to pray and finally must believe. We should note that divisions of this kind lead immediately and necessarily to the position in which we are dealing with a law, in the fulfilment of which the Christian attitude must then consist. The Christian attitude—the Christian knowledge which comes from hearing the Word of God—has nothing whatever to do with a law of this kind, no matter how the sequence may be formulated. The Christian attitude is the being of the Christian as graciously awakened by the Word of God which always gives and always demands. It is his being in the freedom of the Gospel, not his being under a law. But seen in this freedom of the Gospel each of the three forms is also the whole ; each of the three forms include the other two within itself.

We are bold to make the comparison that, as the three trinitarian modes of the divine being do not limit and complete each other as parts of the Godhead, but are the one God in a threefold identity, so that each of the modes includes the other two within itself and is within the others, so the faith and obedience and prayer of the Christian are the one Christian attitude, and they are all individually that which the others are as well. If faith is really the faith of the true Christian attitude, it is also obedience and prayer, and on the same presupposition obedience is faith and prayer, and prayer is faith and obedience. Yet the distinction, i.e., the peculiar emphasis and standpoint and even life of faith and obedience and prayer is just as indispensable as is the distinction between the modes of being in our confession of the triune God, for the unity and totality of the Christian attitude is never actual or visible *in abstracto*, but only in the three forms. A reversion either to the neglect of any one of the forms in favour of the others, or to the totalitarianism of any one at the expense of the others, cannot be justified on the score that we consider them to be identical in essence, just as in trinitarian teaching the doctrine of the *perichoresis* of the three divine modes of being cannot mean that ultimately we are returning to the modalistic heresy.

On this presupposition and with this reservation we shall now expound the three forms of the one Christian attitude to the divine providence and lordship, and therefore the three forms of one and the same Christian knowledge at this point. We will take them one after the other, but in the most intimate connexion the one with the other, first faith, then obedience and then prayer.

1. Faith is the receiving of the Word of God as such. It is the lively confidence in which the Christian perceives and acknowledges the Word as a Word from God and a Word spoken to him, and in which he affirms it to be such, a Word from God and a Word spoken to him. Faith, therefore, is the source of the Christian attitude. As compared with obedience and prayer, it has no primacy in value or importance, but it has a primacy in order : not necessarily a primacy in temporal order ; but necessarily a primacy in actual order. In faith in Jesus Christ a man becomes a Christian. In faith, God in Jesus Christ is his Father, he himself in Jesus Christ is the child of God, and he becomes the particular creature which participates from within in the divine providence and universal lordship. In faith, the particular relation and union which God has established on earth between Himself and His people actually attains its goal on the manward side. Therefore everything which goes to make up the Christian attitude is really grounded in faith and is a form or work of faith.

This is not the place, however, in which to speak fully or in detail of the origin and nature of faith.

We may dismiss briefly, on the one hand the idea that faith is a magical quality imparted to man and enabling him to surpass the nature given him at creation, and on the other the idea that it is an activity which man produces of himself simply by exercising a capacity which belongs to him by nature. The true source of faith is the Word of God. Faith, therefore, is a new activity which man cannot of himself decide to undertake, and which he has no power of himself to undertake. When it takes place, faith is a historical determination of human existence, a determination in the history of salvation. But—in opposition to the first view—it is an awakening of man to his own activity, an activity which as such is not merely within the sphere of his own creaturely nature, but corresponds at every point to the highest natural determination of his creatureliness ; just as the incarnation of the Son of God, which is the great pattern of the origin of faith, means not only a completely unmerited liberation of human nature, but also and for that very reason a restitution of its highest creaturely determination.

We may also dismiss, on the one hand the idea that faith is a blind subjection to a law imposed upon the will and understanding from without, and on the other the idea that it is a conviction of the truth and importance of certain objective facts, a conviction which is established and attained by man himself, and then, and for this reason, chosen and adopted by man himself. As opposed to the second idea, faith is, of course, an arrest and commitment in which man is set free from his own caprices and acquires a Lord whom he must follow. It is a new and strange light shining upon man from above. But—in contrast to the first idea—it not only shines upon human life, and therefore the human will and understanding, from without, but it also illuminates them from within. It does not close our eyes, but opens them. It does not destroy our intellect and compel us to sacrifice it, but it sets it free just as in a definite sense it captivates it, i.e., for itself. It does not break down our will, but sets it in free movement ; just as the incarnation of the Son of God, the pattern of the nature of faith, is actual and visible not only in the perfect obedience but also in the perfect sovereignty of the activity of Jesus Christ.

The reality of faith transcends these antitheses. It includes them. Faith is altogether the work of God, and it is altogether the work of man. It is a complete enslavement, and it is a complete liberation. And it is in this way, in this totality, that it is raised up and lives as it is awakened by the Word of God.

And it is in this way that the Christian participates in faith in the divine providence and world-governance. In the first instance his faith is simple and direct—a participating in Jesus Christ and in His work of grace and salvation. Jesus Christ is in fact the Word of God by which faith is awakened. The Christian lives by Him, and holds fast to Him. In its first and decisive moment his faith is a confidence in what took place and was revealed in this One, in the kingdom of God in Him, in the uniting of God and man accomplished by Him, in the reconciliation of the world with God actualised by Him, in the fatherhood of God and the sonship of man proclaimed by Him. As faith in Him, as faith in the power and obedience of the Holy Spirit, it is Christian faith. And as such, in a movement arising from this first movement, it as it were raises itself and reaches out and becomes confidence in the fact that what occurred in Jesus Christ has precedence over all other occurrence ; that all other occurrence is subordinate to it, having in this occurrence its origin and goal, its norm and standard ; that to the one Jesus Christ all power is given both in heaven and in earth. It is as he participates in Jesus Christ in faith that the Christian participates in the divine providence and universal lordship. The same Holy Spirit who first led him into the narrower and central sphere now leads him out over its periphery into the wider circle. The distinction between the two movements is clear. Believing in Jesus Christ, the Christian enters into a given presupposition, and now he draws out the deductions implicit in that presupposition, but implicit only as deductions. In the former case, faced with the particular occurrence in Christ, his faith is a confidence which is both related to and based upon a definite objectivity. In the latter, faced with creaturely occurrence generally, it is a confidence which ventures out from this basis without any such objectivity. In the one case, it is a light kindled by the light, and in the other a light shining in the darkness. In the one case, it receives the assurance and encouragement and promise which it does not receive in the other, but by which it has to live and conquer. In the one case, it has the character of a present certainty, in the other, of a certain hope. But in both cases it is the same. In both it is altogether the work of God and it is altogether the work of men. In both it is the complete enslavement of man and his complete liberation. It is never present in the one case and not in the other. It cannot participate in Jesus Christ without participating in the divine providence and universal lordship. Again, it cannot participate in the latter without participating in Jesus Christ. It is always our striding from the one to the other : from the place where God is revealed to the place where He is hidden ; from the Here with its Therefore to the There with its Nevertheless.

In the present context our interest in faith is in respect of the second movement in which the Christian is faced with creaturely occurrence generally : not lost and helpless and defenceless, for in faith he participates in Jesus Christ ; but only in the power and protection of that participation. He is called to participate in the divine providence and universal lordship, but it is only as the one who participates in Jesus Christ that he is empowered and equipped to do so. For the rest, he is actually confronted with the world-process in which he cannot expect to meet fresh revelations. The Word alone which he has heard can make it possible for him to accept there too the ruling hand of God, there too the plan of God which is now being executed, there too the active mercy and omnipotence and wisdom and goodness of God, there too the faithfulness of God both generally and in detail. The Word alone can open the eyes of the Christian to the signs and testimonies of the presence and purpose and helpfulness of God, signs and testimonies which are real but hidden, which always need to be re-discovered. The Word alone by which he has known God can enable him to recognise God there. The Word alone can prevent him from creating either on a large scale or a small his own arbitrary and arrogant or it may be despairing or sceptical scheme of things ; from indulging in, or perhaps surrendering to, his own unsubstantial vision of a self-subsisting and self-motivated universe in which there is no place for God ; from becoming a heathen either secretly or openly, either in theory or in practice. The Word alone can hold him over the abyss and lead him across the waves. And the Word alone can give him the necessary courage and patience, and cheerful heart. And by this Word the Christian is awakened to faith. In faith he lays hold of it. In faith he assents to it and affirms it. In faith he holds to the Word and maintains it in face of everything that the world-process can produce, and above all in the face of his own unsettled heart which so consistently opposes and contradicts it. That is why we can and must say that faith alone must make it possible. In faith alone the Christian must have open eyes and see. In faith alone he must despise and dismiss all false systems. In faith alone he must be held over the abyss and be led through the waves. In faith alone he must be courageous and patient and cheerful. In faith alone ; for how may he or can he or ought he to be willing and ready for all these things except in faith ?

But in faith the Christian does all these things. And it is not a matter whether his faith is greater or smaller, stronger or weaker, more instructed or simpler. These are secondary questions. It is a matter whether his faith is a real faith and not a faith only in appearance. It is a matter whether as a real faith it is the source of the whole Christian attitude. And whether it is a real faith depends upon whether it is participation in Jesus Christ, and whether it draws out the deduction implicit in this fact. To put it in another way, it depends upon whether it really draws upon the Word, and is nourished by the Word, and allows itself to be directly and constantly renewed by the Word. If it does not do this ; if in one sense or another the faith of the Christian is faith in himself, possibly an introverted faith in the power and seriousness of his own affirmation of the Word, or very commonly faith in the truth and beauty of Christianity ; or if it is merely borrowed or assumed, a faith which is the imitation of what we believe is faith as perceived in others, then we need not be surprised if it is not the victory which overcomes the world. But to the extent that in some measure or form it does do what is essential to it as faith, participating in Jesus Christ and drawing out the deductions involved in this fact, even if we cannot describe its achievements as perfect or brilliant, it is at least the Christian's participation in the divine providence and universal lordship. And the Christian, the creature which knows first of all that it can only lie in the dust before God, is the man who in faith, even if it is only a pitiable fragment of faith, is with God, and therefore not under or in but above all the wind and waves of world-occurrence. He is with God as a child of the Father and heir of His glory, and here and now a free lord of all things. He can see even where there is nothing to see. He can laugh at false systems and visions even when they are so strong. He can stand and proceed even when his neighbours and he himself expect to see him fall into the abyss. He can be courageous and patient and cheerful even where not just appearances but the massive whole of reality forbids him to be so. He bids defiance, not in an artificial spasm of religious over-exertion, but because in believing he is himself defied, and therefore maintained both against himself and against this whole. He himself has a Lord, and therefore he can and may and must bid defiance and himself be lord with him. From the Therefore there follows at once the Nevertheless, and what is still lacking, what he still awaits, awaits ardently but not anxiously, is simply the revelation of his own Lord as the Lord also of world-occurrence, or, to put it in another way, the revelation that his Nevertheless is also a Therefore. But that is what it means—at any rate in this respect—to live by faith. The just, the Christian, will live by this faith of his.

By this time it should be clear why it is so important that we should maintain that faith is altogether the work of God and altogether the work of man ; that it is the complete enslavement of man and also the complete liberation of man. If it were not all these things, it would not achieve what it does achieve. It achieves it in so far as it is all these things.

If it were not the work of God on man, how could it exalt man as it does ? How could it mean his participation in Jesus Christ, and therefore in the divine providence and world-governance ? How could the creature grasp at such a thing for himself, or maintain it once it had been given ? How could the creature believe of himself, and live by his faith ? What an Icarus-flight faith would be if it were a venture undertaken by man in his own strength ! But with God, and as God gives Himself to man by awakening faith, nothing is impossible. Awakened and moved by God, man can and does believe. But again, faith must also be the work of man if it is really to find him and affect him as the work of God on him, and not merely to hover above him as a kind of hypothesis. If the Christian did not himself believe, himself trust, himself make that first and second movement, himself be caught up in the step from one to the other ; if in all these things he were merely the spectator of God, how could it ever be said of him that he could personally recognise the revealed God even in His hiddenness, that as a child of the Father he could find his way about the house of the Father, that with God he could be the lord of all things ? In this respect he would find himself left on one side, with fine thoughts about the things which might be, but are not for him. But the gift of faith consists in the fact that man himself can believe, that man himself can really accomplish the whole work of faith, that man himself therefore, can really live by his faith.

The importance of the second assertion will also be clear. Faith must consist in a complete enslavement of man. If he believes, he necessarily acquires a Lord ; he necessarily begins to exist in what is for him a new and strange light. He cannot remain in the world as he was before. He must be separated and consecrated to participate in Jesus Christ and the divine providence and lordship. He must accept the fact that the Word of God disposes concerning him, and demands obedience. If he did not do this, how could he ever come to the point of clinging to it and being borne by it ? How could he ever be made by it the friend and confidant of God who recognises Him even where He is now hidden ? How could he ever be made by it courageous and patient and cheerful ? How could he be a free lord over all things with the Lord, if he himself either could not or would not have a Lord ? How could he see light in the darkness if he himself had not come into the light ? If he will not lose his life, he cannot gain it. Therefore faith must always consist in the fact that in Christ he not merely sees himself questioned in the most radical possible way, but he must constantly abandon himself for lost in favour of the One who has found him. But the faith which consists in this is also the complete liberation of man. In the very fact that he is so completely challenged, he is completely established. His being as a creature is not humiliated but supremely glorified by the fact that in faith he experiences this separation and consecration ; that in faith he acquires a Lord and comes to stand in this new and strange light. Again, he would not have acquired this Lord, or come to stand in this light, if his creatureliness had not been revealed by faith, if in faith he had not become alert, one who sees accurately, and thinks keenly, and wills with decision, and acts with knowledge and energy. How could his faith be the victory if it were not also and at all points the warfare, if he were not willing to wage this warfare as a free man, enlisting and participating in it not with more, but certainly not with less, than the whole man ? How could he believe from the heart, and be comforted and established in his heart by faith, if his whole being—for the heart is the whole man—were not thereby made free to live freely ? Faith, then, must always consist in this summoning of the whole heart and soul and mind and strength of man. The Christian is always the man who is challenged in this sense.

From all that we have said, it will be immediately apparent that faith as such contains within itself obedience. The very essence of Christian obedience is subjection by emancipation, emancipation by subjection. And is not this the essence of all obedience ? But does not all other obedience suffer because of its vacillation between subjection to tyranny and emancipation to anarchy ? In Christian faith obedience occurs without being enmeshed in this unholy tension. As included in Christian faith, on both sides it is a critical and genuine obedience. In faith as trust in Jesus Christ, and by implication as trust in the fatherly rule of God in world-occurrence, obedience is not merely necessarily included in it, but it is necessarily included in this genuine and critical form. Faith lives by the Word. The Christian lives by his faith in hearing the Word, but only in really hearing it, only in living by hearing it, only in being obedient to it. Trusting the Word means entrusting himself to it, surrendering himself to its keeping, and therefore to its direction. He would not be trusting it if he did not do this. And if he did not trust it, he would not really believe. And then it would not be at all surprising if what he regarded as his trust in the Word of God were not justified by his life within world-occurrence ; if he failed to make the second uprising and outreaching movement of faith ; if he were not capable of the Nevertheless at the place where God is not revealed but hidden. If he really believes the Word, if he really trusts in it, then he has surrendered himself to its direction, and in so doing he has already become obedient, and genuinely so.

In the same way faith includes within itself prayer. Christian prayer means thanksgiving and praise, then confession and intercession, and then again thanksgiving and praise : all directed towards God ; all offered to Him ; all spread out before Him ; all commended to Him with absolutely empty hands ; all with the intention of committing oneself wholly and utterly to Him. Such prayer is included in faith. Faith itself cannot be without prayer, for, as we have already maintained, faith is neither a possession which is transferred to the Christian from without, nor is it a conviction which he has reached from within, but it is an act which is creaturely by nature, which fulfils itself in those two movements, but the fulfilment of which is anything but self-evident, needing the awakening of man by the Word of God. Therefore it is inevitable that in faith, in the fulfilment of this act, God is always a surprise to man, and man a surprise to himself. Man stands amazed before the divine goodness which gives him the freedom for this act. And he stands amazed before all that it shows him—the fatherhood of God, his own sonship, and the right of sonship in the house of the Father as the Father confers it and he himself receives it. It is in this inevitable surprise that the faith of a Christian as such is also prayer—the prayer of thanksgiving and praise. Again, he stands amazed before the unmerited gift that he himself is actually enabled to believe, to believe this. And he can never understand how it is that he is able to do so, to receive this unmerited gift. Indeed, the more freely he can believe, and the more fully he receives in faith, the more he is conscious of his own inability and unworthiness, his own incapacity. It is in this surprise that his faith as such is prayer—the prayer of penitence and confession of penitence towards the great God who has done such things towards man, and still does so. And again, the Christian stands amazed before the nearness of God, and the superabundant wealth of all those things which call him to faith, and which as the gift of God are calculated to appease his hunger, to cover his nakedness, to make good his deficiencies. He stands amazed at the fact that he has only to ask and to knock, like a child at the nearby and trusted door behind which the Father dwells, and he can believe and live again in faith in the participation in Jesus Christ, and then in the divine providence and universal lordship. And again, it is in this surprise that the faith of the Christian as such is prayer—the prayer of the petition and intercession in which faith ventures to ask about the God who is so near to it and about his benefits which are so near to it, and when it is heard, again receives comfort and blessing, and above all is again given the freedom to be real faith, thus again turning to praise and thanksgiving. This faith would obviously not be the Christian faith if at its deepest level it were not this great surprise in which in and with the two other movements inwards and outwards—and the step from the one sphere to the other is unheard of in its Whence ? and Whither ?—man did not make of himself the movement of prayer, which is a pure movement upwards. For what is this movement in which the Christian can proceed so absolutely from God if in every respect, and therefore in all the inward possibilities of prayer, it does not of itself lead back to God, so that each individual act of faith is at bottom always an act of prayer ?

So much for faith both in itself and in its relation to obedience and prayer. Faith constitutes the Christian attitude. To that extent it is the first form, and we shall have to consider it together with the two others, at which we have already cast a preliminary glance. The Christian believes, and in relation to the divine providence this gives him the knowledge without which all thinking and utterance on the subject is futile. In faith, the Christian has knowledge of the divine providence.

2. Obedience is the doing of the Word of God, the alert response in which the Christian justifies it against himself, against all men, against the whole world, and in which the Christian himself is justified. For the justification of man consists in his having and using the freedom to justify the Word of God. This is what is demanded by the Word of God ; this is what it claims man for. And man hears it—really

hears it—not merely by accepting it as the imparting of information, but by surrendering to and satisfying its claim. In this respect, the activity of the Christian is obedience, the second form of the Christian attitude, and one which again in its own way includes the whole. In believing, a man becomes a Christian ; in obeying, he is a Christian. In doing what he has to do as a man who in Jesus Christ has come to know God as his Father and himself as a child of God, the Christian is the creature which not merely contemplates the work of the divine providence and lordship from without, but co-operates in it from within. What we have particularly to emphasise in this connexion is that the Christian attitude to the divine work does not consist merely in looking at it, but in co-operating with it. The same really has to be said of both faith and prayer. But this is the special feature of the whole Christian attitude which we have to note and describe when we speak of its character as obedience.

In the present context we cannot fully expound the question of Christian obedience : Christian works ; active Christian righteousness ; the Christian life in sanctification. What we can do is to draw two lines of demarcation on the two different sides.

On the one side, Christian obedience is certainly not an achievement which gives the Christain a claim or merit, which enables him to attain or keep for himself a position of advantage in man's relationship to the judgment and promise and assistance of God. And on the other side, Christian obedience is certainly not an achievement which can be either chosen or avoided ; something which he may equally well achieve or not achieve. As opposed to this second view, it is the *obligatorium* under which the Christian is placed by the very thing which makes him a Christian, the necessary content of being as a Christian. But in opposition to the first view, it is so because it is only the fulfilment of a direct obligation, not related to any claim and not carrying with it any distinction for the one who discharges it. It is the direct expression and manifestation of a life for which he will have no claim to thanks and for which he least of all will expect either gratitude or reward.

When the Son of God, who was sent by the Father, does the Father's will on earth, and fulfils it to the end, what advantage or reward or honour does He get because of it ? He does the will of the Father simply because He is the Son. To be sure, He does do it, and He has no choice not to do it. He does it necessarily. He would not be the Son of God if He did not do it. This is the great pattern of Christian obedience as we have to consider and understand it according to this twofold demarcation.

Again, on the one side Christian obedience is certainly not under an outward law. It is not in any sense the fulfilment of a written or unwritten code. It has nothing whatever to do with the maintaining of Christian standards or the setting forth of a Christian way of life.

For it comes from the Holy Spirit, who is the Christian's only Master. But on the other side, because it does come from the Holy Spirit, it is the very antithesis of human whims and caprices, of free-lance fancies and opinions, of conduct based only on sentiment or resentment. For the Holy Spirit rules the Christian, in a conflict in which the Christian's own spirit must always give in and be beaten. The Holy Spirit speaks by the Word of God, binding the Christian to its commands and directions. And ultimately He is the Spirit who is given not as the Spirit of the individual but as the Spirit of the whole community. He leads the Christian in the fellowship of this community, and He orders his actions to obedience within the framework of this fellowship and its mission and service. Yet while we have to remember this on the one side, on the other we have to remember, too, that in His divine authority, on His own basis, and within the limits of His own nature, the Spirit is the free Spirit of God, moving where He Himself wills, demanding of each individual his own individual obedience, demanding of each individual an obedience which is always new, and leading the community as such into new situations and laying upon it new tasks. Therefore there cannot really be any external statutes by which Christian obedience may ever be defined or determined absolutely.

Once again the divine pattern must be normative on both sides. In His procession from the Father and the Son, the Spirit is a particular Spirit, the Holy Spirit. He is always a Spirit of love and peace and order, but now He is the Spirit of the love and peace and order which according to the eternal mystery of the unity of Father and Son will always be a mystery in the ways and works of the Spirit in the created order, and therefore in Christian existence. The Spirit can never be observed or imprisoned by the creature, and therefore by the Christian, but in all His majesty He will always be a free Spirit and therefore the Holy Spirit.

It is in the obedience which has this basis that the Christian participates in the divine providence and universal lordship. But first we have to consider this obedience in the direct form in which it is simply his participation in Jesus Christ ; in the kingdom of the grace which is revealed and active in Him. The Christian is used in this kingdom. When he is incorporated into this kingdom he is enlisted for duty and service. He is given a commission. He is directed to a particular path. That he himself should be delivered and saved is not the final meaning of the grace shown to him in Jesus Christ, or the final aim of the Christian life. He is delivered and saved as he acquires a Lord and a task. He is delivered and saved to the glory of God and for co-operation in the execution of the kingdom which God has purposed. He is bound to this Lord and established for the sake of this Lord. And it is because his obedience is obedience to this Lord that at one and the same time it is so necessary and so voluntary, so bound and so free. The fact that it proceeds from the Holy Spirit means concretely that it is one of the movements in which the lordship of Jesus Christ as the Head of His community is expressed and reflected. The Christian is a member of this community, and therefore his activity is one of the movements which Jesus Christ its Head induces in His body and its members. Christian obedience is therefore the submission of the individual Christian, as a member, to the directions given by Jesus Christ to His community. It is following Jesus. And this means that the obedience of the Christian begins at the cross of Christ where it is decided what man is to be as he belongs not to himself or to an alien power but to God, and what the world is to be as it is not lost to him but loved by Him even in its lost condition. The individual and the world as a whole really begins there. But the Christian who knows what really happened there does what has to be done now that the world as a whole and the individual come from there. As we said at the outset, he justifies the Word of God. This means concretely that he justifies the decision made in Jesus Christ, in the death of Jesus Christ. He takes his stand on this decision. He acts as it demands. This is his obedience. And he is constrained to it by the Holy Spirit, who seeing that he is a member of the community, seeing that he is enabled to believe, indwells and controls him. This is the meaning of the personal sanctification and discipline and purpose to which he is made subject. And this is also the meaning of his incorporation into the life and service of the community and his responsibility for its inward development and outward mission.

But from the first movement of obedience there spontaneously arises a second, which is again an uprising and outstretching movement. The Lord of the community, who as such is the personal Lord of the Christian, is also the Lord of world-occurrence generally, in which the Christian participates at every step, not passively only, but at his own time and place and in his own way actively as well. In the one case the Lord is revealed, in the other He is hidden. But in the latter case no less than the former He is the Lord. Therefore in the latter case no less than the former the Christian can be obedient to Him. Hence the wider sphere of world-occurrence generally is not a sphere in which the Christian is any the less claimed, or not claimed at all by Jesus Christ. In this sphere, too, he has to respect and attest the decision which was made in the death of Jesus Christ, and to justify it by his conduct. It was a decision which was made for all men and for the whole world, and therefore in the case of the Christian for the totality of his being in all its dimensions. This means that he is claimed not only in the religious sphere but also in the secular ; not only in the spiritual but also in the physical ; not only in the ecclesiastical, but also in the political and economic and academic and aesthetic. Here, too, the difference between the two movements is clear. We might say that the one is centripetal and the other centrifugal, or the one direct and the other indirect, or the one basic and the other deduced, or the one original and the other the copy. But here, too, our first task is to see that they belong together, and to see how they belong together ; to see that Christian obedience consists in a single step from the one to the other, so that the Christian can never be engaged exclusively in either the one or the other. The distinctness of the two movements of obedience is conditioned by the fact that God, Jesus Christ, as the Lord of creaturely occurrence, is revealed to him in the one, in the Christian community and his personal life as a member of it, but hidden from him in the other, in world-events generally. But the homogeneity of the two movements is conditioned by the fact that in both cases it is the same Lord and the same claim is made upon the Christian. This means that there is no place for dualism, and that from the very first it is impossible either to neglect or to omit the second form of Christian obedience.

In this context our concern is with the second form, in which consciously or unconsciously, voluntarily or involuntarily, directly or indirectly, on a small scale or a great, the Christian does actually participate in the course and process of creaturely and universal occurrence as a whole. Our concern is with the second form in which the Christian is called obediently to participate in the lordship of God in this more general sphere, and therefore—and this is the real problem of obedience—to participate in it actively, justifying by his conduct that which God Himself is doing in this sphere. Now it is clear that only in a direct participation in Jesus Christ, only in discipleship, only in the life of obedience as a member of His community, is the Christian equipped to do this. At this former point he has to learn to know what will be the bearing of his subjection to the will of God at the latter. At this former point he has to become so familiar with the life and authority of the Holy Spirit in the Word of God as to be able at least in some measure to differentiate Him from all other spirits at the latter. At this former point he has to accustom himself to obedience to Him, and exercise himself in this obedience. Any gap in his development, his schooling in active righteousness, in this inward sphere will necessarily avenge itself at once in a refusal to exercise it in the outward. And the smallest faithfulness at this point will be confirmed a hundredfold at that. But it is, of course, with the equipment that he receives at this point that he must manage and succeed at that. In that sphere, in world-occurrence generally, he will be confronted with all kinds of clear or less clear ordinances and regulations, with all kinds of general rules which interfere with his actions, with all kinds of generally or fairly generally recognised principles which demand both his respect and on sufficiently concrete grounds his compliance. But in that sphere he will not encounter the Holy Spirit in the Word of God. He will not encounter any absolutely binding directions, any divine commands which he can and must observe unconditionally as one who knows both the utter freedom of the subject and the utter subjection of the free man. He will not encounter anything which can be compared even remotely in its unequivocal authority with the will of God as it is actualised and revealed in Jesus Christ. In this respect, he will never find solid ground in that sphere. It is only of the Holy Spirit whom he has received and by whom he is controlled that he is governed at all and not carried one way by this current and another by that like a ship without engine or rudder. It is only of the Holy Spirit that he can take heed when he hears His orders. It is only of the Holy Spirit that he can learn to understand situations, to recognise opportunities, to choose possibilities and to distinguish them from impossibilities. The situations and opportunities and possibilities and impossibilities of the world-process with which he is called upon to wrestle do not as such contain within themselves or proclaim any divine and infallible Word. In the midst of them he can direct his path only with a provisional certainty. It is only the Holy Spirit who can command him, giving the orders and prohibitions which he must and can obey. It is only the Holy Spirit who can really guide him. It is only the Holy Spirit who can give him a good conscience both before and after his actions. It is only the Holy Spirit who can so bind him to his path that he is really bound, and so liberate him that he can tread this path in real freedom. It is only the Holy Spirit who can give him the light for right decisions and the power to make them. It is only the Holy Spirit : but that is to say, it is only the pure and unbroken Word of God accompanying him where God Himself is hidden ; or, from the standpoint of his own attitude, it is only the obedience which he has learned in the school of Jesus Christ and brought out from that school, and to which he can remain faithful in all his decisions. Whether he actually is obedient is measured by the extent to which his obedience is this obedience. It may conform to all the other ordinances and regulations and principles and claims with which he is confronted, or it may be in opposition to them, in a completely isolated opposition to them, but at any rate it is not obedience to other lords, but to the Lord who has at this point the only claim to his obedience because He is the only true Lord. And in relation to the divine providence and governance in world-events, what he does in this obedience is the active righteousness, the good work of the Christian, his life and activity in sanctification.

The Christian actually achieves this obedience. We do not overestimate him when we say that. We naturally reckon with the fact that what he does is only more or less obedience—usually less. Even here there are really substantial differences between an enlightened and an unenlightened obedience, between an obedience which is clearly directed in its origin and one which is not, between an obedience which is bold and one which is timid, between an obedience which is pure and one which is obscure. But however substantial these differences may be, they are only side-issues compared with the question whether it is a real or only an apparent obedience. And whatever else we may have to say about it or against it or for it, this question is decided by whether as a participation in Jesus Christ this obedience is founded and induced by the Holy Spirit, the wisdom and power of the Word of the one true Lord. We may grant that in the actions of a Christian many other lords may constantly exercise dominion side by side with the one who is really Lord. If only the Christian is not entirely unspiritual! If only he is not a complete stranger in the school of Christ! A little that is spiritual can make its way against much that is unspiritual. A little real obedience—even with all the scandal that there is so little of it—can counter-balance and make good a great deal of disobedience. If only it is there in some degree and in some form, then with all its ambiguity and brokenness we can say of the conduct of a Christian that in his decisions and activity, in what he does and accomplishes, he becomes and is a real factor, an active element in the hidden governance of God, along the positive line of this hidden governance. This fact is not altered in the slightest by his being under the lordship of God, by the creatureliness of his conduct. Grasping at the divine sceptre is the very last thing that the Christian will attempt if he is living in obedience. With all other creatures he is still in the dust before God, and the more real his obedience, the more he will be conscious of the fact. But it is still the case that to the small extent that he is obedient, at specific points and in specific ways he is posited and used in the service of the divine lordship, in the fulfilment of the positive divine will. On earth God has in every age elected and created and preserved His community as the people of His own beloved Son, willing both to have and to rule them as His peculiar possession within all other occurrence. And in the last analysis He does not do this in vain. It is not an indifferent matter or an idle pastime that by the Holy Spirit of His Word He establishes their existence as individual members of the community, and determines their decisions and activities. The particular purpose of God rules in all these happenings according to the particularity of the happenings. His community has its commission, and in this community there are commissions for the individual members. And it is in the execution of these commissions that in the midst of world-occurrence Christians are compelled to obedience; that by the commands and prohibitions of the Holy Spirit of the Word of God they are led to recognise and distinguish between the various situations and opportunities and possibilities and impossibilities, selecting some and rejecting others; that they are empowered and consecrated to an active righteousness, to good works in this world. All this is not really for their own satisfaction or profit, or to supply here and there a pious flourish at the wonderful conjunction of events. In the midst of world-events, in all the necessity and obligatoriness, the constraint and freedom of their obedience, in all the poverty of its execution, in all the shame which they heap upon themselves and their Lord, Christians are the children of God, and as such they are the true and proper servants of God, not hired servants, employees, but natural servants, by whose activity God wills at a specific time and place to accomplish something specific in the context of His own activity; something which will attest His kingdom, or recall the revelation which He has already given, or declare this revelation as it has still to be completed. It is as these creaturely acts of attestation, recollection and declaration take place within world-occurrence that the positive will of God is done in this sphere. And as the Christian is obedient, and to the extent that he is obedient, he is used to this end, and is in the service of the will, the positive will of God, and of the divine providence and world-governance. For this to be the case, it is not necessary that he himself should sit in the counsel of God. It is not necessary that he should understand the context, the pragmatics, of the will of God, even as it concerns a single week, let alone years and centuries. It is not required of him, and he himself does not need, to know the great line of the divine purpose for the kingdom, or to be able to assign as it were to himself and his activity their function in the strategic plan of the divine world-governance. He can and indeed he must leave all these things to God. All that he has to do is to listen. But as he does listen, and to the extent that he does, he has his function in the divine world-strategy, doing at some point the duty which is allotted to him as a soldier and servant. Why he has to do it, what he accomplishes or does not accomplish by it, why he was used and posited in this service, he will one day learn when a great light is shed on all things. But all that concerns him here and now is that his work is not really in vain, that he is in this service, and that he has his duty to do, whether he does it well or ill. He is always a very unimportant creature with other creatures. From the point from which he and all other members of the community may come he is referred only to the Holy Spirit in the Word of God. He is a modest creature, and a modest member of the people of God. But as such he is directed to this place; he is posited and used in it; he is given his own particular commission at this point in world-occurrence; he is equipped for it in his own particular way. All that is required of him and all that he needs is faithfulness. And as in some measure and form he is faithful, he has a part—and in all its lowliness a glorious and active part— in the divine providence and world-governance.

Looking back, we can now repeat that the demarcations which we made at the beginning of the discussion were not superfluous. The obedience of the Christian is wholly necessary, but it can never be an acquisition; and, while in this obedience the Christian is not under any statute, he is subject to the strictest authority.

Christian obedience is not an acquisition but a free achievement. It can never look for thanks or merit or reward because in itself it proceeds from what is the highest and at bottom the only acquisition that man can ever know : from the election and call which constitutes a Christian ; from participation in Jesus Christ ; from the gift and operation of the Holy Spirit. The Christian can obey only as he comes from the acquisition which has accrued to him, not as he seeks some further acquisition. He thanks God for the fact that he is a Christian, but he cannot expect any thanks for it. He obeys as God has made Himself meritorious on His behalf—what further merit is to be expected ? He has his reward in the fact that he is a Christian, and that as such he can obey. This reward, which precedes and follows all his own achievement, is now hidden and will one day be revealed. But the man who participates in it has no time to look for any other, because all his time is taken up in simply obeying on the basis of the reward already received in secret. The obedience which he has to exercise in the inward and practise in the outward sphere would obviously be null and void if he could and did maintain it in another way. But to say this is to say already that its free achievement is also necessary. Real obedience has passed the point where there is a possible choice of disobedience. Christian obedience is real obedience because in it this choice was excluded at the source. From the very first it consists in the recognition that God is justified : justified in the incomprehensible mercy of His movement towards man ; justified in His claim upon man ; justified in His will to determine and direct him by the Holy Spirit in His Word. In the light of this recognition the Christian can do no other. He achieves obedience knowing that it has to be achieved. If it were otherwise, if he could disobey, he would *ipso facto* be denying his own origin and being ; the thanks which God can claim for the fact that he is there at all ; the merit which God has gained for him ; the reward which he has already received from God. He is under a personal obligation to God : personal, for this is what makes his obedience a free achievement ; and an obligation, for this is what makes it a necessary one.

And now, to take up the second demarcation, Christian obedience is not under any statute, but takes place under the sole authority of the Holy Spirit in the Word of God, because as real obedience it has only one Lord, because all ordinances and regulations and rules and principles and claims which are encountered by it in the world-process lack the unconditional majesty and validity which might make respect for them a real and genuine obedience. Authorities of this kind can enslave and liberate man only in appearance. And it is a dangerous error if we believe that we have to render them an absolute reverence or compliance. Their majesty and validity are really conditioned, that is, they are measured by the supremacy of the one true Lord, and their recognition or non-recognition is decided by His sentence. If the Christian does recognise them, it is for the sake of this one Lord, because this Lord orders him to recognise them within their own limits. Often enough it can and will happen that in obedience to the same Lord he will not grant them this recognition but will have to oppose that which they enjoin. He would not be obedient to the one true Lord if he were not prepared to do this. He remains free either way, but in this freedom he is under real authority. Having the sovereign choice either to comply or not to comply, as a child and also a servant (or better, a slave) of the heavenly Father, he is wholly at the disposal of the will of his Father ; he is merely an executive instrument ; he is simply caught up in the fulfilment of the function allotted to him. In this very freedom he no longer asks : Why should I• do this ? What will be the outcome of it ? What do I stand to gain by it ? He no longer tries to sit in the counsel of God. He no longer wants to be master and servant at one and the same time. If this were what he wanted, it would be a sure sign that he has not completely escaped the dominion of false gods and their decrees, that he has not yet entered the sphere of true obedience. It is only submission at this point which makes him a free man ; his own whims and caprices can only unfit him to be so. And as a free man, he has to make the most definite submission and observe the strictest discipline.

In this respect, too, we have to bear in mind the unity of the Christian and therefore the relationship of Christian obedience to Christian faith and Christian prayer. In obedience as we have described it faith is necessarily included. We have seen already that as the work of God to man and man's own work faith is translated into an event, an action, a real human existence, only in virtue of the fact that it contains within it obedience, that faith itself is at root an act of obedience. It is only too true that while faith alone is the basis of the Christian's standing, yet without works, without its translation in obedience into an event or action, it would be dead. But in the case of obedience, too, everything depends upon the fact that it contains within it faith. Only as the Christian believes does he participate in Jesus Christ and the community of Jesus Christ, and therefore in the divine providence and lordship in world-occurrence. Only as the Christian believes is it true that he begins his whole life at the cross of Jesus, where the decision of the love of God for him and for the whole world was made. Only as the Christian believes is he summoned to justify the will of God in the one sphere and also in the other. It is as he is able to believe that he enters the school of obedience to which he can then be true and upon which he can bring honour in the realm of creaturely occurrence generally. The command and the power to do this, and the courage to dare it, are the command and power and courage of faith, without which the whole undertaking would simply be a gamble leading inevitably to failure and collapse. It needs a particular confidence to make this venture ; and this confidence is quite simply the confidence that Jesus Christ is Lord of all, and that it is His will that we have always to consult and His interests that we have always to represent. It is not at all self-evident that Jesus Christ is this, that no other lords can dispute His title, that no fate or chance or laws or principles can vie with Him or permit the Christian to turn to anyone else or to meet any other commands but His. To say this, we have continually to utter that Nevertheless, not merely with heart and mouth, but also in deed. To say this, we have always to venture that run and make that leap in a sphere where everything seems to be obscure and where—apart from what the Christian brings with him from this school—it remains always equivocal and uncertain. In this sphere the Christian finds himself in the sphere of the hidden God. He needs a confidence that the one light of revelation will give light and prove reliable even where apart from it there is no light. He needs a confidence which endures, a confidence which renews itself, a confidence which in a sense is new every morning. For the situations in which the Christian has to obey are many, and are constantly changing, and make necessary new insights and new decisions in which he can hardly do other than begin again and again at the beginning. Above all, he needs a confidence to be always alert and ready for such beginnings. Even the little obedience that the Christian can always bring is in fact surrounded by so much of his own weakness and folly and even wickedness, by so much shame, that he has good reason constantly to grow weary of himself, to despair of himself, to abandon himself as utterly unworthy and unfitted to execute his commission, and even to relinquish this commission. In all this he would be utterly lost if it were not for the fact that he is upheld by the assurance that for him, too, there is divine mercy, that he, too, will be forgiven, and that because of this he cannot be weary. He needs Jesus Christ to forbid him to despair of self. He needs to have it impressed upon him that no severity of judgment under which he may see himself authorises him to surrender instead of fulfilling (well or ill, with good report or bad) the function which has been allotted to him in the divine plan. For God in His grace and also with His claim is all the closer to him the more clearly he sees with what fulness he is under the divine judgment. But the confidence which he needs is at all points the confidence of faith, without which there can be no Christian obedience. And to this we must add that the authoritarian Commander and Leader to whom the obedience of a Christian is due is the Holy Spirit and none other. Upon this depends the fact that it is an achievement which is both free and also necessary, which is completely free from all regulations and for that very reason completely under discipline. But there are so many spirits. Above all, there is the spirit of the Christian himself, to which we have to attribute far too great a readiness to substitute itself for the Holy Spirit, and which can far too easily lead the Christian into enterprises which have really nothing to do with obedience and in which he will fulfil anything but the purposes of the kingdom of God and be anything but a dutiful servant of the Lord. Advisedly, then, we have referred again and again to the Holy Spirit of the Word of God. This would imply that the Holy Spirit is not an indefinite or inarticulate spirit, not a vague nor even a vigorous compulsion this way and that, the understanding of which is finally left to the conceits and caprices of the Christian himself. The Holy Spirit is holy in the fact that He does not come from us but to us, and that He does not come to us from our own environment but from above. The Holy Spirit is the wisdom and power of the Word of God. And so Christian obedience differs from an uncontrollable compulsion in the fact that following the guidance of the Spirit means obedience to the Word of God. But this brings us back again to the source of the whole Christian attitude in faith. For we have defined Christian faith as a knowledge and acknowledgment of the Word of God as a Word spoken by God and to us. The Word of God—and in this it is obviously different from all other words—is Jesus Christ Himself in His own work and revelation. The obedience of the Christian means that he gives himself to this specific Word and to the wisdom and power and guidance of this Word. He does not listen to the voices and promptings either of his own heart or of that of others, but only to what the Word itself says, and to what it says to him here and now. But this means that he must return constantly to his faith, to the place where he personally is bound by the Word and made free by it to be truly obedient. If he does not do this he will inevitably go astray at every slightest step. And the Holy Spirit whom he obeys outwardly will be a sinister figure under whose guidance he can only do harm to himself and others, and certainly fail to fulfil the task with which he has been entrusted. The power of his obedience can be only the power of the confidence in which he gives himself afresh to the protection of the Word of God and in which he will continue afresh under this protection. In the power of this confidence, and therefore in the power of faith, but not otherwise, he will be a man constrained by the Holy Spirit, and therefore an obedient man.

And now we must consider the relationship of obedience to prayer. That Christian obedience includes prayer means first that prayer is the most intimate and effective form of Christian action. All other work comes far behind, and it is Christian work, active Christian righteousness, the doing of the will of God, the fulfilling of the function allotted to the Christian in the discipleship of Jesus Christ and the service and execution of the divine purpose of the kingdom, only to the extent that it derives from prayer, and that it has in prayer its true and original form. When the Christian wishes to act obediently, what else can he do but that which he does in prayer : render to God praise and thanksgiving ; spread himself before God in his weakness and sin ; reach out to Him with all that impels him ; commend himself to Him who is his only help ; and again, and this time truly, render to Him praise and thanksgiving. This is Christian obedience *in nuce.* In it there takes place the one thing necessary, the one thing that is demanded of the Christian, the one service that is required of him. For everything else is included in this one thing. It is perfectly true, within limits, that prayer is the renewing and inward empowering of the Christian, a breathing of the soul, and so forth. But it must not be forgotten that prayer is also the true and proper work of the Christian. And the greatest Christian business is only idleness if this true and proper work is not done ; while again, if outward appearances are not deceptive, the most active workers and thinkers and fighters in the divine service in this world have at the same time, and manifestly, been the most active in prayer, and obviously they have not regarded this activity as a waste of time. And on this point we have also to say that the problem of obedience, like that of the permission and necessity of faith, sets the Christian at a place where if his willing and doing is genuine, if it proceeds from faith, it must pass over into this particular form of willing and doing, passing over into prayer, ending and also beginning afresh in prayer. The Christian himself can never simply presuppose that he has the light and the power for genuine obedience. And the faith in which alone he can be obedient is not something which is so readily accessible that he has only to give himself a jolt and he will believe afresh, and in this faith be obedient afresh. In faith, he is dealing directly with God Himself in His freedom and majesty. But in prayer he presents himself to God, the God whom he can always avoid in his activity, but to whom he must always present himself if he is to have a genuine and effective faith and therefore to be capable of a bold and effective obedience. In prayer, he makes use of the freedom to answer the Father who has addressed him, or, to put it in another way, to go to meet the Father from whose goodness he proceeds, or, to put it in yet another way, to give direct and natural expression to his great surprise that God is his Father and that he is the child of God. In all its forms prayer is this answering, this going to meet, this direct expression of the truth of the situation in which the Christian finds himself as a Christian. When he prays, he puts himself in the position in which faith and obedience can always begin again at the beginning. As this primitive movement, prayer, which is the basis of all other activity, is included in obedience. It is itself the act of obedience *par excellence*, the act of obedience from which all other acts must spring.

3. Prayer has just been described as a primitive movement. Indeed, in this third form of the Christian attitude we are dealing with the simple and basic form of the first two. Prayer is the primary thing in faith as well as obedience. Basically, faith is prayer, and obedience too is prayer. Yet we have still to distinguish a third form, and to this form we must now give more specific consideration. For we shall not do justice to the essence of prayer in this context if we simply

think of it as included in faith and obedience as the basic form of both.

When we touched upon it earlier we described it as the sequence of praise and thanksgiving, confession and penitence, petition and intercession, and again praise and thanksgiving—all side by side with or following one another as seen from a distance. This description was not incorrect, but it is insufficient. What is lacking when we think of prayer in this way is a centre ; something which makes it prayer as opposed to faith and obedience. On this view, it could easily merge into those first forms of the Christian attitude. But prayer has and is a form of its own, a form which as such includes within it the other two just as it is included within them. The sequence of acts which we provisionally described as prayer has in fact a centre, one specific act which constitutes the whole, from which all the rest proceeds and to which it returns, from which alone it receives its meaning and power.

To do justice to what takes place in Christian prayer we must not try to bring it under the one denominator of praise and thanksgiving, or more comprehensively, worship. This is a possibility which might well have suggested itself already from the fact that we deduced prayer from the great surprise which is also the source of faith and obedience ; the great surprise of the Christian in the situation in which he finds himself placed by the Word of God and in which he can be a Christian. From this surprise there results very simply a worship of the One who has made this situation and who determines and controls it as the Lord ; a humble astonishment at the mystery of it ; a praising and an honouring and magnifying of God because He has turned and revealed Himself to man in His Word, and because of the form in which He has done so ; a prostration before His incommensurable greatness ; a thankfulness for His incomprehensible favour ; a praising of His glory and unmerited goodness. But the very situation which the Word of God has made for the Christian, and therefore the surprise which it evokes, and therefore the worship of God which results, have all a definite direction and colour, a distinctive Whence ? and Whither ?, which will prevent us from stopping at this point and seeking here the very essence of prayer. The Christian situation is not the abstract one of that which is great encountering that which is small, of that which is exalted encountering that which is lowly, of that which is holy encountering that which is defiled, of majesty encountering creatureliness. It is this ; but it is it in a very concrete form. And that is what distinguishes our surprise in this particular situation from the general surprise which might easily be nothing more than idle gaping. That is what distinguishes Christian worship from a general glancing upwards, from mere reverence at the presence of the numinous, which in a form which is more religious than Christian and more aesthetic than religious might easily be nothing more than the sterile reverence of rapture or terror. To do justice to the specific element in Christian worship we must not try to understand prayer systematically, as it were, as worship, as praise and thanksgiving. This element can never be lacking. And in practice prayer does both begin and end at this point. But it is not at this point that we shall understand the factual order and essence of prayer.

Again, to do justice to prayer we must try not to bring it under the one denominator of confession or penitence. The Christian's surprise at his situation does have this element or aspect. It is a knowledge and acknowledgment of the judgment under which he stands. Therefore Christian prayer is inevitably a confession of his own weakness and inability and unworthiness, of the whole lost condition in which he is discovered in the sight of God. It is an indication that his utterly empty hands are the only offering which he can bring before God and spread out before Him. To pray in the Christian sense means fully and unreservedly to admit and confess to God all our wretchedness. To pray in the Christian sense means to renounce all illusions about ourselves, and openly to admit to ourselves our utter need. The man who will not do this will never pray. The Pharisee in the temple had a heart which seemed to be full of praise and thanksgiving, but he did not do this and therefore he did not pray. We must necessarily pass through this humiliation if our worship of God is not to be self-deception and pretence before God. But again, we must not try to understand prayer at this point. The Christian situation is not the abstract one of the lowliness of man before God, although this forms part of it. Nor is the Christian situation the abstract one of man's horror of himself, although this is included within it. Christian prayer, therefore, is not exhausted by this self-humiliation of man before God. This act must not be lacking in it, but even in this act it has a particular character, a particular direction and purpose, in which it is distinct from a general wretchedness which might be merely pitiable, or from a general self-abasement which might be only that of lassitude or despair or scepticism. The way of prayer does, of course, lead us to this impasse. Prayer does include penitence. But there is no point in trying to understand the essence of prayer in the light of this fact. The short prayer of the publican in the temple was natually a prayer of penitence, but in its decisive content it was something more, and something different.

There remains prayer as petition. And the question arises whether worship and penitence and petition (the centre of all prayer not being found in the latter) are not equally important and urgent and characteristic in the equality in which we have provisionally considered them ; whether they do not form a sequence, the end of which always brings us back again to the beginning. In practice this may well be so. But in substance it is not so. In all languages the word prayer is itself against it. For it speaks only of petition as the constitutive element in what takes place in prayer. It shows us that while prayer is a matter of worship and penitence, it is not so in the first instance.   In the first instance, it is an asking, a seeking and a knocking directed towards God ; a wishing, a desiring and a requesting presented to God.   And the actuality of prayer is decidedly against not merely a precedence of the other two elements but even their equality with petition.   The man who really prays comes to God and approaches and speaks to Him because he seeks something of God, because he desires and expects something, because he hopes to receive something which he needs, something which he does not hope to receive from anyone else, but does definitely hope to receive from God.   He cannot come before God with his petition without also worshipping God, without giving Him praise and thanksgiving, and without spreading out before Him his own wretchedness.   But it is the fact that he comes before God with his petition which makes him a praying man.   Other theories of prayer may be richly and profoundly thought out and may sound very well, but they all suffer from a certain artificiality because they miss this simple and concrete fact, losing themselves in heights and depths where there is no place for the man who really prays, who is simply making a request.   But the first and decisive argument against the subordination or equality of petition is the actual text of the Lord's Prayer, the substance of which is quite clearly and simply a string of petitions, pure petitions, in which the elements of worship and penitence have, of course, their place, which begin and end with worship, but which in themselves and as such are neither adoration nor confession, but simply petition.   If we are to understand the essence of prayer, we may well be asked to follow the Lord's Prayer.   And in the present context, in our survey of the divine providence and universal lordship and the Christian attitude to it, it is essential that we should speak of prayer in detail, because in the first instance—and this controls and includes everything else—prayer, or praying, is simply asking.

And now let us try to understand materially what it is that is primarily and properly surprising in the Christian situation.   It is not simply that God is so great and holy and rich, nor is it simply that in comparison man is so small and unworthy and poor.   Both these things are unmistakeably clear and surprising to the Christian, but they are only the complement to that which is primarily and properly surprising—that by His Word this great and holy and rich God draws so near to the man who is so small and unworthy and poor ; so near, indeed, that in perceiving Him man can only worship, and in perceiving himself he can only abandon himself ; but above all, so near with the nearness of Father and child that in face of Him man now finds himself in the nearness of child and Father.   At bottom, it is this nearness which surprises him, and it is from this that there derive all other things which surprise him both in the heights above and the depths below.   This, and this alone, is the specifically Christian element in the

Christian situation. This is the content of the Word of God by which the Christian finds himself placed in this particular situation. This is the content of the revelation of God in Jesus Christ whose attestation is the task of the Christian community and in the knowledge and acknowledgment of which the Christian is a Christian, a member of this community, participating in its faith and sharing the responsibility for its service in the world. It was for the direct nearness between God and man as between Father and child, and child and Father, that Jesus Christ was born a man and crucified. And this nearness is the light of His resurrection. And when the Christian prays, he does what he has to do in answer to the Word and work of the Son of God. He makes the first available use of the freedom which is given to him by the amazing fact created in Jesus Christ. But this first answer certainly does not consist of thinking high thoughts about the glory of God and deep thoughts about his own unworthiness, and then making the movements which correspond to these thoughts. It consists in simply turning to the God who has drawn so near to him, and to whom he himself has been brought so near, with the intention that God should give to him, and that he should receive from God, all that is necessary to his situation ; that he should receive from Him that which, as he clearly perceives in this situation, only God can really give to him. The freedom of his situation is that he sees the majesty of God, that he also sees himself and what he lacks and what is against him, but that he does not need to be in any way anxious about these things. He does not need to be afraid to draw near to God so that he who is so small and unworthy and poor may receive from Him something, yes much, yes everything. Nor does he need to be afraid to lift up himself to tell God who is so great and holy and rich what it is that he wishes to receive from Him. Something has happened in Jesus Christ, and something has been said in the Word of God, which makes this twofold fear unnecessary. The Christian is able to ask. The mystery that God is the Father of man and man the child of God is a mystery which has been revealed to him. And so he does ask. He says that which corresponds on his side to this happening and this revelation. He takes God as God gave Himself and showed Himself to the world and to him, as a Helper and Giver and Deliverer, as the source of all blessing and power and enlightenment and hope, in short of all the things that he himself lacks, but which God who has drawn so near to him, and is bound to him, will not keep to Himself but will allow him to enjoy as well. It is true that God does not allow any part of Himself to be taken from Him. But how if He gives Himself ? If He does, it is even more true that He does allow Himself to be taken. And God will not allow anything to be taken from Him, not one of all the things that He possesses, and that is everything. But how if He gives man all the things that He possesses when He gives Himself ? Is it not even more true that He allows everything to be taken from

Him, from His own hand ? The Christian is able to take because God gives him Himself and all that He possesses. " He that spared not his own Son, but delivered him up freely for us all, how shall he not with him also freely give us all things ? " (Rom. 8[32]). Thus the most intimate thing in Christian prayer, and therefore in the whole Christian attitude, is the fact that the Christian both may ask and actually does ask. In the praying of a Christian there is no impudence ; no forgetting of distances ; no arbitrary transcending of the antithesis between the one side and the other, between that which is above and that which is below ; no self-seeking. On the contrary, he is doing that which corresponds and answers to the situation in which he finds himself placed by the Word of God. He does that which he is not merely permitted but commanded to do in this situation, seeing that he is obviously placed in this situation in order to do it. We may note that in so doing he makes the most genuine act of praise and thanksgiving, and therefore worship ; and again, that in so doing he makes the most genuine act of penitence. By coming before God as one who asks he magnifies God and abases himself. And this is what God desires of him. This is how God would have him act. In so doing he meets the attitude of God Himself towards him. The true worship of God is that man is ready to take and actually does take where God Himself gives, that he seeks and knocks in order that he may really receive. This receiving is Christian prayer in all its centrality as petition. In this form it does not derive from the self-will of the Christian himself, just as the freedom which is given him is not the freedom of self-will. On the contrary, it derives from what the Christian receives from God, and from the command which is given with this gift. As petition, it is the human fulfilment of this receiving. It is really the basic form of Christian obedience. But we must reverse the proposition. The basic form of Christian obedience consists in the fact that on the basis of what God is and has for him man does not look upon God as so great and himself as so small that he dare not ask ; he looks upon God as so gracious and himself as so genuinely accepted by God that he not merely must in some way dare to come to God as a suppliant, but he may actually do it as the most natural and necessary expression of his life.

If we are to understand the essence of prayer, we must try to be clear concerning this asking. And to do this we shall have to take rather a strange and apparently circuitous path. For however difficult it may sound, the hearing really precedes the asking. It is the basis of it. It makes it real asking, the asking of Christian prayer. It makes it the third and decisive form of the Christian attitude. That is why we said above that prayer derives from what the Christian receives. It is simply the human fulfilment of this receiving, the direct expression of the life of the one who stands amazed at what God is and does for him ; amazed primarily, not at the majesty of God compared with himself, not at his own lowliness as contrasted with this majesty, but at the fact that God is actually for him, and that God acts for him. That is the point where we must begin.   It is there and there alone that we can understand why prayer is permitted and commanded to man as petition.   It is there and there alone that we can understand why together with faith and obedience, and including both, prayer is an integral element in the whole Christian attitude.

Of all the things that are needed by man, and needed in such a way that he can receive them only from God, that only God can give them to him, there is one great gift.   And to all the true and legitimate requests that are directed necessarily to God, there is one great answer. This one divine gift and answer is Jesus Christ.   It is Jesus Christ because in Him it came about that God concerned Himself in the world and man, and in so doing He turned upon the world and man the fulness of all blessing.   It is in relation to Him, in and with His election as Mediator, that the world and man are created.   It is as the Son and Word of God became flesh, man, creature, that God pledges and covenants Himself to the world, and at the heart of the world to man, accepting solidarity with him and accomplishing his deliverance, and directing upon him His own eternal glory.   In Him God has constituted Himself personally the Lord and Guardian and Helper and hope of the world and man.   In Him, in His own beloved Son, in His Word which is a Word of salvation and peace, He controls all occurrence, upholding it, accompanying it and ruling it.   In the fact that Jesus is there, the world is already helped, and everything that creation needs, and at the heart of creation man, is already provided.   In the fact that He is there, the name of the One from whom all things derive and to whom they return, who has moved all things, is declared and revealed and proclaimed as the name of the God who is the Saviour of the world, who is not without or against the creature, and does not work without or against it, but absolutely and utterly for it.   Therefore He is the one great gift and answer in which all that we can receive and ask is not merely determined but actually given and present and available for us.

And Jesus Christ is not an isolated form or figure.   To Him there belong those who are elected in and with Him, His own people, who by the Spirit of His Word are called to faith in Him, and by faith to obedience to Him.   In its historical form He has called forth this body by the message of His prophets and apostles.   This body of His is the community, His community, the Christian community, His people. He has given Himself to this people as the Lord, and revealed Himself as the Lord.   He has shown Himself to this people as the One He is in order that there may be an office and ministry of witness at the heart of creation ; in order that His light may shine in this world even before and up to His final manifestation before all things and on behalf of all things ; in order that the recollection and hope of the divine love may have a concrete location and content. And in this respect He is present now in His people. In Him, it has present within it the one great divine gift and answer. In Him, it knows the name of the One who is the beginning and end of all things, the Lord of all occurrence. In Him, its Creator, the Preserver and Ruler both of itself and of all creation, is actually and personally present within it as the Saviour, so that it looks to Him, it lives in communion with Him, holding fast to Him and fixing all its confidence on Him. This people is born for Him and gathered to Him in baptism. It is nourished by Him and for Him in the Lord's Supper. It is continually called and upheld and enlightened and guided by His Word. It lives, therefore, in the presence of the divine gift and answer which takes place in Him. And this means that it does not lack anything from its Lord. In Him, it possesses already all the grace and hidden glory which God has ascribed and applied to the creature. In Him, it has found already its home, its citizenship, its inheritance : found them in heaven ; and indeed above all heavens, in the immediate proximity of the throne of God, of God Himself. From God it looks back and down upon all that is not yet ordered, all that is not yet solved, all that is not yet liberated, all the disturbances and obstructions and confusions and devastations which we still find in the world-process, all the darkness which still tries to obscure and actually does obscure for us the fatherly rule and determination under which this process stands. In Him, it already sees it unobscured. In Him, it already lives by all the goodness and wisdom and perfection of this rule. In Him, it already breathes at the heart of God. It would not be the Christian community if, as it knew about Jesus Christ, it did not also know about this Already, if in all the weakness and imperfection of its creaturely existence, but looking always to its Lord, and always in faith, and by faith in obedience to Him, it did not really live in this Already, in the full presence and receiving of the divine gift and answer. How could it, and how would it be the witness to Him, the light which He has kindled in the darkness, if it did not know about it and live in it, if it could not bear witness to it ? It can only be a matter for concern—and we must not allow the protestations of a humble realism or a realistic humility to conceal or justify the fact—if things are otherwise ; if it has nothing to say to the world, or only something lame and halting to say to the world, about the full divine gift and answer which is already actualised and present ; if it is not very sure about this matter even so far as it applies to itself. It is precisely about this matter that the living Christian community is absolutely and unconditionally sure. It proclaims it with a loud and not a broken voice.

And the Christian whose attitude we are now considering is a member of this Christian community, the body and people of Jesus Christ. All that we have said in relation to Jesus Christ, and in company with Him the Christian community, also applies to the Christian personally. He personally is baptised into Jesus Christ, and can receive His body and blood, Jesus Christ Himself, in the Lord's Supper, to live by Him and with Him. He personally can hear His Word, to experience its truth for him. He personally is made responsible for the community's mission in the world. It is for him that Jesus Christ is who He is ; for him that the name of God the Creator of heaven and earth is made known ; for him that God is present as Saviour and also as the gracious Lord and Guardian and Helper and all his hope. It is he who can live in this world and participate in the events of this world in the full knowledge that God has taken up its case, that He has finally affirmed this world, that He has pledged Himself to it, that He has entered into covenant and accepted solidarity with it, that He has taken it into His own service. It is for him as a Christian, i.e., as one who has personal knowledge of the prophetic and priestly and kingly office of Jesus Christ, as one who by his membership of the community participates in this office, that world-occurrence is clearly and palpably not abandoned to its own devices, but preserved and accompanied and ruled by God, that it is preserved and accompanied and ruled by Him for good, for salvation, and in goodness and mercy, and that it is moving forward to eternal glory. It is he who in the Lord of the community, who as such is also his Lord, is dealing with the one great gift and answer which have already been manifested for him, which are already clear and palpable. And what does he not have, what can he possibly lack, when he can have Him ? What can disturb or hinder or confuse or devastate him in life as a Christian and a man when he can live with Him, in communion with Him ? What need is not already met in Him, what difficulty is not already removed in Him, what help is not already present in Him, what word of comfort that he needs is not already spoken in Him, what direction that he awaits is not already given in Him ? In Him, he has already attained, he is already at the goal, and he can look back and down upon all his distress as already alleviated, all his complaints as already redressed, all his questions, however they may engage or consume or agitate him, as already answered. And let it not be said that this is to maintain too much or to speak too highly. No formulation can be too bold or far-reaching except when it is made by one who is not yet a Christian or no longer a Christian, except when it is made by one who secretly separates himself from the body of Jesus Christ, from the community which is elected and called by Him, except when it is made by one who perhaps separates the community and therefore himself from Jesus Christ instead of seeing and understanding both himself and the community as they are in Him. And if there is anyone who does do this he ought not to pretend that it is honesty but recognise it as his own weakness. In the honesty which he owes himself as a Christian he will not make separations of this kind, but rather be amazed and horrified that he has not yet realised in what fulness the divine gift and answer is already present and near to hand, and with what joy he can avail himself of it, and in what thankfulness he can acknowledge the fact.

And Christian petition, the meaning of which we are trying to understand, is simply the taking and receiving of the divine gift and answer as it is already present and near to hand in Jesus Christ. In this gift and answer we have to do with the will of God not only over but with the creature. We have to do with His covenant with man. We have to do with His grace directed towards man as an autonomous being distinct from Himself. We have to do with His work, which in man has an animate and not an inanimate subject. We have to do with His Word, which man can hear and answer. In short, we have to do with the freedom in which man himself can live. In this freedom the Christian takes and receives that which God is and does for him, that which God offers him. In this freedom the Christian asks. For what can all that great and divine gift and answer be to him if he does not take and receive ? It is destined for him, and therefore for one who takes and receives. But how can he take and receive that divine gift and answer except by asking for it ? The only possible status of the creature in this matter is that of one who asks. Appropriating, using and enjoying is nothing but a continual and continually renewed asking. It is only in asking that it is not something strange and novel and unattainable to him. Asking is the only thing that he can do, the only spontaneous response that he can make. When he asks for it, when he says to God : I have not, and Thou hast ; Therefore give me what Thou hast and I have not, he acknowledges and magnifies God Himself as the Giver, and he honours the divine nature of that which he is able to take and receive. And when he asks for it, he also perceives and confesses that he himself is a weak and unworthy partner of God, that he is most inadequate in his taking and receiving of the divine gift. In asking for it, he fears God and loves God. Again, in asking for it, he takes up towards this God a position which he alone may and can take up. But in doing this, in entering into a suitable and therefore a right and profitable relationship to the gift and answer already given and present, it comes about that he can actually take and receive it, so that God attains His end with him as the Saviour. The Christian asks, and by this asking the doors are opened wide, and the gates are lifted up, that the King of glory may come in.

To understand this Christian asking as such, it will be our best plan to follow the same order as when we spoke of the divine gift and answer. The first and proper suppliant is none other than Jesus Christ Himself. The Gospels tell us that He taught His disciples to pray, and that He did so by repeating a prayer with them, by being their Leader in prayer. This fact is of decisive practical importance for the meaning and character of Christian prayer. As the Son of God, He was the divine gift and answer, but as the Son of Man He was human asking. In Him, God interceded for the creature, pledging and offering and imparting Himself to it in all His divine wealth. And in Him, the creature entered into the right and profitable relationship to God, and He became the first One properly to take and receive the divine gift. He himself was the King of glory who comes in, but He Himself was also the man who opened wide the doors and lifted up the gates in this world. He is the revelation of the name of God, the name of salvation, but He is also the man who hallows this name, who according to the divine revelation confesses the glory of God and the shame of man, and in so doing proves and demonstrates that He is the man who is elected and favoured and blessed and exalted and glorified by God, the representative man, the One who brings deliverance and bears salvation for the whole race. For what the man Jesus did was the very thing that He told us to ask for in the first petition of the Lord's Prayer : He hallowed the revealed name of God. He took up towards God the relationship that man must take up because God is the merciful Saviour. He justified God, and in so doing He allowed Himself to be put in the wrong. He acknowledged the holiness of God, and in so doing He acknowledged the transgression and misery of man. He submitted Himself to God in all the fulness of a free and loving childlike obedience, and in so doing He was content to suffer the punishment of human sin, and to be delivered up to death because of it. Jesus Christ asks, that is, He takes up towards God the position of One who has nothing, and has claim to nothing, who has to receive everything, and to receive it from God. He trusts in God that He will in fact receive it from Him. He trusts only in God, but He trusts in God fully. He entrusts everything to Him. This is how He lives. This is how He loses His life. This is how He gains and saves it. As a Suppliant and nothing more, as One who in His supplication takes seriously both the holiness of God and the transgression of man, He is already heard and answered. His life is a life which is controlled and upheld by the grace of God. It is revealed by His resurrection to be a life which is delivered and glorified by God. God Himself has moved towards man. In His person the salvation which God has intended for man and the glory which He had predestined and promised to man are made event and presence. Man is caught up in the whole fulness of God. And all this is because He asks, because in all His actions as a man He is only and altogether a Suppliant. Naturally, as the Son of Man He is only and altogether a Suppliant because as the Son of God He is Himself altogether the divine gift and answer. It is, therefore, the love and power of God Himself which breaks through and gains the victory in the existence of this man by becoming a single request. God triumphed in this man. But He did it because this man actually asked, and asking took and received ; because this man sought, and seeking found ; because this man knocked, and as He knocked, it was opened to Him. In this way God triumphed in the asking, and therefore in the individual being and work of this man. And because it was in the individual being and work of this man, it was only by this man that the name of God was hallowed, only by this man that the response to the divine gift and answer became event and reality on the human side, not merely objectively but subjectively. It was, therefore, by this man, as He went through the narrow archway of asking, that the doors were opened wide and the gates were lifted up in this world. This man prayed. He prayed to God for His unspeakable gift.

And we may now add that He is not alone in doing this. He did not do it for Himself. For Himself, He did not need to confess either the glory of God or the transgression of man. In His own person He did it for others, and first of all for His own people, for all those who believe in Him, and who believing in Him can obey Him, because He Himself has called and empowered them to do so, because in this calling and empowering He has willed to send them forth into the world. God's target when His Son became flesh was the world, just as His target when He made the world was His Son's becoming flesh for its salvation. And so in the asking of the Son of Man, in His existence as the one great Suppliant, and as the One who in asking receives, the target was the world. But because it was the world, it was primarily others who can and may and will ask together with the Son of Man. It was primarily His community as the assembly of those who can ask, and who can therefore receive. For His community is the assembly of those whose eyes are open to the fact that in this One the target of God was the whole world, and primarily themselves, and that in Him and with Him they too, as they are assembled by His Word, are elected to ask, and therefore to take and receive, and in this way to be His witnesses to the world. The Christian community sees and knows that this One did not pray for Himself but for them, that they might be His witnesses, and that they might keep themselves as such. The Son of God became the Son of Man, and passed through the narrow archway of asking, in order that He who takes and receives the divine gift and answer might be the Representative and Substitute for all others. There must always be this taking and receiving. But this taking and receiving is beyond the will and capacity of men. It had, therefore, to be done for men. Thus the existence of the Son of Man in which it was done was not merely petition but intercession, i.e., petition on behalf of those who cannot and will not ask for themselves, and therefore of themselves are not in any position to take and receive. But this mighty intercession has already taken place. The community which is elected with Him and called and assembled by Him knows by the Holy Spirit of His Word that it has already taken place. And now this community is called to Him, called into His fellowship and communion. He Himself is in the midst of it. He has attached Himself to it, and it has attached itself to Him. It is constituted by the fact that it knows and acknowledges and affirms His intercession as that of the great High-priest, that it is posited on this basis, that it cannot posit itself on any other. It accepts the fact that the gates are opened for it too, that its incapacity and unwillingness are now at an end, that there has been created and made available for it the freedom to be able and willing, the freedom to ask. The Son of Man teaches it to pray, and therefore to ask. It allows itself to be taught by Him. And as He prays with it, it can now pray with Him. How can it accept that intercession of His by which it lives, how can that intercession ever be made for it or revealed to it, if it will not accept and learn and practise this lesson, the lesson of true prayer, if it will not pray with Him? Naturally, it will always be aware that it needs this lesson, not once, but continually. It will always be aware that it cannot do anything without Him, that it cannot pray unless He prays with it. Therefore it will never regard it as its own work, as a human achievement, if by asking it is able to be true to its election in Him and its calling by Him. It will never ask except " in His name." It will never regard its asking except as the gift and work of His Holy Spirit, something with which it can honour Him alone, without any glory at all for itself. But just because it holds fast to Him, just because it asks in His name, and therefore expects everything from His intercession and nothing at all from its own asking as such, just because in its own asking it relies entirely on the gift and work of His Holy Spirit, it can never be idle—for there is no stronger incentive than the knowledge of the real grace of God. Therefore it will not allow its Lord to be alone in prayer, but it will be at His side with its own asking, however imperfect and perverted and impotent this may be compared with His. And both with heart and mouth the asking of the community which is elected together with Him will be a true and genuine asking, because and in the very fact that it is merely a repetition of His petition, that it is enclosed in His asking, that it is associated with it, that it lives by its seriousness and power, that it is related to the gift and answer of God present within it. It is in this that it has its own seriousness and power, that it is prayer which is answered, even though it is made with all the imperfection and perversion and impotence of all things human. It is in this that it is a real taking and receiving of the fulness of God actual and present in Him. It is in this that the community participates in Him, in His life as the Lord. It is in this that it really is His community. It will ask, therefore, as for the one thing needful : that it may really be His community ; that it may not be in vain that it is founded and maintained and ruled by Him ; that it may not be in vain that it is separated from the world and sent out into the world. It will ask for His love, that in a new way it may be united within itself ; for His Word, that in a new way it may hear and know it ; for His witness, that in a new way it may be effective both in its life and on its lips. It will ask for all that it requires as His community, and therefore as the light of the world which He has kindled. It will certainly not ask for its existence as such, as though that were an end in itself, but for its existence in His service, for its existence in the carrying out of His commission, for its existence with Him and for Him, the One who by His own existence with it and for it revealed Himself so gracious and mighty towards it. It cannot exist at all except as it goes with Him through the narrow archway of this petition for its own existence. Like Him, it lives only and altogether as it asks, as it asks with the recollection that He has asked for it. Like Him, it can keep and gain and save its life only as it risks and loses it in a confession of the glory of God and the sin of man. If it could keep it in any other way it would not be the Christian community. There is no Church which is not an asking Church, a Church which is continually asking for its own existence as such. But the real question is its existence in the service of its Lord. And for this reason its asking, too, is at the deepest level intercession. As it asks for its own existence, it asks for the world from which it is separated and into which it is sent. It knows that help can be given to the world, but actually is given, only by the divine gift and answer for which it asks and which asking it takes and receives. It sees that as yet the world does not know this, and it sees how the world suffers from the lack of this knowledge. And it sees, too, that its own task is to tell the world what the world does not know. And when it asks it does what the world does not do. It does it for the world, on behalf of the world. But how could it presume to do this if it were dependent on its own capacity and willingness, if it were not supported by the intercession of its own Lord, an intercession of which its own petitions are simply the repetition ? It is in this repetition that it is really at His side, above all in the sense that in it it finds its own part in the divine gift and answer which is made to Him, its own part in the fulness of the Godhead which dwells in Him. For the God who answered the request made by His Elect, the God who answered Him as in obedience to Him He humbled Himself even to the death of the cross, is the very same God who answers the request made by those who are elected with Him, His brothers, His community. He is the very same God who answers this request as it is brought to Him in His name and with reference to Him and in full confidence in Him by those who as members of His body live by Him and with Him as their Head. It is as the Church asks in the name of Jesus—however little it may do so—that it exists as a true Church. As it does so, it receives all that is necessary for its existence as such. Its existence as a true Church is to be the light which is kindled by Him and which constantly burns and shines by Him. Therefore as it asks in His name, it is continually at His side in the sense that it acquires a part in the fulness of grace directed upon Him, an active part in His ministry. For the Church there can never be any question of anything more or anything other than the ministry of witness. It can never usurp the place of its Lord. It can only be at His side. The existence of the community is not an extension of the incarnation. But it can be and it is a witness to it. It is a true confessing community, confessing Him, and therefore confessing God to the world by asking in His name. In asking, it attests and confesses Him, not only because it receives that which equips it for its office and activates it, i.e., the Holy Spirit, and together with Him unity in love and the light of knowledge and the capacity for obedience, but also in the simple sense that over against the world it is the most powerful witness to Jesus Christ, the most powerful recollection of Him, and the most powerful intimation of His coming : a community which is gathered around Him in petition ; not therefore in wealth but in poverty ; not with self-consciousness but with humility ; not triumphantly but with the most profound modesty, and yet also a determined and joyful expectation ; looking to Him, and in Him to God ; expecting everything from God, and from God everything. By its very existence this community speaks of Him. And it is only as it does speak of Him by its existence that it can and will do so in other ways as well. It is as an asking community—and basically perhaps only as this— that it is really a new phenomenon in the cosmos ; something which can be understood, if at all, only in the light of its origin in Jesus Christ and relationship with Him. And from this standpoint, there is a third sense in which we can say that in its asking it is at the side of its Lord. As it repeats His petitions, as it asks with Him, it is together with Him before God. It participates not only in His prophetic but also in His high-priestly office and work. Again, this is not in the sense that it can continue or amplify or complete His intercession on the world's behalf, for this is unnecessary, since His work is quite complete and sufficient in itself ; it is in the sense that it attests His asking even before God, that there at the heart of the cosmos it can confirm the fact that His name is already hallowed, His kingdom has already come, His will is already done on earth, and the whole cosmos is caught up in a movement whose end is the meaning of its creation and preservation and of all that occurs within it. Thus the asking community stands together with its Lord before God on behalf of all creation. Not merely is the fulness of all divine giving and receiving present within it, but as it prays there takes place within it something which does not take place anywhere else in the world, where this asking is neglected, or denied, or completely wanting. The asking of this community anticipates as it were that of creation as a whole. It gives voice and expression to the groaning of creation. We can say that whatever may be already present in the world, although unnoticed by it, of the divine gift and answer, of the blessing of the gracious patience of God, is there as an answer to the asking of the community, which is a repetition of that of Jesus Christ. Because the community asks, the world in its godlessness is not simply godless, but God finds in the world and has in it a partner, and the history between Himself and the world—which is not merely a history of judgment but also of salvation and grace—moves forward to its ultimate goal.

And each individual Christian as such is a member of this asking community. In the framework and context of its asking he, too, is both called and empowered to ask. His asking belongs essentially and necessarily to this context of the asking of Jesus Christ Himself and therefore of His community. It is the prayer of Jesus Christ, the Lord's Prayer, which he will repeat in some form or other whenever he asks. And even as his personal and individual asking it will be a We prayer according to the unequivocal direction of the Lord's Prayer. The We are the members of this community, and behind them, not praying but groaning together with them, all men and all creatures. In the fellowship and discipleship of the asking Lord, and in the assembly and sequence of the asking We, it is, of course, a matter of the personal and individual asking of the individual Christian. It is up to him. It is he with his personal sin, but also with his personal union with the supplication of Jesus Christ, who is responsible for the community. Upon his crying to God as one who is poor and modest and humble after his own fashion, everything depends. And everything depends upon his receiving from God that which has already been prepared for him, and for the whole community, as the divine gift and answer. He can and must pray for himself : that the name of God may be hallowed by him, and therefore by his genuine praying, which will itself always be supplication ; that the kingdom of God may be set up, and therefore the lordship of God in his own life ; that the will of God may be done in his life, in his free thoughts and words and actions ; that he may have the daily bread which is necessary if he is to continue to exist both as a creature and as a man ; that he may be forgiven the particular guilt which separates him from God ; that he may be guarded against his own particular temptation ; that he may have all the things which he does not have and of himself cannot have, but can have only from God. He can and must ask these things for himself. How else can he really ask for them ? But he asks for them in this order. He would not really ask for them if he did so in such a way that this order was broken. With the whole community he asks in the name of Jesus, on the basis of His intercession, attaching himself to Him, standing at His side. Therefore in his own prayer he cannot disregard or deny or crowd out the true and proper Subject of prayer who recites the prayer before him. In his own prayer he can desire only to serve and follow Him. In his own prayer he will leave the initiative to this first and proper Subject of true prayer, of the prayer which is heard and answered even as it is offered. And as the Christian follows his Lord with his own most personal and individual petitions, they become holy petitions, petitions which are heard and answered, petitions in which the divine fulness is grasped and received as they are presented to God. But as the Christian prays in this way, his petitions cease to be private petitions, and the more so the more directly they relate to his own needs. They are prayed in the chamber in secret, but they are the petitions of the community. And this means that in the concrete form of his own most personal concerns, the Christian brings before God the concerns of the community; that there—in his life as a member of the community—he may help and rectify and save, proving himself an heir of glory. What the Christian needs, what he can and must legitimately desire for himself both physically and spiritually, including the nature and course and effect of his environment both far and near, and his own relationship to it, is that he himself in each specific situation, and also those around him, should be equipped and usable and ready in the service which Jesus Christ has assigned to His people, and in which they can have their salvation and glory. Therefore in his own form— and it may be a very improbable and external and worldly form— the Christian will pray that he and those around him may be kept worthy and may be able to may remain cheerful in that service. This is what he most legitimately needs and desires for himself, and this is what he also receives as he asks for it in the name of Jesus. From this it will be seen that the asking of the individual Christian includes intercession not merely as an optional extra, but if it follows the order of the Lord's Prayer, and therefore of We prayer, essentially and necessarily. If he prays in the name of Jesus, if therefore he prays after Jesus, then like Jesus he prays for the community. If he prays in the name of Jesus, he can never pray more earnestly for himself than when as a member of it he prays for the community, asking that it may be ordered and equipped for the service laid upon it, that it may discharge it conscientiously and cheerfully, and that it may have the Holy Spirit as the power behind its continuance and work. And because the community lives in its members, the asking of each member as such is necessarily an asking for the others. The particular asking of each individual Christian has its place in that of the community, in the framework and context of it. There- fore all ask for all, and each for each. For in the service of the community each knows that the other is used in the same service, and that no one else is capable of this service apart from the divine gift and answer. And the true and only good that each can wish for the other is that this part in the divine gift and answer may not be denied but may come to him from God, and that on the basis of it he may fulfil his role in the service of the community. But since in each case this is something which only God can answer, no one can pray for himself, and therefore for the community, without praying for others, and indeed for all others who come within the orbit of his vision and understanding. And when he really does this, he will in fact be also praying for those who are outside, for those who do not so far pray, or who no longer pray, but can only groan. He will, in fact, pray for all men and for all creation.

And this is Christian prayer. It is human asking according to this order. In the name and service of Jesus Christ, in the context of the asking of His community, it is the petition of the individual Christian, with its basis and reference in the divine gift as it is directed to that community and to each individual in the same Jesus Christ, in the divine answer which is already given. It is the prayer which as petition of this kind is the taking and receiving of the whole fulness of this gift and answer. It is (1) primarily and centrally an asking. It stands (2) in a basic relationship to the divine answer. And it takes place (3) in this order. These are the three elements which are essential for an understanding of Christian prayer. We shall touch later on the last of these, which gives to prayer its particular importance in the present context. But first let us consider briefly the relationship of prayer to the two other basic forms of the Christian attitude.

It is apparent at once that Christian prayer can only be the prayer of Christian faith. It is human asking in confrontation with God; asking in which man turns to the One who confronts him and expects from Him the fulfilment of his request. The asking of which we are now speaking is not a yearning sigh or cry addressed into the void, into the mystery of a supposed transcendence in which man finally runs up only against his own limitations. That God does actually hear this sighing, that there is a definite answer and gift even for the creature which merely sighs, is a subject apart. The asking of Christian prayer, however, is something more and other than this sighing or groaning. In Christian prayer as the prayer of Christian faith man transcends his own limitations, for in his asking he turns to the God who has posited and given Himself as the One who confronts him. It is because we had definitely to describe it as a taking and receiving of the divine fulness that we had first of all to speak of the divine gift and answer and only then of its character as asking. Christian prayer is participation in Jesus Christ; participation, basically, in the grace which is revealed and active in Him, in the Son of God; and then only, and on this basis, participation in the asking of the Son of Man. Christian prayer is life in and with the community of Jesus Christ; life primarily and basically out of and in the fulness of the Spirit and the hope which Jesus Christ imparted and continually imparts to them in His Word and in baptism and the Lord's Supper; and then only, and on this basis, co-operation with Him in the service to which it is commissioned. Christian prayer is the preservation of the existence of the Christian as a member of the body of Christ which is His community; the preservation, primarily and basically, which is freely granted to him ; the supreme freedom which is given him as a child of God, by God's only Son ; and then only, and on this basis, the fulfilling of the duty to which it is committed by this freedom. In prayer, the Christian is dealing with the merciful God. To be able to pray, he must be awakened and called to prayer by God. He must receive and appropriate the childlike freedom to believe in Him. And this means that God must set him in fellowship with His Son, gathering him into the community of His Son and making him a living member of it. In this freedom, he prays, and therefore he asks, and he can do it as we have described—in the fulness of the divine presence, and therefore with a strong assurance that he will be heard even as he asks. It does not need a great faith to do this. It needs only real faith. But without faith the Christian cannot pray, just as without faith he cannot be a Christian at all.

On the other hand Christian prayer is just as self-evidently related to Christian obedience. We will not labour the fact that the prayer of the Christian to God is the basic act of the obedience engendered in faith. We will simply think of the order in which his asking takes place and affirm that in asking he places himself within this order. His asking, therefore, is not a capricious act which derives from his own needs and desires. It is related—and how else could it be so joyful and assured ?—to the divine gift and answer already present in faith. In asking, he follows the law by which this fulness is showered down upon him. He asks therefore—and how else could he arrive at this point ?—not in his own name, nor relying upon the power and force of his own asking, but in the name of Jesus and in conjunction with His asking. Therefore, although he prays for himself as an individual, he does not pray private prayers. At his own place and in his own way, according to his own part in the community, he prays the prayer of the community, the common prayer of all Christians. Praying for himself, therefore, he prays with and for all other Christians, because he prays for the service and work of the community ; and in so doing he prays for all men. In this way he prays obediently. If he were to pray in any other way he would fall away from faith ; he would not really be dealing with God ; he could not pray with any assurance of exaltation ; his prayer would again be a mere sighing at closed doors and windows ; and in the last resort he would again be alone with that supposed transcendence. The fact that he remains obedient in his praying means that he keeps to this order and therefore to the point. And as he does so, his asking always becomes as such taking and receiving. It is only natural that a disobedient asking should disintegrate like an unbelieving asking, and that there should be no answer to either the one or the other. And it is equally evident that the obedience in which Christian prayer keeps to this order and to the point should be simply the obedience of faith, of the evangelical faith of the free children of God. If Christian prayer is made in this obedience, then from a dead work it will continually and necessarily become a living, from an unprofitable work a fruitful.

In conclusion, our treatment of Christian prayer would not be complete if we described it as a living and fruitful work but were merely thinking of something which is no doubt very important but takes place entirely within the Christian himself as he prays in the obedience of faith. There are certain theories of prayer which finally amount to little more than an understanding of prayer merely as the highest form of religious or Christian self-edification, a living and fruitful dialogue between the Christian and himself. By thinking of it centrally as petition, and understanding it wholly in the light of the divine gift and answer, and therefore strictly in that order, we have necessarily parted company with theories of this type, and tried from the very outset to bring out its objective bearing. In our whole study of the Christian under the world-governance of God the Father, it was, of course, our very first task by way of general elucidation to make it quite clear once again that there is a creaturely subject, the Christian man, who recognises the relation in which he and all other creatures are placed, who participates in the great events of the divine world-governance inwardly as well as outwardly, who is in sympathy with this governance, and who has a real knowledge of the whole matter. But we could not describe this Christian knowledge as a mere seeing and knowing. On the contrary, the knowledge of which we spoke presented itself in the guise of a particular attitude—the attitude of Christian faith, Christian obedience and Christian prayer. And as we tried to understand this attitude in the form of prayer we were led far beyond any idea of a merely subjective basis of our knowledge of the objective events of the divine world-governance, far beyond any idea of a merely subjective reality. There can be no doubt that at this point too—as at every point in our description of the Christian attitude—we find ourselves at the very heart of creaturely occurrence and therefore under the universal lordship of God. But it must not be overlooked that in this supreme form of prayer the whole Christian attitude, although it has its place below as a creaturely movement within all creaturely occurrence, does also point upwards, above all the immanence of the creaturely subject, above all the supposed transcendence within this immanence. It does so because in this supreme form it has the character of petition, of an asking which has to be understood in the light of the divine gift and answer, of an asking which is done in this order. And even less must it be overlooked that occurrence in this higher sphere, far above all creaturely occurrence and therefore above the Christian attitude even in the form of prayer, inclines as it were towards this attitude, merging into and fusing with it, so that although the Christian attitude is still a creaturely movement it acquires a share in the universal lordship of God, so that that lordship has a place and is actualised not merely in the higher sphere but also in the attitude of the Christian. Not that the creature itself, man, the Christian, could do this. Not that the Christian could of himself secure a share in this high matter. He simply believes, he simply obeys, and even his prayer is simply an asking. Not that the universal lordship of God has ceased to be wholly and entirely His own work. The creature, man, the Christian acquires a share in the matter simply by believing, by obeying, and finally and supremely by praying, and therefore by asking. The share is given him by God. It is a share which is quite incomprehensible from his own standpoint. He cannot deduce it from his own capacity or volition and activity. It is not in any way effected or conditioned. Yet it is still a genuine and actual share.

It is a genuine and actual share in the universal lordship of God. The will of God is not to preserve and accompany and rule the world and the course of the world as world-occurrence in such a way that He is not affected and moved by it, that He does not allow Himself to converse with it, that He does not listen to what it says, that as He conditions all things He does not allow Himself to be determined by them. God is not free and immutable in the sense that He is the prisoner of His own resolve and will and action, that He must always be alone as the Lord of all things and of all occurrence. He is not alone in His trinitarian being, and He is not alone in relation to creatures. He is free and immutable as the living God, as the God who wills to converse with the creature, and to allow Himself to be determined by it in this relationship. His sovereignty is so great that it embraces both the possibility, and, as it is exercised, the actuality, that the creature can actively be present and co-operate in His overruling. There is no creaturely freedom which can limit or compete with the sole sovereignty and efficacy of God. But permitted by God, and indeed willed and created by Him, there is the freedom of the friends of God concerning whom He has determined that without abandoning the helm for one moment He will still allow Himself to be determined by them. There is no autonomous and rebellious counter-activity of the creature in opposition to the eternal activity of His own will and action ; but on the model of His own will and action there is an individual activity of the creature which is planned and willed and demanded and made possible and actual by His own eternal activity, since it is included within it. There is no divine surrender to the creature, but in the very fact that God maintains and asserts himself as King and Lord there is a divine hearing—on the basis of the incomprehensible grace of God an incomprehensible hearing—even of the creature which is sinful. The grace of God to sinful man is that He encounters him as the hearing God ; that He calls him not merely to the humility of a servant and the thankfulness of a child but to the intimacy and boldness of a friend in the immediate presence of the throne, His own presence ; that He not merely permits but commands him to call upon Him in the definite expectation that He will both hear and answer, that his asking will have an objective as well as a subjective significance, i.e., a significance for his own will and action. The will of God is done even as the creature calls and presses and prevails upon it to be done. It is done as the converse with the creature established by this will is entered into by the creature in the form of this calling and pressing and prevailing. It is done as God participates in the creature, and enables it to participate in Himself, and in the purpose and direction of His works. It is done on this condition. And in this way it triumphs as the sovereign will of God which is living even in its divine sovereignty.

This is what takes place in what we have described as the Christian attitude, and ultimately and supremely as the asking of Christian prayer. We do not rightly describe even Christian faith and Christian obedience if we do not think of them as a human co-operation in the doing of the will of God. To be sure, it is a co-operation here below under the universal lordship of God. But none the less it is a real co-operation. And this is absolutely and unequivocally the case in the supreme form of the Christian attitude, which is prayer as petition. In obedience the Christian is the servant, in faith he is the child, but in prayer, as the servant and the child, he is the friend of God, called to the side of God and at the side of God, living and ruling and reigning with Him. To be sure, he is only a suppliant. He acts only as a suppliant, and as a suppliant down below, under the universal lordship of God. It is only as a suppliant that he is called to God's side. It is only as God stoops down to him and sets him there that even as a suppliant he is actually called to His side, and is there and can live and rule and reign there with God. It is only as God has intervened for him, with the fulness of the divine gift and answer to him, that he can actually present his request to God, that as a suppliant he can actually be the friend of God. It is all the divine condescension of grace, and there can be no question of human possibility or attainment, of human right or merit, of human autonomy or presumption. But grace is creative and active in the sphere where a man can believe and obey and finally pray as a Christian. And grace is creative and active to make it possible for a Christian to be actively present in the divine lordship as the friend of God : present not merely as one of many objects nor as a spectator or critic ; but present as a subject, which in its own place and within its own limits has an actual voice and responsibility in the matter.

It is clear that we cannot understand this except within the order apart from which we cannot say anything worth while about

Christian prayer, or even faith and obedience, because apart from it they would not exist at all. Originally and properly the Christian who is at the side of God and has His own voice and responsibility in the divine rule is the one Son of Man, Jesus Christ. It is He who sits at the right hand of the Father Almighty. It is He who with God is the Lord and King of all things. It is to Him that there is given all power in heaven and on earth. It is His asking which is answered, which is the work of the creature which includes within it the fulness of the divine presence and gift, and therefore helps to determine the divine will and action. Far be it from us to ascribe to the Christian creature, and his piety, and the strength of his faith, and the seriousness of his obedience, and the depth and fervour of his prayer, the power to rule and reign with God. Without Christ there are no Christians and there is no Christianity. But by and with Christ there are Christians and there is a Christianity, and it is to these that we refer. There is a discipleship of Christ. There is a faith in Him, and through Him in God. Likewise there is an obedience to Him. Likewise there is prayer or asking together with Him, and on the basis of His asking. Likewise there is a participation of the Christian not merely in His prophetic and high-priestly but also in His kingly office. In Him God came to our side and entered into our humility. And in Him we are set at God's side and lifted up to Him and therefore to the place where decisions are made in the affairs of His government. And this is what takes place in Christian faith and Christian obedience and Christian prayer. We are set there ; we are lifted up to that place. To deny this or to question it is just as fatal as to deny or question the full humanity and creatureliness of the Christian's activity. It is not the Christian in and for himself, but the Christian in Christ, who is at God's side and has a say and a part in the place where those decisions are made. It is not the Christian in himself, but the Christian in Christ, who is the servant and child and also the friend of God, and as such a free lord with him over everything.

In relation to this order we have also to say, of course, that he is all this as a member of the body of Christ and therefore as a member of His community. He is it in the most personal sense. He can lead his own life in this freedom, and he has to lead it in the responsibility which it involves. But he cannot do it as a free-lance. He personally is called to God's side. But he is not called as it were in his private but in his official capacity. And it is his personal but not his private needs and demands and petitions which can there confidently await an answer and determine the will of God. The friends of God are the creatures to whom He has given His grace and also a definite commission in the world. It is for the sake of His business, and therefore—because His business concerns the whole of creation—for the sake of creation as a whole, that God calls them to faith and obedience and also to prayer. It is in their official capacity in this respect that He allows Christians a voice and a part in the formulation and execution of His will. This share in the kingly office of His Son, and therefore in His lordship, is not granted to the I in isolation, but to the We of those who are gathered to His people and service, and to the I within the We. The individual can expect and experience an answer in so far as he believes and obeys and prays as a member of this people, as one who is called to this service. If he is not this, or if he thinks that he ought to believe and obey and pray in some other context, he need not be surprised if he is left groping in the void. But the moment he does it as a Christian, and therefore as a member of this community, he will be amazed at the fulness of the divine answer in which he participates.

Presupposing that it is done within this order, we can never rate too highly the objective significance of the Christian attitude, even if we are thinking only of the individual Christian as such. Nor can we reject too strongly those theories which seek to restrict the significance of prayer to the subjective sphere alone. If this presupposition can be made, then whenever the Christian believes and obeys and prays there does not merely take place a creaturely movement. But concealed within the creaturely movement, yet none the less really, there moves the finger and hand and sceptre of the God who rules the world. And what is more, there moves the heart of God, and He Himself is there in all the fulness of His love and wisdom and power. We then find ourselves at the very seat of government, at the very heart of the mystery and purpose of all occurrence. The subjective element, which ultimately can never have more than the form of a bloodless and impotent asking, of hands which are empty although stretched out to God, conceals and contains and actualises the most objective of all things, the lordship of the One who as King of Israel and King of the kingdom of grace holds all things in His own hands, and directs everything that occurs in this world for the best : *per Jesum Christum, Dominum nostrum.*

§ 50

GOD AND NOTHINGNESS [1]

Under the control of God world-occurrence is threatened and actually corrupted by the nothingness which is inimical to the will of the Creator and therefore to the nature of His good creature. God has judged nothingness by His mercy as revealed and effective in Jesus Christ. Pending the final revelation that it is already refuted and abolished, God determines the sphere, the manner, the measure and the subordinate relationship to His Word and work in which it may still operate.

1. THE PROBLEM OF NOTHINGNESS

There is opposition and resistance to God's world-dominion. There is in world-occurence an element, indeed an entire sinister system of elements, which is not comprehended by God's providence in the sense thus far described, and which is not therefore preserved, accompanied, nor ruled by the almighty action of God like creaturely occurrence. It is an element to which God denies the benefit of His preservation, concurrence and rule, of His fatherly lordship, and which is itself opposed to being preserved, accompanied and ruled in any sense, fatherly or otherwise. There is amongst the objects of God's providence an alien factor. It cannot escape God's providence but is comprehended by it. The manner, however, in which this is done is highly peculiar in accordance with the particular nature of this factor. It is distinct from that in which God's providence rules the creature and creaturely occurrence. The result is that the alien factor can never be considered or mentioned together in the same context as other objects of God's providence. Thus the whole doctrine of God's providence must be investigated afresh. This opposition and resistance, this stubborn element and alien factor, may be provisionally defined as nothingness.

So far we have only perceived on the margin that something of

[1] Many terms have been considered for *das Nichtige*, including the Latin *nihil* which has sometimes been favoured. Preferring a native term, and finding constructions like " the null " too artificial and " the negative " or " nonexistent " not quite exact, we have finally had to make do with " nothingness." It must be clearly grasped, however, that it is not used in its more common and abstract way, but in the secondary sense, to be filled out from Barth's own definitions and delimitations, of " that which is not."—Ed.

this kind exists, that in view of it we must reckon with a serious complication of our knowledge and exposition of the divine providence, and that amplification is perhaps required in this direction. We do, of course, remember one occasion at least when the alien element in question had already to be expressly named, i.e., when we were trying to understand the divine preservation of the creature. We saw this to be God's preservation of His creature from being over-thrown by the greater force of nothingness. We then considered how God confirms and upholds the separation between His creature and nothingness as effected in creation, halting the threatened and commencing enslavement of the creature. We saw that He does this because His will for His creature is liberation for a life in fellowship with Himself, because He wills to be known and praised by the creature as its Liberator and because He thus wills its continuation and not its destruction. He preserves the creature. For He has executed His will. He Himself has become a creature in Jesus Christ. And therefore He has set Himself in opposition to nothingness, and in this opposition was and is the Victor. Nothingness then met us as this total peril which is not actual in this form but is warded off by God's preservation. In that context, however, we gave only an incidental account of its existence and nature. We considered it only in the form in which it is a final peril warded off by the divine preservation. We did not consider it in the other form in which, though unable to overwhelm and destroy the creature, it constantly threatens and corrupts it. We did not take into account that it is not only inimical to the creature and its nature and existence, but above all to God Himself and His will and purpose. Neither did we answer the question how there can exist side by side the will and purpose of God and this opposition and resistance, the providence of God and the menace and actual operation of this alien factor, and even more radically the divine creation and the fact that this alien factor can exist and operate at all. All these questions must now be asked and answered.

It would be comparatively easy to understand and state the doctrine of God's providence if it involved no more than the relation-ship between the lordship of God and creaturely occurrence as such. So far we have understood and stated the doctrine in this basic form. There would be no difficulty if only creaturely occurrence, though ruled by God, did not also stand under the determination of this alien factor, of nothingness. There would be no difficulty if only a careful consideration of this factor which also determines creaturely activity were not absolutely unavoidable if the doctrine of God's providence is not to ignore its most urgent question and to desist from giving its most important answer. Perpendicular lines from above can render it in some measure intelligible and clear, as we have already demonstrated, what takes place between God the Creator and the creature as God's royal dominion on the one side, and creaturely existence, life and occurrence under this dominion on the other. " Of him and through him, and to him are all things : to whom be glory for ever. Amen " (Rom. 11³⁶). This thought has already been developed. With regard to the good Creator and Lord, and the creature created good by Him, it could indeed be developed in straight (or apparently straight) lines. The truth of this scriptural saying must stand. Yet what does " of him, through him, and to him " mean in view of the fact that " all things," i.e., man first, but through him and for him all things, are also affected by nothingness, being enmeshed in and bound up with it, sharing its nature, bearing its marks, and in some degree, directly or indirectly, actively or passively, overtly or covertly, being involved in the existence and operation of this alien factor ?   What is the meaning of " of him, through him, to him " from this standpoint ?   Is not the question of what is meant by God's lordship posed afresh and very differently against this background ?   Can the question be regarded as answered as long as it remains open to enquiry in this respect ?   Does not even the best which emerges from God's Word concerning His lordship over the creature remain unsaid if it is not also stated from the particular standpoint that it also belongs to the existence of life and activity of the creature to be involved in nothingness, and always to be partly determined by it in its present form ?

We again recall the exemplary answer of the *Heidelberg Catechism* to the question of God's providence, and the writings of Paul Gerhardt, and all the classic hymns of trust and comfort of the older Protestantism. The strength of these texts obviously lies in the fact that they do not evade but face that which might destroy or at least disturb and weaken trust in God's providence and the comfort of its knowledge, namely, the whole complex of sin, guilt and punishment, the whole reality of calamity, suffering and death in the world-process, in short, the factor of nothingness. They bear witness to the lordship of God not by concealing but by openly acknowledging the dreadful fact that this factor exists. These texts are obviously based on the insight that only if this fact is taken into account with genuine sighing, in " confident despair " but also " despairing confidence," can the lordship of God be attested, but that in this way it may and must be proclaimed the more powerfully and triumphantly. In face of this fact the question of God's providence is obviously a serious one and their witness to it is real and credible. Apart from it the question cannot be seriously put nor can a significant answer be given. It has thus been realised in the dogmatics of all confessions that here more than anywhere a special account of the faith is due to the community and the world, and that here more than anywhere special attention to God's Word is unavoidable.

In this instance, however, we do not make any advance by drawing straight lines from above, i.e., by thinking and speaking in direct statements concerning the action of the Creator on and with His creature. It is true that here also there is involved a repetition and confirmation, i.e., a particular application, of the simple recognition that God is Lord over all. But the peculiar factor now to be considered is that between the Creator and the creature, or more exactly the creaturely sphere under the lordship of the Creator, there is that at work which can be explained neither from the side of the Creator nor from that of the creature, neither as the action of the Creator nor as the life-act of the creature, and yet which cannot be overlooked or disowned but must be reckoned with in all its peculiarity. The simple recognition that God is Lord over all must obviously be applied to this third factor as well. Where would be the real situation of the real man or the real way of real trust of the real Christian, where would be the decisive truth and power of the doctrine of God's providence, if the knowledge that He is Lord over all were not applied especially to this element ? But if God's lordship is applicable here too, how are we to avoid error on the one side or the other ? We stray on the one side if we argue that this element of nothingness derives from the positive will and work of God as if it too were a creature, and that the Creator Himself and His lordship are responsible for its nothingness, the creature being exonerated from all responsibility for its existence, presence and activity. But we go astray on the other side if we maintain that it derives solely from the activity of the creature, in relation to which the lordship of God can only be a passive permission and observation, an ineffectual foreknowledge and a subsequent attitude. In the one case, the obvious error is to misinterpret the fact that God is Lord, to fail to understand that for that reason His lordship cannot be affected by nothingness. In the other case, the error is to misinterpret the meaning of lordship, namely, that God rules in sublime and unlimited majesty over every sphere, and therefore over that of nothingness as well. But how is it possible to avoid the one error without falling into the other ? How can justice be done both to the holiness and to the omnipotence of God when we are faced by the problem of nothingness ? How can the simple recognition that God is Lord over all be applied to this sphere ?

We may well understand the sighs of many of the older dogmaticians as they take up this subject. This is a *quaestio perceptu difficillima*, says F. Burmann (*Syn. Theol.*, 1671, I, 44, 52). It is a *quaestio intricatissima et maxime ardua*, complains F. Turrettini (*Instit. Theol. el.*, 1679, VI, 7, 1). And A. Heidan (*Corp. Theol.*, 1686) says : *Maximus labor restat, ut dispiciamus, quomodo, providentiae divinae sua tum veritas tum certitudo constare possit, etsi malum et peccatum sit in mundo.* They saw the difficulty precisely in the dilemma to which we have alluded : of failing either *in excessu* or *in defectu* ; of either speaking, with Manichaeans, Priscillianists and similar early heretics, of a *causalitas mali in Deo* and thus violating the holiness of God (a possibility Calvinists were particularly careful to guard against), or of joining with Pelagians old and new in ascribing evil solely to the creature, thus putting evil more or less outwith the providence and lordship of God and becoming guilty in consequence of an overt or covert denial of the omnipotence and omnicausality of God ; in short, of vitiating either one way or the other the nerve-centre of the doctrine of divine providence, the recognition of God Himself as Lord over all.

Yet it is also possible to go astray here in an entirely different manner. For it is clearly wrong to apply the basic recognition of God's lordship in such a way that nothingness in its relation of opposition and resistance to God's world-dominion assumes the form of a monster which, vested with demonic qualities, inspires fear and respect instead of awakening the Easter joy that even in all its power as sin and evil it is no more than the nothingness which as such is already judged in Jesus Christ and can therefore injure but no longer kill or destroy. Again, it is no less clearly wrong if this victorious might of faith is treated as if it were a principle at our own disposal, or if it is forgotten that the victory over nothingness can be ours only through hope in Jesus Christ, or if we think and speak of this adversary, who was certainly not defeated by us, in any other way than in the fear of God and the seriousness of faith. We describe the same dilemma when we say that in considering the manner in which God disposes even of nothingness, letting it have its course and yet overruling it for good, there is the danger either of an uneasy, bleak and sceptical overestimating of its power in relation to God, or of an easy, comfortable and dogmatic underestimation of its power in relation to us. How are we to avoid both an easy pessimism on the one side and a no less easy optimism on the other? How are we to think and speak of God's lordship even over nothingness with the necessary confidence and yet also the required humility, the required humility and yet also the necessary confidence? Nor is the truth to be sought in a central position of neutrality between these claims; for all are of equal urgency. Nor can we overcome the contrast between God's holiness and His omnipotence by mediation. How, then, is this matter to be seen and stated? How can the simple recognition of God's lordship be rightly applied?

It may be said at least that it can be so only as we soberly acknowledge that we have here an extraordinarily clear demonstration of the necessary brokenness of all theological thought and utterance. There is no theological sphere where this is not noticeable. All theology is *theologia viatorum*. It can never satisfy the natural aspiration of human thought and utterance for completeness and compactness. It does not exhibit its object but can only indicate it, and in so doing it owes the truth to the self-witness of the theme and not to its own resources. It is broken thought and utterance to the extent that it can progress only in isolated thoughts and statements directed from different angles to the one object. It can never form a system, comprehending and as it were " seizing " the object. That is true of all theological assertions. It is true even of the perpendicular lines from above in which we have developed the general doctrine of God's providence with regard to the relationship between the good Creator and His good creature. But if we failed to see this there and elsewhere, here at last we must surely see and acknowledge that our knowledge is piece-work, and that only as such can it stand and make sense in relation to its theme. But why is this true here, and therefore universally ? The reason is obvious. The existence, presence and operation of nothingness, which we are here concerned to discuss, are also objectively the break in the relationship between Creator and creature. The existence, presence, and operation of nothingness are not only the frontier which belongs to the nature of this relationship on both sides and which is grounded in the goodness of the Creator and that of the Creature. They are also the break which runs counter to the nature of this relationship, which is compatible with neither the goodness of the Creator nor that of the creature and which cannot be derived from either side but can only be regarded as hostility in relation to both. We are not now dealing with the break itself, but with God's relation to it, with His providence and the extent to which it comprehends this break as well. In this context, however, this break is our particular concern. For theology as a human activity, and under the presuppositions of the present dispensation, knows its object solely under the shadow of this break. Objectively, it must always receive it from beyond this break. Hence it cannot even be aware of its object without also being aware of this break. And this means that theological thought and utterance must always be broken. Not even objectively is the relationship between Creator and creature a system. It is always disrupted by this alien element. Hence there can be no system in the subjective knowledge of this relationship, and therefore in theology. Does not this emerge with particular clarity when we have to deal specifically with God's providence in its relation to the nothingness with which His creature is involved ? Here if anywhere it is imperative that theology, which is also a creaturely activity, should acknowledge that it is bound up with nothingness, and cannot and must not try to escape it. Here if anywhere theology as the subjective reproduction of objective reality ought not to impose or simulate a system. Here especially theology must set an example for its procedure generally, corresponding to its object in broken thoughts and utterance.

When P. van Mastricht (*Theol. pract. theor.*, 1699, VI, 10, 18) treats of this particular problem, he says, not without a hint of complaint, that it is the *imbecillitas captus nostri* which prevents us from unifying what really ought to be unified. He is thinking especially of the unification of God's holiness and omnipotence, which is so difficult in face of the existence and presence of nothingness. But what ground is there for saying that here we have something which ought to be unified ? What ground is there for saying that a sober and radical acknowledgment of the *imbecillitas captus nostri* which reveals our incapacity to achieve and demonstrate certain unifications is not more in keeping than all the alleged or real cleverness and skill which might permit us to achieve these unifications ?

This does not mean, of course, that we ought not to proceed here and everywhere with the greatest intellectual probity and with rigorous logic and objectivity. Here however—and not only here, but here with particular urgency by reason of the particular aspect of the theological object—the meaning of objectivity is that we must be prepared simply and without diminution to accept and take into account, each in its own place and manner, all the conflicting claims : the claim that God's holiness and omnipotence should be equally respected ; the claim that we should think and speak of this matter with joy and also with seriousness ; the claim that the power of nothingness should be rated as low as possible in relation to God and as high as possible in relation to ourselves. If we do this, it does not mean that we shall be led to a system nor to the complete and compact sequence of thoughts and statements yielded by a principle. On the contrary, the break itself and as such will be reproduced and reflected in our knowledge and its presentation ; and not only the break, but in, with and above it the history in which it is after all—for God is Lord—no more than an alien, disruptive and retarding moment—the history of the Creator's dealings with His creature, of the doing of His will as it was in His counsel and as it will finally and ultimately be fulfilled. This history, in the course of which this break occurs, is the object of theology. Theology is the record of this history. Hence it must consider all those claims in their place and manner. It must not be intent on unifications or mediations which are not to be found in the history. It must not degenerate into a system. It must always be related to that history. It must always be a report. It must not strain after completeness and compactness. Its aim must simply be to make the right report. This is the general and formal answer to the question how the simple recognition of God's universal lordship is rightly to be applied in view of the presence of nothingness as opposition and resistance to that lordship.

But what is the nature of this opposition and resistance ? What exactly is nothingness ? It is to this question that we must now address ourselves.

2. THE MISCONCEPTION OF NOTHINGNESS

We must indicate and remove a serious confusion which has been of far reaching effect in the history of theology. Light exists as well as shadow ; there is a positive as well as a negative aspect of creation and creaturely occurrence (cf. *C.D.*, III, 1 § 42, 3). When the first biblical account of creation distinguishes and opposes day and night, and land and water, it unmistakeably indicates this twofold character and aspect of creaturely existence. Viewed from its negative aspect, creation is as it were on the frontier of nothingness and orientated towards it. Creation is continually confronted by this menace. It is continually reminded that as God's creation it has not only a positive but also a negative side. Yet this negative side is not to be identified with nothingness, nor must it be postulated that the latter belongs to the essence of creaturely nature and may somehow be understood and interpreted as a mark of its character and perfection. It belongs to the essence of creaturely nature, and is indeed a mark of its perfection, that it has in fact this negative side, that it inclines not only to the right hand but also to the left, that it is thus simultaneously worthy of its Creator and yet dependent on Him, that it is not " nothing " but " something," yet " something " on the very frontier of nothingness, secure, and yet in jeopardy. It thus follows that though its existence is under doubt and shadow it is not of itself involved in opposition and resistance to God's creative will. On the contrary, this will is fulfilled and confirmed in it. The creature is natural and not unnatural. It is good, even very good, in so far as it does not oppose but corresponds to the intention of God as revealed by Him in the humiliation and exaltation of Jesus Christ and the reconciliation of the world with Himself effected in Him. For in Him God has made Himself the Subject of both aspects of creaturely existence. And having made it His own in Jesus Christ, He has affirmed it in its totality, reconciling its inner antithesis in His own person. The creature does not have the character of nothingness as and because it is a creature and partakes in this antithesis. On the contrary, this is its perfection and the proof of its creation in and for Jesus Christ. In this it is determined for its place in the covenant of God. In this it is energized and equipped for life in fellowship with its Creator, for work in His service, for faith, obedience and prayer. In this it is given a place for its praise. For God Himself has revealed and shown that this is the determination of His will by Himself becoming a creature under this determination. There is thus no common ground between it and nothingness, the power inimical to the will of the Creator and therefore to the nature of His good creation, the threat to world-occurrence and its corruption. To be sure, the negative aspect of creation is a reminder of this threat and corruption. But it is not the case that because creation has this shadowy side it is itself their victim and therefore belongs to nothingness. When Jesus Christ shall finally return as the Lord and Head of all that God has created, it will also be revealed that both in light and shadow, on the right hand and on the left, everything created was very good and supremely glorious.

It is difficult to attack a slander on creation which is so old, multiform and tenacious. Yet it is imperative that we should do this at the very outset. No protest can be too sharp or emphatic. It is true that in creation there is not only a Yes but also a No ; not only a height but also an abyss ; not only clarity but also obscurity ; not only progress and continuation but also impediment and limitation ; not only growth but also decay ; not only opulence but also indigence ; not only beauty but also ashes ; not only beginning but also end ; not only value but also worthlessness. It is true that in creaturely existence, and especially in the existence of man, there are hours, days and years both bright and dark, success and failure, laughter and tears, youth and age, gain and loss, birth and sooner or later its inevitable corollary, death. It is true that individual creatures and men experience these things in most unequal measure, their lots being assigned by a justice which is curious or very much concealed. Yet it is irrefutable that creation and creature are good even in the fact that all that is exists in this contrast and antithesis. In all this, far from being null, it praises its Creator and Lord even on its shadowy side, even in the negative aspect in which it is so near to nothingness. If He Himself has comprehended creation in its totality and made it His own in His Son, it is for us to acquiesce without thinking that we know better, without complaints, reproach or dismay. For all we can tell, may not His creatures praise Him more mightily in humility than in exaltation, in need than in plenty, in fear than in joy, on the frontier of nothingness than when wholly orientated on God ? For all we can tell, may not we ourselves praise Him more purely on bad days than on good, more surely in sorrow than in rejoicing, more truly in adversity than in progress ? It can, of course, be otherwise. But need it always be ? If not, if there may also be a praise of God from the abyss, the night and misfortune, and perhaps even from the deepest abyss, the darkest night and the greatest misfortune, why should we doubt the hidden justice which apportions the distinctions and contrasts to ourselves and others ? How surprised we shall be, and how ashamed of so much improper and unnecessary disquiet and discontent, once we are brought to realise that all creation both as light and shadow, including our own share in it, our puny and fleeting life, was laid on Jesus Christ as the creation of God, and that even though we did not see it, without and in spite of us, and while we were shaking our heads that things were not very different, it sang the praise of God just as it was, and was therefore right and perfect. We aspire to be Christians, and no doubt in some small measure we are, but is it not strange that only in our few better moments can we make anything either theoretically or practically of the truth that the creation of God in both its aspects, even the negative, is His good creation ?

I must again revert to Wolfgang Amadeus Mozart. Why is it that this man is so incomparable ? Why is it that for the receptive, he has produced in almost every bar he conceived and composed a type of music for which " beautiful " is not a fitting epithet : music which for the true Christian is not mere entertainment, enjoyment or edification but food and drink ; music full of comfort and

counsel for his needs ; music which is never a slave to its technique nor sentimental but always " moving," free and liberating because wise, strong and
sovereign ? Why is it possible to hold that Mozart has a place in theology,
especially in the doctrine of creation and also in eschatology, although he was
not a father of the Church, does not seem to have been a particularly active
Christian, and was a Roman Catholic, apparently leading what might appear
to us a rather frivolous existence when not occupied in his work ? It is possible
to give him this position because he knew something about creation in its total
goodness that neither the real fathers of the Church nor our Reformers, neither
the orthodox nor Liberals, neither the exponents of natural theology nor those
heavily armed with the " Word of God," and certainly not the Existentialists,
nor indeed any other great musicians before and after him, either know or can
express and maintain as he did. In this respect he was pure in heart, far
transcending both optimists and pessimists. 1756–1791 ! This was the time
when God was under attack for the Lisbon earthquake, and theologians and
other well-meaning folk were hard put to it to defend Him. In face of the
problem of theodicy, Mozart had the peace of God which far transcends all the
critical or speculative reason that praises and reproves. This problem lay
behind him. Why then concern himself with it ? He had heard, and causes
those who have ears to hear, even to-day, what we shall not see until the end
of time—the whole context of providence. As though in the light of this end,
he heard the harmony of creation to which the shadow also belongs but in
which the shadow is not darkness, deficiency is not defeat, sadness cannot
become despair, trouble cannot degenerate into tragedy and infinite melancholy
is not ultimately forced to claim undisputed sway. Thus the cheerfulness
in this harmony is not without its limits. But the light shines all the more
brightly because it breaks forth from the shadow. The sweetness is also bitter
and cannot therefore cloy. Life does not fear death but knows it well. *Et
lux perpetua lucet* (sic !) *eis*—even the dead of Lisbon. Mozart saw this light no
more than we do, but he heard the whole world of creation enveloped by this
light. Hence it was fundamentally in order that he should not hear a middle or
neutral note, but the positive far more strongly than the negative. He heard
the negative only in and with the positive. Yet in their inequality he heard them
both together, as, for example, in the Symphony in G-minor of 1788. He never
heard only the one in abstraction. He heard concretely, and therefore his
compositions were and are total music. Hearing creation unresentfully and
impartially, he did not produce merely his own music but that of creation, its
twofold and yet harmonious praise of God. He neither needed nor desired to
express or represent himself, his vitality, sorrow, piety, or any programme. He
was remarkably free from the mania for self-expression. He simply offered
himself as the agent by which little bits of horn, metal and catgut could serve as
the voices of creation, sometimes leading, sometimes accompanying and sometimes in harmony. He made use of instruments ranging from the piano and
violin, through the horn and the clarinet, down to the venerable bassoon, with
the human voice somewhere among them, having no special claim to distinction
yet distinguished for this very reason. He drew music from them all, expressing
even human emotions in the service of this music, and not *vice versa*. He himself
was only an ear for this music, and its mediator to other ears. He died when
according to the worldly wise his life-work was only ripening to its true fulfilment.
But who shall say that after the " Magic Flute," the Clarinet Concerto of October
1791 and the Requiem, it was not already fulfilled ? Was not the whole of his
achievement implicit in his works at the age of 16 or 18 ? Is it not heard in what
has come down to us from the very young Mozart ? He died in misery like an
" unknown soldier," and in company with Calvin, and Moses in the Bible, he
has no known grave. But what does this matter ? What does a grave matter
when a life is permitted simply and unpretentiously, and therefore serenely,

authentically and impressively, to express the good creation of God, which also includes the limitation and end of man.

I make this interposition here, before turning to chaos, because in the music of Mozart—and I wonder whether the same can be said of any other works before or after—we have clear and convincing proof that it is a slander on creation to charge it with a share in chaos because it includes a Yes and a No, as though orientated to God on the one side and nothingness on the other. Mozart causes us to hear that even on the latter side, and therefore in its totality, creation praises its Master and is therefore perfect. Here on the threshhold of our problem—and it is no small achievement—Mozart has created order for those who have ears to hear, and he has done it better than any scientific deduction could. This is the point which I wish to make.

But there is another and very different reason for rejecting this confusion. The confusion itself and as such is a masterpiece and even a triumph of nothingness. This is so not merely because it entails a slander on creation, and an act of stupidity and ingratitude towards the Creator who seeks His own likeness, but also because it implies a most subtle concealment of genuine nothingness, because in this confusion with what is not null but perfect the latter fabricates a kind of alibi under cover of which it cannot be recognised and can thus pursue its dangerous and disruptive ways the more unfeared and unhampered. For what happens when we wrongfully indict the Creator and the creature? What happens when we seek, localise and apprehend the real source of danger and distress to the creature, perhaps lamenting and bewailing and taking it tragically, but openly or secretly adapting and preparing to use it, at a point where in actual fact no more is involved than this negative aspect of creation and existence? What obviously happens is that we neither perceive nor evaluate it as true nothingness, but accept it, incorporate it into our philosophical outlook, validitate and exculpate it, and thus, if we are consistent, finally justify it, not regarding and treating it as null, but as an essential and necessary part of existence. This is inevitable, for no reality corresponds to this confusion. Though we may err and deceive ourselves and others by seeking nothingness in the negative side of creation, this does not alter the fact that this negative side also belongs to God's good and perfect creation. It does not alter the fact that the real or supposed antithesis between the negative and the positive side is a relative and provisional one which is basically not only innocuous but even salutary in view of the orientation of creation on Jesus Christ. Our confusion is wrecked on the rock of this truth. But this means that, no matter how serious and solemn and tragic we may be, and even if we may identify ourselves theoretically or practically with Marcion and Schopenhauer (and *Auch Einer* [1]), we do not really come to grips with true nothingness, with the real adversary which menaces and corrupts us so long as we look in this direction. Entangled in this confusion, we can never achieve the seriousness which is required in

---

[1] *Auch Einer* is a novel by F. T. Vischer—Translator's note.

face of true nothingness. What is not dangerous *in re* simply cannot be treated as if it were *in cognitione*. However serious we may pretend to be, and even in the spasms of real seriousness occasioned by this great deception, we shall still come to terms with it somehow. We shall encounter it as an adversary with whom we contend but may at a pinch capitulate and come to terms, indeed, with whom we must come to terms, because with it we are " in the same boat " as the whole of creation and finally the good Lord Himself. We shall encounter it with a bad conscience and without joy, yet temporarily lulled by these considerations; whereas Mozart encountered the inner antithesis with joy and a good conscience. What we wrongly regard as nothingness will be considered in the context of God's good creation, or rather what we arbitrarily think to be good in it. We shall then find some way of showing that it stands in a dialectical relationship to the so-called good, and therefore assume that we can see a higher unity of both. On the wrong assumption that it is genuine nothingness, we shall then be able to ascribe to it a certain goodness, a certain participation in good. In short, nothingness suddenly becomes something which is ultimately innocuous, and even salutary. Real sin can then be regarded as a venial error and mistake, a temporary retardation, and *comprendre c'est pardonner*. Real evil can then be interpreted as transitory and not intolerable imperfection, and real death as " rest in God." The devil can then be denied or described as the last candidate for a salvation which is due to him too by reason of a general *apokatastasis*. Nothingness can then be tidily " demythologized," although in actual fact what is in question is not real nothingness, but only the misconceived negative side of creation, which is not null *in re*. Nor must we fail to realise that, while we indulge in this formidable confusion, real nothingness, real sin, evil, death and the devil, are no less present and active, although not where man in his folly seeks and thinks to find them. The whole trouble is that they are overlooked, forgotten, unnoticed, unexpected and disregarded. While we look in the wrong direction, and there hope to hear ultimate harmonies and to accomplish ultimate syntheses, they are not taken seriously in their reality. Is not the consequence clear ? Do not all the seriousness in face of sin and the grave, all the tragedy, all the fear of the devil, to which we think we must give way in virtue of this confusion, seeking the adversary where he is not to be found, and not seeking him where he is, constitute not only an empty calumniation of the Creator and creature, but also direct co-operation with what is attempted against them by true nothingness ? The more tidily the latter is " demythologized," i.e., the more it is interpreted as an element in a philosophical system in which things are not really so dangerous, and what is dangerous is only what occasions a little fear and sadness, tragedy and remorse, the more this confusion establishes itself ; or, conversely, the more the strange mystery of the true nothingness between Creator and creature is reduced to fantasy, the more freely and surely nothingness can take its course and exercise its power. Is it not manifest that in the masquerade and camouflage of this confusion and the concurrent insult offered to Creator and creature, in the infamous trick which is played upon us and which we ourselves help to play, we have the most palpable self-revelation and self-demonstration of genuine nothingness ? The very existence and essence of the latter is that this can and does happen. In this way nothingness deceives us, we let ourselves be deceived by it, and we deceive ourselves. In this way true nothingness irrupts into God's good creation. In this way we ourselves come to have a part in its nullity.

Where is the error in this confusion, and why must we avoid it ? We call it an insult to Creator and creature because it contradicts God's self-manifestation in Jesus Christ. Since God's Word became flesh, He Himself has acknowledged that the distinct reality of the world created by Him is in both its forms, with its Yes and its No, that of the world which He willed. He has thus revealed its right to this twofold form, and therefore the goodness of creation. We cannot believe in Jesus Christ and repudiate this right of the Creator and creature proclaimed in Him. We cannot ignore the fact that in Jesus Christ God has again and expressly claimed the whole of creation as His work, adopting and as it were taking it to heart in both its positive and negative aspects. In the knowledge of Jesus Christ we must abandon the obvious prejudice against the negative aspect of creation and confess that God has planned and made all things well, even on the negative side. In the knowledge of Jesus Christ it is inadmissible to seek nothingness here.

But in this confusion an error is also made in relation to nothingness itself. Being sought where he is not to be found, the enemy goes unrecognised. He assumes a form, a relatively and ultimately innocuous form, to which he has no right and in which he cannot be taken seriously. Being understood as a side or aspect or distinctive form of creation, nothingness is brought into a positive relationship with God's will and work. Its nature and existence are attributed to God, to His will and responsibility, and the menacing and corruption of creation by nothingness are understood as His intention and act and therefore as a necessary and tolerable part of creaturely existence. We cannot really fear and loathe nothingness. We cannot consider and treat it as a real enemy. We have already decided to make terms with it, and thus unconsciously to give it power and honour. Without desiring to do so, we already serve it most effectively, for how could we better serve it than by this misapprehension ? But why must we avoid this confusion as a misconception of nothingness itself ? Why is a very different seriousness demanded in face of nothingness from that which is required in face of the negative aspect of creation and which, because God's creation is good even on this side too, can only be a relative seriousness and can have nothing whatever to do with real fear or loathing ?

3. THE KNOWLEDGE OF NOTHINGNESS

To answer this question we must revert to the source of all Christian knowledge, namely, to the knowledge of Jesus Christ, though now in a different sense. For in Him there is revealed not only the goodness of God's creation in its twofold form, but also the true nothingness which is utterly distinct from both Creator and creation, the adversary with whom no compromise is possible, the negative which is more than the mere complement of an antithetical positive, the left which is not counterpoised by any right, the antithesis which is not merely within creation and therefore dialectical but which is primarily and supremely to God Himself and therefore to the totality of the created world. This antithesis has no substantive existence within creation, i.e., it is not a creaturely element confronted by others as elements of good. It is the antithesis which can be present and active within creation only as an absolute alien opposing and contradicting all its elements, whether positive or negative. It is the antithesis which the creature (which it does of course greatly concern) cannot possibly envisage, comprehend and explain within creation, even though it is present and active within it. It is the antithesis which cannot be synoptically viewed, or reduced to a common denominator, or reconciled, with what is opposed to it. It is the antithesis whose relationship to creation is real but absolutely negative, offering only menace, corruption and death, so that it must never be expressed in terms of synthesis. For a real synthesis, which must always be the criterion of an ideal or intellectual, cannot be effected except by the surrender of creation to the negation, menace and corruption offered by this antithesis. It is the antithesis which is only comprehensible in correlation with creation not as an equilibrating but an absolute and uncompromising No. For it is in opposition primarily and supremely to God Himself, and therefore necessarily and irrevocably to all His work and creation. Yet God Himself comprehends, envisages and controls it. This is the insight which in the context of the doctrine of providence we seek to attain in this whole section. For God is Master of this antithesis. He overcomes and has already overcome it. The negative content and significance of His saving decree and act in Jesus Christ are that this antithesis should be finally routed and the creature liberated from it, as His sovereignty requires. But we have not yet reached this point. God alone, the God who from all eternity has decreed its defeat, transcends the antithesis, comprehending, envisaging and controlling it. For us it remains the antithesis which we can neither conquer nor comprehend, neither envisage nor master and control either in theory or practice. It is the antithesis which is impatient of any legitimate synthesis. God, but He alone, can deal with it and has already done so, in accordance with the fact that He transcends it from all eternity in His essence as God. But it must be clearly understood that He has treated it as His adversary, as the No which is primarily and supremely addressed to Himself, as the nothingness which is the true nothingness in opposition to Himself and His will and work. But if this is the relationship between God and nothingness, we cannot and must not include it in the creaturely world, in the divine creation, or in any way relativise or subtly minimise it. Any theoretical synthesis we contemplate between creaturely existence and genuine nothingness can only be a description of its triumph over creaturely existence, and therefore blasphemy. Our only option is to refrain from any such attempt in the radical fear and abhorrence which alone are appropriate. In face of this antithesis, this adversary, genuine nothingness, there is place only for the seriousness which we cannot exercise even in face of the negative side of creation. For here we are confronted by what is not only abhorrent to ourselves but also primarily and supremely to God Himself, and therefore terrifying to His creature faced with its ultimate and mortal threat. If we are weak and inclined to conciliation or appeasement, we treat God's enemy as our friend, thus renouncing our one hope of deliverance from the danger which overhangs us. For the sake of God nothingness can only be nothing worth. Against it, God is our one hope. For it is His enemy no less than ours.

How do we know this? How do we know that nothingness really exists, and does so in such a way, in such radical superiority, that it cannot be legitimately incorporated into any philosophical system, that we must not try to treat it as one element in the world among others? We know all this clearly, directly and certainly from the source of all Christian knowledge, the knowledge of Jesus Christ. It must be clearly grasped that the incarnation of the Word of God was obviously not necessary merely to reveal the goodness of God's creation in its twofold form. To be sure, it gives us this revelation too. When God Himself became a creature in Jesus Christ, He confirmed His creation in its totality as an act of His wisdom and mercy, as His good creation without blemish or blame. Yet much more than this was involved. It is written that " the Word became flesh," i.e., that it became not only a creature, but a creature in mortal peril, a creature threatened and actually corrupted, a creature which in face and in spite of its goodness, and in disruption and destruction of its imparted goodness, was subject not to an internal but to an external attack which it could neither contain nor counter. The Word became a creature which had fallen under the sway of a possessive and domineering alien, and was therefore itself alienated from its Creator and itself, unable to recover or retrace its way home. The Word became a creature to which it was of no avail to be the creature of God, or to receive confirmation of its creation by Him, or to remember the wisdom and mercy in which it was created, because it was betrayed and *nolens volens* subjected to a determination inimical to its creation in wisdom and mercy. That the Word became flesh means that the Word became a creature of this kind, a lost creature. That God's Word, God's Son, God Himself, became flesh means no other than that God saw a challenge to Himself in this assault on His creature, in this invading alien, in this other determination of His creature, in its capture and self-surrender. It means that God took to heart the attack on His creature because He saw in it an attack on His own cause and therefore on Himself, seeing His own enemy in this domineering alien, intruder, usurper and tyrant. God therefore arose, and in His Son gave and humbled Himself, Himself becoming flesh, this ruined and lost human creature, setting Himself wholly in the place of His work and possession. To be sure, He did this in confirmation of His goodness as Creator and of that of His creature. But for this reason He did so in His own most proper cause, repelling an injury and insult offered to Himself. He did so in necessary and righteous wrath, not against His creature but against its temptation and destruction, against its deviation, defection and consequent degeneration. He did so as a Judge asserting His own right and therefore restoring that of His creature. And therefore in His Son He exposed Himself with it to this assault, to this alien, to this hostile determination, yielding to this adversary in solidarity with His creature, and in this way routing it, achieving what the creature, who was and is only secondary in this matter, could not accomplish but yet required for its deliverance.

Our present interest in all this is that it is obviously the decisive ground of our knowledge of the whole problem with which we are concerned. Here we can see what nothingness is. Here we can see its true nature and reality. Here we can see that it is an antithesis not only to God's whole creation but to the Creator Himself. What challenged Him and provoked His wrath, what made Him come forth as the Judge, what made Him yield to nothingness in order to overcome it, was obviously nothing that He Himself had chosen, willed or done. It was nothing that He would or could previously have affirmed. It was nothing—day or night—that He as Creator had declared to be very good. It was nothing that could be considered the end and aim of His creation. That which rendered necessary the birth of His Son in the stable of Bethlehem and His death upon the cross of Calvary, that which by this birth and death He smote, defeated and destroyed, is that which primarily opposes and resists God Himself, and therefore all creation. It is obvious that this neither can nor may be understood as something which He Himself has posited or decreed, and that it cannot be subsumed under any synthesis. It thus demands on our part a wholly different seriousness from that imposed by life and the world—the seriousness of a radical fear and loathing founded on hope in the God who is primarily affected but who is omnipotent and supreme and therefore our only hope. What is nothingness, the real nothingness which is not to be confounded with the negative side of God's good creation behind which it seeks to shelter for greater strength? What is nothingness unmasked and deprived of that camouflage by which it seeks to deceive us, and we ourselves? In plain and precise terms, the answer is that nothingness is the "reality" on whose account (i.e., against which) God Himself willed to become a creature in the creaturely world, yielding and subjecting Himself to it in Jesus Christ in order to overcome it. Nothingness is thus the "reality" which opposes and resists God, which is itself subjected to and overcome by His opposition and resistance, and which in this twofold determination as the reality that negates and is negated by Him, is totally distinct from Him. The true nothingness is that which brought Jesus Christ to the cross, and that which He defeated there. Only from the standpoint of Jesus Christ, His birth, death and resurrection, do we see it in reality and truth, without the temptation to treat it as something inclusive or relative, or to conceive it dialectically and thus render it innocuous. From this standpoint we see it with fear and trembling as the adversary with whom God and God alone can cope. But it is to be noted that in this we see it where our one real hope against it is grounded and established. If there is confusion concerning it, we obviously do not see it from the standpoint of Jesus Christ.

It is evident that the concept may at once be developed in many different ways against this background. We can and must ask and say what real evil is, real death, the real devil and real hell—questions to which we can give only the most summary answers in this context. Above all, although it is not our present theme, our eyes are opened to the most important of all its forms, i.e., the real sin of man, its source and its several manifestations and consequences. When seen in the light of Jesus Christ, the concrete form in which nothingness is active and revealed is the sin of man as his personal act and guilt, his aberration from the grace of God and its command, his refusal of the gratitude he owes to God and the concomitant freedom and obligation, his arrogant attempt to be his own master, provider and comforter, his unhallowed lust for what is not his own, the falsehood, hatred and pride in which he is enmeshed in relation to his neighbour, the stupidity to which he is self-condemned, and a life which follows the course thereby determined on the basis of the necessity thus imposed. In the light of Jesus Christ, it is impossible to escape the truth that we ourselves as sinners have become the victims and servants of nothingness, sharing its nature and producing and extending it.

Nevertheless we must be careful not to relinquish the position that the objective ground of our knowledge of nothingness is really Jesus Christ Himself. We must be careful not to transfer this ground to the consciousness of our own existence and sin as though this were our direct consciousness of nothingness. We must be careful not to postulate a knowledge of human sin, whether immediate or mediated or occasioned by an abstract law, as the real source of the truth required.

For the knowledge of sin it is formally decisive that it should be recognised as man's personal act and guilt, that man should be and be made responsible for it, and this in such a way that he can neither renounce his liability nor impute it to others nor to an inexorable fate. It is essential that the direct climax should be seen which compels man to confess that alien and enemy, and to acknowledge his own treachery in giving entrance to the enemy. This is indeed the only serious knowledge of nothingness. But this knowledge is assured only if God Himself, and God in His Word and work, and therefore Jesus Christ, is its basis. We must remember that what we know of ourselves is necessarily relative to our creatureliness. Therefore even our most sincere and serious self-consciousness, even our profoundest experience of our own existence, cannot reveal sin except as an element in our creatureliness. The consciousness of sin of which we are immediately capable in mere self-understanding can consist only in the ultimate realisation that the twofold determination of creation runs through our own lives, that in us, too, the Yes is confronted by the No, the light by shadow. It can consist only in this realisation because the consciousness of sin itself cannot amount to more than an awareness of the deficiency of our spontaneity and activity, and therefore of our action, and to that extent of our existence in the true sense. But this deficiency is not our true sin. Even when we are conscious of our deficiency we are still able to take a detached view of ourselves, and to correlate the evil in us with the good which is certainly not lacking. We are still able to make favourable comparisons of ourselves with others, and to reflect on the general contrariety of creaturely existence, its intrinsic tension and distinctive dialectic. When the knowledge of sin derives from man's self-communion it cannot possibly be a knowledge of real nothingness, of real sin, because in the knowledge of sin acquired in this way there can be no indictment of the existence of man in its totality, including its Yes and No and light and shadow, as one which involves a repudiation of the grace of God and its command, a breach with the neighbour, and a perversion of creaturely nature. Why should man accuse himself? Why should he accept this accusation ? What we say to ourselves on this ground can never be this total indictment, nor consist in the saying : " Thou are the man." I can and will be told that I am a real sinner, responsible for the reality of nothingness because I am its bearer and doer, only when I am told it by God Himself. And it can be told me by God Himself only as He reveals Himself to me in His opposition to real nothingness, to sin, as His real adversary, so that I see that He Himself is contradicted and resisted by this enemy and opposes to him His own more powerful contradiction and resistance, and thus abolishes and overcomes him. No abstract law of God, if such were possible, could reveal this to me—only the law of His grace and judicial action, the law of His covenant. These alone can speak to me of sin, of my real sin, which is not an attribute or defect of the creature, but an insult to the Creator and therefore its guilt. This guilt cannot be estimated, assessed, evaluated or classified by the creature, since the creature itself permits and participates in it, bearing and committing the offence against God. It can be revealed to me only by the God who Himself became flesh in His Word, yielding to the adversary in the flesh and judging sin in the flesh (Rom. 8³). It can be revealed to me only by Jesus Christ, because in Him alone and in His light real nothingness, the real sin that wages war with God and is assailed and overcome by Him, stands revealed as the sin of man, and so revealed that I may no longer regard it as a defect or as something natural but must rather recognise in it the alien and adversary to whom I myself have given place. Again, only in Him did the Word of God become flesh, flesh of my flesh, to judge sin in the flesh, executing this judgment for me as my Brother. Only in relation to Him as my Substitute do I know myself as the man who is also smitten by this judgment. Only in relation to what reality is in or in face of Him can and must I confess myself to be such a man, and acknowledge that I am a sinner, a real sinner before God. In relation to Him I can and must do this. But we must be clear that all our knowledge and acknowledgment of sin can be genuine and related to our own real sin, to true nothingness, only when it is clearly apprehended that sin and nothingness are primarily and properly known in Jesus Christ and acknowledged by Him, so that in this respect, too, we can only follow Him, adding our indirect and secondary knowledge and acknowledgment to His. Unless Jesus Christ is their objective basis, our own knowledge and acknowledgment will bear no real relation to the alien and adversary here involved, nor to the insult which it is his very nature to offer to God ; and we ourselves shall certainly accept no responsibility for this insult. This is the first and formal reason why, to understand the nature of nothingness, we must not turn elsewhere than to the heart of the Gospel. But there are also two material reasons.

The reality of nothingness is not seen sharply enough, even in its concrete form as sin, if sin is understood only generally as aberration from God and disobedience to His will. This is true enough, but we cannot stop at this generalisation. Otherwise we might escape and extricate ourselves with the assertion that we are men, creatures, and not God, and that therefore our aberration from God, and to that extent our disobedience, and therefore sin and nothingness, are basically no more than our essential and natural imperfection in contrast with His perfection. Even in the bitterness of self-accusation we might still excuse and even justify ourselves by arguing that there can obviously be no real conformity between creature and Creator, and that this cannot be expected, so that the divine demand for obedience is robbed of its ultimate rigour and its transgression is not quite so serious a matter. In sin as the concrete form of nothingness we should then be dealing again with merely the negative aspect of creation. This is the point where it becomes particularly clear and definite that, even if such be possible, no abstract law of God, whether revealed or natural, can possibly be the objective ground of the knowledge of real sin. An abstract law can no more make us conscious of the true nature of our sin or the seriousness of our situation than the most conscientious self-examination. In face of a stark demand of God we might well be conscious of the imperfection of our actions, but we should not find our escape cut off. This is the case only when we realise that as disobedience to the will of God sin is a repudiation of His grace and its command, and therefore on the one hand a refusal of the gratitude which is naturally due to the gracious God, and on the other a rupture of the relationships with our neighbours which are normal and natural because this gracious God is our Creator. In relation to his gracious Creator man ought to be both free and bound by nature, not to a divine or even a heavenly but to a creaturely and earthly perfection, corresponding though not equal to the perfection of his Father in heaven. In relation to his gracious Creator man could and should live in this righteousness. His sin consists in the fact—and this is why it is so real and inexcusable—that he repudiates this possibility and imperative, and therefore the grace of God and its command. Hence he can no longer claim that he is only human and therefore fallible and not God. He cannot interpret his sin as mere retardment. God has not required too much of him, nor was he unable to meet His demand. God in His goodness required no more of him than his adherence to this goodness, and man was free and bound by nature to meet this demand. In all its majesty, the sovereign will of God which he resisted was His merciful, patient and generous will. It was this will that he rejected, preferring to go his own way. This is what gives such seriousness to the opposition between God and human sin, between God and the sinner. This is what reveals the true nature of sin and nothingness as our repudiation of the goodness of God.

But how can we maintain that this is the case? How do we have knowledge of the gracious Creator? How do we know, then, that our fellowship with Him is our true and natural state? How do we have consequent knowledge of our real sin and real nothingness? How do we perceive that the command or law against which we sin is the command or law of God's grace? How does this command or law so judge us that we are left with no avenue of escape? The answer is obvious if Jesus Christ is the objective ground of knowledge of sin and nothingness. For the incarnation of the Word of God was not the revelation of a mere requirement or abstract divine law, and therefore of an abstract indictment and condemnation which man might evade by pleading the severity of God and his own human frailty. But when the Word of God became flesh, God took up the cause of sinful man enslaved to nothingness and subject to sin, putting His creative will into operation and revealing it as the will of His mercy. In the incarnate Word God has shown that His goodness to His creature is His persistent attitude. With His right to the creature He has vindicated and restored its own natural right. Himself becoming a creature, and attacking and overcoming that which offended Him, He has dealt with it as also an offence to His creature, and completely destroyed it. The cause which He assumed in the flesh as the Judge of sin was the cause of man as well. Thus the incarnation of His Word is the new and ultimate revelation of His grace, the ratification of the faithfulness which He pledged to the creature when He made it. It proves that His mercy is not conditional but unconditional, and that it cannot be reversed even by sin and nothingness. But all this is proved in His confrontation with sin and in the confrontation of sin with Himself as the One who is essentially the gracious God. Yet it is only in Jesus Christ and not in an abstract divine law, however founded and formulated, that we have a revelation of real sin, of its nature as real enmity against the grace of God, and of man's refusal of the gratitude natural to him. The sickness is disclosed with the cure. How else could we see it? As the grace of the covenant, i.e., as the requirement which results from the covenant established, maintained and fulfilled by Him, as the command imposed on us by God's faithfulness and mercy, the Law in this concrete form confers the knowledge of sin. It "worketh wrath" and "killeth" with the irrefutable verdict that the disobedience of man does not consist in imperfection but in guilt. If it were not the command of the gracious God, how could man be conscious of his guilt, indeed how could he be guilty at all? Why should he not justifiably plead the weakness of his humanity? But he cannot do this in face of the command of the gracious God, the God who is unconditionally for him, who from the very outset is his God and Father. He cannot do it in face of the command of the God revealed in Jesus Christ. The command of the gracious God invalidates any such plea, convicting man of an opposition and resistance for which there can be no explanation, excuse or justification. This command which exposes the real nothingness served and effected by man is the command of Jesus Christ. No shifts or turns can alter the fact that without this objective ground of knowledge there can be no real insight in this matter, and the result will necessarily be some form of that major confusion.

The other material reason for strict adherence to this source of knowledge is as follows. We have called sin the concrete form of nothingness because in sin it becomes man's own act, achievement and guilt. Yet nothingness is not exhausted in sin. It is also something under which we suffer in a connexion with sin which is sometimes palpable but sometimes we can only sense and sometimes is closely hidden. In Holy Scripture, while man's full responsibility for its commission is maintained, even sin itself is described as his surrender to the alien power of an adversary. Contrary to his will and expectation, the sin of man is not beneficial to him but detrimental. He is led astray and harms himself, or rather lets himself be harmed. He is not merely a thief but one who has himself fallen among thieves. Sin as such is not only an offence to God ; it also disturbs, injures and destroys the creature and its nature. And although there can be no doubt that it is committed by man, it is obviously attended and followed by suffering, i.e., the suffering of evil and death. It is not merely attended and followed by the ills which are inseparably bound up with creaturely existence in virtue of the negative aspect of creation, but by the suffering of evil as something wholly anomalous which threatens and imperils this existence and is no less inconsistent with it than sin itself, as the preliminary experience of an absolutely alien factor which is radically opposed to the sense and purpose of creation and therefore to the Creator Himself. Nor is it a mere matter of dying as the natural termination of life, but of death itself as the intolerable, life-destroying thing to which all suffering hastens as its goal, as the ultimate irruption and triumph of that alien power which annihilates creaturely existence and thus discredits and disclaims the Creator. There is real evil and real death as well as real sin. In another connexion it will fall to be indicated that there is also a real devil with his legions, and a real hell. But here it will suffice to recognise real evil and real death. " Real " again means in opposition to the totality of God's creation. That nothingness has the form of evil and death as well as sin shows us that it is what it is not only morally but physically and totally. It is the comprehensive negation of the creature and its nature. And as such it is a power which, though unsolicited and uninvited, is superior, like evil and death, to all the forces which the creature can oppose to it. As negation nothingness has its own dynamic, the dynamic of damage and destruction with which the creature cannot cope.

Knowledge of these important features is attained when it is seen in these forms, i.e., the forms of evil and death. Evil and death may be distinguished from sin in so far as they primarily and immediately attack the creature but indirectly and properly the Creator, whereas sin primarily and immediately attacks God and only indirectly the creature. Yet both attack the creature no less than God. And it is also a common feature that they are necessarily incomprehensible and inexplicable to us as creatures. It is absolutely essential that nothingness should be seen in all these forms and aspects if we are to understand what is at issue and to what we refer.

But in this totality, in the form in which it is not merely evil but the supreme adversary and assailant, in the mode in which it must be suffered by the creature, nothingness is to be known only at the heart of the Gospel, i.e., in Jesus Christ. In the incarnation God exposed Himself to nothingness even as this enemy and assailant. He did so in order to repel and defeat it. He did so in order to destroy the destroyer. The Gospel records of the miracles and acts of Jesus are not just formal proofs of His Messiahship, of His divine mission, authority and power, but as such they are objective manifestations of His character as the Conqueror not only of sin but also of evil and death, as the Destroyer of the destroyer, as the Saviour in the most inclusive sense. He not only forgives the sins of men ; He also removes the source of their suffering. He resists the whole assault. To its power He opposes His own power, the transcendent power of God. He shows Himself to be the total Victor. He works as the perfect Comforter. This emphasis is unmistakeable in the New Testament, and if for any reason we erase it we necessarily annul its testimony and silence the voice of Him to whom it testifies. For here there not only speaks but acts the One who has come to hurl Himself against the opposition and resistance of nothingness in its form as hostile and aggressive power. Here there speaks and acts the One who for the salvation of the creature and the glory of God has routed nothingness as the total principle of enmity, physical as well as moral. He is not only the way and the truth ; He is also the life, the resurrection and the life. If He were not the Saviour in this total sense, He would not be the Saviour at all in the New Testament sense. It is a serious matter that all the Western as opposed to the Eastern Church has invariably succeeded in minimising and devaluating, and still does so to-day, this New Testament emphasis. And Protestantism especially has always been far too moralistic and spiritualistic, and has thus been blind to this aspect of the Gospel. In this respect we have every cause to pay more attention rather than less. We certainly cannot afford to make arbitrary demarcations, and therefore not to see, or not to want to see, the total Saviour of the New Testament. According to the New Testament, the last and true form in which Jesus exposed Himself to this total enemy is that of His crucifixion.

He did it by suffering death, this death, the death of condemnation. The New Testament says that He suffered death for the forgiveness of the sins of many, but it also says, and the two statements must not be dissociated, that He did so in order to take away the power of death, real death, death as the condemnation and destruction of the creature, death as the offender against God and the last enemy. In His resurrection from the dead God reveals that He has done this. His resurrection sums up the whole process of revelation. It is the manifestation of the divine act which according to the New Testament was effected in His work, the work of His person. According to this witness, it shows that His death is God's own reconciling and liberating act against nothingness, in all its scope and dimensions. But since this may be affirmed only of Him, only of the divine act which, according to the witness of the New Testament, was effected and revealed in Jesus Christ, from this standpoint too the only knowledge which includes a knowledge of true nothingness is that of Jesus Christ. In Him, i.e., in contradistinction to Him, nothingness is exposed in its entirety as the adversary which can destroy both body and soul in hell, as the evil one which is also the destructive factor of evil and death that stands in sinister conflict against the creature and its Creator, not merely as an idea which man may conceive and to which he can and does give allegiance but as the power which invades and subjugates and carries him away captive, so that he is wholly and utterly lost in face of it. In the incarnation Jesus Christ, God Himself, has exposed Himself to this real nothingness. And He has proved Himself to be its Victor. In so doing He has disclosed and revealed its true nature and threat, its impotence against the creature, and its utter impotence against the Creator. This being the case, we have every reason to adhere to the truth that Jesus Christ Himself is the objective ground of our knowledge even of nothingness.

In dealing with this whole question of the objective ground of our knowledge of nothingness, I have been engaged in implicit controversy with the most significant literary work which has as yet been specifically devoted to this difficult theme. I refer to the famous book by the Halle theologian Julius Müller first published in 1838–44, *Die Christliche Lehre von der Sünde* (E.T. *The Christian Doctrine of Sin*, 2 Vols., 1885). In this work we have one of those phenomena in 19th-century Protestant theology which reflect a partial yet very definite movement in opposition to the general trend. J. Müller was of the view that there is a point at which contemporary Christian Monism, the synoptic view of God and the world, God and man and sin and redemption classically represented by Schleiermacher and Hegel, comes up against a frontier where it either ceases to be Christian or must cease to be monistic. Other theological individualists of the time found the same frontier at different points. Kohlbrügge found it in the problem of justification in Christ ; the elder Blumhardt in that of Christian hope ; Vilmar of Marburg in that of ecclesiastical order. But the specific point where Müller found it, where as a Christian theologian he felt obliged to employ Christian and not monistic categories, was the problem of sin. At this point he largely repudiated the widely adopted views and ideas of his time, accepting a Christian doctrine of evil only as a " conception of its inconceivability " (E.T. II, p. 172), only as the assertion of an utterly alien factor which is radically opposed and resistant to the nature of God and of man and their mutual relationship, for the existence of which man alone must bear responsibility, and the derivation and explanation of which from a higher principle are to be resolutely rejected. It is another matter that Müller does not remain wholly true to his own insight when in the second volume he introduces the curious theory of a " pre-temporal fall " of which the temporal reality of human sin must be regarded as a consequence or at least an epiphenomenon. But, as we shall see, it is difficult and even impossible to make any meaningful final or initial pronouncement on this alien and entirely negative reality without incurring the suspicion of covertly seeking to expound it in a " speculative " manner, incorporating it into a system and thus misrepresenting its nature. We may ignore these doubtful features in Müller's exposition in view of the fact that he so sharply perceived and propounded the problem itself, and that he was the first and only scholar of his day to do so.

The implicit controversy with him in my own statement is in respect of the decisive and objective ground of knowledge normative in this question. Müller was a product of his age, and followed almost all earlier tradition, in accepting it as axiomatic and incontestable that the reality and nature of the factor which separates God and man can be established and discussed as it were in a vacuum, in the mere analysis of evident facts. His apparent rule is that, if we consider human existence in its psychological, sociological and historical reality, a little serious reflection will necessarily lead us to the conclusion that man is a sinner. The words with which he introduces his great exposition (I, p. 28) plainly characterise what he regards as a self-evident procedure : " It requires no special profundity of reflection but only a moderate degree of moral earnestness to prompt us thoughtfully to pause before one great phenomenon of human life, and ever and anon to turn towards it a scrutinizing look. I refer to the phenomenon of evil ; the presence of an element of disturbance and discord in a sphere where the demand for harmony and unity is felt with peculiar emphasis. It meets us at every turn as the history of the human race in the course of its development passes before us ; it betrays its presence in manifold forms when we fix our eyes upon the closest relationships of society ; and we cannot hide from ourselves its reality when we look into our own hearts. It is a dark and dismal shadow, casting a gloom over every department of human life, and continually pervading its fairest and brightest forms." The lofty moral earnestness which like so many before and after him Müller exhibited in discussing this phenomenon is indubitable. He was deficient neither in deep and comprehensive insight into human reality nor in scrupulous consideration of earlier thought and opinion. In this regard the monograph he devoted to this unrewarding theme leaves nothing to be desired. On the contrary, the outstanding and enduring significance of his work is that he confronts this dark stain on the psychological, sociological and historical picture of man with greater thoughtfulness, perplexity and alarm, that he investigates and explores this sphere with greater thoroughness, and that he weighs and evaluates the dialectics and limitations of the various ancient and modern theories with greater exactitude, not only than his contemporaries, but also than most of the representatives of the earlier tradition. There is only one question which he apparently neither contemplates nor pursues. It is the radical question whether this dark stain can be so directly perceived, identified, analysed and assessed as though it were one phenomenon among others, or whether knowledge of this phenomenon is not a question of faith and therefore in the strict sense a theological question. Müller assumes the existence of sin as a matter of common knowledge, and he believes that a conscientious and comprehensive investigation and consideration must inevitably conduce to a knowledge of its nature. By this apparently direct approach he can come to the conviction that sin is that which stands in absolute opposition, and that as such it cannot have its source or justification either in the nature of God or in that of the creature or in their natural inter-relation, but can and must be understood only as man's evil act and guilt. Even before Müller, at the beginning of his *Religion within the Limits of Pure Reason* and on or even outwith the periphery of his own system, Kant claimed to be capable of demonstrating sin as a reality of this kind. He speaks, for example, of the " indwelling of the principle of evil alongside that of good." He refers to the evil which opposes good very differently from the way in which sensuousness opposes reason or folly wisdom. He says that its foundation is not inherent in the natural instincts of man, but in the " malice of the human heart." He speaks of the " bias " towards evil ; of the " inscrutable reason for the acceptance of unlawful maxims " ; of the corruption of the loftiest subjective ground of all maxims which is characteristic of man and his whole species, which in its way is just as much a matter of his freedom as of his obedience to the law, and for which he is responsible. He speaks of " radical evil." Kant does not state the source of his knowledge of this curious, perverted " freedom." Probably he would not have called it a " phenomenon," as Müller does. But he assumes that this perverted freedom is as patient of direct perception as true freedom, the freedom for good. And this is also the view of Müller. The remarkable accuracy of their main thesis invites the conjecture that perhaps their only failure is not to see that they actually accept the Christian insight and look from the heart of the Gospel. Since even a theologian like Müller was guilty of a radical failure at this point, and could not exploit all the possibilities offered, there are inevitably some serious gaps and weaknesses in his investigation and presentation.

1. He did, of course, try to understand evil as " absolutely alien and repugnant to our nature, to whose existence no higher standpoint and no clearer perception can ever reconcile us " (I, p. 30), so that we can only explain and acknowledge it as our guilt. In this respect, contrary to the prevalent trend of his age, he formally returned to the fundamentals of the Reformation and older Protestant theology. But when asked : " Whence knowest thou thy misery ? ", older Protestant theology could give a plain answer like that of the *Heidelberg Catechism* : " From the Law of God " (*Qu.* 3). Müller, too, refers at once to the Law, but for him it is only the idea of human life as voluntarily conditioned, so that the impression made upon an unbiassed mind is necessarily that of transcendent majesty. It is the " moral law," and in opposition to it evil is revealed as the deviation and perversion of the actual orientation of the will. " In this sense " (I, p. 43) he then seeks to apprehend what the Bible calls Law, sin and the knowledge of sin. But Müller does not make clear that the Bible speaks of the Accuser and Judge who transcends and confronts man, of God the Lawgiver (Christ according to the *Heidelberg Catechism*, *Qu.* 4) whose judgment reveals sin as sin and whose Word compels man to acknowledge himself a sinner. Therefore, although Müller's intrinsically correct assertions concerning the absolute enmity of sin and man's responsibility for its commission are impressive and important, they remain mere assertions and no more. They lack the authority which such exceptional declarations require and which alone can give weight to such unusual intelligence concerning the reality of this alien element. We can only surmise and suppose that both Müller and Kant based their theses on postulates which they suppress but which would give them the strict validity that a mere reference to the " moral law " is quite unable to do. However emphatic Müller's presentation and defence of his view, the result may simply be to estrange, as happened in the case of Goethe when confronted by Kant's assertion of " radical evil."

2. Conversely, Müller was only too faithful to the general trend of older Protestant theology in failing to understand the Law which reveals sin in the

light of the Gospel. He conceived of it as a stark abstract imperative rather than the Law of the covenant and grace. And it was in the light of this imperative that he then showed sin to be disobedience to God, selfishness, worldly affection etc., and finally guilt. He did not ask, however, how far God and man are so related that this imperative is reasonable, possible and necessary, and its non-observance is abhorrent and absurd. He was thus unable to show the true incomprehensibility, iniquity and culpability of sin. He was unable to show that sin is no mere formal but a material transgression, that it is not the breach of a high and difficult but a near and easy command—the requirement of the gratitude which is natural to man because the God who requires it is beside him, is covenanted to him in His mercy, has identified Himself with him and has freed and bound him to do His will. Müller was unable to show that it is the goodness of God which makes His Law binding on man, and therefore makes sin abhorrent as a loathsome product of nothingness. He was unable to show the invalidity of the familiar excuse that God is too exalted and his command too excessive and extraordinary for man in his frailty to fulfil it. He was unable to show the fact and extent that even as a sinner man is still indebted to the Law (i.e., in virtue of God's faithfulness), or that this is not so much a threat as a promise. He persisted in the dialectic of Law and sin, which, if they were based on a genuine understanding of the Epistles to the Romans and the Galatians, could only lead to the conclusion that Paul's experience on the road to Damascus did not consist in a manifestation of Christ but in a revelation of the Old Testament Law as understood by the Pharisees—the very thing from which Paul assures us again and again that he was then delivered. Müller completely obscured the fact that only the sweetness of the Old and New Testament Gospel and its command can make man conscious of the bitterness of his transgression, whereas a command which is wrongly called bitter, and is thus godless from the biblical standpoint, may certainly embitter man against an unknown and exalted God, but cannot reveal to him his personal bitterness, the bitterness of his transgression.

3. Again in agreement with theological tradition, at any rate in the West, Müller did not realise that human sin is not an isolated phenomenon but only one important aspect of the fundamental phenomenon of nothingness. Among the older theologians Polanus (*Synt. Theol. chr.*, 1609, VI, 7) was an exception when he devoted a special treatise to the *malum afflictionis*, and even placed it before his discussion of the *malum peccati et culpae*. In Müller the question of the *malum afflictionis*, of evil and death, arises only in connexion with the judgment and punishment of sin. He does not really seem to see anything but the *malum peccati et culpae*. For him the New Testament accounts of the acts of Jesus on behalf of the sick, the bewildered, the hungry, the dying and even the dead, and indeed the resurrection of Jesus Himself, seem to have no significance. It seems never to have occurred to him that in the physical evil concealed behind the shadowy side of the created cosmos we have a form of the enemy and no less an offence against God than that which reveals man to be a sinner. Hence Müller was incapable of any serious recognition of the power of this adversary or of this adversary as a power. He was entirely unaffected by the discovery made in this matter by the elder Blumhardt in his own lifetime. He thus restricted his monograph to the doctrine of sin. Nor could it have been otherwise. When the total Saviour and perfect Comforter is not the primary source of knowledge, it cannot be expected that there will be knowledge of the full misery of the creature, or of the absolute negation which is the source of this misery.

There are, of course, excuses for Müller, particularly in respect of the second and third points, for neither his contemporaries nor the authoritative tradition in which he stood had anything better to offer, and in his attempt to understand sin as a given factor apart from Jesus Christ he was simply following the general tendency. If I dissociate myself from Müller in his attempt and the resultant inferences I do so because he does not go to the heart of the matter, because one might have expected a new and better approach to the basis and to these three questions in view of the material accuracy of his main thesis, and because his conclusions especially show that a new and better approach is imperative.

We shall now consider some of the most important of the historically influential theories which we have implicitly rejected in our discussion. And first we must recall the mighty figure of G. W. Leibniz (cf. *C.D.*, III, 1, p. 388 ff.), who in his *Theodicy* and kindred works elaborates the following view of this matter. To the absolutely perfect God as the being who is self-consistent and who integrates in Himself absolute wisdom, power, freedom and goodness, there corresponds in perfection, although a relative perfection, this actual world of ours which, created and governed by Him, has been selected from an infinite range and is thus the best of all possible worlds. Yet while this is the case, and in this sense it is relatively perfect, the world still presents us with a problem. In short, it confronts us with the fact of metaphysical evil, and more extensively with the facts of physical suffering, moral evil, and death. These facts are as such incontrovertible. Yet they do not constitute a final or insoluble enigma, but one which is patient of satisfactory explanation.

The explanation offered is as follows. Metaphysical evil, as the sum and source of all others, is simply the essential non-divinity of the creature. That the divinely created world is the best possible world does not exclude but includes this imperfection, for the world is not God. God could not endow the world with absolute perfection except by making it another god. He has really blessed the creature and endowed it with an appropriate perfection by refraining from performing what is impossible for Himself. Thus the creature is perfect within the limitations of its non-divinity. If this non-divinity entails imperfection, this merely consists in creaturely limitation. It is not, then, a positive evil, nor should it be described as evil but only as a deficiency or " privation " proper to the creature. Privation is so conjoined by God to creaturely perfection as not to diminish but rather to augment it. The possible and actual evils of sorrow, sin and death proceed from this necessary metaphysical evil (which is not really an evil) and are explicable in like terms.

Sorrow is the pain which is no less unavoidable to the human spirit than pleasure, because the spirit is what it is only in conjunction with a material body and therefore, in conjunction with its perfection, shares all the positive and negative sensations of this body. Sorrow is meted out to human life and individual persons in accordance with the innate excellence and salutary benevolence of the cosmic order. It may be a just punishment or more generally a profitable educational process. But reason and patience will always make it essentially endurable. And in any case, in relation to the total realisation of the world order, there are more and greater grounds for pleasure than for pain, for joy than sorrow. As a later poet sang : " Hand in hand joy and woe, Together down the ages go." Finally, it must be said of sorrow that it is merely a partial and passing privation in the intrinsically though relatively perfect cosmic order governed by the absolutely perfect God. In the light of this, we must realise that sorrow is supportable even when and where we cannot understand its wider setting or see how it is to be endured in any particular instance.

The case is ultimately the same with moral evil and therefore with sin. God has made man capable of sin. He had to do so, for otherwise He would have deprived him of free will, thus denying him his spiritual and moral nature and therefore his distinctive perfection. Evil arises because the limitation innate in the creature emerges also in the region of the will. Naturally God does not will this. He does not will that man should sin. He does not cause or compel him to do so. Leibniz did not teach a necessity of sin in this sense. Yet God allows man to sin, and He does so in His beneficence. Man could not be a free and reasonable creature, living dutifully and to the glory of God ; he could not be the man whom the grace of God encounters and assists, if he were not a creature which can and does sin. Grounded in the innate imperfection of the creature, sin is likewise conjoined with its creaturely or relative perfection. This is possible because it, too, is in itself a mere privation which is not grounded in a *causa efficiens* but only in a *causa deficiens*, only in the defective clarity of our conception and the defective certainty of our decisions, or again only in a natural inertia, so that the good and bad attributes and actions of men may be likened to a number of boats which, though conveyed by the same current (that of the divine activity), still move downstream at greatly differing rates because they carry different weights of cargo and therefore the force of inertia inhibits their motion to varying degrees. But again, the relationship between sin and creaturely perfection is an actual one because there can and must be sin within the context of the whole. Without the possibility of sin there could be no creaturely good. By its inexcusable and culpable committal it necessarily serves to augment the sum total of good in the creaturely order in a way which would otherwise be impossible. If this specific man did not now commit this specific sin, the whole world order would be entirely different. It would no longer be this real order which is the best. God Himself, its Creator and Governor, would then necessarily be different, and could not be the absolutely perfect being. This means that it is indispensable that God should create and posit the possibility of sin and allow its realisation.

The case is also finally the same with death. For individual souls and their physical organisms subsist eternally, and are therefore indestructible. At the beginning of life there is expansion, and at its end merely contraction. Hence the latter, and consequently death, is merely a passing privation, an unfortunate compression of life, the disintegration of a distinct and notable function of the living creature. Yet the creature survives this transformation both in soul and body, and thus attains to a new life. Hence even in death there is no real disruption or disintegration of the continuity of creaturely existence, so that even on the ground of mortality no rational objection may be raised to the perfection of the created world.

Now it must be allowed that Leibniz' view has an obvious advantage over those of a critic like J. Müller and most other theologians. It is universal, and does not restrict itself to the moral problem but tries to take a loftier synoptic view of sin, evil and death and therefore to understand the whole of what we mean by nothingness. In this sense the *Theodicy* might be regarded as a masterly Western representation of the Eastern conception. But unfortunately this is its only praiseworthy characteristic.

For it would be a mistake (cf. *C.D.*, III, 1, p. 406 ff.) to think that, though Leibniz is obviously guilty of confusing nothingness with the intracosmic antithesis or negative side of creation, he is at least right in relation to this negative aspect, so that his doctrine is illuminating and useful in our approach to this preliminary problem. The fact remains that, even if his doctrine is applied only to the preliminary problem, it necessarily results in a repudiation and abrogation of the antithesis, i.e., in the absorption or at least the assimilation of the negative aspect of creation by the positive. The negative side becomes the mere periphery of the positive. This is of a piece with the fact that there is in Leibniz' system no adequate criterion by which to establish that which opposes it, namely, the " perfection " which is obviously the positive aspect. There is clear lack of a higher principle by which to select, decide and discriminate between the two, and therefore to say an unequivocal Yes which includes and expresses but also overcomes and transcends the unequivocal No. For Leibniz' concept of God is a resplendent reflection of the strong human self-sufficiency which later found even more massive expression in the philosophy of Hegel. But it is no more than this. It does not describe the real God who is the Lord of creation but the man who aspires to be. Yet this man cannot even visualize the intracosmic antithesis. The man who conceives this idea of God, or rather this idea of his own self-sufficiency, and who with the help of it considers and judges the perfection and imperfection of God's creation, is a spectator and observer of God and His creation, and even of himself. He is not a properly cited and sworn witness to the truth. Clarity to distinguish between the right and the left, and positive perception that this is essential, are lacking in his vision and judgment. That is why even in the region of this preliminary problem Leibniz' *Theodicy* cannot be an adequate instrument.

Yet the *Theodicy* makes an even greater claim. It purports to offer an explanation of real sin, evil and death, and therefore of real nothingness. Confusing it with the twofold aspect of the world, it has in view the antithesis in which God and the totality of the world created by Him stand on the one side and the counterpart of both on the other. It could be conceded that Leibniz had this counterpart in view and in his own fashion took it seriously. We can as little contest this as that in formulating his concept of God and of the world he had God and His creation in view and was anxious to magnify them both to the best of his ability. But from the Christian standpoint it is impossible to say that the adversary is in any sense recognisable in Leibniz' exposition. With what may be described as a truly fantastic thoroughness the great Leibniz successfully undertook to domesticate the adversary. This domestication is such that the wolf not only dwells with the lamb, as depicted in Is. 11⁶, but actually becomes a lamb. There can be no thought of redemption or liberation, since there is nothing or no one from whom the created world needs to be redeemed and liberated. Again, there is no place for a reconciliation of the world with God, since the peace between them has never been broken. The decisive concept of privation makes this clear. He took it from Augustine : *malum est privatio boni.* Augustine used the term quite correctly to define the purely negative character of evil, i.e., the nullity of sin, evil and death, its nature as opposition both intrinsically and in relation to God and His creature. For Augustine privation is *corruptio* or *conversio boni.* It is not only the absence of what really is, but the assault upon it. Evil is related to good in such a way that it attacks and harms it. It seeks to destroy and consume it, *tendit ad non esse*, as the fire threatens to consume fuel, and is in process of doing so. It is another matter whether evil has the power to succeed, whether good is actually destructible as that which really is. Augustine rightly replies in the negative. Nevertheless, evil in its relationship with good has this aggressive and hostile character. But when Leibniz took over the Augustinian concept, privation became in fact mere negation ; the creaturely imperfection which consists in the fact that the creature is a creature and not God, and does not therefore possess the divine attributes. Because of this essential metaphysical imperfection, the creature may be and is subject to suffering, sin and death. But this metaphysical imperfection is natural to the creature. There can thus be no question of disruption, deprivation and corruption, and therefore of privation in the Augustinian sense. Anxiety, fear and especially despair, are superfluous in face of what is natural to the creature as such. And Leibniz consistently and necessarily proceeded yet a stage further on his chosen path when he saw in the negation to which the creature is subject one of the determinations of its perfection. For him evil is so related to good that it is only a particular form of good, not opposing, disrupting or threatening it, but rendering it an indispensable service, contributing to it as the necessary vacuum which permits its fuller expansion, the indispensable darkness which it needs to shine forth as light. For Leibniz nothingness cannot have the character of true nothingness in the sense of that which has been and is thus consistently to be rejected, of a danger to be constantly shunned and avoided, of an awful thing to be continually deplored. It cannot be real nothingness. For as sorrow it is only passing and partial pain, as evil only deficient intellectual perspicuity and power of moral decision, as death only the transition of a being intrinsically indestructible from one state of existence to another. Under all these aspects it is something which is necessarily allowed by God and may and must therefore be accepted by us. Hence only a limited dejection, opposition and resistance are legitimate in face of it. For Leibniz it cannot have the character of an originating and active force. For it is not just nothingness but nothing, i.e., the absence of something, the absence of divine perfection, and therefore pain, the lack of good, and in the form of death a mighty contraction of creaturely existence, but not its destruction or extinction. It neither owns nor effects anything ; it is merely a deficiency. It neither has nor is a destructive, extinguishing or consuming energy. It has no position from which it can rebel against God and invade the world and establish " negative positions." It is purposeless and immobile. It cannot affront God. It cannot conquer or capture any one, enslave or victimise any one. It had absolutely no function. It has merely the force of inertia, so that the more heavily laden boats are conveyed by the same stream with less momentum than those whose load is lighter. Yet individually all these boats proceed in the same direction. It is not to be gainsaid that we do have here a feeble echo of the biblical message that God has brought to nought all the powers opposed to Him and His creation. But how faint and easily misheard this echo when the reference is to a powerless nothing which God cannot fight and overcome as a real enemy ! How trite and jejune is that which in the New Testament is not at all self-evident but a costly reality and truth ! Nothingness as understood by Leibniz cannot even be set aside or removed. For in spite of the use of the term it is not real privation at all but merely a necessary negation which is innate in the created world and therefore intrinsic to its perfection, which is not, and is not to be rejected, which has neither initiative nor function, neither power nor potency. A defeat of this nothing in the sense of its abolition by the Creator and the creature's liberation from it is not only unnecessary but even impossible. Its defeat in the sense of its abolition would mean that the creature becomes God and partakes of His absolute perfection, thus losing its own nature and therefore its own perfection. The most that can be considered and is actually entertained by Leibniz in this respect is only an infinite approximation to the abolition of creaturely imperfection. It is in this sense that he defines the created spirit as the " *asymptote* of the Godhead." Creaturely bliss presumably consists in the *progressus infinitus* of this approximation. For it is clear that according to Leibniz what awaits us beyond death will not be a new life in the sense that the creature is no longer involved in the metaphysical imperfection natural to non-divine being and therefore ceases to carry within itself the seeds of suffering, evil and further death. Since man is an *asymptote* of the Godhead and the process of approximation is infinite, the consoling truth to which he may cling will be the same to all eternity, namely, that he must always be imperfect, and that his imperfection is necessary to his perfection. It is particularly clear at this point that the question whether or not nothingness is rightly understood is not in any sense peripheral but basically affects our understanding of the positive truth concerning the relationship between Creator and creature. Those who like Leibniz convert nothingness into something positive—and in this respect Leibniz is the classic representative of the many lesser men who followed him—need not be surprised if they can perceive and understand what is really positive only in the strange relativity to nothingness which characterises it in Leibniz' great exposition.

In further illustration of what we must repudiate we select the doctrine developed in §§ 65–85 of his *Glaubenslehre* (E.T. *The Christian Faith*, 1928) by F. E. D. Schleiermacher. These sections belong to the second main part of his work, in which he discusses religious self-consciousness antithetically determined as a consciousness of sin and grace. They constitute a sub-division on " the first aspect of the antithesis," namely, the " explication of the consciousness of sin," and are succeeded by a contrasting discussion of " the second aspect of the antithesis," namely, the " explication of the consciousness of grace."

Since even our statements about sin have their source in our immediate self-consciousness, " which as the truth of our being cannot be in contradiction with itself " (§ 65), we must assume from the very outset that, whatever else may have to be said, there can be only an apparent contradiction between man's innate disposition to God-consciousness and the resultant statements concerning the eternity, omnipresence, omnipotence and omniscience of God and the original perfection of the world and man on the one hand, and what must be said about sin and consequent evil on the other. For seen from the standpoint of the consciousness of grace sin is simply that " which would not be unless redemption was to be " (§ 65). The crucial point with which we are confronted in Schleiermacher's teaching is the resolution of this " apparent antimony."

What is sin ? Schleiermacher's answer is that it is a particular determination of our self-consciousness by our God-consciousness, namely, the determination in which we are conscious of the relative impotence or obstruction of our God-consciousness, or, in other words, of the obstruction of the determinative power of the " spirit " by the continuing independence of the sensuous functions, of the incapacity of the " spirit " in relation to the " flesh," or of the more rapid development of our insight as compared with our willpower in relation to our God-consciousness. God-consciousness itself determines our self-consciousness as the consciousness of this condition as pain. It must thus be said at once that consciousness of sin never exists in the soul of the Christian without the consciousness of the power of redemption (§ 66). The awakening of God-consciousness in us renders us conscious of sin as resistance to it. But even prior to this awakening this resistance germinates in us, and to this extent it takes precedence of our God-consciousness. Yet just as a trace of sin-consciousness lurks in even the most exalted moments of religious experience as awakened God-consciousness, conversely the sinful condition anterior to the awakening of our God-consciousness presupposes an original perfection not abrogated by it. Moreover, the awakening of our God-consciousness, at all events in its Christian form as the knowledge of the absolute sinlessness and perfect spiritual power of the Redeemer, includes the assurance that the end of its development is sinless human perfection. From both standpoints sin must be conceived of as a derangement of human nature but no more (§§ 67–68). It offers a twofold aspect. We experience it both as our dependence on the form given to life by preceding generations, and therefore as " original sin," and also as our own self-grounded act, and therefore as " actual sin " (§ 69).

In its first form as " hereditary " or " original sin " it is universal human " sinfulness," i.e., the total incapacity for good which is prior to every act of the individual and which is thus grounded outside his being and can be removed only by the influence of redemption. " Incapacity for good " does not signify incapacity to appropriate redemption, as though man were born without human nature. It means incapacity to develop or even to desire the state of complete and victorious God-consciousness which is the goal of the process of redemption (§ 70). In this first form sin is not only already accepted and admitted but committed by every individual. His sinfulness perpetuates itself in his will and is thus his guilt. But in the first form sin is also the " corporate act and corporate guilt of the human race." Thus it is " in each the work of all, and in all the work of each." Every man sins in and with his own generation, and " what appears as the congenital sinfulness of one generation is conditioned by the sinfulness of the previous one, and in turn conditions that of the later." In this first form, therefore, consciousness of sin is a " corporate feeling," and is thus connected with the consciousness of the universal need of redemption (§ 71). The question how this universal sinfulness originated is irrelevant. It certainly did not originate in an alteration in human nature in our first parents, for it is surely inconceivable that " to such an extent God should have made the destiny of the whole human race contingent upon a single moment, the fortune of which rested with two inexperienced individuals who, moreover, never dreamt of its having any such importance." This sinfulness must rather have been present along with original perfection in our first parents as the presupposition of their sinful act, as the " idiosyncrasies " of sex were already present in them and they were subject to " changes of mood " (§ 72).

In its second form sin is the sinful act, or " actual sin," which, beginning with a sensuous appetite or sloth, derives in all men from that universal sinfulness. In some individuals the first form of sin is more predominant, in others the second, but apart from redemption no individual is wholly secured against any of its forms (§ 73). All sins rank equal as manifestations of universal sinfulness and momentary or partial victories of the flesh over the spirit, though the power of the God-consciousness obstructed in them and the force of the external attraction to sin and occasion for it can be greater or less. But involved in all forms of sin is the reciprocal action of a predominant desire or sloth and a vitiation of the God-consciousness. A real distinction of degree between different sins only arises because man's relationship to redemption may be positive or negative. In the first case the sin committed is venial, being already broken, shadowy, impotent, and no longer dominant but waning, while in the second it is the " sin of the unregenerate " and will grow and rule, consolidating and extending itself, though it must always be remembered that here, too, it will never occur without a deeper or fainter shadow of the good, without " an acquiescent presentiment or imagining of a state free from inner conflict " (§ 74).

Nothing could properly be reckoned as evil if there were no sin. It is sin alone, the repression of the God-consciousness, which destroys the harmony between originally perfect man and the originally perfect world, and makes an evil of those aspects of the world which limits man's spatial and temporal existence. If there were no sin, what we know as " natural " evil, e.g., disease, or " social " evil, i.e., the obstruction imposed by one man on the life of another, might well be understood partly as inevitable imperfection and partly as incentive to future control of natural forces and intensive amelioration of the social order (§ 75). Since it is because of sin that they both seem to be evils, they are its direct and indirect punishments (§ 76). But sin and evil involve the whole structure of corporate human life, so that the evils experienced by an individual must not be traced back directly to his sins as their cause (§ 77). The godly resignation which endures " evil " on account of its connexion with sin will necessarily include and not exclude resistance to sin as the cause of evil, together with practical measures in the realm of nature and society (§ 78).

Even as we trace the annulment of sin by redemption to the divine causality, so we are bound to ascribe attributes to God in virtue of which even sin, not in abstract isolation but in so far as redemption from it is due to Him, is ordained by Him as its author (§ 79). To be sure, God is the author of sin in a very different way from what He is of redemption. Yet there is no doubt that we know the power of the God-consciousness and therefore of redemption only in co-existence with our continuing incapacity for good, so that we can understand the good will of God only if we conceive of the sin which yields before grace as posited in it and therefore by God. Both these points must be seen and stated. The practical interest of religion in the integrity of the divine will must be conserved no less than its theoretical interest in the divine omnipotence (§ 80). It is to be particularly noted that even sin does not entail a complete cessation of the God-consciousness, that even in sinful nature evil is always accompanied by good, that no moment is entirely pervaded by sin. Why should not the limitation of grace, and therefore sin, be grounded in the same divine will as its impartation? Why should not the shortcoming in us, and again therefore sin, be grounded in God's efficient as distinct from His commanding will (§ 81, 1)? Sin could not be grounded in human freedom if it had no divine causality. Sin, too, is posited with free self-development and therefore in virtue of the divine ordination, just as it proceeds as man's guilt from the universal sinfulness that is part and parcel of the principle of his individual will (§ 81, 2). Purely from the standpoint of God and His omnipotence, there is no divine causality of sin ; it simply does not exist for God. But in so far as the consciousness of sin is a true element in our being, and to that extent sin is a reality for us, it is ordained by God as that which makes redemption necessary. It comes from God, not only in the form of the sensuous natural impulse which rests on divine causality and with the ascendancy of which it gains an entry, not only in the form of the God-consciousness which rests on the same divine causality and which yields before it, and not only in the form of the weakness of this God-consciousness, but also in the sense that, although the God-consciousness is impotent in face of the sensuous impulse, to the extent that it is effected in us by God as the recognition of His commanding will, and as the consciousness of this will, it negates this impotence and thus makes it sin to us. It is due to God's decree that " the continually imperfect triumph of the spirit should become sin in us," a state of weakness which must be transcended, a state of opposition which must be annulled, a state which ought not to be, and must therefore end. Is sin not to be attributed to the divine causality merely on the ground that it is a negation ? It has this in common with all finite nature, which is as such a blending of being and not-being but even in its not-being rests on the efficient will of God. Or is it not of God because it does not correspond to the divine will which commands the good ? But it has this in common with all the good undoubtedly effected by God, in which there are always elements of evil and yet it is no less the work of God. Only if sin were an absolute contradiction of the commanding will of God, and thus utterly annulled this will in us, would it be impossible to think of the efficient will of God in relation to it. But the commanding will of God still remains within us, and it is by this that the weakness of our God-consciousness is made sin, and sin is thus ordained by God (§ 81, 3), but with a view to the redemption in whose light it cannot even be regarded as injurious, since " the merely gradual and imperfect unfolding of the power of the God-consciousness is one of the necessary conditions of the human stage of existence " (§ 81, 4).

What has been said concerning the divine causality with regard to sin also applies to evil in virtue of its connexion with sin. The notion that the entrance of sin caused a pejorative change in the physical world is, of course, " fantastic." But the religious self-consciousness advances two equally essential propositions. We must ascribe evil to ourselves as the consequence of our sins, and therefore not to God as the Author of the original perfection of the world. And we must acquiesce in all the evils of life as an expression of a divine decree passed upon us, seeing them so far as possible in relation to the atoning sufferings of Christ. When viewed in this light they cease to be evils for us, but become calls and incentives to a spiritual activity to be embraced with joy. An " origin in God " is obviously to be ascribed to evil itself in its relationship to sin. Evil too, to the extent that like sin it is grounded in our freedom, is ordained of God. In the measure in which God-consciousness is not yet dominant in us, and we are doers of the " corporate action " of evil, we must regard natural and social imperfections as evils and share in " corporate suffering " (§ 82).

The holiness and righteousness of God are to be understood as the divine attributes which correspond to our consciousness of God as the Author of sin and evil, as the modes of the divine causality in this particular respect (§ 82 postscript).

The holiness of God is the " divine causality through which conscience is found conjoined with the need of redemption." It is the conscience by which, as already described, a certain state is made sin for us as our own act. Conscience is the voice of the commanding will of God within us. It is thus " the sole and whole causality which sin as such implies." Conscience is related to man's need of redemption, and is therefore to be ascribed to the whole human race for which redemption is ordained through Christ. Yet it is also related to redemption itself, for it is through conscience as consciousness of their incapacity that men are held for and to redemption. Conscience can cease to exist only in a consciousness in which the will is perfectly at one with the God-consciousness, which means that Christ Himself can have had a conscience only in the form of fellow-feeling and not as something personally His own. Through the operation of God's holiness, conscience belongs to the human consciousness as antithetically determined by grace and sin. As it appears in corporate life, it is identical with the moral law. The holiness of God, in so far as it is effectual in man as grace, redemption and the power of God-consciousness, is man's displeasure at his own sin as effectuated by means of conscience and law. But if God's holiness is also directly apprehended as His own absolute displeasure at sin, it inevitably follows that sin cannot exist or be a divine thought as the object of the divine displeasure opposed to the good. Thus there is no reality nor idea of sin. For finite being cannot generate sin of itself. Therefore sin as a real antithesis to the good has no existence at all, and strictly speaking our displeasure at sin as effected by God is merely our displeasure at the fact that the effective power of the God-consciousness falls short of the clearness of the apprehension it gives us (§ 83).

The righteousness of God is the divine causality through which, in the state of universal sinfulness, a connexion is ordained between evil and actual sin. At this point Schleiermacher understands by God's righteousness only His retributive or punitive justice. This justice consists in the fact that the whole constitution of the world, to the extent that evil is also conditioned in it, is related in a particular way to the sin grounded in human freedom, and that this relationship is also present in our consciousness in such a manner that all sin, corporate as well as individual, is reflected in evil, and evil is explained by sin. In this sense evil is the operation of God's punitive justice, but the latter has nothing to do with retribution for an offence. " What has all along been preached, sometimes with apparent profundity, regarding the mysterious nature of the divine wrath and the fundamental necessity of divine retribution cannot be made clear to the mind." God's ordination of evil as an activity of divine justice is simply the preservation of man with a view to a future strengthening of the God-consciousness : " the object being to prevent his dominant sensuous tendencies from meanwhile attaining complete mastery through mere unchecked habits." But as a real opposition to the original perfection of the world, evil cannot exist at all. Divine holiness and justice are both essential elements in our God-consciousness, for we can know the absolute power and predominance of the latter only as we know the state and culpability of sin as removed by redemption (§ 84).

On the other hand, Schleiermacher holds that the concept of divine mercy is more appropriate to the language of preaching and poetry than to that of dogmatic theology. The reason is that this concept speaks of " a state of feeling specially evoked by the sufferings of others, and finding outlet in acts of relief." Being definitely anthropopathic, it cannot be applied to God without bringing Him under the antithesis of the agreeable and disagreeable. In any case, we do not speak of mercy in a close fellowship such as that between father and children, and therefore the object of God's mercy cannot be those who are already enjoying their part in redemption. Finally, mercy could mean " the repression of jealousy by compassion," and therefore " readiness to remit punishment." But apart from the fact that God is neither wrathful nor jealous, the punishment in question is ordered by the divine justice. Mercy would have to begin where justice ceased and *vice versa*, " a relation that cannot subsist between divine attributes." In short this concept cannot be used in relation to sin and evil and the divine being and attitude towards them (§ 85).

Schleiermacher's doctrine of sin and evil has been frequently and severely criticised. Older writers such as K. Rosenkranz, J. Müller and W. Bender reduced it to shreds, and E. Brunner has condemned it outright. It is true that his teaching is untenable as a whole and thus contains much that is obscure and artificial. His answer to the problem of nothingness is no more satisfactory than that of Leibniz. But it is also true that merely to indicate the failings of his teaching is insufficient. A careful study of his doctrine is rewarding, though this may not be apparent after the destructive criticism to which it has been subjected. In certain respects this destructive criticism was unjustified, for his teaching (like that of Leibniz) has certain definite and positive merits. Once these are recognised, we can still reject it, and the reasons for our rejection will be better understood. I shall begin by mentioning some of the points in Schleiermacher's teaching which have been most unjustly criticised.

We cannot object that what he calls sin is only the consciousness of sin, and therefore no true reality. Schleiermacher's procedure was to examine and expound the religious self-consciousness of the Christian. He was unable to avoid the perils of this procedure, but it must not be disregarded that his doctrine might well be adapted and developed in a very different direction as a theology of the subjective reality and possibility of revelation which is not exclusive but inclusive of its objective reality and potentiality—a theology which, beginning with man, is intended as a theology of the Holy Spirit. To be sure, Schleiermacher himself did not regard his theology of the consciousness in this way but viewed it wholly subjectively as an historical exposition of specific states, the inner religious states of the Christian. These were for him realities as such. Grace was real as the consciousness of grace, and he attributed a definite reality to sin as the consciousness of sin. For him sin had reality within the framework of his theology of consciousness—and therefore not as it should and would have done if he had realised that the grace which confronts it in objective transcendence is the grace of God in Jesus Christ, and that therefore sin is opposition to God. Yet it is not to be denied that, within the limitation of his purely subjective examination of Christian consciousness, sin was for him a reality. His error is not that he confounded sin with consciousness of sin, but that he failed to interpret the Christian self-consciousness first as a consciousness of grace and then of sin, in the antithesis in which grace and sin manifest themselves in the work of the Holy Spirit in man as a subjectivisation of the objective Word of God, or, if we must use the term, in the "Christian self-consciousness." He was thus unable to exhibit the peculiar reality of sin, for he was unable to exhibit the reality of grace. But it must not be denied that he did exhibit as a reality that which he was able to apprehend as sin in contradistinction to grace.

Moreover, the common charge cannot be sustained that he equated sin with sensuality (" beloved sensuality," Rosenkranz), as the essence of the natural appetites in opposition to the higher spiritual life of man ; or that he erroneously identified sensuality with the Pauline concept of " flesh," thus overlooking the fact not only that sensuality is not intrinsically sinful, but also that the higher spiritual as well as the natural being of man is involved in sin. For sensuality as Schleiermacher understands it is not only man's specifically natural impulses, but the whole of his being or consciousness including his capacity and activity of mind and will, in so far as it may be distinguished as his world-consciousness from his God-consciousness. And what he calls sin is world-consciousness as opposed to God-consciousness, for which he here employs the Pauline term " spirit." This is certainly rather confusing, since by " spirit " he usually understands the higher spiritual life which is here classified in the category of sensuality or world-consciousness. World-consciousness is to be regarded as sinful, and therefore called " flesh " in the Pauline sense, to the extent that it dissociates itself from God-consciousness (the Pauline " spirit ") and thus opposes it instead of being governed and pervaded by it. Sin is sensuality paramount and predominant but—because will is outstripped by knowledge—inwardly divided. It is world-consciousness evading or resisting the majesty and claim of God-consciousness or spirit, and therefore falling into disorder and becoming flesh. Augustine had already portrayed sin in this way. And even in Schleiermacher

3. *The Knowledge of Nothingness*   325

sin is definitely not identical with sensuality, i.e., with world-consciousness as such. In view of his plain assertions in this respect, and of his basic dialectics of nature and spirit, the physical and the ethical, it is rather surprising that any other opinion can ever have been entertained.

Again, it cannot be that for Schleiermacher sin merely consists in the fact that man is " not yet spirit," or that it is " nature which is not yet spirit." According to the presuppositions of Schleiermacher, it is impossible that nature should ever become spirit, for this would entail the transformation of man's world-consciousness into pure God-consciousness. But Schleiermacher's ideal of human consciousness is not pure God-consciousness or purely spiritual being. It is world-consciousness governed, pervaded, filled and fashioned by God-consciousness, i.e., world-consciousness with all the attributes and tokens of God-consciousness. His concern is that man should cease to be " flesh," i.e., to be implicated in his world-consciousness, in that opposition to God-consciousness. According to Schleiermacher, sin is man's continuing implication in this opposition.

Again, it is wrong to attack Schleiermacher on the ground that he defines sin, and especially original sin, as a mere condition, and the " incapacity for good " as a natural determination of man. He certainly describes sin as something " original " in man, innate in our first parents even before their evil deed. It may well be that this is an unfortunate suggestion. But it must not be overlooked that on his own presuppositions Schleiermacher could not entertain a merely passive conception of the " sinfulness " which precedes all actual sin, or think of sin as simply a condition. On the contrary, he expressly described this " hereditary " or original sin as a specific form of the human will, as act and therefore guilt. Although the " corporate act and corporate guilt of the human race," these are none the less real act and guilt, and although in " each the work of all," they are none the less " in all the work of each."

Hence the absurd accusation falls to the ground that Schleiermacher discards the concept of sin as guilt, replaces it by " the psychological concept of voluntary action," and transfers it from the individual to the entire race. That he so emphatically indicated men's universal solidarity in sin, and therefore did not see the individual only in isolation but in the sequence of the generations of men, surely does not restrict the definition of sin as guilt. In line with the general Christian tradition, this insight is intended rather to emphasise and strengthen it. To anticipate any misapprehension, he describes sin (§ 69, 2) as not only grounded outwith the life of the individual but also as his own " voluntary action." As he himself explains, Schleiermacher's purpose is to state that as individual sin it has the basis of its reality in the man himself. What else could sin as guilt be, within his system of theology of consciousness, but voluntary action (the self-grounded action of the individual) in opposition to the God-consciousness? Do we not have here the misunderstanding as merely " psychological," and lacking in ethical content, of a statement in Schleiermacher which, if not exhaustive, is not inaccurate as an exposition of the point at issue, and cannot really be avoided in any description of the matter or definition of " guilt " ?

It is also manifestly unjust to argue that Schleiermacher tries to " evade " the issue of punishment. His whole doctrine of evil and divine retribution refutes this. He is open to criticism on the ground that he links the concept of evil too closely to that of sin, envisaging it exclusively from the standpoint of retribution and handling it in such a way, i.e., as the mere misapprehension (in sin) of an intrinsically perfect world, as ultimately to deny its existence. But he cannot be accused of blindness to the gravity of evil in the form of this misapprehension, and even less of evasion of the issue of punishment. For as he sees it, this misapprehension is the inevitable result of sin, and it is God's punitive justice that it must establish itself in the consciousness of sinful man. Schleiermacher's contention in the passage (§ 71, 4) against which this indictment is preferred is simply a Christian truth which we must all uphold, namely, that fear of punishment cannot in itself either awaken or deepen man's sense of the need of redemption, because the desire to liberate the God-consciousness from obstruction, and therefore to obtain what redemption offers, differs from the desire to attain to certain conditions of sensuous self-consciousness and to avoid their opposites (i.e., to exclude evil), so that it is impossible to have a genuine sense of the need of redemption which derives solely from a consciousness of the culpability of sin.

It is a considerable testimony both to the formal originality and the material value of Schleiermacher's conception that, though its rejection is patently necessary, this cannot be accomplished without conceding its great merit and following up as it were some of its insights. We are forced, indeed, to agree with Schleiermacher against himself, as J. Müller once said in a very different sense and on very different grounds (I, p. 359). If we look closely, and dismiss every false accusation, the remaining objections present themselves as a vast complex which curiously enough confronts us at the exact point where we cannot but first and foremost acknowledge and admire his positive achievement. In other words, he is extremely weak where he is so very strong ; he is catastrophically wrong where he is most convincingly and instructively right. One is tempted to say that controversy with him, and the implied relationship of acceptance and rejection is almost forced to reflect his own dialectical views of the relationship between grace and sin. Yet the important difference remains that controversy with him demands a differentiation and decision between acceptance and rejection which are unfortunately impossible in his doctrine of grace and sin.

We must first state what is to be learned from Schleiermacher, and rather strangely from Schleiermacher alone. It may be reduced to a proposition with two cognate parts—that the nature and being of nothingness consists in the fact 1. that God in His omnipotent grace has negated it, and therefore 2. that it exists only in this relationship to His grace.

We may begin with the first point that it is that which God has negated. And at once we remember Schleiermacher's doctrine of sin. Consciousness of sin is not fortuitous. It is not a determination of our world-consciousness nor generated by ourselves. We are conscious of sin because our God-consciousness determines our self-consciousness in a particular way, as displeasure at self. We are conscious of sin because we are conscious of our implication in a " positive antagonism of the flesh against the spirit," and consequently must be displeased at ourselves. We have here a definite being and action of man that is realised in a particular relationship between his " sensuality," i.e., his world-consciousness and his God-consciousness. Why and how far are this being and action sinful in this relation, and man himself within it ? Schleiermacher's answer is that man is sinful because the relationship is made sin as the tyranny of his sensuality and the weakness, impotence and obstruction of his God-consciousness. But why is it made sin ? Schleiermacher's answer is that this weak, impotent and obstructed God-consciousness, not in virtue but in spite of its impotence, i.e., in the power which it has as God-consciousness even in its impotence, negates the being and action of man. In its very impotence it does not cease to command, to own and exercise the power of the commanding will of God which makes demands on men. It is consciousness of the divine holiness. How does God-consciousness do this ? Schleiermacher's answer is that the holy God in His omnipotence has given conscience to man as a sign of the God-consciousness of which the " moral law " is the corresponding universal human form. Because God-consciousness exists in the form of conscience, because in God's omnipotence God-consciousness is indisputably and irrefragibly conscience as well, it negates the being and action of man and determines that this particular relationship between human world-consciousness and God-consciousness is sin, man's incapacity for good and his evil act. In this way God " makes " his being and action sin. In this way it " becomes " sin. Schleiermacher clearly states that conscience, or the divine causality operative in it, is the " whole and sole causality which sin as such implies," and that beside it there is no other (§ 83, 1). This assertion of Schleiermacher's has often been overlooked, and his formally most audacious proposition that God is the Author of sin has been taken quite wrongly and in a sense quite contrary to his intention. God is its Author as He negates it. He is its Author solely because consciousness of Him is the cause of our displeasure at ourselves, of our being and action. In this sense He is certainly the Author of sin. The fact that we are sinners and commit sin is not in dispute. We become conscious of the sinfulness of our being and action by reason of the negation to which we are subjected through our God-consciousness. That our being and action are sinful and we ourselves sinners, that the relationship between our sensuality and God-consciousness is discordance, opposition and resistance and therefore culpable and punishable, is neither explicable in terms of human nature nor is it caused by ourselves, but it is " ordained " for us, and ordained by God in the form of this negation, in the omnipotence of His holiness in which He has posited conscience. Without this divine ordinance sin would be incapable of either reality or being. In Schleiermacher's view and exposition, this ordination is not to be abstractly apprehended in isolation from the fact that God's will for men is redemption and therefore good. Why, then, does God make this negation ? The answer of Schleiermacher is that He does so to hold man firmly for and to redemption ; to make and keep him aware of the need of redemption without which he would be incapable of attaining to or continuing in the consciousness of redemption itself. Hence the negation is in fact an additional decree of salvation. It is made by the omnipotent grace of God. Sin has reality and being by reason of this decree of salvation, i.e., of this irrefutable and irrefragible negation to which we and our being and action are subjected by our God-consciousness but which by the omnipotent grace of God is positive in its end. Sin in itself is our being and action in the relationship between sensuality and God-consciousness which we can only understand, in the light of our God-consciousness, as the superiority of the former and the corresponding weakness of the latter, as the victorious antagonism of the flesh against the spirit, so that it inevitably becomes the object of our self-disapproval of which we can be conscious only in the form of a " displeasure " which will be emphasised and augmented by the evil which corresponds to this relationship and is entailed by it as its punishment. Sin exists as our being and action are actually determined in this way by our God-consciousness, and are thus negated by the omnipotent grace of God. It exists as we ourselves exist.

Do we not have to say : So far so good ? Within the most dangerous limits of Schleiermacher's basic outlook and terminology, we may certainly do so. As we shall see later, the limits were not only dangerous, but there took place within them a theological catastrophe of the first magnitude. Yet it is not only right but also rewarding to affirm that Schleiermacher has here made a contribution to the apprehension of sin and nothingness which we usually seek in vain even in orthodox theology, but which is absolutely indispensable in relation to the doctrine of providence. Nothingness is what it is, and is real as such, because it, too, owes its existence to God in the sense that He has not elected and willed, but ignored, rejected, excluded and judged, or, as Schleiermacher would say, " negated " it. Whatever else must be said of nothingness, e.g., that it opposes and resists God, or disturbs and destroys man and world, is a corollary of the initial truth that it is that which is first opposed by God. This is the Alpha and Omega of what Schleiermacher says in his hundred and twenty pages on sin. He introduces other necessary matters, but they follow on this initial statement. He makes it within the limits prescribed for or selected by him. But within these limits he might well have described sin, like Leibniz, as mere negation and therefore as a mere imperfection which as such necessarily conduces to the perfection of all creation. Why was Schleiermacher incapable of such a simplification of his thesis ? Why did he attribute or at least try to attribute a certain substantiality and gravity to sin by consistently expounding it not only as that which negates but also as that which is negated by the God-consciousness and has reality by reason of this divine negation ? Is this not obviously related to the fact that in spite of everything, and in contrast with Leibniz' *Theodicy*, we have here a real doctrine of the Christian faith, and one in which Christology is given the important place, the function of one pole in the whole discussion, which Schleiermacher accords it ? To be sure, the compulsion of his monistic thinking is such as to inhibit him from according to Christology even the complementary significance which is his obvious intention. The first pole, the religious experience of the individual, is from the very outset stronger than the second. In his teaching Christology ultimately becomes a purely transitional point, a kind of objective reflection of the portrayal of subjective Christian experience. Thus the defect of his Christology is its ultimate superfluity. For Jesus Christ is in no sense adapted to function as the second pole in Christian thought. If He is treated in this way, He can only disappear as in Schleiermacher's systematics. Nevertheless, in contrast with his contemporaries Schleiermacher does try to honour Christ by making Him the historical point of connexion with the religious consciousness of the Christian. He reckons with Him in a manner in which Leibniz does not do, at least in his system. And it is to be suspected that, though Schleiermacher himself was unconscious of it, this was of great consequence for his distinctive doctrine of sin. Christology can indeed show that sin must first and foremost be apprehended from the standpoint of God, namely, as the work of a powerful divine negation, as a reality which is not created but posited or, as Schleiermacher says, " ordained," by God's opposition to it. In the light of Jesus Christ, this reality may be perceived as that which is excluded by omnipotent grace, so that, while it has no basis in itself, it acquires and temporarily enjoys a sinister basis in and through this antithesis, and can work itself out as the basis, origin and sum of all the contradiction in which alone it exists like all evil opposition, being subjected from the very outset, as mere nothingness, to the omnipotent grace of God and finally succumbing and falling to it at the end of the way on which God accompanies His creature and its adversary. Schleiermacher does not put it like this. Christology is not the real point of departure in his development of the doctrine of sin. All that can be asserted is that on the one hand he actually intended to exalt the position and significance of Christology more than was possible on his premises, and that on the other the form actually assumed by his doctrine of sin is only explicable in terms of a christological point of departure. But although Schleiermacher does not formulate it as we do, he does actually say it. And it cannot be denied that within the limits prescribed and adopted by him his statement is supremely true and important.

Unfortunately however—and this brings us to our first criticism—he did actually succumb to the danger of his limits, and made a further assertion, or rather a definite denial, which inevitably compromises the whole truth and importance of the first insight. In other words, he tried to understand the divine " ordination " of sin in the form of its negation—this is where his monism betrayed him—as an inner process effectuated only in the Christian religious consciousness and therefore exclusively subjective. There was no recollection of the Jesus Christ who is more than the embodiment of a serene and supremely potent human God-consciousness pervading and governing world-consciousness. There was no recollection of the Jesus Christ in whom God covenants with man and therefore genuinely confronts him, negating, judging and condemning sin and thus opposing it as an objective reality. Just as Schleiermacher denies that real encounter and real history are involved in the relationship between God and man, or God and creation, so he refuses to admit them in the relationship between God and sin. It is not, of course, fortuitous that the concepts of transgression, rejection and judgment are absent from his exposition of sin, and that he almost entirely avoids the term " evil " to denote that which resists God and is negated by Him. In Schleiermacher's teaching, the negation and therefore the ordination of sin are real only in our consciousness of God. For God Himself they are unreal and irrelevant, and are treated accordingly. As Schleiermacher sees it, God has no part in this matter, but stands inviolate above it. He merely sees to it that we become conscious of it, of His grace and therefore in contradistinction of our sin. In virtue of His holiness, He causes the discordance of our existence to become sin for us through conscience. God Himself has neither adjutant nor adversary. He is not assailed. He is neither offended, nor does He suffer. He is neither wroth against sin nor merciful to sinners. He is merely the Physician who prescribes a medicine for the patient with no intention of testing or taking it Himself. We and we alone are really implicated in sin. It is instructive to note what Schleiermacher says concerning Jesus Christ. As the vehicle of supremely potent God-consciousness, He possesses no personal conscience of His own, but simply a fellow-feeling with those who must needs have one because they are actually implicated in sin. Do we not have to conclude that there is no place for the holiness of God in the supremely potent God-consciousness of Jesus ? Is there really a place for holiness in God Himself ? The case is naturally the same, and even more so, with evil. Divine justice ordains that as a mis-apprehension due to sin evil should be very painful to us. But from God's standpoint and for Him it has no existence. In creation itself there is no alien element capable of being the result or object of His wrath. Evil is operative in our consciousness simply as opposition, as disruption of the perfection of the world, and as the inevitable subjective consequence of the disunity of our nature which is made sin for us. Again God has no part in it, nor is there any question of the divine mercy as " a state of feeling specially evoked by the sufferings of others finding outlet in acts of relief." J. Müller has rightly seen and described (I, 35 f.) the resultant dilemma in the following terms.

If it is really God who " ordains " sin for us ; if it is true that as sinners we must become and be conscious before Him of the culpability of our being and action ; if God has actually " shut up all unto disobedience " (Rom. 11^{32}), justly indicting and branding them for their disobedience ; if men must acknowledge this to be true and just ; if there can be no escape except by the avenue of His grace, how can all this be the case unless sin is first and foremost a reality for God Himself ? Has He or has He not accomplished anything by its mighty negation ? But if He has, and His act is not without purpose but of real significance for us, how can it have no significance for Him ? How can His holiness and justice be described as divine attributes which we attribute to Him, not because they are characteristic or essential, but because we find that in our consciousness we are confronted by the truth of the disunity of our existence and are negated, judged and punished by Him in consequence ? How can any place be found for the proviso that God is untouched by what we apprehend as the antagonism between our sensuality and our God-consciousness ?

On the other hand, if it is really the case that God is untouched by our sinfulness and actual sin ; if it is not primarily God's own adversary who is at work ; if He Himself is not engaged ; if there is neither wrath nor mercy in God ; if the work of His holiness and justice is simply to render us conscious of our need of redemption, why is there any true need of this consciousness ? Can anything less than God Himself, can our mere consciousness of God, suffice to make this need clear and certain, especially when we are clearly informed that God has no personal interest in the matter but is concerned only as the Author of our consciousness, for whom it is suggested that neither sin nor evil has any reality. Where, then, is the veracity of God to which we must be able to cling if we are to take the accusation of our conscience seriously ? How can anything have reality for us if we are convinced that it has none for God ? Does not the fact

that it has no reality close the question ? How can anything have existence
if it is nothing for God ? How, then, can we be capable of a real consciousness
of our sin as guilt, and of the evil to which we are subject as punishment ? Why,
then, should we have any real desire for grace and redemption ? If this is how
matters stand, how can dogmaticians speak of an essential, serious and stringent
insight ? On these presuppositions is not the insight nullified even before it
presents itself as a problem ? How can anything move us either theoretically
or practically to anxiety and repentance, prayer or even consideration, if we
are informed that God views it not only as nothingness but as nothing, as in no
sense an object, but for some reason seems to think that it should be of concern
to us ? Surely if it is of no concern to Him, it cannot be to us !

This is the great dilemma which Schleiermacher's doctrine cannot avoid
as he himself propounded it.

If it is his serious contention that God Himself is not concerned with sin and
evil, then man need not take them seriously nor acknowledge his own need of
redemption from them.

But if he believes in man's need of redemption, in the culpability and punishment of sin, in the divine holiness which imputes it to him, and the justice which
subjects him to evil as its consequence, then God Himself is supremely involved
in this mighty negation of nothingness, it is His own most intimate concern, He
is holy and righteous not merely for us but in Himself, and He is the God of
wrath and mercy.

If Schleiermacher cannot be understood in the sense of the second alternative,
i.e., if he cannot be radically rectified by the elimination of the first, then it is
hard to see—and this is the crucial point—why the grace and redemption of
God should not also be regarded as mere phenomena of the consciousness, as a
sense of exaltation and deliverance which is communicated by God in opposition
to the sense of sin and its consequence, but in the experience of which we accept
the fact that God Himself is not involved, that He is self-evidently not gracious
in Himself, but remains aloof from our conflicting senses. He is certainly their
Author, but has in Himself no fundamental reality corresponding to them and
making them genuinely necessary for us. It is unfortunate that we cannot take
Schleiermacher in the sense of the second alternative. But if his doctrine were
radically rectified in this way, and the first alternative eliminated, he would
cease to be Schleiermacher. The limits of his theology are such that he was
neither able nor willing to look beyond the facts and emotions of the Christian
consciousness ; that even Jesus Christ was for him merely one, though a most
important, subjective fact and emotion among others ; that " God Himself,"
even in relation to Jesus Christ, could not be for him a necessary, let alone a
decisive theological concept, but only an enigmatical figure who stands above
the human emotions He causes and of whom it can basically be said only that
He is alien to the antithesis of our emotions. Within these limits Schleiermacher's
doctrine of nothingness as that which is negated by the omnipotent grace of God
cannot be developed as a Christian perception which is tenable by the biblical
standard. Therefore we can only state that within these limits he does offer
the remarkable beginning of a true Christian understanding.

But we should be well advised to consider the matter in the light of the fact
that Schleiermacher has expressed that which makes his doctrine so remarkable
within its limits in a second form, namely, that nothingness does not exist at
all except in relation to redemption. In other words, since there is a consciousness of redemption, and this contains a consciousness of our original human perfection, then, estimated in relation to the end held out to us with the consciousness
of redemption, and to the origin thus revealed, there are such things as sin and
evil. As by our God-consciousness we become simultaneously aware of a future
victory over the disunity of our existence and of its original unity, we also become
aware of the disunity itself and its culpability, and we thus come under the

negation which is as it were a mere addendum to the affirmation to which we must primarily accede. The consciousness of sin follows that of grace, and serves it by conducing to our sense of the need of redemption. The negation is not in fact injurious to us. On the contrary, it is provisionally and incidentally advantageous. The same is true of the punishment meted upon us in the form of our great misconception of the intrinsically perfect world, i.e., in the form of evil. Indeed, punishment is only our preservation for and in redemption. It was to demonstrate this that Schleiermacher defined sin in terms which are decisively negative—that it is not so much the resistance and rule of the flesh (though in fact it is this too) but the state of the spirit no longer or not yet capable of ruling, subduing and renouncing the flesh as flesh. Sin is the impotence, obstruction, limitation, withdrawal and non-development of our God-consciousness. The consciousness of sin, the dissatisfaction with it, the " displeasure " which our knowledge of it entails, is decisively the dissatisfaction of our God-consciousness with itself, with its weakness and impotence, with its failure to pervade and sanctify our world-consciousness instead of being defiled by it. Strictly speaking, then, there is no essence or idea of sin. As it is only that which is negated by our God-consciousness, it has reality only in so far as it constitutes the frontier of our God-consciousness, and as we become conscious of it in that capacity.

Again we might say : So far so good. For it cannot be contested that Schleiermacher has seen and said here something which is true and important. And within the limits of his theology he has seen and said it in such a way that we are forced to listen and able to learn from him, even though a more scrupulous study must reveal that the standpoint which he assumed is untenable. Here, too, he has perceived something which the majority of the exponents of a purer doctrine failed to perceive, to the detriment of themselves and of the Church. We are again surprised that it did not occur to him to establish his view christo-logically. But we must immediately add that his own Christology rendered this impossible, and that if he had established it on another and better Christology it would have been embodied in another and less fallacious form than that in which it exists. Yet it is a no less astonishing fact that on another and better Christology, and in another and more valid form, we necessarily come to the same view of the relationship between grace and sin as that of Schleiermacher. If at the outset we realise that we are not free to formulate our own serious and profound opinions on the whole complex of nothingness and therefore on sin, evil and death, nor to determine the existence, nature and importance of this matter in a vacuum, i.e., speculatively, as is finally the case with the otherwise rigorous Müller ; if we must maintain that here, too, Jesus Christ the incarnate Word of God is the only objective ground of knowledge, then the conclusion is inevitable that real nothingness does not reveal its existence to us at random points, e.g., in an abyss within ourselves, or in face of a personal or general calamity, or in our pretended understanding of transcience and death. It is an error to suppose that we can seek and find nothingness in this way. We encounter it in the relationship that God has established between Himself and us and all creation by becoming man to deliver us and creation. We encounter nothingness as the reality that God confronted in Jesus Christ. It is real in relation to God, and not with an absolute reality. And its nature is also revealed at this point. Nothingness is not something malign, sinister and monstrous. It is not endowed with invented negative qualities, but with the specific and authentically evil character of the antithesis to the grace of God. That which it wills to be it cannot, and therefore here too it is not absolute. Its nature corresponds to the relationship in which it exists. It is the antithesis to the good, kind, benevolent will of God which He exercises and manifests by not abandoning His creature but by identifying Himself with it in His Word. What confronts Him in us and all creation, what is alien and opposed to His gracious will—that and that alone is true nothingness, sin, evil, death in their true form as that which is bad. And this relationship also reveals the scope and therefore the limitation of its power. The extent of our gravity and fear in face of nothingness is not to be determined by our free choice and opinion. When nothingness is seen in this relationship, in its opposition to Jesus Christ, it cannot be for us either a legendary monster of unlimited power or a second and negative God. In this respect, too, it is not absolute. God is first and last in action against it. It exists only through God, in the power of the divine negation and rejection, of the divine judgment. Its place is given it by God. It is never over God, but always under Him. It does not limit God, but is limited by Him. God's grace is mightier than sin, evil and death. They are together the enemy of whom it can be said : " One word shall quickly fell him." No morality however earnest, no pessimism however sincere, can possibly exonerate us here. We do not honour the truth but compound a falsehood and make common cause with the enemy if even momentarily we fail to see nothingness otherwise than in its relativity. Schleiermacher is quite right to maintain that from the standpoint of creation and the covenant the total force of the enemy is far from absolute. It is only the object of the victory which God has gained over it. To be sure, Schleiermacher did not and could not express it in this way. But in his own terminology and within his own limits, did he not assert the same thing ? Before any objection to the development of his idea is advanced, must he not be credited with the fact that he justly opposed a foolish dualism in the consideration of the relationship between sin and grace, an unbiblical absolutisation of nothingness by Christian theology as though it could be apprehended and existed in a vacuum ? Did he not try to exhibit against this the sovereignty of the grace of God ? When he says that " evil is only correlative to good," is this statement false because it is actually reminiscent of Leibniz' conception, or because it is unfortunately a statement in his monistic philosophy and is thus accompanied in his teaching by other propositions which completely compromise its Christian character ? We cannot accept the other propositions, but are forced to say that evil is the one entity in Christian knowledge and confession which cannot be affirmed absolutely but only in relation and subordination to the grace of God. Nothingness is radically but not autonomously opposed to the creation and covenant of God. It does not exist in itself, but only in this state of antithesis. It is thus merely " correlative to good." This proposition is not in itself the doubtful element in Schleiermacher's teaching. On the contrary, his powerful advocacy of it is the illuminating feature which must not be ignored or denied even in the most necessary and justifiable criticism.

The criticism which we are forced to bring is that Schleiermacher understood this intrinsically correct proposition in such a way that he thought he could reverse it like an hourglass and say that good is only correlative to evil. He was thus guilty not only of a serious consolidation of evil but of an even more serious disintegration of good quite contradictory to what the proposition that evil is only correlative to good should signify in a truly Christian sense. What does he affirm ? He affirms that the power of our God-consciousness, of our consciousness of grace and redemption, subsists only in relation to our incapacity for good and our sin yielding before grace. It is in some sense essential that sin should also be posited as an element in human development, which without it would be inhibited. Were it not so, man would not be a free agent and therefore would not be man. All being as divinely caused is a compound of being and non-being. There is evil in all the good wrought by God. Therefore, in virtue of relationship to redemption, sin can be no true " injury," because " the merely gradual and imperfect unfolding of the power of the God-consciousness is one of the necessary conditions of the human stage of existence." Because of this necessity sin was posited and ordained for man by God. We cannot possibly accept this view. While sin may justifiably be regarded as relative in confrontation with grace, Schleiermacher's proposition goes further. It includes sin in the same category as grace, and thus esteems, justifies and even establishes it as the counterpart and concomitant of grace. Sin is given a legitimate standing in relative grace. It presents itself as an agent whose reaction to grace fulfils a function no less accredited than that of grace, and just as lawful and necessary and divinely ordained. This is a real return to Leibniz. Sin is now understood positively. Without sin grace could not exist. That evil is correlative to good now means that it balances it. At this point we can only protest. When sin is understood positively, when it is esteemed and justified and established, when it counterbalances grace and is indispensable to it, it is not real sin. For real sin cannot be vindicated in this way. We cannot say of it that it is in any sense necessary to a stage of human existence and therefore willed and posited by God. How can sin be grounded in human freedom, the freedom of man created perfect by God ? How can it be indispensable to man ? But our protest goes even deeper. For the grace which is conditioned by the presence of sin, living by its antithesis and therefore bound to it, is not real grace. Grace cannot possibly be subject to this necessity, require to be counterbalanced in this undesirable way, or need this indispensable " accomplice." How can it ever be averred of the real grace of God that it can be true only in conjunction with our incapacity for good and the resultant evil actions ? What kind of a grace is it which is obviously unable to cover, forgive and cancel sin ? What does the justification of the sinner mean if his sin is already justified as sin ? At this point we are confronted by an abysmal error in Schleiermacher's teaching. For he either does not see or completely forgets that the relationship between grace and sin in which sin can have only a relative existence and power is not a positive relationship but one of opposition and conflict, of the victorious conflict of grace against sin and the futile conflict of sin against grace, but of real conflict, and therefore not in any sense of peace. In Schleiermacher's teaching the nature and character of the two concomitants are forgotten, and it is thus overlooked that there can be no mediation nor arrangement between these two adversaries. It goes unheeded that their relationship is an encounter and history in which all the honour and justice and dignity pertain to the first partner, whereas the existence and being and power of the second have no basis, so that they cannot competently be classified together, and first and last theology can define their interconnexion only in terms of a conflict which is favourable to the first and not to the second. How could Schleiermacher fail to see this ? How could he venture to reverse his proposition, and thus give nothingness the favourable report of being essential to man's existence, though injurious to it ? How could he dare compromise in this way the cause of God in relation to it ? Well, he not only could do this, but his presuppositions left him no alternative. We understand the whole tragedy when we consider that, faithful to his historico-psychological methodology, Schleiermacher means by grace and sin no more than two corresponding states in the religious consciousness of the Christian. It is true indeed that in our consciousness the antithesis exists only as a variable juxtaposition and not an exclusive encounter of good and evil. The good in our consciousness is always correlative to evil, and *vice versa*. The grace of God is never present with us as absolutely antagonistic to or triumphant over our sin, but sin is always too firmly entrenched against it. We cannot actually know grace without a simultaneous acknowledgment of our sin. In our own consciousness, and in relation to that of the race as a whole, there are good grounds for the notion that the impotence of our God-consciousness is a prerequisite of our existence and is thus divinely ordained. The fallacy of Schleiermacher was to absolutise the historico-psychological actuality of the Christian religious consciousness, and therefore to regard the sin apprehended within its limits as real. If he had been free to transcend the self-imposed limitations which circumscribe his conception, and to consider sin where it can be recognised as real sin in its relativity to real grace, he would have been compelled to take seriously his own definition of sin as that which is negated by our God-consciousness and is only real as such, and therefore to refrain from minimising it. Even the religious consciousness itself, opened to the Word of God and instructed by it, should have given him a different view of sin. Even in relation to this subjective sphere, it should have been possible to speak of sin with far greater dismay and of grace with far deeper joy. The trouble is that the religious consciousness as Schleiermacher understood it was not opened to the Word of God. In the restricted sphere in which Schleiermacher was cramped the divine No to sin could not be revealed as God's own No, nor the divine Yes as His Yes. In this sphere, therefore, the threat of sin, the nullity of nothingness and the glory of grace could not be seen in their reality, i.e., in their encounter and history, but only in a peace which is really spurious and not the peace of God that passes all understanding.

It is on these grounds that, for all the credit due to Schleiermacher and our debt to him, we must categorically repudiate his concept of nothingness.

We may conclude our review by turning to two contemporaries, Martin Heidegger (b. 1889) and Jean-Paul Sartre (b. 1905). Although their work is not yet complete, the main features are already distinct, and are highly pertinent to our present investigation. I am aware that exception might be taken to classifying Heidegger and Sartre together (cf. Max Müller, *Existenzphilosophie im geistigen Leben der Gegenwart*, 1949). It is true enough that they only stand together as it were back to back ; yet the fact remains that they do stand together. And both must be heard if we are to wrestle with the view of nothingness which, approximately two centuries after Leibniz and one after Schleiermacher, has emerged as characteristic of our own time, the decades of the two world wars. Modernity with its obtrusion of seemingly indispensable viewpoints and criteria is not the measure of all things. And the so-called existentialism of our own day, in this or any other form, is certainly not the philosophy *par excellence* which will have no successor and therefore merits our special or even exclusive attention. Let it not be forgotten that in the time of Hegel it was held with even greater conviction, and perhaps with greater internal justification, that a similar delusion might be entertained regarding the conclusive significance of his teaching. And the position which Roman Catholicism gives to Aristotle as the philosopher *par excellence* was and is a very remarkable but also a very questionable matter. In theology, at least, we must be more far-sighted than to attempt a deliberate co-ordination with temporarily predominant philosophical trends in which we may be caught up, or to allow them to dictate or correct our conceptions. On the other hand, there is every reason why we should consider and as far as possible learn from the typical philosophical thinking of the day. As we have listened to Leibniz and Schleiermacher, so now we listen to these modern thinkers at a point which is particularly important for them and in which they may be able to teach or warn us in our own understanding of the theme.

With regard to Martin Heidegger we are in the fortunate position of being able to consult the short essay which he delivered as his inaugural lecture at Freiburg in Breisgau in 1929, *Was ist Metaphysik ?* (E.T. *What is Metaphysics ?* in *Existence and Being*, 1949). This is a summary of what he says on the present theme in his greater work *Sein und Zeit* (or rather in the first and so far the only volume published in 1927). I shall not try to follow Heidegger's process of thought, but to describe the concept which dominates his exposition and then to show how it is developed in his teaching and how an answer is finally given to the question under discussion.

The predominant concept is that of nothing. According to Heidegger, the question of nothing is raised, and ultimately already resolved, by the fact that science repudiates and rejects nothing as nothingness (the only time this term is used), but in so doing admits it (p. 358). Science is related to the world as to that which is, and to nothing more (p. 358). That which is determines its attitude, and nothing more. It deals with that which is, and nothing more (p. 358).

Science seeks no knowledge of nothing. We know nothing by seeking no knowledge of it (p. 359). The question : " What is nothing ? " is meaningless, and even more so is any answer which might try to begin : " Nothing is . . ." Nothing is merely admitted and repudiated as that which " is not " (p. 359). It is the negation of the totality of that which is. It is that which is not absolutely (p. 361). On the other hand, it is not grounded either in our rational act of negation or in our " not." It does not exist because of this negation. Our negation can only be subsequent to our rational act. In this act we acknowledge nothing (in the form of its admission and repudiation). Nothing itself is prior to our " not " and negation. Heidegger believes that he may justifiably regard this thesis as crucial (p. 361). While he offers neither ground nor proof for it, it is obvious that as he advances it he regards " nothing " not only as a " something," a factor, which has to be reckoned with, but as an original factor which precedes our negation and affirmation, which is dynamic and active, and which operates with an original dynamism and activity. We cannot set ourselves before it by our own resolution and willpower (p. 374), but it " obtrudes " upon us as being as a whole escapes in a mood of dread. In face of it, it is impossible to say " is " (pp. 366–367). It thus discloses itself in dread, not as a being or object, nor in isolation from that which is, but in unity with it. In dread that which is falls away altogether. It is not annihilated, but it eludes us (p. 368). In dread nothing is manifested as that which essentially refers aside, but yet which refers us to elusive and evanescent being. It is this work of nothing Heidegger calls its " nihilating." But as it nihilates, rejecting and reprimanding elusive being, it discloses that which is in all its hitherto undisclosed alienation as that which is absolutely other, in its utter differentiation from itself, as that which really is and is not nothing. The essence of nothing as original nihilation thus consists in the fact that it sets the existence of man face to face with being as such, confronting man with that which is (p. 369). Only on the basis of the original disclosure of nothing can the existence of man approach that which is. Apart from the original disclosure of nothing existence can have neither self-hood nor freedom. Not only, then, does nothing belong to the essence of being—since the nihilation of nothing occurs in the being of that which is—but existence, which is essentially related to that which is, derives always from manifested nothing. " Existence means being projected into nothing " (p. 370). It is indeed true that we do not always but only very occasionally live (or are " suspended ") in a state of dread because of it. The primary reason is that nothing is continually " distorted " out of its original state by the fact that we wholly immerse ourselves in that which is, not allowing it to elude us, and thus intruding ourselves into the " open superficies " of existence. Yet this perpetual if equivocal aversion from nothing " accords within certain limits with its own essential meaning." Nothing itself refers us to that which is. But this does not alter the fact, unapprehended by ordinary perception, that it continuously nihilates (p. 371). In sum, it can be generally agreed with Hegel that " pure being and pure nothing are one and the same." The older affirmation : *ex nihilo nihil fit* must be amended to read : *ex nihilo omne ens qua ens fit* (p. 377). On this basis we shall now try to understand the details.

The initial question concerns (human) existence. We are informed that there is a " basic event " in which all that which is is disclosed to existence. The basic event in which this occurs is comprehensively described as the " affective state " (p. 364). It is of interest to observe that this basic event is assumed to be identical with metaphysics (p. 379). The mood involved in the disclosure of all that which is might be joy. But for Heidegger another form of this disclosure seems to be more significant, namely, " true boredom." " Profound boredom, drifting hither and thither in the abyss of existence as in a silent fog, gathers all things and all men, and oneself with them, into a strange indifference. This boredom is the totality of that which is." Yet when our moods thus bring us face to face with this totality, they still conceal nothing. Materially, the revelation of nothing which is truly constitutive for existence occurs prior to this revelation and as it were at a deeper level. It, too, occurs in a mood, but in the basic mood of dread (pp. 364-365). On the very basis of the revelation of nothing which occurs in the mood of dread, existence itself, being projected into nothing, reaches the stage of approaching and entering that which is, but also passes beyond the totality of being, thus " transcending it " (p. 370). " Projection into nothing on the basis of hidden dread is the overcoming of the totality of that which is— transcendence " (p. 374). Projected into nothing, existence has self-hood and freedom (p. 370). As existence is not only capable of logical negation, but more generally is pervaded by a nihilating attitude, being constantly engaged in the acrimony of opposition, the violence of loathing, the painful responsibility of refusal, the cruelty of interdiction and the bitterness of renunciation, there is present the constant but much concealed revelation of nothing (p. 373). Finally, it falls to be said of man, whose existence is involved, that the projection of his existence into nothing on the basis of hidden dread makes him " the *locum tenens* for nothing " (p. 374). Necessarily brought into the question concerning nothing, existence itself is inevitably called in question by this question (p. 378).

But what is the basic mood of dread which is so obviously decisive for the basic event of existence as well as for the action and revelation of nothing ? We have seen that nothing itself stands as the agent behind this key-mood into which we are brought, if only very occasionally, by it. This mood is not to be confounded with fear, which is always the fear of this or that. Dread is not this confusion of fear. On the contrary, it is pervaded by a peculiar kind of peace. Dread is dread of the indefinite as that which is essentially impatient of definition. In dread, " one feels something uncanny." But what is meant by " some-thing " and " one " ? We cannot say what occasions this uncanny feeling. " One just feels it generally." Everything merges into a kind of indifference. Yet this does not mean that everything disappears, but that in the very act of withdrawing it returns to us. It is the withdrawal of the totality of that which is which oppresses us in dread as it surges around us. There is nothing to cling to. That which eludes us, and we can cling only to this nothing. What happens ? Dread reveals nothing. In dread we are suspended, or more exactly dread holds us in suspense by causing the totality of that which is to elude us. This is because we ourselves, as these men who are, elude ourselves in the midst of that which is. Hence it is not thou or I but one who has this uncanny feeling. In the trepidation of the suspense where there is nothing to cling to, the only thing which remains is pure existence. Dread strikes us dumb. In the uncanniness of dread we may often try to break the silence by random words, but this only proves the presence of nothing. And what happens when we have overcome our dread ? We are forced to say that that of which we were afraid was " actually "—nothing ! Indeed, we are forced to say that nothing itself and as such was there (pp. 365-367). And what happened as dread was there ? What happens as it is basically always present ? Although it is powerless as dread in face of the totality of that which is, nothing declares itself in it in and with that which is, and that which is reveals itself in it as a totality which eludes us (p. 368). Again, we ourselves in dread are engaged in a withdrawal which is not a flight but a conjured rest. That before which we withdraw, or by which we are conjured to rest, is nothing. Our withdrawal or rest in dread thus proceeds from nothing, from its nihilation (p. 369). It is true that only in the clear night of dread does the original " disclosure of that which is, and is not nothing, emerge." It is true, then, that we " distort " nothing as we follow its reference to that which is, and lose ourselves in it (p. 371). But this does not alter the fact that dread is present, and with it nihilating nothing in its original disclosure. Dread is always present, though sometimes dormant. Its breath palpitates through all existence, most feebly through the pusillanimous, imperceptibly through the active, most readily through the introverted, and most firmly through the valiant. The dread felt by the valiant, which is the most real dread, is not patient of contrast with joy, or even with the easy enjoyment of life in tranquillity. Beyond all such contrasts, it stands in mysterious union with the serenity and tenderness of all creative longing. Yet it is always there as dread, and can awaken at any moment. It needs no extraordinary event to awaken it. Its action is so deep that the shallowness of its possible cause genuinely corresponds to it. If it seldom plunges, it is always on the brink, so that when it does plunge it drags us again into the state of suspense (pp. 373–374).

That which is, then, is to be apprehended from the standpoint of the revelation of nothing which occurs in dread. In the mood of joy, or supremely in that of boredom, that which is discloses itself to us in totality. But it is still not manifested to us in its actuality, i.e., in its distinction from nothing. For the manifestation of that which is nothing and its nihilation are indispensable, since it is in virtue of this nihilation that that which is discloses itself as recessive, elusive and evanescent, yet in this way as that which is. Only as nothing is disclosed at the basis of existence is it possible for the utter strangeness of that which is to dawn upon us. Only when this utter strangeness intrudes itself upon us does it excite our wonder, and the question of its ground and its nature springs to our lips, so that we can ask and answer, i.e., prove and explain, and therefore investigate (pp. 369 ; 378–379). Nothing is that which renders the disclosure of that which is possible for human existence. It is nothing, therefore, which makes science possible. Nothing belongs to the essence of that which is. It is in the being of that which is that the nihilation of nothing takes place (p. 370). Under this determination there is not only an attitude of (human) existence to that which is, but there is to be ascribed to that which is itself a definite dynamism and activity which is very real even if secondary in its relationship to that of nothing. There is thus attained in the objectivity of scientific enquiry, definition and proof a subjection of existence to that which is in which the latter must disclose itself. What is achieved in science, then, is not only the irruption of a particular entity called man into the totality of that which is, but also in and through this irruption an eruption of that which is itself, so that in its own way science as an " erupting irruption " helps that which is to itself (pp. 357–358). All this rests, of course, on the original disclosure of nothing in which that which is is revealed as elusive and evanescent, but in this way as that which is.

The rational act of negation is also to be apprehended from the standpoint of the revelation of nothing which takes place in dread. It does not lead to nothing, since, as the rational negation of a theory, of a conception of the totality of that which is, it offers only the formal concept of an hypothetical nothing and not real nothing itself (p. 363). Nothing itself is of necessity prior to our negation ; the latter can only follow it. In this way our negation attains significance and justification. The fact that in negating we repeatedly utter a Not which is not generated by our own negation, since that which is to be negated must as a negative entity precede our negation, is more impressively demonstrative than anything else of the revelation of nothing in our existence. That they may utter the Not our negation and human cognition are already expecting a Not—a Not which can only manifest itself with the disclosure of its source in the great nihilation of nothing and therefore in nothing itself. Thus negation is based on the Not which derives from the nihilation of nothing. Thus it is merely a mode of the nihilating behaviour of our existence based on the nihilation of nothing itself. The rational act of negation is not alone. Nor is it a chief witness either for the disclosure of nothing which is an essential part of existence, nor for its nihilation which shakes our existence everywhere. More abysmal is the multitude of negations unrelated to rational acts—opposition, loathing, refusal, interdiction, renunciation. In short, the exact apprehension of the rational act of negation demonstrates precisely that the sovereignty of reason in the field of enquiry into nothing and being is demolished, and that the fate of the rule of logic in philosophy is determined. " The very idea of logic disintegrates in the vortex of a more fundamental questioning " (pp. 372–373).

On the basis of these propositions, we now come to Heidegger's answer to his thematic question : What is metaphysics ? In his exposition he was trying to raise and answer one metaphysical question in order to make metaphysics possible. Metaphysics consists in the investigating and therefore the passing beyond being which takes place in the essence of existence, in its basic event which we have learned to know as the " affective mood." Metaphysics is transcendance. The enquiry concerning nothing is an enquiring and passing beyond of this kind in which we men are already actually engaged. Enquiry concerning nothing is therefore a metaphysical question (p. 374) which, though it is only one, embraces and occupies all metaphysics because it is obviously concerned with the being of that which is (pp. 374–377). It is a genuinely metaphysical question because it integrates our questioning existence with itself and thus calls our existence in question ; for scientific existence is not possible unless " projected at the outset into nothing." Existence can only apprehend its own nature if it does not repudiate nothing. The pretended sobriety and superiority of science become ludicrous if they fail to take nothing seriously. Science can exist only on the basis of metaphysics, indeed on the basis of the metaphysics which is penetrated and embraced by this particular metaphysical question concerning nothing and which in so doing takes science into itself (pp. 374–378). The task of philosophy is to instigate metaphysics, this metaphysics. But philosophy itself is only instigated when the philosopher plunges his own being into the basic possibilities of being as a whole. In this plunge these points are of vital importance : first, to allow room for the totality of that which is ; secondly, to let oneself go into nothing ; and finally, to give free play to this suspense " so that it may continually revert " to the basic question of metaphysics wrested from nothing itself : Why is there being at all and not just nothing ?

In relation to Jean-Paul Sartre we again have the advantage of having his own commentary on the position and message advocated by him in *L'Etre et le Néant* (1943) and other works, for the most part literary. This commentary is *L'Existentialisme est un humanisme* (1945), in which he not only answers his opponents but also offers an exact and definitive statement of his system, discarding the intentionally exasperating attitude of his other works, and clearly adumbrating his essential interest. If by reason of the consistently exasperating attitude of the author, or our exasperated failure to take his part, we have not seen it in his other works, in this work we cannot but realise that Sartre presents us with a view which is completely self-consistent and finally simple, and for all the differences very much of a piece with that of Heidegger.

In passing from Heidegger to Sartre our first main impression is that Sartre has behind him (as though obsessed by nothing and unable to see anything except in the light of it) what Heidegger still has before him (as though obsessed by nothing and unable to look to any other goal). In other words, while nothing is the basic concern of both, there is this difference in their respective attitudes towards it. In Heidegger we are concerned with the premise of Sartre, in Sartre with Heidegger's conclusion. Both deal with nothing as a principle, dimension and imperative. But whereas Heidegger's purpose is almost entirely to demonstrate the potency of nothing against existence, that of Sartre is almost entirely to demonstrate human existence as conditioned by it. In both cases I have said " almost entirely," for naturally there is overlapping. Heidegger's own teaching foreshadows the inevitable and ultimate tendency of the development of his thought if his conclusions regarding the constraint and compulsion of nothing are accepted and human existence is positively interpreted in accordance with his view. Indeed, this tendency is already evident in his own thought. But his true passion is revealed in relation to the " disclosure " of nothing which is ready to leap out in the basic mood of dread and which is always on the verge of possible awakening. It is thus revealed in connexion with the evanescence of that which is and the concomitant dubiety of human existence itself. Sartre again does not fail to indicate his point of departure, i.e., the absolute impotence of what lies behind human existence. He even gives to the initial perception of nothing a sharpness which is implicit and necessary but not explicit in the thinking of Heidegger. Sartre's decisive presupposition is a regretful but emphatic and forceful denial of the existence of God. For this reason he has a radical awareness of dread, *délaissement (expression chère à Heidegger*, p. 33), and despair. In 1938, when the French were faced by a probable war which was only postponed, Sartre depicted it in *Le Sursis* in all the colours of a mythical monster : *on était solidaire d'un gigantesque et invisible polypier*. His description of hell in *Huis Clos* is overpowering just because it is ultimately no more than a portrayal of the dreadful banality that prevails in man's relationship with man. And many more examples might be given. Because he is so eloquent and illuminating on this subject Sartre has often been misunderstood. It has often been thought that he could be dismissed with the assertion that—like a second Zola—his sole concern was the realistic exposure of the sordid, ugly and base side of human life. Though there is no ambiguity in either his writings or his explicit defence of them, it has been completely overlooked that his passionate concern is to be sought in his description of man : the man whose point of departure and therefore background is nothing with its constraint and compulsion ; the man who realises that he must live without God ; the man who knows dread, *délaissement*, despair, war and hell ; the man who knows and reckons with all that to which Heidegger looks as though he were obsessed, and who in this way and for this reason is man, and is absolutely resolved to be and become and remain such. As though he also were obsessed Sartre looks forward from this point. If the source of Heidegger's philosophy is to be found in the First World War in retrospect, Sartre is a very definite and in his way magnificent type of the man of the French Resistance in the Second. But even before the Second World War Sartre was a *résistant*—one who saw the adversity of the age and was fully resolved to reveal it to the blind, but who also meant to assert himself, to caution others against all collaboration and to inculcate in them a similar self-assertion. He emerged from the Second World War immeasurably purified and strengthened in this positive purpose. The awful No derived from nothing is an actuality, but out of it there strangely grows the peculiar and categorical Yes of human existence. This Yes is Sartre's concern. In my view, he is the most virile of modern existentialists. The core of his teaching is not that man must be somewhere " in suspense," or vacillate in the famous " frontier situations," but that he should stand and advance to a goal.

We can understand his derivation from Heidegger and the relationship of the two if we also consider the connexions in Heidegger's teaching, in which we are surprised to learn that the real dread in which nothing is revealed to us is not without a " peculiar peace," not being a flight but a " conjured rest " in mysterious union with the serenity and tenderness of creative longing, or that the valiant experience dread most surely and the introverted most readily, or that this dread is not patient of contrast with joy, " the easy enjoyment of life in tranquillity." We must also remember that Heidegger's ultimate intention in his doctrine of dread and nothing was to establish a positive basis not only for metaphysics but also for the quiet purpose, outlook and labour of science. Heidegger is not and never was a " Nihilist." His statement that man is the " *locum tenens* for nothing " can be interpreted positively. This is where Sartre comes in, but on a broader basis. He does not ignore dread, and the nothing which underlies it. He submits them to a careful scrutiny. But he will not allow them to prepossess, hamper, or obstruct him. He performs at this point a resolute *volte face*. He turns to his true theme, i.e., the depiction of man as he comes from dread and nothing, and the positive message of the existence of this man. Is his intention already tantamount to what Heidegger condemns as " distortion " of nothing ? Be that as it may, the all-embracing question and questionability which form the horizon for Heidegger are not ultimate for Sartre. To be sure, his writings speak with eloquence and agony of the *ignominie humaine*, of the intolerable confusion of weakness, brutality, triviality, folly, mendacity and dread which we call human life, and of the inevitable impasses and labyrinths into which man ineluctably wanders, however noble his intentions and efforts may seem to be. Yet there is always somewhere in Sartre the sudden flash of a kind of Nevertheless, a defiance which is defeated yet does not accept defeat, but always reveals in some way that man has finally grasped and overcome everything with a smile, and is sovereignly transcendent. It is precisely this sovereign transcendence of lost but self-reliant man which is, if I understand him aright, the existential viewpoint of Sartre, and the call to final resolution for this movement is the core of his teaching. To put it summarily, Sartre contrasts with the ponderously reflective German Martin Heidegger as a type of the perennial French *débrouillard*. It is for this reason and in this sense that he can and must make what many find the surprising explanation : *L'Existentialisme est un humanisme*.

For Sartre existentialism—and this is what he means by *humanisme*—is *une doctrine, qui rend la vie possible* (p. 12). His existentialism is a doctrine of freedom. Man *hic et nunc*—this or that particular man—cannot and may not find freedom anywhere at all. But he can and may exercise and therefore possess it. Indeed, he can and may become it himself. Hence his freedom is not an idea. It is not a potentiality which he controls. It is not a gift which he is granted. It is not an assumption on which he may proceed. It is not a capital sum on which interest accrues and with which he can start something. He cannot start anywhere or with anything. There is no corresponding something. He can start only with nothing. The ground is taken from under his feet. For as there is no God, so there is no human nature. There are no eternal and historical realities, nor conventions and ideals, to which he may cling, which he may believe and respect, which can help, secure or deliver him. He cannot take others as examples and imitate them. He is given no directives. Even in himself he is and has and finds absolutely nothing of any significance, authority, power or value, so that he cannot even fall back upon himself. There is nothing on which he can fall back. What is behind him is always nothing. In the light of what is behind he has no prospect but hell. *Continuons !*—as he says just before the final curtain in his *Huis Clos*. There remains only one true case of precedence in which life is possible and there is prospect of a genuine future. This is existence itself : *l'existence précède l'essence* (p. 17). But man is the being who can live and be this case of precedence. He can first be nothing and then something. He can be as he wills to be, as he imagines and makes himself (p. 22). What is man ? *Ce qui se jette vers un avenir et ce qui est conscient de se projeter dans l'avenir*. What is man ? *Un projet, qui se vit subjectivement, au lieu d'être une mousse, une pourriture ou un choux-fleur ; rien n'ex ste préalablement à ce projet ; rien n'est au ciel intelligible.* Let it be clearly understood that he is not what he wills. What he wills (e.g., to join a political party, to write a book, to marry etc.) is only the manifestation of a more original decision. He is that as which he wills himself (p. 23 f.)— himself before all his thoughts, inclinations, passions and decisions, and self-evidently before all the external circumstance of his life, and above all before what is usually called his " destiny." He has not created himself. He is " projected into the world." But he is projected in order that he may choose, will and create himself. *L'homme est condamné*, but *condamné à être libre* (p. 37). He has no advisers. Even to choose possible advisers he must first have chosen himself, and every true and genuine adviser can only say to him : *Vous êtes libre, choisissez, c'est-à-dire inventez* (p. 47). It is to be noted that even the *essence* before him can only be what he can and will choose, will, invent and create as he chooses himself. *La vie n'a pas de sens a priori ; avant que vous ne viviez la vie, elle n'est rien* (p. 87). Man has no future prospect apart from what he is, lives and does. For example, he cannot take part in a general kind of "progress." All that he can and may do is to act. *Il n'y a pas de réalité que dans l'action* (p. 55). What is man ? He is *l'ensemble de ses actes ;* he is *sa vie ;* he is *une série d'entreprises* (p. 58). *Ce qui compte c'est l'engagement total* (p. 62). It is always on man himself that there is laid the ineluctable necessity of this *engagement total* with every positive or negative possibility, with every acceptance and self-assertion, with every great or small decision, with all that is called either good or bad. This is inevitably the case. *Autour de lui les choses s'étaient groupées en ronde ; elles s'attendaient sans faire signes, sans livrer la moindre indication, il était seul, sans aide et sans excuse, condamné à décider sans retour possible, condamné pour toujours à être libre* (from *L'âge de raison*).

Sartre denies the charge that his existentialism is naturalism. He is not concerned with how man is, but with how as such he is the being which freely chooses himself in his life. He also maintains that his existentialism is not materialism, but the only doctrine which does not make man into an object : *nous voulons constituer précisément le règne humain comme un ensemble des valeurs distinctes du règne matériel* (p. 65). Again, he claims that his existentialism is not pessimism, but points to the freedom of man and thus a genuine humanistic optimism. Above all, it is not libertinism. This is the point at which he has been most widely misunderstood, and therefore close attention must be paid to his own explicitly expressed desire that his concept of freedom should be understood as responsibility. One might, of course, ask to whom man is responsible ? Who calls him to account for the life he has actually lived ? But we must not overlook the fact that Sartre wishes the freedom of his new man to be ethically understood. In his strictly subjective action man is responsible for all men (p. 24). *En se choisissant il choisit tous les hommes.* With each of his actions —and here his agreement with Kant cannot but be observed—he creates an image of man as he thinks he ought to be (*une image de l'homme tel que nous estimons qu'il doit être*). *Choisir d'être ceci ou cela c'est affirmer de même temps la valeur de ce que nous choisissons.* What we choose is never the worse but the better, and can anything be " better " for us unless it is better for all ? In consequence, our action at any time is a commitment not only of ourselves but of the whole of mankind (p. 24 f.). We ought always to ask ourselves : What would happen if everyone did as I am doing just now ? This question provides the standard of truth according to which we choose and will ourselves (p. 29). Finally Sartre definitely repudiates the charge of subjectivism. For a man does not discover himself only in himself, but in relation to his fellows. And in himself he does not only discover himself, but his fellows too. *Pour obtenir une vérité quelconque sur moi il faut, que je passe par l'autre. L'autre est indispensable à mon existence, aussi bien d'ailleurs qu'à la connaissance que j'ai de moi . . . la découverte de mon intimité me découvre en même temps l'autre comme une liberté posée en face de moi. . . . Aussi découvrons-nous tout de suite un monde que nous appellerons l'inter-subjectivité et c'est dans ce monde que l'homme décide ce qu'il est et ce que sont les autres* (p. 65 f.). What, therefore, Sartre desires is not merely individual freedom, *la liberté pour la liberté*, but freedom which depends entirely on the freedom of others and on which the freedom of others depends. Only within this corporate freedom does the individual act *de bonne foi ;* otherwise he acts *de mauvaise foi* and is *un lâche* or even *un salaud* (p. 83 f.). While there is nothing that can be called " human nature," there is nevertheless an *universalité humaine de conditions.* There are the great unvarying necessities of being in the world, of having to labour, to live with other men and to die (p. 67 f.). Freedom is freedom within the order of these conditions. But what man is or shall be under these conditions is not a given reality but always requires (and this is what his existence means) to be imagined, produced and built up (p. 70). It is to this that every man is committed : *Chaque homme se réalise en réalisant un type d'humanité. . . . Chacun de nous fait l'absolu en respirant, en mangeant, en dormant ou en agissant d'une façon quelconque* (p. 71 f.). In short, *il n'y a aucune différence entre être librement, être comme projet, comme existence qui choisit son essence et être absolu ; et il n'y a aucune différence entre être absolu temporairement localisé, c'est-à-dire qui s'est localisé dans l'histoire et être compréhensible universellement* (p. 72).

Sartre clearly wishes existentialism to be understood as *un effort pour tirer toutes les conséquences d'une position athée cohérente* (p. 94). Unlike the radicals of the 18th and 19th centuries, he is not particularly concerned to demonstrate the non-existence of God. He can even say *qu'il est très gênant, que Dieu n'existe pas* (p. 35). The existence of God simply falls away because nothing of value, significance and capacity can precede human existence. Even if a proof of the existence of God were possible it could not alter the fact that there is nothing to precede the existence of man, to keep him from the " damnation of freedom," to spare him his responsibility for himself and for mankind, to deprive him of the magnificent defiance or defiant magnificence with which he conquers the nullity of everything which is not of his own will and invention, leaves all else behind and below, and fashions a new world, his own world, the world of his own human values. *L'existence précède l'essence.* Even a God whose existence could be proved could only be added as an element in the essence which follows existence. Sartre shows real discernment in the fact that he cannot admit God even at this point, as a *valeur* among other *valeurs*. The real conclusion of his case against the existence of God is that He is absolutely superfluous where He should matter most, i.e., prior to human existence. For every " prior " can only be human existence itself. Hence God's place is already filled. The man who is projected into the world, who is necessarily active in it, who necessarily lives among his fellows, who is mortal, but who is free, who imagines, chooses and wills himself, who lives reasonably—this man is himself God. I cannot imagine how Sartre's existentialism can possibly be understood without the realisation that from first to last it involves the extraordinary but typically mythological spectacle of a theogony. To be sure, it is a strange, short-lived and stunted God who is conceived and born—a God for whom many allowances must be made before the claims which he advances, the powers which he assumes and the role which he tries to fill can be accepted. Nevertheless the position and significance claimed—*l'existence précède l'essence*—are indisputable evidence that we are confronted by a God, or at least by something resembling the conventional Western conception of God. To be sure, this being is only man. Yet we see something of the passion of a monotheistic conception of God in the way in which man excludes and rejects the existence of God, of any other God. Sartre thought that in this way he could give man his proper place. But this obviously means that he gives him the place and function of God, i.e., of the true God as distinct from all others. Naturally, we hardly ever find in his writings a specific equation of man with God. There are times when he almost makes this equation, e.g., when he says : *si j'ai supprimé Dieu le père, il faut bien quelqu'un pour inventer les valeurs* (p. 89). But he only borders upon it. For all that he despises the positivism of the older French radicals, he is too deeply imbued with it to be speculative or even dialectic at this point. He can accomplish the apotheosis of man without God. It is as man that man assumes the functions of deity, and in spite of the strangeness of his form is clotted with the attributes of at least the conventional Western conception of God, existing of and by and for himself, constituting his own beginning and end as absolute actuality without potentiality, unique, omnipotent, and certainly omniscient. If I am not mistaken, not even the favourite attribute of infinity is lacking, for it may be seen in the unlimited nature of the claim which Sartre's man-God advances for himself. All that is lacking is the slightest trace of the biblical concept of God. Yet the conventional Western figure of God is almost completely delineated, with the one difference that the existence of God is denied, and " atheistic " man, man discarding acknowledgment of any Supreme Being other than himself, stands forth clothed in the garments of the conventional figure of God.

Our first question concerns the position of God in these thinkers. We shall put it to Heidegger first, whose starting point is not quite the same as that of Sartre. Sartre regards Heidegger as a fellow-representative of atheistic existentialism (p. 17). It is to be noted, however, that Heidegger has recently denied that his doctrine is atheistic. Nevertheless, if he is no atheist, in the same sense although in a different way Sartre is not one either. He is perhaps an atheist in the sense that it is difficult to envisage any possible function and place for a God outside his threefold postulate of that which is (human) existence and nothing. But he is not an atheist in the sense that in his teaching the nature and functions of deity are not absent but are in fact transferred to another dimension. He, too, has not made an actual equation. But he cannot be understood unless it is realised that his teaching involves such an equation, not identical with but corresponding to that of Sartre. In Heidegger nothing is actually the pseudonym which conceals the Godhead. He considers it from the standpoint of man, whereas in Sartre it is itself the standpoint from which man is considered. In what is Heidegger a believer in the sense that Sartre is undoubtedly a believer in man ? We have already seen that the basic question of metaphysics as wrested from nothing is why there is anything at all and not nothing. We have seen the underived and comprehensive dynamism and activity of this nothing : how it actually compels, obtrudes, repels and nihilates ; how it can never be discovered by us, yet reveals itself in dread as the basic mood of existence ; how our existence itself is a projection into nothing and is constituted by our enquiry into it ; how to be open to nothing is the fundamental virtue of existence, and " distortion " of nothing its fundamental sin ; and finally how even that which is, is only as nothing pervades and is present with it, and discloses itself to existence only as it becomes elusive and evanescent. We have seen that it is nothing that exhibits the nature and mode of that which is, and the fact that it is. We have seen that it is the whence and whither of transcendence, the basis and pure content of human science. We have seen that " pure being and pure nothing are one and the same," and that *ex nihilo omne ens qua ens fit*. Must we not say that just as it is irrelevant that Sartre explicitly denies the existence of God, His place being taken and filled by man, so it is irrelevant that Heidegger does not explicitly deny it, His place being fully and finally taken and filled by the all-dominant and dynamic depth of nothing ? We might easily say that if Sartre were not to deny God, and Heidegger to deny Him, it would not modify in either the essential fact that God is not dead, but that a substitute is provided and therefore He is suppressed, and put as it were " on the retired list." Heidegger differs from Sartre only in choosing a different substitute for God : " My cause on nothing is founded." [1] But in his teaching this substitute has actually arrogated the place and function of deity. Thus his doctrine, too, is really a mythological theogony. He is not concerned to interpret it in this way, or to make the express equation : " Nothing is God." He is content with nothing itself without the apotheosis of this designation. Nevertheless, after the suppression of God the Father he, too, required someone *pour inventer les valeurs*. The " someone " that Heidegger discovered, approved and adopted to fulfil this function is nothing. Nothing is the basis, criterion and elucidation of everything, and in relation to it that which is can be only elusive and evanescent, and man can only be a *locum tenens*. In Heidegger's thought, nothing seems lacking in none of the essential features of the conventional figure of God (aseity,

---

[1] Parody of Johann Leon's Hymn : " Ich hab' mein Sach' Gott heim estellt " (My cause on God is founded).—Trans. note.

uniqueness, omnipotence, omniscience, infinity etc.), but nothing has of course no relation to the biblical concept of God, which is not taken into account by either Heidegger or Sartre in their respective mythologies. It might well be said, then, that the God of the Bible, the living God, is entirely unaffected by the suppression and pensioning off of " God " in terms of these two mythologies. In the " God " whom Heidegger and Sartre suppress by providing a substitute for Him, the Church cannot possibly recognise the One whom it calls God. Nor can it recognise Him in the positive aspects of these mythologies, in their proposed substitutes for Him, whether it be said that man or that nothing is the first and the last word, the being from which all things derive and in which they find their end. From the standpoint of the biblical conception of God these alternative postulates between which we have to choose are only mythological fabrications in respect of the character, place and function attributed to them by Heidegger and Sartre.

But in our present discussion of Heidegger and Sartre we are concerned to learn about nothingness rather than God. It would seem that with the necessary reservations already made Heidegger turned towards and Sartre away from nothingness in order to press on in their different ways to absolutisations and therefore to their substitutes for God. What is this nothingness which is Heidegger's goal and Sartre's starting-point ? What do they know of that which is obviously the conclusion for the one and the premise for the other ? Is it or is it not identical with the nothingness with which we are here concerned in its relation and opposition to God ? Is there anything to be learned from them, and if so, what ?

We have observed that Heidegger and Sartre alike have remarkably little to say about God. And the God whom explicitly or implicitly they deny, or at least try to ignore and actually replace, is not the God whose relation and opposition to nothing we are considering. Even less so is the substitute for God which they venture to offer either in the form of man emerging from nothing or of nothing itself claiming man, in both cases with an actual though not an explicit identification. We are thus tempted to assume that, though Heidegger and Sartre are both in different ways concerned with nothing, they are concerned with something very different from the nothingness which we have here considered as nothingness before God. And indeed, in view of the state of their knowledge of God, we cannot expect from these two philosophers a knowledge of nothingness which is finally acceptable. But it would be an error to leave out of account the compulsion of the thing itself operative to some extent, and sometimes with remarkable force, in all human systems, and therefore the fact that for all the speculation something instructive and worth while is introduced. We can surely see its compulsion in the fact that even in their atheistic blindness Heidegger and Sartre could not escape the problem of God, that they could not remove, let alone deny Him with their actual replacement and denial. In this respect do they not see something they would rather not ? And in view of that which confronts both the one and the other as nothing, are we not forced to ask whether they do not see something of that which, because of their ignorance of God, they could not really see, but which still seems in some sense to be quite manifest to them ? I should like to call it the pure presence and operation of nothingness, in correspondence with what I have said about both seeming to be obsessed by it, so much so that it is for one the only end and for the other the only starting-point. It may well be that what they know in this obsession, and what they have to say about it, is all false and ineffectual. It may well be that their knowledge of nothingness is vitiated by the fact that both are unable freely to direct their thoughts towards God, or to think from His standpoint, and are thus obsessed, constrained and captivated by and to this subject. But, the fact remains that from their thought and its expression as determined by this obsession an inference may be drawn which cannot be drawn from the teaching of Leibniz or Schleiermacher, namely, that nothingness is really present and at work. It is no mere fiction or theme of discussion. It is no mere product of our negations to be dismissed by our affirmations. It is there. It assails us with irresistible power as we exist, and we exist as we are propelled by it into the world like a projectile. We are forced to consider it, for it already confronts us. We experience nothingness, and in so doing we experience ourselves and all things as well. Heidegger's astonishment is no less eloquent of this than Sartre's defiance, nor does the latter bear lesser witness. Their thought is determined in and by real encounter with nothingness. They may misinterpret this encounter and therefore nothingness, but not for a moment can they forget it. They misunderstand what they read, but this is the text which they undoubtedly read. Their thought and expression are determined in and by the considerable though not total upheaval of Western thought and expression occasioned by two world wars. They have completely abandoned the optimism and pessimism, the quietism and activism, the speculation and positivism of the 18th and 19th centuries. While the " road back " may not be closed altogether to them, for we cannot tell what the ultimate development of their systems will be, it is nevertheless heavily barred. For the moment at least they cannot deny that nothingness—and it might well be the true nothingness—has ineluctably and unforgettably addressed them, that the question of nothingness has emerged from the plenitude of problems and that it has become for them the real problem. We may certainly learn from them, if we have not learned it already, a more intense and acute awareness. In this sense, whether taught by Heidegger and Sartre or elsewhere, no one to-day can think or say anything of value without being an " existentialist" and thinking and speaking as such, i.e., without being confronted and affected by the disclosure of the presence and operation of nothingness as effected with particular impressiveness in our day. Whoever is ignorant of the shock experienced and attested by Heidegger and Sartre is surely incapable of thinking and speaking as a modern man and unable to make himself understood by his contemporaries. For we men of to-day have consciously or unconsciously sustained this shock. In our time man has encountered nothingness in such a way as to be offered an exceptional opportunity in this respect. More than that may and must not be said, for at all times man has his being within this encounter, and no more than an exceptional opportunity of realising this is offered us even to-day. Even to-day we have no reason to boast that " we have looked in the face of demons." Although an exceptional opportunity is offered us to-day of recognising nothing in encounter with it, it does not follow that this has actually taken place. There are grounds for believing that it has not really done so in the case of Heidegger and Sartre. But it cannot be denied that in an outstanding way they have grasped an outstanding opportunity to do so. And their positive value is to direct their age to this outstanding opportunity, to introduce the subject of nothingness with such urgency. In this respect they reach a point unreached in much ancient and modern—and even Christian—literature.

But in spite of our indebtedness to them for bringing us to the point, to *this* point, we cannot agree that, with their doctrine of nothing, our existentialists have even entered the dimension in which nothingness is to be seen and described as true nothingness by Christian insights. This is naturally of a piece with their ignorance of God, in consequence of which they cannot adopt the standpoint from which one must see and think and speak in this matter. They see and think and speak as true, alert and honest children of our time who have experienced themselves the shock sustained by modern man. Yet they still resemble Leibniz and Schleiermacher in the fact that they do so from an arbitrary human standpoint and in the unshakeable confidence that they themselves can and should assume such a standpoint, that they are free to choose it, and that, from it they are able to see things as they really are. In a fine sentence Heidegger says of science that " its distinction lies in the fact that, in an altogether specific manner, it and it alone explicitly allows the object itself the first and last word. In such objectivity there is a submission to what is, so that this may reveal itself " (p. 357). But in respect of the choice and assumption of the scientific standpoint there is no such " submission to what is " by Heidegger and Sartre. At this point " the object itself " has neither a first nor a last word nor anything at all to say to them. The one thing that has not been affected, let alone broken, by the upheaval of the age—and it cannot be effected by purely secular upheavals— is the self-reliant assurance of the *ego cogito* as the presupposition of their whole systems. From the standpoint of the *ego cogito* true nothingness cannot be discerned, no matter how powerful the impression of its presence and operation may be. From this standpoint nothingness cannot be interpreted in any other way than it has been and always will be when the Christian basis of knowledge is left out of account. It is futile to deny that what the existentialists encounter and objectively perceive is real nothingness. Yet it must be stated most emphatically that seeing they do not really see. What they see, describe and proclaim is not real nothingness, just as the God whom, denying or not denying, they ignore and replace by surrogates is not the real God.

We shall first take the case of Sartre. We have said that nothing is behind him. He has definitely apprehended it as evil and bad. He has really recognised it as calamity and misery. He has experienced so powerfully its actuality that he constantly reverts to it and confronts himself and his contemporaries with it. He is so deeply engrossed in it that one might easily misunderstand his position and think that his only concern is to " debunk " man and the world. Yet nothing is actually behind him. His threefold advantage is that he sees it (1) in its reality, (2) in its actuality, and yet also (3) as behind and beneath. Here a distant recollection of Christian perception might almost be seen. Badness and evil exist in full actuality, yet in such a way as to be behind and below, sterilised, vitiated and overthrown. We cannot but admire the virile address and resolution with which Sartre sets this matter behind him. But at the same time it is here that the most serious problem confronts his system. For who is it that sets the matter behind him ? It is the man who in the midst of cor- .ruption and ruin defiantly chooses, imagines and wills himself ; who, projected into the world, projects himself into the future, his own future ; who undertakes to live his life in full and sole responsibility for himself. We are moved to say to this man : " Well done, we are with you." But have we not heard the same before ? Was not the ancient watchword of the Stoics : *si fractus illabatur orbis impavidum ferient ruinae* ? There is not much to be said against this slogan, and a good deal for it. But it is to be noted that real nothingness cannot be set aside by a pinch of indifferent resolution. If " I " can cope with it, opposing " myself " to it victorious in defeat ; if I can acknowledge and resist it by defying it, it is not true nothingness. It may well be significant, violent, threatening and extremely aggressive, but if I can confront it with sovereign power, if I can deal with it, if I can even play with it in changing situations, if I can set it behind me, I cannot convince myself that I have to do with the true and deadly dangerous adversary of myself and man and life. As I project myself into my future, disposing of the enemy who can be disposed of in this way, i.e., of adverse circumstances, of human folly and evil and their consequent entanglements, of all the calamities of the age, might it not be that in the course of this most courageous and success- ful conflict of St. George with the dragon, the true and deadly dangerous enemy quietly leers over my shoulder from behind and mocks my manliness, the more secure because I have obviously forgotten him in learning and then happily out- growing a little terror ? As I project myself into my future, might it not be that the true enemy accompanies my flight, and easily overhauls me, and is at the goal before me ? Might it not be that in real nothingness I have an adversary who is quite unimpressed by my vaunted sense of responsibility for myself and mankind, the more so as I do not know to whom I owe this responsibility, and who is my judge ? Might it not be that I have to do with a refutation and abolition of the very existence which I boldly assert to precede all essence ? This enemy and adversary, this one who refutes and abolishes my existence, this No which strikes and brackets the Yes with which I try to overcome it, might well be real nothingness. And Sartre does not have the slightest inkling of it. Otherwise he could not have fabricated the myth in which man is in effect the God who can master and control nothingness. The paltriness of this God, or rather the fact that Sartre is capable of thinking that he is not paltry but a majestic deity well equipped to fight the dragon, indicates that the dragon envisaged by him is comparatively innocuous. In the conflict with it a truce is possible, but decisive victory can never be gained. This dragon may be handled as Sartre handles it. It may be made a subject of literary elegance. It may be continually presented and represented as a spectacle which affords the public enraptured dread or dreadful rapture. The public may be taught how to overcome it. Or with a cynical sneer the attempt may be made to teach it. Those who have the gift, like Sartre, can make existentialism fashionable as a humanism, as the old but ever new gospel of the free sovereignty of man. By this existentialism some slight encouragement may be given to man as with two world wars behind him he faces the second half of the strange concluding century of the second Christian millennium. The intention is good. So, too, is the act. To inject morphia is often a good act. Yet the fact that it can be effected or attempted is itself evidence that the case is not as severe as at first supposed. If it were realised that this is a case of " sickness unto death," a syringe of morphia would not be used. That Sartre uses it is evidence that the sickness unto death, real nothingness, is as unknown to him as the true God.

We return to Heidegger. His case is different to the extent that nothingness, or what might seem to be such, is before him. He is in no sense a *débrouillard*. He has not mastered this factor, neither does he trifle with it. He handles it with religious solemnity. The effect which he produces is therefore immeasurably more serious than that of Sartre. His apparent aversion to Sartre is thus comprehensible, as is the indignation of his friends at the idea that he should even be named in the same breath as Sartre, let alone be considered beside him. We are undoubtedly in a different milieu. But when we address to him the same question as to Sartre, enquiring concerning nothingness, we can only say that his blindness regarding it is as great as Sartre's. Although it cannot be without significance in a writer so word-conscious as Heidegger, the fact might easily escape our notice that only once in his study on metaphysics does he explicitly define nothing as nothingness, and this only by way of introduction and in definition of its a-logical nature. For him it is in no sense nothingness. That it discloses itself in the basic mood of dread might indicate a trend in this direction. But in its most real form this dread (and this is a direct agreement with Sartre) is already overcome. It is peace, serenity and even daring. And that as which nothing reveals itself in dread, Heidegger's nothing in itself and as such, has no power to awaken dread at all. Otherwise how could it arrogate the functions of God and become a substitute for Him, as in Heidegger's myth ? Otherwise Heidegger would surely have had to say that the devil is the true God. But he never dreams of saying this, because for him nothing is not a dreadful, horrible, dark abyss but something fruitful and salutary and radiant. In face of Heidegger's nothing, acceptance and not exclusion is demanded. For without such acceptance there can be no metaphysics or science. Indeed there can be no existence except as a projection into nothing. What possible relationship can there be between the nothing which in this positive sense can replace God and arrogate and exercise His functions, and true nothingness ? Heidegger's nothing is an ambivalent concept. Heidegger was quite serious when as early as 1929 he accepted the Hegelian identification of nothing with being. In this writing the leading concept might well be replaced throughout by that of being without modifying in any way the sense and substance of his exposition. In a letter on humanism written in 1946 to one of Sartre's French followers, and published in 1947 in the appendix to *Platons Lehre von der Wahrheit*, Heidegger does in fact effect this replacement, introducing the " truth of being " as the subject of exactly the same assertions as in 1929 were made concerning nothing. In place of the " nihilation of nothing " there now emerges with equal intensity and like effect the " affirmation of being " (*das Lichten des Seins*), and existence as projection into nothing is now " ecstatic " *ek-sistere*, " entry into the truth of being." All the negative inferences drawn by disciples or critics of the earlier form of his teaching in respect of humanism, logic, values, transcendence, the highest and holiest good of men, and even God, are now dismissed as false with an air of contempt for such pedantries of logic (p. 95 f.). Indeed, a place is now found for God (or at least for " God and the gods " p. 85) as a dimension of being, namely, the " dimension of the Holy " (p. 102), and in the history of being there is the prospect or possibility of the dawning of a " day of the saints " (p. 85). We are tempted to say : " Behold all things are made new," but this would involve another and more radical misunderstanding of Heidegger. For if the earlier work is intelligently read, it is obvious that even there nothing is also being, that in some dimension it may be the holy or even God, and that it does actually arrogate and exercise a divine function. On the other hand, his concept of being in 1946 is still ambivalent, and therefore does not cease to comprehend the nothing of 1929. When being asserts itself positively, wholeness is accompanied by that which is evil and horrible. Being itself is " that which is disputed." " In it is concealed the origin of the essence of nihilation from which every Not derives and which gives to every genuine negation its legitimacy and necessity " (p. 112). There is really nothing new. Heidegger is thoroughly consistent. In 1946 he merely reverses his concept of nothing. But even in 1929 is not the concept reversible and actually reversed ? Nor is there anything original in this. Heidegger himself tells us that in his dialectic he is pursuing the path of older philosophy, gnosticism and mysticism. It is not for us to estimate the legitimacy of this dialectic. But one conclusion is inevitable. The nothing of Heidegger, which may also be called being and under either title arrogates the function of God, can never be identified with nothingness in the Christian sense. Whatever it may be that Heidegger perceives and expounds (and he and the tradition which he obviously follows must accept responsibility for this), it is absolutely certain that his nothing is not real nothingness, but is comparatively innocuous as compared with it. The concept of real nothingness is in no sense ambivalent. If Heidegger had perceived real nothingness, he would not have described the dread in which his nothing discloses itself as though it were not basically dread but peace, serenity and daring. The sickness unto death in which man is confronted by real nothingness has a different aspect. The dialectic in which nothing may reveal itself as being and being as nothing is a useless instrument in face of it. If Heidegger had seen it, he might well have spoken of the relativity, inferiority, subjugation and vitiation of nothing, and shown that in spite of its nature it can be subordinated to the service of being and brought under its control. But in so doing he would have established and authenticated it as nothing, and could not have conceived of its identification with being, nor even dreamt of attributing to it of all things the sovereign role and function constitutive of being and existence. He would have realised that to do this is to proclaim the devil to be the principle of all being and existence. The unhesitating confidence with which he did what he could not possibly have done if he had perceived real nothingness is conclusive evidence that he did not perceive it. Thus by a different route we reach the same conclusion as in the case of Sartre.

Credit must be given to both that in so striking a way they looked and pointed in the direction in which real nothingness can actually be perceived in other circumstances. Yet we cannot but say of both that their accounts of what they have seen in this direction have so far been a false alarm.

4. THE REALITY OF NOTHINGNESS

Forearmed and forewarned by these discussions, we may now attempt a comprehensive statement. What is real nothingness? 1. In this question objection may well be taken to the word " is." Only God and His creature really and properly are. But nothingness is neither God nor His creature. Thus it can have nothing in common with God and His creatures. But it would be foolhardy to rush to the conclusion that it is therefore nothing, i.e., that it does not exist. God takes it into account. He is concerned with it. He strives against it, resists and overcomes it. If God's reality and revelation are known in His presence and action in Jesus Christ, He is also known as the God who is confronted by nothingness, for whom it constitutes a problem, who takes it seriously, who does not deal with it incidentally but in the fulness of the glory of His deity, who is not engaged indirectly or mediately but with His whole being, involving Himself to the utmost. If we accept this, we cannot argue that because it has nothing in common with God and His creature nothingness is nothing, i.e., it does not exist. That which confronts God in this way, and is seriously treated by Him, is surely not nothing or non-existent. In the light of God's relationship to it we must accept the fact that in a third way of its own nothingness " is." All conceptions or doctrine which would deny or diminish or minimise this " is " are untenable from the Christian standpoint. Nothingness is not nothing. Quite apart from the inadmissibility of its content, this proposition would be self-contradictory. But it " is " nothingness. Its nature and being are those which can be assigned to it within this definition. But because it stands before God as such they must be assigned to it. They cannot be controverted without misapprehending God Himself.

2. Again, nothingness is not simply to be equated with what is *not*, i.e., not God and not the creature. God is God and not the creature, but this does not mean that there is nothingness in God. On the contrary, this " not " belongs to His perfection. Again, the creature is creature and not God, yet this does not mean that as such it is null or nothingness. If in the relationship between God and creature a " not " is involved, the " not " belongs to the perfection of the relationship, and even the second " not " which characterises the creature belongs to its perfection. Hence it would be blasphemy against God and His work if nothingness were to be sought in this " not," in the non-divinity of the creature. The diversities and frontiers of the creaturely world contain many " nots." No single creature is all-inclusive. None is or resembles another. To each

belongs its own place and time, and in these its own manner, nature and existence. What we have called the " shadow side " of creation is constituted by the "not " which in this twofold respect, as its distinction from God and its individual distinctiveness, pertains to creaturely nature. On this shadow side the creature is contiguous to nothingness, for this " not " is at once the expression and frontier of the positive will, election and activity of God. When the creature crosses the frontier from the one side, and it is invaded from the other, nothingness achieves actuality in the creaturely world. But in itself and as such this frontier is not nothingness, nor has the shadow side of creation any connexion with it. Therefore all conceptions and doctrines which view nothingness as an essential and necessary determination of being and existence and therefore of the creature, or as an essential determination of the original and creative being of God Himself, are untenable from the Christian standpoint. They are untenable on two grounds, first, because they misrepresent the creature and even the Creator Himself, and second, because they confound the legitimate " not " with nothingness, and are thus guilty of a drastic minimisation of the latter.

3. Since real nothingness is real in this third fashion peculiar to itself, not resembling either God or the creature but taken seriously by God Himself, and since it is not identical either with the distinction and frontier between God and creation or with those within the creaturely world, its revelation and knowledge cannot be a matter of the insight which is accessible to the creature itself and is therefore set under its own choice and control. Standing before God in its own characteristic way which is very different from that of the creature, the object of His concern and action, His problem and adversary and the negative goal of His victory, nothingness does not possess a nature which can be assessed nor an existence which can be discovered by the creature. There is no accessible relationship between the creature and nothingness. Hence nothingness cannot be an object of the creature's natural knowledge. It is certainly an objective reality for the creature. The latter exists objectively in encounter with it. But it is disclosed to the creature only as God is revealed to the latter in His critical relationship. The creature knows it only as it knows God in His being and attitude against it. It is an element in the history of the relationship between God and the creature in which God precedes the creature in His acts, thus revealing His will to the creature and informing it about Himself. As this occurs and the creature attains to the truth—the truth about God's purpose and attitude and therefore about itself—through the Word of God, the encounter of the creature with true nothingness is also realised and recognised. Of itself, the creature cannot recognise this encounter and what it encounters. It experiences and endures it. But it also misinterprets it, as has always happened. Calumniating

God and His work, it misrepresents it as a necessity of being or nature, as a given factor, as a peculiarity of existence which is perhaps deplorable, perhaps also justifiable, perhaps to be explained in terms of perfection or simply to be dismissed as non-existent, as something which can be regarded as supremely positive in relation to God, or even as a determination of God Himself. All these conceptions and doctrines, whatever their content, are untenable from a Christian standpoint if only because they are contingent upon an arbitrary and impotent appraisal of what can only make itself known in the judgment of God, and is thus knowable only as God pronounces His sentence, while its malignity and corruption find supreme expression in the assumption of the creature that of itself and at its own discretion it is able to discover its nature and existence.

4. The ontic context in which nothingness is real is that of God's activity as grounded in His election, of His activity as the Creator, as the Lord of His creatures, as the King of the covenant between Himself and man which is the goal and purpose of His creation. Grounded always in election, the activity of God is invariably one of jealousy, wrath and judgment. God is also holy, and this means that His being and activity take place in a definite opposition, in a real negation, both defensive and aggressive. Nothingness is that from which God separates Himself and in face of which He asserts Himself and exerts His positive will. If the biblical conception of the God whose activity is grounded in election and is therefore holy fades or disappears, there will also fade and disappear the knowledge of nothingness, for it will necessarily become pointless. Nothingness has no existence and cannot be known except as the object of God's activity as always a holy activity. The biblical conception, as we now recall it, is as follows. God elects, and therefore rejects what He does not elect. God wills, and therefore opposes what He does not will. He says Yes, and therefore says No to that to which He has not said Yes. He works according to His purpose, and in so doing rejects and dismisses all that gainsays it. Both of these activities, grounded in His election and decision, are necessary elements in His sovereign action. He is Lord both on the right hand and on the left. It is only on this basis that nothingness " is," but on this basis it really " is." As God is Lord on the left hand as well, He is the basis and Lord of nothingness too. Consequently it is not adventitious. It is not a second God, nor self-created. It has no power save that which it is allowed by God. It, too, belongs to God. It " is " problematically because it is only on the left hand of God, under His No, the object of His jealousy, wrath and judgment. It " is," not as God and His creation are, but only in its own improper way, as inherent contradiction, as impossible possibility. Yet because it is on the left hand of God, it really " is " in this paradoxical manner. Even on His left hand the activity of God

is not in vain. He does not act for nothing. His rejection, opposition, negation and dismissal are powerful and effective like all His works because they, too, are grounded in Himself, in the freedom and wisdom of His election. That which God renounces and abandons in virtue of His decision is not merely nothing. It is nothingness, and has as such its own being, albeit malignant and perverse. A real dimension is disclosed, and existence and form are given to a reality *sui generis*, in the fact that God is wholly and utterly not the Creator in this respect. Nothingness is that which God does not will. It lives only by the fact that it is that which God does not will. But it does live by this fact. For not only what God wills, but what He does not will, is potent, and must have a real correspondence. What really corresponds to that which God does not will is nothingness.

The first and most impressive mention of nothingness in the Bible is to be found at the very beginning in Gen. 1² (cf. *C.D.*, III, 1, p. 101 f.), in which there is a reference to the chaos which the Creator has already rejected, negated, passed over and abandoned even before He utters His first creative Word, which He has already consigned to the past and to oblivion even before the beginning of time at His command. Chaos is the unwilled and uncreated reality which constitutes as it were the periphery of His creation and creature. It is that which, later depicted in very suitable mythological terms and conceptions, is antithetical both to God Himself and to the world of heaven and earth which He selected, willed and created. It is a mere travesty of the universe. It is the horrible perversion which opposes God and tempts and threatens His creature. It is that which, though it is succeeded and overcome by light, can never itself be light but must always remain darkness. Note that the first creative work (Gen. 1³f.) is simply separation—the separation of light from darkness, of the waters on the earth from the threatening waters above the firmament, of the dry land from the seas. Note also that with this separation there arises even within the good creation of God a side which is as it were the neighbour and frontier of chaos. But chaos is not night, or the waters above the firmament, or the earthly sea. It still remains not merely distinct from the works of God, but excluded by the operation of God, a fleeting shadow and a receding frontier. Only in this way can we say that it " is." But in this way it undoubtedly " is," and is thus subject to the divine sovereignty. In this way it is present from the very outset with God and His creature. In this way it is involved from the very outset in the history of the relationship between God and His creature, and therefore from the very outset the biblical witness to this history takes its existence into account. The sin of man as depicted in Gen. 3 confirms the accuracy of our definition. It is purely and simply what God did not, does not and cannot will. It has the essence only of non-essence, and only as such can it exist. Yet the sin of man also confirms the real existence of nothingness. Nothingness is a factor so real that the creature of God, and among His creatures man especially in whom the purpose of creation is revealed, is not only confronted by it and becomes its victim, but makes himself its agent. And all the subsequent history of the relationship between God and His creature is marked by the fact that man is the sinner who has submitted and fallen a victim to chaos. The issue in this whole history is the repulse and final removal of the threat thus actualised. And God Himself is always the One who first takes this threat seriously, who faces and throws Himself against it, who strives with chaos, who persists in His attitude, who continues and completes the action which He has already undertaken as Creator in this respect, negating and rejecting it. As He affirms and elects and works His *opus proprium*, the work of His grace, God is always active in His *opus alienum* as well. And He is always holy. Therefore He always wills that His creature should be holy. He wills to take part in its conflict. Since it is really His own cause, He wills to place Himself alongside it in this conflict.

Nothingness " is," therefore, in its connexion with the activity of God. It "is " because and as and so long as God is against it. It "is " only in virtue of the fact that God is against it in jealousy, wrath and judgment. It "is " only within the limits thus ordained. But within these limits it "is." From the Christian standpoint, therefore, any conception must be regarded as untenable if it ascribes to nothingness any other existence than in confrontation with God's non-willing. It would be untenable from a Christian point of view to ascribe autonomous existence independent of God or willed by Him like that of His creature. Only the divine non-willing can be accepted as the ground of its existence. Equally untenable from a Christian standpoint, however, is any conception in which its existence in opposition to the divine non-willing is denied and it is declared to be a mere semblance. Within this limit nothingness is no semblance but a reality, just as God's non-willing in relation to it, and the whole *opus alienum* of the divine jealousy, wrath and judgment, is no semblance but a reality.

5. The character of nothingness derives from its ontic peculiarity. It is evil. What God positively wills and performs in the *opus proprium* of His election, of His creation, of His preservation and overruling rule of the creature revealed in the history of His covenant with man, is His grace—the free goodness of His condescension in which He wills, identifying Himself with the creature, to accept solidarity and to be present with it, to be Himself its Guarantor, Helper and King, and therefore to do the best possible for it. What God does not will and therefore negates and rejects, what can thus be only the object of His *opus alienum*, of His jealousy, wrath and judgment, is a being that refuses and resists and therefore lacks His grace. This being which is alien and adverse to grace and therefore without it, is that of nothingness. This negation of His grace is chaos, the world which He did not choose or will, which He could not and did not create, but which, as He created the actual world, He passed over and set aside, marking and excluding it as the eternal past, the eternal yesterday. And this is evil in the Christian sense, namely, what is alien and adverse to grace, and therefore without it. In this sense nothingness is really privation, the attempt to defraud God of His honour and right and at the same time to rob the creature of its salvation and right. For it is God's honour and right to be gracious, and this is what nothingness contests. It is also the salvation and right of the creature to receive and live by the grace of God, and this is what it disturbs and obstructs. Where this privation occurs, nothingness is present ; and where nothingness is present this privation

C.D.—III.–III.—I2

occurs, i.e., evil, that which is utterly inimical first to God and then to His creature. The grace of God is the basis and norm of all being, the source and criterion of all good. Measured by this standard, as the negation of God's grace, nothingness is intrinsically evil. It is both perverting and perverted. In this capacity it does not confront either God or the creature neutrally. It is not merely a third factor. It opposes both as an enemy, offending God and threatening His creature. From above as well as from below, it is the impossible and intolerable. By reason of this character, whether in the form of sin, evil or death, it is inexplicable as a natural process or condition. It is altogether inexplicable. The explicable is subject to a norm and occurs within a standard. But nothingness is absolutely without norm or standard. The explicable conforms to a law, nothingness to none. It is simply aberration, transgression, evil. For this reason it is inexplicable, and can be affirmed only as that which is inherently inimical. For this reason it can be apprehended in its aspect of sin only as guilt, and in its aspect of evil and death only as retribution and misery, but never as a natural process or condition, never as a subject of systematic formulation, even though the system be dialectical. Being hostile before and against God, and also before and against His creature, it is outside the sphere of systematisation. It cannot even be viewed dialectically, let alone resolved. Its defeat can be envisaged only as the purpose and end of the history of God's dealings with His creature, and in no other way. As it is real only by reason of the *opus Dei alienum*, the divine negation and rejection, so it can be seen and understood only in the light of the *opus Dei proprium*, only in relation to the sovereign counter-offensive of God's free grace. It " is " only as the disorder at which this counter-offensive is aimed, only as the non-essence which it judges, only as the enemy of God and His creation. We thus affirm that it is necessary to dismiss as non-Christian all those conceptions in which its character as evil is openly or secretly, directly or indirectly, conjured away, and its reality is in some way regarded or grouped with that of God and His creature. Where God and His creature are known, and His free grace as the basic order of their relationship, nothingness can only be understood as opposition and resistance to this basic order and cannot therefore be regarded or grouped with God and His creature.

6. The controversy with nothingness, its conquest, removal and abolition, are primarily and properly God's own affair. It is true, of course, that it constitutes a threat to the salvation and right of the creature, but primarily and supremely it contests the honour and right of God the Creator. It is also true that in the form of sin nothingness is the work and guilt, and in the form of evil and death the affliction and misery, of the creature. Yet in all these forms it is first and foremost the problem of God Himself. Even the man who submits

to nothingness and becomes its victim is still His creature. His care for His creature takes substance as its work and guilt and affliction and misery engender such rebellion and ruin, such disturbance and destruction. It is true, again, that God does not contend with nothingness without allowing His creature a share in the contention, without summoning His creature to His side as His co-belligerent. Yet the contention remains His own. His is the cause at stake, His all the power, His all the wisdom, His every weapon profitable and effectual in the strife. His free grace alone is victorious even where it is given to His creature to be victorious in this conflict. Everything depends upon the performance of His *opus proprium*. Only with the operation of His election and grace, and only as its converse, is His *opus alienum* also performed, and the sovereign No pronounced by which nothingness is granted its distinctive form and existence. Only within the limit of His No does nothingness have its reality, and in its reality its character as that which is evil, alien and adverse to grace, and therefore without it. And the limit of His No, and therefore of nothingness, is His Yes, the work of His free grace. As God performs this work, espousing the cause of the creature, He engages in controversy with nothingness, and deals with it, as is fitting, as that which separated, passed over and abandoned, as the eternal yesterday. He exercises the non-willing by which it can have existence, and His jealousy, wrath and judgment achieve their purpose and therefore their end, which is also the end and destruction of nothingness. It is God's *opus proprium*, the work of His right hand, which alone renders pointless and superfluous His *opus alienum*, the work of His left. This penetration and victory of His free grace as the achievement of the separation already recognisable in creation, and therefore as the destruction of chaos, is the meaning of the history of the relationship between God and His creature. He alone, His activity grounded in His election, can master nothingness and guide the course of history towards this victory. God alone can defend His honour, ensure His creature's salvation, and maintain His own and His creature's right in such a way that every assault is warded off and the assailant himself is removed. God alone can summon, empower and arm the creature to resist and even to conquer this adversary. This is what has taken place in Jesus Christ. But it has taken place in Him as the work of the creature only in the strength of the work of the Creator. The creature as such would be no match for nothingness and certainly unable to overcome it.

It is not insignificant that the story of the creature in its relationship to God begins in Gen. 3 with a disastrous defeat, and that in the terrible form of human sin the chaos separated by God becomes a factor and secures and exercises a power which does not belong to it in relation to God but can obviously do so in relation to His creature. The creature had neither the capacity nor the power to effect that separation. It neither could nor should be God, judging between good and evil. It could and should live only by the grace of God and in virtue of the judgment already accomplished by Him. It could not and should not deal with nothingness as God did, nor master and overcome it like God. Only in covenant with God could it and should it confront nothingness in absolute freedom. And even in covenant with God, where God never fails, there could be and has been failure on the part of the creature. It is worth noting that in Gen. 3 the failure of the creature consisted in the fact that, succumbing to the insinuations of nothingness, it desired to be like God, judging between good and evil, itself effecting that separation, unwilling to live by the grace of God and on the basis of the judgment already accomplished by Him, or to persist in the covenant with God which is its only safeguard against nothingness. It did evil by desiring to do in its own strength the good which cannot be done save by God alone and by the creature only in covenant with Him. The creature sinned by thinking, speaking and acting in a way alien and adverse to grace and therefore without it. We are certainly not to say that man was capable of sin. There is no capacity for nothingness in human nature and therefore in God's creation, nor is there any freedom in this direction as willed, ordained and instituted by God. When man sinned he performed the impossible, not acting as a free agent but as a prisoner. We can and must say, however, that the creature in itself and as such did not and does not confront nothingness in such a way as to be exempt from its insinuation, temptation and power. It cannot, then, be secured against it apart from the grace of God, nor is it a match for it in its own strength. If it tries to meet and fight it in its own strength, as in Gen. 3, it has already succumbed to it. This is the disastrous defeat of the creature by nothingness as typically described in Gen. 3.

The incredible and real mystery of the free grace of God is that He makes His own the cause of the creature which is not even the equal of nothingness, let alone its master, but its victim. There is a grain of truth in the erroneous view that in virtue of His Godhead God Himself has absolutely done away with nothingness, so that for Him it is not only nothingness but nothing. In Him there is room only for its negation. And as the Creator He has effected this negation once and for all. In creation He separated, negated, rejected and abandoned nothingness. How, then, can it still assail, oppose, resist and offend Him? How can it concern Him? But we must not pursue this thought to its logical end. We have not to forget the covenant, mercy and faithfulness of God, nor should we overlook the fact that God did not will to be God for His own sake alone, but that as the Creator He also became the covenant Partner of His creature, entering into a relationship with it in which He wills to be directly and primary involved in all that concerns it. His grace as the basis of His relationship with His creature means that whatever concerns and affects the creature concerns and affects Himself, not indirectly but directly, not subsequently and incidentally but primarily and supremely. Why is this so? Because, having created the creature, He has pledged His faithfulness to it. The threat of nothingness to the creature's salvation is primarily and supremely an assault upon His own majesty. That is to say, He whom nothingness has no power to offend is prepared on behalf of His creature to be primarily and properly offended and humiliated, attacked and injured by nothingness. For the sake of the creature which of itself can be no match for it, He Himself is willing not to be an easy match for it. He thus casts Himself into this conflict which is not necessarily His own. Where His creature stands or succumbs, He comes and exposes Himself to the threat of assault, to the confrontation with nothingness which the creature cannot escape and in which it falls an easy prey. God is not too great, nor is He ashamed, to enter this situation which is not only threatened but already corrupted, to confess Himself the Friend and Fellow of the sinful creature which is not only subject to the assault but broken by it, to acknowledge Himself the Neighbour of the sinful creature stricken and smitten by its own fault, and to act accordingly He Himself inaugurates the history of His covenant with this impotent and faithless partner. His grace does not stop short because it sees that, in spite of the nature which He has given it and the freedom for which He has determined it, the creature is alien and adverse to grace and therefore without it. Though Adam is fallen and disgraced, he is not too low for God to make Himself his Brother, and to be for him a God who must strangely contend for his status, honour and right. For the sake of this Adam God becomes poor. He identifies His own honour and right, which nothingness is obviously unable to contest, with the salvation and right of His creature, which is not only exposed but has already succumbed to its threat. He lets a catastrophe which might be quite remote from Him approach Him and affect His very heart. He makes this alien conflict His very own. He does this of His free grace. For He is under no compulsion. He might act as the erroneous view postulates. He might remain aloof and detached from nothingness. He need not involve Himself. Having given free course to His jealousy, wrath and judgment once and for all in creation, He might have refrained from any further exercise of them. He might have been a majestic, passive and beatific God on high. But He descends to the depths, and concerns Himself with nothingness, because in His goodness He does not will to cease to be concerned for His creature. He thus continues to act in relation to nothingness with the same holiness with which He acted as the Creator when He separated light from darkness. He continues to be the Adversary of this adversary because His love for the creature has no limit nor end. He does not will to be faithful to Himself except as He is faithful to His creature, adopting its cause and therefore constantly making the alien problem of nothingness His own.

Thus it follows that the controversy with nothingness, its conquest, removal and abolition, is primarily and properly the cause of God Himself. At first sight we might regard the converse as true. Nothingness is the danger, assault and menace under which the creature as such must exist. Therefore the creature as such is surely the hero who must suffer and fight and finally conquer this adversary, and the conflict with it is the problem of his destiny and decision, his tragedy and courage, his impotence and comparative successes. But there can be no greater delusion nor catastrophe than to take this view. For it would not be real nothingness, but only an ultimately innocuous counterfeit, if the attack were primarily and properly directed against the creature, and its repulse could and should be primarily and properly the creature's concern. And while the creature is preoccupied with the assault and repulse of these counterfeits, it is already subject to the attack of real nothingness and its defence against it is already futile. In face of real nothingness the creature is already defeated and lost. For, as Gen. 3 shows, it regards the conflict with it as its own cause, and tries to champion it as such. It tries to be itself the hero who suffers and fights and conquers, and therefore like God. And because this decision is a decision against the grace of God, it is a choice of evil. For good—the one and only good of the creature—is the free grace of God, the action of His mercy, in which He who has no need to do so has made the controversy with nothingness His own, exposing Himself to its attack and undertaking to repel it. He knows nothingness. He knows that which He did not elect or will as the Creator. He knows chaos and its terror. He knows its advantage over His creature. He knows how inevitably it imperils His creature. Yet He is Lord over that which imperils His creature. Against Him, nothingness has no power of its own. And He has sworn fidelity to His threatened creature. In creating it He has covenanted and identified Himself with it. He Himself has assumed the burden and trouble of confrontation with nothingness. He would rather be unblest with His creature than be the blessed God of an unblest creature. He would rather let Himself be injured and humiliated in making the assault and repulse of nothingness His own concern than leave His creature alone in this affliction. He deploys all His majesty in the work of His deepest condescension. He intervenes in the struggle between nothingness and the creature as if He were not God but Himself a weak and threatened and vulnerable creature. " As if "—but is that all ? No, for in the decisive action in the history of His covenant with the creature, in Jesus Christ, He actually becomes a creature, and thus makes the cause of the creature His own in the most concrete reality and not just in appearance, really taking its place. This is how God Himself comes on the scene.

But it is really God who does so in His free grace. And therefore it is He as the first and true and indeed the only man, as the Helper who really takes the creature's place, lifting from it all its need and labour and problem and placing them upon Himself, as the Warrior who assumes the full responsibility of a substitute and suffers and does everything on its behalf. In the light of this merciful action of God, the arrogant delusion of the creature that it is called and qualified to help and save and maintain itself in its infinite peril is shown to be evil as well as foolish and unnecessary. So, too, is the arrogant illusion that it is the principal party affected, that its own strength or weakness, despair or elation, folly or wisdom, modicum of " existential " insight and freedom, is the problem in solution of which there takes place the decisive encounter with nothingness, the repelling of its assault, and perhaps its defeat. In the light of the merciful action of God, only God Himself, and trust in Him, and perseverance in His covenant, can be called good, even for the creature too. Hence the creature has only one good to choose, namely, that it has God for it, and that it is thus opposed by nothingness as God Himself is opposed, the God who can so easily master it.

In this way, in this trust and perseverance, in this choice of God's help as its only good, the creature can and will have a real part in the conflict with nothingness. It is certainly no mere spectator. But only in this way does it cease to be such. Only in this way is it rescued from illusory struggles and strivings with what are only counterfeits of nothingness, and from inaction in the event in which the onslaught of nothingness is real but its repulse is effective and its conquest in sight. In this way alone is the situation of the creature, its fall and rehabilitation, its suffering, action and inaction, full of meaning and promise. As the action of God is primary, the creature can and will also play its part. For it is the salvation of the creature which God makes a matter of His own honour. It is for the right of the creature that He establishes and defends His own right. The *opus alienum* of divine jealousy, wrath and judgment is no less for the creature than the *opus proprium* of divine grace. For it is the sin and guilt, the suffering and misery of the creature that God makes His own problem. The creature is not its own. It is the creature and possession of God. It is thus the object of His concern. And therefore conflict with nothingness is its own problem as it is the cause of God. The full intervention of God is needed, and this action of His mercy is the only compelling force, to make the creature willing and able to act on its own behalf in the conflict with nothingness. As God takes action on its behalf, the creature itself is summoned and empowered. It has no arrogant illusion as to its own authority or competence. It really trusts in God, perseveres in His covenant and chooses His help as the only effective good. But if it does this it can and will take action in the conflict with nothingness. It is not under the wings of divine mercy but in the vacuum of creaturely self-sufficiency that the laziness thrives which induces man to yield and succumb to nothingness. And it is not in the vacuum of creaturely self-sufficiency but under the wings of divine mercy that the fortitude thrives in which man is summoned and equipped to range himself with God, so that in his own place he opposes nothingness and thus has a part in the work and warfare of God.

The concluding delimitation which must be made is self-evident. We must reject as non-Christian all conceptions of nothingness which obscure or deny the fact that God Himself is primarily affected by its contradiction and opposition and primarily confronts it with His own contradiction and opposition. There are few heresies so pernicious as that of a God who faces nothingness more or less unaffected and unconcerned, and the parallel doctrine of man as one who must engage in independent conflict against it. We know well enough what it means to be alien and adverse to grace and therefore without it. A graceless God would be a null and evil God, and a self-sufficient, self-reliant creaturely subject a null and evil creature. If a doctrine of nothingness is not unyielding on this point, nothingness itself will triumph. But from another angle, too, we are here at the heart of the whole question. If God Himself were not the primary victim and foe of nothingness, there would be no reason for the unyielding recognition (1) that nothingness is not nothing but exists in its own curious fashion, (2) that it is in no way to be understood as an essential attribute of divine or creaturely being but only as their frontier, (3) that we are capable of knowing nothingness only as we know God in His self-revelation, (4) that nothingness has its being on the left hand of God and is grounded in His non-willing, and (5) that it is evil by nature and therefore we cannot regard or group it in any sense with God and His creature. All these insights, and therefore the whole theological concept of nothingness, depend upon the fact that the primal antithesis or encounter in which it has its being is its confrontation with God Himself, which God freely allows because His freedom is that of His grace and love and faithfulness, and His glory is that of His condescension, to His creature. Everything ultimately depends on this one point, and we remember that it is not a theory or notion but the concrete event at the core of all Christian reality and truth—the self-giving of the Son of God, His humiliation, incarnation and obedience unto death, even the death of the cross. It is here that the true conflict with nothingness takes place. And it is here that it is unmistakeably clear that it is God's own affair. All the statements and delimitations which we have made rest on this point and can be made only on this noetic and ontic basis.

7. On this one point, again, rests our final and decisive insight that nothingness has no perpetuity. God not only has perpetuity, but is Himself the basis, essence and sum of all being. And for all its finiteness and mutability even His creature has perpetuity—the perpetuity which He wills to grant it in fellowship with Himself, and which cannot be lacking in this fellowship but is given it to all eternity. Nothingness, however, is not created by God, nor is there any covenant with it. Hence it has no perpetuity. It is from the very first that which is past. It was abandoned at once by God in creation. He did not even give it time, let alone any other essence

than that of non-essence. As we have already pointed out, in all the power of its peculiar being it is nothing but a receding frontier and fleeting shadow. It has no substance. How can it have when God did not will to give it substance or to create it? It has only its own emptiness. How can it be anything but empty when it is only by God's non-willing that it is what it is? It is thus insubstantial and empty. Only in this way does it have being, form and space on the left hand of God as the object of His *opus alienum*.

But this *opus alienum Dei* is jealousy, wrath and judgment. It does not confer substance and fulness on nothingness but prevents it from assuming them. It gives it only the truth of falsehood, the power of impotence, the sense of non-sense. It establishes it only as that which has no basis. It admits it, but only as that which can have no perpetuity. Nor is this *opus alienum Dei* an interminable process. It moves towards a definite goal and end. It is not effected for its own sake. Unlike the *opus proprium Dei*, the work of His grace, it does not take place by an inner and autonomous necessity. On the contrary, it is subsidiary and complementary to the divine *opus proprium*. The *opus alienum Dei* can have only the significance, weight and scope proper to it as the inevitable divine negation and rejection. If it is inevitable, i.e., as the obverse of the divine election and affirmation, it is nevertheless as such a basically contingent and transient activity. As God fulfils His true and positive work, His negative work becomes pointless and redundant and can be terminated and ended. It is of major importance at this point that we should not become involved in the logical dialectic that if God loves, elects and affirms eternally He must also hate and therefore reject and negate eternally. There is nothing to make God's activity on the left hand as necessary and perpetual as His activity on the right. It takes place only with the necessity with which it can take place according to its nature and meaning—not with the higher, true and primary necessity with which God is gracious to His creature, but only with the subordinate and transient necessity with which, in virtue of His grace, and to establish its rule, He wills to keep it from evil and save it from its power, and has thus to reckon with evil and take it seriously. This negative activity of God has as such, in accordance with its meaning and nature, a definite frontier, and this is to be found at the point where it attains its goal and accomplishes its purpose. With the attainment of the goal the *opus alienum* of God also reaches its end. God is indeed eternally holy, pure, distinct and separated from the evil which is nothingness. But this does not mean that He must always strive with this adversary, enduring its opposition and resistance, and Himself exercising His jealousy, wrath and judgment upon it. Surely He will also be holy, and all the more so, when judgment is executed, when the triumph of His love is unchallenged and boundless, and therefore when He is the God who no longer has to do with an enemy but only with His creature. If He now has to do with nothingness, it is only that He may have to do with it no more, but only with His creature in eternally triumphant love. No eternal enemy is needed for this. And because nothingness is *His* enemy, because it is *He* who allows it to be this, because He has made the controversy with it *His* affair, it cannot be an eternal enemy or have perpetuity.

It is true that God concerns Himself with it. How else could He take up the cause of the creature which is menaced by and subjected to it ? He does this by giving Himself in His Son, by Himself becoming a creature and as such taking on Himself the sin, guilt and misery of the creature. It is true that in the person of the man Jesus He becomes the bearer of the creature's guilt and shame, and as such causes His burning jealousy and kindling wrath and righteous judgment on nothingness to concern and affect Himself. It is true that in what befalls this man God pronounces His No to the bitter end. But it is no less true that this divine *opus alienum*, the whole activity of God on the left hand, was fulfilled and accomplished once and for all, and therefore deprived of its object, when it took place in all its dreadful fulness in the death of Jesus Christ. Nothingness had power over the creature. It could contradict and oppose it and break down its defences. It could make it its slave and instrument and therefore its victim. But it was impotent against the God who humbled Himself, and Himself became a creature, and thus exposed Himself to its power and resisted it. Nothingness could not master this victim. It could neither endure nor bear the presence of God in the flesh. It met with a prey which it could not match and by which it could only be destroyed as it tried to swallow it. The fulness of the grace which God showed to His creature by Himself becoming a threatened, even ruined and lost creature, was its undoing. In the encounter with God Himself it could only fulfil its true destiny of having no perpetuity, of ceasing to be even a receding frontier and fleeting shadow. This is what happened to it in the death of Jesus Christ, in the justification and deliverance of sinful man in this death. If it is true that in humbling Himself in the man Jesus God had to do not only with His creature but with nothingness for the sake of His creature, it is also true, and even more so because definitively and conclusively, that in the exaltation of the same man Jesus God has to do only with His creature and no longer with nothingness. The purpose of His *opus proprium* is the termination of His *opus alienum* and therefore the elimination of its object. Where God exercised His jealousy, wrath and judgment, He does so no more ; but where He does so no more there is no enemy against whom to do so. Where God has said No, He has done so and need do so no more ; but where He no longer does so that which He negates no longer exists. Nothingness is deprived of even the transient, temporary impermanent being it had. Even the truth of falsehood, the power of impotence, the sense of non-sense and the possibility of the impossible which it is accorded on the left hand of God are withdrawn from it in the victory of God on the right. Even the permission by which it existed there is revoked. This is what has already been fulfilled in Jesus Christ, in the exaltation of this creature to the right hand of God. However audacious it may seem to be, we cannot deviate from it by a hairsbreadth. In the light of Jesus Christ there is no sense in which it can be affirmed that nothingness has any objective existence, that it continues except for our still blinded eyes, that it is still to be feared, that it still counts as a cogent factor, that it still has a future, that it still implies a threat and possesses destructive power.

What is nothingness? In the knowledge and confession of the Christian faith, i.e., looking retrospectively to the resurrection of Jesus Christ and prospectively to His coming again, there is only one possible answer. Nothingness is the past, the ancient menace, danger and destruction, the ancient non-being which obscured and defaced the divine creation of God but which is consigned to the past in Jesus Christ, in whose death it has received its deserts, being destroyed with this consummation of the positive will of God which is as such the end of His non-willing. Because Jesus is Victor, nothingness is routed and extirpated. It is that which in this One who was both very God and very man has been absolutely set behind, not only by God, but in unity with Him by man and therefore the creature. It is that from whose influence, dominion and power the relationship between Creator and creature was absolutely set free in Jesus Christ, so that it is no longer involved in their relationship as a third factor. This is what has happened to nothingness once and for all in Jesus Christ. This is its status and appearance now that God has made His own and carried through the conflict with it in His Son. It is no longer to be feared. It can no longer " nihilate." But obviously we may make these undoubtedly audacious statements only on the ground of one single presupposition. The aspect of creaturely activity both as a whole and in detail, our consciousness both of the world and of self, certainly do not bear them out. But what do we really know of it as taught by this consciousness? How can this teach us the truth that it is really past and done with? The only valid presupposition is a backward look to the resurrection of Jesus Christ and a forward look to His coming in glory, i.e., the look of Christian faith as rooted in and constantly nourished by the Word of God. The knowledge and confession of Christian faith, however, inevitably entails the affirmation that by the divine intervention nothingness has lost the perpetuity which it could and must and indeed did have apart from this intervention. It can no longer be validly regarded as possessing any claim or right or power in relation to the creature, as though it were still before and above us, as though the world created by God were still subject to and dominated by it, as though Christians must hold it in awe, as though it were particularly Christian to hold it in the utmost awe and to summon the world to share in this awe. It is no longer legitimate to think of it as if real deliverance and release from it were still an event of the future. It is obvious that in point of fact we do constantly think of it in this way, with anxious, legalistic, tragic, hesitant, doleful and basically pessimistic thoughts, and this inevitably where we are neither able nor prepared to think from the standpoint of Christian faith. But it is surely evident that when we think in this way it is not from a Christian standpoint, but in spite of it, in breach of the command imposed with our Christian faith. If our thought is conditioned by the obedience of Christian faith, we have only one freedom, namely, to regard nothingness as finally destroyed and to make a new beginning in remembrance of the One who has destroyed it. Only if our thought is thus conditioned by the obedience of Christian faith is it possible to proclaim the Gospel to the world as it really is, as the message of freedom for the One who has already come and acted as the Liberator, and therefore of the freedom which precludes the anxiety, legalism and pessimism so prevalent in the world. We need hardly describe how throughout the centuries the Christian Church has failed to shape its thought in the obedience of Christian faith, to proclaim it to the world in this obedience, to live in this freedom and to summon the world to it. For this reason and contrary to its true nature, so-called Christianity has become a sorry affair both within and without. It is shameful enough to have to admit that many of the interpretations of nothingness which we are forced to reject as non-Christian derive their power and cogency from the fact that for all their weakness and erroneousness they attest a Christian insight to the extent that they do at least offer a cheerful view and describe and treat nothingness as having no perpetuity. It ought to be the main characteristic of the Christian view that it can demonstrate this more surely because on surer ground, more boldly because in the exercise and proclamation of the freedom granted to do so, and more logically because not in a venture but in simple obedience. We must not imagine that we serve the seriousness of Christian knowledge, life and proclamation by retreating at this point and refusing to realise and admit that the apparently audacious is the norm, the only true possibility. The true seriousness of the matter, and we may emphasise this point in retrospect of the whole discussion, does not finally depend upon pessimistic but upon optimistic thought and speech. From a Christian standpoint " to be serious " can only mean to take seriously the fact that Jesus is Victor. If Jesus is Victor, the last word must always be secretly the first, namely, that nothingness has no perpetuity.

Our only remaining task is briefly to indicate how the reality of nothingness as we have expounded it is to be conceived in relation to the doctrine of God's providence and world-government. We began by defining it as the sinister alien factor in the sphere of the fatherly rule of God. Our fuller enquiries have confirmed the fact that it must indeed be regarded as an alien factor, that it cannot be anything else, but that even as such it cannot be envisaged and apprehended as outside the jurisdiction of the fatherly rule of God, but only as within it. A few remarks must still be made on the final formulation.

The problem of nothingness primarily arises in a consideration of the relationship between Creator and creature, and therefore of general world-occurrence under the rule of God. In this connexion there comes to the forefront a disturbing and destructive element which casts doubt on the goodness and the being of either the Creator or the creature or possibly of both. The resultant problem of theodicy is usually presented as follows. God is either good, but obviously neither divine nor omnipotent in relation to this element, or He is divine and omnipotent, but obviously not good in relation to this element. And the problem of the perfection of the creature, of being as distinct from God, is presented in this way. The creature is either good, but obviously imperfect in relation to this element, or perfect, but obviously good only in a limited sense in this regard. And the problem of the co-existence of Creator and creature is given the following form. This co-existence is either orderly, but not good in relation to this element, or it is good, but disorderly at this point. But where does it lead us to pose these alternatives? We obviously pose them in this way only if the relationship between Creator and creature, general world-occurrence under the divine government, is considered abstractly and as it were detachedly, in forgetfulness of the fact that this relationship and general world-occurrence under the divine government are centred in the history of the covenant, grace and salvation, that decisions concerning the meaning of this relationship and the goodness and right of Creator and creature, and their co-existence, are taken at this central point, and that therefore truth will be attained in this matter only as we take this concrete centre as our starting point and goal. What reason have we to disregard this fact and to begin with an abstraction?

The older orthodoxy is vitiated at the very outset by the fact that it begins with this abstraction and thus admits these alternatives in all their captiousness, which indeed is inevitable if this centre is not accepted as our starting-point and goal. The older orthodoxy did not make use of the simple and obvious possibility of considering this matter from a Christian standpoint, but treated Creator, creature and their co-existence, and the intrusion upon them of the undeniable reality of nothingness, as if they were philosophical concepts which had to be resolved or brought into a tolerable relationship. The result was that even its most careful labour could not produce definitive statements and acceptable findings in any respect, whether in respect of Creator, creature and their co-existence, or even in respect of nothingness itself, its nature, recognition, ground, character, location and final conquest. It necessarily lost itself in academic discussions which from the very first were of doubtful value for theology and the Church and which as a general consideration of the relationship between God and the world could not even claim any final originality over later philosophical developments, let alone superiority as an authentic interpretation of the revelation committed to the Christian community.

Here we ourselves have tried to avoid this abstraction. We have not sought to apprehend the relationship between Creator and creature philosophically and therefore from without, but theologically and therefore from within. Hence we have not accepted the alternatives posed by an abstract and external view. Even in the general relationship between Creator and creature, even in general world-occurrence under the divine government, we have sought the problem of nothingness where it is raised in its true form and is authentically answered. It is in the mighty act of salvation in Jesus Christ as attested by Holy Scripture that the question of the reality, nature and function of this alien factor is seriously raised and seriously answered. Only what is shown to be true there in the central fact of all history is true in relation to this alien factor even in world-occurrence generally.

From this standpoint—and our final word must really be the first —we must say first and supremely of nothingness that basically it can be reviewed and interpreted only in retrospect of the fact that it has already been judged, refuted and done away by the mercy of God revealed and active in Jesus Christ, or, in other words, that basically it can be reviewed and interpreted only in prospect of the fact that this refutation and termination will be generally revealed in the return of Jesus Christ. Nothingness has its reality and character, and plays its past, present and possibly future role, as the adversary whom God has regarded, attacked and routed as His own enemy. All that makes it threatening and dangerous, all that it can signify as disturbance and destruction in the relationship between Creator and creature, all its terrible features, all the hostility to God and nature which characterises and proceeds from it, can be summed up in the fact that it is that which God did not will and therefore did not tolerate but which He has Himself removed. Indeed, we may say that if nothingness is not viewed in retrospect of God's finished act of conquest and destruction, it is not seen at all. It is confounded with the negative side of God's creation, and viewed only in its negative and not in its privative character. A notion of the dreadful is feared but not the thing itself. And strangely enough, the dreadful is feared only when it is realised that God has denied and deprived nothingness of perpetuity and therefore it is no longer to be feared. It is to be really feared only in retrospect and prospect of Jesus Christ, and therefore only in the fearlessness which is founded on the act of God.

But secondly it also follows that no true or ultimate power and significance but only a dangerous semblance of them are to be attributed to the existence, menace, corruption, disturbance and destructiveness of nothingness as these may still be seen. Whatever its actuality and potentiality, that which it is and does is only in the power of a fragmentary existence. It is only an echo, a shadow, of what it was but is no longer, of what it could do but can do no longer. For the fact that it is broken, judged, refuted and destroyed at the central point, in the mighty act of salvation accomplished in Jesus Christ, is valid not merely at that point but by extension throughout the universe and its activity. This is not yet visible or recognisable, but it cannot be doubted and does not need to be repeated, fostered, augmented or extended. It took place once and for all, and is universally effective. Nothingness may still have standing and assume significance to the extent that the final revelation of its destruction has not yet taken place and all creation must still await and expect it. But its dominion, even though it was only the semblance of dominion, is now objectively defeated as such in Jesus Christ. What it still is in the world, it is in virtue of the blindness of our eyes and the cover which is still over us, obscuring the prospect of the kingdom of God already established as the only kingdom undisputed by evil.

Third, it follows that nothingness can have even its semblance of validity only under the decree of God. What it now is and does, it can be and do only in the hand of God. How can it be otherwise when it can never escape the divine grasp ? There is a legitimate place here for a favourite concept of the older dogmatics—that of permission. God still permits His kingdom not to be seen by us, and to that extent He still permits us to be a prey to nothingness. Until the hour strikes when its destruction in the victory of Jesus Christ will be finally revealed, He thus permits nothingness to retain its semblance of significance and still to manifest its already fragmentary existence. In this already innocuous form, as this echo and shadow, it is an instrument of His will and action. He thinks it good that we should exist " as if " He had not yet mastered it for us—and at this point we may rightly say " as if."

Finally, because in this form still left to it nothingness exists and functions under the control of God, we must say that even though it does not will to do so it is forced to serve Him, to serve His Word and work, the honour of His Son, the proclamation of the Gospel, the faith of the community, and therefore the way which He Himself wills to go within and with His creation until its day is done. The defeated, captured and mastered enemy of God has as such become His servant. Good care is taken that he should always show himself to be a strange servant, and therefore that his existence should remind us who and what he used to be, and therefore that at the sight of him we can never cease to flee to the One who alone has conquered him and has the keys to his prison. Yet it is even more important to reflect that good care is taken by this One that even nothingness should be one of the things of which it is said that they must work together for good to them that love Him.

THE KINGDOM OF HEAVEN, THE AMBASSADORS OF GOD AND THEIR OPPONENTS

God's action in Jesus Christ, and therefore His lordship over His creature, is called the "kingdom of heaven" because first and supremely it claims for itself the upper world. From this God selects and sends His messengers, the angels, who precede the revelation and doing of His will on earth as objective and authentic witnesses, who accompany it as faithful servants of God and man, and who victoriously ward off the opposing forms and forces of chaos.

1. THE LIMITS OF ANGELOLOGY

The dogmatic sphere which we have to enter and traverse in this section is the most remarkable and difficult of all. Why do we have to give ourselves at all to this part of biblical and ecclesiastical tradition? And if we do, how are we even to put the right questions, let alone give the right answers? And if we are successful in putting the right questions and giving the right answers, what results, what lessons, what enrichment of Christian knowledge and proclamation, what solid gains for the Christian life, are we to expect from it? In this sphere there has always been a good deal of theological caprice, of valueless, grotesque and even absurd speculation, and also of no less doubtful scepticism. *Vestigia terrent*—the lack of any sense of humour on the part of those who know and say too much, and the equal lack of any sense of humour on the part of those who deny or ignore too much. How are we to steer a way between this Scylla and Charybdis, between the far too interesting mythology of the ancients and the far too uninteresting "demythologisation" of most of the moderns? How are we to advance without becoming rash, exercising discretion without overlooking what has to be seen, not saying too much and yet not failing to say what has to be said? How are we to be both open and cautious, critical and naive, perspicuous and modest? There are no spheres of dogmatics where we are not well advised to take note of these questions. But there are reasons why they are particularly dark and oppressive in the doctrine of angels which must now concern us.

At all events, this sphere brings us to the very limit of what can be the subject of necessary, sure and helpful Christian impartation and therefore of Church dogmatics. The limit is to be seen in the fact that the name and concept of angels denotes a reality which is distinct both from God and man, and therefore distinct from the true and central content of the Word of God although intimately related to it. The problem of angelology, the character of the kingdom of God as the kingdom of heaven, and the being and activity of heavenly messengers of God border on problems which are necessarily alien to the task and purpose of a dogmatics grounded on the Word of God. The step over this frontier is undoubtedly a step into the sphere of the superfluous and uncertain, which as such might also be both dangerous and even corrupt. But it is illegitimate, and it might be equally dangerous and corrupt, if we allow a fear of failing to halt at this frontier to exclude from our dogmatic investigation the remarkable sphere of the kingdom of heaven, ignoring and even denying it. We have thus no option but to take up the questions which crowd so thickly upon us at this point.

Traces of an awareness of this frontier are clearly discernible in the Early Church at any rate in the centuries prior to the epoch-making *Hierarchia coelestis* of Pseudo-Dionysius. Even Origen (*De princ.*, I, *praef.* 10) said of angels that although they belong to the proclamation of the Church (*ecclesiastica praedicatio*) there is no sure knowledge *quando isti creati sint, vel quales aut quomodo sint.* Similarly Gregory of Nazianzus(*Or.*, 28, 31) said that it is difficult to find the right words in which to speak of angels. Similarly Augustine (*ad Oros*, 11, 24) admitted that it is difficult to say how matters stand with the orders of the angelic world (concerning which Pseudo-Dionysius thought that he knew so much)—*quo me contemnas, quem magnum putas esse doctorem, quaenam ista sint et quid inter se differant nescio. Dicant, qui possunt, si tamen possunt probare, quod dicunt ; ego me ista ignorare confiteor* (*Enchir.*, 15, 58). And Thomas Aquinas could also concede : *Nos imperfecte angelos cognoscimus et eorum officia* (*S. theol.*, I, *qu.* 108, *art.* 3c). But there could, of course, be no question of abandoning the problem. At a later date Calvin was even more radical and pointed (*Instit.*, I, 14, 4), claiming that most of what *ille Dionysius, quicunque fuerit* wrote concerning the nature and order and number of angels was ματαιώματα *absque Dei verbo tradita*, the *mera garrulitas* of one who seemed to imagine that he had come to earth with first-hand knowledge of heaven, in sharp contrast to the apostle Paul, who according to 2 Cor. 12[2f.] had really been caught up into the third heaven, yet nowhere spoke of it in this way, but expressly stated that we have to do here with mysteries which it is not appropriate for man to discuss. But this does not mean that Calvin was trying to avoid the task of speaking of angels according to the guidance and rule of Scripture (*ib.*, 14[3]) : *quia si Deum ex operibus suis agnoscere cupimus, minime omittendum est tam praeclarum et nobile specimen.* How far the limit of theology generally must form that of angelology in particular was finally and almost classically stated by Calvin, both negatively and positively, in the dictum (14, 4) : *Theologo autem non garriendo aures oblectare, sed vera, certa, utilia docendo conscientias confirmare propositum est.* As we address ourselves to this theme we cannot pay too much attention to the restraint as well as the compulsion to which he made reference.

But there is another and more specific reason why the questions are so urgent in this connexion. As we have seen, it belongs to the nature of the case that the doctrine of angels, unlike that of predestination, creation, or man, has in the strict sense no meaning and content of its own. Angels are not independent and autonomous subjects like God and man and Jesus Christ. They cannot, therefore, be made the theme of an independent discussion. Directed to God and man, and belonging particularly to the person and work of Christ, they are only the servants of God and man. They are, only as they come and go in this service. They are essentially marginal figures. This is their glory. It is in their subordination to the great events enacted between God and man that they are that *praeclarum et nobile specimen* of the creaturely world. Hence they have to be considered in our present context, namely, in the consideration of God's lordship over the creature, which has its meaning and centre in its exercise in Jesus Christ. And this is the task which we must now take up. But in this context they can only be considered together with other things. Strictly speaking, every angelological statement can only be an auxiliary or additional statement, an explanation and elucidation of what is not to be said properly and essentially of angels but—corresponding to the ministerial nature and work of angels—of the divine action in Jesus Christ and therefore of the divine lordship in the creaturely world. The only thing is that, since angels belong to the divine action and lordship in this incidental and ministerial fashion, we cannot omit this explanation and elucidation, but have to make it as definitely and precisely as possible.

I hope that I understand Erich Schick correctly if in this connexion I refer to the fact that on p. 9 of his book *Die Botschaft der Engel im N.T.*[2], 1946, he says that he wishes to speak of the relevant truths only " incidentally and in passing " and " very softly," " just as there is something essentially fleeting and transitory about the beings under discussion." I do not think that the same general validity can be ascribed to the saying of Kierkegaard which he adduces, and which is to the effect that in religious matters the speaker is always a whisperer. Even the speech of angels never seems to take the form of a whisper. Yet there is no doubt that what is intended is right enough in this particular sphere. When we undertake to think and speak about angels we have to remember that they are not leading characters and that we can thus speak of them only incidentally and softly. And the " incidentally " and " softly " have to be taken with the greatest seriousness and force. After all, it makes a great difference whether we treat a theme independently or in connexion with something else. And it is the latter which must obtain in relation to the kingdom of God as the kingdom of heaven and therefore to angels as the heavenly messengers of God.

From this standpoint, too, it should be obvious that all the questions of appropriate procedure on both sides, of what to do and not to do, of what not to do and to do, are particularly pressing in the sphere of domatics to which we now turn, so that we have no option but to allow them to be put.

In the first sub-section, then, we shall attempt some basic and methodological clarifications in relation to these questions.

1. The first of these clarifications must necessarily consist in the

proposition that the teacher and master to which we must keep in this matter can only be the Holy Scriptures of the Old and New Testament, that we must not accept any other authority, that we must listen exhaustively to what this guide has to tell us, and that we must respect what it says and what it does not say. It will be seen that in this matter we have to claim a specific freedom in relation to all tradition both orthodox and liberal in order to be the more obedient to Holy Scripture. What we mean is Holy Scripture as the human and historical but unique and normative witness to the revelation and work of God in His dealings in Jesus Christ and therefore in His lordship in the creaturely world. According to the witness of the Old and New Testaments, to this revelation and work of God there belongs also the character of the kingdom of God as the kingdom of heaven, and the angels as His heavenly messengers. They belong to it in a particular way, not as leading but subsidiary characters, and these not as autonomous subjects but merging as it were into their function, which is wholly and exemplarily that of service. It is only in this way that they belong to it. But in this way they do belong to it. Concerning the basis and reach and meaning and importance of the fact that they do so we shall have to speak when we take up the theme itself. For the moment it is enough to maintain that in certain contexts the biblical witness to the revelation and work of God includes the witness to angels, and that in the sense of its authors it would not be right, but a definite dimension would be lacking, if this witness were lacking. This is the fact which forms our starting-point. The dogmatics of the Christian Church has no other reason or cause to enter the sphere apart from this fact, which is not merely indisputable but springs at once to our notice and demands that we take up some sort of attitude to it. We are not concerned with angels in general, or with higher angelic beings which may be possible or actual, postulated or in some way confessed. We are dealing wholly and exclusively with what are described and introduced as angels in the witness of Scripture and in connexion with the revelation and work of God. In this respect our procedure is similar to that which we had to follow in relation to God, where we were not concerned with a real or supposed deity, a personal or impersonal cosmic or redemptive principle, but only with the One who is attested as God and Saviour in Holy Scripture under the name of Father, Son and Holy Ghost ; and also in relation to man, where we were not dealing with a generalised picture of man but only with the real man who according to the witness of Holy Scripture is the reflection of Jesus Christ. The fact which is our starting-point is co-extensive with the fact that according to the witness of Holy Scripture the revelation and work of God also have this dimension, that this witness also includes the strange existence or function of angels, and that it thus presents it unavoidably for discussion, no matter how it is to be understood or explained. So far as the task of dogmatics is concerned, we cannot imagine that we have any knowledge of this sphere of ourselves or on the basis of any philosophical freedom or compulsion. We can only keep to the fact that the biblical witnesses say that they know something of this sphere : something which stands in what is for them a necessary connexion with their true theme, God and man and the history of God with man ; and something which in this context is very definite and contrasts with all philosophical parallels. It is with this alone that we must concern ourselves at this point.

I again quote Calvin (*Instit.*, I, 14, 4) : *Meminerimus hic, ut in tota religionis doctrina, tenendum esse unam modestiae et sobrietatis regulam, ne de rebus obscuris aliud vel loquamur, vel sentiamus, vel scire etiam appetamus quam quod Dei verbo fuerit nobis traditum.* And negatively Quenstedt is even clearer (*Theol. did pol.*, 1685, I, cap. II, sect. 1, th. 3) : *Existentia angelorum nititur non tam argumentis probabilibus ex philosophia petitis sive a gradibus entium et complemento universi . . . sive a testimoniis humanis sive ab experimentis variis, quam apodictico, clara nimirum et crebra scripturae assertione.*

2. In this respect we do really have to wrestle with the witness of Holy Scripture. That is to say, we have to ponder what it presents for our consideration, understanding and explaining it so far as the limits of the matter itself and of our own capacity allow. There can be no question of a blind acknowledgment and acceptance of something perceptible in the Bible. If it would be bad biblical scholarship to stop at this kind of acknowledgment and acceptance, this type of attitude is totally impossible in relation to the special task of dogmatics. If according to the witness of the Bible the function of heavenly messengers belongs incidentally to the revelation and work of God, and therefore incidentally to the faith of the Church, and incidentally and softly to its proclamation, we do not have here a *pistis* which does not press forward to *gnosis*, a *fides* which is not as such a *fides quaerens intellectum*. We cannot, then, merely affirm the fact and describe it as such. We must really *start* from this fact. That is to say, we must press on to what is denoted by this witness. And we must do so to the point of exhausting its knowability and therefore our own possibility of knowing what we say when we are not silent concerning it, when we do not deny or ignore it, but try to say something about it. We do not honour the authority of Scripture with due obedience, indeed, we are not dealing with its authority at all, if on its authority we try to hold a biblical doctrine of angels without taking the trouble to ask what it is that we really hold and how far we do so. The Church has no right to appeal to this authority for continually speaking about angels in its songs and prayers and pictures if it is not prepared to consider what this means, sparing dogmatics the effort involved, or concluding that it is not worth while. Even to-day the Church gives many

signs that it has not accepted a simple denial of angels. But if we agree that the effort is worth while it must obviously be made, not merely for reasons of personal honesty and conscientiousness, but even more so for the sake of the credibility of the Church's proclamation. How can this be credible to the world and itself if, because there is some correlate in the Bible, it proceeds to say something—even if only on this margin—without knowing, or perhaps trying to know, what it is saying? To be sure, an angelology which is dogmatic as well as historico-exegetical is a difficult and dangerous undertaking. But a dogmatics which tried to escape the task of angelology would be guilty of an indolent omission which might well jeopardise the whole Church. A *sacrificium intellectus* is thus the very last thing which is justified or demanded by the reference to the witness of Scripture in this matter. On the contrary, we are summoned to ponder what the witness of Scripture presents for our consideration in this respect.

In saying this, we take consciously and expressly into account the fact that when the Bible speaks of angels (and their demonic counterparts) it always introduces us to a sphere where historically verifiable history, i.e., the history which is comprehensible by the known analogies of world history, passes over into historically non-verifiable saga or legend. That is to say, when it is a matter of angels in the Bible, we are in the sphere of the particular form of history which by content and nature does not proceed according to ordinary analogies, and can thus be grasped only by divinatory imagination, and find expression only in the freer observation and speech of poetry.

There is real, spatio-temporal history which has this form or that of transition to it. The fact that it has this form is not a compelling argument for rejecting as less valuable or even worthless its narration in the corresponding genre of saga or legend. Why should not imagination grasp real history, or the poetry which is its medium be a representation of real history, of the kind of history which escapes ordinary analogies and cannot therefore be verified historically, but is real history all the same? Not all saga or legend deals with real history, nor can this be said of all narratives which cannot be verified historically. But there is true saga or legend as well as false. To turn to the Bible, if we have reason to see in a history narrated in the Bible an element in the revelation and work of divine grace, and therefore real—we might almost say the most real— history in time and space, then the fact that we must regard the account as a saga or legend does not mean that we can deny the history this character. Whether it can be verified historically or is saga or legend does not affect its credibility in this respect. If we believe it, it is because we see that it has happened as the revelation and work of divine grace, and this is the gift of our enlightenment by the Holy Spirit. If this recognition and gift be presupposed only for a moment, the fact that a biblical history cannot be verified historically but has only the form of saga or legend cannot deprive it of this character or make it incredible as real history. Thus, although we must regard the relevant sphere as saga or legend, we must accept it as true and not false legend in the relevant sense, and therefore treat this history too as credible in its distinctive form. Once this is grasped, it obviously makes no odds that in the construction of these accounts the active imagination of the biblical authors, as is only to be expected, lived with images and conceptions which were stamped by the outlook and mythology of their day and which we can no longer accept, but which it was not the purpose of the texts in question to impart or to force on us. If it is a matter of scholarly understanding, we may always try to translate them, so far as possible, into the current images and conceptions of our own outlook and mythology. But if we really want to know and understand the accounts, it will not help us to translate them into the language of the outlook and mythology of any age either present or future, but we too shall have to make that divinatory crossing of the frontier of historicism and enter the sphere of imagination and poetry. It cannot be a question of translating the saga or legend into verifiable history, but of repeating (in whatever language) the saga or legend as such, of a renewal of the form commensurate with the history envisaged in these accounts. On the pretext of a translation from antiquated to more modern language we cannot put another history in the place of this history. Otherwise the translation is a falsification. And it is a safe rule in cases of doubt to narrate this history in a language which is less clearly understood to-day than to narrate another history in a language which is supposedly or actually better understood. The history of the revelation and work of God recounted in the Bible, while it intends to be and is real spatio-temporal history, passes over into the sphere in which (in whatever language) we can obviously think and speak only in the form of saga or legend. At all events, it will always have this form in a faithful translation of the biblical account, and every faithful rendering of what is narrated by it will necessarily reveal the historical sphere into which it passes.

To this sphere there undoubtedly belong all the biblical passages in which angels appear. On grounds still to be discussed, we are even forced to say that the appearance of angels is always a distinctive sign of the basically continuous proximity of the biblical history to this sphere, and of its continual secret tendency in this direction. There is reason for surprise that angels are not more frequently mentioned in the Bible. The whole history of the Bible, while it intends to be and is real spatio-temporal history, has a constant bias towards the sphere where it cannot be verified by the ordinary analogies of world history but can be seen and grasped only imaginatively and represented in the form of poetry. How can it be otherwise when it is the history of the work and revelation of God, which as such, as the history of the action and lordship of the Lord of heaven and earth, although it can also take place in the comparatively narrow sphere of historically verifiable occurrence, is not confined to the sphere of ordinary earthly analogies? To some extent the angels mark this transition, this reaching of the incommensurable into the commensurable, of mystery into the sphere of known possibilities. For this reason they particularly are figures of biblical saga and legend. This does not count against them. It is a factual explanation of their distinctive being and action. Nor is it a concession to modern thought. The distinction between documented history and saga is a possibility of modern thought. We make use of it. But we do so in the very free sense indicated, and only because it is peculiarly adapted to set the nature of the object under discussion in a light in which it could not stand for the older theology which did not know this distinction. In general and formal terms, the angels are the particular representatives of the mystery of the biblical history. If we are to understand this history as the work and revelation of divine grace, even on this general and formal ground we cannot dismiss the angels as of no consequence. It is to this that we point when we describe them as figures of biblical saga and legend.

But this assertion cannot mean that *fides quaerens intellectum* has to halt at the angels, or that the question of theological truth has not to be raised in this matter. If this were the case, there would be no question of theological truth at all, and therefore no theology, no *fides quaerens intellectum*. For in some way, we repeat, almost the whole of the biblical history is engaged in that transition to saga or legend, and the angels in particular can only make this clear. But in dogmatics it is a matter of trying to understand both the fact and the extent that in the whole sphere of biblical history—whether it be documented history or saga—we have to do with the work and revelation of divine grace, and to that extent with real, with the most real history. To understand this, and to put the question of truth in this sense, is our task in relation to the angels too. Hence we are not released from this task by the fact that we regard the angels as figures of biblical saga or legend. This does not mean that we are in the sphere of Red Riding Hood and her grandmother and the wolf, or the stork which leaves babies, or the March Hare and Father Christmas ; in a sphere in which the biblical authors gave free rein to their poetic imagination, and in which we can give ourselves up with abandon to the same indulgence. This is not the case. For there can be meaningful as well as meaningless imagination, and disciplined as well as undisciplined poetry—this is the difference between good saga and bad. Both imagination and poetry can be ordered by orientation on the subject and its inner order. Both can be truthful, and in their own way the knowledge of the truth, in virtue of the truth of the subject. But the subject of the imagination and poetry of the biblical authors is not an ocean or mist of obscure possibilities. It is the spatio-temporally real history of the revelation and work of divine grace. This subject orders what they think and say in terms of saga no less than in terms of history. It establishes the meaning and discipline of their divination, of their imagination and poetry. This subject is the truth which in all circumstances they seek to attest and to which in some form they subject themselves. If we really hear them, we hear them speak of this subject. And if we accept their witness, it can only be for us the witness to the truth of this subject. As and because the question for us can only be that of repeating the history narrated by them as the history of the work and revelation of God, we are summoned to think and speak as they did, not without the divination, imagination and poetry which they found necessary in view of the fact that this history is continually engaged in that movement of transition, yet not with any divination, imagination and poetry, but like them with the divination, imagination and poetry which are ordered and filled with meaning and disciplined by this particular history. Even in relation to the angels we are not left without any thoughts at all, or in the sphere of dreams or day-dreams, but we are summoned to think with the true theological knowledge in which it will be shown that no indolence is possible in this sphere, that divinatory thinking and speech are indispensable, but that we are not allowed to think and speak anything and everything, that the angels and the March Hare are two different things, that in relation to the angels we are commanded to think and say something very definite—*vera, certa* and *utilia,* to use once again the terminology of Calvin.

It may be instructive to give a particularly bad example of what we must not do. For this purpose, I select the doctrine of angels which Carl Hase, a church historian distinguished not least of all by his gushing style, presented in the volume of dogmatics to which he gave the title *Gnosis* (1827, 2nd edit. 1869). His biblical disquisitions concerning angels are completely devoid of any deeper understanding, and his historical observations are amused and in their own way amusing (Vol. I, pp. 485 f.). He crowns them with the following concluding judgment. Beings of a spirituality by nature and grace higher than that of man, and which may be either angels or demons, are certainly conceivable but problematical. Yet the conception is unfortunately quite impossible, having perished with a " past and childlike outlook," of a heaven with the throne of God surrounded by singing angels (" and surely on this view it must have been very wearisome for the Lord to let His praises be sung so continually.") Whether they exist or not, these beings do not really belong to religion, and so " faith does not need to decide concerning them any more than it does concerning other heavenly bodies or the man in the moon." " If we confidently entrust ourselves to the providence of God, what does it matter to us whether or not it is exercised through an angel ? " Goethe was right when he wrote to Lavater : " Let me call nervous calm what you call an angel." What place is there then for these problematical beings ? " By their possible existence, their poetic content, their religious associations and the manner in which they have been handed down they constitute a circle of sacred saga." If there is no religious interest in the question whether they exist, they embody certain ideas which are either religious or related to religion, and hover in the pleasant twilight between poetry and history. " Those who have a heart for the beautiful and the ideal will gladly think of angels. It was the desire for a living creature better than ourselves yet benevolently participating in our human joys and sorrows which first heard the angel-song in the quiet night : ' Glory to God in the highest . . .'." In particular the belief in a personal guardian angel is not regarded by Hase as completely reprehensible. " In intercourse with oneself, the protection of one's own spirit presents itself to youthful phantasy. High above every worthy man there stands his idea. The man usually contemplates it in self-awareness and sees himself in it ; the maiden, in unconscious innocence as regards her own spiritual beauty, is disposed to love it in the man." The philosopher F. H. Jacobi is quoted : " The object of the noble love of Heloise certainly deserved this love ; for he formed her tender soul, adorned her and gave her wings—and it was not Abelard ! " But Hase knows better : " And yet it was Abelard ! Not the one whose aspiring spirit was torn in the conflict with his age, but a higher, eternal spirit which in both his theology and his love gave only an inkling of what he was and was to be." And again : " Our own future, and the conception of transfigured friends, take on angelic form. The thought of a mother, or some other loved one, becomes a guardian angel in the hour of temptation." It is objected against the scholastic doctrine of angels that in it the angels became " metaphysical bats," and in face of all biblical and ecclesiastical tradition it is finally taught that " the angels belong to the poet and painter for the ideal representation of youthful and childlike beauty. The angels of Thomas Aquinas cut a poor show compared with the two heavenly children which resting on their little arms look pensively on Raphael's virgin mother of God, reflecting in their childlike eyes the most beautiful thing that this world ever saw. Art can as little portray heaven without angels as spring without flowers." With similar eloquence Hase in a final burst of generosity found a place for the devil as a " heroic and humorous " figure of poetry, art, rhetoric and especially the forceful speech of the people.

What are we to say to all this ? Naturally it represents the 19th century in full blast, as in the *Trompeter von Säckingen*. And we need hardly be surprised that, having dismissed the real angels and substituted these paper pomposities, Hase did not see how comical he himself was, and therefore saw no reason to apply his witticisms to himself and his own products. But there is a serious side to the matter. How did Hase reach this strange conclusion ? The decisive point was that, although he knew the relevant texts of the Old and New Testaments, of " Hebraism " and " primitive Christianity," he merely recorded their contents without any interest in their relationship to the biblical message and without putting the question of theological truth, but with a superior smile which could only become broader as he turned to the statements of the Early Church, the Middle Ages, the Reformation, Orthodoxy, the Enlightenment and Romanticism, and everywhere with the inquisitive and ironical detachment of the pure historian making his discoveries, until at last he came to the conclusion which had been obvious from the very first, that philosophically and religiously there was nothing of any practical value in the whole history as he had unravelled it in the Bible and in previous ages in the Church. But in this particularly bad case of intellectual self-complacency Hase did not attempt either a speculative reconstruction like some of the theologians whom we shall consider later or a complete dismissal of the whole sphere like his contemporary D. F. Strauss or more ruthlessly R. Bultmann in our own day. What remains in his case is a doctrine of angels which is that of a not very bold but rich, home-baked, aesthetic enthusiasm, the " circle of sacred saga " and the " pleasant twilight " in which the theologian, trying to improve on the Bible and Church history, lights on the idea which hovers above the worthy man, on Abelard and Heloise, on transfigured friends, on the thought of a mother, on the childlike eyes of Raphael's cherubs, and what have you. It was these new curiosities which he substituted for the old in solution of the problem. And if we are not to end in the same way we must take up a different attitude from the very beginning. The strange thing is that Hase gave to his dogmatics the title *Gnosis*. But if we are merely summoned by the Bible to record and not to ponder and understand, we shall necessarily regard what is said in the Bible and elsewhere on this topic as so much arbitrary nonsense, and we shall even more certainly demonstrate that we ourselves cannot do better than produce even more arbitrary and greater nonsense ourselves. If we are merely clever and are obviously not prepared from the very first to practise the *credo ut intelligam*, we are well advised not to venture into this sphere, or that of dogmatics generally. For we can have no prospect of success.

3. If the doctrine of angels is to be theological in character ; if,

then, it is to be significant for the faith and proclamation of the Church ; or more simply, if it is to rest on solid ground, it is necessary that we should strictly respect the sequence, relationship and consequence disclosed in the statement *credo ut intelligam.* It is not a matter of any *intelligere,* but of that whose theme is the angels to the extent that they belong to the context of Christian faith, so that the *intelligere* does not arise from a general need to know but is demanded by Christian faith, nor does it rest on any basis but on that which is given to Christian faith in this respect as in all others. But this means that we have to wrestle with the view and concept of angels as they come before us in Holy Scripture as the witness to the work and revelation of God in Jesus Christ. It is no use erecting on general grounds a conception of something that angels might be, then persuading ourselves that these are the angels to which Holy Scripture refers and of which we have to accept that their nature, existence and action are related to the work and revelation of God and therefore to the theme of Christian faith, and finally deducing that *credere* means to have some kind of belief in these beings and that the real task of theology, applying the *intelligere* consistently to these beings, is to understand and explain them. We must not be guilty at this point of the πρῶτον ψεῦδος, taking up the matter with a preconception of what angels might be or must be which we have formed on some very different grounds, no matter what these grounds may be. But we must be ready to be instructed concerning them *ab ovo* from the source from which theology must always learn if it is not to degenerate into that gnosis in the bad sense which hovers either in the heights or the depths. If we are guilty of that πρῶτον ψεῦδος, we need not be surprised if we are entangled in all kinds of questions and difficulties which secretly hampered the angelology of older orthodoxy, which were merely increased by the sun of the Enlightenment that lit up so many other things, and which have finally brought the whole subject into the disrepute from which it still suffers to-day. These do not derive from what is discernible in the Bible as a witness to the work and revelation of God which also includes the existence and work of angels, but from the preconception by means of which it was hoped even in early days to provide rather than to facilitate an understanding of this witness instead of applying the required concern for the *intelligere* directly to the witness itself. They derive from the false translation with which even in early days, and with the best intentions, the biblical view and concept of angels were to be made more readily accessible. There is every reason to be particularly strict in our application of the Scripture-principle in this field because tradition has been unhelpful in this respect, not merely preparing the catastrophe which broke later and still affects us to-day, but doing something which was far worse, i.e., binding and obscuring the positive instruction to be gained in the matter. We must avoid both these errors. The doctrine of angels is difficult to understand like all the other things that we have to understand in faith in the Word of God attested in Holy Scripture. It may even be said that, although it is not more difficult to understand, it is difficult in a particular way. Even if we keep strictly to Scripture, and make its witness the theme of our endeavour, we shall have our work cut out and find plenty of questions to engage us. But this legitimate, necessary and unavoidable difficulty is to be distinguished from that which besets us if in what we think and say about angels we look in a different direction from that to which we are directed by Scripture. We can and must jettison the ballast which has accumulated in consequence of the latter aberration, and we shall then see that there is no reason to take part in the stampede from the whole subject which has become general in our own day. But it is not merely a question of freeing ourselves from difficulties. It is a question of bringing to light the truth which has been buried not so much by that catastrophe and the common denial of the whole subject but by the way in which it was earlier affirmed and made the theme of positive discussion.

In both respects, however, our only course is to keep to the original form of the subject in our attempt to understand and explain it. The angels have an original form in the witness of Holy Scripture. In it they belong to the theme of Christian faith. In it they are not an absurdity or curiosity which we are at liberty to reinterpret, to deny, or to replace by curiosities of our own invention. In it they open up vistas of a dimension of Christian faith which this should not lack. At a pinch and in the forbearance of God, which sustains it in spite of its defects, the Church and its proclamation may well survive without this dimension of faith, although not without hurt, and not without an underlying awareness that something is missing. Yet when it opens up, the knowledge of this dimension will not be something to be evaded ; it will be found to be a liberation and enrichment which once discovered is no longer dispensable. And it is hard to estimate what it might mean for Christianity and the world if in faith it could really become aware again of the distinctive reality of this thing which at best it does not abandon but somehow brings in for reasons of piety. But this depends upon its becoming aware again of its original form. It is to this, and therefore to the biblical witness to angels, that we must direct our attention and endeavours.

In this introduction we are well advised to consider some concrete instances of the possibilities which must be avoided.

In the Apologists of the 2nd century it is more than equivocal that in answer to the charge of atheism brought by pagans against the Church Justin (*Apol.*, I, 6) can give a reassuring account of the many divine authorities which Christians actually reverence and worship (σεβόμεθα καὶ προσκυνοῦμεν) : the true God as the Father of righteousness, prudence and all virtues, who is free from every taint of evil ; the Son who teaches us, and the host of other angels which follow and resemble Him ; and finally the prophetic Spirit. And Athenagoras is even more suspect when he says (*Leg. pro Christ.*, 10) that Christian theology is not exhausted in the confession of the triune God, but that we also confess the πλῆθος ἀγγέλων καὶ λειτουργῶν which God the Creator of the world set by His Word over the elements, the heavens, the cosmos, and all that is in it, and over the order of this totality, subordinating the latter to them. And in another place (*ib.*, 24) he says that as we confess God and the Son (His Word) and the Holy Ghost . . . so we reckon with other δυνάμεις which rule in and over the ὕλη. Already we have here many features which are new and strange in relation to the doctrine of angels in the Old and New Testaments. In Justin there is the conception of Christ as an ἄγγελος at the head of a host of similar beings (cf. *Dial. c. Tryph.*, 128). In Justin and Athenagoras there is the assumption that the angels are a subject of Christian confession, reverence and worship together with the triune God. And in Athenagoras there is the presupposition as self-evident (cf. also the *Shepherd of Hermas, Vis.* III, 4, 1) that angels have the function of mediatorial cosmic principles.

In the Church fathers there is a whole series of similar conceptions which plainly deviate from the Bible and obviously derive their nourishment from another source. Decisive for all that follows is the emergence and the rapid domination of the assumption that it is possible, legitimate and necessary to seek the existence and nature of angels elsewhere than in their function as God's heavenly messengers. Certainly this took place in answer to a natural require-ment of formal logic. But it did not take place in the sense and according to the pattern of the biblical witness. It was under the sway of an alien interest that there was an increasing desire to know about the nature of angels and an in-creasing belief that it was possible to know what these beings are in themselves, and therefore prior to and apart from the fact that they are *angeli*, the messengers of God. The basic innovation involved, although not introduced by Augustine, receives at his hands its classical formulation (*Enarr. in Ps.* 103[1, 15]) : *Spiritus autem angeli sunt ; et cum spiritus sunt, non sunt angeli ; cum mittuntur fiunt angeli. Angelus enim officii nomen est, non naturae. Quaeris nomen huius naturae, spiritus est ; quaeris officium, angelus est ; ex eo quod est, spiritus est ; ex eo quod agit, angelus est.*

There was now an interest in angels as a particular species of creaturely being which at an earlier time it was thought possible to group in one genus with man according to his psychical components. Irenaeus (*Adv. haer.*, IV, 37, 1) thought that this common grouping was possible only for the one reason, maintained by all who followed, that angels and men are both endowed with freedom of choice (*potestas electionis*) between good and evil. Eusebius, however, took the wider view more typical of the age which followed that each is a λογικὴ κτίσις, a *rationalis creatura*, created by God for fellowship with His own rational and spiritual being (*Demon. evang.*, IV, 1). This common rational and spiritual nature is imparted (according to Gregory of Nyssa, *De or. domin.*, 4) to the ἀσώματος and the ἐνσώματος φύσις, i.e., to angels and men, who both have their true and supreme destiny (Gregory the Great, *Moralia*, IV, 3, 8) in the fact that they may know God. The peculiarity of the nature of angels as compared with that of men is that they are non-corporeal or non-material, or at least that this is almost the case (Greg. of Naz., *Or.*, 28, 31), i.e., that it is so in relation to us though not in relation to God, since God alone is absolutely non-corporeal and non-material (J. Dam., *De fide orth.*, III, 2). The fact that—with this reservation —they are purely spiritual and therefore self-evidently invisible and immortal now became the dominant view, and it was usual to compare them with the purity of fire. With both philosophical and mythical splendour Gregory of Nazianzus (*Or.*, 38, 9) described how the eternal goodness was not content to move alone in its own θεωρία; how its good, corresponding to its nature as goodness, had to flow out and be spread abroad ; how, active in the Logos and perfecting in the Spirit, it conceived angelic and heavenly powers ; and how in the work of this conception of the Godhead, and subordinated to it, they were created as λειτουργοὶ τῆς πρώτης λαμπρότητος the νοερὰ πνεύματα, the *intelligentes spiritus*, which we have to think of as fire or as non-corporeal and non-material nature or something similar. And Augustine (*De Gen. ad lit.*, IV, 32, 49) character-ised the reason of angels as one which clings in pure love to the Word of God because it is adapted to know all things first in this Word and therefore *a priori* (as *cognitio matutina*), and not merely as created by this Word and therefore *a posteriori* (as *cognitio vespertina*). Their reason embraces both these forms of cognition. As a created reason, it cannot, of course, know God as He is but only in accordance with its capacity (Cyril of Jerusalem, *Cat.*, 6, 6). Therefore right up to the days of Protestant orthodoxy (e.g., J. Wolleb, *Theol. chr. comp.*, 1626, I, *cap.* 5, 3) the definition could be accepted that angels are *spiritus intelligentes a corpore liberi*. If in the later parlance of the Church God is often called the Creator of the *creatura spiritualis et corporalis*, the reference of the *creatura spiritualis* is to the *creatura angelica*, according to the express elucidation of the Fourth Lateran Council of 1215 (*Denz.*, 428). But this basic definition obviously gave rise to further questions and the corresponding answers, and these could only lead even further away from the Bible. For example, how is it that these beings are holy and stand essentially in a particular relationship to God ? A trace of biblical reminiscence may be found in the answer given by Basil (*De spir. s.*, 16, 38 etc.) and others, that this was not by nature but as they received and maintained a special sanctification by the Holy Spirit. Or again, what is their relationship to space ? *Momento ubique sunt, totus orbis illis locus unus est*, was the rather over-confident assertion of Tertullian (*Apol.*, 22). But the view expressed by Athanasius (*Ad. Serap.*, I, 26) became the dominant one, namely, that they are not omnipresent like God but for all their freedom of movement are always in one particular place. As J. Damascene put it (*De fide orth.*, II, 3), they are neither corporeal nor material, and therefore unlimited and unrestricted, yet they are always in a definite and therefore a limited place, in heaven and not on earth, or *vice versa*. According to Didymus Alex. (*De trin.*, II, 6, 2), they have a πέρας, an ὡρισμένη ποσότης. Or again, are there differences and degrees of dignity and power as between these beings ? Is there an order intrinsic to them ? In the light of the different biblical descriptions of angels and the biblical refer-ence to angelic hosts (although not merely on these grounds), Dionysius Areopagita had long since answered this question in the affirmative, and if Augustine declared that he did not know this order Jerome (*Apol. adv. Ruf.*, I, 23) intimated that he knew something about it. There seems at first to have been a certain restraint in this matter, which the Areopagite was the first to penetrate. Again, if angels for all the difference of their nature were to be counted as part of the known constitution of that which is outside God and therefore of the creaturely world, the question arises why there is no mention of them in the Mosaic account of creation, and at what point in this account their creation is tacitly assumed. If appeal was not made to Gen.2¹ with its recapitulatory reference to heaven and earth " and all the host of them," or if their creation was not found in that of light in Gen. 1³, then it had to be explained, as by Ambrose (*Hex.*, I, 5, 19), that although as creatures they were not without beginning they were already present at the creation of the rest of the cosmos (as suggested by Job 38⁷ : " When the morning stars sang together, and all the sons of God shouted for joy "). Or on the basis of the same text it was said (cf. Epiphanius, *Adv. haer.*, 65, 5) that although they could not have come into being after the stars they could not have preceded heaven and earth, because in the beginning God created heaven and earth, prior to which there was nothing apart from Himself. Or it was thought with Gennadius (*Libr. eccl. dogm.*, 10) that their creation should be put

in the space of time when darkness was upon the face of the deep in Gen. 1² :
ut non esset otiosa Dei bonitas, sed haberet in quibus per multa ante spatia bonitatem ostenderet. The final problem was to explain the existence of demons. This was usually done by the theory of the fall of a number of angels, created good like men but gifted with *liberum arbitrium*, and their consequent corruption. This apostasy took place under the leadership of the *Diabolus* as the great *angelus apostata* (Irenaeus, *Adv. haer.*, V, 24, 3). What was his sin ? Not licence, theft or the like, but pride, was the answer of Athanasius (*De virg.*, 5), and the wickedness of the other bad angels was that, although they should only be orientated on the supreme being, instead they *ad se ipsos conversi sunt* (Augustine, *De civ. Dei*, XII, 6). Following the first, and voluntarily forfeiting the blessedness they might have enjoyed, a greater or lesser number of other angels became transgressors and therefore bad angels—a final and irrevocable decision because quite inexcusable in view of the high nature of angels as compared with weaker man. On the other hand, those who did not do so stood fast in the truth in virtue of their *liberum arbitrium*, being finally established after their victorious withstanding of this once-for-all temptation (Augustine, *De corr. et grat.*, 10, 27 ; *In Joann.*, 110, 7 ; Fulgentius, *De fide ad Petr.*, 3, 30 ; Gregory the Great, *Mor.*, IV, 3, 8). As Tertullian saw it (*De carne Chr.*, 14), the reason why Christ became a man and not an angel was because the Father could neither promise nor commission the redemption of fallen angels. Much later Anselm of Canterbury (*Cur Deus homo*, I, 16–18) could use this theory of the fall of angels, which he regarded as a revealed truth, as an argument in his doctrine of atonement. As he saw it, the original number of angels as citizens of the *civitas superna* had to be restored. The gap could not be filled by the creation of new angels, because the number had been laid down in the plan of creation. Thus, to overcome this disruption of cosmic harmony, God had to elect a corresponding number of other rational beings, i.e., of men. Since they are elected and ordained to replace angels, they must themselves be like angels, i.e., freed from their sins. For this satisfaction was needed, and since God alone would supply this satisfaction He had to become man.

It is obvious—and it confirms the fact that what we have here is a basic aberration—that in the fathers relatively less attention is devoted to what claims the exclusive interest of the Old and New Testaments, namely, what Augustine called the *officium angelicum*, than to the far more widely discussed question of the *angelica natura*, in which the Bible seems to have no interest at all. Nor can we say of the comparatively few statements of the fathers on the former point that it follows the line of the biblical witness. We seem to be nearest to this when we read in Chrysostom (*in Ep. ad Hebr. hom.*, 3, 2) that the λειτουργία of angels consists in serving God to our salvation ; that it is the ἀγγελικὸν ἔργον to do everything to save the brethren ; that this is the true work of Jesus Christ Himself ; that He Himself as the Lord is the real Saviour ; and that the angels can only be His servants in this work. In what does their διακονεῖν consist ? According to Hilary (*Tract. sup. Ps.*, 129, 7), it consists in a *ministerium spiritualis intercessionis* which was needed by man though not by God for the effectiveness of his prayer and meritorious work. The surest and most general conception is that of the guardian angel given to each individual on his way, of an *angelus in custodiam delegatus* (Jerome, *In Matth.*, 3, 18, 10). This is to be found already in Origen (*In Luc. hom.*, 12), although with the dubious addition that we all have a bad angel as well. Then according to Hilary (*loc. cit.*), on the obvious basis of Rev. 2–3, there are also *spirituales virtutes ecclesiis praesidentes*, and according to J. Damascene (*De fide orth.*, II, 3) and others there are national angels which " keep watch over the different parts of the earth, presiding over nations and regions, controlling our history and giving us their aid." But even if this or that passage in the Bible seems to say something of this kind, the question arises where in the Bible the ideas of guardian and national angels are so substantial and important as to compel or even to allow us to understand the function of angels according to this norm.

A very different aspect of the angelic office is opened up if the theory developed by Erik Peterson (*Das Buch von den Engeln*, 1935, pp. 39–81) really represents the general conception of the Early Church. As he sees it, the decisive function of angels consists in the worship which they offer in heaven and in which the worship of the Church on earth has only an imitative part, although conversely the angels participate in the worship of the Church on earth. With the ascension of Christ, and as Christians have left the earthly Jerusalem and " come unto . . . the heavenly Jerusalem, and to an innumerable company of angels, to the general assembly and church of the firstborn " (Heb. 12$^{22f.}$), the temple of Isaiah 6 has been transferred to heaven, and it is there that the glory of God and the *Sanctus* of the seraphim are now located. But all the angelic hosts now stand behind the seraphim, and that isolated cry has become an unceasing hymn. This is the worship which embraces the whole cosmos. Its central and most spiritual part is that of the angels in heaven. But the sun and moon and stars all have a share in it. And the worship of men can only be added to this worship of angels and all creation. The earthly liturgy can only be integrated and fused into the great order of the heavenly. For this reason the worship of the Church has a tendency to change into a ministry similar to the worship of angels. And it is the hymn of monks (as distinct from the mere acclamation or *Sanctus* of the people) which in its constant repetition of the offices, its unison, and its renunciation of any musical instruments apart from the human voice, is obviously closest to the worship of the angels and comes nearest to actualising that change. And there is a corresponding participation of the angels in the worship of the Church on earth, a sharing in the administration of the sacraments, a particular presence of angels in the services of monks, Church synods etc.—always with the particular intention of lending to the actions of the Church a public character in the emphatic and almost political sense of the term, the character of a participation in the worship of the cosmos. Peterson has been able to find support for this view in numerous passages, especially from the Egyptian Liturgy of St. Mark, but also from the Syrian Liturgy of St. James and many of the fathers and other ecclesiastical writers. But the question remains whether it will stand up to detailed scrutiny. Something which is so far-reaching, if it had been a dominant view, would surely have exercised a plain and general influence on the whole picture presented by patristic theology. Is it not surprising that a devotee and expert in this whole field of heavenly and ecclesiastical hierarchy like Pseudo-Dionysius, who actually wrote about the two hierarchies, while he certainly knew the relationship between the two and the imitation of the one by the other, should not really base his presentations on this mutual relationship, and that the specifically cultic or choral function of angels, although he certainly touches on it, does not seem to constitute for him the essence of their office ? Again, how is it that neither Pseudo-Dionysius nor the other fathers seem to have thought of using the biblical passage (Rev. 4–5) to which Peterson makes basic reference on pp. 19–38 to explain the ministry of angels along the lines which he has propounded ? Why have they not even exploited in this sense the verse in Heb. 1^{14} where angels are expressly called λειτουργικὰ πνεύματα ? But I am in no position to contradict a scholar like Peterson. In the Early Church there may well have been such views and systems with many other secret traditions which are poorly attested from the literary standpoint. Yet if Peterson is right, and the angelology of the Early Church was really dominated by this aspect, we can only come to the unfortunate conclusion that it departed further from its biblical basis than was actually the case according to its clear pronouncements concerning the *natura* and *officium* of angels. For the basic term *angelus*, messenger, is reduced to almost utter insignificance in this system. Even in Pseudo-Dionysius the term is sometimes given its proper weight. But how can the task of a messenger consist decisively in the singing of hymns ? And how can the sight and sound of the choir office of the Benedictines give the impression that this can have anything whatever to do with the service of messengers ? What is said in Revelation 4-5 will certainly call for consideration. But we can say already that even if these chapters do in some sense point in this direction we shall certainly not recognise the angels of the biblical witness in its entirety if we confine ourselves to a doctrine which looks abstractly in this direction.

But it is high time that we considered the most famous of all the early monographs on our present subject, the *De hierarchia coelesti* of the supposed Dionysius the Areopagite. This is the work of an unknown writer who probably lived and worked in Syria about 500 A.D. He pretended to be the disciple of the apostle Paul who bore the name of Dionysius in Acts 17³⁴. In reality, however, he was a Christian Neo-Platonist well-versed in the Greek fathers from Clement to Cyril of Alexandria and particularly influenced by the philosopher Proclus. Under the same pseudonym he wrote a series of other writings of which the most important extant are *De hierarchia ecclesiastica* and *De divinis nominibus*. We have here the work of one of the greatest frauds in Church history (which seems to have had more than its share of this type of author), and one who made such a material impression on the ages which followed that for a long time he was recognised as one of the official saints of the Catholic Church and it was only in the period of Humanism that the first doubts were raised as to the authenticity of his writings—doubts which have now been confirmed even by Catholic scholars. But forged or otherwise his writing achieved a historical significance which it is impossible to contest and which remained long after the discovery of the imposture. For in it we have a first and epoch-making climax in the angelology of the Early Church.

As the title indicates, it is specifically concerned with a question which the earlier fathers had touched on but never developed—that of the hierarchy of the heavenly world. In the process, however, it gives us a very definite doctrine of angels generally.

The word " hierarchy " seems to have been given a new sense by this Dionysius. As he uses it, it means generally the order of salvation executed by God as the original and proper " Hierarch " or sacred Ruler. This order consists in the outpouring and outshining of the primal divine light. It is thus to be understood essentially as revelation, as intellectual illumination and irradiation for the purpose of knowing God and all things in Him and from Him and to Him. Its meaning and goal is to lead the beings which are reached by it, which receive it, and which become its active bearers and mediators, each at its appointed stage and to its allotted degree, to likeness to God, union with Him and participation in His work, i.e., to cause them to become mirrors of the primal divine light and therefore those who have genuine knowledge. In this process, according to the specific stage and in relation to those above and below, " some are purified and others purify, some are enlightened and others enlighten, some are perfected and others perfect," but all are made capable of contemplation and participant in knowledge, and therefore all are elevated to participation in God and co-operation with Him. In different ways this is true of every hierarchy, of the ecclesiastical and other terrestrial hierarchies. As used by Dionysius, hierarchy is not a static but a supremely dynamic general term to denote the manner in which the Godhead participates in manifold ways in the created world and the created world in the Godhead. But the specific hierarchy on which Dionysius proposes to inform us on the basis of Holy Scripture is the heavenly hierarchy—that of angels.

In the second chapter of his work he interposes a remarkable epistemological discussion. Holy Scripture speaks of angels, as of God, by means of images, thus taking into account our human capacities and at the same time concealing its mysteries from profane eyes. This concealment with a view to true and legitimate disclosure consists sometimes in homogeneous images (e.g., word, spirit or essence), sometimes in less similar (e.g., light or life), and sometimes in those which are openly dissimilar and incommensurate (especially where the images are corporeal and material). The language is always to be understood and expounded anagogically, i.e., according to the spiritual sense, and not according to what is conveyed directly by the images. When we speak of " wrath " in relation to God, to spiritual natures and to angels, we mean their resolute wisdom and inflexibility ; when we speak of " desire," their inconceivable divine love for the spiritual ; when we speak of " excess," their undivided and unalterable love for divine beauty ; and when we speak of " irrationality " (for some of the biblical images belong to the inorganic and animal world), their superiority as supraterrestrial spirits to our discursive rational and emotional capacities, which are tied to matter. The fact that these descriptions of the divine and heavenly have a discordant and offensive element not only conceals that which is holy from those who are not initiated, but prevents those who are from clinging to the truth of the images, frightening them off as it were, and directing them to the way of true knowledge, which in its purity is always apophatic, and therefore negative.

On this presupposition Dionysius believes and maintains that Scripture has taught him as follows. It corresponds to the goodness of God to call creatures according to their nature to participation in His own being : inorganic creatures to participation in His mere being as such ; organic but irrational to participation also in His living power ;. and rational spirits to participation also in His eternal wisdom. It is obvious that the creatures are closest to Him which participate most diversely in Him. But of these rational beings those are closest of all to Him, i.e., the angels, which are engaged in forming His image in a way which·is purely spiritual. They are called angels because it is to them first that the divine illumination comes directly, being mediated to all others only through them. In this connexion Dionysius thinks that he can refer to the statement in Gal. 3[19] that the Law was given by angels. On his interpretation this means that there was and is for man no direct manifestation or vision of God, but that this was and is always accomplished by the intervention of heavenly powers. Thus we men, as members of a lower order, are lifted up to the divine by angels as members of a higher. And this process necessarily finds consistent repetition in human orders, e.g., in that of the Church. Hierarchical order is thus essential to the Church. For instance, it was the angels who first learned of the incarnation of Christ, and they then communicated it to Zacharias, Mary, Joseph and the shepherds. Even the man Jesus subjected Himself to the directions of His Father and God as mediated by angels. " Angel " is a basic term to denote all heavenly spirits, even those of a higher order which in their particularity bear other names. In the stricter sense the " angels " are merely the spirits which stand at the foot of the heavenly hierarchy and are thus responsible for the direct conveyance of messages to us men. They do not have the prerogatives of higher spirits, and cannot therefore bear their names. But the general title is valid because the higher spirits all possess, and possess to a supreme degree, the illuminations and powers of all the lower and even these lowest spirits. All of them, therefore, can be described as angels.

In Chapter 6 there commences the famous detailed description of the angelic hierarchy as such. It is the names given to angels in the Bible which rightly understood declare the peculiarity of the different classes of angels and also their mutual order and relationship. A divine teacher—it is not quite clear whether the apostle Paul is meant or not—has introduced Dionysius to the resultant knowledge, and on the basis of this knowledge he is able to pass on the following information. There are in the Bible nine names of angels, and therefore nine angelic choirs, which are mutually related in three triads, each of which has also its own order. The first and highest of these consists of the three choirs of the seraphim, the cherubim and the throne. These are the direct recipients of the divine revelations, outpourings and initiations : the seraphim as the flaming movers ; the cherubim as those who first see and know ; and the throne, it seems, as the principles of the relative sovereignty of these first three angelic choirs. For it is the particularity of the first order to be sovereign (relatively, of course, to God) ; to be removed from every suggestion of weakness and inferiority ; to be incapable of any kind of lapse. It is filled with a light which surpasses even immaterial knowledge. It is the reflection of God in the sublimest sense. It is perfect because engaged in a direct upsoaring to primal deity. It is grouped immediately round God, and in unceasing praise the simple mediation of these supreme spirits is occupied in the eternal knowledge of God. As the first and supreme triad, raising the first *trisagion*, it is the direct witness of the triad and monad of the Godhead. The second and middle order consists of the dominions (κυριότητες), powers (δυνάμεις), and authorities (ἐξουσίαι). It is hard to extract from the fulness of his eloquence the details of what he has to say concerning this triad. It emerges, however, that by these three choirs he means instruments of heavenly rule which exercise their power in noble freedom, with no taint of tyranny, yet inviolably, unconquerably and in perfect harmony. We have here spirits which are led mediately to perfection, and are therefore less full of light as compared with those of the first triad. But in their particular function and to their own degree they have indirectly both a passive and an active part in the divine irradiation. The third and lowest triad consists of the principalities (ἀρχαί), the archangels ἀρχάγγελοι) and the angels in the stricter sense, which form the lowest choir of all. The transition from the second to the third order, and the distinctive features of this final triad, are not at all clear. But it is evident that at this point the order of heaven draws near to events on earth and the hierarchies which control them. Again it is a question of instruments of rule—and here as in the second order we have to remember that for Dionysius rule consists in an enlightenment, in an impartation of knowledge. But now we have to do with instruments of a more concrete kind. The principalities look to the source of all rule, seeking, finding and giving a certain orientation. The angels are heavenly interpreters in the sphere of the more visible and the earthly world. And the archangels occupy a midway position, reflecting the attitude of the principalities on the one hand and prefiguring, directing and co-ordinating the action of the angels on the other. It is indicative of the peculiar conception of Dionysius that he finds the direct activity of angels in earthly occurrence wholly in their influence on earthly hierarchies (ecclesiastical and otherwise), and not in their influence on individuals, so that for him guardian angels are exclusively national angels.

In nature, structure, task and function, touching Godhead at the one end and the human sphere at the other, yet distinct for all the intensity of the contact, the heavenly hierarchy is a harmonious whole, hovering as heaven between God and earth. All the angelic choirs are revealers, proclaimers and messengers, each from and for the others, all directly or indirectly from God, all directly or indirectly for the world of man, all engaged in descent and ascent. When by their mediation the illumination of divine revelation finally comes down to man, again by their mediation it mounts back to God as its origin. All angels of all degrees can be called heavenly powers as well as angels to the extent that on their level and to the appropriate degree they all participate in the distinctiveness and purpose of the whole dynamically motivated system. It is to be noted, however, that the law of hierarchical sequence admits of no exceptions. Although Isaiah 6 seems to speak of a direct encounter between the seraphim and the prophet, Dionysius takes this to imply that a vision was given to the prophet through a lower angel and that it was in this vision that he saw the supreme angels and God. His work concludes with a mystical analysis, on the basis of his earlier epistemological theory, of the corporeal and material images used by the Bible when it speaks of angels, concealing and disclosing at one and the same time.

What was it that Dionysius attempted and achieved ? His work plainly claims to be a reduction of the angelology of the earlier fathers. It is to be noted that it leaves on one side the questions and answers of his predecessors concerning the relationship of angels to space, the fall of angels, or individual guardian angels. This is because he is not really interested in the existence and history of angels as such, but only in their existence and function in that heavenly hierarchy. And this orientation of interest allowed and demanded a remarkable concentration of the elements which he took over from the earlier angelology. What his predecessors said about the nature of angels as *spiritus intelligentes puri*, about their peculiar knowledge, about their gracious sanctification and about their ministry, is comprehended or rather subsumed or submerged into the one consideration and depiction of the heavenly hierarchy as that order of salvation, i.e., of revelation and knowledge, which proceeds from God. In this he was not, of course, absolutely original, for he made use of hints which he may have found in Gregory of Nazianzus, and he obviously borrowed a good deal from his Neo-Platonic teacher Proclus in respect of the famous triads in his system. Since the unmasking of the literary imposture of which he was guilty many justifiable objections have been raised against the bombast of his style and language and against the garrulous obscurity or obscure garrulity of his mode of presentation. But this does not alter the fact that within its limits his work is one of those original and masterly ventures which do not often occur in the history of theology. It was not by accident, nor due only to the pseudonym, that it made such an impression on its own age and the whole of the Middle Ages, whose thinkers had ultimately a good eye for quality. The one who made this venture was no ordinary man. He did not need to masquerade as a disciple of Paul to gain a hearing. As angelology his heavenly hierarchy is a remarkable and instructive enterprise. Nor is this a tribute merely to its formal aspects.

There are, of course, obvious material objections to his teaching. Nor do they relate only to his annoying—and in detail not very clear or helpful—omniscience concerning the three triads and their choirs, and the names and natures of the various classes of angels ; nor to the arbitrariness of his spiritual exposition of the biblical terms and the images used in the Bible—a matter on which we have touched only briefly in the present context. They must be brought against his view of the heavenly hierarchy as such, against that wave of light which as revelation comes cascading down from above and as knowledge climbs up again from below, which in the last resort is obviously cyclic, and within which the angels after their manner are all transitional elements. That this intellectual cycle between deity and humanity is identical with what is described as God's revelation and the knowledge of this revelation in the Old and New Testaments is something which we can hardly accept, and this means that we cannot recognise the real angels attested by the Bible in the figures which bear this name in Dionysius, i.e., in the hypostatised transitional points in that ascending and descending wave. Was Dionysius trying to lay the metaphysical foundation for a definite cosmology, anthropology and above all noology alien to the witness of the Bible, and did he find it helpful to use certain fragments of the biblical revelation and its transmission, and therefore the figures of the biblical angels, in demonstration of this underlying system ? Or was he trying to find and display a metaphysical basis for a definite hierarchical but again unbiblical conception of the Church, and in the establishment and development of this basis was forced to make what he did of the biblical revelation and especially the biblical angels ? Who can say whether he was trying to do the one or the other, or perhaps with this or that emphasis both ? The one thing which is incontestable is that in Dionysius the biblical concern for its subject and therefore for angels finds no place but is replaced by another. And since in his angelology we have to do with a joyfully and gratefully attempted reduction and concentration of that of the Early Church in general, the problem of Dionysius is that of all early angelology. For what kind of an angelology is it if it can culminate in his teaching, and if in the period which follows right up to the Reformation, and in Roman Catholic circles right up to our own day in spite of agreement on the literary question, Dionysius can be regarded as the outstanding representative of primitive angelology ? Does not this mean that from the very outset unbiblical and materially unchristian attitudes, questions and answers dominate this whole doctrine ? If its interests and concerns are the same as those of Dionysius, are we not forced to ask whether in this whole teaching we do not have either a metaphysical speculation—we might almost say a secular myth—or the justification by means of such a myth or speculation of a conception of the Church and revelation and faith whose authenticity is brought under suspicion by the very fact that it needs this basis or justification ?

But when all this is said against Dionysius, we cannot deny him the specific merit of having tackled this doctrine. It is a truth which has to be asserted in relation to the history of theology that none of the many philosophical systems which have been brought in as a foundation, and have always come to dominate and determine it, has ever failed to damage and corrupt it, enticing it away from its orientation by the Word of God and falsifying it in its processes of thought and forms of representation, but that on the other hand none has ever served only to damage and corrupt and not also to provide a very real opportunity. Both these things are true of the Neo-Platonism of Dionysius. It sounds strange, but it is true, that his heavenly hierarchy gives us easier access to the biblical witness to angels than what was written on this subject either by the earlier fathers before him or Thomas Aquinas after him. The reduction and concentration to which he subjected the tradition of the 3rd to the 5th centuries was a good thing to the extent that it removed the figures of the angels from the isolation in which they were then conceived and understood. According to Dionysius it is no longer the case that somewhere below God (or suspiciously near Him according to the Apologists) and above man, with their own nature and history and a function which does not rightly correspond to their elevation, there are angels. But according to him they appear in a great and necessary context which, even though it is neo-platonically conceived, seems to be, or to be seen in the place of, that of the divine work of salvation on behalf of man, the economy of grace. The hierarchies of Dionysius in their totality unmistakeably represent or caricature or replace what the Bible in a narrower circle describes as the history of the covenant of grace between God and man and in a wider circle as the rule of divine providence. Seen in this context, the angels lose their interest as distinctive beings existing for themselves and acquire instead a genuinely necessary function as dynamic factors in that occurrence between God and man, thus becoming really interesting. Even in the Bible account has to be taken of the created heaven between God and man, and the problem of angels is that of the participation of this sphere of creation in the history of the covenant and salvation as it concerns man, and in this context of the divine governance of the world in general. Dionysius did not see this, but he saw something very like it, whereas the earlier fathers may have suspected it in part but did not really see or state it. And because he saw it, for him the angels were not just heavenly beings which God willed to create and did create as He also created earthly creatures, and concerning the nature, meaning and history of which theology has the task and the capacity to seek information. In and with what he called the heavenly hierarchy, he saw something corresponding formally to the participation of heaven in God's action and work on earth as attested in the Bible. And therefore, in a way which was impossible both for his predecessors and his successors, he was not only able to make use of the biblical concept of angels as servants and even revealers, announcers, witnesses and messengers, and therefore of the basic understanding of Scripture, but also, within the sphere of his Neo-Platonic view of the cyclic movement of intellectual being, and for all the remarkable arbitrariness of his development of it, to reproduce something of the significance and dignity which it enjoys as the predominant motif in the Bible. In spite of all our reservations in respect of the form and content of his doctrine, this is a serious point in favour of Dionysius.

The Neo-Platonic key which he used was unsatisfactory. But it was not unserviceable. The Neo-Platonic temptation to which Christian theology was acutely exposed in Dionysius also gave it a definite opportunity. It was not impossible to move back from the view of Dionysius to the Bible and therefore to the matter itself, to the knowledge of angels in the context of the divine work of salvation. And the great aberration of which he was undoubtedly guilty both in detail and (as the representative of ancient angelology) in general, is less lamentable than the fact that the period which followed did not accept the summons to move in this direction. What happened both in the age which immediately followed with Gregory the Great and John Damascene, and throughout the Middle Ages when he was quoted as so eminent an authority, was that he was used as a kind of quarry for all kinds of treasures of knowledge in respect of the difference and gradations in the angelic sphere as expansively described by him, so that his triads in particular came to constitute the central core of the Church's doctrine of angels. Moreover, his reduction and concentration of the whole problem was tacitly abandoned and the dynamic purpose of his hierarchy forgotten, the discarded elements in tradition being readopted, and his doctrine being understood as if he had made to the description of the heavenly cosmos and its inhabitants—even " hierarchy " was now taken to suggest a static reality—a contribution which was particularly interesting and which surpassed the work of his predecessors in a way which was highly significant. With the remarkable addition that their names and degrees were now known, the angels were again given a particular and rather curious place in the inventory of the created world, and their meaning and necessity could be considered as far as possible in the light of selected standards. Materially, the way proposed by Dionysius was itself alien to the biblical witness. But it had the advantage that for all its alien character it still indicated the way in which thinking must proceed in this matter. In the Middle Ages his Neo-Platonism was limited, if not replaced, by the Aristotelian counter-movement. In the process, however, the important stimulation which might have come from Dionysius was completely lost. Even the Reformation made no decisive difference in this respect. In its controversy with mediaeval Scholasticism, orthodox Protestant dogmatics was content to jettison the extravagancies of Dionysius and other repellent and over-subtle elements, and it spoke of angels very much after the matter of the fathers before Dionysius and much mediaeval theology. But unfortunately it was not merely the shock of the discovery of the literary fraud which prevented Evangelical theology from asking whether there was not to be learned from Dionysius something which his successors and the Scholastics did not learn from him—an understanding of the existence of angels in the context of the history of salvation as the basis and order of their ministry.

In view of developments after Dionysius, it is only with the gravest anxiety that we can turn to the other great climax in the history of angelology, i.e., the doctrine developed by Thomas Aquinas in relation to this question (*S. theol.*, I, *qu.* 50–64, 106–114, and *S. c. gent.*, II, *cap.* 91–101). The distinction of his treatment is to be found in the scholarly acuteness, fulness and comprehensiveness of the investigation which he pursues and the information which he gives concerning the questions which are to be posed in respect of angels, the answers which can be given either in logical development of the concept or its application, and that which is to be gleaned from Scripture and tradition with reference to their nature, history and function. If the *Hierarchy* of Dionysius reads more like a dithyramb, in the two *Summae* of Thomas we enter the sphere of the most calm and sober enquiry and teaching, of the strictest method and of corresponding statement—a sphere where nothing unnecessary, but everything necessary is said, and what is said is controlled by everything else and by its more immediate and remote contexts, so that there are no mere assertions, but every statement ventured is proved with refreshing conscientiousness. But in this respect Thomas Aquinas is too great to need any particular praise from us. In relation to his doctrine of angels, two things are clear from the very outset. The first is that consciously and of set purpose he pursues an abstract angelology. In considering the world created by God, either primarily as in the *S. theol.* or finally as in the *S. c. gent.*, we must think of these beings which are called angels, and investigate and portray their particular being and nature and activity. As God is after His own manner, and physical things and psychico-physical men after theirs, so too it is with the angels. It is with them as such that the doctrine of angels has to do. This is assumed as self-evident. Many very acute questions are posed, and handled in great detail. But the decisive question is not even seen whether a Christian understanding of this matter can pursue an abstract investigation, or reach any useful goal if it attempts to do so. The second point is that with relentless determination a definite conception in respect of the nature of angels, a particular definition, is presupposed, introduced and applied as a canon to the whole material, being assumed to be self-evident and tirelessly repeated and victoriously confirmed at each stage in the investigation and presentation. Again the central question (perhaps the question of all questions) is not even perceived, let alone considered, whether this is really the Christian conception, and therefore really in keeping with a *Summa theologica* or a *Summa contra gentiles* bearing the sub-title : *De veritate catholicae fidei.* Both decisions emerge at once at the beginning of both tractates on the theme as irrevocable and indisputable decisions. *S. theol.*, I, *qu.* 50, *art.* 1 is an answer to the question : *Utrum sit aliqua creatura omnino spiritualis et penitus incorporea ?* i.e., whether and to what extent there really is a creature of this kind beside God and among other creatures. And *S. c. gent.*, II, *cap.* 91 stands under the thesis : *Quod sint aliquae substantiae intellectuales corporibus non unitae.* The existence of these substances among others, under God and above man and purely physical things, can and will be proved. They exist as do the others. There are such beings, created but distinctive. The task is thus to see and explain them in their autonomy. What kind of beings are they ? And it is clear that we have to do with purely spiritual, intellectual and non-corporeal creatures, with " substances " (autonomous beings) which have this peculiarity. In the *S. theol.* they bear from the very first the accepted name of *angeli.* But it is only incidentally in *qu.* 112, which speaks of the *missio angelorum ad homines*, that attention is drawn to the material significance of this name. Elsewhere it merely covers what is indicated by a definition which does not in the very least correspond to it. And in the *S. c. gent.*, perhaps out of regard for the *gentiles*, the name is used only on very few occasions, while the abbreviated designation of the subject treated, in closer correspondence with the matter as envisaged by Thomas, is simply *substantiae separatae.* These are the considerations which compel us first and last to treat with the greatest reserve the famous angelology of Thomas. Its character is too unequivocal not to demand an equally unequivocal attitude. It is interesting as the classical opposite of the only procedure which we can regard as theologically meaningful. This work of probably the greatest angelogue of all Church history unfortunately has nothing whatever to do with the knowledge of the *veritas catholicae fidei*, or with attention and fidelity to the biblical witness to revelation. Far from accepting the inspiration which might have been received from Dionysius, it has made a principle of all the more doubtful features of earlier angelology, reducing them *ad absurdum* by its very exactitude. In its misguidedness we can compare it only with the foolish explanations which many modern theologians have given for their complete scepticism or indifference to the whole problem. And we must add that the negations of the moderns are explicable if not excusable against the background of the assertions of the ancients as classically codified and systematised by Thomas. Even the angelological views of Protestant orthodoxy have nothing to offer in the last resort except Thomas weakened and modified. But on this basis no one could or can be brought face to face with the real question.

In proof of this judgment I will cite as an example the way in which Thomas gives his basic demonstration of the existence of these *substantiae separatae* in *S. c. gent.* (II, *cap.* 91). He knows and develops no less than 8 grounds for maintaining their existence. 1. From the survival of the human soul on the dissolution of the body it follows that there is a non-corporeal existence of intellectual substances. This existence is proper to the human soul only *per accidens*. But what in this case can accrue to the intellectual substance only *per accidens* must first, in a higher form than the human soul, belong to it *per se*. Thus there are intellectual substances higher in character than the human soul to which it belongs to exist as such and therefore apart from the body. 2. It does not belong to the species of the human soul, but to the genus of intellectual substance to which the human soul belongs, to exist independently and not in conjunction with a body. From the fact that the human soul, which exists in conjunction with a body, belongs as a species to this genus, it follows that there is in the same genus another species of beings which do not exist in this conjunction, i.e., intellectual substances without bodies. 3. On its lowest level, as *anima intellectiva*, which is the purest form of the human soul, higher, i.e., intellectual nature finds itself in contact with the highest stage of lower, i.e., physical nature. But if the *anima intellectiva* in its relationship to a body is the lowest form of intellectual substances generally, there must be higher forms which do not have this relationship and which are therefore non-corporeal substances. 4. Being in the form of matter is imperfect. But being in a body is a being in the form of matter. Thus being in a body, even though it be that of a *substantia intellectualis*, is imperfect. But where there is the species of something imperfect in a genus, there must also be the species of something perfect, and therefore in the genus *substantia intellectualis* there must be the species of a *substantia separata a corpore*. 5. A corporeal substance has quantity. But it does not belong to the essence of every substance to have quantity. There can thus be substances which are without quantity and therefore non-corporeal. God Himself is an example. But the universe created by Him would be incomplete if it lacked any possible substance. Since it was created perfect, it cannot actually lack substances which are without quantity and therefore non-corporeal. Hence there are substances of this kind. 6. In the case of something composite, there is an autonomy of the individual components. Man is a being composed of intellectual and bodily substances. It is recognised that bodily substance can and does exist independently. If this is true of the lower substance, how much more is it true of the higher ! Hence there are intellectual, non-corporeal substances. 7. The distinctive activity (*operatio*) of intellectual substance consists in cognition (*intelligere*). Conjoined with a body, it can exercise this activity only as it apprehends objects (*intelligibilia*) in sensual form. But this is an imperfect form of cognition. The perfect consists in knowing objects in their own nature. If there are intellectual beings with a capacity of imperfect cognition, there must also be such as are capable of perfect cognition and are not therefore conjoined with a body. 8. Where there is a regular, continuous and unceasing movement (*motus*), according to Aristotle there must also be an unmoved mover (*motor*), and where there are many such movements there must be many such movers. " Astrological " knowledge proves that there are actually many such movements, and therefore there must be many movers. But a bodily mover, or one which is conjoined with a body, cannot be an unmoved mover. There must thus be many movers which are neither bodies nor conjoined with bodies. This, then, is the eight-fold demonstration with which Thomas believes that he has not only proved the existence of his *substantiae separatae*, but also refuted the Sadducees who according to Acts 23[8] questioned the existence of spirits and angels, the scientists of antiquity who would accept as substance only that which was corporeal, the doctrine of Origen who would concede non-corporeality only to the triune God-head, and all the fathers who wished to ascribe some slight measure of corporeality to angels.

It cannot be contested that in a specific sphere and on a specific assumption proof is here given of the existence of a specific object interesting to the one who conducts the proof. It might be asked whether this sphere is real, and if so accessible, and if so able to be marked off in this way and approached with this assumption. It might be asked whether the proof furnished on this assumption and in this sphere is really conclusive and convincing either in detail or as a whole. But if we assume that everything is in order in this respect, and that Thomas has legitimately proved what he really could prove, there can be no doubt that with this assumption (or with the criticism or partial or total rejection of his demonstration) we are merely making philosophical and not theological decisions. Whether there are intellectual substances without bodies, and whether their existence can be proved in this or some other way, may be a question which is interesting and important in the sphere of philosophy. It may be one which can be discussed and even decided in this sphere. It may even be one which is decisive. But it is purely philosophical. On the basis of the Word of God attested in Holy Scripture we are not asked whether there are or are not substances of this kind, nor are we required to prove their existence in some way. If there are, and if their existence can be proved, this does not lead us to angels in the biblical sense of the term. And if there are not, and their existence cannot be proved, this is no argument against angels in the Christian sense. What are called angels in the Bible are not even envisaged in Thomas' proof of the existence of these *substantiae separatae*, let alone is anything said for or against their exist-ence, or anything meaningful stated about them at all, with the eight proofs. And what Thomas later constructed upon the demonstrated existence of these *substantiae separatae* is very different from a doctrine of angels in the Christian sense of the term. In his demonstration Thomas has given us philosophy and not theology, and he has done so far more exclusively than Dionysius. He does occasionally refer to Holy Scripture, and therefore it may be asked whether he does not incidentally and in some sense contrary to his own intention make some contribution to theological knowledge. But fundamentally and as a whole he simply offers us a classical example of how not to proceed in this matter.

Yet his doctrine of angels is so classical a statement that we cannot refrain from a brief glance at the most notable features in its extensive treatment. For this purpose we shall confine ourselves to the S. *theol.*

The first part (I, *qu.* 50–64) stands in the context and (as distinct from the S. *c. gent.*) at the beginning of his doctrine of created being. Its main point is as follows. Angels are non-corporeal and non-material, and therefore incorrupt-ible (50, 5). But in execution of their functions among us they can assume bodies from the air which they condense in the power of God, and in these bodies they can be really and not merely apparently seen by men (51, 2), having something similar to the corresponding vital operations (e.g., eating, moving and speaking), although not really fulfilling the activities themselves (51, 3). The number of angels is greater than that of all material beings put together (50, 3). And none of them is a mere specimen, but each has his own individual nature (50, 4). They are always at a particular point, although not limited by it (52, 1 f.). Yet only one angel can be at the one point at one and the same time (52, 3). In accord-ance with this, they really move from one place to another, and claim a span of time (53, 1 f.). Unlike that of God, their cognition is not identical with their essence ; it is an activity (54, 1 f.). It is also distinguished from that of God by the fact that for knowledge angels have need of certain images (55, 1 f.). Yet their cognition differs from ours in the fact that these images are not received from things, but are given them with their nature as the essential images of all things in the Word of God (55, 2), the degree to which they enjoy them varying with their status in the angelic world (55, 3). This is how they know themselves, incompletely in respect of their creation by God, which is inconceivable to them (56, 1). This is also how they know one another as naturally related (56, 2). This is how they know God, not the divine essence, for no created image is adequate to represent this, but—*quia imago Dei in ipsa natura angeli impressa*—in this image which is directly given to them as opposed to us (56, 3). And this is how they know material things in their individuality (57, 1 f.), although not knowing the future or the inward thoughts of the human heart as God does (57, 3 f.), and having to be instructed by the special revelation of God, and actually being instructed (to some extent from the very first), concerning the mysteries of divine grace and particularly the incarnation (57, 5). Thomas takes up the doctrine of Augustine that the cognition of angels is both *a priori* and *a posteriori*. To the extent that they know all things in the Word of God and therefore *a priori*, *cognitione matutina*, the knowledge of angels is an actual and simple knowledge embracing all things at once and altogether (58, 1–4). To the extent that they know all things in their own created being and therefore *a posteriori*, *cognitione vespertina* (58, 6 f.), their knowledge is potential, discursive and syllogistic as ours is (58, 1–4). But it is never mistaken or false (58, 5). Since they are perfectly disposed by nature to good, we must ascribe to angels a volition distinct from their knowledge and carrying with it the capacity to choose (*liberum arbitrium*, 59, 1–3), but in this respect there can be no question of any strife of different passions (49, 4). Both by nature and on the basis of their free choice and decision their volition is distinct inclination (*inclinatio*), a love (60, 1 f.), in which they first love themselves (like men according to Thomas), then other angels as themselves (60, 3 f.), and finally more than themselves God as the *universale bonum* to be loved for His own sake (60, 5). Now that the question of the nature of angels is answered (*qu.* 50–60), the next question to arise is that of their creation. That this is not explicitly mentioned in Genesis Thomas ascribes to the fact that Moses was speaking to an uncultured people which was unable to comprehend *incorporea natura* (61, 1). But this does not mean that they existed from all eternity. They, too, are created out of nothing, and (for the sake of the necessary co-ordination of the universe) at the same time as the physical creation (61, 2 f.). The place of their creation is in the highest of all spheres, the *coelum empyreum* or whatever else we may call it, but not the *coelum sanctae Trinitatis* (61, 4). Concerning the standing of angels in grace, and therefore their participation in beatitude and the glory of God, the following points are made. A first and natural beatitude belongs to angels by creation, but not the final and supernatural beatitude to which they too must attain by their activity (62, 1). To do this they too need sanctifying grace, *gratia gratum faciens* (62, 2). In fact, however, they were created in this state of grace (63, 3). Yet this does not exclude the fact that they must merit supernatural beatitude as empowered by this grace (62, 4). But as non-corporeal beings they attain it at once and definitively with the first of their acts of volition (62, 5), although with different degrees of fulness according to their grade in the angelic order and the measure of the grace imparted to them (62, 6). The fact that they have attained beatitude does not mean, of course, that the activity corresponding to their nature (their cognition and volition) ceases : *Quamdiu manet natura aliqua, manet operatio eius. Sed beatitudo non tollit naturam, cum sit perfectio eius. Ergo non tollit naturalem cognitionem et dilectionem* (62, 7). Holy angels, those which have their first act of will behind them as an act of appropriate love for God, cannot again fall into sin. They still maintain a freedom of choice, but without the imperfection of a freedom which carries with it the choice of deviation. They lie in the perfect freedom in which free choice and volition is as such that of the good (62, 8). And the definitiveness of their beatitude also means that this cannot be increased by any further merits, but may consist in pure joy at the reward already received (62, 9). Concerning the exceptional fall of a number of angels we learn the following. Angels could sin in virtue of their natural freedom of choice (63, 1). According to their nature, their sin could only be spiritual, but for this reason it was all the more serious, consisting in pride and envy against God (63, 2). This was the terrible sin committed by the devil and a number of other angels. What was it that the devil wanted in committing this sin ? He was like an ass wanting to be a horse. That is to say, he was not content with his own stage of being, but wanted to be like God. But what does it mean to want to be like God ? He sought as the highest goal of bliss (as only God can do) that which he could himself attain in virtue of his nature, instead of striving as a creature on his own level of being for the supernatural beatitude which derives only from the grace of God (63, 3). Like bad men, he and the other wicked angels neither were nor are bad by nature, but if their sin took place at the moment of their creation it did so contrary to their nature and the grace imparted to them in an act of free choice. But in this way there took place once and for all, immediately after their creation, the division of angels into good and bad (63, 4–6). Thomas believes that the chief of the fallen was a cherub, whereas the rest belonged to the lower angelic orders (63, 7) and were seduced by him (63, 8). Concerning the numerical proportion of good angels and bad it can be stated in the light of 2 Kings 6[16] that the good are more numerous (63, 9). Finally, it may be said of the status of bad angels after the fall that their natural knowledge as angels remains intact, but that their knowledge of divine things is diminished and they are completely deprived of the knowledge from which love for God proceeds and which is essential to true wisdom (64, 1). And as good angels persisted and will always persist as such in perfect freedom after that first act, so the bad are committed to wickedness by that definitive choice. Thomas believed that a contrary opinion would necessarily jeopardise the beatitude of the holy angels and men, and was therefore quite intolerable. Once he has made his choice, the will of an angel is immutably fixed on that which is chosen. Thus evil angels are as such finally incapable of repentance, and cannot be reached or liberated by the divine mercy (64, 2). They can only suffer eternal torment, kicking at that which is for them but not for them (64, 3). As to their location, we are told that in expiation of their guilt they are in hell but for the testing of man in the *caliginosus aer*, in the clouds (64, 4). This is what we learn from Thomas concerning the inner drama of the angelic cosmos (*qu.* 61–64).

In the context of his doctrine of divine providence Thomas returns to the subject (I, *qu.* 106–114) and speaks of the activity corresponding to their nature, i.e., of what we might almost call their historical existence. What is it that the good angels do ? The higher angels enlighten the lower, and, since the light which illuminates them all is God, this can only mean that they strengthen them (not unlike human *doctores* their pupils) by passing on, distinguishing and giving concrete form to the truth as it is better known to themselves (106, 1). Thus one angel can incite the will of another (*inclinare eam ad amabile quoddam*) but not move it—which only God can do (106, 2). And there can be no question of the enlightenment of the angels of a higher degree by those of a lower. For the *ordo qui convenit spiritualibus substantiis nunquam a Deo praetermittitur*. By their very nature the higher angels are nearer to God, and therefore they can pass on the knowledge directly received in this closer proximity but cannot receive knowledge from the member of a lower order as in the hierarchy of the Church (106, 3). Instead the lower angels receive from the higher a full impartation of the very light which the latter have received, of all that they know. The only thing is that they cannot grasp it with the perfection with which it is mediated, so that the distinction of degree remains (106, 4). The speech of angels is then investigated. Angels speak with one another in the simple form of definite acts of will in virtue of which what they carry within themselves as *verbum internum* can be revealed at once to other angels (107, 1). In this process one or more angels can be addressed to the exclusion of others (107, 5). In this sense the lower angels can speak to the higher (107, 2). And in this sense the angels can speak with God, for although they have nothing to tell Him which He does not know already they speak in order to receive from Him, or to seek His advice, or to give expression to their admiration of His inconceivable majesty (107, 3). And because this speech of the angels is a purely intellectual occurrence, it cannot be hampered by distance in space or time (107, 4). In the eight articles of *qu.* 108 Thomas takes up the question of hierarchy in the angelic world, and it is here that we can see how he adopts and understands and amplifies what is said by Dionysius. In general, he is clearly not interested by the heavenly hierarchy as a whole, but by the hierarchies (as he calls the triads of Dionysius), and within these by the *ordines* (as he calls his choirs). Again, these hierarchies and *ordines* do not interest him as the moments of a heavenly movement and history, but as the elements of a stable heavenly system. Finally, they do not interest him decisively as the heavenly *prius* of an earthly order of salvation, but in their relationship to the world-order, to the *ratio* of created being in general and as such. The distinction of three triads or hierarchies, with three choirs in each, is to be kept, for illumination, even of angels, is from the threefold standpoint of the divine origin of things, their relation to *causae creatae universales* and their contingent individuality (108, 1), and even in earthly states there are the *optimates*, the *vilis populus*, and between the two the *populus honorabilis* (108, 2). It is interesting that for Thomas this collective distinction of the angelic *ordines* cannot be the last word. On a closer knowledge of these beings than we are given we should have to recognise that there are as many angelic *officia* and therefore *ordines* as there are angels (108, 3). Undoubtedly it is both ordained by grace and also in keeping with their nature that angels should exist in these gradations (108, 4), continuing to do so even after the last judgment (108, 7). The explanation of the individual choirs and their relationships from their names is adopted by Thomas with the modification that fundamentally all angels participate in all angelic perfections, the angels of the higher choirs with a greater portion in the higher of these and the lower a less, so that the giving of specific names to specific *ordines* is always to be understood *a parte potiori* (108, 5–6). Finally Thomas thinks that he can show that men who attain to blessedness by the grace of God, without losing their distinctive nature, will be " as the angels of God " (Mt. 22[30]), and therefore ranged with the angelic *ordines* according to their merits, departed saints being already active among us in fulfilment of angelic functions (108, 8). We also have to reckon with a corresponding order in the kingdom of demons. For all their perversity they have not lost their angelic nature and therefore their character as ordered beings which are either superior or subordinate. In this sphere, too, there is ruling and obeying (109, 1–3). But the order of good angels is superior and victorious in face of this opposing sphere (109, 4). Particular attention is now paid to the operation of angels *ad extra*, to and in the rest of the created world. Even if only indirectly, angels control all bodily things : *Et hoc non solum a sanctis doctoribus ponitur, sed etiam ab omnibus philosophis, qui incorporeas substantias posuerunt* (110, 1 f.). That they control them means that they set them in movement from place to place (110, 3). The only restriction is, of course, that they cannot perform miracles (110, 4). Again, they illuminate men, according to their capacity, by mediation of the truth in the form of sensual images and by the strengthening of their subjective power of reception (111, 1). They can stir up but they cannot move the will of man. The latter, like the performance of miracle, is a matter for God alone (111, 2). But both bad and good angels can set in motion the imaginative power of man, and thus determine the character of his outward experiences (111, 3–4).

Finally in *qu.* 112, under the title *De missione angelorum*, Thomas comes to the theme which in the light of the Bible ought surely to have been the controlling if not the exclusive theme. But we do not gather that Thomas was even remotely aware of this. The question of this real sending of angels does not interest him except as one of their possibilities of action in relation to corporeal things and men as treated in the two preceding questions, and he is more interested in the question of the existence and action of guardian angels to which he will come later. Indeed, even in respect of this *missio* his concern is with purely formal questions, questions of competence as it were. Thus some angels are actually sent by God as *particularia agentia* for specific tasks. That is, they are transferred from their own sphere to that of man. God Himself is always the *principium* and *finis* of their action. They themselves are His *instrumenta intelligentia*. And since their action remains purely intellectual as distinct from ours, their contemplation of the divine wisdom as the true and proper activity corresponding to their nature cannot be disturbed by this action *ad extra* but is conducted through it (112, 1). Not all angels, however, are sent in this way. The higher angels do not take part in this work (112, 2), but only the lower *ordines* ; and Thomas thinks that he can know and prove in even greater detail that it is undertaken only by the five lower and not the four higher of these *ordines*, a distinction which does not really seem to tally with that of the three hierarchies (112, 4). Conversely, not all angels stand in the immediate presence of God, for they are not all capable of what this involves, i.e., of grasping the depth of the divine mystery with the immediate clarity of the present divine essence. This can belong only to the higher angels, as in the entourage of an earthly monarch there are both constant *assistentes* and *administrantes* who come and go. By the higher angels preferred in this way Thomas means specifically the highest hierarchy (112, 3). But what about the first *ordo* of the middle hierarchy, which also has no part in the *missio* ? However that may be, this is all that Thomas actually has to say on the point.

For in *qu.* 113 we are already dealing with guardian angels. Is it that Thomas thought of the particular activity of angels *ad extra* mainly or even exclusively in these terms ? At any rate, it is only here that he comes to speak of any concrete activity of angels *ad extra*. Does man need a guardian angel ? Can he not protect himself ? Ought he not to do so ? Is not the protection of God sufficient ? Does not the fact of the daily sin of many suggest that they have no guardian angels, if the latter are not to come under the accusation of negligence ? In spite of all these difficulties, Thomas assures us that as the providence of God moves all corporeal things by spiritual substances and all the lower among them by the higher, and as in our thinking we must be guided by immutable principles, so men with their fallible insights and emotions must be assisted by angels by whom they can be directed and inclined to the good. For this purpose it is not enough that man has freedom of choice and a knowledge of the natural law. And although the immediate protection of God works itself out in the form of the general direction of man to the good through infused grace and virtue, it does not have the form of special instruction concerning the concrete paths which he has to tread. For the latter purpose, he is given a guardian angel. If he still sins, this is not due to the negligence of the angel but to his own wickedness (113, 1). As there are different angels for the different types of corruptible things, so there are for the higher and lower human collectives and even for individual men (since each individual is a *creatura incorruptibilis*), and higher or lower angels according to the higher or lower determination given to each individual (113, 2). By " higher " angels, in so far as we are referring to men, Thomas does not mean those from the higher hierarchies, which have nothing whatever to do with this ministry, but higher angels within the lowest hierarchy, through whom the powers of the higher can be mediated to man (113, 3). Does every individual really have his own particular angel ? Yes, says Thomas, in the *status viae* and *quamdiu viator est*. In the eternal kingdom he will not have an *angelus custos* but an *angelus conregnans*. Even those appointed to perdition, even unbelievers, if only to protect them from some of the harm they might do to themselves and others, have a guardian angel. Even Antichrist will have his guardian angel. This angel is just as indispensable as the assistance of natural reason. Adam had his guardian angel even in the state of innocence. As the sequel showed, he was under serious enough threat from without, if not from within. The only exception to this rule is the man Jesus in virtue of His direct relationship to the Word of God. The angels who attended Him could not be *angeli custodes* but only *angeli ministri* (113, 4). Is the guardian angel assigned to man at birth or at baptism ? The answer is that he is assigned at birth, for he is one of the gifts of the providence directed to man as *natura rationalis*. If prior to baptism he cannot help man to eternal salvation, if he cannot instruct an infant in divine truth, he can ward off demons and preserve it from spiritual and physical harm. How about the child in the womb ? The answer is that since at this stage it still belongs to the person of the mother we may assume that prior to birth it stands under the protection of the guardian angel of the latter (113, 5). Can a guardian angel abandon the man allotted to his care ? The answer is that he cannot do so strictly and totally, for nothing can escape the providence of God. There can only be a temporary and local abandonment, and even then the angel still keeps his ward in view from heaven, and the efficacy of his protection is not impaired (113, 6). Can angels bewail the evil which their wards commit and bring upon themselves ? The surprising but logical answer is in the negative. They can certainly rejoice over them, e.g., over the sinner repenting. But sorrow and pain are alien to the angels in perfect bliss. Sorrow and pain can be felt by a being only when his will is crossed. But the will of the angels is at one with that of the divine righteousness without the operation or permission of which nothing can take place, not even the sin and punishment of man. Hence the latter cannot be contrary to the will of the angels. Hence it cannot be an object of their sorrow and pain. Hence angels cannot bewail the evil which their wards commit and bring upon themselves (113, 7). The final question is whether there can be disunity and strife amongst the angels. The answer is again surprising, for this time it is in the affirmative. For Thomas does not accept the view of Jerome that the " prince " of the kingdom of Persia, of whom we read in Daniel 10[13] that he withstood for 21 days the angel sent to Daniel, was really a demon, but he agrees with Gregory the Great that he must be regarded as a good angel, as one of the collective guardian angels, and his exposition is then as follows. All angels obviously agree that the will of God should be done. But there are relative contradictions within created things and relationships as such, and therefore between the *merita* and *demerita* of individual men and kingdoms. For the resolving of these contradictions even the angels must be instructed by divine revelation. In their functions as guardian angels they may, therefore, be involved in temporary disunity and even conflict, i.e., in a different reading and seeking of the one will of God. In the less drastic language of a modern Thomist (Franz Diekamp, *Kath. Dogm.*[6], Vol. II, 1930, p. 70), " the independence with which guardian angels have to fulfil their commission explains why there can be differences of opinion and opposing movements among them as indicated in Daniel 10. This passage also shows that their measures, although always proceeding from the holiest intention, may sometimes be objectively unsuitable."

To the work of guardian angels there corresponds *in pejorem partem* the *impugnatio daemonum*, the devilish assaulting of man. Thomas' doctrine of angels closes with his consideration of this sinister theme. What is the source of temptation ? It derives wholly from the malice of demons. But while it has this origin, it is ordered by God and takes place according to the measure of His ordering. To the extent that it is temptation to sin, it is only permitted by Him. To the extent that it serves as a chastisement, it is expressly sent. But either way His righteousness is its basis and aim. Is God unjust to expose weak man to a conflict which is so unequal in view of the power of demons ? He is not unjust because He provides for man in His grace a force which is more than adequate compensation. Are not the assaults of the flesh and the world enough to test man ? They do not satisfy the demons in their malice, and under the superior *ordinatio divina* this additional temptation can serve only to the glorifying of the elect (114, 1). In its truest and purest sense, demonic assault consists in temptation as an inducement to sin. God Himself " tempts " man, not to corrupt him, but to reveal to him and to others what He Himself knows concerning him. But the devil, using the flesh and the world and its good or ill fortunes, tempts to sin. Taking upon himself something which is the prerogative of God alone, i.e., to search and reveal the inner secrets of man, he wills the corruption of man, and he tries to accomplish this by influencing his will, which he cannot control, through the lower impulses of his nature, thus guiding him to that which is evil (114, 2).

Is all sin to be traced back to temptation by the devil ? Indirectly yes, in the sense that the burning of pieces of wood can be traced back to the one who sets them aside for this purpose. To this extent the one who led the first man into sin is the seducer of all sinners. But not all sin can be attributed directly to the devil. Much sin has its direct cause only in the free will of man and the corruption of his nature, the flesh. To be sure, man is capable of good and meritorious action only with divine assistance and through the ministry of angels. But this does not mean that all his evil acts are to be explained directly by demonic action (114, 3). Can demons perform miracles to serve their evil ends. The answer is that they cannot do so in the strict and proper sense of the term. They cannot do anything *quod fit praeter ordinem totius naturae.* No creature, no angel and therefore no demon can perform miracles in this sense, but only God. There are, however, miracles in a relative and improper sense, i.e., happenings which are beyond the capacity and understanding of man. Demons no less than angels are capable of these, just as some men can evoke the astonishment of others by doing things which the latter can neither do nor understand. These miracles have their own distinctive reality and effect and are not to be dismissed as mere *phantasmata*, although in the case of those which are demonic we also have a determination of the human imagination and even the senses so that under this influence things seem to be very different from what they really are. Yet there is more to it than this. As Thomas sees it, demons like angels have access to the *semina quae in elementis mundi inveniuntur* by which natural forces, although they cannot be destroyed or altered, can be moved in a particular direction. And as they themselves, like the angels, can assume definite shape and form from the air, they can invest other things (objectively) with bodily shapes in which they can be seen by man. What they produce— we remember the signs of Pharaoh's magicians—are *signa mendacii*, but they are *vera prodigia* by which man can be really deceived. *Diverso fine et iure* their operations are technically the same as those of the saints and good angels. They do for their own glory and in pursuit of their private ends that which the latter do for the glory of God : *publica administratione et iussu Dei* (114, 4). The last question is whether demons can renew their attack on a man when it has been repulsed. The answer is given by Luke 4[13] : " And when the devil had ended all the temptation, he departed from him for a season." Victory over a demon gives a certain security against him, but it does not give an unlimited security. Does not the unclean spirit cast out of a man (Mt. 12[43f.]) say when he has wandered through desert places and not found the rest which he seeks : *revertar in domum meam, unde exivi* (114, 3) ? With this not very consoling prospect Thomas closes his final round of questions and his whole doctrine of angels.

No less than 118 individual questions are raised and answered by Thomas on this theme. It was probably because of this series, prominent both for quantity and material interest, that Thomas earned the particular title in the Middle Ages of the *Doctor angelicus*. We gladly accept this style. The only thing is that in all his 118 enquiries we do not find an answer to the question on which the theological relevance and serviceability of his doctrine of angels depends. As Evangelical theologians, committed to the witness of the Bible, we are ill-advised to treat the subject on the ground which he was not the first to select but which he did so with a radicalness that can hardly be surpassed. And because we cannot do this, we cannot follow him in the detailed questions which he poses or answers which he gives.

Let us take a retrospective glance. In his " Die Engel und Wir " (*Kirchenbl. f. d. ref. Schweiz*, 1937, No. 18–19)—to my mind the most useful modern contribution to the subject—Gerhard Spinner has given us an excellent appraisal of the results of Aquinas' investigations which we can accept apart from a final reservation. His assessment is as follows : " The angelic world of Thomas functions to some extent as a powerful co-ordinated system by which the place of man is determined in the universe. The scholastic system resembles a gigantic ladder set up to heaven, on which the heavenly messengers do not ascend and descend, but all have their appointed places with the rigidity of the utmost objectivity. Catholic man needs this objectivity of forces reaching up to the supreme point of the universe if he is not to hang in the unknown or plunge into the abyss. The much admired objectivity of the Catholic Church in its doctrine and cultus rests finally on the objective cosmos of supra-sensual powers as depicted in the scholastic doctrine of angels which has so prominent a place in the whole system of Thomas. . . . Thomas' assertion that beings which are intellectual and supernatural greatly surpass in number those which are bound to matter serves to shift the whole emphasis onto the heavenly cosmos, to which the world of the visible, and man within it, cannot be regarded as more than an almost insignificant annexe. The man who knows that he is in this co-ordinated system can hardly be in danger of thinking of himself and his fellows as the central point in the universe and thus adopting an anthropocentric and egocentric view of the world or mode of life. . . . Angels as understood in Scholasticism perform the service of again setting man under the heavenly cosmos, and therefore in his true place before God, humbled and redeemed." With regard to this final statement, it is to be noted that it is not the angels as understood in Scholasticism which really do us this service. What is needed to-day is not that " behind the high peaks of the Reformation the ice-cold summits of Scholasticism should again enlighten us as summits of our Church." Angels as understood in Scholasticism are those *essentiae spirituales*, those *substantiae separatae*, and the objectivity of the heavenly cosmos in the scholastic sense is only that of an artificially and arbitrarily separated, i.e., abstracted and hypostatised, intellectual being as opposed to a material and to our own intellectual conjoined with matter, which Thomas like Plato and Aristotle regarded as relatively less perfect and essentially earthly. Armed with this criterion, Thomas could certainly disclose ice-cold summits of objectivity. But this objectivity of the spiritual or intellectual is much too equivocal for us to want it to shine again in our Church. If another age, armed with a different criterion, were to set up another system, orientated less by spirit and more by the matter which is here despised, it might easily be exchanged for another and no less ice-cold objectivity. And was the scholastic view really so free from anthropocentricity and egocentricity that it could effectively oppose an exchange of this kind ? When the new age came, it did not actually do so. Is it really so certain that on this view man has any genuine knowledge of the heavenly cosmos ? May not the converse be true ? May it not be that the second part of the Thomistic doctrine of angels is only the attempt at a gigantic self-projection of the *anthropos* or the ego into an objectivity in which it thinks to find in the angel its desired and in the demon its dreaded superior *alter ego*, i.e., itself supremely magnified ? Only one of the lowest angels has to do directly with man, says Thomas, not on any biblical ground but with notable humility, and he affirms that above this there are higher and supreme angels which are far too exalted to be directly concerned about man. Yet directly or indirectly is not man the goal of the whole of the heavenly cosmos ? At any rate, it is he who has sketched and devised it as a titanic counterpart of his own social and individual existence. With his knowledge and recognition of this higher cosmos, has he really done anything but magnify the intellectual side of his own nature ? And has he not crowned this by seeing in God Himself, beyond this objective world of the spirit and spirits, a purely intellectual being which is merely self-grounded, self-resting and self-motivating in contrast to all creatures, himself being far below this God and all angels, and yet the product of this God and on this side divine by nature ? No, to build on the rock of this system is as little advisable as to construct a materialistic or for that matter any system at all. All systems, and therefore this too, have a tendency to tip over and turn into their opposite. To God and therefore to angels as understood in Scholasticism there cannot be denied an objectivity which is remarkable in its own way. But we have no real cause to admire the objectivity of the Catholic Church and its doctrine and cultus to the extent that it rests on the objectivity of the scholastic doctrine of angels. For this is not the objectivity with which we have to do in Christian faith when it speaks of God and the angels. Real humility and redemption are not to be expected from these ice-cold summits. Christian theology asks concerning another God, and therefore concerning other and less equivocal angels.

But with his praise of Thomas, Gerhard Spinner had something very true in mind, as the continuation of his work reveals. An open-minded reader of Thomas cannot escape the impression that—no matter how—we are here pointed with imperative urgency in a direction in which Christian theology has genuine cause to look, i.e., to the heavenly cosmos above our earthly, and to its participation in the history which is enacted between God and man, this creature of the earthly cosmos. If Thomas missed the mark when he thought that this heavenly cosmos should be described as specifically spiritual, and if his whole doctrine of angels necessarily became in consequence the depiction of an unreal heaven and unreal angels, yet by treating the matter as he understood it in a way which is quantitatively so prominent and also so concentrated and meticulous, he set up a sign and bore a witness for which we must always be grateful to him. The same is true of the angelology of the fathers. The same is true of Pseudo-Dionysius. But it is particularly true of Thomas in view of the monumental form which the matter took in his case. The problem must be differently posed and treated from the way in which he posed and treated it. But he was and is the man who so handled it that we either do not know him or we are complete philistines if we think that there is nothing in this subject which moved him so strangely, and that we can thus ignore it altogether. In this sense the angels as understood in Scholasticism can render us a genuine service, and we cannot refuse to their great interpreter the title of *Doctor angelicus*.

4. We return to the *Credo ut intelligam*. We have so far applied it to our present subject in two ways : 1. that by the *credo*, i.e., by the witness of Scripture to which faith refers, there is given us in this question of angels, too, a task of knowledge ; and 2. that this task must be taken up and pursued only on the basis of the *credo*, i.e., of the witness of Holy Scripture. Our next statement is the sharper and more emphatic one that we must view the task exclusively in this light, confining ourselves to the *intelligere* which it offers, and not

turning back or aside to other grounds, motives or concerns alien to the *credo* or the witness of Holy Scripture, to freely selected constructions which might also cause us to put this remarkable question concerning angels and suggest this or that answer to it. We have considered and illustrated the great possibility that the term angels might lead us quickly to forget or push into the background the preceding *credo*, and in the task of knowing angels generally to move off in a different direction—in the direction of a view or concept concerning which we are convinced from some other source than the Bible that it stands for something true and valid and describes approximately or even precisely what an angel is. On the whole the angelology of the primitive and mediaeval Church gives us an example of this possibility. But there is also another possibility. We may seriously ask concerning the angels of Holy Scripture, and really receive the instruction of Holy Scripture concerning them. In theology orientated by the Reformation it is inevitable that the Scripture-principle should be basically and theoretically accepted in this matter too. And yet, even though we may recognise this principle and go out from Egypt, we may still long after its flesh-pots. We may in fact proceed with one eye on the angels of the Bible and the other on a real or invented complex which we assume to be identical with these angels.

We may do this in all innocence and for no precise reasons. Why should not angels exist otherwise than in the contexts and sense of the biblical witness ? And why should they not be seen and known in this other form ? Are not two threads stronger than one ? Must we not deal with God in such a way that, although we know how important the *credo* is, we set beside it a little *intelligo* in order to press on the more surely in respect of the intended and decisive *ut intelligam* ? But usually those who adopt this course have good reasons for doing so. Perhaps in this little *intelligo* set alongside the *credo* it is a matter of persuading oneself that the latter cannot be understood except with the help of the former. The Bible is consulted, but if it is not to be consulted in vain a hermeneutical principle must first be sought. The biblical ciphers concerning angels are so obscure. They must be solved if they are to be understood. For this purpose a key is needed. To secure and use this key one has to look both to the Bible and also elsewhere where information can be gleaned which, if it is not so authentic, is at any rate clearer and more accessible and direct, and therefore helpful in this whole question of biblical angels. Or again, the looking aside might be more for the sake of apologetics than hermeneutics. That small *intelligo* is set beside the *credo* because there is no assurance that full confidence can be placed in the Bible in this matter. At any rate, the witness of the Bible is surely more powerful if it can be shown to be confirmed by the witness of other observations, considerations and deliberations, and to have at least a degree of probability. Indeed, the confirmation of these witnesses is perhaps regarded as essential if credence is to be given to that of the Bible. Or more sharply still, the witness of the Bible cannot be accepted at all without this confirmation.

Well, these are all processes of thought which here as elsewhere we must rule out in dogmatics. Neither at this nor at any other point can we trifle with the *credo*. At this point, too, we can attain to an *intelligere* worthy of the name only if we give to the *credere* our full and exclusive attention and confidence. *Credere* is to believe. But we cannot believe and yet at the same time not believe but want to know. This is not to believe at all. In dogmatics as in life, and at this point in dogmatics no less than any other, the comfort of faith is linked with the fact that it is the only comfort, and that as such it is accepted with the appropriate joy. And faith relates to the witness of Holy Scripture. It is the willingness and readiness to be taught from this source, referring all the concern for *intelligere* to what is said there, because there we have to do with the origin and object of faith. Faith is the confidence that what we are told there will be intelligible in terms of itself, i.e., of the context in which it is said. Or negatively, it is radical mistrust in face of the supposed understanding of what we are told there in terms of insights and criteria acquired elsewhere. And faith is the confidence that what we are told there is grounded in itself, i.e., in the matter attested. Or negatively, it is radical mistrust in face of the supposed grounding of what we are told there on that which is not identical with the substance of the biblical witness. Faith is thus free from any anxiety lest the biblical witness should not be intelligible in itself ; and it is certainly free from any anxiety lest it should lack any basis or certainty without external confirmation. Faith has only one anxiety, namely, lest it should cease to be this free faith. It does not therefore try to find any other comfort or clarity or certainty than that which it abundantly receives at this source, from this object, and by the biblical attestation of this object. Faith is confident that it will not be left in the lurch either hermeneutically or apologetically if it confines itself to this witness. It also knows that every supposed enrichment by another hermeneutics or apologetics can only mean impoverishment, any assurance of this kind uncertainty, and any extension in this direction the jeopardising and loss of the one thing needful. Faith dares to trust the Holy Spirit. But even in this matter of angels we must dare to trust the Holy Spirit, and for good or evil we must dare to trust Him alone. Here too, then, we must rule out all those processes of thought.

The consequence of a failure to do so are almost always fatal. To look in two directions is not to see straight in either. In the matter of angels it is better to look resolutely and exclusively in a different

direction than to try to look at the Bible and other sources of knowledge at one and the same time. In so doing, as may be seen from the
example of Thomas, we shall at least find something orderly. But
if we try to find angels both in the Bible and elsewhere, we shall only
see hazy pictures. Our philosophy will spoil our theology, and our
theology our philosophy. Our present concern is with the first point.
The knowledge which does not dare to be wholly and exclusively
theological and therefore in faith and therefore based on the witness
of Holy Scripture will as such be a pale and uncertain knowledge
and erroneous at the decisive point. As theological knowledge it
could be free. Bound to other concepts, even though only incidentally
for hermeneutical or apologetic reasons, it is unfree, and therefore
an unfaithful half-knowledge estranged from itself and its object.
A key is found to the dark ciphers of Scripture, but the results are
either artifical or platitudinous. And the statements of Scripture
may seem to be well-grounded, but what they say is robbed of any
relevance or significance by the fact that they are grounded elsewhere.
Yet this threat can only be of secondary importance at this point.
If we do not accept the promise of the Holy Spirit, and on this promise
dare to look with both eyes at Holy Scripture and not to look aside
with either, we shall not even realise how fatal is the threat to which
we expose ourselves. There are many theologians who have
succumbed to this threat and never even noticed the consequences for
their theology. But if we dare to be content with Scripture alone, it
can only be because the promise of the Holy Spirit has itself been given
us by Scripture. The risk is not then a real risk, but simply the
obedience required of us. If we are to have the freedom and to be
compelled to see this limit, like all the limits of a Christian angelology
it must be drawn by a higher hand. It is perhaps as well to be clear
at this point that in angelology too the theological question is a
spiritual one. And it is at this point that we must realise it because
the promise of the Holy Spirit is the only force between heaven
and earth which has the power to direct us wholly and exclusively
in a particular direction, enforcing the prohibition of deviation to
the right hand or the left which is primarily at issue under this fourth
head.

Some historical illustrations will show clearly what I have in mind.
As we have seen, the patristic and mediaeval angelology inevitably made
frequent allusion to the Bible, either adducing passages to support the theses
adopted, or accepting the questions and limits posed by it. But the example
of Thomas makes it quite clear that these references belong only to the apparatus
of scholarship and not to the matter itself. The Bible is a particularly important
element in the guidance offered by antiquity. But it is introduced formally in
the same sense and with the same diligence as the fathers, Pseudo-Dionysius,
and above all Aristotle, the supreme *philosophus*. In this respect an appalling
ignorance is revealed. With disarming innocence it is decided to work out one's
own view of angels, but nothing is seen against, and much in favour of, accepting

the stimulus and control, the compulsion and restraint, of the Bible as of many other books of recognised authority.

Evil vacillation or aberration is not yet a problem in the early and mediaeval period, but it is the great problem in the post-Reformation epoch with its conscious awareness that the Bible is not merely one respectable text-book among others but the witness of the concrete divine revelation which constitutes the Church and therefore the text to which Christian doctrine has to keep, on the content of which it must base its thinking, and to which it is always responsible. In Protestantism there was posed for the first time the question of belief or unbelief in respect of the sufficiency of this revelation and its attestation, and there has to be a clear decision between the venture, the act of obedience, in which theology is ready to be free as it is bound to Scripture, between the well-known command and the transgression of this command, the looking past Scripture, the drawing on other sources of knowledge.

We have already seen with what distinctness Calvin saw and drew the limit of angelology in this direction, and how Quenstedt spoke of the *apodicticum argumentum scripturae* in contrast to every other. But if Calvin's doctrine of angels (*Instit.*, I, 13, 3–19) is in fact an attempt along these lines which must be taken seriously, and if even in J. Gerhard (*Loci*, 1610 f., V, *cap.* 4) we have the impression that not without a certain measure of success he was engaged in resistance to the penetration of alien standpoints, Quenstedt no less than other orthodox Protestant divines did in fact make unthinking use of a non-biblical knowledge of angels derived from Scholasticism. And in the great work of J. W. Baier (*Comp. Theol. pos.*, I, 3, 3) which appeared a year after that of Quenstedt we can see clearly the beginning of even a theoretical cleavage in theological consciousness. Scripture shows us *disertissime* that angels exist as a species of creatures (*species creaturarum*) different from men and all others by their nature as *spiritus completi*, as *substantiae simplices, spirituales, incorporeae.* That this is the case cannot be clearly proved *lumine naturae, quamvis suaderi possit rationibus probabilibus.* It is worth noting that a diligent search has now begun for these *rationes probabiles.*

In the supranaturalist F. Volkmar Reinhard (*Vorl. üb. d. Dogm.*, 1812, § 50) we read the following. Observation and physics teach that species of creatures are "uncommonly varied and numerous" on our earth. "Since, then, the heavenly bodies, whose number and size are almost immeasurable, cannot possibly have been left untenanted by God, but are incontestably filled with creatures appropriate to their nature, we are freely justified in assuming a host and variety of creatures infinitely surpassing all human conception." And if we are taught by natural science that there is an ascending series of earthly classes of creatures, in which the human race is commonly accepted to be the last and final link, it is "easily seen that we may not be the most perfect creature, but that the series may well reach up to infinity through higher and more excellent natures." The divine wisdom, power and goodness, and the immeasurable span of creation, make this so probable to reason that it may take it as proved and perfectly clear. But it is not evidently confirmed by Scripture. Yet this undoubtedly speaks of angels. "Hence it is necessary that we should gather what the Bible says on this theme, and complete from this source what reason only suspects, as we shall now proceed to do. . . ."

In the rationalist K. G. Bretschneider (*Hand. d. Dogm. d. ev.-luth. Kirche*, Vol. I, 1838, § 104) we find an excellent expansion of this proof from reason into a conception of angels which serves as a canon for the understanding of Scripture. It is established by a series of postulates. To the arguments of Reinhard, Bretschneider adds that the perfection of God makes it probable that apart from the soul of man there are other kinds of rational creatures, spirit and reason and virtue being called into being by God in every possible form in spiritual and moral individuals. Moreover, the doctrine of " immortality " leads unavoidably to the thought that the men who lived centuries ago must now constitute a much more exalted class of rational beings than we are. Again, as our earth and solar system " stand in the closest physical relationship " to the universe, so it is to be expected that the invisible kingdom of reason throughout the universe should stand in a moral relationship of which we can have a fuller conception only when we die. Nor can reason regard it as unlikely that God uses these higher rational creatures to mediate certain effects, " thus exercising their gifts and perfecting them." Bretschneider, too, thinks that he can maintain all this with a " moral probability tantamount to certainty." The resultant conception of angels is then compared with " the form of the doctrine of angels as present two thousand years ago," i.e., that of the Bible, the latter being regarded as a form, temporally conditioned and associated with a defective world-view, of this intrinsically valid and important conception. It is hardly necessary to state in detail how much or how little he is ready and able to appropriate of this biblical form.

Further on in the 19th century, within the framework of later Idealism, Richard Rothe (*Dogm*. Pt. I, 1870, p. 205 f.) declares that speculative (for him scientific) theology not only does not take offence at the idea of an angelic world but is necessarily led to it (p. 244). There can be no doubt that it is biblical, and the scriptural foundation of the older dogmatic concept is to be recognised in its main features. But quite apart from this Rothe reckons on the existence of a " higher world of spirits." What are good angels ? They are personal creatures which have been perfected, i.e., which have become pure spirit. That these exist is proved by the fact that there are perfect worlds. According to Rothe, this earthly and imperfect creation of ours cannot be the first or the last. Hence there are earlier spheres of creation, or worlds, which are already perfect, and to which there belong personal creatures which are already perfect. And these are our angels, concerning which Rothe thinks that he may say : " Even angels have had to serve in the ranks and make their way up from below. From material or sensually personal creatures they have become by way of moral development perfected and purely spiritual persons, i.e., angels " (p. 232). To these perfected beings of earlier spheres of creation there are continually added the perfected human individuals of our own. Yet the fact that all these beings have become perfected spirits does not mean that they are absolutely non-corporeal. At this point Rothe has gone back behind the customary doctrine and even Thomas, and adopted the view of Origen and the other Greek fathers, teaching that each of these perfected persons is the absolute unity of a personal I and a natural organism, a spiritual body, distinctively belonging to this I. Unrestricted by space and time as they are, the universe is opened up to them without limitation, and we can only assume that they exercise a specific influence on our as yet imperfect sphere and particularly on its imperfect personal creatures. In this sense, then, the good angels have a part in the divine rule. Indeed, they are the specific organs to mediate it. As each sphere is produced and determined by God through the mediation of those which precede, " these individual worlds organically proceed from one another as mediated by one another " (p. 245). Thus the mutual relationship of these higher beings is necessarily that of a completed organisation. And this organisation is held together by the " absolute, creaturely-spiritual, central individual of the universe, which must be thought of as a collective individual, namely, as the absolute, personal unity of the spiritual individuals which are the sources and centres of the individual spheres of creation—the endlessly increasing axis of the whole world of spirits. Quite uncapriciously, therefore, we agree with the doctrine of Holy Scripture that Christ (in His completion) is the Head of the whole world of good angels." Uncapriciously indeed ! And in the same uncapricious way Rothe agrees with the teaching of the Bible concerning the devil and demons. It is worth noting that J. C. Blumhardt (*Schriftauslegung*, ed. 1947, p. 160) refers not unsympathetically

to this angelology, obviously thinking of Rothe's presentation, though not mentioning him by name.
With less certain tread J. A. Dorner (*Syst. d. chr. Gl. lehre²*, Vol. I, p. 534 f.) moves in the same direction as Rothe. We shall return to an instructive hint to be found in his doctrine of angels. His exposition as a whole is as follows. The concept of the angelic world not only contains no contradiction, but angels can actually be described as a necessary class of creatures. Their existence or recognition in the form of a doctrine of angels constitutes a safeguard against a false this-worldliness, namely, on the one side against an exaggeration of the earth and the earthly spirit, and on the other side against a depreciation of the infinite significance of the spirit in face of the apparent preponderance of material quantities. The doctrine of angels sets our mind in a great perspective, calling it back from restriction to our planets, widening our consciousness of the world by the consideration of a higher and infinitely rich world of spirits, and assuring to the consciousness of God a powerful point of contact for the religious consideration of the universe. If on this side it resists the pride and defiance of the human heart, on the other it resists the pusillanimous doubt of the spirit. It forces us to think of other regions as filled in a manifold ascending series by rational creatures. As a doctrine of the participation of higher spirits in our history it contains an indication of the fact that in the world of the spirit nothing is isolated, but that what takes place on this earthly body, this drop in the bucket, has a significance for the totality of spirits. Beyond this, following traces already known to us, Dorner thinks that he can give to the doctrine of angels the following positive significance. If our earth and history are not eternal, but the thought of a temporal beginning of the divine work is impossible, the doctrine of angels gives us the possibility, as a " necessary postulate," of reckoning with circles of creation which, in relative independence but mutually intersecting, precede our own. Even the beginnings of the human race " seem to need the doctrine of angels." The spiritual in man required for its development spiritual stimulation by a more powerful spirit outside. As this could not be mediated through men, " the beginning of human development points to the fact that our race is not a self-enclosed and self-sufficient totality, but remains a place where the ring of our species expects to be penetrated by that of another." In this other we recognise the biblical angels, who in many different ways serve the divine impartation to the world. Dorner tried to represent angels, if not as non-corporeal, at least as unrestricted by space and unburdened by matter. And he thought that the doctrine of angels brings before us " the wealth of the spirit in the most manifold forms," the possibility of unsinful development and a cheerful fulfilment of the divine will, and finally the already present reality of the Church triumphant.

The matter took a more original and bolder turn, with some instructive points, in Dorner's Danish friend, Hans Lassen Martensen (*Chr. Dogm.*, 1856, p. 118 f.). As he saw it, the angels are one of the presuppositions of human existence. They are pure spirits, not bound to bodies or the conditions of space, but also not subject to space. " An angel cannot become old." It cannot have a history in the sense of development, progress and maturity. The home of angels is the intelligible heaven, and from here they come into the world of men, as spirits of light working for the furtherance of the kingdom of God on earth. And now Martensen ventures the astonishing statement—a genuine Columbus' egg, far more tempting than anything which has preceded—that when we think of the world of angels we cannot avoid thinking of that of ideas. Does not the description of angels in the Bible and Church doctrine tally fairly exactly with these mediatorial beings between God and the real world, these bearers of light, which bring to man the message of God ? Angels are ideas, not as they appear to abstract thought, but " as they are seen as living powers and active spirits." That is why they are called by Paul " principalities and powers," " forces which rule in certain circles of the divine providence, dominions to which different regions of creation are subject." Furthermore, " when we think of angels under this aspect, we have to think of what mythology calls gods. What philosophy calls ideas and mythology gods, revelation calls angels," namely, to the extent that they are active for the kingdom of God. Martensen favours the LXX text of Deut. 32[8] (as in the Zurich Bible) : " When the most High divided to the nations their inheritance, when he separated the sons of Adam, he set the bounds of the people according to the number of the angels. But the Lord's portion is his people ; Jacob is the lot of his inheritance." Thus in distinction from Israel with whom He came to dwell in person, God set angels, finite mediators, subordinate deities, over the nations of the Gentiles. It was His goodness, His revelation, that even the Gentiles should not be left destitute of ideas, even though they did not know the one to whom the world of ideas belongs. Their mythical deities are in truth the ministering spirits of providence, the angels of God. Confused with God, and turning man away from the true God, they are of course idols or demons. But at all events they are powers or forces—whether as angels or demons depends on their attitude to the kingdom of God. And even in paganism we always have to do with both. Have angels as understood in this way personalities ? No unequivocal answer can be given to this question. There are impersonal, semi-personal and personal spirits of this kind, and according to Martensen this is what is meant when the older doctrine maintains that there are different grades and classes of angels. In the winds and flames of fire which execute the will of the Lord according to Ps. 104[4], and in the angel which according to Jn. 5[4] stirred the water in the pool of Bethesda, we obviously have to recognise " personified forces of nature." The national spirits and mythical deities are to be construed as " beings half-way between personification and personality." In addition there is a third class of cosmic powers which constitute a free and personal kingdom of spirits. In relation to men angels have both advantages and disadvantages. Their chief advantage is that they are more powerful spirits. But men are richer. " The angel in all his power expresses only one side of what man in the inwardness of his soul and wealth of his individuality is to comprehend in microcosmic totality." Angels are spirits, but they are not souls ; they are not points of unity between spirit and nature. They can participate only in the majesty of God. They cannot be genuinely united with God as man can—Jesus in the incarnation and Christians in the sacrament. " This superiority of men to angels is expressed by Scripture in the fact that the Son of God did not become an angel but a man." Do we still have to reckon with the reality of angels to-day ? Certainly, for angels continue to be active throughout history. And if belief in angels is muffled in these days, in current ideas about " powers of cosmic life " we have a point of contact for this faith. It is only a matter of understanding these ideas " in a sacred sense." Once they are stated in the light of the Christian doctrine of providence, " we enter the sphere of belief in angels." Have not " national angels been active in the introduction of Christianity " ? Are not the ideas under whose dominion the nations are naturally set the natural points of transition for holy things, and have they not conditioned and determined the distinctive appropriation of Christianity by these nations ?

And now the remarkable fact may be noted that in the extra-biblical demonstration of angels two well-known modern theologians are met who are very different from each other and whom one would hardly expect to come across in this field. Yet there is nothing fundamentally new or clearer in what they say.

The first is none other than Adolf Schlatter (*Das chr. Dogma²*, 1923, p. 85 f.), whose view has also been adopted by Paul Althaus (*Die christliche Wahrheit²*, 1949, Vol. II, p. 69). We seem to be back in the world of Reinhard and Bretschneider when he tells us that for those who speak to us in Scripture man did not stand at the head of creation, " but that they saw above him a multiple kingdom of spirits. Confirmation is to be found in the fact that a sober self-evaluation forbids us to think of ourselves as the supreme and final product of God's creative activity." There are many things below us. " Then we come with the narrow limitation of our spirituality—and surely it cannot be that there is nothing above us." It cannot be said that in our world-view with its infinite space filled with the elements and forces of nature there is no room for anything beyond us. " In truth our natural view makes the thought of angels even more indispensable. Can it be that in this infinity of spaces and powers there is no other life but that of beasts and men, or that the power of the world-basis which fashions persons is exhausted in the formation of the intellect which we have ? " Since God has created space and localised all things in it, since He has thus a positive relationship to space, why should there not be for angels too a positive relationship to space ? " Our incapacity to think of any other relationship to space than that which we men have is subjectively grounded ; it arises through the limitation of our thinking by our being."

Pointing unmistakeably in the same direction, but more enigmatically and in the style of the postulates of an angelology of the beginning of the 19th century, Ernst Troeltsch (*Glaubenslehre*, 1925, p. 255 f.) asked whether the cosmic purpose of salvation or ethical communion with God which is accepted by faith can be regarded as the only cosmic purpose. That this is " absolutely impossible for the lower spiritual " creation has become all the more certain with the extension of our knowledge of the greatness of the universe. And on the same basis it has become continually more impossible to maintain that man and his salvation are the centre of faith in the divine government of the world. What then ? A first point is that there must be a purpose of the lower spiritual creation in the revelation of divine power and the outliving of its vital impulse which can be conjoined with the supreme purpose of spirit only as its preliminary stage and presupposition. And a second is that " there must be a plurality of spiritual realms beside man." There must—this is the view which we meet in almost all these angelologies. Yet it was a more respectable and better founded " must " that we found in Richard Rothe. Rothe did at least know what he was saying and could explain what he meant when he spoke of his kingdoms of spirits, whereas Troeltsch simply tossed off the term and was quite unable to say what he understood by it. Rothe did at least consult the Bible and early Church doctrine before he proceeded to his really Gnostic speculation, whereas Troeltsch does not give a moment's thought to either. At this point the dogmatics of Troeltsch is formally the nadir of the Neo-Protestant development which commenced at the beginning of the 18th century.

Everywhere, in Troeltsch no less than a serious theologian like A. Schlatter, we meet that " must." What is it that " must " be ? The angels as inhabitants of the other heavenly bodies (Reinhard). The angels as moral and spiritual individuals in the invisible kingdom of reason within the universe (Bretschneider). The angels as the spirits of preceding spheres of creation perfected after undergoing a kind of angelic course (Rothe). The angels as stimulators of spiritual life at the beginning of the human race (Dorner). The angels as identical with intellectual forces and mythical deities (Martensen). The angels as supreme and final products of the creative activity of God (Schlatter). And finally, if the unexplained reference is really to angels, the angels as the members of a " plurality of spiritual realms " (Troeltsch). In each case everything depends upon the great assertion that there must be such things. *Quamvis suaderi potest rationibus probabilibus*, maintained J. W. Baier in 1685. And here in the bright light of the 18th, the 19th and even the 20th centuries we are given *rationes probabiles* for the existence of angels which do not derive from Holy Scripture. Do I need to prove that it was all a mere groping in the dark, and that only the hazy pictures of a scattered and uncertain knowledge, only artificialities and platitudes, can result when the attempt is made, as in the case of angels, to learn from other sources as well as from the Bible ? Everything leads into the void, and by comparison the doctrine of angels taught by Thomas appears respectable. Is it not plain that at this point philosophy has been corrupted by theology, not to speak of the corruption of theology by philosophy? But this brings us already to the fifth and final point in our introduction.

5. We have only to add that if we keep to the rule stated and emphasised in 3 and 4 we need not be anxious concerning the knowledge required in 2, whether in respect of the possibility or the correctness and importance of a theological knowledge of the reality of angels. Theology has only to be theology at this point too. It has only to be on its guard against unwittingly becoming philosophy. It has only to accept the discipline of being wholly and exclusively theology. It has only to refrain from seeking *rationes probabiles*, from also trying to be a little philosophy, whether on hermeneutical or apologetic grounds. If it does this, it cannot be lacking in a concrete objectivity of theme. And in some degree, and in a way which is basically worthy, it will do justice to it. And the theme itself will be sufficiently important to claim it seriously and profitably. Holy Scripture gives us quite enough to think of regarding angels. And it is something positive. We have only to consider what it says in its distinctiveness, and to try to assess it without pre-judgment. Nor does it do so in such a way that we can quickly leave the problem on the pretext that it is merely peripheral. If we wholeheartedly accept angels in the position and role assigned to them in the Bible, in their own place and way they make themselves so important that we can no longer ignore them when we consider the centre and substance of the biblical message. Again, the Bible is not so obscure in respect of angels that we cannot responsibly draw out certain notions and concepts which are quite adequate for a Christian understanding. All that is required is a firm resolve that the Bible should be allowed both to speak for itself in this matter, i.e., in the course of its message, as a witness of what it understands by the revelation and work of God, and also to be very impressively, and in its own way very eloquently, silent.

For example, we must not take offence or stop short at the fact, as already indicated, that there are undoubtedly passages introducing angels which are saga or legend or poetry. On the contrary, we have to see and understand that this is of a piece with the matter, with the nature of angels in the biblical sense of the term.

Again, we need not be surprised that in a whole series of points which arouse particular interest, and in which it has been promptly and fully augmented, the biblical doctrine of angels gives us no information whatever. It tells us nothing, for example, about the much ventilated question of the " nature " of angels, whether they are persons, or what is their relationship to the physical world and to space, their number and order, their creation, their original unity, their ensuing division into angels and demons, and many other things which later there was both the desire and a supposed ability to know. Is it not supremely instructive to start from the fact as from a very eloquent circumstance that in the Bible itself nothing is to be known about these matters? Is not positive light shed by the fact that certain questions in respect of the existence and history of angels which may seem very pressing to us are not to be put if angels are rightly understood?

Again, we must not be misled by the fact that in the Bible, as there is no independent doctrine of God or man, so there is no independent doctrine, i.e., no independent definition, depiction or account of angels, and that this is particularly true in the case of angels because in the sense in which they are introduced in the Bible it is obviously essential to them to be only in the movement from God to man, i.e., only in the history between these two factors which are not dogmatically rigid, existing as it were incidentally beside them, or rather in their common history, the history of the divine covenant of grace. Hence they cannot be regarded as independent objects, nor constitute an independent theme. That this is the case does not mean that we cannot have any true knowledge of them, but that we know that in a sense yet to be determined they exist in this way, in this relation, and in this way are to be apprehended as an object of knowledge and teaching. The angels cannot conduct themselves in accordance with what may be desired of them for the purpose of an orderly angelology, but to be genuinely orderly an angelology must keep to the angels as they encounter us in the Bible, whether they fit in easily with our theories or not.

Again, when we have grasped the fact that in the Bible the angels exist only incidentally with God and man in the history between them attested by Scripture, the further question arises what we are to make of them, what significance they have for us, whether, and in what sense for our understanding of the Word of God as it comes to us and for our faith, they have a bearing on our world and our view of the world, and may thus be a practical, significant and determinative factor in relation to our existence and the greater and lesser happenings in our age and environment. On this point it is to be noted that the history between God and man as attested in the Bible is the Word of God here and to-day in our world and time and environment; that the point at issue in Christian faith is that we should have a part and in some sense find ourselves caught up into this history; and that what counts in Christian preaching is that this history is the centre, mystery and meaning of all that happens on earth. If, then, the angels belong incidentally but genuinely to this history; if they are not really general elements in the world; if they cannot be separated from the concrete event of Christ as attested in the Bible; if for all that they are incidental they are elements which cannot be overlooked in this happening,

the decisive point of which we have to take account in our doctrine
of angels is that the Word of God by which we take part in this
happening also speaks to us concerning the existence and work of
angels. Thus the real question is not what we can make of angels.
It is whether in our supposed Christian faith and proclamation
we really have to do with the Word of God attested in the Bible if
we can easily ignore angels and regard them as superfluous, or
cheerfully and confidently ask what we are to make of them. In
other words, there may well be given here a *testimonium paupertatis*
in respect of our Christianity and churchmanship. We may be
forced to note that we have not really noted the Word of God as it
is really given. We may have to affirm that we have cause to regard
not the angels, but ourselves with our obviously precarious understanding of the Word of God, as superfluous and in need of correction.
If the existence of angels stands indeed in a once-for-all relationship
with the once-for-all event attested in the Bible, and if we believe
that this once-for-all event has some reference to us, this can only
cause us the more seriously to consider the angels in their distinctive
once-for-allness. Angelology will then have to build not only on the
once-for-allness of God in Jesus Christ but also on the related once-
for-allness of angels, and in this way to prove its truth and relevance.

But all this depends upon whether the condition proposed in 3
and sharpened in 4 is really fulfilled and not allowed to drop. The
Scripture-principle must obtain in all its exclusiveness. Angelology
cannot be confused with a philosophy of angels, nor what the
Bible says about angels interpreted in terms of such a philosophy.
Otherwise we cannot reach the *intelligere* demanded in 2. Instead,
everything becomes uncertain, equivocal, suspect and superfluous.
Imagination is used, and a bad conscience is created by the fact that
the resultant product is undisciplined, ill-defined and basically
unnecessary. Questions are accepted, and answered with notions,
which may be very illuminating for the horizon and taste of one age
but which will arouse the scorn of the next at its sophistries and
metaphysical obscurity. We are then lost in impossible hypotheses
with whose conceptual construction we only advance the more surely
our own scepticism and that of others, the more reflectively and
solemnly we conduct ourselves. We only further the question what
is the point of it all and what is to be made of it, if we do not begin with
a genuinely necessary " must," with the vitally important material
offered by the Word of God, but begin instead with the " must "
of an arbitrary postulate, and then look for reasons to show that this
postulate—assuming a corresponding reality—is vitally important.
What can be built by hands can be destroyed by hands. Behind this
kind of " must " there lurks near or far the " must not " which at
some point and in some way will revolt against it. If angelology
ignores the conditions of 3 and 4 it hastens to the point where one

day it will become the angelology of the weary shrug of the shoulders. If in this matter we desire or do anything but the one thing demanded in theology, sooner or later we shall prefer not to desire anything more, not to put any more questions or to desire any more answers, and therefore to abandon the task of *intelligere* with a tired sigh. We may do this. Indeed we must. But if we do we must not imagine that it corresponds to or is required by the matter. It simply rests upon the fact that we have not allowed ourselves to be warned and kept to the matter itself.

We may fitly conclude this introduction with a little warning picture of this angelology of the shrug of the shoulders.

"Heaven may be left to angels and sparrows," was how Heinrich Heine once put it. Theologians may have something similar in view, but they do not usually express themselves so crudely. Yet D. F. Strauss (*Die chr. Glaubenslehre*, Vol. I, 1840, p. 670 f.) is almost as frank. When humanity "freed itself from the Middle Ages, and laid hold of the principle of the modern world in its different relationships, the notion of angels which had flourished on very different soil was bound to wither on this alien territory." We now trace back occurrence as a whole and not its individual parts to the divine causality, and have thus no further use for a particular activity of angels in the world. "The Copernican view of the world has robbed us of the place which Jewish and Christian antiquity thought of as the throne of God surrounded by the angels. For us the suprasensual world is not beyond and above but in the sensual. We immediately treat that which is not yet explained on the assumption that it will yield to explanation by natural causes. Hence we not only cannot accept the possibility of such beings as angels, but we cannot even leave the question undecided. If the modern idea of God and conception of the world are right, there cannot possibly be beings of this kind." And "these basic notions of the modern age as fashioned by our increasing knowledge of nature undoubtedly rest on better grounds than the Church's belief in angels, the primary source of which is simply popular thinking and saga which Jesus and the men of the New Testament undoubtedly shared in all seriousness and which we must leave to them, but by which we must not be bound, as they themselves never thought of taking our views from us." This is clear speaking. It has all the clarity of a man who thinks with axiomatic certainty upon the basis of what he takes to be the only possible picture of the world and who can speak for believers in this view (his " we ") with genuinely apostolic authority, but who finds it impossible to give an unprejudiced account of the meaning and importance of the biblical message, and in this context of the biblical meaning of this particular matter. We have only to compare D. F. Strauss with Thomas or R. Rothe to see the common source which in his case could give rise to such an expressive shrug of the shoulders.

Other theologians were more reserved. This is especially true of Schleiermacher, whose famous two theses concerning angels (*D. chr. Glaube* § 42 and 43) are very typical. The first of these is as follows : " Since this conception native to the Old Testament has passed over into the New, and on the one side neither contains anything impossible nor contradicts the basis of all God-fearing consciousness, but on the other is never brought into the circle of true Christian doctrine, it can be present in the language of Christianity without imposing any necessary affirmations concerning its reality." And the second : " The only thing which can be represented as a doctrine of angels is that whether angels exist can have no influence on our conduct, and that no further revelations of their being are to be expected." G. Spinner (*op. cit.*, p. 276) has summed this up in the formula : " The reality of angels is questionable ; their influence none ;

their revelations to us none." And he adds : " We shudder at the empty spaces which open up at this point." For Schleiermacher himself these empty spaces were filled by a reference to the private and liturgical use which we still accord to the idea. On this point he made the following statement in the first edition of his work (Vol. I, p. 218) : " The private use is limited in the first instance to a materialising of the divine protection in circumstances where there is no scope for dutiful activity and concern. The liturgical—which each can of course make his own in the free place of his religious impulses—consists supremely in the fact that God is to be represented as surrounded by pure and infinite spirits."

There were many who followed Schleiermacher in the view that the doctrine is neither established nor relevant. We may refer to W. M. L. de Wette (*Lehrb. der chr. Dogm.*, Part II, 1821, p. 89) : " This doctrine, which derives from pious yearnings and symbolic imaginations, is enriched by an alien mythological metaphysics and has been falsely introduced into the sphere of Christian dogmatics, has only doubtful value as a subject of conviction," while " the doctrine of bad angels is to be totally rejected, since the idea of a purely bad spirit is quite impossible."

We may refer to R. A. Lipsius (*Lehrb. d. ev. prot. Dogm.*[2], 1879, p. 418 f.) : " The notions of angels and devils are quite impossible for scientific thought, but may be used in the symbolic speech of religion so long as we take care to see that they are of no practical significance for the religious relationship itself, and are thus never invested with dogmatic importance." To ban them even from the speech of religion Lipsius regards as misplaced pedantry in view of the symbolic nature of this speech. " The only thing is that they are to be used in this field in keeping with a purified dogmatics, as transparent symbols and not as metaphysical truths."

We may refer to Julius Kaftan (*Dogm.*[3-4], 1901, p. 268) : " Angels are not an object of faith, for this is true only of God in His revelation. Consequently they are not an object of the knowledge and doctrine of faith." But does the postulation of angels help to make more conceivable the divine providence ruling in the world ? Even this is not the case : " The secret of the divine rule is not lessened by such a doctrine. And for this reason dogmatics has nothing to say concerning angels." This is not meant as a denial of the existence of angels. " On the basis of Scripture it will still be a pious opinion that there are such creatures as angels. And there is nothing to disprove this." Kaftan has no objection to the postulation of spiritual beings on a level above that of man, but a doctrine of angels cannot be built upon this assumption. " This mention of the topic is quite enough in dogmatics, so long as we make it clear that our relationship with God is not in any case mediated by angels, and that the doctrine of angels becomes a dangerous error if deductions of this kind are drawn from it."

We may refer to Otto Kirn (*Grundr. d. ev. Dogm.*[8], 1930, p. 72). He sees no possibility of giving to the idea of angels the certainty and clarity which can be guaranteed only by a connexion with the central Christian experience of salvation. This connexion cannot be ascribed to the " notion of superhuman servants of God." This notion does not belong to the essential content of the revelation of salvation itself. But Kirn does not want it excluded from the speech of religious contemplation. Its use is to be left to religious taste, particular care being taken " that it never encroaches on the direct relationship between God and man."

We may refer to T. Haering (*Der chr. Glaube*, 1906, p. 261 f.) Angels are not an object of pious experience like sin and grace. Angelic manifestations are not necessary to the Christian. The belief of Jesus in angels is not bound up with the innermost core of His self-consciousness, His filial belief. Have we then to recognise the authority of Jesus in matters which are not indissolubly connected with the heart of the Gospel ? We cannot use the belief in angels as a necessary element in saving faith, or regard it as the measure of a particularly strong faith.

Yet some value may with a good conscience be ascribed to it as a living representation of inexpressible truths which are in themselves independent of it, and particularly as a representation of divine help through means as yet unknown to us.

We may refer to F. A. B. Nitzsch (*Lehrb. d. ev. Dogm.*, 1889, ed. Horst Stephan, 1912, p. 443 f.). What Scripture tells us concerning angels does not constitute an adequate basis for a connected doctrine. If it cannot be said that the reality of angels is impossible, there can be no proof of it. There are no historically demonstrable facts to compel belief in the existence of angelic beings. The idea of angels may well have been no more than a passing notion of Judaism and early Christianity. Nor is the suggestion to be dismissed that Jesus linked the proclamation of the infallible truth which belongs to His calling with national concepts which do not themselves form any part of objective truth. Still, the doctrine of angels can be highly estimated, whether in its connexion with the idea of the glory of God or as a means of stimulating faith in divine providence. " The idea of angels maintains this significance even when no real existence can be ascribed to them. For even a poem can serve to embody and present objective truths."

We may refer to Reinhold Seeberg (for forty years the head of the modern positive school, *Christl. Dogm.*, Vol. II, 1925, p. 91). The idea of angels comes from the Israelite view of things, and is taken over by the men of the New Testament. But since they have no significance beyond the divine rule, they do not belong to Christian dogmatics. On the other hand, the notion is not in any sense dangerous for Christian piety if understood in its biblical sense. Thus there is no reason to contest it. " But a doctrine of angels cannot possibly be regarded as one of the tasks of dogmatics."

And we may refer to Horst Stephan, who echoes the same views in his *Glaubenslehre*, 1928, p. 125 f. The idea of angels is inherited from pre-Christian religion. If the older dogmatics developed a doctrine of angels, " in so doing it did not obey its knowledge of faith but its external biblicism. For this reason it may be left out of account." This is not meant to be a verdict on the existence of angels. But Christian piety has no need of the idea. " The proximity of God is so vital through Jesus and the community, and the modern picture of the universe with its infinity and severity has so transcended all geo- and anthropocentrism, that pre-Christian means are no longer necessary to represent it."

The consensus of all these modern dogmaticians, both among themselves and with their master Schleiermacher, is overwhelming. But in theology there can be agreement even in aberration. And this is what has happened in the present instance. For in what consists the general consensus of opinion at this point ?

First, it obviously consists in a definite negation. These modern thinkers are not prepared to take angels seriously. It does not give them the slightest joy to think of them. They are plainly rather peevish and impatient at having to handle the subject. And if we are told in Hebrews 13[2] not to be neglectful of hospitality, since some have entertained angels unawares, these theologians are almost anxiously concerned to refuse the angels a lodging in their dogmatics, and think that all things considered they should warn others against extending hospitality to them. They are obviously of the opinion that they have never had any dealings with angels. At any rate, they show themselves quite determined to direct the attention of Christianity as far as possible away from them.

What is the reason for this negative attitude ? Here, too, they are agreed. Angels are dispensable and superfluous for the religious relationship, for faith, i.e., saving faith. The Christian has to do with God alone, with the will and presence of God. What, then, is the point of angels ? We cannot believe in them as we do in God. They cannot even be an object of our pious experience, nor can it be maintained that they stand in any necessary connexion with this.

In deed, it is to be feared that if their existence is accepted they will be venerated and even worshipped, and that they will prejudice the immediate relationship to God in other respects as well. It is for this reason that they cannot be " invested with dogmatic importance." In a serious undertaking like a doctrine of faith, they are unworthy of any positive consideration, discussion and presentation. Thus the door is shut against them, and they remain without.

But no, the door is not completely shut. With common consent, something else is said. All these dogmaticians agree in some sense that they are not denying the existence of angels. Nor do they ever speak of them with the negativity of Strauss or the mockery of Heine. There is no reason to contest their existence (Seeberg). Even the formulation of de Wette is regarded by some as rather too severe. Angels are not desired in dogmatics. But a kind of internment camp (or is it a nursery?) is opened for them in which they are tolerated. They are allowed to stay for the present as objects of pious opinion, as elements in the symbolic speech of religion, as symbolic representations. On the assumption that tact will be exercised by those who receive them, they are accepted as visitors if not as residents. Not without some shaking of the head, a certain value is ascribed to them, just as Schleiermacher himself had given them free scope in the sphere of private and liturgical usage.

The fact that there is this consistent unity is striking and gives rise to questions. If these dogmaticians were putting the question of truth ; if in their own way, by the analysis of the religious consciousness or faith, they came to the conclusion that angels are not to be accepted and that there is no serious place for them ; if they were sure of themselves, why did they not, as responsible teachers of the Church, maintain that even pious opinions and the symbolic speech of religion should not cling to the assertion of angels, but that this superfluous element ought to be banished even from liturgies and hymn-books and the quiet chamber of the private religious life ? This is what the Reformation did in relation to Mary and the saints and purgatory once it was seen that these were elements which were not true according to the Word of God and were thus necessarily alien to faith established upon this Word. When the length is reached of seeing that something is erroneous, in no serious period in the Church's history has it then been described as valuable and left to religious taste ; it has been called an error and rejected and no longer practised even as a transparent symbol. Following his own critical canon, i.e., the modern view of the universe, D. F. Strauss drew this conclusion in respect of angels. Why, then, did not modern Liberals and Ritschlians draw it ? Why did they not simply deny the existence of angels, and declare all further references to them to be unlawful superstitions ? Why were they not purists in this matter ?

It would be excellent if we could explain it as follows. They were prevented by a serious theological reason, by their relationship to the source and norm of all theological knowledge. The Bible always stood in their way. They had not been able to dismiss it. They could not follow its own interpretation of angels. They could not deduce from it with certainty how it stands with angels. They could not see from the Bible what angels really have to do with God's revelation and faith in it. And therefore, in order not to say what they could not say responsibly, they preferred to be silent concerning them, and to leave undiscussed the *locus De angelis*. But again they were not so sure of their knowledge in this respect as to be able to say with a good conscience that the Bible leads us to a negative decision, that there is nothing in the matter at all. They were not so sure as to feel capable of a direct denial and a general cleansing of the temple. Hence they did not deny the existence of angels like Strauss because they did not find in the Bible a final negative. And they were so reserved and patient in respect of the private and liturgical use of the idea of angels because they did not wish to forestall a final positive which might be reached on the basis of the Bible. It would be excellent if we could interpret in this way the restraint and mildness which we see exercised by these theologians in contrast to their basic attitude.

But unfortunately this interpretation is not possible. They are quite clear as to the negative result of their conception of the biblical testimony. They are all agreed that the biblical doctrine of angels belongs to the Old Testament or more generally to pre-Christian religion. They are all agreed that it is an idea of the time which stands on or beyond the margin of the biblical witness to revelation. From their understanding of the Bible they can understand its doctrine of angels only as a representation, historically transparent to us, of truths in respect of the divine providence etc. which are quite independent of the existence and work of angels. What they find in the Bible is once and for all the revelation with which angels have basically nothing to do and the faith for which angels are strictly superfluous. Hence Haering is quite certain that belief in angels does not belong to the inner core of the self-consciousness of Jesus. None of these thinkers is really prevented from dismissing angels just as energetically as Strauss did on his basis, and from drawing the practical deductions from this dismissal. Indeed, they really ought to have done so on the basis of their understanding of the Bible.

But the revolution which they underwent was not so deep, nor the question of truth so urgent, as to force them to do so. The power of the negation was not by a long way so great as that of the Reformation in relation to Mary, the saints and purgatory. It was great enough only to make them very definitely refuse to invest the idea of angels with dogmatic importance. Yet the fact that it was not greater has nothing whatever to do with their understanding of the Bible, the question of truth raised by it, the *docta ignorantia* possibly imposed, or openness to a final word still to be spoken. The painful thing about the position of these modern theologians is that in each of them one can fairly easily lay one's finger on the point where there was restraint from a very different quarter, and consideration was given to the possibilities of a non-biblical and speculative demonstration of faith in a spirit-world as more or less impressively exploited by Bretschneider, Rothe and Dorner, Schlatter and Troeltsch. The thinkers to whom we refer could not accept ideas and constructions of this kind. They did not find them convincing. Yet the fact remains that they were illumined by these conceptions, even to the point of a certain coquetry with them on the part of more than one of those mentioned. If the spirit-world could not be proved ; if it could not be seen what significance it might have for the religious relationship and faith ; if nothing could be erected on such hypotheses any more than on the biblical doctrine of angels, their possibility could not be flatly denied. *Hinc illae lacrymae*—hence the mildness and restraint ! There was no doubt as to the understanding of the Bible. On this side the verdict was negative. The decision did not rest on the authority of the Word of God and it was not therefore so categorical as to involve an absolutely unconditional No, but it had at any rate been taken. There could thus be no restraint from this angle. In respect of the general possibility, however, the matter was not quite so simple. Perhaps from this standpoint there was something in it after all. Who could tell ? Who could really deny it ? This is what constituted the barrier. They were not prepared for exclusion on this side. They had no confidence in the possibility and did not use it, but they could not reject it altogether as a possibility. And it was this possibility which dictated the ultimate ambivalence. It was this which separated them from Heine and Strauss, with whom they ought to have been at one in substance if not in basis and tone. Their understanding of the Bible would never have prevented this agreement, but it was prevented by the consideration that a philosophical demonstration of the doctrine of angels was not perhaps wholly out of the question.

The painfulness of the whole situation is obvious. We might have had confidence in the theological seriousness of these dogmaticians if their understanding of Scripture had led them either to a strict and full rejection of the doctrine of angels, or if it had led them to an acknowledgment not merely of their inability to make anything of the doctrine but also of their inability to oppose to it a simple negation in theory and practice. A *Non liquet* of this kind might well have been a theological decision which is formally at least in order. And I do not wish to be so unjust as to question that this was perhaps the true opinion of at least some of those mentioned. But what in fact they all did in concert is quite impossible. If they were as sure as they made themselves out to be of their understanding of Scripture in the matter, they ought not to have been prevented from carrying through to the last the full negation which they obviously had in view. Or, on the other hand, they ought not to have refrained from showing from Scripture why they could not do this and restraint and mildness were demanded. Yet even as and although they appealed to Scripture, they allowed themselves to be halted, not by Scripture, but on the ground of the consideration that there might be something about this spirit-world which others if not they themselves thought they knew quite apart from Scripture. It was this possibility which arrested them. Hence the fact of the matter is that the poor angels, excluded from dogmatics yet not contested, denied or abolished, owe their shadowy existence, like that of the dead in Hades, to the circumstance that these dogmaticians will not close if they do not open the door to a philosophy of angels, but out of a final respect for this possibility (not for the Bible) try to leave it on the latch. We hardly dare contemplate what they themselves think of these dealings with them in the studies of theologians. No, this *Non liquet* was and is profoundly unsatisfactory.

This, then, is the angelology of the shrug of the shoulders, the weary sigh, which is the necessary consequence when an attempt is made in this matter to do something other than that which is alone possible in theology. Now that we have tasted this cup, and considered this limit of angelology, we can turn to the matter itself.

2. THE KINGDOM OF HEAVEN

The dialectic of the concepts God and man, or rather the real dialectic of the factors denoted by these concepts, has in the thought and speech of the biblical witnesses to revelation its exact correspondence in the dialectic of the concepts, or again in the real dialectic of the circles of being denoted by the concepts, of heaven and earth. What the biblical witness says concerning angels, and what the angels are and signify in the context of the work and revelation of God, can be understood only if we are open, and remain open, to this twofold dialectic. If we insist that theology is exclusively and abstractly a matter of God and man, or, in other theological schemes, of God alone or man alone, then obviously there will be no place for, or understanding of, angels. But obviously, too, we shall not be dealing with the work and revelation of God as attested in the Bible, with Jesus Christ, and therefore with God and man in the form in which they are normative for the Christian Church and its faith and proclamation. For where it is a matter of God and man in this normative form, in the sense of the biblical concepts of these two factors, it is always a matter of heaven and earth. And the converse is also true—that where it is a matter of heaven and earth, it is also, and decisively, a matter of God and man. But this follows from the former truth. Its validity is secondary. Hence it does not need to be emphasised in the present context. The first truth is what calls for emphasis. To say God in the biblical sense and therefore with a responsible Christian understanding is also to say heaven ; and to say man in the same sense and with the same understanding is also to say earth. Hence if we are to speak of God and man in this sense and with this understanding, if we are to say something theologically relevant, we must remember that explicitly or implicitly we have also to speak of heaven and earth. If we think in this twofold dialectic, we are necessarily led to the concept of angels appropriate to the context of the biblical witness and therefore true in the Christian sense. For in the relationship first between God and heaven, then between heaven and earth, and then and decisively between God and man, the angels have their specific place. In the history of angelology many devious and erroneous paths, much confusing play with alien presuppositions, much wasted effort in blind alleys, and above all the angelology of the shrug of the shoulders, might well have been avoided if there had been a fundamental realisation of this fact and further thinking had been based upon it.

It is self-evident, but we must begin with the assertion that in this twofold dialectic—it is a genuine dialectic which cannot be resolved—we are not dealing with two equal terms. Our present interest in this assertion is that God and heaven are naturally not identical or of equal essence. The same cannot be said of man and earth. Jesus Christ is in His own person identical and of one essence with God, but this is not true of anything or anyone apart from Him, not even of heaven. Heaven with earth—and in this sense it is not different from earth—is the creature of God, posited by Him, called into being from nothing by His Word, needing to be sustained by Him, and absolutely subject to His rule. As this is to be said of heaven, it is implicitly said of the angels too. And the decisive negative and positive determination of their existence and being is that they are not God and not divine, but creatures. Heaven is not, therefore, under God as earth is under heaven, but it is under God as earth is under Him. We shall have to speak of a difference between heaven and earth, of a precedence of heaven over earth in their relationship to God. But this difference and precedence are within the radical equality in which they are both the creatures of God. As the bracket which encloses everything else, this must also be said of the angels. There is a correspondence, a similarity, of the relationship between heaven and earth to that between the Creator and the creature. We shall have to speak of this. It gives to heaven and the angels a dignity in relation to earth and to man who is of the earth and on the earth. But this dignity is not to be confused with that of the Creator in relation to the creature. Compared with this it is littleness. And the supreme glory and true honour of the Creator are displayed in the fact that in Jesus Christ He has not taken to Himself heaven and the angels in their majesty but man and the earth. The secret of this glory is so great that in the unity between Him and man in the person of Jesus Christ, and in the promise which this One is for all men, the distinction is not merely removed, but man who is of the earth and on the earth is exalted, not only to heaven and to fellowship with the angels, but above these to fellowship with his Creator. The free, electing grace in which this is the case is the majesty and glory with which God is exalted even above heaven. We must make use of this decisive key of Christian knowledge from the very outset. For we should be merely speculating without rhyme or reason if we tried to measure the majesty of God above heaven and the angels, or the depth of heaven and the angels under God, by anything but the mercy of God which is in Jesus Christ.

The Old Testament does not use the term " world " to denote the sum of the reality distinct from God and posited by Him. It speaks of " heaven and earth," and in this way it describes the world within that twofold dialectic, in the differentiation in which it reflects the distinction between God and man. When the New Testament was written the word " cosmos " had long since come into current usage, but for the most part it follows the Old Testament in speaking of heaven and earth. Thus the Bible as a whole understands the world in the light of its meaning and purpose. Its meaning and purpose is the relationship of God and man. Jesus Christ, in whom both are one, is its goal and its basic order. This basic order is reflected in the fact that it is " heaven and earth." But it is only reflected. Heaven is not God. Heaven did not create earth. But " in the beginning God created the heaven and the earth."

The Old Testament lays emphasis on the fact that Yahweh created heaven too (Ps. 96⁵). " By the word of the Lord were the heavens made ; and all the host of them by the breath of his mouth " (Ps. 33⁶). They are the work of His hands (Ps. 102²⁵) or fingers (Ps. 8³). Thus the perfection of the Almighty is not only deeper than the underworld but higher than the heavens (Job 11⁸). God is exalted above the heavens (Ps. 57⁵). Jesus Christ has ascended above all heavens (Eph. 4¹⁰). Heaven and the heaven of heavens cannot contain God (1 K. 8²⁷). Even the heavens are not pure in His eyes (Job 15¹⁵). Heaven itself is shaken when He acts (Joel 2¹⁰). " The pillars of heaven tremble and are astonished at his reproof " (Job 26¹¹). One day " the host of heaven shall be dissolved, and the heavens shall be rolled together as a scroll : and all their host shall fall down, as the leaf falleth off from the vine, and as a falling fig from the fig tree " (Is. 34⁴). Yes, " the heavens shall vanish away like smoke " (Is. 51⁶). Heaven no less than earth will flee from the presence of God, " and there was found no place for them " (Rev. 20¹¹). It will perish with the earth as it came into being with it (Mk. 13³¹, Rev. 21¹), and God will create both a new earth and a new heaven (Is. 65¹⁷, Rev. 21¹). For this reason it is forbidden to worship it (Deut. 4¹⁹). Even in heaven the pious man can find no consolation but in God Himself (Ps. 73²⁵).

All this refers implicitly and explicitly to the angels too. They are unquestionably κτίσις (Rom. 8³⁹). The θρόνοι, κυριότητες, ἀρχαί and ἐξουσίαι are all created in and by and to Jesus Christ, so that He is before them all and they all consist by Him (Col. 1¹⁵ᶠ·). They are the Old Testament host of heaven to worship which can only mean apostasy and abomination (Deut. 17³, 2 K. 17¹⁶ and *passim*). Hence the scene in Rev. 22⁸ᶠ· between the seer and the heavenly interpreter : " And when I had heard and seen, I fell down to worship before the feet of the angel which shewed me these things. Then said he unto me, See thou do it not : for I am thy fellowservant, and of thy brethren the prophets, and of them which keep the sayings of this book : worship God." Hence the scene in Rev. 4⁹ᶠ·, where the four and twenty πρεσβύτεροι fall down before Him that sits on the throne, and worship Him who lives to all eternity, and cast their crowns before the throne and say : " Thou art worthy, our Lord and God, to receive glory and honour and power : for thou hast created all things, and for thy pleasure they are and were created." Hence the warning in Col. 2¹⁸ against the θρησκεία τῶν ἀγγέλων introduced by those early Gnostic errorists. What are angels before God ? " Behold, he put no trust in his servants ; and his angels he charged with folly " (Job 4¹⁸ cf. 15¹⁵). And in accordance with what we are told concerning heaven, there is no heavenly ἀρχή or ἐξουσία or δύναμις which will not some day be removed and as it were dismissed from service (1 Cor. 15²⁴). Any anxiety lest the existence and study of angels might entail injury to the direct relationship between God and man and man and God, or a jeopardising of the knowledge of the uniqueness of God and respect for it, is quite unfounded. Indeed, it is the very thing which is made impossible by what emerges from the very outset in the witness of Holy Scripture to angels. When we have to do with heaven and therefore with angels, we are wholly within the sphere of the creature.

But what is to be seen and learned concerning heaven and the angels cannot really be reduced with a good conscience to this necessary reservation. If the distinction between heaven and earth is not identical and cannot be equated or confused with the distinction between Creator and creature, or the decisive distinction between God and man, it cannot be seen and understood in abstraction from the latter. Biblical thinking knows also this dimension of heaven and earth. Only as we follow it into this dimension do we come up against the reality to which it refers. And the first point which we have to notice in this connexion is that the created world in its totality (and therefore heaven and earth) corresponds to that for which it was created ; to the encounter, history and fellowship between God and man. In its twofold form it is the home, and recognisable as such, which God chose and willed and posited for this purpose because we were to be called His children. In what does the correspondence consist ? In the fact that here too and already there is an above and below, an earlier and later, a more and less. For the sake of precision, we must add that this is not an absolute antithesis, of which there can be no question. It lies within the relativity appropriate to an intracosmic relationship. But there is a real distinction, and indeed a fundamental and essential distinction, and it consists in the fact that there is in the one cosmos an above and a below, and to that extent an upper and a lower cosmos. And these are heaven and earth. They only reflect, but they do reflect, the true and proper and strict above and below of Creator and creature, of God and man. They attest the manner of this confrontation and conjunction ; the relationship which is at issue in that encounter, history and fellowship and therefore in Jesus Christ ;

the relationship in view and for the sake of which the one whole cosmos is created. They only reflect and attest, but this they do. The heavenly above can no more be effaced than the earthly below. They are both creatures, but they cannot be interchanged or confused. The world would not be the world without this above and below, this earlier and later, this more and less of heaven and earth. This dialectic steadily accompanies that of Creator and creature, of God and man. We do not experience or know the second and decisive dialectic—which is that of the history of the covenant and salvation—apart from the first dialectic grounded in the nature and constitution of the created world. Indeed, the latter is the form in which, noetically and ontically, we participate in the former and decisive. Man is on earth under heaven. In no way and on no pretext can we abstract from the fact that we have the earth to which we belong beneath us and the heaven which is not as such our place above us. That which did and does and will take place between God and man is an event which, willed and accomplished by God and relating to us, is both heavenly and earthly. In this way alone is it an event of revelation and salvation, of which God is the basis and in which we participate. Only in this correspondence does it speak. Only in this mirror can it be apprehended. Only in this witness is it manifest. Only in this likeness does it come from God and apply to us. We cannot try to go behind this likeness to a true reality which can be detached from it. We cannot treat this likeness as a cipher which can be dispensed with once it has been solved. To dismiss the reality of this likeness is to dismiss the reality of the event, its divine origin and human goal. It is the event between heaven and earth, or it is not the event between God and man, the event of Christ. To exclude oneself from the former is to exclude oneself from the latter. And all that is left is a little morality and mysticism, a little psychology or existential philosophy. This can be avoided only if we have an active concern for the realism of Holy Scripture with its basic law that we should give the serious attention which it deserves to the subordinate but indispensable dialectic of the antithesis between heaven and earth in its relationship to that between God and man.

To take up first this question of understanding, why is it that we are compelled to think of heaven as an above and earlier and more, and earth as a below and later and less ? The answer which the Bible gives to this question is simply that within the one cosmos God is nearer to one of the spheres, i.e., heaven, than He is to the other, i.e., earth. It is better not to say that heaven is nearer to God than earth, although this inversion may seem to be both possible and necessary. In the greater nearness of heaven and the lesser nearness of earth it is not a question of qualities proper to heaven and earth as such, but of an action and attitude of God in which He draws and is nearer to heaven than earth. We are thus dealing with a qualification of the two spheres in which they are posited in this distinct relationship to Him and the corresponding relationship to one another. It is for this reason that heaven is superior to earth. It is for this reason that heaven is the upper cosmos and earth the lower ; that heaven is before and more than earth. It is not these things in itself and as the creature of God. But it is made these things by the divine action.

It is always an abstraction to think of God apart from the fact that, as the One from and by whom the creature is, He is also its Lord, Preserver and Ruler, and above all, as the meaning of His lordship, preservation and rule, its Saviour, the God of grace and the covenant. It is in the light of this that we have to understand His action and attitude to the world and therefore to heaven and earth. But if for the sake of conceptual clarity we momentarily allow ourselves this abstraction and therefore do not take into account the history of the Creator with the creature, we can only say that God has not created heaven and earth in this superiority and subordination ; that He has not made heaven the upper and earth the lower cosmos ; that He has not created both creaturely spheres in this qualification and mutual relationship. It is not, therefore, proper to them by nature. It does not belong to their creaturely constitution.

Yet they receive and have it as and because there begins with their creation the history of God with them, the history of His grace and covenant, and therefore the history of His cosmic rule. As this takes place, they receive and have and maintain this qualification. In the biblical view of things, heaven is in every respect the upper cosmos and hierarchically superior to earth as the presupposition of the biblical witness to the revelation and work of God. A theology based on this witness cannot evade the concept of this intracosmic hierarchy. But we have to realise that in accepting this concept we are already thinking in terms of the grace and revelation and work of God. Hence we must not be surprised if thinking which is not cast in these terms stumbles at this concept. And the fact that we are continually inclined to stumble at it makes it clear that it is not at all self-evident that in our own thinking we should really think in these terms. The action and attitude of God to the creature are the basis of this hierarchy. From what is to be said concerning heaven and earth in themselves and as such there does not follow the superiority of heaven to earth as a likeness of that of God to man. If it is this likeness, it is not on the basis and in the power of the nature which it is given at creation. We can say only that in this nature it is destined to become this likeness. But it does become or receive it only on the basis and in the power of the divine action to and in and with the creaturely world.

Concerning heaven itself and its nature a first cautious statement which we can make is that, as earth exists as the sphere of man, heaven also exists, thus constituting the inalienable counterpart of earth. What exists and takes place in our sphere exists and takes place in the presence and with the participation of this other sphere, this counterpart, heaven. It belongs to earth as our sphere to be open to the other. And it belongs to happenings in our sphere to be set against that other sphere and thus to take place in relationship from and to it.

To the outlook of man in the Old and New Testament there belongs the consciousness of existing as an earthly creature in the presence and with the participation of this other sphere. Even apart from his relationship to God this man is not alone. With his cosmos which he can see and in which he is at home he is not alone even apart from God. Another cosmic sphere has also been created by God and is also present in addition to his own. There are celestial as well as terrestrial σώματα, even though the glory of the celestial is one and that of the terrestrial another (1 Cor. 15⁴⁰). There are knees which can bow in heaven as well as on earth (Phil. 2¹⁰). There is a binding and loosing in heaven corresponding to what takes place on earth (Mt. 16¹⁹ and 18¹⁸). There is a connexion, a relationship, a common tie. The prodigal son does not sin only before his father but also against heaven, and he sins against heaven first and only then before his father (Lk. 15¹⁸). Similarly in 2 Chron. 28⁹ we read of a transgression which cries aloud to heaven. As the earth can mourn, heaven too can wrap itself in darkness (Jer. 4²⁸). And heaven no less than earth can rejoice and be glad (Ps. 96¹¹, Is. 49¹³, Rev. 12¹² and *passim*). Together heaven and earth grow old and are renewed. And if in Eph. 1¹⁰ the end of the ways of God is described as the process in which heavenly and earthly reality come to have their Head (ἀνακεφαλαίωσις) in Christ, this is to be understood as a confirmation of their mutual relationship and confrontation as grounded in their creation (Col. 1¹⁶).

A second thing which we may cautiously maintain concerning the nature of heaven is that as this counterpart of earth it is the sum of all that which in creation is unfathomable, distant, alien and mysterious in creation. Earth is the sphere of man ; the sphere of his vision and comprehension ; the sphere of his access and capacity. But this is not true of heaven. Heaven is the boundary which is clearly and distinctly marked off for man. It exists. But in distinction from earth it exists as invisible creaturely reality. It is invisible and therefore incomprehensible and inaccessible, outside the limits of human capacity. If man reaches this frontier even in his own sphere ; if the really invisible or the invisibly real meets him even on earth, this is of a piece with the fact that earth is under heaven, having its counterpart in heaven, and standing in this relationship to it. To the extent that it encounters man on earth, heaven is not to be equated, of course, with the heights and depths and other mysteries of the earthly sphere which have not yet been fathomed but are not basically unfathomable. Obscure, i.e., unexplored parts of the earth are not on this account heaven. The unknown is not as such the unknowable. But the unknowable waits at the limits of the knowable. The definitive and essential mystery of all creaturely being waits at the limits of the provisional. Again there must be no false equation. Even this final mystery is not the mystery of God. But it is the mystery of heaven as the sum of that which is really invisible or invisibly real. The frontier which separates God and creation is thus higher. It embraces both heaven and earth, both the visible and the invisible. But across that which is outside God and has its reality from God there also runs the frontier between the visible and the invisible. And we exist before this frontier as well as that of creation. It is not merely God who is incomprehensible ; the same can also be said of heaven within the creaturely world.

In saying this I have followed in the first instance the Nicene definition (A.D. 325). On the basis of Col. 1¹⁶ this brings together earth and heaven under the phrase πάντα ὁρατά τε καὶ ἀόρατα (*omnia visibilia et invisibilia*), Almighty God being the ποιητής (*factor*) of both. It may well be said that in effect this is in agreement with the biblical definition of their relationship. For biblical man, too, heaven is not merely the supreme but the proper notion of what he does not see and understand ; of the sphere of creation which is basically inaccessible and outside his control, yet not identical with God even in its incommensurability, but created by Him and therefore distinct from Him, even though it represents and reveals the mystery of creation to man as a creature of earth. The only point is that the biblical view is more naive and radical in the sense that when it speaks of heaven it first thinks of the visible (atmospheric or astronomical) heaven, being led from what it sees in these far heights and distances to the reality of the invisible. It is also more naive and radical in the sense that it finds the same invisible and incommensurable no less on earth than in heaven. If heaven above cannot be measured, the same is true of the foundations of the earth (Jer. 31³⁷). " Who hath measured the waters in the hollow of his hand, and meted out heaven with the span ? " But then the verse goes on : " And comprehended the dust of the earth in a measure, and weighed the mountains in scales, and the hills in a balance ? " (Is. 40¹²). And if it is asked in Job 38³¹ᶠ· : " Canst thou bind the sweet influences of Pleiades, or loose the bands of Orion ? Canst thou bring forth Mazzaroth in his season ? or canst thou guide Arcturus with his sons ? Knowest thou the ordinances of heaven ? canst thou set the dominion thereof in the earth ? ", these questions belong to a whole series of similar challenges in respect of the earth and sea and underworld, and later of a list of puzzling animals from the lion and goat to such semi-mythical figures as Behemoth and Leviathan. To climb up or journey to heaven is one impossible venture, and to break through into hell and dwell there another (Deut. 30¹³, Amos 9², Ps. 139⁸). Thus the frontier between the visible and the invisible is not co-extensive in the Bible with the frontier between heaven and earth. For in heaven there is also that which is visible, the sun and moon and stars, the wind and the clouds, and it is in face of these visible things that we are set before the invisible. Similarly, even on earth in the direct sphere of man there are many things which cannot be seen or measured or counted or weighed or reckoned or brought under human apprehension, so that apart from the mystery of God man is continually occupied with that of creation. Yet we cannot fail to see that for the Bible heaven is in this respect, even perhaps as *pars pro toto*, a particular factor in virtue of its particular nature, and stands with its own mystery in some sense at the head of all mysteries. Quite apart from the special relationship of God to heaven, there are passages, constantly recurring from Gen. 1¹ onwards, in which the correlation and distinction of heaven and earth can mean only that the sphere of man is accompanied and preceded by another sphere which is not in any sense his. The folly of men which leads to their dispersal and the confusion of their languages is typically expressed in the fact that according to Gen. 11⁴ they tried to build a tower whose top should reach to heaven. That the excellency of the godless mounts to heaven and his head touches the clouds (Job 20⁶) ; that Babylon mounts up to heaven and fortifies the height of her strength (Jer. 51⁵³) ; that in a dream Nebuchadnezzar sees himself as a tree high in the midst of the earth and growing and becoming strong until its height reaches heaven (Dan. 4⁷ᶠ·) ; that the little horn waxes great even to the host of heaven (Dan. 8¹⁰) ; that the sins of men reach to heaven (Rev. 18⁵)—these are all the extreme limits of pride rising to a supreme height before it falls. In the same way the fact that the godless and corrupt speak loftily is one of the signs that God has set them in slippery places (Ps. 73⁸, ¹⁸). Heaven is the epitome of the limit set for man. And the height of heaven above earth is obviously calculated as such to serve as a likeness of the height of the ways and thoughts of God over those of man (Is. 55⁹), or of the incomprehensibility of His goodness and faithfulness (Ps. 36⁵) or of His grace to those who fear Him (Ps. 103¹¹). Heaven thus seems to be the norm of that which is inconceivable to man.

This is what is to be said concerning the nature and essence of heaven as such, and therefore concerning its ordination to be this likeness. But it can be stated only with great reserve. It is no accident that though the witness of Scripture in respect of the character of heaven as the counterpart of earth, and as the world of the mystery which encounters us, is not obscure or ambiguous, it is certainly sparing. The fact is plain to see that the men of the Bible have no intention of instructing us concerning the nature of heaven, and that they are as little occupied with heaven as such as they are with earth as such. Indeed, it is only in the context of the witness to the divine Word and attitude that heaven emerges with decisive clarity either as that counterpart or as the world of mystery. And in all that we have said on this topic we have been guided from the very first by the fact that the nature of heaven as we have attempted to indicate it can be seen only in the light of the divine action and attitude. This reveals it for what it is, i.e., the mysterious counterpart. That the divine creation is actual in this form, with this duality and crossed through by this frontier, is something which man has to be told by the Creator Himself and His work and revelation. He can recognise it in creation only as he is first told it in this way.

And this is particularly true of the subject of our investigation : of the hierarchy in the relationship of heaven and earth ; of the superiority of the former to the latter ; of the characterisation of heaven as the upper and earth as the lower cosmos. Even if we could assume (as we cannot) that we have behind us a kind of demonstration of the nature of heaven in relation to earth, this would not mean that heaven is above earth or earth below heaven. This involves something more than an assertion of the nature of heaven. It involves a judgment ; the recognition of a dignity, function and significance of heaven in relation to earth. It tells us that God is nearer to heaven than earth. It makes heaven in its relation to earth a likeness of God in His relation to man. It gives it a specific precedence in the history of God's dealings in and with and to the world created by Him. It compels us to bring at once into our thought of God the thought of heaven, and to connect at once the thought of God with that of heaven. But no presentation of the nature of heaven, of that counterpart and mystery, can compel us to do this. The knowledge of the nature of heaven does not include that of its superiority. According to the description of its nature as here attempted, heaven could only be the partner, a duplicate as it were, of earth. There might well be another or many spheres alongside our own, different yet corresponding and interconnected, and yet we are not forced to speak of a hierarchy in which our sphere is necessarily below and the other or others necessarily above. And the limit which has been drawn, the radical separation of that which can be measured and controlled from that which cannot, might well be a very real one, and yet not signify more than that we must quietly venerate what is incommensurable but without being compelled to add to this veneration genuine awe and humility and adoration because in this limit we have a greater proximity to God and in the mystery of creation a likeness to His mystery. Even if the question of superiority and subordination necessarily arises, why should not the converse be true that earth is the first and upper and true cosmos and heaven only a monstrous shadow or reflection of earth, that counterpart and limit being perhaps a determination and the supreme work of the human spirit, an unavoidable idea or a superfluous fiction? No concept of the nature of heaven can exclude this. None can place us under the compelling judgment that in heaven we have to do in a serious and definitive sense with an upper cosmos and in our own sphere with a lower. It would thus be an impossible act of caprice if we were to assume that in our deliberations thus far we have already answered the question before us, demonstrating the hierarchy in which heaven is more than earth.

It may well be that the two statements which we have cautiously advanced with regard to the nature of heaven can receive illumination, concretion and enrichment from certain aspects of the cosmic picture of modern physics on the one side and from an impartial historical appraisal of the so-called magical view of antiquity, the Middle Ages and the early Renaissance on the other. But it would still be the case that the decisive foundation for these statements can only be the theological, and that in themselves these statements do not provide what is needed to make heaven a magnitude which is theologically relevant.

If in this question of the superiority of heaven to earth we are to emerge from obscurity to light, and if we are to set on solid ground that which we have provisionally stated concerning its nature, we must abandon this attempt to consider and define and describe it abstractly, and press on resolutely to survey it in the position and function which it is specifically allotted in the context of the activity of God as the God of grace and the covenant. We took up the attempt only to bring into focus as such the problem of the heavenly, i.e., of that counterpart to our creaturely sphere, of the limit which is set for us by the existence of another creaturely sphere. And we had to do this in order to make it clear that it is not the nature of heaven, so far as we may speak of this, which makes it theologically relevant and gives it that distinctive superiority to our own sphere of existence. To know the latter, we must now speak of what we have already called the qualification which it is given by God. It is this alone which gives heaven the character in virtue of which it is above and before and more than the earth. And it is this alone which unequivocally reveals its nature and makes it the counterpart and limit of the earthly sphere.

We are now at the end and goal and climax of the whole doctrine of creation, and here if anywhere it ought to be evident that the first article of the creed can be understood and explained only in the light of the second, which speaks of the turning of God in His free mercy to the world created by Him ; of the faithfulness of the love in which, when He had created the world, He did not abandon it, but, in accordance with the fact that it is His, willed to be its God and Saviour and as such its Lord ; of His kingdom, the kingdom of His almighty Word and living Spirit, which He causes to come and break into the creaturely world, which He establishes within it, and as the King of which He comes in person to be its Ruler, Helper and Deliverer. It is in this setting that we must understand creation, the Creator and the creature, or we cannot understand at all this whole tract of dogmatics. It is here and here alone that the different views and concepts of this sphere acquire relief and colour and contour. For here it is a matter of the sense in which God is called the Almighty and the Father in the creed. But the same holds good in a very particular way of our enquiry concerning heaven and the angels. By means of certain biblical references or even without them—for God is the Creator of heaven and earth—we can have some idea of what is meant by heaven. We can give the kind of answer already attempted. But we cannot really know at all why the formula and its biblical patterns always speak of heaven and earth rather than earth and heaven. Nor perhaps can we be certain why there is this mention of another sphere than that of earth, or what is involved in this sphere. This is possible only when we see how heaven and earth, in this hierarchical order and in their particularity and differentiation, are implicated in that great movement of God, in His turning in free mercy to the world, in the work of His faithfulness, in the coming of His kingdom, and, as we must also say, in the history of His covenant of grace, which secretly from the very first and publicly in its consummation bears the name of Jesus Christ. If this happening is seen, even in its recapitulation in the second article of the creed, there may be seen in this happening not only creation and the Creator but also the creature and man as God created him (although rather strangely there is no reference to him in the first article of the creed). There may be seen heaven and earth, which in the first article comprehend the whole, in their differentiation, their reality and their obviously irreversible order ; and in and with heaven the angels of heaven. If we are to see all this, we must not fall back into the other and in some sense naturalistic mode of contemplation. Otherwise all that is to be seen in the sphere of the first article will lose its clarity and credibility. We must continue steadily to see everything—the Creator and His work, the creature in general and man in particular, and therefore heaven and earth, and in and with heaven the angels—in this movement and history. When we do this, we can know this whole sphere theologically. In respect of the problems which are our particular concern we shall thus have no need to resort either to philosophy or to mythology, but with a genuine necessity and propriety we may reach certain dogmatic conclusions.

We shall first consider in its most general form the happening between God and the creature which transcends the act of creation. In it we have to do with a movement which has its origin in God and its target and goal in the creature. We may think of it in terms of the content of the second or even the third article of the creed, or more explicitly of the whole history which is partly reported and partly announced in the Bible. We may think in terms of what is envisaged in divine service, in preaching, baptism and the Lord's Supper, as the objective content, as the divine response confirming what is done by man. In the same sense, i.e., in relation to what is done on God's side, we may think in terms of the personal dealings of each individual Christian with God, or of the divine guidance of the Church both as a whole and in detail, or finally of the cosmic rule of God in its most comprehensive sense. But always we have to do with a movement in which God Himself is the *terminus a quo* and the creature the *terminus ad quem*. God speaks and is heard ; He reveals Himself and is known ; He comes and is present ; He goes and comes again ; He acts and effects ; He gives and takes ; He hastens and waits. Christian witness must and will be conscious that, because God Himself is the Subject, the reality behind all these statements, and the many other statements which give them their fulness and content, far surpasses any ideas or concepts which we might link with the terms used. But it must either be silent or become a denial if it refuses to speak in such statements ; if it will not venture affirmations of this kind ; or if it does so otherwise than with reference to the movement really executed by God. The God who did not really execute this movement would not be the living God of Christian witness. And to take up towards this movement an attitude of silence or denial is to do the same to the living God

Himself. In this movement we have to do with a divine will and a divine way. We have to do with a divine intervention and a divine execution. We have to do with something begun and something accomplished. We have to do with a Whence and a Whither. Nor is the movement only in one direction. As God turns to the creature, there is also a turning of the creature to Him, not in its own strength, but in virtue of what God does in and with and to it. Thus, when it reaches its goal, the divine movement returns to its origin. The *resurrexit* follows the *conceptus* and *natus*, the *mortuus* and *sepultus*. An *ascendit* follows the whole *descendit*. The faith, obedience and prayer of the Church and of Christians follow the outpouring of the Holy Spirit. The only thing is that the cycle does not end as it were ; the last word again becomes a first : *unde venturus est*. Remission of sins, the resurrection of the flesh, eternal life, everything which can only be ascribed and given to the creature, which can only come upon it—all this comes as God Himself comes to the creature, speaking and acting, saving and resurrecting, in exclusive omnipotence and glory. The content of Christian witness is this movement. Otherwise it is not Christian witness.

But as the creature, man, is the goal and object of this movement, it is characterised as a movement executed within the creaturely world. God Himself is its Subject and Author. But this could also be said of the movement of intra-divine life of which we have to speak in the doctrine of God's triunity. That God the Father begets the Son and sends the Holy Ghost ; that the Son is begotten of the Father and with Him sends the Holy Ghost ; that the Holy Ghost proceeds from the Father and the Son—this is how we describe the inner life of God, the *opera Dei ad intra*, in which the movement to which we now refer has its basis and model. But this movement is an *opus Dei ad extra*. It is a work in which God does not remain alone, in which He is not alive and active merely in Himself, but in which, as the One He is and will be to all eternity, He enters space and time, and the structure and conditions, and even the perceptibility and conceptuality of the created cosmos distinct from Himself. In His free mercy the One who made us has elected to be our God, God for us and with us. And in the execution of this decision He enters our world and makes its form His own. How else could He be our God, God for us and with us ? How else could that movement of His concern us ? How else could it reach and profit us ? How else could we take part in it ? How else could we be called by it and made responsible, humbled and exalted, judged and blessed ? How else could it be the theme of Christian and therefore a human and creaturely witness ? If it is a reality for us, then irrespective of the fact that God is its Subject and Author it really takes place where we really are, and therefore in our world, in the world created by God. It is here that it has its origin and goal.

It is here that there takes place that *descendit* and *ascendit*, that divine intervention and execution. It is here that the Holy Spirit is outpoured and returns to its origin in the form of the faith, obedience and prayer of the Church and of Christians. The height and depth of the free grace of God is that He has chosen Himself and the created world for the fact that He should be wholly alive and active within it, that He should wholly rule and initiate and fulfil His will within it, that He should speak and cause Himself to be heard within it, that He should promise and perform and plan and execute within it. As He causes His honour to dwell in the world created by Him, this becomes the theatre of His glory. We cannot ignore, deny or restrict this. If we did, we should violate the reality of the movement, its basis in God's free grace, and the living God Himself who is so gracious and who in His grace has such genuine dealings with His creature.

But if we see all this, and therefore see the divine history of the covenant and salvation, the event of Christ, and this as God's action in and with and to us, and therefore as His dealings in our creaturely world, with many other things we also see how the two great cosmic spheres of heaven and earth emerge distinctly and confront one another and then come together again in a genuine hierarchical order. And we see this with a clarity which obviously could not be imparted by even the most profound or exalted knowledge of the nature of the two spheres. It is from God's gracious action in the world, from this movement within it of His turning and faithfulness and kingdom, that we receive this clarity.

We shall take a first glance at earth. What is earth as seen in this historical context ? Our starting-point is that it is the place of the man to whom this divine action refers, and therefore the goal and end of this action. Even though there is a return to its origin, the fact is not abolished but confirmed that earth is first and last the *terminus ad quem* of the divine action. The promise of God refers to man and must be fulfilled in him. The command of God refers to man and must be observed by him. But man is a creature of earth. Therefore it is for the earth's sake that God fulfils the movement to the world created by Him. It is on earth that His faithfulness is to be demonstrated and His kingdom established. For God wills to be for us and with us. We are the target of His whole movement to the creature. And we are of earth and on earth. Hence the divine qualification or distinction of earth consists in the very fact that it is the depth below to which God condescends in free grace ; our sphere to which the God who reigns in the world stoops and comes down—and all this is in order that the secret will of God which was from the very first should have open and effective consequences in what He does here. In this context, therefore, there can be nothing derogatory or disgraceful in the fact that earth is below.

It is not thereby disqualified. Its glory as this particular sphere of God's creation is not contested. It is no less glorious than other real or possible spheres may be in different ways. It is below because the man to whom the free mercy of God is addressed is below. It is below in the light of the majesty of the God who is active for and to man in the world. Since this is what is at issue in the universe, or rather in the divine activity in the universe, what else could it be but the lower cosmos ? It is to this sphere that the Word of the Most High is given. It is to this sphere that the Son of God humbles Himself, being born and obedient and dying on earth, accepting solidarity and unity with the creature of this sphere in order to exalt it in His own person beyond this sphere, drawing all men after Himself. It is in this sphere that the Holy Spirit is outpoured, in order to return to His origin in the form of the faith, obedience and prayer of the Church and Christians. Is it not really a distinction for the earth to be the lower cosmos in this sense and context ? It has at least the advantage over every other created sphere of being the goal of the free grace of God and therefore below.

But our present concern is with heaven. In that historical context, our first statement concerning it is simply that it is the place in the world from which God acts to and for and with man. If the great movement of the living God which is at issue is a movement within the created world, then a place within the world must be allotted to its *terminus a quo*, its origin, no less than to its goal and end. As the One who is at work in the world, God, who is the only Subject and Author of this movement, does not work above the world, but in the world, even in the sense that in fulfilment of His earthward action He occupies another place from which He may really come to man and have real dealings with him. Without this special place of God, and the distance therewith posited between Himself and man in his own place, there could obviously be no genuine intercourse between them. There could be no dialogue, but only a monologue on the part of God (or perhaps of man). There could be no drama, but either God or man could only live in isolation with no relationships to others or significance for them. If this is not the case ; if the theme of Christian witness is neither the life of an isolated God nor isolated man, but the history enacted between them of isolation, estrangement, reconciliation and fellowship ; and if this history is really enacted in our world, then this means that God as well as man has a distinctive sphere in this real world of ours. This distinctive sphere of God is heaven. Self-evidently this does not exclude but includes the fact that as the Creator and Lord of heaven and earth He can also enter and occupy particular spheres on earth which give to that movement its concrete—or, in the narrower sense, historical— forms. But heaven is primarily, originally and properly that which all God's particular spheres on earth become in virtue of the fact that

God comes from it to speak and act on earth. Heaven is the Whence, the starting-point, the gate from which He sallies with all the demonstrations and revelations and words and works of His action on earth. And this is what distinguishes it from earth. This is what makes it genuinely and validly and definitively the upper cosmos in relation to earth. This is what gives it its own distinct and higher nature. God in the omnipotence of His grace is first in heaven to come down from heaven to man and earth. It is from heaven that He speaks and works. It is from heaven that His majesty encounters us. It is from heaven that His mystery limits us. Hence this place, heaven, is before earth and more and higher than earth. The mere fact that it is heaven does not bring this about, making it so superior to earth, and constituting it an exalted mystery for us who are on earth. No, this is due to the fact that it is from heaven that the kingdom of God comes to us, so that as such the coming kingdom of God is also the kingdom of heaven.

We adopt at this point an expression which is dominant in St. Matthew's Gospel and which characterises his theology. Outside the First Gospel there is only one reference (2 Tim. 4[18]) to the βασιλεία ἐπουράνιος of the Lord. In the New Testament the word βασιλεία does not denote the institution or state or sphere but the act and exercise of kingly rule by the being and activity of a royal person. If in Matthew the phrase ἡ βασιλεία τοῦ θεοῦ is usually replaced by ἡ βασιλεία τῶν οὐρανῶν, this certainly does not mean that the existence, action and dignity of God as this royal person are pushed into the background, let alone denied. In Mt. 12[28], and 21[31, 43] there are express references to the kingdom of God, which is also called the kingdom of the Father in Mt. 13[43] and 26[29]. " Thy kingdom come," is also the prayer of Mt. 6[10]. In Matthew, therefore, heaven does not take the place of God. But in the distinctive language of the First Gospel the divine rule is described as a heavenly, so that we are continually invited by these passages to consider that where God rules heaven is also involved. It is to be noted that the Hebraic plural οὐρανοί is always used in this connexion.

In the LXX and the New Testament (I say this on the authority of E. Lohmeyer, *Das Unservater*, 1947, p. 78), the word " heaven " is always in the singular when it is explicitly or implicitly conjoined with earth to describe the totality of creation, whereas the plural is consistently used where it is linked with βασιλεία to denote the sphere and world of God, the reference being to heaven " in the form in which it is dissociated from everything earthly and related to God." If, then, in Mt. 6[9] (as distinct from Lk. 11[2]) God is addressed as " Our Father in the heavens," and if in many other passages in Matthew He bears this name (Mt. 5[16] and *passim*) or the adjectival alternative " heavenly Father " (Mt. 6[14] and *passim*), this serves to emphasise that, apart from His own being as God and Father, God has in the relationship to us men indicated by the word " Father " (as my, our or your Father) the particular nature and essence of heaven. Or rather, His own divine and fatherly essence encounters us men—as though to be both near and distant, both knowable and unsearchable, He had invested Himself with an alien but not inappropriate or unworthy cloak—in the nature and essence of heaven.

In this sense His kingdom, and therefore His action as Ruler in the world which He has created and the covenant which He has instituted, can and must also be called the " kingdom of heaven." The fact that His kingdom has drawn near (Mt. 3^2, 4^{17}, 10^7), i.e., that it has come to earth, to the sphere of men, to us, includes within itself (as it is called the kingdom of heaven) the fact that in and with the being and speech and activity of God on earth, the reality of which is the content of the New Testament kerygma, there have also appeared and are active on earth the created but decidedly supraterrestrial possibilities and illuminations and powers of heaven. The μυστήρια of the kingdom of heaven (Mt. 13^{11}) are naturally the mysteries of God, i.e., the divine orders executed on earth and revealed to some but concealed from others. But how can these be seen by man at all ? The answer is that although they are divine, they are also decidedly supraterrestrial and therefore heavenly, and now that the kingdom of God as the kingdom of heaven is nigh, they are reflected in the natural relationships and processes of earth. Hence the kingdom of God as the kingdom of heaven can be likened to (ὁμοιώθη) or like (ὁμοία) good seed (Mt. 13^{24}), or a grain of mustard seed (Mt. 13^{31}), or leaven (Mt. 13^{33}), or the king (Mt. 18^{23}), or the more than dubious οἰκοδεσπότης (Mt. 20^1), etc., and in this ὁμοιουσία it can be known by those to whom it is given and missed by those to whom it is not, but either way it is in the circle of human vision. As the kingdom of God is known or missed in these parables, heaven is also known or missed. But the converse is also true. As heaven is known or missed, necessarily and *per se* God is also known or missed. To be a scribe instructed in matters of the kingdom of heaven (Mt. 13^{52}), to enter the kingdom of heaven (Mt. 5^{20} and *passim*), to have a share in the kingdom of heaven (" Yours is . . . ," Mt. $5^{3, 10}$, 19^{14}), to sit down to meat in the kingdom of heaven with Abraham, Isaac and Jacob (Mt. 8^{11}), to be the least (Mt. 5^{19}) or great (Mt. 18^1) in the kingdom of heaven, to do violence to the kingdom of heaven (Mt. 11^{12}) or to close it *per nefas* to men (Mt. 23^{13})— all these are expressions in Matthew which have certainly to be understood as metaphors and comparisons, but as such they are to be regarded as of supreme reality, for here the kingdom of God is also called the kingdom of heaven, so that although it is a supraterrestrial it is not a supracosmic but a cosmic kingdom. God Himself undertakes to speak and act and give His help on earth, to be God for and with the man who lives on earth. But in so doing He steps down from the heaven created by Him, and as He does so heaven becomes a plurality of heavens, and He moves from these heavens in the direction of earth. Thus, when His kingdom comes to us, to earth, in this way, as its circumference and in its service, as the cosmic attestation of His distance in our proximity, or of His proximity as the One who is so radically distant from man on earth, there also comes to earth, if not all heaven, at least its essence, something of heaven, something of its cosmic possibilities and illuminations and powers ; and His kingdom on earth acquires the character of the kingdom of heaven. In other words, when this Gospel uses the term " kingdom of heaven " it describes the kingdom of God as a kingdom which, because it is real in the divine, is also real in the cosmic sense, and has really entered the circle of human vision.

It may be responsibly affirmed that in this usage of the First Gospel we already have to do in principle and *in nuce* with the biblical view and doctrine of angels. In this sense the title and theme of this basic sub-section can and must be " The Kingdom of Heaven." But if we are to advance with any degree of certainty, we must examine this initial concept in rather greater detail. We have understood it in the light of the divine action in the world. And conversely we have understood the divine action and therefore the kingdom of God as the kingdom of heaven. Yet the linguistic usage of St. Matthew's Gospel might not seem to afford a sufficient scriptural basis for this interpretation. It is confirmed in substance, however, by the proposition that the royal measures of God as the Lord of earthly history are frequently described in the Old and New Testament as events which proceed from heaven and move earthward with the participation of heaven.

This is first true of all the external and spiritual benefits which God confers on man. A general biblical view and insight is formulated in Jas. 1[17] : " Every good gift and every perfect gift is from above, and cometh down from the Father of lights." The same truth is negatively stated in the saying of John the Baptist in Jn. 3[27] : " A man can receive nothing, except it be given him from heaven." The pious man of later Old Testament days knows that " God hears him from his holy heaven " (Ps. 20[6]). He thus prays that God will send His goodness and truth from heaven to save him " from the reproach of him that would swallow him up " (Ps. 57[3]). A plastic representation of this divine help which comes right down from heaven to human need and folly is to be found in the narrative of Ex. 16[2f.], where God answers the murmuring of the people in the wilderness, and its ridiculous hankering for the fleshpots of Egypt, by causing the bread called " manna " to fall from heaven. It is no accident that this passage is so solemnly taken up and given a new meaning in Jn. 6[30f.]. Similarly, in Deut. 28[12] heaven is the rich chamber opened up by the Lord " to give the rain unto thy land in his season, and to bless all the work of thine hand." The fact that the divine benefits are already fixed and ready as it were in heaven, and have only to come down to the recipient, is also a distinctive New Testament conception, the meaning being that although the men have to receive the divine benefit they are already its lawful possessors and have already tasted the heavenly gift (Heb. 6[4]). It is not the end but the beginning of the apostolic proclamation that God has already blessed us with all spiritual blessings (Eph. 1[3]) and even set us (Eph. 2[6]) ἐν τοῖς ἐπουρανίοις. Disciples who are despised and persecuted and calumniated on earth have in heaven the reward in which they may genuinely rejoice already (Mt. 5[11f.]). They are to heap up to themselves treasures in heaven, in contrast to the ephemeral treasures of earth (Mt. 6[20]). Their names are already written in heaven (Lk. 10[20], Heb. 12[23]). Their reward is reserved and secure for them in heaven (1 Pet. 1[4]). When our earthly tent perishes, we have a building prepared by God in heaven, an eternal house not made with hands (2 Cor. 5[1]), the better country to which men of God have always been on the way in faith (Heb. 11[16]). There in heaven is our Jerusalem : the free woman which is the mother of us all (Gal. 4[26], Heb. 12[22]) ; the πόλις which will come down from thence "prepared as a bride adorned for her husband " (Rev. 3[12], 21[2, 10]) ; the heavenly πολίτευμα in relation to which our present status is that of colonists who live in this world but are lawful members of that which is above (Phil. 3[20]).

There is also a heavenly dimension and scope, however, in the fact that to the divine measures there also belong judicial warnings and punishments. Heaven can remain closed and refuse the expected rain (1 K. 8[35], Deut. 11[17]). It can be as iron (Lev. 26[19]) or brass (Deut. 28[23]) over man. The wrath of God can be " revealed from heaven against all ungodliness and unrighteousness of men " (Rom. 1[18]). In Is. 34[5] we find the astonishing expression that the sword of the Lord has become drunk in heaven : " Behold, it shall come down upon Idumaea, and upon the people of my curse, to judgment." Or again, the windows of heaven can be opened (Gen. 7[11]), and it is no longer a treasure-house but the firmament of waters (Gen. 1[7]), which come plunging down in a flood, as they also arise from the deeps, to destroy all life on the earth. Or again, it is from heaven that fire and brimstone are rained on Sodom and Gomorrah (Gen. 19[24] cf. 2 K. 1[10f.]), as also hail-stones upon the routed Amorites (Josh. 10[11]).

But all these divine benefits and judgments are only the epiphenomena of what comes primarily and centrally from heaven to earth, namely, the Word which the God who is gracious in His holiness and holy in His grace addresses to man as the Lord of the covenant ; the Son in whose person He Himself becomes man and therefore earthly for our salvation. The earlier and later Hebrew traditions in this matter are probably not so different as often supposed when the statutes which according to the former are given to the people by the God who dwells and encounters Moses in the darkness of Sinai (Ex. 20[22], Deut.

4³⁶, Neh. 9¹³) are said by the latter to have been spoken from heaven. In accordance with the later view the prophet of the exile (Ez. 1¹) ascribes his visions to the fact that " the heavens were opened." Similarly, the series of visions in the New Testament Apocalypse begins with the fact (Rev. 4¹) that a door is opened in heaven through which the seer can perceive everything which follows. What we have here is not merely a development in the history of religion, but at the same time, and as the material basis of this movement, a development in the history of revelation. The intensity, clarity and concreteness of the voice and Word of God are not lessened as heaven is increasingly described as their origin and they are increasingly separated from everything which might encounter man from within his own sphere and claim him with earthly authority and power. And as the voice of God is regarded as a heavenly voice, it is not idealised but genuinely seen in its reality. It is obviously envisaged as a final word regarding both the majesty and the urgent proximity of the directly divine mission and appearance of Jesus when the evangelical tradition (Mk. 1¹⁰ and par.) says of the beginning of His Messianic way in the baptism in Jordan that heaven was opened and the Spirit lighted upon Him like a dove and there came a voice— again from heaven—proclaiming : " Thou art my beloved Son, in whom I am well pleased." To this there corresponds the saying of Jesus (Jn. 1⁵¹) : " Verily, verily, I say unto you, Hereafter ye shall see heaven open, and the angels of God ascending and descending upon the Son of God." Not merely the majesty of God, but the reality with which He finally became man and earthly, seems to make necessary so emphatic a stress on the participation of heaven in the events of earth. For these sayings are not to the effect that an earthly man is approved and applauded from heaven, but that One has come from God and therefore from heaven, and has become man and earthly. The Jesus who receives Stephen when he too sees heaven opened (Ac. 7⁵⁶) is the Son of Man standing at the right hand of God. As we see from the vision of Daniel 7¹³ᶠ·, even the latest parts of the Old Testament know something more than the man over whom heaven opens. Now that the preceding beast-empires have been overcome, this man who comes on the clouds of heaven and therefore from heaven is One " like the Son of man " to whom as such there is granted power and glory and an indestructible kingdom. Again, in Rev. 12¹ᶠ· the birth and youth of the boy who is threatened by the dragon that appears at the same time, but who is " to rule all nations with a rod of iron," are described as " a great wonder in heaven "— not on earth. Again, in Acts 26¹⁹ Paul describes as a heavenly ὀπτασία the appearance of Christ which came to him on the Damascus road. Again, he tells us in 1 Cor. 15⁴⁷ that Christ is the second man who is from heaven. The Fourth Gospel also tells us that Jesus is from above (8²³), that He comes from above (3³¹), or that He has come from above (3¹³). He is " the true bread from heaven. For the bread of God is he which cometh down from heaven, and giveth life unto the world. . . . I am the bread of life " (Jn. 6³²ᶠ·). And as He has come from heaven, and in confirmation of the fact that this is so, He ascends into (Ac. 1¹¹) and is received by heaven (Ac. 3²¹), entering into heaven " to appear in the presence of God for us " (Heb. 9²⁴), and traversing the heavens (Heb. 4¹⁴). It is from heaven that He has poured out His Spirit upon the community (Ac. 2², 1 Pet. 1¹²). It is from there that He now speaks with it (Heb. 12²⁵). It is from there that it now expects Him (1 Thess. 1¹⁰). And it is from there that He will come again, conclusively revealing Himself as the Lord (2 Thess. 1⁷), appearing " in the clouds of heaven with power and great glory " (Mt. 24³⁰, 26⁶⁴, Mk. 14⁶²). In Him we are already blessed with all spiritual blessings in heaven (Eph. 1³). In Him we are already set in heaven (Eph. 2⁶). And if even Christian exhortation can sometimes take on a cosmic character, so that James 3¹⁵ᶠ· can oppose to an earthly wisdom which is described as earthly and even demonic, a σοφία ἄνωθεν κατερχομένη which is not contentious but peaceable, and Col. 3² can apparently sum up all Christian ethics in the antithesis : τὰ ἄνω φρονεῖτε μὴ τὰ ἐπὶ τῆς γῆς, the context of the latter passage makes it clear that there is no question here of the establishment of ethics upon something cosmically higher, but rather of its establishment upon the higher One who, as and because He is God coming in Him to men, does in fact confront men as One who is cosmically higher, so that *per se* the establishment of man upon Him necessarily implies a cosmic *Sursum corda*.

This then, or this One, is the substance of what according to the biblical witness comes down (with blessing and punishment in its train) from heaven to earth because from God to man. It is He who bears the movement of God to the cosmos. In Him there is fulfilled that turning of God. He is the faithfulness of God in person. He is the kingdom of God and therefore the kingdom of heaven. For this is what it is only in relationship to Him. Thus heaven is decisively the place where and from and to which He is. For this reason we have still to receive conclusive instruction concerning it from Scripture.

We have not so far considered all the biblical statements from which it emerges that the Old and New Testaments see heaven as a cosmic reality constituted and consolidated by the fact that, as there is an operation of God from heaven, so there is a being of God in heaven. It is obvious that if we are speaking of the living God of the biblical witness the distinction is only provisional. For this God is as He works and works as He is. But even in this context we cannot dissolve or ignore the second statement that He is as He works. It is to safeguard this that we make the provisional distinction. God will not be dissolved into a relationship in which we find ourselves. Otherwise He is no longer God, and the relationship itself is dissolved into the mere idea of it. To the real Whence of the divine activity there necessarily corresponds a real Where of its origin, a real place of God as its Subject and Author. This real place of God as the Lord acting in the world is heaven. Even heaven would not be a cosmic reality in the biblical sense if it were only the Whence of the divine activity and not as such also the Where, the place of its Subject and Author. The former itself would not be true without the latter. Heaven is a place : the place of God in view of which we have to say that God is not only transcendent in relation to the world but also immanent and present within it ; the place of God from which His dealings with us, the history of the covenant, can take place in the most concrete sense, and His majesty, loftiness and remoteness can acquire the most concrete form, where otherwise they would simply be a product of human fantasy. As the place of God heaven is, of course, a place which is inconceivable to us. It cannot be compared with any other real or imaginary place. It is inaccessible. It cannot be explored or described or even indicated. All that can be affirmed concerning it is that it is a created place like earth itself and the accessible reality of earth which we can explore and describe or at least indicate ; and that it is the place of God. The final point is the decisive one. And for good reasons the Old and New Testaments do not hesitate to speak of the fact that God is in heaven and heaven is the place of God.

We cannot pray the Lord's Prayer without saying at once : " Our Father ὁ ἐν τοῖς οὐρανοῖς (Mt. 6⁹), and this is continually emphasised : " Flesh and blood hath not revealed it unto thee, but my Father which is in heaven " (Mt. 16¹⁷). " If two of you shall agree on earth as touching any thing that they shall ask, it shall be done for them of my Father which is in heaven " (Mt. 18¹⁹). " Love your enemies . . . that ye may be the children of your Father which is in heaven " (Mt. 5⁴⁴ᶠ·). If we take seriously the words " Father " and " my " and " our " and " your " in these verses, surely we must do the same with the phrase " in heaven." But if we do we are forced to say that God is in heaven as His place. And there is also the witness of the Old Testament at any rate in the later books. If we ask where God is, we seek in vain for the banal answer that He is everywhere. The omnipresence of God in the biblical sense (cf. Ps. 139⁸ᶠ·) really means something more spiritual and dynamic than this "everywhere." What we are told is that " God is in the heavens " and therefore that " he hath done whatsoever he hath pleased " (Ps. 115³). He is " above," " on high " (Job 31²), " in the height of heaven " (Job 22¹²), and in this sense ἐν ὑψίστοις (Lk. 2¹⁴). " God is in heaven, and thou upon earth," we are told in Eccles. 5² in an intentionally sharp antithesis. He is thus called the " Lord of heaven " (Ps. 136²⁶, Jon.1⁹, Dan. 2¹⁹). Heaven is His holy and glorious habitation (Is. 63¹⁵). Perhaps in the saying in Jn.14² about the Father's house in which there are many mansions we have also to think of heaven. It can also be called the upper storey (Amos 9⁶) from which He beholds everything that is done on earth (Ps. 14², Job 28²⁴ and *passim*), so that the tempted man may boast : " And now, behold, my witness is in heaven, and one who knows on high " (Job 16¹⁹).

The decisive view, however, is the one according to which heaven itself is the throne of God (Ps. 2⁴, Ez. 10¹, Is. 66¹ and *passim*). Hence to swear by heaven is to swear by this throne and the One who sits on it (Mt. 5³⁴, 23²²). Yet this throne is not a place of rest. It is rather the official seat of God. The sense emerges clearly in Ps. 103¹⁹ : " The Lord hath prepared his throne in the heavens ; and his kingdom ruleth over all." From the fact that God is enthroned in heaven (Ps. 33¹⁴, 123¹) we learn that He is not merely present or looks down from there, but that He reigns there, exercising authority and rule. The sovereignty with which He does so is drastically stated in Ps. 2⁴ ; " He that sitteth in the heavens shall laugh : the Lord shall have them in derision, " i.e., He shall mock the raging of the nations, the futile imaginations of the peoples, the pretensions of earthly rulers and the counsels of the rulers. This divine laughter is not to be thought of merely as the amused laughter of a disinterested spectator. But when God sees and laughs, there takes place something corresponding on earth. In the idea of God seated on His heavenly throne the being and work of God in and from heaven merge into each other and are one. There is no suggestion that He is there in a kind of frozen immobility. The One who is enthroned in heaven can also be called the One " that rideth upon the heaven of heavens, which were of old " (Ps. 68³³). And how He can come from thence to be mightily near to His own—we shall hear more about this later—is very powerfully described in Ps. 18⁶⁻¹⁸ and especially in v. 13 : " The Lord also thundered in the heavens, and the Highest gave his voice," or v. 9 : " He bowed the heavens also, and came down : and darkness was under his feet," or v. 16 f. : " He sent from above, he took me, he drew me out of many waters. He delivered me from the strong enemy."

The New Testament gives fulness and precision to this view by describing Jesus Christ not merely as the One who has come from heaven, has ascended to heaven, and is to be expected from heaven as the definitive revelation of God, but also as the One who is in heaven. These points are all gathered up in the remarkable saying in Jn. 3¹³ : " No man hath ascended up to heaven, but he that came down from heaven, even the Son of man which is in heaven." In view of this the saying in Col. 3¹ may well be regarded as the normative biblical definition of heaven : Εἰ οὖν συνηγέρθητε τῷ Χριστῷ, τὰ ἄνω ζητεῖτε, οὗ ὁ Χριστός ἐστιν ἐν δεξιᾷ τοῦ θεοῦ καθήμενος. Where is this whole strange " above " from which we are told (not without the accompanying warnings) that all good gifts come, where our names are already written, our house or city or country awaits us, our reward or treasure or inheritance is already prepared, and we ourselves are secretly present ? Where is this heaven ? The answer is that it is where Christ is. But Christ sits at the right hand of God. We cannot explain the ἐστίν without at once considering this καθήμενος, which leads us at once *in media res sc. gestas et gerendas*. For the session and therefore the right hand of God are explained by the fact that a consideration of the Christ who is in heaven brings us again and this time fully into the historical context of the divine activity. To " sit " is to be enthroned and therefore to enjoy and exercise power, to rule or

passim) : " Sit thou at my right hand, until I make thine enemies thy footstool. The Lord shall send the rod of thy strength out of Zion." Only on this presupposition can the Psalm continue : " Rule thou in the midst of thine enemies." When Christ sits at His right hand in that plenitude of power, God does not cease to be the living and omnipotent God. He is God in supreme activity in the fact that He gives Christ this sovereignty and institutes Him into this fulness of kingly rule. And the kingly rule of Christ is simply His own, and its exercise His own action. When He gives Him all things, He does not deprive Himself of anything. Nothing is taken from Him. But in this way He comes fully into His own—His glory and right and the goal of His will. Being wholly in Christ (2 Cor. 5¹⁹), and putting all things under Him (Ps. 110), He is no less the Most High. In Christ, indeed, He is it in full force and majesty. He rules as Jesus Christ rules as King. The relationship between Him and Christ is that which the Fourth Gospel and Paul in his commentary on Ps. 110 (1 Cor. 15²⁴ᶠ·) expressly describe as that of Father and Son. But this Father can as little be limited, rivalled or even effaced by the Son as He for His part can limit, rival or efface the Son. It is only when the Son works that He really works. They are not two persons in our sense of the term, i.e., two different subjects which will and work independently, so that their activities might cut across and restrict one another, and necessarily give rise to a conflict of priority and authority. But as the ancient doctrine of the Trinity had it, they are two modes of being (τρόποι ὑπάρξεως) of the one divine Subject, two times the one God, the one omnipotent will, the one eternal righteousness, goodness and mercy. What, then, is the difference ? God the Father is the one true God in so far as He is this and only this, and as such is in heaven. The Son is the same true God in so far as He became and was and is also as such true man to all eternity, having come on earth to be born and to suffer and to die. And the exaltation of the Son to the right hand of the Father is that in heaven as on earth the one true God will and can be no other than the One who is also true man and was born and suffered and died on earth. He wills to be this in heaven and in the whole cosmos. The fulfilment and revelation of this will of the one true God is the resurrection of Jesus Christ from the dead, which forms the explicit or implicit presupposition in all the passages in the New Testament which speak of the elevation of Jesus Christ to the right hand of the Father. For in His resurrection, completed in the ascension, it took place that as true God and true man He was taken from earth and set in heaven. And it is simply this one event seen from different standpoints —now as the act of the one true God who is the Father, and now as that of the one true God who is the Son—if the Easter-event is sometimes described as His resurrection in the power of the Father and sometimes as the resurrection which He Himself has accomplished ; if in Ac. 2³³ and 5³¹ and Eph. 1²⁰ we are told that He was exalted by God or by the right hand of God, and in Heb. 1³, 10¹² and 12² we read that He seated Himself at the right hand of God. Again, it is only a question of standpoint if in Heb. 10¹² (with reference to Dan. 7¹⁴) we learn that Christ seated Himself for ever (εἰς τὸ διηνεκές) at the right hand of God, and in Eph. 1²⁰ᶠ· that His kingdom will last into the future aeon as well as the present, whereas in 1 Cor. 15²⁴ᶠ· Paul takes the beginning of Ps. 110 to mean that when everything is subject to the Son He will hand over His completed and manifested kingdom to the Father who has subjected everything to Him and is thus excepted from this subjection, so that when it is accomplished " the Son also himself will be subject unto him that put all things under him." And this leads us to the well-known conclusion at the end of v. 28 : ἵνα ᾖ ὁ θεὸς πάντα ἐν πᾶσιν. If our former deliberations are correct, it would be foolish to relate this saying merely to the last link in Paul's exposition, and therefore to the subjection of the Son. On the contrary, it sums up the whole passage. God is all in all in His subjecting of all things to the Son. And He is again all in all in the Son's subjecting of Himself to the Father. In both cases, in the action of Father and

Son alike, it is a matter of all things in heaven and earth, in the heights and depths of the created universe, in the whole history of all created spheres and individuals. And in both cases, in the action of Father and Son alike, the one true God Himself is all in all : the beginning, middle and end ; the origin and goal ; the fulfilment and limit ; the power and the effect. This then, the glory of the one true God, constitutes the relationship between Father and Son, between Him that sits on the throne and Him that sits at His right hand.

But to return to our previous question, where is this above ? Where is heaven ? The answer of Col. 3¹ has now been filled out. " Where Christ sitteth on the right hand of God," there is the glory of the one true God who is not merely this, not merely the Father, but who as the Son also became true man, and who even as this Son, and therefore as true God and true man, was not only once on earth, but is also with the Father in heaven, ἐν ὑψηλοῖς (Heb. 1³).

It is this one true God who dwells and is enthroned and rules in heaven, who looks down from this upper storey on the children of men, who laughs at His enemy, and who is not merely the Witness but the Judge and Helper and Deliverer of His own. How concrete everything which is said by the Old Testament along these lines becomes when we are told by the New Testament that it is this God who is in heaven, and works there, and thence also on earth ; that it is this God who is the θεὸς ἐν ὑψίστοις (Lk. 2¹⁴) !

At this point we might quote the solemn words of *Qu.* 49 of the *Heidelberg Catechism*. " Of what value to us is the ascension of Christ ? First, that He is our Advocate in heaven in the presence of His Father. Second, that we have our flesh in heaven as a sure pledge that He as the Head will take us to Himself as the members. Third, that He sends us His Spirit as an earnest by the power of which we seek those things which are above, where Christ is seated at the right hand of the Father, and not those things which are on earth." What is said here concerning the ascension is also the final word concerning heaven itself. For it is the fact that He, the Son, the one true God who became one with our poor flesh, the omnipotent mercy of this one true God, is there for us above in heaven, which confirms this above, which makes heaven higher than earth, which distinguishes it as the upper cosmos, and yet which also sets it in indissoluble union with earth. Is He only in heaven ? Of course not ! For the *inde venturus* is also true ; and the end and goal of all earthly history is the definitive revelation of His glory and therefore that of the Father, the one glory of the one true God ; and already by His Holy Spirit He is not remote from His community on earth in the present course of earthly history, but by His Word (*kerygma*, baptism and the Lord's Supper), He is genuinely present as very God and very man. Again, He is not only in heaven because in His exaltation He has traversed the heavens (Heb. 4¹⁴), ascending up " far above all heavens " (Eph. 4¹⁰), and becoming ὑψηλότερος τῶν οὐρανῶν (Heb. 7²⁶). God Himself and His right hand or side are not merely in heaven. The heaven of heavens cannot contain Him. And Jesus Christ shares fully in this transcendence of God over heaven which is merely His throne. But neither this nor His presence on earth alters in the very slightest the fact that even as the Giver of His Spirit and in His presence on earth He is still for us in heaven, in this created above, and therefore truly in our world, and in this world truly above us. And the fact that He is there, that His work from there is effective for us, that He, this One, the Son in His unity with the Father, is for us the one true God, constitutes and consolidates heaven as the counterpart of earth, as the mystery, the upper cosmos, which limits but is for this reason near to us as creatures of earth. He rules, and He rules in the kingdom of heaven.

God rules in the kingdom of heaven. This means that His work, His speech and action, the whole execution of His omnipotent mercy, commences in heaven, and then comes down from heaven to us on earth in a form which is partly determined by its commencement in heaven. By the fact that it comes to us in this way, in a form which is partly determined by its heavenly commencement, we are invited to consider first this heavenly commencement, and with the required reservations to say what is necessary and possible concerning it.

Reserve is demanded because, although heaven as the place of God is known as a place, as another created place, as a higher cosmic sphere confronting our own, beyond these delimiting definitions it is unknown and inconceivable, and therefore a mystery. Even the revelation of God does not give us any further information. This means that as we direct our attention to this heavenly commencement of the Word and work of God we cannot expect and we shall not try to amass data concerning heaven as such or the relationship of heaven and earth. In any such attempt we should be building on sand, missing what we could attain, and failing to attain what we cannot. How much or little we shall know of heaven in itself and heaven and earth as such when we come into the presence of God and look on the new heaven made earthly and the new earth made heavenly, remains to be seen. But here and now—and surely there and then too—it is wisely arranged that we cannot know what we do not need to know and for our own good ought not to try. Because it is the place of the God who is and works there, the nature of the upper cosmos can be known to us only to the extent that it is illumined for us by the heavenly commencement of His Word and work with reference to us. For the rest, i.e., in itself and as such, it is a mystery, and here and now at least will always be so. In the further step which we have now to take we shall have to respect this mystery. Respect for this belongs essentially to the knowledge which is possible, salutary and necessary at this point. Any attempt at an independent ontology of heaven would at once estrange us from this knowledge and lead us into the realm of an impossible, dangerous and forbidden desire for knowledge. We must keep strictly to the fact that we have only to see and know of heaven what may be seen and known as it is illuminated by the kingdom which comes from heaven. Hence we have not really been led to the threshold of an ontology of heaven by our deliberations thus far.

On the other hand, they have set us the task of giving methodical consideration to the heavenly commencement of the kingdom of God which comes on earth, and therefore to the kingdom of heaven in the original and strictest sense of the concept, i.e., in so far as it is first in heaven and only then on earth. To the extent that it subsequently comes to us on earth, we can and must say that by the revelation of God which consists in the coming to us of His kingdom we are taught concerning the commencement of this kingdom, and therefore empowered and summoned to give it this consideration. Our reserve cannot, therefore, go to the point of evading this consideration or refusing the necessary and accessible thoughts on what can be seen and known in this connexion. There is indeed a visible and perceptible illumination of the upper cosmos as the Word and work of God which refer to us find their commencement there. And if it is impossible, dangerous and forbidden to try to know more of this upper cosmos than is visible and perceptible in this illumination, in another sense it is also impossible, dangerous and forbidden not to see what is to be seen or know what is to be known. At this point, again, we must err neither *in excessu* nor *in defectu*, i.e., neither in the direction of misplaced speculation nor in that of an equally misplaced scepticism. The objection that the heavenly commencement of the divine Word and work, and that which is to be seen and known in the light of heaven, is not a proper object of faith and cannot therefore be a true theme of dogmatics, is without substance. The theme of faith and dogmatics is the proclamation of the Christian Church. But the theme of this proclamation is the kingdom of God come on earth. If this kingdom of God is in fact the kingdom of heaven, i.e., the royal speech and action of God which commences in heaven and come from heaven to us, the heavenly commencement, and therefore that which is to be seen and known of heaven in the light of this happening, certainly belongs to the theme of faith and therefore of dogmatics. If we refuse to know anything of what is to be seen and known at this point, it might be tragically the case that we refuse to know anything of the kingdom of God which really comes to us. For this reason, we are genuinely invited, summoned and empowered to attain even in this respect the clarity which is both necessary and possible.

We may begin by affirming that heaven, the above where Christ sits at the right hand of God, the whence of the kingdom which comes to us, is certainly not a vacuum, however inconceivable it may be to us. It is not nothing. It is inaccessible and unknown, but it is a real context of being. In its own very different way it is just as real as the earth which is ontically and noetically our sphere. The place where God is as He turns to the world created by Him itself belongs to this world of His creatures. It has, therefore, a creaturely and as such a true being ; a being under very different presuppositions and conditions from our own, but a true being. And in this true being it is heaven under God, at His disposal, and therefore obedient to Him. In the first instance, this is true in the general sense in which it is true of all creatures. Like all creatures heaven was created good, i.e., according to His own purpose and for His own ends. He gave it the form and constitution which adapt it to serve Him and to be perfect in this service. But there is also a special sense in which this is true. Heaven is under God and at His disposal in the sense that it has a particular place and function in the historical context, in the plan and execution, of the divine purpose of salvation and grace for man. The being of heaven is concretely determined by the fact that Christ is seated there at the right hand of God. It is the creaturely place of that unity of the Father and the Son ; of the one true God in His might and majesty as such ; and of the same one true God who is also true man. That it is the creaturely place of this unity, and the creaturely whence of occurrence on earth, is grounded in this unity and will find fulfilment in it ; and this is the peculiarity of its being which we may and can and must know for all the incomprehensibility with which it otherwise confronts us. Heaven cannot remain unaffected but is supremely impelled and determined and fashioned by the fact that it is this place, this whence. In face and as the witness of this presence of God, this commencement of His Word and work, it cannot be neutral, let alone inimical or antithetical to this Word and work. Whatever may be the manner in which heaven was created good, as God is over and in it in fulfilment of His purpose of grace and salvation, it cannot express and actualise itself except in acts and attitudes which acknowledge the right and necessity, the supreme glory, the true wisdom and beauty, of that which commences in its presence, in proof of its willingness and readiness for helpful participation in this commencement. Whatever the manner of heaven, its being is an obedient being.

Thus our first point is that something is done in heaven, so surely is it the place of God, and so surely is something done on earth as subsequently and from heaven it too becomes the place of God. And as this occurrence on earth in correspondence with what God does is creaturely, so that which takes place in heaven in accordance with the divine action is creaturely. And we may go on to say that this heavenly happening is not neutral, independent, opposed or arbitrary in relation to the divine will and action. It is the fulfilment of the will of God. That is, it is a happening in which the creature, the heavenly creature, whatever its manner and kind, is obedient to and actually serves the will of God. The presence of God in heaven, the origin and commencement there of His action in the world, makes it necessary that He should find there the obedience of His creature ; that His creature in heaven should do His will. This corresponds exactly to the fact that the coming of God from heaven to earth, if His action in the world is to attain its goal and end in man (thus involving for man a new origin and commencement), makes it necessary that God should find on earth the obedience of His creature ; that His will should be done on earth too ; and that here too it should be done in definite acts and attitudes on the part of His creatures.

In saying this, we have brought ourselves into tacit relationship with a verse which cannot but be regarded as of central importance, namely, the third petition of the Lord's Prayer : " Thy will be done in earth, as it is in heaven " (Mt. 6[10]). In codex D and some old Latin manuscripts, which omit the ὡς, this is made into a prayer that the will of God should be done both in heaven and on earth.

It thus becomes a petition for the triumph of the will of God throughout the universe, opposition being presumed in heaven as well. Now although the New Testament nowhere suggests that heaven itself can have anything to do with opposition to the will of God, it does refer to opposition which takes place in heaven too. This interpretation cannot, therefore, be described as materially impossible. On the other hand, the ὡς in Matt. 6¹⁰ is so overwhelmingly supported that we must accept the common rendering, i.e., that the will of God should be done on earth as the end and goal of the divine purpose and activity as it is done in heaven as its origin and commencement ; that it should be done on earth to-day and to-morrow as it was always done in heaven ; that it should be done on earth by the obedience of the earthly creature as it is done in heaven by the obedience of the heavenly ; that it should be done on earth with the same self-evident necessity as it is done in heaven. Lohmeyer (*op. cit.*, p. 87) seems to leave it an open question whether the meaning is that earth should be raised to heaven or heaven should descend to earth. In the light of the second petition the latter seems to be more obvious, i.e., that from heaven God should cause His will to be done on earth as in heaven. Lohmeyer is certainly right when he says that the petition presupposes that heaven and earth are still divided or at least distinct, and asks therefore that this differentiation should cease in the day of consummation. But its material presupposition is that the will of God is done in heaven. Heaven is the sphere of the created world where God has always found the obedience which he has still to find in our sphere, so that we in our sphere, where it is not found, have to orientate ourselves by that in which it is, and we can thus know what we ask when with Jesus (who had no need of such orientation) we pray : " Thy will be done." Hence we can and should think of heaven as the creaturely sphere in which the will of God, which we pray should be done on earth, takes place already, and has always done so. Not incorrectly, Chrysostom (quoted from Lohmeyer, p. 88) has given us the following paraphrase : " O Lord, let us be so zealous for the heavenly kingdom that we may will as it does."

The idea of heavenly occurrence is not unknown in other parts of the Bible, especially the Old Testament. And in the relevant texts it is always a happening which is initiated by God in His gracious and judicial action as the Lord of the covenant with Israel, and must therefore serve Him, but which also has its correspondence in an earthly history which runs parallel with it or follows it. It is part of the description of the coming terrible day of the Lord in later prophecy that God causes heaven as well as earth to be shaken and to tremble. In Is. 13¹³, for example, this is one of the many signs of the divine judgment executed on Babylon ; in Joel 3¹⁶ the voice of God which goes out from Jerusalem brings this and many similar things to pass in the great moment when world-wide judgment and the beginning of a new age of salvation for Judah and Jerusalem are to take place in the valley of Jehoshaphat, in the valley of decision ; and in Hag. 2⁶, ²¹ it forms part of the promise of a new and more splendid temple as this is given to Zerubbabel, Joshua and the whole people. The remoteness and height ascribed to heaven in the language and thinking of the Old Testament must be remembered if we are to assess what is involved when we are told that it cannot remain intact or neutral in the day of judgment and salvation, but must undergo with men and beasts and land and sea and sun and moon and stars the great convulsion which this day means not only for the history of the nations but for the whole earth and therefore, and especially, for heaven. It is no accident if we find this view of the eschatological shaking of heaven expressly adopted in certain passages of the New Testament (Mt. 24²⁹, Ac. 2¹⁹, Heb. 12²⁶). And even more forceful than this view of the shaking of heaven with the consummation which dawns on earth is the tumultuous cry of Is. 64¹ᶠ· : " Oh that thou wouldest rend the heavens, that thou wouldest come down, that the mountains might flow down at thy presence, as when the melting fire burneth, the fire causeth the waters to boil, to make thy name known to thine adversaries, that the nations may tremble at thy presence! When thou didst terrible things which we looked not for, thou camest down, the mountains flowed down at thy presence. For since the beginnings of the world men have not heard, nor perceived by the ear, neither hath the eye seen, O God, beside thee, what he hath prepared for him that waiteth for him."

The fiery apocalyptic of these passages must not blind us to others which speak of a cosmic occurrence, a shaking of heaven and earth, of a very different character, namely, those passages in the Psalms in which heaven and earth are summoned to praise the Lord as though they were a choir or orchestra (Ps. 69[34], 148[4]), or in which it is said of them that like chroniclers or court poets they recount the glory of God, and like messengers proclaim His handiwork (Ps. 19[1f.]), or declare His righteousness, since " God is judge himself " (Ps. 50[6]), or praise His wonders (Ps. 89[5]). In this praise of God which is sung or played by the heavens we are not to think of the sounding of a cosmic organ like the Greek harmony of the spheres, outside time and unrelated to anything or related to all things. The One whom the heavens praise is the God of Israel who led His people through the Red Sea ; the God of Abraham, Moses, David and the Son of David. It is His glory which they tell and His wonders and righteousness which they declare. They themselves are the work of His hands. It is incontestable that in these passages creaturely nature, in its supreme form of heaven, is summoned to be the witness of God. But it is highly contestable whether these passages, like others in the Psalms and Job which refer to the rest of creation, represent or reveal an abstract natural theology. There are no " nature-psalms " in the pure sense in the Old Testament. As the contexts show, what these Psalms tell us is that the cosmos, and therefore the upper cosmos, attests the God who called the fathers, and revealed Himself to His people at Sinai, and gave it an inheritance in Canaan. And the wider setting in which we have to see it is naturally the poor praise on earth which, even as the heavens extol Him, is offered to God, or still withheld from Him, by this people of His. Hence in the praise and declaration of heaven referred to in these Psalms we are not so far removed from the shaking and rending of the heavens on the day of the Lord as attested by the prophets. They, too, speak of an obedient being of heaven, and particularly of a participation of heaven in the history of the great acts of God on earth. The attempt to harmonise them in detail with the prophets is, of course, both hopeless and irrelevant. All these passages speak of the heaven which, because God dwells in it, is as incomprehensible to us as God Himself. Their contradictions cannot and do not need to be resolved. It is enough that in their different ways they say that which is succinctly summarised in Mt. 6[10], namely, that there is done in heaven the will of God which, in fulfilment of what God has resolved and commenced in heaven, is to be done on earth.

What Luke tells us concerning the entry of Jesus into Jerusalem (19[37f.]) is a solemn acknowledgment and welcoming of this heavenly fulfilment by the earth which is affected by it : " And when he was come nigh, even now at the descent of the mount of Olives, the whole multitude of his disciples began to rejoice and praise God with a loud voice for all the mighty works that they had seen ; saying, Blessed be the King that cometh in the name of the Lord : peace in heaven, and glory in the highest." All the details in this description are significant. What is at issue is an entry—the entry of the King into the royal city which belongs to but is estranged from Him. This entry takes the form of a descent (κατάβασις). There are verbal reminiscences of the manifestation of the angels in Lk. 2[13f.], the angelic host being now replaced by a multitude of disciples singing the same praises of God. By the inversion of the phrases the song of the disciples becomes genuinely antiphonal to that of the angels. What is done on earth, the fulness of the acts of power which have now taken place, is crowned and confirmed in the Messianic entry. And behind all these things in the foreground there are seen the heavenly presuppositions in the background. The man of the divine εὐδοκία has become the one King manifesting Himself with the divine εὐλογία. The peace of God, which has come on earth according to Lk. 2¹⁴, is now magnified as the peace which rules in heaven. The glory to God in the highest, in general correspondence to the change of place, is no longer the first phrase but the last, and therefore the horizon of the whole. It would be hard to imagine a finer commentary on Mt. 6¹⁰ than Lk. 19³⁷ᶠ· taken in conjunction with Lk. 2¹³ᶠ·, especially when we compare these passages with those in the Old Testament which speak of the movement of heaven in relationship to that of earth.

God rules in heaven as in a creaturely sphere. We have thus to reckon with a happening which takes place in this sphere. But this heavenly happening is determined by the fact that the goal of the lordship of God by which it has to orientate itself is a happening in our sphere, on earth. If we can assume this, we can venture the next step—not forgetting the high incomprehensibility of the whole subject—and say that this heavenly happening is one which is ordered, harmonious and integrated, but also differentiated. If its nature is unknown, we are not wholly ignorant of its purpose, function and direction. It takes place under the lordship of God, and therefore, because the lordship of God is that of the One at whose right hand Christ is seated, under the determination that it should find its continuation and correspondence in a happening on earth. It serves this continuation and correspondence in advance. It precedes it, as it were, in heaven. For this reason, it is unitary but not formless, collective but not without individuation, total but not uniform or monotonous. This conclusion might be based on the wealth of the essence of God, which surely finds no less expression in His being and work in heaven than on earth. But possibly this smacks of a mere hypothesis. And weight is given to it only by the fact that the lordship of God as that of the Father and the Son has as its goal man and the multiplicity and mobility of his history and existence, or of earthly history and existence generally. It is the lordship of His omnipotent grace, which is concerned with the order, harmony, integration and differentiation, the reorganisation of our earthly history and existence according to the model and plan of His wisdom and goodness. Because as heavenly occurrence it is determined by this model and plan, it cannot lack form, individuation and multiplicity, but is already ordered, harmonious, integrated and differentiated in its unitariness, collectiveness and totality. If we do not know what might be called the sub-stratum of this happening ; if we do not know as such either heavenly being or its qualities, this does not mean—for God Himself stands before us as its Creator and Lord, and the goal of His will is perceived—that the obedience which He finds in this heavenly occurrence is not the obedience of a subject which can be understood as a single subject but also in its singleness as a multiple, and as a single in its multiplicity. And it is thus that the kingdom of God comes to earth as the kingdom of heaven, not at a single stroke, on a single note, or in a single shade or form, but in a concentrated multiplicity of revelations and declarations, of events and relationships, of individuals and societies, which have their constitutive centre in God Himself, namely, in Jesus Christ as very God and very man, but which all the same, or for this very reason and in this very way—otherwise grace would not be grace—form this concentrated multiplicity addressed to the history and existence of the creature. But since the kingdom of God comes from heaven to earth in this way, this is tantamount to saying that in heaven and in its commencement there it has and is itself this concentrated multiplicity—an organisation.

In this respect our first reference is to the fact that according to the usage of the Old Testament heaven is a plural term. To this there corresponds the notion discernible in 2 Cor. 12² of three heavens one upon the other : the firmament above the stars ; the heavenly ocean ; and heaven in the true sense, in or above which is the throne of God. We have already noted that the plural is always used in the New Testament where the reference is to the sphere and world of God.

But the Bible leads us a decisive stage further when in the Old Testament it gives to God the title of Yahweh (or less frequently Elohim) Sabaoth, the Lord of hosts, which entails the corresponding notion of a host of Yahweh or of heaven. The title does not occur in the Hexateuch, Judges or Ezekiel, but it is found in the Books of Samuel and Kings, comparatively infrequently in Psalms, more often in Amos and Jeremiah, and predominantly in Isaiah and Zechariah. In the first instance, it excludes any idea of a lonely God sitting on His heavenly throne in an empty or formless heaven. By this name Yahweh is described as the Sovereign of a multitude, and of a multitude constituted as a host, and of a heavenly multitude constituted in this way. So surely as He is in or above heaven as His throne, and rules there or thence, so surely is He surrounded by the multitude of this heavenly host of servants. The saying of the prophet Micaiah in 1 K. 22¹⁹ and 2 Chron. 18¹⁸ is particularly illuminating in this respect : " I saw the Lord sitting on his throne, and all the host of heaven standing by him on his right hand and on his left "—an armed and disciplined force standing at His disposal for instant use. Instead of a host of God Ps. 82¹ speaks of a congregation, and Ps. 89⁷ of an assembly of the saints. It is obvious that we have here what we described as the organisation, order, integration but also differentiation of what is done in heaven ; and that this is the master-concept under which the Old Testament groups the beings which in their decisive function bear the name of angels. We must keep strictly to the fact that our concern is with that organisation and differentiation of heavenly being and occurrence—we know of no other— which are grounded in the fact that it is from heaven and therefore the character of the kingdom of heaven that the kingdom of God comes to us men and therefore to earth. This is finely expressed in Rev. 19¹¹⁻¹⁶ in the description of the sallying forth of the Rider on the white horse whose name is " Faithful and True " (v. 11) and " The Word of God " (v. 13), who is clothed with a vesture dipped in blood, from whose mouth there goes a sharp sword, and who bears inscribed on His thigh the further name : " King of kings, and Lord of lords " (v. 16). What we have here is a description of the parousia of Christ. But we are also told in v. 14 : " And the armies which were in heaven (τὰ στρατεύματα τὰ ἐν τῷ οὐρανῷ) followed him upon white horses, clothed in fine linen, white and clean." They obviously have and reveal their true being as the host of heaven in the Word of God whom they follow and accompany as He comes from heaven to earth. Similarly, the picture in Rev. 4—the great heavenly doxology offered by the four and twenty elders, the seven spirits and the four living creatures gathered round the throne of God—is only as it were made actual and concrete, or at any rate explained, by that of Rev. 5, in which the Lamb slain (v. 6), the Lion of the tribe of Judah, the Root of David (v. 5), comes forward and takes the book with the seven seals (v. 8), and a corresponding doxology is offered to Him by that assembly, accompanied this time by ten thousand times ten thousand angels, and thousands of thousands (v. 11). It is also of a piece with this that there is only one passage in the Bible, namely, in the account of the nativity (Lk. 2^{13}), which speaks of a manifestation and function of the $\pi\lambda\tilde{\eta}\theta o s$, i.e., of the fulness or totality of the heavenly hosts on earth.

This connexion of the existence of the heavenly host with the event of salvation of earth gives to this master-concept, especially in the Old Testament, an ambivalence which is at first sight confusing. This host does not always have the direct meaning of the heavenly host, and even when it does it does not always mean the host of truly angelic beings around the throne, the organisation and differentiation of the upper cosmos. In Gen. 2^1 for example (" Thus the heavens and the earth were finished, and all the host of them "), the most that we can say is that it includes this reference, and the same is true of Neh. 9^6. It is true, of course, that a particular creation of the heavenly host might be envisaged in Ps. 33^6 : " By the word of the Lord were the heavens made ; and all the host of them by the breath of his mouth " ; and also in Is. 45^{12} : " I, even my hands, have stretched out the heavens, and all their host have I commanded." But in some of the passages which warn against worshipping the host of heaven instead of God (Deut. 4^{19}, 17^3) it is expressly stated, and in others of like content it may be inferred, that the sun and moon and stars are meant by this host. This is certainly the reference in Is. 40^{26} where man is challenged to " lift up his eyes on high, and behold who hath created these things, that bringeth out their host by number : he calleth them all by names. . . ." And on the other hand it has to be taken into account that in 1 Sam. 17^{45} the divine name " Lord of hosts " is equated with " the God of the armies of Israel," and that even in Is. 13^4 the army mustered by the Lord of hosts seems to be an army of men. On this point it is to be noted that the heavenly assembly of elders, spirits and beasts in Rev. 4–5 has at least an affinity to human gatherings on earth, although it is only with great caution that we must see in it a direct prefiguration even of the Church. We shall meet the same ambivalence when we come to deal with the concept of the individual heavenly beings within these hosts, and especially of the angels which exist and work on earth.

Yet there can be no doubt that this concept of a host is more than a description of the stars or a term for the armies of Israel or any other human array. In 1 K. 22^{19} the heavenly host on the right hand and the left cannot possibly be the stars or human warriors. And there is a clear distinction in Ps. 148. After the general call : " Praise the Lord from the heavens ; praise him in the heights," we have the specific summons : " Praise ye him, all his angels : praise ye him, all his hosts," then again specifically : " Praise ye him, sun and moon : praise him, all ye stars of light," and yet again specifically : " Praise him, ye heavens of heavens, and ye waters that be above the heavens." Similarly, the host of God in Gen. $32^{1f.}$ cannot have any direct connexion with a Hebrew or any other army. Indirectly the different applications of the notion are naturally inter-related, and in such a way that the idea of God's host or assembly as the direct *entourage* of His throne forms the basic concept reflected in that of the stars and then of the armies of God's earthly people, but with all kinds of cross-references as in the Song of Deborah in Jud. 5^{20} : " They fought from heaven ; the stars in their courses fought against Sisera." If only we keep to the fact that, as in our general view of the heavenly world, so in our consideration of its discipline, order and integration, we have to do with a movement under the lordship of God from above to below, to earth and to human history, we shall not regard as in any way strange this peculiar interchange of meanings in virtue of which we are at one moment really above with God, then in the sphere of a very earthly heaven, and finally on earth itself, where the heavenly hosts are very definitely earthly. These hosts exist at all only as they follow the Word of God (Rev. 19[14]) in His movement to this goal in earthly existence and history. This is true already of the organisation, the concentrated multiplicity of heavenly being and existence, which is the immediate point at issue.

We must now venture a further step. If the kingdom which as the lordship of God comes from heaven to earth, and therefore commences and is first in heaven, is an order, then it embraces certain elements ordered within it and adjusted to its order. If there is integration, there must be members. If there is concentrated multiplicity, there must be simplicity and individuality. If there is a collective, there must be individuals. If heaven, known to us as the kingdom of heaven, is a creaturely sphere, it must embrace creatures. And however strongly we must emphasise their unity and fellowship, the plurality of these creatures cannot be submerged in identity. An army is made up of soldiers, an assembly of participants. This is no less true of the host or assembly around the throne of God.

We must remember the incomprehensibility of the heavenly sphere of being, and therefore exercise the greatest caution, if we dare to draw these conclusions in relation to the biblical view. As the Bible sees it, these elements or members or units or individuals or different creatures of heavenly being and occurrence appear only (1) in the course and context of the history which commences in heaven and aims at earth, and therefore only in this movement, and their distinctive functions within it ; (2) in clear relationship to the order, the collective, the fellowship and unity which they enjoy with others of their kind ; and (3) with the unmistakeable stamp of elements, members, units or individuals which are heavenly by nature. But this constitutes a threefold warning against any attempt to define these creatures on the assumption that we are in a position to consider them in their abstract essence and to make pronouncements concerning them on the basis of this consideration.

This is where the fathers go astray, and the scholastics, and all angelology which—whether its answer is positive, or negative, or critical—puts the question as if it were a matter of understanding the existence and manner of certain beings which can be known apart from their function in that history, their membership of that collective and therefore their mutual unity and fellowship, and finally the fact that they are heavenly beings and cannot be grasped in earthly terms. We cannot ignore these things. To maintain the existence of angels and describe their nature as the ancients did is to try to limit the sea with a handful of sand. And to deny them, or reduce them to a comical state of immobility, like the moderns, is to tilt against windmills. To be sure, these beings are distinct creatures, different from the other creatures of earth known to us, and also distinct both in numbers and nature among themselves. But it is a mistake to range them schematically with other creatures as the older dogmatics usually do with the sequence *De homine* and then *De angelis* (or *vice versa*), for we cannot know how these beings are different as creatures from the earthly creatures known to us, nor how they exist, nor what is their particular nature, nor how they are inter-related in unity and plurality. We cannot know these things because as they appear in the Bible they can be known to us as elements, members, units or individuals of the kingdom of heaven only in the movement of the coming of this kingdom to earth, only in their adherence to an order which we cannot survey, and only as heavenly and therefore incomprehensible beings. In consequence, we can only regard it as a mistake for which we have no warrant in the Bible to concern ourselves with the famous question of their creation, and to adopt one or other of the answers given to this question.

They are known to us not in their abstract but in their concrete nature as the heavenly *entourage* of the God who acts from heaven to earth, and therefore not as an abstractly existent heavenly collective of abstractly existent heavenly individual beings but as the concretely operative heavenly collective of concretely operative heavenly individual beings. At this point, of course, the caution demanded of us reaches its limit. In this form they are indeed known to us, for God's coming kingdom on earth is the kingdom of heaven and is revealed to us as such. If the kingdom of heaven were not a collective, and if it did not consist of individuals, it would not be the kingdom of God coming on earth and bursting into earthly nature and human history with all its universality and particularities. Our present emphasis is upon the latter. If it comes to us, it does not come only in universality, but also in particularity; it does not come only as a totality, but also as a multiplicity. And if as God's kingdom it comes into this world and therefore from heaven, as the kingdom of heaven, it is itself characterised by both universality and particularity, totality and multiplicity, collectivity and individuality. Hence when we consider it we have not to think only of heaven and its heavenly essence, or globally of the heavenly host and assembly, but also of the heavenly being and therefore of the angels who are comprehended in this unity.

We knew nothing of their essential being and its particular nature. We know nothing of the mode of their mutal relationship and distinction. We know nothing of the way in which they are a totality and yet distinct. But we do know that even in the mystery of their being they exist in and with the kingdom of God coming and revealed to us. And we do know that they are both inter-related and distinct, both a totality and individuals.

They are in and from heaven in the service in which they precede, accompany, surround and follow the coming kingdom. This is all that we know concerning them. But we can and must define them in these terms. And the definition can be explicated as follows. They are in the service of God. It is their existence and nature to observe the will of God and stand at His disposal. Their heavenly glory consists solely in this determination. Moreover, they are in the service of the merciful God, for whom there are no problems, and in the strict sense nothing to will and do, where He is with them in heaven, but who is confronted on earth by the illimitable need of an existence of the creature which is not only threatened but assaulted, disturbed and destroyed by the forces of negation, so that He has resolved and is willing and ready to take up its cause and be its Saviour. This is the will which they observe. This is the God at whose disposal they stand. It is in the service of this mercy of His that they are glorious. Moreover, they stand for this reason and to this extent in the service of the earthly creature, not to give it help in things in which it might very well help itself or receive help from its fellows, but as the heavenly witnesses and messengers of the Saviour God, i.e., as the special heralds of His mystery as of the necessary form of His revelation and work. This will be our express theme in the next sub-section. Moreover, they fulfil this service perfectly. They stand before the throne of God. They are at the place where the speech and action of God commence in the created world. They are its direct *entourage* and original witnesses. They follow the Word of God as riders on white horses. They have no part in the confusion and contradiction and opposition of the earthly sphere which they enter with God Himself and as His following. Their only *raison d'être* as heavenly beings is to render this service. They have no neutral place in view of which they might be something other than God's servants. Finally, whatever this may mean for their mutual inter-relationship, they are something distinctive in this service. In correspondence with the concreteness of the saving will and work of God, and notwithstanding their integration and subordination under the one God, but in this subordination, their service is not one and the same, but a service in fulfilment of different commissions and therefore of varying character. They are not therefore one, but in distinction from God, yet corresponding to what He wills and establishes on earth, they are many, the plurality of angels which has its necessary basis in the universality of heavenly being as this is concretely related and fashioned. This is what may be legitimately said in general definition of these beings.

In Heb. 1¹⁴ we are given what is virtually a definition of the nature of angels, and one which might almost be called the *locus classicus* for the biblical view : οὐχὶ πάντες εἰσὶν λειτουργικὰ πνεύματα εἰς διακονίαν ἀποστελλόμενα διὰ τοὺς μέλλοντας κληρονομεῖν σωτηρίαν. The question is formulated with the intention of bringing out the transcendence of Jesus Christ over these beings. No matter from what height they come, what functions they exercise, or what dignity they may enjoy, when they are compared with Him they cannot be described as anything more than the λειτουργικὰ πνεύματα of this verse. But it may well be that the positive thing which has to be said concerning them cannot be better said than by extolling against them the more excellent name of Jesus Christ (Heb. 1⁴). To be sure, we must exercise care in our reading of the decisive statement. The main point is not that angels are πνεύματα, but that as such they receive from the adjective λειτουργικὰ and the participle ἀποστελλόμενα a distinctive character and activity which differentiate them from Jesus Christ but also set them in a positive relationship to Him. It was the exegetical error of Thomas Aquinas to show far too lively an interest in the equation of ἄγγελοι and πνεύματα, and the results were catastrophic when with the help of a concept of spirit alien to Old and New Testament alike he tried to find in these πνεύματα his *substantiae spirituales separatae.*

The same mistake was later responsible for leading J. C. K. Hofmann (*Der Schriftbeweis*, Vol. I, 1852, p. 274 f.) to the brilliant but impossible and finally quite intolerable doctrine that there is a plurality in the unity of the concept God (*Elohim*); that since God is a Spirit this is a plurality of spirits; that the one essence of God, the supracosmic Creator, resolves itself into multiplicity in terms of the presence which He exercises in the world by His Spirit; and conversely that the world of spirits, to the extent that in it the one essence of God resolves itself into the multiplicity of His qualities exercised in the world, is enclosed in the Spirit of God and gathered up in its self-multiplying unity (cf. esp. p. 354 f.). In this exposition far too much weight is laid on the term πνεύματα in Heb. 1¹⁴, and the decisive statement in the verse is completely neglected. It is true that when God is described as the Father of spirits in Heb. 12⁹ the reference is probably to the angels, and that the seven spirits of the Apocalypse (3¹, 4⁵, 5⁶), and also the four and twenty elders and the four living creatures, are to be understood as angelic forms. But in the Apocalypse not all angels are called πνεύματα as they are here. Indeed, the fact that it is here an ἅπαξ λεγόμενον ought to restrain us. The context does not give us any compelling reason for calling angels πνεύματα. And the description is only a negative characterisation, telling us that the angels are not beings which can be conceived or grasped or controlled by us, but that like demons, which are often called πνεύματα in the New Testament, they can be understood in their movements and impulsion only from a very different standpoint. It is thus better to leave this definition rather colourless. The essential determination of πνεύματα is not the fact that they are πνεύματα, but the fact that they are λειτουργικὰ πνεύματα, i.e., incomprehensible beings which have a sacred office. And as the bearers of this office they are εἰς διακονίαν ἀποστελλόμενα, i.e., despatched to fulfil this office. It is the twofold fact that they have this office and this mission which makes these incomprehensible beings ἄγγελοι in the sense of this passage. Their relationship to Jesus Christ in their sphere is like that of the apostles in the human sphere. This is both their greatness and their limitation.

In this connexion we may recall the interesting exposition of this verse by Erich Schick (*Die Botschaft der Engel*, p. 30 f., *Vom Dienst der Engel*, p. 18 f.). His rendering of λειτουργικὰ πνεύματα is "liturgical spirits." By liturgy he means "standing in adoration before the presence of God," and by διακονία "service in the world and to men." He thus gathers from the verse that in time, inner meaning, rank and essential significance there is a twofold ministry of angels, liturgy and diaconate, in which both are bound together in an indissoluble unity, but of which it may be said that for the angels (and Schick obviously thinks for us too) there can be liturgy without diaconate, but not diaconate without liturgy. Yet I am not convinced that this is the real meaning of Heb. 1¹⁴. That the sacred office which is integral to the essence of angels includes their being as λειτουργικὰ πνεύματα in the sense of standing in adoration before the presence of God is certainly to be gathered from the express statement of the angel Gabriel in Lk. 1¹⁹ and from the general context of Rev. 4–5. But is this to be regarded as a first ministry of angels from which their διακονία can be distinguished and even divided as a second? Is it really possible to think of a purely liturgical being and action of angels (or men) addressed only to God, of a pure being and action in sacred office which is not as such a being and action in the corresponding service, but can take place quite apart from this service? Can any created being do God a service which does not at once take the form of a service in the world and to man? Schick is prepared to maintain that there is no service in the world or to man which does not proceed from service to God, i.e., that there is no diaconate without liturgy. But can he really contend for a liturgy without diaconate? What kind of a God would it be—surely it could not really be the God of grace and the covenant, God in Jesus Christ—to whom heavenly or earthly beings might turn even momentarily in such abstraction, without *eo ipso* becoming His messengers and going forth as such? In Heb. 1¹⁴ does not the very transition from the adjective (λειτουργικά) to the participle (ἀποστελλόμενα) exclude even linguistically any such separation of ministry? Does not the accent of the statement plainly rest on the fact that in practice angels have their sacred office, and stand before the presence of God, in the fact that they are sent to the ministry corresponding to this office? Is not the emphasis on this side strengthened by the fact that this ministry is expressly stated to be " for them who shall be heirs of salvation," whereas we look in vain for a similar explanation of what Schick supposes to be a distinct and primary " liturgical " ministry. In view of these doubts, I prefer to take it that this passage describes all angels unequivocally as ἄγγελοι, as the host of those who are appointed and commissioned to the service of God, and therefore to service in the lower cosmos. It describes them by speaking of the sacred office which they are given and of their commission in execution of this office. It thus describes the movement in which they exist and have their distinctive being. The fact that in origin and execution this movement is one of service distinguishes them from the One who in this matter, in what is to take place " for them who shall be heirs of salvation," is Lord and King.

It is within this framework that the other general names, definitions and descriptions of angels, and such other statements as are made concerning them in the Bible, are to be correlated and become relatively intelligible.

In the context of our whole exposition we can see at once why in Zech. 14⁵ and Ps. 29¹ they are called " the heavenly ones," and in Phil. 2¹⁰ the ἐπουράνιοι in contrast to the ἐπίγειοι and καταχθόνιοι. They are given this title as the individual members of the kingdom of heaven and its order, of the occurrence which commences in heaven and aims at earth, and in which they have a part with their ministry. On account of its connexion with the kingdom of heaven we might well be tempted to make this designation both exegetically and dogmatically a leading concept. We often enough read of the coming down of an angel from heaven (e.g., Dan. 4¹⁰), or more briefly of an angel from heaven (e.g., Gal. 1⁸), or of the angels in heaven (e.g., Mk. 12²⁵). But to make this the leading concept might well involve an undesirable emphasising of the ontological side of the matter. It is wiser, perhaps, not to adopt any main concept, but to treat the usual word " angel " as a *tabula rasa* to which to relate the many other things which are said of them, including the fact that they are " heavenlies." This is the more advisable because the word " angel " will also prove to have the fullest content at the decisive point.

In Ps. 89⁶, ⁷ and Job 5¹ and 15¹⁵ (and perhaps also in 2 Thess. 1¹⁰) they are called the saints. In accordance with the general usage of the Bible this means that they are selected, ordained and separated by God for the ministry. What we called the discipline of heavenly occurrence is expressed in this designation of the individual figures. And if in Dan. 4¹³, ¹⁷, ²³ these saints are equated with watchers, we can see in this an indication that their holiness is not merely related passively to what they are on the basis of the divine order, but also to their active function in the history of salvation. They guard the frontiers, as in their opposition to the pretensions of Nebuchadnezzar in Dan. 4.

In a third series of passages (Ps. 89⁶, Job 1⁶, 2¹ and 38⁷), they are called the sons of God, and even " gods " in Ps. 82¹. (The difficult passage in Gen. 6, which speaks of the sons of God in v. 2 and v. 4, is a special case which probably does not belong to this series and cannot therefore be adduced in this connexion.) It would be foolish to allow these passages to tempt us on to the thin ice of Martensen's theory, which would have it that the angels are identical with the pagan deities, or of that of Hofmann, which treats them almost as self-emanations of God. There can be no question of angels being sons of God in the sense in which this is said of the Son of God in the New Testament, just as no rivalry with Christ is entailed if in the New Testament Christians are also called the υἱοὶ θεοῦ. Men are also addressed as " gods " or " sons of the Most High " (Ps. 82⁶, cf. Jn. 10³⁴). Both terms have a sense in which they can also be applied to creatures. Like " saints," they tell us that these creatures belong and are pledged and committed to God in a special sense. This is what is said of angels when they are called the sons of God or " gods." As the individuals of heavenly being and occurrence and its order they are impressed into God's service, and are thus made these individuals and members of the heavenly family.

In an isolated but important passage (Is. 6¹ᶠ·) we hear tell of seraphim, and it seems as though this term denotes the totality of the heavenly *entourage* of God. There is more frequent mentions of cherubim. In Gen. 3²⁴ we are reminded of Daniel's description of the angels as the watchers of Paradise, or of the way to the tree of life, but for the most part the reference is to God enthroned (1 Sam. 4⁴ and *passim*) or riding upon them (2 Sam. 22¹¹). In this function they figure prominently in the ornamentation of the ark. The linguistic sense of the two terms is so disputed by the experts that it is better for a mere layman to ignore this question, and the same is true of their material role and significance. In respect of the seraphim it is plain that their activity (the threefold *Sanctus* by which the foundations of the temple are shaken, and their purification of the lips of the prophet) points in the direction of " saints " in the active as well as the passive sense. And Gen. 3²⁴ indicates that the same is true of cherubim, while we learn from the other references to them that they are thought of partly as representatives of the subordination of even the heavenly world to God, and partly as accompanying elements in the comprehensive movement executed by God from heaven.

In some passages individual angels are given specific names. Dan. 10¹³, 12¹, Jud. 9, and Rev. 12⁷ speak of Michael, Dan. 8¹⁶, 9²¹ and Lk. 1¹⁹, ²⁶ of Gabriel, and the Book of Tobit of Raphael. Michael means " Who is like God ? ", Gabriel " the man of God," and Raphael " God heals." With a whole series of other phenomena of angelic manifestation in the Bible, these names show us that the host or assembly of God in heaven, the heavenly ones or saints or sons of God, and therefore the seraphim and cherubim, must not be thought of merely as a collective but also as individuals. As we shall see, they do not appear and act only *in corpore*, but also as individuals ; they do not speak only in concert, but personally. But we do violence both to the historical character of the texts and to the matter itself if we try to press ontologically what is said more or less clearly concerning angels in this respect. For all the vitality with which it speaks, the biblical doctrine of angels is more sober in this respect than what was later fashioned from it. Heavenly individuals are no more earthly than the heavenly collective. But as the πνεύματα exist only in virtue of the predicates λειτουργικά and ἀποστελλόμενα εἰς διακονίαν, as the heavenly host exists only as it is assembled around the throne of God and sent out from it, so individual figures, to the extent that their names and speech and action are mentioned, exist only as they are specifically summoned and separated from the rest with a specific commission and in a specific relationship to the earthly history of salvation, disappearing again into the general body as soon as their work is accomplished.

Hence it is futile to ask what Gabriel did or was between the role ascribed to him in Daniel and his part in the events of the nativity. All that we are told concerning the individual existence of angels is that they are there as the mighty ones " that do his commandments . . . ministers of his, that do his pleasure " (Ps. 103²⁰ᶠ·), and we do well, therefore, to picture their individual existence, if at all, only in the actuality with which it is presented in this Psalm. The more strictly we do this, the more the angels lose the character of a curious gallery of legendary figures, the more clearly we see their practical significance, and the more clearly above all we see their existence in direct relationship to the reality and will of the living God. The specific names of specific angels are themselves a clear challenge to think along these lines. They are eloquent in the very fact that they slip between our fingers, what they say individually being merely a declaration about angels generally and their relationship to God, and in this way about the nature of angels. The name Michael : " Who is like God ? ", is particularly interesting in this connexion. It may be compared with Ps. 89⁶, ⁸ : " For who in the heaven can be compared unto the Lord ? who among the sons of God can be likened unto the Lord ? . . . O Lord God of hosts, who is a strong God like unto thee ? " Thus what is said of Michael in particular is to be said of all angels generally. They all can and must be called Michael, and by this name they propose the question to which the only answer is that even in heaven there is none like God.

This brings us to the problem whether and how far there is an inner order of the angelic world on the biblical view. We have seen what the theology of the primitive and mediæval Church thought it knew concerning a ranking and therefore a hierarchy of angels. Is this a tenable idea from the biblical standpoint ?

It results from the notion of the heavenly host or assembly only if we believe that what is true of human and earthly phenomena of this kind may be postulated of the heavenly reality. But the passages which speak of the numbers of angels are a warning in this connexion : " Thousand thousands ministered unto him, and ten thousand times ten thousand stood before him " (Dan. 7¹⁰, Rev. 5¹¹). These are not statistical but hyperbolical statements. They simply tell us that numbers fail. But how can there be any ranking without numbers ?

Allusion has been made to Job 33²³, where after the reference to other ways and means by which God can speak to man we are told that " if there be a messenger with him, an interpreter, one among a thousand," who can both explain to man the chastisement which has fallen upon him and also pity him and make intercession for him, it may well be that " twice and thrice " (v. 29) he will be helped and enlightened with the light of life. But why should this one among a thousand be higher than the other nine hundred and ninety-nine ? That he is separated from them is obvious. But it is equally obvious that this is only on the ground and in the sense of the special commission which he is given in relation to this man, and not of a higher rank proper to him *in se*.

More illuminating perhaps in this connexion, although not wholly clear in context or preserved in wording, is the passage Joshua 5¹³⁻¹⁵, where outside Jericho a man with a drawn sword meets Joshua, and when Joshua asks him : " Art thou for us, or for our adversaries ? ", he answers : " Nay, but as captain (*sar*) of the host of the Lord am I now come." The only thing is that, as so often in the Old Testament, this angelophany shows itself to be really a theophany : " And Joshua fell on his face to the earth, and did worship, and said unto him, What saith my lord unto his servant ? And the captain of the Lord's host said unto Joshua, Loose thy shoe from off thy foot ; for the place whereon thou standest is holy. And Joshua did so." It was obviously to characterise the angelophany as an occasion of the first order, to declare the power of the host of Yahweh and in and with it of its true Lord, and to show that the angelophany was a theophany, that the heavenly being made itself known to Joshua under this title. But the passage hardly gives us to understand that there are *sarim* by birth or commission in the host of Yahweh. The same is true of the two passages in Daniel which are often quoted in this respect : Dan. 10¹³, in which Michael is called one of the chief *sarim* ; and Dan. 12¹, in which he is called the great *sar*. We have already stated that the specific name of this particular angel is against a view which would give him any inherent distinction as compared with others. If he is here called a *sar*, and one of the chief, the obvious context of the chapter shows that the reference is to his function. He is the angel who, in the fulfilment of the earthly events of salvation history, is associated with the people of Daniel, i.e., the elect people (as a heavenly *sar* is also active in relation to Persia, 10¹³, ²¹, and another in relation to Greece, 10²¹). According to the clear statement of Dan. 12¹ Michael is " the great *sar* which standeth for the children of thy people " ; and according to Dan. 10²¹ he is " your *sar*." It is in honour of his commission as distinguished by the divine election of grace in history, and not in relation to any inherent rank of his in the angelic hierarchy, that these emphatic statements are made. Here as in Joshua 5 the term *sar* is not to be taken as a *nomen numeri* but as a *nomen officii*. Nor is a higher rank ascribed to Michael in Jude 9 when he is called Μιχαὴλ ὁ ἀρχάγγελος. An archangel is not like an archbishop or an archduke— not even the archangel whose voice will be heard at the return of Jesus Christ (1 Thess. 4¹⁶) ! The term ἀρχάγγελος obviously derives from the Septuagint version of Daniel which has εἷς τῶν ἀρχόντων for *achad hasarim* (10¹³), ὁ ἄρχων ὑμῶν for *sarekem* (10²¹) and ὁ ἄρχων ὁ μέγας for *hasar hagadol* (12¹). The Vulgate uses *princeps* in all three passages. An ἄρχων or *princeps* is one who exercises power, and therefore an angel which is called ἄρχων is one to whom a specific authority is given in history, as in the case of Michael in relation to Israel (Dan. 10 and 12). He is the bearer and representative, not of any power and least of all of his own, but of the power of God over this people. It is this power which is proclaimed by the ἀρχάγγελος of 1 Thess. 4, and an inherent dignity is as little ascribed to him by the fact of this office as is a higher rank to the accompanying trumpet in relation to other trumpets. The distinction of both angel and trumpet is to be found in what they say and blow, not in what they are. Hence we cannot speak of a higher dignity of Michael, or of a general hierarchy of heaven, merely on the basis of the term ἀρχάγγελος.

In the light of all that has been said we obviously cannot agree with the militarists that when Rev. 12⁷ speaks of Michael and his angels making war against the dragon which has invaded heaven we are to think of the ἄγγελοι αὐτοῦ as a force commanded by Michael and Michael himself as the officer at their head. They are called " his " angels because now, in contrast to the Book of Daniel and perhaps in view of the accession of the ἔθνη to Israel, they share his commission and are responsible with him for its execution.

What is true of Michael is no less true of Gabriel. His name " Man of God " might well be that of any other angel and does not give him any pre-eminence. According to Dan. 8¹⁶ and 9²¹ his commission and service are to explain the vision which Daniel has seen. In Luke 1 it is he who announces to Zacharias the birth of John (1¹¹f·) and to Mary the birth of Jesus (1²⁶f·). From the fact that he is called ὁ παρεστηκὼς ἐνώπιον τοῦ θεοῦ (v. 19) we are ill-advised to deduce that there is ascribed to him " a higher, extraordinary rank " within the angelic hosts (E. Schick, *op. cit.*, p. 30), for according to Rev. 4³f· κυκλόθεν or ἐνώπιον τοῦ θεοῦ seems to be used of all angels (and according to Rev. 7¹⁵) of all the perfected saints), and in Rev. 8² the seven angels with trumpets are described as οἱ ἐνώπιον τοῦ θεοῦ. It is hard to see, therefore, why any ontic dignity should be ascribed to Gabriel on the basis of this expression. His honour is great enough if understood in the light of his commission in Luke 1.

And now finally in this connexion we must consider the terms or realities in the Pauline Epistles especially which once claimed the interest of Pseudo-Dionysius and contributed so largely to the construction of his hierarchy : the ἀρχαί and ἐξουσίαι (1 Cor. 15²⁴ ; Col. 1¹⁶, 2¹⁰ ; Eph. 1²¹, 3¹⁰, 6¹² ; Titus 3¹) ; the δυνάμεις (1 Cor. 15²⁴ ; 1 Pet. 3²²) ; the κυριότητες (Col. 1¹⁶, Eph. 6¹²) ; the θρόνοι (Col. 1¹⁶) ; the κοσμοκράτορες (Eph. 6¹²) ; and θάνατος, ζωή, ἐνεστῶτα, μέλλοντα, ὕψωμα and βάθος (Rom. 8³⁸). The term ἀρχαί is used in all these passages with the exception of 1 Pet. 3²². Mention might also be made of the ἄρχοντες τοῦ αἰῶνος τούτου (1 Cor. 2⁶ᶠ·). The term ἐξουσία is present in each case except Rom. 8³⁸ᶠ·, and in Romans it seems instead to be given a particular application in 13¹ᶠ·. It is obvious that all the terms are used to denote power. In view of the context (" Who shall separate us from the love of Christ ? ", Rom. 8³⁵) this is true even of the extended list in Rom. 8³⁸ᶠ·. In the other passages the terms have a ring and scope which are political in the widest sense. They speak of the powers which control and fashion human history. Three meanings intersect in these passages and must be given greater or lesser prominence in their exegesis. (1) In Rom. 13¹ and Tit. 3¹ (cf. Lk. 12¹¹ and Jn. 19¹⁰ᶠ·) the reference is plainly to the powers of state instituted by God but exercised by men. Indeed, 1 Pet. 2¹³ speaks expressly of an ἀνθρωπίνη κτίσις. (2) In Col. 1¹⁶ and 2¹⁰, Eph. 1²¹ and 3¹⁰ and 1 Pet. 3²², where the same words are used, it is a matter of the heavenly powers created and established for the sake of Christ and in His service (δι' αὐτοῦ καὶ εἰς αὐτόν) and therefore controlled by Him—powers whose function and service will attain their goal with His coming again, and will thus be " put down " by Him. (3) In the other passages, the same terms refer to the illegitimate and perverse demonic powers which imitate and rival the heavenly and of which it is said that they have already been taken prisoner by Christ and will be marched in His triumphant procession (Col. 2¹⁵), so that although we have still to fight (Eph. 6¹²) we do not need to fear them (Rom. 8³⁸ᶠ·). Our present concern is with the second interpretation, and there can be no doubt that the words ἀρχαί, ἐξουσίαι, θρόνοι, κυριότητες and δυνάμεις do also denote the heavenly powers which are subject to Christ and have in Him their Head (1 Pet. 3²², Col. 2¹⁰). It is plain that in this connexion we are basically on the same territory as that of the heavenly *sarim* of the Old Testament. If for the time being we ignore the existence of demonic powers of the same name, these heavenly powers, directly determined from heaven by the action of God, stand over against the earthly formations, and especially the powers of state, instituted by God but fashioned by men. They are not identical with them, yet they are also related to them as their divinely marked originals. If we can say of earthly powers that they are ὑπὸ θεοῦ τεταγμέναι (Rom. 13¹), we owe this to the fact that they correspond on earth to these powers in heaven. As God speaks His Word from heaven, He reveals and exercises His power to make peace on earth. The heavenly ἀρχαί and ἐξουσίαι are this revelation and exercise of His power to make peace on earth, and they find their counterpart in the earthly powers of state as forces for the maintenance of a relative peace. The fact that the same terms are used for both the heavenly originals and their earthly counterparts shows us (as we may gather from the political terminology) that the former first and properly, because determined by the divine action in respect of the covenant and salvation, are powers of order, and that they are not merely obscure *potentiae* but definite *potestates*, salutary forces for the establishment of a relative peace, the relative aversion of chaos and therefore in this sense the furtherance of the kingdom of God. Whether they are called ἀρχαί, ἐξουσίαι, or anything else, they have in Christ their Head, and, in the phrase which J. C. Blumhardt used of the angels, they represent the power of order in the covenant and grace. As and because there are these representations of the divine power of order from heaven, earthly history can never be given up wholly to chaos, but there can always be within it, as poor but genuine replicas, real forces of peace and order ; and it is by these powers, and as their imitation, that the forces of disorder live—the demonic powers with their specific human replicas. Yet because in the case of all these terms we have to do with the representation, revelation and expression in human history of the one divine power of order differentiated in form and action by time, place and circumstance, we are completely wide of the mark if we try to conclude from the different terms or descriptions an inner gradation in these forces, various sections or departments of the kingdom of heaven, and therefore the existence of a heavenly hierarchy. The exegesis of these terms by Pseudo-Dionysius reached the very limit of arbitrariness and futility. There is absolutely nothing to authorise or compel us to regard the ἀρχαί as higher than the ἐξουσίαι, the δυνάμεις as lower than the θρόνοι, etc. All these terms denote in their own place the one whole power of the kingdom of heaven. There can be no question of any ranking of the realities indicated by them because the power which they represent, reveal and express is in each instance the power of the one God, and because Christ is the Head of them all, and they would not be powers apart from the power of this Head. To be sure, their distinction, and their integration in this distinction, are also real. But as the kingdom of heaven as a whole is a historical reality, so it is with its integration and with each of the powers which these terms show to be different from others. Their difference is to be understood from the sequence and differentiation of the divine Word and act coming down from the heavenly sphere to the earthly. It is to be understood as the outworking of the πολυποίκιλος σοφία τοῦ θεοῦ from the knowledge of which, as it attains its goal and is revealed in the existence of the community, even the angels in heaven have something new to learn (Eph. 3¹⁰). If there is order in heaven, it is not the order of rank, but of function and service. And with this conclusion we may bring this excursus to a close. As we have seen, it is not impossible to understand Pseudo-Dionysius in this sense, or at least in this direction. He has not made it easy for the Church to understand him meaningfully. But his concept of the heavenly hierarchy is sufficiently dynamic not to exclude the possibility that for all his mistakes in detail he should be understood as a whole as a man who unfortunately spoke of an order of rank but perhaps had in mind an order of service.

And now within the framework of this general survey of our subject we may venture a final question and answer. What is the order to which heavenly occurrence is subject both as a whole and in detail, and by which it is both differentiated and integrated ? What is it that commences above and then comes down to earth with the kingdom of God ? What is the purpose in which these heavenly hosts have their being, i.e., stand in their ministry ? In what does the service of angels consist ? Here, too, we must be on our guard against thinking that we know too much, but also against the stupidity which refuses to know what is to be known. As we have stated, it is a question of the service of God, of the merciful God, and therefore of the earthly creature to whom He has turned ; of a perfect and a highly specific service. If we gather up these various threads, the answer to the question in what this service consists is so obvious that no speculation is needed to see it, for only wilful blindness can fail to receive it. If we have rightly described the ministry of angels as their vital function in relation to Christ their Head, or more expressly as the perfect and highly specific assistance which they give to God as the Lord of the covenant and grace in His relationship to the earthly creature, it is evident in what their ministry can alone consist materially, and does in fact consist.

But first a brief mention must be made of that in which it naturally cannot consist. It cannot consist in their doing what God alone can do, It has no basis here. Angels cannot, then, speak words which as their own are the words of God. They cannot do works which as their own are divine works. They cannot save, redeem or liberate the earthly creature. They cannot forgive even the smallest sin, or remove even the slightest pain. They can do nothing to bring about the reconciliation of the world with God. Nor are they judges of the world. They did not create it. They can neither be wrathful nor gracious toward it. They did not establish the covenant between God and man, and they cannot fulfil, maintain, renew or confirm it. They do not overcome death. They do not rule the history of salvation, or universal history, or any history. Otherwise they would not be the angels of God. They would have nothing whatever to do with the kingdom of heaven coming on earth ; they would deny their own nature ; they would be apes of themselves, demons, if they did anything along these lines, òr rather if they tried to do (for these are things which no creature can do), if on the pretext and with the appearance of being helpers, saviours, comforters, prophets, priests and kings, they assisted the earthly creature with their own word and work, directed its attention, adoration and gratitude to themselves, and approached it as lords in their own right and with an autonomous claim. And how terribly they would be misunderstood by the creature if they were seen in this role, and on the basis of any consideration or presumed experience, or in any form, independent expectations, hopes, appeals and thankgivings were addressed to them ! We really do not know what we are about if we treat them in this way. For we confuse them with their express opponents. We do not really have to do with them at all, or with the kingdom of heaven, but with their express opponents and with the kingdom of falsehood and darkness. The heavenly beings, the saints, the sons of God, the seraphim, Michael and Gabriel, neither are nor do these things that they are falsely assumed to be and do. They are heavenly creatures, but they are creatures no less strictly than all earthly creatures. If they speak the Word of God and do the work of God, it is never as their own. If they have power to do so (as they have) ; if they themselves are heavenly powers, it is as representatives, in the revelation and exercise of the one power of God Himself. They never take the central position, but always leave it open for the One who alone can occupy it. They merely come and go again, having maintained this freedom of God. They never catch the eye. They always look away from themselves, and they invite and command others to look away from every creature, themselves included, to the One who alone is worthy that the eye of every creature should rest on Him, and from whom alone they can really see themselves and their fellow-creatures. How could their ministry be genuine ministry if things were otherwise, if it were in any sense their own rule or partial rule ? How could it then be the service of God ? Or what God would they then serve ? It would certainly not be the merciful God. Nor would they serve the earthly creature whom the merciful God wills to adopt and has already done so. And far from being perfect their being and action would always be total and desperate rebellion, and all its particularity would resolve itself into a wild anarchy in which the individual would be lost instead of honoured. In no circumstances, therefore, can the ministry of angels consist in this usurpation of the position and function of God. And it is obvious that any presumed dealings with angels or discussion of their reality cannot avoid the test whether it keeps within or has long since crossed the fine but very definite limit beyond which we enter at once the sphere of a mythology which is not harmless but savage and destructive. Here as elsewhere, for example, Christian art has almost always rendered poor service, demonic rather than angelic, to the cause of Christian truth.

The true service of angels, like that of all other creatures to God, is that of witnesses. Whether heavenly or earthly, the creature can render assistance in relation to God and its fellows by being the witness of God. That is to say, it can exist in such a way that in its existence, while it cannot usurp His functions or take His place, it gives an appropriate response to His existence, Word and work. In their existence they can render and be a response which corresponds to Him as their Creator and Lord. In this correspondence they can declare Him, and their declaration can have the character of thanksgiving in relation to Himself and proclamation in relation to their fellow-creatures : the more powerful as proclamation the more radically it is thanksgiving ; and the more sincerely as thanksgiving the more seriously as proclamation. The creature may praise God. It cannot do this on its own initiative, but solely at His behest and in obedience. It cannot do it in well-meant disclosures, but only as it corresponds to His Word and work. It praises the Lord as it obeys this behest and is this correspondence. And praising Him in this way, it is His witness. This is the one thing required of it. When it does this, it does not trangress its limits but respects them, doing within them that which is possible to it, for which it is free, and which is required of it as it has this freedom. When it does this, it serves God, and as and because it serves God it also serves its fellow-creature. This is what is required of it. God expects the praise of His creature, for He does not will to remain alone in His Word and work, but, as He speaks and acts, to be together with the creature, and in this way, in this covenant with it, to be its God. This expectation of God makes the praise of God necessary. But all creation waits to hear the praise of God and to be summoned to take part in it. It needs to do this to achieve its true nature and thus to be itself a correspondence of the Word and work of God. And in so doing it does not will to be alone. It cannot strike up the praise of God—no creature can do this —but only join in the praise of God as it hears it already in the existence of other creatures and is thereby summoned to it. Thus the expectation of the fellow-creature also makes the praise of God necessary. And where God is praised, He is served and has His witnesses.

All this is true equally and primarily of angels. That " He rules in the kingdom of heaven " is a phrase which we have already used at the appropriate point, and we may now continue the quotation : " Ye strong angels, discharge His praise, and magnify the great Lord, and set forth His holy Word." Nor should we omit the conclusion : " My soul, increase His praise in every place." The ministry of angels is the supreme ministry of witness, to the increase of which our praise of God and ministry, and all service of God, can be added only as a secondary ministry attaching itself to it. The will of God is first done in heaven, and then on earth. We can paraphrase this to the effect that it first takes place in heaven and then on earth that God is praised by the creature, finding His creaturely correspondence and witnesses., He has found these in heaven before He finds a single one on earth. They exist in plenitude and perfection there even when there seems to be or are only a few on earth, and these are all extremely feeble witnesses. And because His kingdom comes from heaven to earth, this means that in those who come with Him He will always have many trustworthy witnesses on earth, namely, in the existence of His strong angels who are always present and active in full numbers, willingness and readiness even where the earthly creature seems to be sadly lacking with its praise both in quantity and quality, and in view of whom we can never find completely intolerable and hopeless the apparently or genuinely troubled state of things on earth. The heavenly witnesses to God's rule of the Church and the world, these witnesses of the first rank, are always and everywhere present. And when we have the insight into the protocols of ecclesiastical and universal history which is denied to even the most perspicacious of ordinary historians and students of human affairs, we shall probably find the most unexpected traces of the way in which the angels have been present and effectively spoken and acted, not as demigods or fabled creatures, but simply in the heavenly power of their witness and praise.

We must insist that their ministry is a ministry of witness. God alone rules. God alone is holy and gracious, sovereign and merciful, kind, omnipotent and glorious. Jesus Christ alone is the Lord of all things. Creatures, including the angels, can only praise Him and be His witnesses. But in the course of the divine speech, action and rule the angels as heavenly creatures are His primary, authentic, constant, inflexible and infallible witnesses. Their praise of God is pure praise. Their existence corresponds perfectly to His Word and work. The service which, in praising Him, they render both to Him and to their fellow-creatures is always an authentic, a fully authentic service. It is this because it is quite free from any personal desires for power or lordship. What is represented and present in the angels is always the whole secret of God. And it is the genuine secret of God, poles apart from any mystagogy or pseudo-mystery, and finally consisting only in the simple, but in its simplicity inaccessible and unfathomable reality that He, God, is with us and for us : He, the Lord, who alone can command but does command ; He, the Lord over every difficulty, and always in some way the Lord who leads us out of every difficulty ; He, the Lord of life and death ; He, the Lord who imputes and does not impute sins ; He, the Lord who in all things is to be feared and loved ; He, the Lord even of nature and history ; He alone, but He totally and infallibly. This is the great and genuine mystery of God. What do we know already of this mystery ? How stupid even the best of us are in face of this simple " He " ! What are all our theology and liturgy, preaching and piety, when we realise that they must deal with this total and genuine mystery of God ? And what is the praise of our soul and existence, what are we ourselves, when we measure ourselves by the fact that we are to correspond to this mystery ? But the angels know and praise and attest Him in this mystery. As those who do, they are present when heaven comes down to earth, and He speaks and acts and rules on earth. They observe and sanctify this mystery, declaring it in all its glory, as first in heaven, then between heaven and earth, and finally on earth they form its accompaniment and circumference. They are not blind or deaf or without feeling for this mystery. They exist in contemplation of it, from afar but steadily and openly. And for this reason they are not dumb or indolent. They exist as they declare it, and therefore as they are faithful in relation to God and their fellow-creatures. Their existence is thus exemplary. This is not because they are heavenly creatures, but because as heavenly creatures they are ordained and summoned by God Himself to exist in this way. They do so in obedience to this calling. This is, in general terms, the service of angels. The fact that they are real servants in this sense, that they are nothing but servants, is what makes their existence exemplary in a way in which this cannot be said of any saint, let alone of any of the other great men in the earthly sphere.

We can best illustrate the biblical presuppositions of what is said from the main themes of Revelation 4 and 5, where we have an authentic general depiction of the ministry of angels. The two chapters exercise a retarding function in the context of the apocalyptic narration (E. Peterson, *op. cit.*, p. 19). In 4[1] the seer is told : " I will shew thee things which must be hereafter." But in the first instance he is not shown these things. Through the open door of heaven he first sees (c. 4) the throne of God, then—in highly characteristic movement— its immediate *entourage*, then (c. 5) in the midst of the throne and those around it the Lamb to whom there is given the book with seven seals in which these future events are inscribed, and finally the renewed movement of the whole *entourage*, which is now illimitably extended. " The invisible background of world history is disclosed " (J. T. Beck, *Erkl. d. Off. Joh.*, 1884, p. 92). It is from this that the eschatological events later revealed to the seer acquire their true relevance. Our interest must now be particularly focused on this background to the extent that to it there also belongs the heavenly *entourage* of God and the Lamb, and its distinctive movement.

The controlling centre of what the seer is shown is the throne with its lightnings, thunders and voices (4⁵) and He who sits on it (vv. 2–3). But He who sits on it is not named. He does not need to be named. There is only One who can sit on it. And what He is, is indicated by the radiance which streams from Him and which is compared with that of particularly bright diamonds and the rainbow. We are reminded of 1 Jn. 1⁵ : " God is light, and in him is no darkness at all." He is the Holy One who reveals Himself, to whom everything is revealed, and who reveals all things in what He does. There then follows the description of His immediate *entourage* in vv. 4–8.

It begins with the 24 πρεσβύτεροι sitting on thrones, clothed in white robes and bearing crowns. Irrespective of any questions of superiority or subordination, these obviously form the outer circle around the throne of God. They are not glorified men, and therefore they cannot be identified with ecclesiastics, whether Roman cardinals, Lutheran pastors or Presbyterian elders. According to the place, speech and action ascribed to them, they are undoubtedly angels, so that the seer can address one of them as κύριος in 7¹⁴. Already in Is. 24²³ the term " ancients " seems to be used for angels. But the fact that they are given this designation does not mean that they are to be thought of either as old men or as counsellors. It has often been suggested that the heavenly assembly is a kind of privy council around the throne of God, but this rests on a conception which here as elsewhere is quite alien to biblical angelology. There is not a single trace of any such function in their conduct in Rev. 4–5. And Is. 40¹³ (and possibly Rom. 11³⁴) is quite conclusive in this respect : " Who hath directed the Spirit of the Lord, or being his counsellor hath taught him ? " We cannot deduce from their name more than that they are exalted and authoritative beings, as suggested by the fact that they sit on thrones and bear crowns. A sober but possibly the best translation is " representatives," which brings us at once into proximity to the terms used by Paul to denote the heavenly beings. Of these we are particularly reminded of θρόνοι. It would be a mistake, of course, to think of them as representing the earthly community, or a perfected community translated into heaven. If they represent anything or anyone, then, in accordance with their general function, it is God in His relationship to a specific earthly sphere of reality. To which sphere is decided by the interpretation of the number 24. Is this the number of the tribes of Israel doubled with the accession of the Gentiles ? Does it represent the 12 patriarchs together with the 12 apostles ? Are we to think of the 24 priestly classes and their " princes " in 1 Chron. 24⁴ᶠ· ? If these suggestions are correct, the 24 are the representatives of God in relation to the fellowship of the old and new people of God. In other words, they are in plurality what in the Book of Daniel Michael is said to be in particular. Or are they the 24 hours of the day as determined by the movement of the firmament, thus representing on a Pythagorean interpretation the totality of the astronomical heaven ? This suggestion has the advantage of establishing a clear relationship between the 24 elders and the 4 living creatures, which are obviously the representatives of God in relation to the sub-lunary or earthly sphere. But in the text itself there is no direct indication that the 24 have this astral character.

Possibly the text itself ought not to be read in such a way as to entail a clear decision between these alternatives, but something of all of them ought to be found in the number 24. The important thing, however, is that they are clothed in white garments. We remember that in Rev. 19[14] the heavenly hosts who follow the Word of God are also clothed in white and ride on white horses. Again, the head and hair of the Son of Man—and this has nothing to do with old age— are said to be " white like wool, as white as snow " (Rev. 1[14]). Again, we are told that at the transfiguration the raiment of Jesus " became shining, exceeding white as snow ; so as no fuller on earth can white them " (Mk. 9[3]), or " white as the light " (Mt. 17[2]). This whiteness is the appropriate response of the creature to the multicoloured radiance of God (v. 3). The fact that the 24 elders wear white clothes means that they reflect this δόξα of God. They do not owe these clothes to their own nature, or to the fact that they are heavenly beings. These are not the robes of earthly kings or priests, but the festal garments with which they are invested in virtue of the fact that God has sat on this throne among them. It is He alone who makes heaven and its creatures bright.

The question arises whether we are to take it that the " seven lamps of fires burning before the throne, which are the seven Spirits of God " (v. 5), are angelic beings. They are not mentioned again. And it cannot be denied that the context in which the phrase is introduced in Rev. 1[4] supports the view that this is perhaps a distinctive designation of the Holy Spirit Himself. Rev. 5[6] points in the same direction with its reference to the seven eyes of the Lamb " which are the seven Spirits of God." But the images and terms used by the writer are so elusive that we cannot rule out the possibility that in this case, where it fits the context better, the seven spirits are not the divine Spirit in His activity and manifoldness, but heavenly creatures, described as λαμπάδες πυρὸς καιόμεναι in correspondence to the radiance of God and in analogy to the white clothes of the elders, and certainly to be understood as representatives of the divine lordship in process of establishment over the whole cosmos.

Finally—beyond the crystal sea, in which we have probably to see the heavenly ocean of Gen. 1[7] now made transparent and robbed of its terrors—there are the four living creatures of v. 6 f., in whose depiction we seem to have a combination of the seraphim of Is. 6 and the four similarly described creatures of Ez. 1, the first like a lion, the second like a calf, the third with a face as a man, the fourth like a flying eagle, and all with six wings and full of eyes within. In the fact that we have here a wild beast, a domestic animal, a man and a bird, there is a clear reference not only to the earthly but to the sub-lunary sphere. It would be even clearer if we were to relate their number to the four parts of the day, or the four seasons of the year, or the four quarters of heaven, or to all these things in conjunction. And it is remarkable, and to be noted in our exposition, that these earthly beings in the narrowest sense stand in an innermost circle around God almost like an immediate bodyguard, just as later they will have a most important part to play. On the other hand, it must be pointed out that their description bursts the limits of all observation or even conception of earthly creatures. They are not earthly creatures. We cannot, then, regard them, as I was once tempted to do, as the " representation and concentration of creaturely life in the world in the original form of paradisal perfection " (W. Hadorn, *Die Offb. d. Joh.*, 1928, p. 72). Certainly the reference is to creaturely nature on earth, but what we have here is the representation and relationship of God to it, of the representation of His lordship even in this sphere. The four living creatures are creatures ; but they are not earthly creatures. They are quite definitely heavenly beings.

The point is now reached where the whole picture comes to life, or where it is shown to the seer to be already caught up in a secret movement. For while the 24 elders continue to sit on the thrones, and the lamps only burn, it is said of these creatures in the innermost circle that " they rest not day nor night."

It is as though they were the perpetual motion by which the earthly sphere in the narrowest sense, the sub-lunary world, but latently too the astral and even the heavenly, is constantly kept in unrest, or tension, or expectation of things to come. It is as though the whole historical drama in which all heaven is later engaged were initiated at this point by what the four creatures, as the heralds of the eternal vitality of God Himself, have always done and will obviously do up to a certain moment in the process of that general movement, when they are themselves caught up in it (5^8). At any rate, we can see in them first what is meant by the ministry of angels : the praise which is offered to God but in this way is also proclaimed to the whole earthly and heavenly cosmos ; the praise of God in His absolute uniqueness, superiority and lordship in relation to all His creatures. In other words, they strike up the well-known, threefold *Sanctus* of Is. 6^3. They confirm and express the fact that the angels are holy ones by looking away from themselves and again and again praising God as the Holy One. They are characterised as heavenly beings by the fact that they can and self-evidently do do this, not being a people of unclean lips as the prophet confesses in Is. 6^5, but a people of clean lips.

We must go on at once to comment on v. 9 if we are to understand this *Sanctus*-cry. The concept of a heavenly cultus-act continued in all kinds of corresponding earthly actions is surely far too narrow to describe what is here represented as the heavenly liturgy commencing with the call of the four creatures. They " give " glory and honour and thanks to Him who sits on the throne and lives from aeon to aeon. This means that they render or ascribe to Him that which belongs to Him. They acknowledge that all these things are His, and cannot belong to any other. They acknowledge Him as God. Hence they do not do anything which is strange, but that which is natural and self-evident to their nature as creatures. They do not do anything which is particularly solemn or festal, but that which is supremely everyday. They do that which is proper to them and to all creatures from the very first. They do not know any other creaturely act but that which they fulfil with the threefold *Sanctus*. To be sure, this is a liturgy, but it is the kind of liturgy which can find a true correspondence on earth only when earthly creatures join the heavenly with the same self-evident totality as is actually described in 5^{13}. For this reason we should bring it into indirect and not into direct relation (like Peterson) with the liturgy of the Church in its isolation and separation from the natural and everyday events of life. The thought expressed in Rev. 4^8 by the term ὁ παντοκράτωρ is found already in Is. 6^3 : " The whole earth is full of his glory." Not the earthly Church, or a monastic or congregational choir, but the earthly cosmos as such and in its totality is the true and proper participant in the heavenly song of praise initiated by the four living creatures. What the earthly Church can do in this respect will surely be done the more joyfully and solemnly and festally the more consciously it is done with the incumbent modesty.

A further point to be noted in the *Sanctus* of the four living creatures is that the call of the seraphim in Is. 6^3 is visibly expanded in v. 8. The doxologies of Rev. 4 have often been brought into specific relationship to the first article of the creed : *Credo in unum Deum* (W. Hadorn, p. 68, 73). There is a grain of truth in this. Only in Rev. 5 do we see the Lamb in the midst of the throne. But it must not be overlooked that the God whose uniqueness, superiority and lordship are first confessed by the four living creatures is He who " was, and is, and is to come." The ontological sequence of praise is obviously broken in the third link where instead of the expected " who will be " we have " who is to come " (Peterson, p. 24). God is the Creator, but He is not only the One who as such always will be, as He always has been and now is, the Lord of the creature. He is also the One who has set off and is in process of coming as such. The fact that in the answering chorus of the 24 elders He is expressly praised as the Creator (4^{11}) must certainly be taken to mean that He, this One who comes, who does not abandon the creature but is on the way to it as Judge and Saviour, is the Creator of the universe by whose will it was created. He is thus worthy that all δόξα, τιμή and δύναμις should be ascribed to Him. The song struck up in 5⁹ is, of course, a new song in the sense that it explicitly proclaims this coming of the Lord, or rather the fact that He has already come in what the Lamb has done on earth. But even so it only confirms what is implicitly declared and proclaimed to the heavenly and earthly world by the four living creatures. Did not their praise of God in v. 9 expressly add to δόξα and τιμή the εὐχαριστία which goes beyond anything we meet with in Is. 6³ ? Is not their song already a true *Benedictus qui venit in nomine Domini*, and to that extent an anticipation of that new song ?

If this were not the case, the 24 elders could not do what they twice do later (5⁸, ¹⁴). They could not fall down and worship (προσκυνεῖν) before the Lamb, thus repeating exactly the action which is their present answer to the praise of the 4 living creatures (4¹⁰). This, then, is the action with which they too are set in motion. It is plainly presupposed, although not explicitly stated, that they come down from their thrones. They then prostrate themselves before the One who sits on the throne, worshipping the One who lives for ever, and casting their crowns before the throne.

It is to be noted especially that according to the plain sense of vv. 9–10 it is the praise of the 4 living creatures which sets the 24 elders in motion. The former precede and the latter follow. Yet according to the whole depiction the former are angelic beings in which the lordship of God over the depths of earth is particularly represented, so that as compared with the 24 crowned heads on their thrones we might well regard them as lower angels. We have already seen, however, that the whole conception of higher and lower angels is quite untenable. And how we should be thrown into confusion in this passage if we tried to apply it, and thus regarded the 4 as inferior and the 24 as superior, but then suddenly found that the 4 came first and the 24 only second and for the moment last ! But it would be equally false to reverse the classification. All that we can and must say is that the 4 precede the 24 because they are angelic beings which stand in particular relation to the depths of earth. As they look into these depths with their countless eyes, they see something which evokes their *Sanctus*-cry. In anticipation of what will be expressly said in the hymn of 5⁹ we might well expand this from Eph. 3¹⁰. In these depths they see the ἐκκλησία, and there is thus revealed to them the πολυποίκιλος σοφία τοῦ θεοῦ. At all events, in His relation to this sphere in the depths they recognise Him who sits on the throne as the Holy One, as the παντοκράτωρ, as Him who was, and is, and comes. We can and must hazard the statement that what the 4 living creatures proclaim is the evident mercy of God in relation to this lower sphere. And in this respect the 24 elders, the crowned heads on their 24 thrones, which seem to be superior in their significance for salvation history or their astral character, can only follow them. It is as they hear this proclamation that they too are summoned and set in motion.

It is also to be noted that in the first instance their movement takes the form of a silent action and only later finds expression in the corresponding word or song. They first perform a simple act of humility. We are not told that the 4 living creatures performed a similar act, perhaps because their particular nature and position made such an act superfluous, whereas it was natural for the 24 in authority to express their supremacy by placing their powers so dramatically at the disposal of God. But quite apart from the meaning of this action it is worth noting that here (and again in 5⁸, ¹⁴) there is such explicit reference not merely to the speech or singing of angels but also to their action. This is of a piece with the fact that in 5⁷ there is brief reference to something which takes place between the Lamb and Him who sits on the throne. One might have supposed that the two chapters would have consisted only of a description of the encounter between God and the heavenly world and an accout of the doxologies pronounced or sung by the angels. How easily heaven might then have been regarded as a kingdom of spiritual truths and eternal ideas, as a static background to world history ! Yet this is not the case. For it is in heaven that the occurrence originates which then takes earthly form as cosmic and eschatological occurrence. The angels in heaven do already what will also be done on earth by earthly creatures.

Their action consists, however, in the fact that they leave their thrones and worship and cast their crowns before the throne, unequivocally acknowledging before God and all other heavenly creatures and even earthly creation in the person of the seer that there can be no question of any rivalry between their being and majesty and greatness and distinction and rule, and the being, activity and rule of God Himself. They let it be known that they cannot occupy or claim the position of viceroys or regents in their relationship to God. If we can say this of a happening within heaven itself, they go down into the depths. The movement which they execute is an act of solidarity with the rest of creation. They first associate themselves with the four living creatures, and then indirectly with the host of earthly creatures to whom these have addressed themselves from heaven. We are reminded of Lk. 1⁵¹ᶠ·: " He hath shewed strength with his arm ; he hath scattered the proud in the imagination of their hearts. He hath put down the mighty from their seats." But in this case there are no tyrants to be deposed nor is there any pride to be broken. The proud become humble and the great small in the glorious liberty of the children of God. There is an imitation of God Himself, whose majesty is proclaimed in the song of the 4 liviug creatures as a majesty of His mercy and condescension. The prostration of the 24 conforms to this pattern. It is this that they praise when they cast their crowns before the throne of God.

It is in this sense, too, that we are to understand the hymn of the 24 as recorded in v. 11. We can hardly agree with Peterson (p. 26) in describing it as " acclamation," for this suggests that formally at least they were engaged in passing a resolution (like an ancient crowd at a public election or the like). But this is not the case. The ἄξιος εἶ with which the hymn opens has the following significance—that it is intrinsically proper, that it belongs or corresponds to Thee, to. . . . Hence that which is stated of God in what follows is not a predicate ascribed to Him, nor a title conferred by others. It is to be understood analytically as the recognition of what He is originally and essentially in Himself before any other being can resolve or approve or confer it, and of what He would still be if no other being attributed it to Him. The λαβεῖν is to be understood along similar lines. It corresponds to the δώσουσιν of v. 9. What can be given to Him who sits on the throne ? What has He still to receive ? This hymn, as in v. 9, tells us that δόξα, τιμή and δύναμις belong to Him, and to Him alone, and to Him in fulness from all eternity. If the heavenly creation here says that He is worthy to receive these things, this does not mean that He needs to receive them from it, but that it is its own honour and greatness to be able to " give " them to Him, i.e., to acknowledge Him as the One to whom they belong. Doing this, it actualises and increases its own glory and honour and power. It has this in the acknowledgment that what it is and has—this is the expl ination of the descent from the thrones and casting of the golden crowns before His throne —is His. He has created all things, including the heavenly creation. All things, and therefore this creation too, are and were created by His will. As it recognises this, it exists in its own particularity. And we remember what impelled it to this recognition, and therefore what aroused the 24 to their action, thus causing them to expand and to find their true being in what they do and say and sing. They heard the voices of the 24 living creatures ; their *Sanctus*-cry *e profundis*. They accepted the statement that εὐχαριστία as well as δόξα and τιμή belong to Him who sits on the throne. They recognised His mercy, and in this they saw His majesty and His glory as the Creator. This is what brought them into motion, summoning them down from their thrones and opening their mouths in this hymn. This is what integrates them into the ministry of angels. Indeed, this is what makes them angels. What they were before, or would be in themselves, and apart from this, it is difficult to see. But at least they would not exist in their particularity as angels if they merely sat on their thrones and bore their crowns and in the heights gazed dumbly at the even greater height of God, or merely looked straight in front of them, not entering into solidarity with all other creatures or participating in their own way in the service and praise of God. The fact that they fulfil this act of humility and offer their hymn is the climax of Rev. 4 from the standpoint of the *entourage* of God which is our present concern.

If our view of Rev. 4 is correct, the following chapter is not to be regarded as the description of another event but as a deeper and more specific consideration of the event already recorded in *c.* 4. What is implicit in the earlier chapter is now made explicit. But for this purpose a new picture is introduced and a new song has to be sung.

Something already before the seer, but not yet noted or named by him, now claims his attention (v. 1). In the right hand of Him who sits on the throne there is the roll of a book. That it is written on both sides is an indication of the fulness of what is designated in it. It is hardly a happy description to call it the "book of destiny" (K. L. Schmidt, *Aus der Joh. Apok.*, 1944, p. 8). The fact that it is sealed with seven seals characterises it as a will, or at least as a document which has to be executed as well as noted. Thus the opening of the book means that what is written in it takes place in history. This is what will be shown to the seer in Rev. 6–7. But we have not yet reached this point. How will the book come to be opened and these events set in train ? The book is in God's hand. It obviously contains His will and counsel, which will be executed when it is opened. And vv. 2–3 make it plain that it is in the hand of God alone. Who is worthy to open it ? Who can and may and will be in a position to open it ? This is the question of a "strong angel" which rings out through heaven and down to earth and to the depths under the earth. It is a task genuinely worthy of an angel to put questions like this. But even in heaven there is no answer. No one can or may or will execute what God has resolved. No one can even know it. No one can even look into the book in His hand. No creature can do this, not even the strong angel who addresses the question to his fellow-creatures. God is always sovereign. He alone decides and effects, and He alone knows the things which must be hereafter (4¹). "And I wept much," says the seer (v. 4), namely, because this is how matters stand between the Creator and the creature. The creature is implicated in what God proposes and will execute. It is a matter of itself and its future, of His judgment on it, of its salvation or perdition. Surely, then, it ought to have some say, or at least to know something about it. But this is denied to it. No one can open the book (v. 3). No one is found worthy to do so (v. 4). This is a startling thought for at least the earthly creation represented by the divine who here sees and hears what goes on in heaven. It is startled to think that its future is so wholly in the hands of God. It is startled that it is so completely abandoned to that which comes and which it can neither influence nor foresee. It is startled to think of events which it cannot control or even foreknow. And human creatures which have sinned against God have every cause to be terrified on these counts. But possibly the text is merely suggesting that quite apart from any fear or weeping there is dreadful suspense even in heaven in relation to this closed book. For heaven, too, belongs to the cosmos. It thus participates in what God causes to take place on earth, in the sphere of man, and in the expectation of these coming things. But it, too, is quite unable to open the book or even to look into it.

What follows in v. 5 is in the first instance a word of comfort addressed by one of the heavenly beings—one of the 24—to the terrified human seer, but it is also an announcement which is new and important not only to him and the earthly creation represented by him, but to all the heavenly creatures gathered round the throne of God, both ending the weeping of man and preparing the angelic world for a resolving of the tension which oppresses it. The announcement is to the following effect : " Behold, the Lion of the tribe of Judah, the Root of David, hath prevailed to open the book, and to loose the seals thereof." This news of the victory of the Lion of Judah and Root of David is obviously the Easter message of the resurrection of Jesus Christ from the dead, in which it has been revealed at a specific time and place in the earthly sphere that God Himself has closed the gap between Himself and the creatures in the person of this Jewish man, and that He has exalted this Jewish man to participation in His lordship over all creation. It is a victory of God, and for this reason and in this way of man too ; a victory from above, and therefore from below. It is God who has raised this Jewish man from the dead, and it is therefore this Jewish man who has passed through and over the abyss of death. It is God who has placed this man at His side, and it is therefore this man who has become equal to God. What is the reason for all this ? It is in order that He, the human Victor in the grace and power and glory of God, or the divine Victor in the grace and power and glory of this man, should open the book, and thus set in train the future events still concealed from all creatures. It is in order that He should stand at the beginning of these events as their Lord. It is in order that He should resolve and know the things which must be hereafter. And because this is true the seer need not weep and the heavenly creation may rejoice at that which will come to pass.

It is to be noted that the saying of the elder in v. 5 only contains this announcement as such. The declared Victor is not yet seen. The book is still closed and in the hand of God. Hence the seer has every reason to continue weeping. That which holds the heavenly world in tension has not yet been objectively removed. There has been no perception of the revelation of God and of that Victor, the Lion of Judah. The elder himself is not God, nor is he the Lion of Judah, but only his creaturely witness and herald. So far only the witness is to hand. The seer can only be comforted, and the solution of the tension which causes the upper cosmos to hold its breath prepared. This is the provisional accomplishment of the elder with his announcement. He cannot do more. Having done this, he will take his place with the rest and have no further claim to special attention. What we see him fulfil is the typical ministry of angel and witness, in all its greatness and with all its limitations.

The new and decisive vision and occurrence are to be found in vv. 6–7. " And I beheld," we are told in v. 6. But according to v. 8 the whole of heaven beheld, and it then struck up a new song from which we gather that it had seen something new and decisive (v. 9). The author of the early Christian hymn quoted in 1 Tim. 3¹⁶ had perhaps something of the same picture in mind as that described here when he said : ὤφθη ἀγγέλοις. No angel has a part in what is seen by the divine and all angels. There takes place that which is announced in v. 5 : the revelation of the Lion of Judah, the Root of David, as the One who will receive and open the sealed book ; His revelation before all the creatures of heaven, with whom there is associated the earthly creature as a dumb and distant participant. But the surprise is twofold. The Lion was indicated, but what is revealed—" in the midst of the throne and of the four beasts, and in the midst of the elders," as we are forced to translate—is the Lamb. The Lamb is the Lion, the divine and human Victor, who has crossed the abyss between God and man and made the unprecedented step from man to God. The earlier reference to the Lion had the Lamb in view. And it is the self-revelation of the Lamb which declares and confirms that the Lamb is the Lion. We are in heaven and not on earth. The description of the Lamb is thus beyond normal apprehension. It is " as it had been slain," which means that it is a sacrificial animal still bearing the marks of its immolation. But in Rev. 1[18] we are told concerning the One who is here called the Lamb : " I was dead ; and, behold, I am alive for evermore." Seven horns are the marks of His power, and seven eyes of His manifold knowledge proceeding from Him in countless ways. Although He is only a Lamb, and " as it had been slain," He is well equipped to undertake and execute what is later committed to Him. It is clear that the reference is to Jesus Christ : to Jesus Christ Himself and not merely to the witness who declares Him ; to Jesus Christ, not as resurrected, but as suffering, crucified, dead and buried for the sin of human creatures ; to Jesus Christ in His humiliation and sacrifice, in the event of Golgotha. But humiliated and sacrificed, He was the victorious Lion announced in v. 5. As such He accomplished that which is revealed in the event of Easter and attested in the Easter message. As the Humiliated and Sacrificed He declares and confirms this witness. The offering of the Lamb is the triumph of the Lion, the victory of God and man, the closing of the gap between them, the elevation of man to the side of God. This is how the divine sees Him. This is how the heavenly creatures see Him. But they see more. They see how this Lamb " came and took (ἦλθεν καὶ εἴληφεν) the book out of the right hand of him that sat upon the throne." He came—this is His enthronement. He took— this is His seizure of power. For what He received and took is obviously the closed book. As yet there is no word of the opening of the book, but the Lamb takes up the position in which this will follow. The closed book is now in His hands. He will break its seven seals one after the other. The execution of all God's secret counsel will be His affair. Is God dead ? Or has He gone into retirement ? Far from it ! The Lamb is not a second and different God. He is the one God. He will not change the counsel of the one God but execute it faithfully. What is revealed in His enthronement and seizure of power is that from all eternity the secret counsel of God, whatever may be its content in detail, has had the meaning which finds form and reality in the fact that this Lamb is the Lion, the all-powerful and all-wise Executor of His will and plan. The majesty of God as His mercy was the outline and shadow of the divine mystery as indicated already in Rev. 4. And now at the climax of Rev. 5 we are confronted by the form and reality of the same mystery.

But for creation this entails a basic alteration of the picture. And first the angelic world is set in new and decisive and comprehensive motion at the sight of the Lamb (v. 8 f.). In 4[8] it was angels who set other angels in motion. But this time these and all angels are stirred to action by the revelation from the throne itself. Only when the secret of God is present as the Lamb which is the Lion can the majesty of God even over the heavenly creation be unequivocally seen, i.e., that He does not merely receive its praise but evokes it ; that it can be only the answer to His Word ; that the word and ministry of angels can be only a witness to Him which He Himself commissions and empowers. The divine summons is the enthronement of the Lamb and His seizure of power.

Its first effect in v. 8 is the common prostration of the four beasts and the four and twenty elders, self-evidently before the throne of God, but specifically before the Lamb as the Executor of the will of God and therefore as the divine King in whom the substance of the will of God is seen. And something new is now said concerning them. It is not quite clear whether it is said of the 4 beasts too, or only of the 24 elders. I prefer the former view. But at any rate we are told that they all (ἕκαστος) have " harps, and golden vials full of incense." The harps are to be particularly noted, for in spite of Rev. 15[2] as well as this passage, Peterson (p. 62), obsessed by his monastic choirs, is rash enough to say that there is only vocal music in heaven. Nor should we ignore what we are told concerning the vials—that they are the " prayers of saints " (cf. Ps. 141[2]). The " saints " (cf. Rev. 8[3] and *passim*) are members of the Christian community on earth to which there is an immediate and most important reference in the new song of v. 9 f. That their προσευχαί penetrate to the throne of God only through the mediation of angels is a thought which is quite alien to this context and to the whole biblical doctrine both of prayer and of angels. According to Rom. 8²⁷ it is the Spirit who intercedes for the saints according to the will of God. And the biblical angels do not work from below upwards, but from above downwards. Yet what encounters them from below, the prayers of the Christian community, may well serve to adorn and distinguish and demonstrate their downward operation as its fruit and result. To that extent we can say with Hadorn (p. 79) that there is at least an indirect reference at this point to a uniting of the community of God on earth with the adoration of the creatures of heaven. Where there is a praying community on earth, the angels are also present (cf. 1 Cor. 11¹⁰). And where the angels are present, as they are orientated on earth, there are also present—hence the golden vials in their hands—the prayers of the saints. And there too, also evoked by the angels, are the voices of the rest of the lower cosmos which can neither sing, pray, nor even speak, but which yet has voices which in something analogous to the prayer of saints, in longing and gratitude, in pain and joy, can come to the angels and to God Himself, sounding before Him and being heard by Him. Peterson is quite wrong to speak so unkindly of mechanical instruments of music. Surely the playing of musical instruments is a more or less conscious, skilful and intelligent human attempt to articulate before God this sound of a cosmos which is otherwise dumb. Surely the perfect musician is the one who, particularly stirred by the angels, is best able to hear not merely the voice of his own heart but what all creation is trying to say, and can then in great humility and with great objectivity cause it to be heard by God and other men. Hence the harps in the hands of these angels. As they cast themselves down before the Lamb in the midst of the throne, they are adorned not merely by the prayers of saints but by the general sighing of creation articulated in the instruments invented and played by man. We are well advised not to draw hasty conclusions from this fact as to the form of divine service (e.g., the use of organs). The praying community and the sounding cosmos are two very different things. So, too, are divine service and a concert. If the angels may have harps and vials, this does not mean that it is legitimate for us. But the fact remains that it does seem to be right for the angels to have both, to offer divine service in the form both of worship and of the concert, and thus to fall down before God with this twofold adornment.

And now we come to their new song in v. 9 f. It is a new song because it is addressed to the form and reality of the One whom they have previously hymned only in outline and shadow (Rev. 4). Hadorn has justly observed (p. 79) that " in days of small things no new songs emerge, but we have to make do with the old." And it might be added that we usually display an understandable but anxious concern for the oldest possible songs and liturgies etc. The concept of the new song seems to refer even in the Old Testament (Ps. 96¹, 149¹; Is. 42¹⁰) to the coming and crucial time of the Messiah. But here it is a matter of the incomparable new song. Again we hear the ἄξιος εἶ. Again, and here particularly, the idea of a popular assembly with its advice or resolutions or acclamation is quite out of place. What is ascribed to the Lamb is only the subsequent assertion and recognition of what has not merely been resolved by God from all eternity but has actually taken place on earth. The Lamb has taken the closed book. He will open this book and set in train the events resolved by God. It is now only a matter of time and of His own free decision. And the event which makes Him worthy to do so, because in it the majesty of God has taken concrete form and reality in the work of His mercy, and the Lion is the genuinely victorious Lion as the Lamb, is an event which has already taken place. " Thou wast slain." It is an ἐφ' ἅπαξ which can never be reversed and which needs no acclamation. It can only be affirmed and acknowledged and attested, first in heaven, and then on earth. And this is the service of the angels in their new song. As they fulfil it, they look at the Lamb in the midst of the throne. But we have to realise that what they really see is the event which took place on earth. It was on Golgotha, before the gates of Jerusalem, in the reign of Tiberius Caesar, that this Lamb was slain. But it is decisively important that for all its finality and uniqueness this earthly event did not take place in isolation. This point is the middle of a circle. For when this Lamb was slain He did something particular on earth. He created a particular situation. He thus initiated a specific chain of corresponding events. By His blood (by giving His life) He redeemed for God. This sentence has no object. We are simply told, and this shows us unmistakeably that we are involved in the affairs of earth, that He redeemed " out of every kindred, and tongue, and people, and nation." This obviously means men from all these different spheres. And since they are redeemed, it means men who were imprisoned and enslaved. And since they are redeemed for God, it means men who in their imprisonment and slavery were estranged from God. The slaying of the Lamb has put an end to this state of affairs. They are liberated by this event. They are now free for God and for His service. This is the first thing which takes place in and with the slaying of the Lamb, and like this slaying it takes place on earth. The second is an act of creation. It is again the Lamb who accomplishes it. He has made these prisoners who have now been redeemed and set in the service of God " a kingdom and priesthood unto our God," so that they " shall reign on the earth." This is the positive aspect of what has taken place on earth in the light of Golgotha and around this central point. It might properly have been expected that in correspondence with the centre the reference would have been to the community despised, persecuted and suffering for the sake of Jesus Christ. A choir of mystics, ethicists and aesthetes could then have sung much the same song. And the earthly view of this earthly reality would correspond to it. But it is the angels who are singing, and they see and assess the community as it is in heaven and in truth. The little collection of the baptised, scattered among the nations, has hardly escaped the intoxication and stupidity, the blasphemies and blunders, of its heathen past. It is exposed on all sides to oppression and menace. As Paul says in Rom. 8[36] : " For thy sake we are killed all the day long ; we are accounted as sheep for the slaughter "—and the quotation seems to be particularly apt. Yet this harassed flock is the kingdom of God and its members are His elect priests. They and not the *senatus populusque*, or Caesar and his representatives, shall reign on the earth. For it is to be noted that we are not told that they for their part shall one day reign in heaven, but that—in correspondence with what is real in heaven—they shall reign on earth. We must not miss the correspondence. As they are seen from above, and therefore as they are in reality, they are there below what the Lamb is here above, the risen Christ seated at the right hand of God. According to Col. 3[1] they are not only dead with Christ but also raised with Him. And what is called in Col. 3[3] their hidden life with Christ in God is here described as a concrete, earthly reality, concealed from earthly beings but revealed to heavenly, and no less a compact reality than the lordship of their risen Lord at the right hand of the Father. This, then, is what the angels have seen according to their new song. They have seen that centre, but they have also seen this circumference. They have seen the Lord, but they have also seen His people. They have seen the glory of Jesus Christ in heaven, but they have also seen it streaming back from earth where He did this for God (note the twofold $\tau\hat{\omega}$ $\theta\epsilon\hat{\omega}$), redeeming this people for God by His blood and refashioning them as God's incontestable possession. Again, and this time unmistakeably, the depths of earth have the advantage over heaven that it was here below that the decisive event took place, that the Lamb gained the victory as the Lion which He is now seen to be in heaven, that the will of the divine majesty attained its goal in the mercy with which God took earth to Himself. It is for this reason that the angels can and must sing that the Lamb is worthy to take the book and open the seals. It is for this reason that they can and must see and praise Jesus Christ (*vere Deus vere homo*) as the One who stands in the power and wisdom of God at the beginning of all cosmic occurrence and who will initiate and control all cosmic occurrence. It is for this reason that according to the new song the tension is broken with which even angels considered the closed book and contemplated things to come. It is for this reason that even man, the divine, who sees and hears things in the opened heavens, who may see with heavenly eyes what the angels saw, can no longer weep. That He has wiped away and will wipe away all tears from their eyes (Rev. 21⁴) is something which has already taken place, and taken place perfectly and irrevocably, in that which is here seen by the angels and man.

And now we read in v. 11 f. that this man saw and heard the heavenly horizon and the heavenly choir extend into infinity. Many angels—we are reminded of the πλῆθος στρατιᾶς οὐρανίου of Lk. 2¹³—are revealed to the seer, in numbers which defy all calculation, as the outer circle of the heavenly assembly, joining " with a loud voice " in the ἄξιος εἶ. That their hymn, too, is addressed to the Lamb slain shows that they have all seen what has taken place on earth and then been revealed in heaven and attested first by the acts and words of the two angelic choirs in the immediate proximity of the throne. They too, the many angels, are witnesses of this happening. There is no angel who does not have and even receive his particularity in the service of witness to this event. But there is no more explicit reference, either here or in the final verses of the chapter, to the particular theme of the previous hymn, the taking of the book by the Lamb and His commissioning to open it. This is not forgotten, but it is caught up in the adoration of the Lamb as the Bearer of all the divine predicates of power and lordship (in a way reminiscent of the praise of Him that sits on the throne in 4⁹, ¹¹). In the light of this it is surely imperative that Rev. 4 should be understood as we have tried to expound it. And if the same predicates of power and lordship are there ascribed to the one God and Creator, it is evident, now that Jesus Christ appears as their Bearer, that in Him we do not have to do with another but with one and the same God. The only difference is that not without cause a greater number of predicates is now mentioned. And it is no accident that the number is seven, but this indicates the perfection of the One to whom they are ascribed. And they seem to mount as it were to a climax. All the same, it is a little artificial to try to see in the seven predicates, as J. T. Beck does (p. 98), the seven means in the divine economy placed at the disposal of the Lamb for the opening of the seven seals, the four first serving to prepare and the three last to consummate the universal lordship committed to Him. The decisive point is not the difference or peculiarity of these predicates, but their character as moments and designations of the divine essence, and of the divine as the royal essence, superior to all created power and uniting in itself the plenitude of all power. It is this royal essence of God which all angels ascribe to Jesus Christ the Crucified and Resurrected and find united in Him. We remember the report which in the 2nd century the astonished Pliny sent to the emperor Trajan concerning Christians : *carmen Christo quasi Deo dicere*. According to the text, this was first done by the hosts of heaven.

And now the circle opens again in v. 13. The divine does not see other creatures, but he certainly hears them. So far the reference has been only to the heavenly κτίσμα and its movement and witness. But now, unseen but heard by the divine, the κτίσμα on earth, under the earth, in the sea and within all these lower spheres, stands at the side of the heavenly creation. Πᾶν κτίσμα, both heavenly beings and earthly now unite in a final song of praise.

It is worth adding with Hadorn (p. 80), however, that man is excluded. Man's praise of God forms a separate chapter and is not included here. Man is the target of the witness of all creation. If and to the extent that he takes part in its action, he is not simply one with all other κτίσματα. Thus it is not without reason that he is not mentioned here. He is all ears and eyes, but he does not take part. It is a little surprising, perhaps, that there is no reference at least to the earthly community of the saints, who are clearly mentioned in v. 8 and especially v. 10. According to the thesis of Peterson that there is a cultus in heaven in which the Church participates (p. 37), it ought to have appeared at this point. For here at the very latest it ought to have emerged that what is described in these chapters up to 5¹² as the ministry of angels has its response and continuation in specific cultic actions of the earthly Church. The fact that there is no glimpse of this even in v. 13 shows how hollow is the thesis. Those in whom we find this response and continuation as participants in the heavenly cultus are the dwellers of earth and air and sea, the earthly cosmos as such and in its totality. What we are told is that in its own way, which differs from that of angels and men, it has a voice and language formally to join in the ministry of angels in a great cultic act. To be sure, the fact that there is no mention either of man generally or of the earthly Church in particular does not mean that they cannot sometimes join in the ministry of angels in the form of such acts. Yet it does not seem likely, indeed there is not the slightest indication, that the participation of man and the Church in the ministry of angels is either exhausted or consists essentially in the kind of action which is here described as the participation of the earthly cosmos in this ministry. In other words, there is not the slightest indication that the fulfilment of such acts is the decisive action required of man and especially of the earthly Church on the model of what takes place in heaven. Man, and therefore the earthly Church, is certainly the target of the witness of heavenly beings and of all creation. But this does not mean—at any rate primarily and essentially, let alone exclusively—that man and the Church are required to join with the heavenly and earthly creation, to take part in their harmony and to conform to their action. What it does mean is that they are summoned by this ministry to enter the service of God in a way corresponding to their own nature. This is not ensured merely by their joining other earthly creatures in the heavenly cultus and thus participating in the harmony of the universe, no matter how faithfully they may reproduce the heavenly in their earthly cultus. For the ministry of angels is addressed to the God who did not become an angel but man, and who took man to Himself. This means that the service of God to which the angels summon man and the Church is one which is proper to them and different from their own. Imitation of angels is not what is demanded of man and the Church by the ministry of angels. Thus the earthly Church will never see its decisive task in copying the cultus of heaven. May it always be restrained from doing so ! It must never cease to hear the ironical warning of Amos 5²¹ᶠ· : " I hate, I despise your feast days, and I will not smell in your solemn assemblies. . . . Take thou away from me the noise of thy songs ; for I will not hear the melody of thy viols. But let judgment run down as waters, and righteousness as a mighty stream." When the witness of heavenly beings and all creation really reaches the ear of man, and is taken seriously by the earthly Church, it will be realised that from the Church there is demanded a service which is perhaps more strict and stringent but also more full of promise, and certainly its own and not just a replica of what is done by others. This is the point which we have to make in relation to the striking silence of v. 13 concerning man and the Church, and in opposition to the thesis of Peterson.

But now we must emphasise the positive truth that there is an important conjunction of the lower with the upper cosmos in the same praise of God. It is addressed in common " unto him that sitteth upon the throne, and unto the Lamb." There is a confluence of the two apparently separate streams of the doxologies of *cc.* 4 and 5. With the conjunction of the earthly and heavenly choirs there is this conjunction in the theme of their praise of God. But the converse is also to be seen and stated that it is because there is already this conjunction in theme in the hymns struck up in v. 9 f. and v. 12 that the earthly

3. THE AMBASSADORS OF GOD AND THEIR OPPONENTS

The kingdom of God coming to us on earth is the kingdom of heaven. And when the will of God is done on earth as in heaven, this is not merely a divine happening, established, controlled and brought to its goal by God, but also a heavenly happening, executed on earth in the presence and power and with the co-operation and accompanying revelation of heaven. We may state at once that it is primarily, substantially and centrally a divine happening, and only secondarily, accidentally and peripherally a heavenly. Thus the fact that it is both divine and heavenly does not mean that it is twofold, that there takes place an autonomous heavenly happening side by side with the divine, and that this claims independent consideration and appraisal. The fact that it is both divine and heavenly means rather that the one divine happening has also as such the character, the (self-evidently) creaturely form and vesture, of a heavenly. But in this sense it is genuinely heavenly, and the visitation of the earthly creation by God its Creator means its visitation by its heavenly fellow-creation, and its encounter with God—whether it is aware of it or not—its encounter with angels. Where God is—the God who acts and reveals Himself in the world created by Him—heaven and the angels are also present.

The last and best sentence in the rather short and dubious doctrine of angels advanced by A. Schlatter (*Das chr. Dogma*[2], 1923, p. 87) is clear and pointed : " The mystery is near to us." Correctly understood, this statement tells us all there is to be said concerning the reality and significance of angels in the earthly sphere and concerning their relationship to the presence and act and revelation of God. Perhaps Calvin had something similar in mind when he said of angels : *quod in suo ministerio, velut in speculo, divinitatem aliqua ex parte nobis repraesentant* (*Instit.*, I, 14, 5). The mystery would not be near but distant if the divine happening were not also a heavenly. And the appropriate representation of deity would be lacking if it were not given us *velut in speculo* by the ministry of angels. And the lack would probably be much more than one of mere beauty. At bottom a piety or theology in which there is no mystery, which lacks the mirror of self-representing deity, and in which there are therefore no angels, will surely prove to be a godless theology. To quote Calvin again : *Quia Dominus, pro immensa sua clementia et facilitate vult huic nostro vitio subvenire, non est, cur tantum eius beneficium negligamus* (*ib.*, 14, 11).

We must leave aside the foolish question whether and how there is or may be a special experience of angels. It is a foolish question because it is wrongly put. There can be no question of any special, autonomous or abstract experience of angels in and for themselves. The subjects of this kind of experience could not be the angels of God, but only ideas or ghosts or figments of the imagination or even demons and therefore the opponents of the genuine angels. It is best not to speak of any experience of angels at all. For the point at issue in the Bible is always an experience of God and of Jesus Christ, and not an independent experience of angels. The real question is whether and how far there can be any experience of God and His Christ, any encounter and co-existence with Him, which does not take place in supreme truth and reality—whether we are aware of it or not—in the presence and with the participation of His angels. Is God really present and does He really work and speak, help and save, awaken and nourish and consummate our faith and obedience, rule the Church and the world both as a whole and in detail, if in all these things His angels are not present and at work in His service? What would we earthly creatures be before Him, and how could we be before Him and with Him, if He were to visit and encounter us only in divine and not also in creaturely form, in the heavenly vesture which as such is the representation of His mystery and deity, and therefore in angelic mode?

What is the meaning of the presence and operation of angels in the doing of the will of God on earth? It certainly does not mean that there is any competition with the presence and operation of God Himself. But it is not for this reason without any significance at all. It means the presence and operation of God Himself in the heavenly-creaturely form which, because it is heavenly, is appropriate to God and able to represent and attest Him, and, because it is creaturely, appropriate to man and the earthly creation generally and able to make God accessible and His representation and attestation apprehensible. Thus to say that where God is present we shall also find His angels is to say that where God is engaged in the work and revelation of His mercy, there—in order to be genuinely God to the earthly creation, but to be genuinely *its* God—He is surrounded and accompanied and served and attested by the heavenly creation which as heavenly belongs radically to Him and as creation belongs radically to the earthly creation. Where the God who acts and speaks in His grace is present, it is in this mediation. It is not that in this mediation He has beside Him a second acting and speaking subject, or a plurality of such, but that He always acts and speaks Himself in this mediation. In this mediation, by the ministry of the heavenly creation, He is great and powerful and holy but also gracious and merciful and patient on earth. In this mediation the doing of His will on earth is His work, the work of the living God, and therefore wholly divine, but as such it is addressed quite concretely to our creaturely sphere. That His will should be done on earth as in heaven necessarily implies that it should be done on earth in a heavenly way, in this heavenly mediation. God would not be Himself in the granting of this request, nor would the answer correspond to the request, if His will were not done in this mediation.

This then, is, what we must say generally concerning the being and action of angels on earth and therefore in what we call the history of salvation and the Church, in world history, in the histories of individual lives, and in all earthly occurrence. It carries with it two delimitations. We avoid both the over-estimation of angels on the one side and their under-estimation on the other. We contend for the sole lordship and glory of God, but we contend for the lordship and glory of God through the ministry of angels.

Cautiously laying one stone upon the other, we shall now try to understand in detail the second and undoubtedly more difficult but also more practically important aspect of the matter. But where are we to begin? We certainly cannot begin with a definition of angels in their relationship to the earthly creation with which they undoubtedly come into contact as God takes this to Himself and as they are present where God is. If they were definable like earthly creatures they would not be angels, heavenly creatures. Even to have any prospect of success in venturing to explain the name or concept "angel" as "ambassador," we first make the necessary presupposition. But this consists in an answer to the question in what the service properly consists in which alone angels can have their essence and existence on earth as in heaven, and to which they owe their name. Only then can we consider when and where they are present on earth, and what opposition they have to encounter. The worst possible blunder that we could commit would be to try to understand them in terms of this opposition, and therefore to begin by describing them as the enemies of the devil and demons. There can be only one starting-point for our discussion of all these problems, namely, to consider more precisely something which self-evidently impressed itself upon us as the main problem in our short introduction, namely, what is the nature and manner of angels in their relationship to God.

We may begin with a simple assertion which is not likely to fail for lack of adequate support. This is that in all the biblical passages which instruct us most precisely concerning the relationship of angels to God and therefore concerning their own essence and existence the word "angel" does not stand alone but is linked with God or Christ either by a genitive or by a possessive pronoun.

A few illustrations may be given. In Ps. 34[7] we read: "The angel of the Lord encampeth round about them that fear him, and delivereth them"; in Gen. 28[12]: "And he dreamed, and behold a ladder set up on the earth, and the top of it reached to heaven: and behold the angels of God ascending and descending on it"; in Gen. 24[7]: "The Lord God of heaven . . . shall send his angel before thee"; and in Mt. 16[27]: "For the Son of man shall come in the glory of his Father with his holy angels; and then he shall reward every man according to his works." And we might also add the unforgettable conclusion of the evening blessing in Luther's *Smaller Catechism*: "Thy holy angel be with me, that the evil foe have no power over me! Amen. And then quickly and happily to sleep." It might almost be said of this sentence that it contains the whole doctrine of angels *in nuce*, and decisively so on account of the address: "Thy holy angel."

Each angel stands in relationship to God, and is an angel, and has his being and is present as such, in the fact that he is God's holy angel. The only thing is that no possessive pronoun or genitive of human speech has the force adequately to express the relationship, the distinction and the connexion which call for expression at this point. The angels are not emanations of God. They are creatures. But as heavenly creatures they are in an exemplary and perfect way that which constitutes the essence of all creatures and characterises earthly creatures as their origin and goal. That is to say, they belong to God, as belong to Him strictly. They are, only as He is and they are His. But He, God, is in His omnipotent mercy. He is as from heaven He speaks and acts on earth. They are His, and therefore are, as He takes them with Him on His way from heaven to earth as His precursors, companions and followers, giving them a share in His own speech and action on earth. They are, as they are given this share. What makes heaven heaven, and heavenly beings heavenly, giving heaven precedence over earth and heavenly creatures a greater dignity than earthly, is the fact that God is in heaven and not on earth, that He has His dwelling and throne among them and not among us, that His way does not lead from here to there, but from there to here. He thus gives to the There, and to those who are there, a share in Himself which earth and those who are on it do not and cannot have. To this particular participation there corresponds, of course, the fact that, unlike earthly creatures, they have no standing of their own in relation to Him. As the recipients of this incomparable and non-transferable participation, but with no standing of their own, taken by God in this strictly heavenly mode, they come with Him to earth, genuinely distinguished above all the creatures of earth, but only in this way, without any different being or existing differently. Their high advantage in relation to the earthly creation is also their disadvantage. They have no definable being in re.ation to it. They do not exist and act independently or autonomously. They have no history or aims or achievements of their own. They have no profile or character, no mind or will of their own. They have all these things, yet not as their own possession, but wholly and exclusively as God is so rich in relation to them. They are themselves only a possession, His possession. The lowliest creature of earth has an advantage over even the highest of angels to the extent that while it belongs to God it may also belong to itself. But conversely even the least of the heavenly hosts is more than the most perfect of earthly creatures to the extent that it belongs so fully to God and in no sense to itself.

Where an angel appears and is and speaks and works, God Himself appears and is and speaks and works. The angel derives no benefit at all from being a creature and different from God, although he is is this, and is indeed an exemplary and perfect creature in the fact that he belongs so fully and exclusively to God. He would be a lying spirit, a demon, a being which deceives both itself and others in respect of its heavenly character, if he were to try to profit from his nature and position, deriving any personal benefit, cutting an individual figure, playing an independent role, pursuing his own ends and achieving his own results. A true and orderly angel does not do this. He has his honour, dignity and joy, and all that earthly creation has in its autonomy, in the fact that he has these things only in dependence, that he only stands before God and is at His disposal, that he is only an element in the creaturely sphere of being in which God has His dwelling and His throne, that he has himself only as he participates in Him, and exists for himself as he is there for Him. He triumphs and exults in this absolute humility before God.

And wherever the being and action of an angel are perceived, there the Word of God is heard, the doing of His will is contemplated, and gratitude, faith and obedience to Him are awakened or confirmed or rekindled. The part of the angel, then, has merely been to serve, to give his witness, to help. Although he is a creature, and an exemplary and perfect creature, his task as such has simply been to come and then to go again, to pass by. He would again be a lying spirit, a demon, if he were to tarry, directing attention and love and honour and even perhaps adoration to himself, causing even momentary preoccupation with himself and enticing man to enter into dealings and fellowship with Himself instead of through him into dealings and fellowship with God. Again it must be said that a true and orderly angel does not do this. The truth in which he is perceived will always be the truth of God. The work which he accomplishes will always consist in the fact that the majesty and mercy of God are better, more seriously and more gladly seen and acknowledged by man. He is accepted and glorified exclusively as God is accepted and glorified. He can himself be honoured only as he causes man to look away from himself to God.

We again recall the ἄξιος εἶ λαβεῖν of the doxologies of Rev. 4–5, the prostrations, the casting of the crowns before the throne of God, the remarkable " giving " ascribed to heavenly creatures, the thoroughgoing ascription of all δόξα and τιμή and δύναμις and πλοῦτος, of all σοφία and ἰσχύς, of all εὐλογία and εὐχαριστία to Him that sits on the throne and to the Lamb. This ascription which looks away from self, this witness that everything belongs to God alone and not to them, is the ministry of angels not only in heaven but also on earth. And it is because there are not and cannot be such pure witnesses of God among earthly creatures independent even in their relationship to God—for earth is not heaven—that when the will of God is done not only in heaven but also on earth He does not come to us alone but with His holy angels. It is for this reason that where He is they too are present, and as He causes Himself to be perceived and is perceived, there is also a perception of the angels who serve Him.

In this connexion we must make a last incidental reference to the work of E. Peterson, and especially to the dreadful third part (p. 83 f.) in which he brings the being and activity of angels in their relationship with God into connexion with that of the mystic Gnostic (or *vice versa*). If we could adopt to his historical presentation of the relationship between the heavenly cultus and that of the Church a rather distant attitude, and to his supposed scriptural proof from Rev. 4–5 an attitude of gentle repudiation, a very definite protest is now demanded. His doctrine of the quasi-angelic mystic is a refined heresy. It is refined because, presupposing a partially correct view of the being and activity of angels in their relationship with God, it does the very worst thing which can possibly be done in a doctrine of angels, causing these angels who are in some sense rightly perceived and understood to direct the attention and concern of man to themselves instead of to God. According to this teaching, the angels which exist only in relationship to God and for Him do not summon and invite man to give to God the service appropriate to him as an earthly creature but rather to imitate the angels as heavenly creatures. And according to this doctrine, the point of the being and activity of angels is not that we should see and know and express ourselves as creatures in the incarnate Word of God but in a higher, angelic creatureliness, in the being and essence of angels.

As Peterson sees it, the real mystic Gnostic reaches out above purely conceptual knowledge to the metaphysically higher form of being attained only by *apatheia*—to being in the order of being which as that of the angels is above that of man. This elevation of man takes place in the cultus when the number of angelic choirs is swelled, not by those of all the lower cosmos as in Rev. 5^{13}, but by those of quasi-angelic priests and monks (p. 84). For mystic Gnostics participating as esoterics in the cultus of the Church, namely, in the mass, this participation has the metaphysical significance (rather than that of faith) that the archetypal import of the being and life of angels—not of all angels, for there are some which " leave them cold," but of the supreme angels, the cherubim and seraphim—is made actual for them. " The man of angelic likeness desires to be taken up into their ranks, and so in gnosis he begins to rise above the world, flying above everything visible and invisible in heaven and earth to a world which bears no more relationship to the perceptible cosmos but is orientated solely on God," to the fellowship of beings which are what they are as they " pour forth " in praise of God (p. 87 f.). His desire is to participate in their being directly orientated on God, and therefore in their praise of God ; and this is something which he can actually attain. But can man really draw near to the angels in this way ? He can do it no less surely than the angels can draw near to him, and have actually done so in the birth and temptation and resurrection and ascension of Christ. As Christ was above all angels prior to His abasement, and was again exalted above them with His elevation, so the quasi-angelic man stoops down from his being with the cherubim and seraphim to the orders of earth, to priest and people, to the earthly *ecclesia*, to the theological virtues of faith and love and hope which are a model for him too, only to rise again continually to the fellowship of these heavenly beings (p. 90 f.). Their being signifies " a possibility of our being, an enhancement and intensification of our being " (p. 93) ; the possibility of " man's constant rise, not in a moral but in a metaphysical sense, until he becomes the companion of angels and archangels, and attains the frontier where the cherubim and seraphim stand. And there, where even they are halted, he begins to make music with the spheres and to sing with the archangels " (p. 94)—a song which " breaks forth from his innermost being " and in which his coming to himself is completed as he is present with the angels and archangels, and is poured out before God, only as a song (p. 95), so that with the very lowest and the very highest of creatures he expresses his own lowliness, and " can say only that he is absolutely nothing " (p. 96). The grace of the Crucified has awakened the last depth of his creatureliness, " so that he does not merely stand there as the sinner who has experienced mercy, but also as this poor creature, related to the ass, which has no other possibility but to pour forth in praise of God " (p. 97).

Peterson is right in two respects : first, in describing the being of angels as one which is directly orientated on God ; and second, in calling it a pouring forth before God, namely, in His praise. But he is wrong already—although we can leave this point aside—when he limits this description to a supposedly higher class of angels. It is, of course, this class which interests his mystic Gnostic, who takes the liberty of saying that other angels " leave him cold." And this brings us to the basic error of Peterson, for, as he sees it, these supposedly higher angels whom the Gnostic desires and is able to resemble are directly orientated on God in the sense that they and their praise of God have nothing whatever to do with the service of God on earth. They turn to God in such a way that they turn their backs on the earth and man. The saying of Heb. 1[14] that all angels are ἀποστελλόμενα seems not to apply to them. That God's will is to be done on earth as in heaven seems not to concern them. Their outpouring in praise of God seems to have another and in some way more excellent meaning. The will of God to which they are supposedly obedient seems to be a majestic will which is not that of His mercy. What gladdens Peterson in these angels, what his mystic Gnostics hope to attain and actually do attain, is something which is wholly alien to the φιλανθρωπία, to the resolve and act in which God has taken man to Himself and Himself become man. In their orientation on God and outpouring before Him these angels have a metaphysically higher form of being. In this they are " archetypal." For this the esoteric yearns when he takes part in the mass of the earthly Church and condescends to concern himself with the theological virtues. In this he thinks he has found a possibility : that of the enhancement and intensification of his own being ; that of fulfilling the being of the creaturely to its utmost limit. In its own way the angel does this, and in its very different way the ass. But man—the man who is mystically called and endowed—finds that even though he is still related to the ass he is summoned and equipped to rise constantly like the angel, sharing his metaphysical form of being and thus coming to himself and attaining true creatureliness before God. Yet it is surely a false coming to himself when he becomes more lowly even than the sinner who has experienced mercy. It is surely a false ascent. Let those who value their eternal and temporal welfare steer clear of it ! For it raises us past the God who in His Son came down to us men, and will come again. It raises us past His holy angels, who are directly orientated on Him and have their whole being in outpouring before Him, not in the fact that they say that they are nothing, but in the fact that they come down with Him to us as the servants of His mercy. In this kind of ascent we merely disturb the angels by making the humility in which they exist only for God and therefore for us into a creaturely honour, a goal of human yearning. And whether we think to fulfil the being of the creaturely in relationship with the angel or with the ass, we fail to make use of the possibility which is given to man as man by the grace of God and the ministry of angels, i.e., that of being serviceable to God in our own human metaphysical form of being (which is neither that of the angel nor that of the ass), as the angels are serviceable to Him in theirs. What is said in Col. 2[18] about the angelic piety and theology of the false teachers who had arisen in Colossae is too scanty and obscure to give us any clear picture of the point at issue. But we are not malicious if we affirm that the little which is said might well be applied in detail to Peterson's mystics competing with the angels. And after consulting this doctrine of angels it is certainly refreshing to read the exposition of the third petition in the *Heidelberg Catechism* (*Qu.* 124) : " Thy will be done on earth, as it is in heaven, that is to say, Grant that we and all men may renounce our own will and obey without contradiction Thy will which alone is good, each of us fulfilling his office and calling as willingly and faithfully as the angels in heaven."

We now turn to the positive fact that the angels are God's pure witnesses, beside whom there is none to compare on earth, who are therefore needed on earth, and who by the goodness of God are given to us in their reality. They are pure witnesses because they are heavenly beings. They are heaven itself coming with God to earth and invading the earthly world. The essence of heaven consists in the fact that within the created world it is the dwelling-place and throne of God from which He comes to us. Heavenly beings are distinguished by the fact that they are in and from heaven. They lack the autonomy of earthly creatures. Instead, they see the face of the Father—of the Father of Jesus Christ—in heaven (Mt. 18[10]) ; the face which cannot be seen by any earthly creature. They can thus give pure witness of God. Pure has the positive meaning of absolutely genuine and authentic witness as compared with the earthly witness which can have its full truth only in that which it attests and not in itself. And it also has the negative meaning of unalloyed with alien elements of its own, which are always to be found in even the best and most sincere and fitting earthly witness, which are always heard in it and must always be expressly or tacitly discounted by the hearers. It will be seen that the very thing which makes the angels seem essentially weak and feeble as compared with earthly creatures, the fact that they are what they are so exclusively in their relationship with God and in that outpouring, is also the thing which elevates them above earthly creatures and makes them pure witnesses whose service is indispensable. When an angel is present, although he is not God, it is *eo ipso* the case that God is present. When an angel says anything, although he is not God, it is God who speaks. When an angel acts, for all the infinite difference between God and heaven or God and the angel, it is God who acts. To the apparent ontological weakness of the angel there corresponds the fulness, the authority, the incontestability, the divine glory of his functional reality. The angel is not merely an emissary ; he is a plenipotentiary. He is the kind of emissary which no man can ever be, even though he be a prophet or apostle. The witness of the latter is also genuine witness. And in its own place, as the witness of man to man, it is, of course, absolutely indispensable. But like all earthly witness to God, it draws its strength directly or indirectly, consciously or unconsciously, explicitly or implicitly, from the fact that before, above and beside it there is the pure witness to God which it can never be even as the best of earthly witness.

All genuine witness to God lives by the witness and therefore the ministry of angels. For by this it becomes in a sense technically possible and real that God is genuinely present and may be genuinely known as God in the earthly sphere, that He genuinely and recognisably speaks and acts, and that He is genuinely honoured and loved and feared. In their so utterly selfless and undemanding and purely subservient passing, in their eloquently quiet pointing to

God which is always a pointing away from themselves, heaven comes
to earth. And this means that even here there is a real above, a real
distance, a real whence of God. It means that even here the dimension
is opened and perceptible in which God exists and in which alone He
can be known and feared and loved as God. In the being and work
of angels, whether notable and noted as such or not, there lies the
basis of the fact that the mystery of God can have a place on earth.
If God cannot be confused with any static or dynamic, spiritual or
material circumstance of the created cosmos ; if above all man
cannot equate Him with himself, this is something which is unfortunately not guaranteed by any theological or philosophical art,
nor by any internal power and purity of faith, nor by any desperate
or apparently promising extreme situation in which man may find
himself ; but it is very definitely guaranteed by the ministry of angels,
by the heavenly-creaturely essence by which God is surrounded
when He comes to us. To be sure, it is God Himself and He alone
who guarantees it, His almighty Word and Holy Spirit. And it is
obvious that in His divine work as such angels no more than men
can replace or even represent Him or support Him or contribute to
His action in such a way that they stand beside Him or take His place
as the acting and speaking subject, as though they had the Word and
were the moving spirit. Self-evidently even angels can only be the
witnesses of God. But where the revelation and work of God take
place, it is a cosmic occurrence. Thus heaven dawns on earth. The
witness of angels is given. There is established as pure witness that
which no man can establish for himself or others, namely, that on
earth and in its internal or external situations there is disclosed
and perceptible the real above, the real distance, the real whence,
the real mystery of God, in a word the dimension and category of
the divine. Without the angels God Himself would not be revealed
and perceptible. Without them He would be hopelessly confused
with some earthly circumstance, whether in the form of a sublime
idea or a golden calf. But by means of His holy angels He sees to
it that this dimension is always open and perceptible. And we have
to realise that if we do not perceive it we are not merely abandoned
by God but by all good spirits and angels, being entangled not merely
in a spiritual but a cosmic disorder and catastrophe, for which God
and the angels certainly cannot be blamed. But above all we have
to realise that if we have the grace to perceive it we do not owe this
in the slightest to our work, but all our theology and philosophy and
seriousness and depth and soul-shattering experience can only serve
at very best to confirm and illuminate the heavenly as the token of
the divine, the mystery in which God alone is God, thus providing us
with earthly marks by which to recall it when we are in danger of
forgetting it and making God an idol. Within cosmic reality, and
therefore apart from God Himself, there are always the angels to prevent

this and to see to it that we do not lose contact with the living God. They alone are God's pure witnesses.

As such, although creatures as we are, they stand over against us at the side of God. The very thing which they lack in comparison with us includes within itself their infinite advantage over us. In face of God they have no cause of their own in the espousing of which they have to submit to His will. They do not exist in any reciprocal relationships which have to be conformed to the divine model. They do not sing any hymn of praise which well or badly they have to strike up. They are themselves an eternal hymn of praise. And their existence is not tedious, as tedious theologians usually imagine, because as the *entourage* accompanying God they have their hands full with what He wills and does and therefore with us. Their liturgy is their service to Him and therefore to us. But in this service they stand over against us at the side of God. They exist in His glory, speak in His truth and work with His power. We cannot rely on them as we do on God. But we must not forget that when we rely on God we can rely on them. We can as little dispute with them as with God ; we can as little deny them as we can deny God. In faith in a God of theory or ethics or aesthetics we may well deny the angels, because in the company of this kind of God it makes no odds whether there are angels or not. But in faith in the heavenly Father of Jesus Christ, whose majesty is operative and revealed in His mercy ; in faith in the God of Abraham, Isaac and Jacob, the case is very different. To deny the angels is to deny God Himself. For it is an implication of His greatness and condescension that He comes to us in His angels. Although in the smallest no less than the greatest matters He keeps the reins in His own hands, the angels represent Him to us with the plenary authority appropriate to them as pure witnesses.

This is perhaps the point to consider one of the most difficult concepts in biblical angelology, that of the *maleak Yahweh*. We do so within the limits of what is important and necessary for our present purpose (cf. for what follows, Walter Baumgartner, " Zum Problem des Jahwe-Engels," *Schweiz. Theol. Umschau*, 1944, p. 92 f.). In brief, we are confronted with a figure which is not unusual in the world of the Old Testament, but this time it is called *the* angel rather than merely *an* angel of the Lord, thus seeming to unite and represent in itself the essence of angels generally and their essential functions, and therefore to merit the title of ἄγγελος κατ' ἐξοχήν. Our question concerning the relationship between God and angels and angels and God is more insistently posed in the passages in which there is brief and simple or more extended and complicated reference to this angel.

The exposition of the Early Church succumbs to the obvious but very real temptation of seeing in this angel simply the pre-existent Logos, the second hypostasis of the Godhead. Even F. Deliztsch (*Komm. über d. Genesis*⁴, 1872, p. 290 f.) was prepared to understand him as at least a prefiguration of the future incarnation of God, a real angel but as such made by Yahweh an extraordinary organ and phenomenon, i.e., an angel in human shape. H. Cremer

(R.E., Art. *Engel*, Vol. 5, p. 367 f.) advanced an even more attenuated version of the same view when he maintained that a replacement of the presence of God by the ministry of angels, and a mediation of His revelation through them, are just as essential to the period of the old covenant as His revelation and presence in Christ and the Holy Spirit to the essence of the new. In all this, however, no real justice is done to the incomparable and irreplaceable nature of the speech and action of the covenant God of the Old Testament and later of the Word incarnate in Jesus Christ, nor indeed to the specific features of the ministry of angels. Because they are so intimately related, these ought not to have been identified ; nor should the latter have been brought into relationship with the former even as a prefiguration or a temporary substitute. Christ is far more than can be embraced merely by the concept of ἄγγελος κατ' ἐξοχήν. He is more than a pure witness of God. Like the covenant God of the Old Testament (and as His reality concealed in the Old Testament but proclaimed in the form of pure promise), He is the Godhead Himself speaking and acting on earth. He is the Son of God and Son of Man with whom as such no heavenly being, which is neither God nor man, is identical, who cannot be prefigured by any such being or set alongside it as a fulfilment. And quite apart from these basic considerations, we are closer to the meaning and text of these Old Testament passages if we accept purely as an angel this one angel of God which is given such prominence, learning from it the supreme relevance of the existence and ministry of angels in their connexion with the incomparable and irreplaceable Word and work of God.

The suggestion of G. v. Rad (*ThWBzNT*, I, p. 75 f.) seems worth considering that we start with the passages of what he calls folk-lore in which the *maleak Yahweh* is simply an " organ of the particular relationship of grace to Israel," the personification of God's assistance of this people. According to Ex. 14[19f.] he stands protectively between the host of Israel and the pursuing army of the Egyptians. According to Num. 22[22] he is an adversary to Balaam in the way when the latter intends to curse Israel. According to Jud. 6[11f.] he salutes Gideon : " The lord is with thee, thou mighty man of valour," and according to Jud. 13[2f.] he announces to Manoah and his wife the birth of Samson. According to 1 K. 19[5] he restores the weary Elijah. According to 2 K. 19[35] he smites the 185,000 men in the camp of the Assyrians. According to Zech. 1[12] and 3[1f.] he appears before God as the advocate for Israel and the opponent of Satan. It is true that in 2 Sam. 24[16f.] he can appear as the destroying angel, standing between heaven and earth with his sword drawn and stretched out against Israel (1 Chron. 21[15f.]). But this is the exception which proves the rule, for, from the standpoint of salvation history, this does not take place against Israel but for it. In all this it is natural to think of the position and role of Michael in Dan. 10[13, 21] and 12[1]. *The* angel of God is very obviously the angel of God for Israel, the heavenly form in which God turns to this people of His. He is called *the* angel of God because Israel is His chosen people.

In the Acts of the Apostles, too, there seem to be reference to *the* angel in the frequently mentioned ἄγγελος τοῦ θεοῦ or τοῦ κυρίου (without the article). At any rate, the position and function of this angel in relation to the New Testament community seem to be not dissimilar to those of the *maleak Yahweh* in relation to the covenant people of the Old Testament. He opens the prison for the apostles in 5[19f.] and for Peter in 12[7f.]. He orders Philip to the place where he will meet the Ethiopian eunuch (8[26]), and tells Cornelius to get into touch with Peter (10[3f.]). He comforts Paul in the storm (27[23]), and smites Herod, the enemy of the community, at the very moment when the people say of him that his voice is that of a god and not of a man (12[23]). And even here it seems to be the case that he owes his singular position and designation to the singular task ascribed to him. The well-known passage in Mal. 3[1] is particularly helpful in relation to both Old and New Testaments to the extent that it refers to the coming to the temple of a preceding messenger, of the Lord Himself, and of the angel of the covenant (*maleak berith*). If the latter, too, is " a functionary of Yahwek's particular relationship of grace " (v. Rad), it cannot very well be otherwise than that he is identical with the angel who elsewhere is called the angel of Yahweh and who in Jud. 2¹ is expressly said to be concerned with the covenant of Yahweh with Israel. We can thus see how the whole conception came to be taken up by the authors of the New Testament. We are surely dealing with the same angel, for example, in the ἄγγελος κυρίου of Lk. 2⁹ who proclaims the nativity. *The* angel is *the* witness of God. With his appearance, words and acts he attests the work of God as such in the history of salvation and therefore in primal and eschatological history. He attests the election of Israel, the election of the Church, the election of the covenanted community. Hence it is no accident that the name of this angel does not proclaim anything specific but only that which denotes the essential nature of all angels. What angel could be anything other, anything more or less, than an angel of God ?

But now in relation to these simpler passages which treat of the angel of God we must consider that what is ascribed to him in the way of word and act and achievement might just as well—we are almost tempted to say, better—be said of Yahweh Himself, as similar things are actually ascribed to Him in other passages. Indeed, similar and even the same things, as, for example, all that takes place in connexion with the Exodus and the wilderness wandering, are more frequently described and honoured as Yahweh's own words and acts without any mention of the angel of Yahweh. There can, of course, be no question of any rivalry between God and His angel. A pure and transparent witness is one who when he acts does not in any sense introduce himself but only the one whom he attests. It is not for nothing, then, that in the passages mentioned the presence of the angel means that of the Lord. Even the exposition of the Old Testament in terms of religious history, which is particularly honest in such matters, has never, so far as I am aware, found any indications that in Israel any particular sphere of operation was allotted, or any cult dedicated, to the angel of the Lord side by side with that of Yahweh. Where he appears, he is absorbed, as it were, by his speech and action, which are none other than those of Yahweh Himself. The story in Jud. 13²ᶠ· is particularly instructive in this respect. " I asked him not whence he was, neither told he me his name," says the woman to her husband (v. 6). And when the man later asks the angel : " What is thy name ? ", he is given the answer : " Why askest thou me thus after my name, seeing it is wonderful ? " (v. 18). And when the man detains him to offer a burnt offering, the angel refuses : " If thou wilt offer a burnt offering, thou must offer it unto the Lord " (v. 15 f.). And when the man offers it to the Lord who does wondrously, " the angel of the Lord ascended in the flame of the altar. And Manoah and his wife looked on, and fell on their faces to the ground. But the angel of the Lord did no more appear to Manoah and to his wife. Then Manoah knew that he was the angel of the Lord. And Manoah said unto his wife, We shall surely die, because we have seen God. But his wife said unto him, If the Lord were pleased to kill us, he would not have received a burnt offering and a meat offering at our hands, neither would he have shewed us all these things, nor would as at this time have told us such things as these " (v. 19 f.). This is what happens when this angel appears. He obviously appears only to efface himself in favour of the One on whose behalf he appears to man. But how effectively and impressively he does so ! It is understandable that in the Old Testament world he is not a constant, regularly occurring or systematically comprehensible figure ; that he can appear, but can equally well not appear, and often does not do so. We have to see and understand that it is in this very front that he is so important and indispensable. We have only to imagine that he were always present where there is mention of the appearance and Word and work of God, and the impression would be unavoidable that he is an intrinsically important being or principle side by side with God. On the other hand, we have only to imagine that there were no references to his appearance, but obvious mention were made only of God and not of His angel, and the prosaic reader and theologian would be spared a great deal of trouble, but the mystery of God would also be lost. For it is the mystery of God which is concretely revealed and set before the reader in these constantly recurring references to the angel of God. It is the unmistakeable fact that the presence of the God of grace and mercy is very different from that of a harmless supreme being. In these passages, with their happenings which are so strongly cosmic in form but so absolutely supracosmic in meaning, we can see what is meant whenever there is reference to God and His Word and acts, even though there may be no mention of the angel of the Lord. Where the angel of the Lord appears, the dimension of the divine is disclosed and the category of the divine imposes itself. God can no longer be equated with an intellectual or sentimental or aesthetic epitome. He presents Himself as a divine factor which genuinely occupies space and time even in the earthly sphere. Earthly beings cannot fail to see that God is God, and that only fools can say : There is no God, and that those who take one another for God are even greater fools. Worship and sacrifice are demanded, as in the story of Manoah. Man must die, as Manoah rightly perceives. No, he may live, as he learns from his better instructed wife. Not the angel of the Lord is superfluous, but the man and especially the theologian who crossly strikes out these passages, and misses the fact that in them there sounds the great bell which we ought to hear in other apparently—but only apparently—less striking places. What we are told by the intervention of heaven as God's witness as revealed in these passages is that the covenant of grace, the election and calling of Israel and the Church, the Gospel, are not historical events like others on this earth of ours, and that they do not establish ordinary historical relationships, with well-planned theologies, well-intentioned systems of piety, well-run institutions, well-weighed conclusions of assemblies and commissions under the well-meaning oversight of a wisely invisible supreme God. This is what is declared by the angel of the Lord who is the angel of the covenant, and it is declared in such a way that man can see and hear even though sight and hearing fail.

And now we come to the more complicated passages in which the angel of the Lord appears. We refer to the angel in the story of Hagar (Gen. 16[7f.], 21[17f.]), to the visit of the three men to Abraham at the terebinth of Mamre (Gen. 18[1f.]), to the two angels who come to Lot in Sodom (Gen. 19[1f.]), to the angel in the story of the sacrifice of Isaac (Gen. 22[11f.]), to the angel in Jacob's dream before his parting from Laban (Gen. 31[11f.]), to the angel of the burning bush (Ex. 3[2f.]), and to the introduction of the angel as the leader of the people in the wilderness when God is incensed with them (Ex. 33[1f.]). All these passages contain more or less obtrusively the great difficulty, which is brought out rather than removed by source-criticism, that the angel of Yahweh can hardly be distinguished from Yahweh Himself but seems very clearly to be one with Him. The angel appears and speaks and acts, but the appearance and word and action are those of God. Or conversely, God appears, and man has to do with His angel. For example, in Gen. 18[1-16] we are told that God appears (v. 1). But we then go on to read that Abraham " lift up his eyes and looked, and, lo, three men stood by him " (v. 2). He then greets them : " My Lord, (*adonai*) if now I have found favour in thy sight, pass not away, I pray thee, from thy servant " (v. 3). But the invitation to rest and eat is addressed to " them " (v. 4), and it is they who answer : " So do, as thou hast said " (v. 5). We may ignore the additional difficulties that in this case we are dealing with three instead of one, and that this time, unlike the story of Manoah, they (or God Himself) actually eat cakes and a " calf tender and good," and drink butter milk and fresh milk (v. 6 f.). It is " they " again who ask concerning Sarah (v. 9 f.). But then in v. 10 we read : " And he said, I will certainly return unto thee according to the time of life;

and, lo, Sarah thy wife shall have a son." Who is this " he " ? Is he one of the three men ? Obviously not, for in v. 13 we are told expressly : " And the Lord said unto Abraham, Wherefore did Sarah laugh . . . ? Is any thing too hard for the Lord ? " And when Sarah denies that she laughed : " I laughed not ; for she was afraid," the reply is again in the singular : " And he said, Nay ; but thou didst laugh " (v. 15). But then the concluding verse tells us that " the men rose up from thence " (v. 16). The same problems confront us in the other passages mentioned.

The question arises whether they are really so very difficult after all. On the one hand, in Gen. 18 and the other passages we may adopt the explanation of early exegesis that these are not appearances of angels but of the Holy Trinity in which the Logos is obviously the spokesman. On the other, we may follow v. Rad in seeing and applying a definite system by which Yahweh is referred to when something is said concerning Him apart from His connexion with man, and the angel when He enters the field of human apperception. On the latter view, however, we are forced to assume that a later redactor, concerned for the strict transcendence of God, has concealed the original tradition of a sensual appearance of God by interposing the figure of the angel as a form of manifestation. V. Rad himself recognises that this " literary theologisation " is " highly speculative for Old Testament relationships," and no matter how subtly it may be done we can hardly say that it achieves its purpose for subtle readers. The insoluble riddle is also posed why it is done only in these passages and not in the many others in which there is undeniable reference to the appearance, speech and action of God in the sphere of human sense, e.g., His walking in the garden (Gen. 3[8]), His personal closing of the ark behind Noah (Gen. 7[16]), His smelling of the sweet savour of sacrifice after the Flood (Gen. 8[21]), or His coming down at the building of the tower of Babel (Gen. 11[7]). We can hardly overlook the fact that there is a good deal more material for literary theologisation in the Old Testament, and that many more difficult passages would have been eased by the interposition of the angel of Yahweh. And in any case, if this is really what took place in the present passage, it has increased rather than alleviated the difficulty of interpretation. If we have understood the matter aright in the simpler passages, it surely ought not to be all that obscure in the present instances. May it not be that these texts seem to be more complicated merely because the same matter is for definite reason more palpable than in the simpler passages ?

For what is the matter in question in these texts ? As in the earlier series, we have here depictions of the encounter between God and man and man and God ; representations which are characterised by the fact that by the introduction of the figure of the angel of the Lord there is underlined and emphasised the urgency of these encounters, the directness and concreteness with which man is claimed by God and for God, not merely in his thoughts, and certainly not merely subjectively, but objectively, with all his senses, as one who hears and sees in the ordinary sphere of life. It may be by a well in the wilderness on the way to Shur (Gen. 16[7]), or by the terebinth in the heat of the day (Gen. 18[1]), or at evening in the gate of Sodom (Gen. 19[1]), or on Horeb the mount of God (Ex. 3[2]), but always the man who is confronted with the angel of God, and therefore with God Himself, is man as he is in the normal course of life. What the angel attests in these passages, too, is that God speaks in a way which cannot be missed, that He acts in a way which cannot be resisted, that He is present in a way which is quite incomparable, that He both captures man and frees him, that He takes him into His own hands and therefore places him in His service. The angel has the character and task of a perfect mirror of God, in which He whose face no man has seen is disclosed, and He, the High and Hidden and Eternal, is present. He has this character and task even when he is expressly described as a visionary figure, as in Gen. 31[11].

A further point which may be made concerning these particular texts is that they all belong to the period of the patriarchs or the early history of Moses, and therefore to the temporal establishment of the covenant of grace as it takes place in these stories. And it is understandable that in this sphere the narrators should find themselves placed, with respect to the point at issue in angelic appearance, in a state of increased and sharpened attention which has to be divided between the divine theophany as such on the one side and the cosmic or heavenly form in which it is both concealed and revealed on the other, between *God* in His mystery on the one side and God in His *mystery* on the other. We have to consider that we have to do here with the unprecedented beginning of the extraordinary existence of Israel within the history of the nations ; with the one thing which constitutes the *raison d'être*, the dignity and the hope of this people. Something very different might have stood at this beginning : perhaps a God without mystery, with no real attestation of His deity ; perhaps a mystery without God, a powerful impression and claim which were only accidental or links in an earthly causal series. But in that case it would not be this particular, unprecedented beginning. It would not be the calling of Israel in the eternal election of grace. And what would Israel be then ? In the event, however, it was not something different which stood at this beginning. It was the One, *God* in this other, *God* in the mystery, *God* in the angel, *sicut in speculo*. And through this One it was also the other, God in the *mystery*, God in the *angel, sicut in speculo*. The two, God and His angel, do not always have to be spoken of in the Old Testament as they are in these passages. But they can be. And perhaps they have to be in these passages. Perhaps these appearances of God and encounters with Him, on which all the rest depend and by which the whole fellowship of God with Israel is conditioned, have to be depicted in this half-light : now God, now the angel, and now God again ; both in the same place and with the same function and as the same subject confronting man. Everything depends on the fact that this is so, that at the calling of Israel God and His angel, His angel and God, are both genuinely present. Everything depends on the recounting of this fact. But if this is so, we need hardly be surprised that the account of the angel of the Lord takes the form it does. The contradiction in the statements is the appropriate form for indicating at least what has to be said. The apparent obscurity of these presentations is the real clarity with which the matter has to be presented. Their complication is merely a reflection of the great simplicity of the narrators in face of the basic phenomenon of Israelite history. And we must not forget that this is the basic phenomenon of all Israelite existence, not merely of its origin, but of its continuation and future in the light of its origin. And it is also the basic phenomenon of Christian existence, its beginning, continuation and future. If it does not always have to be presented in the same way, it is the same phenomenon as that which demands this presentation here. And the only real cause for surprise is that it has not demanded this presentation more frequently.

It may be noted concerning this angel of Yahweh that he is mentioned in the singular. He seems to be unique. In this respect, too, he seems to stand in a remarkable correspondence and affinity with God Himself. He seems to represent His uniqueness *sicut in speculo*. There is an exception to this rule, of course, in Gen. 18 and 19, where mention is made of three and then of two angels. But at any rate the angel of Yahweh does not seem to be one of many. His relationship to the hosts of Yahweh is not elucidated. As far as I know, there is only one place where they are mentioned together, and significantly this is in the story of the nativity in Lk. 2¹³ : " And suddenly there was with the angel a multitude of the heavenly host praising God, and saying . . ." It is only capriciously that we can ascribe to him a hierarchical relationship to the many angels. No mention is made of this in the texts. But because no general or systematic use is made of this figure we are warned against playing off this angel in his singularity against the rest in their plurality, or interpreting their plurality as a development of his unity. The converse is also untenable. The fact that he is called the ἄγγελος κατ' ἐξοχήν does not mean that he is merely the epitome of all angels. We cannot number the angels in terms of our arithmetic, or assess them against each other. A wise reader will not remember that there are other angels when he reads of the angel of the Lord, nor will he consider that the one angel can replace all the rest and make them superfluous when he reads of the many. Both are true in their own place, but it is neither possible nor necessary either to compare them or to bring them under a common denominator. It is more fitting that this remarkable relationship should show or remind us that in the being of God Himself unity and plurality, simplicity and wealth, not only do not form any contradiction, but co-inhere and together constitute the ineffable glory of God. This is what the texts palpably bring to our notice concerning the angel of Yahweh. It will not prevent us from proceeding quietly, and with no attempt at harmonisation, to a consideration of angels generally in the light of what is said of *the* angel.

It may also be noted concerning the angel of Yahweh that when we have once read carefully the texts which treat of him, like those in Judges, or 1 Chron. 21[15f.], or the story of Moses at the bush, or any of the others, we shall lose all desire to understand the notion or doctrine of angels, whether our attitude towards it be positive or negative, either preferably or even essentially in terms of certain playful, trifling, ornamental, or in a word childish conceptions. If I am right, these have obtruded into the matter by way of Christian art, which here as elsewhere is responsible for so much that is inappropriate. There are tolerable and in their way moving and instructive representations of the specifically childlike angel, as, for example, in the famous angelic chorus in Altdorfer's picture of the nativity. But it was obviously out of place when so many painters of his own and a later age surrounded the infant Jesus with a veritable kindergarten of prancing babies amusing themselves in different ways and yet all contriving in some way to look pious. Even more offensive are Raphael's little darlings, which were so much to the taste of even an adult Protestant like Karl Hase. And it is to be noted that it was obviously for the sake of the rhyme that Martin Schelling asked that God's dear little angels (*Engelein*) should carry his soul (*die Seele mein*) to Abraham's bosom, for he found no warrant for any such conception in Lk. 16[22]. We may certainly think of the angels as little to the extent that they are ministering spirits. In this sense they are inconceivably little in relation to God and finally to man. But it would be a good thing if diminutives like the German *Engelein* and the English " cherub," with all the false associations which they evoke, could be banished from current usage. The same holds good of the common conception of angels as charming creatures. We need not agree with R. M. Rilke, who after many changes in outlook finally wrote (in his *Duineser Elegien*) : " Every angel is terrifying." This may be true of what Rilke finally understood by an " angel," and it may be far better than what he once thought. But the biblical angel is not always terrifying. Even the angel of Yahweh is not merely terrifying. He can also be sweet and charming. He is this. But again he is more. He can also be terrifying. And he is. The angel is what God orders him to be. And this may mean that he is both small and great, both terrifying and charming. After the sea of sweetness in which angels have been engulfed, especially—be it noted—since the beginning of the modern period in the 16th century, it is a real boon to see them portrayed again as dark and stern and lofty figures, e.g., on the nativity fresco of Fritz Pauli in the Antonierhaus in Berne. But it must be remembered that they are neither great nor small, terrifying nor charming, dark nor radiant, by our conceptions. They are to be respected as the angels of God which attest His holiness and goodness, His majesty and lowliness, His mercy and judgment. We must not overlook the fact that there are some representations especially of the annunciation, like that of M. Grünewald, in which we seem to see approximations to what must be done and left undone in this respect, and to the transcendent reality which has to be indicated. The same may be said of the great angel on Pauli's fresco. If we could teach all the poets and artists who have taken up the matter the twofold respect required, we could perhaps concede them a good deal of liberty in these matters. But the Christian doctrine of angels must not be influenced by their failures in this regard. And there is no sense in letting ourselves be led astray by their failures in our attempt to work out a sober Christian doctrine of angels. The Old Testament conception of the *maleak Yahweh* ought to be an effective reminder in this respect.

What angels do, the manner and meaning of their ministry, is obviously to be understood from what they are in relation to God.

A first and general statement must be to the effect that with the commission and in the name of God they do exactly, neither more nor less nor other than, what God wills with the coming of His kingdom to earth. And in their way they do it exactly as He wills it to be done. What distinguishes their doing of it from that of other obedient creatures is that in it there is no question of creaturely autonomy. The possibility of deviation or omission does not arise. Their obedience does not have to come into being, and it has no limit. Their creaturely freedom is identical with their obedience. Their heavenly nature consists and expresses itself in their perfect willingness and readiness, but also in their capacity to speak and act from and with and for God. We can thus have unlimited confidence that their speech and action is always and in every respect that of God Himself. On the other hand, we cannot expect to find in their speech and action anything specific or new or distinct as compared with that of God, anything extraordinary in this sense, and therefore anything particularly angelic as opposed to divine. The divine action is not exhausted in theirs, but theirs is in the divine. God is not bound to them, but they are to Him. Thus their action is not a mystery alongside that of God. It is not a magical world between with its own laws and history and outstanding features. The angels are remarkable only in the fact that in distinction from all earthly creatures they stand first and perfectly in the service which forms the determination of all creatures. They see the face of the Father. They come direct from His throne. They are directly involved in His action on earth. They live and move and have their being in preceding and accompanying and following this action. In this sense they come on earth. They enter the sphere of man. They approach him, and he is conscious of them and experiences their existence. Yet in all this they are different and stand apart from him and all earthly creatures. Neither he nor any other earthly creature is or works as they do. They do not confront him as God does. They, too, are creatures. But as God confronts man, the same is true of the heavenly beings which form his *entourage*. And as they confront man with God, God's relationship to man acquires a cosmic contour and concreteness. It becomes a reality for man in the deity of God, in His mystery. This is the general point which must be made concerning the ministry of angels.

In relation to God and man and the earthly creation as a whole, what they do in this ministry can and will be only indirect. In the first instance, this clearly means that it is not they who establish, maintain and direct the covenant of grace. It is not they who rule the course of the world or any of its spheres. It is not their affair to exercise mercy and judgment, and the life and death of the earthly creature, the limitation of its existence and its form between its beginning and end are not in their hands. This must be taken in the strict sense that they do not even co-operate with God in all these things; that not even to the smallest degree are they willing and speaking and acting subjects side by side with Him; that they are not even commissioned as His delegates to do things while He is resting or otherwise engaged, so that these things are not His work but theirs, and are to be ascribed to them. That it is God who reigns is a rule to which there is not the slightest exception even in His relationship to heavenly creatures. What they do in their service does not violate His sovereign right to which they too are subject and which He certainly does not confer on them. What they do can be only the confirmation of His sovereign right. In their action they do not make the divine movement, but as creatures an intra-cosmic movement which is subordinate and corresponds to the divine. And it is as this movement consists only in a confirmation of the sovereign right of God over man and all earthly creatures that they do that which is specifically angelic, giving to God's relationship to man the contour and concreteness in which it can be perceptible and actual for him as the new creation of God. It is for this that the angels are perfectly willing and ready and fully empowered as heavenly beings, the saints and sons of God. But by doing this they do not add anything new or distinctive or peculiarly their own to the divine action. They show themselves to be creatures of His hand, subjects of His sovereign lordship over all things. In no sense, then, are they lords, or fellow-lords. They are simply servants. In their own way they are wholly what the most modest blade of grass waving on the earth by the will of God is in its very different way. The only thing is that they are not blades of grass; they are heavenly beings. Their movement in accordance with the will of God is thus the movement which He has allotted to them and for which they are determined as such.

Even the frequently heard expression that the ministry of angels consists in mediating between God and earthly creatures is to be used, therefore, only with the greatest caution. God mediates Himself, and does not need a third party for this purpose. He mediates Himself through His own Word and through His own Holy Spirit, and thus

needs no assistance either from earthly or even from heavenly creatures. He Himself throws a bridge across the gulf, and secures it on both sides. He Himself speaks, and sees to it that He is heard. He Himself disposes, and sees to it that His will is done. In these things He is quite adequate in Himself, and man is referred to Him alone. This is made clear in the central point of His work on earth : in the incarnation of His Word and in the reconciliation of the world with God accomplished therein ; in what took place on Golgotha and was revealed on Easter Day. It is obvious that in these matters even the angels can only note and watch and wonder and adore and praise, unable and unworthy to plan or will or accomplish anything of themselves. It was not they who devised and executed this work. They did not co-operate in it either above or below. They did not contribute anything to it. As the heavenly creatures they are, they were simply present. But what is true at the centre is equally true on the circumference. There are no contiguous spheres in which they have to mediate various things in the sense that these things are even momentarily committed to them and are thus to be expected from them ; in the sense, then, that they are agents or middle-men to whom independent attention, gratitude and obligation must be granted as such. We can say that they mediate between God and the earthly creation only to the extent that, as the heavenly creatures they are, and according to the will and command of God, they are actually present in that which He alone does both in the centre and on the circumference when He mediates Himself ; and that, since God does not will or command anything in vain, they are not present for nothing but to His glorification. It is exactly the case with the angels as with earthly creatures too, and especially with some men, of whom we can and must say that according to the will and command of God they are present with their action in that which God does, and that they are not present for nothing but to His glorification. But the glorification of God by the ministry of angels consists in the fact that their presence at what God alone does, as the presence of the heavenly creation, gives to the relationship between God and the earthly creation its cosmic character, the concrete form of the divine mystery perceptible on earth.

Understood in this way, the action of angels cannot be valued too highly. Their presence is not in any sense, not even partially, a presence of lordship. It is wholly the creaturely presence of service. But all the same it is a genuinely powerful presence. It is not for nothing that when God speaks and acts they are present at His will and command, and as heavenly creatures. This is something which counts on earth. The glorification of God by their ministry takes place. The relationship between God and the earthly creation acquires and has this character.

God is present on earth even without the angels. How can it be otherwise? But where His presence becomes event, experience and decision for the earthly creature, this is realised in the action of the angels. As He is present Himself, He shows Himself through the angels. They do not make God present to man. Their own presence as such would be meaningless. But as and when God is present for man, it is through their presence that man may and must perceive it. By their presence He makes it impossible that He should be overlooked.

It is God Himself who speaks with man, and not a heavenly voice, however powerful or mysterious, however worthy of respect or attention, trying to cry or whisper something of its own alongside His Word. But when God speaks, when His Word becomes enlightenment, consolation and direction to man, it is by His angels that He makes His voice distinct from all others, giving to His Word the sound and form of the divine direction by which He places man unmistakeably in the unique responsibility which he owes to Him.

It is God Himself and God alone who is the Lord in the covenant of grace and in the community which recognises and proclaims this covenant to be concluded, and therefore the Lord of the cosmic process, the innermost meaning of which is the history of this covenant and this community. But when He exercises this lordship, when He continually evinces His might and power in the execution of His covenant, in the gathering and maintaining and renewing of His community and its service, but also in the process of cosmic and natural occurrence, this demonstration of His lordship takes place in the presence of His angels. It is not that He abdicates in favour of them even for a moment or in a single respect. It is not that any might or power ceases to be directly His own. But as His own these powers are also heavenly powers and in this form cosmic, really active in the world. They are here and now valid orders and precepts, determinations and directions. They are this by the ministry of His angels.

Neither as a whole nor in detail are there any finally true, valid and effective divine acts, preservations, demonstrations, assistances or deliverances in which the angels co-operate with God or act as His vice-gerents. But in all these acts of God the angels are present, and both as a whole and in detail their ministry is that within earthly occurrence they give to them the character of divine acts; that by preceding, accompanying and following them they distinguish them from other events for earthly creatures; that they make them eternally noteworthy. The presence of angels means that these events are distinguished both from the dispositions of fate or chance and from the best works of human self-help or brotherly assistance. The presence of the angels means that even in that which seems to belong only to the nexus of creaturely occurrence, or to be his own or some other creaturely act, man is summoned to see the intervention of

God Himself, and therefore an element in His plan and its execution. an element of the salvation history or universal history directed by Him, and within this context an element in his own life-history as controlled by God. It is the angels who impress this stamp as it were on the acts of God. They serve God in this sense. They work with Him in this sense. And in this sense we can and must speak of a mediating ministry of angels between God and earthly creatures.

We now return to our principal thesis that the angels are God's witnesses. In a supreme sense, therefore, they are that which God, when He speaks and acts, wills to make and does actually make certain men and finally all men, and indeed the earthly creation in its totality as He espouses its cause. To restrict ourselves to the narrowest circle, the angels are the originals of the prophets and apostles to whom they often seem to approximate, indeed, with whom they often seem to merge, in the biblical text.

The fact that they are witnesses has on the one side the modest implication that they are actually there when the will of God is executed. They see and hear, and are thus in a position to confirm what they have seen and heard. They are there when the will of God is *executed*. The use of the term " witness " brings us face to face with the limitation that they were not present in the eternal counsel of God, either as advisers, or even as spectators. They are creatures, and therefore they are not eternal. They do not know the Father as the Son knows Him, or the Son as He is known by the Father. They do not know, then, either the ground or the goal of the will of God. Between the beginning and the end they cannot foreknow either as a whole or in detail what God wills or how He will accomplish it. In face of the fact that on the basis of His eternal counsel God speaks and does such and such things, they are no less novices than other creatures. To know His eternal counsel, they are no less referred than other creatures to its continual revelation in what He actually says and does. They have only two advantages over earthly creatures. The first is that as the heavenly *entourage* of God they have primary and original knowledge of what He says and does Because the kingdom of God comes from heaven to earth, they are the first to know the doing of His will, the Word and work in which He reveals it. The Word and work of God are not directed to them. They are directed to earth. Their target is man. But the angels are there, and see and hear, when God comes down from heaven to take man to Himself. They know and revere and praise the Word and work of His mercy before any man can do so. And because they are heavenly creatures they have the second advantage that their seeing and hearing of the divine movement is not only primary but perfect. They are genuine and reliable witnesses—crown-witnesses. It is not really necessary to ascribe to them marvellous qualities. Their being and existence is summed up in this seeing and hearing. All heaven is simply the place from which God comes to man. Hence it is not a meritorious achievement on the part of angels that they are perfect witnesses of this happening. Because their being and existence is really exhausted in this seeing and hearing, and as heavenly creatures they have no room for a deviation or reserve which would mean imperfection, they have no option but to be perfect witnesses of God. I repeat that their freedom consists in their obedience. This is a further reason to extol, not themselves, but the God who made them thus, with this nature. But with this nature they are in this first sense of the term not only the primary but the best witnesses, crown-witnesses, witnesses of the Word and work of God, seeing and hearing spectators of the first and supreme rank.

On the other hand, however, the term "witness" implies the high dignity of angels as those who are ordained, as the primary and perfect spectators they are, to attest or confirm to earthly creatures the Word and work of God, guaranteeing and pledging by their existence that the will of God which commences in heaven is about to be done on earth. They are ordained to do this as the kingdom of God comes from heaven, as it is thus the kingdom of heaven on earth, and as they form the accompanying *entourage* of God on earth. On this side, too, the term "witness" carries with it a limitation. This time it is a limitation in relation to earth. The angelic ministry of witness cannot replace the prophetic and apostolic witness, or the witness of the community. Nor can it replace the witness to which all the lower creation is summoned, and not summoned in vain, by the Word and work of God. The beginning of the doing of the will of God is when it takes place on earth that the Word and work of God are so manifest that even men can see and hear and thus proclaim them, guaranteeing and pledging that His Word is the truth and His work the salvation of the world ; so manifest, indeed, that all earthly creation can then join in the praise and proclamation of God. Where and to the extent that this happens, the last time dawns on earth and the consummation comes. That this takes place, that there is this calling and action of earthly creatures, is God's own work, the fruit of His manifestation in the flesh, the fruit of the offering of His Son at Golgotha, the fruit of the Spirit outpoured on all flesh after His resurrection. It is not, then, the work of angels, nor can it be replaced nor anticipated by their work. Their work has its limit in what is finally to be done by men, by earthly creatures generally, as they are moved by God. They can only prepare for this with their witness, as they can only follow and confirm the eternal counsel of God in the light of its execution. In this respect they are below even the least of earthly creatures which God wills to make His witnesses. But when God is on the way to this goal in His Word and work, they mightily precede and accompany and follow Him. They powerfully

issue the summons with which He calls earthly creatures and men
to be His witnesses. In so doing they serve God and man and the
whole earthly creation. It is in this connexion that we speak of their
co-operating and mediatorial action. Their witness is not the thing
which is finally to take place on earth. In the purpose and end and
goal of His action, God is not dealing with them. He is dealing with
man, with the earth. All the emphasis falls on the witness of the
prophets and apostles and those who are called by and with them,
and none at all on the witness of the angels. Yet as heavenly witness,
primary and perfect and therefore pure, their witness is important
and even indispensable to the extent that it forms the necessary
presupposition for the human witness with which the doing of God's
will on earth begins. Man cannot of himself cause it to happen that
God encounters and may be perceived by him in His deity, that He
sees and hears Him, that even cosmically He becomes a reality for
him as a cosmic being, and that man as a cosmic being is thus enabled
to be His witness in the cosmos. This is something which he must
be given, and because he is below he must be given it from above.
And in order that he should be given it from above, his great visitation
by God does not take place without cosmic form, without the heavenly
entourage accompanying God, without His crown-witnesses the angels.
Their proper office is to be as it were the atmosphere in which there
can be a witness of men and earthly creatures, their seeing and hearing and therefore their proclamation of God. That is why there is
so much about angels in the Bible. That is why the people of the
Bible have so many dealings with them. That is why it is so important for them to affirm that they are not merely in the presence
of God but—because in the presence of God, because in His real
presence—they are also in the presence of His angels. That is why
the biblical authors must continually indicate and mention and
frequently record that men are surrounded by angels, experiencing
their power, hearing their voices, knowing their protection and
guidance. This simply means that, as the earthly creatures they are,
they know that they share in a witness to God which they cannot
give themselves and which no other earthly beings can give them,
but which permits and commands them even as earthly beings to be
themselves witnesses of God, hearing and seeing Him, and proclaiming Him in His service. This witness from which the men of
the Bible proceed and which the authors of the Bible must take into
account is the witness of angels. It is the self-witness of God
accompanied by the witness of angels and by this witness confirmed
and demonstrated to be divine.

In our exegesis of Rev. 4–5 we have already considered the powerful and
comprehensive picture of the way in which angels as the heavenly *entourage* of
God are made witnesses of the will of God as it commences above and is fulfilled

below. We can find a similar depiction in the fine saying in Job 38[7], which tells us that at the creation of the earth the morning stars sang together and the sons of God shouted for joy. In the New Testament we may again recall the hymn to Christ in 1 Tim. 3[16], in which the third of the six phrases tells us that He was " seen of angels." This appearance to angels is preceded by the decisive work of God—that He was " manifest in the flesh " and " justified in the Spirit." Hence even the angels are confronted by something new. They, too, need and receive a special revelation. But it is given to them first. Only then do we read that He was " preached unto the Gentiles," " believed on in the world," and finally " received up into glory." But this passive witness of angels has obviously to be augmented, and this takes place. Even when God has appeared in the flesh and in the Spirit, they have much to learn. In Eph. 3[10] we are told, indeed, that the heavenly principalities and powers are instructed concerning the manifold wisdom of God by the existence of the ἐκκλησία on earth. In this phenomenon, they are again surprised as it were by something new. Again, 1 Pet. 1[12] tells us that the Gospel preached by the apostles on earth is something which the angels desire to look into (παρακύψαι), their knowledge being obviously dependent upon events. Along the same lines we read in Lk. 12[8] (cf. Rev. 3[5]) that the Son of Man will confess before the angels of God those who confess Him before men, and in Lk. 15[7, 10] that there is joy among the angels of God over one sinner who repents. Again, Paul tells us in 1 Cor. 4[9] that the apostles are made a θέατρον to the cosmos and angels and men. According to all these passages, what takes place on earth is for the angels a current experience in the course of which they have still to become witnesses. That they are in some way present to see and hear what takes place in the community is shown by 1 Cor. 11[10], where women are called to order by the recollection of the angels, obviously as representatives of the respect due to God, and also by 1 Tim. 5[21], where Timothy is charged to act prudently in matters of Church discipline " before God, and the Lord Jesus Christ, and the elect angels."

Yet all this is only the presupposition for a consideration of the true and active witness of angels in the service of the saving and cosmic events overruled by God. We shall best proceed if we keep to that which is directly stated in the New Testament concerning the relationship of the action of angels to that of Jesus Christ. It is self-evident that radically and finally all the action of angels attested in both Old and New Testaments can be meaningfully understood only in this context, in its relationship to this centre of the divine action. This is unforgettably expressed in the strong statements in Col. 2[10], Eph. 1[22], 1 Pet. 3[22] and Heb. 1[6] about the lordship of Christ over heavenly dominions and powers. It is in the relationship to Jesus Christ, in which they are subordinate to Jesus Christ but real in this subordination, that all the things are true which we have said about their presence, their speech, their might, their operations under, before, with and after that of God, their ministering but perfect witness as a movement of the heavenly world consequent upon the divine movement, their greatness and their limitation both above and below. To be sure, angelology is not, like anthropology, a consequence and analogy of Christology. For God did not become an angel in Christ. It is possible that Heb. 1[5-14] is specifically directed against such a conception. On the other hand, angelology must be understood as an annexe to Christology. For when God passed by the angels and became man in Christ, the angels entered the sphere of man with Him. When He became man among men, and as by His Spirit, concealed instead of revealed, He is still man among men, His presence includes that of the angels. It is a matter for some surprise, perhaps, that in the Bible there are not far more frequent references to angels in connexion with Jesus Christ and in relationship to Him. In fact, however, the number of these references is very limited, and they are to be found only in specific contexts.

We must begin with a surprising negative fact. In none of the four accounts is there any reference to the appearance, speech or action of angels in the centre of the evangelical record of Jesus. Their last appearance at the beginning is the story which is given in such compressed form in Mark (1¹²ᶠ·) : " And immediately the Spirit driveth him into the wilderness. And he was there in the wilderness forty days, tempted of Satan ; and was with the wild beasts ; and the angels ministered unto him " (διηκόνουν αὐτῷ). This reference is to be found in Matthew too (4¹¹), but is lacking in Luke, who instead is the only Evangelist to tell us at the end, in the story of Gethsemane (22⁴³), that " there appeared an angel unto him from heaven, strengthening him." In neither case is there any indication of what is meant by " ministering " or " strengthening." Since both passages emphasise the tempted humanity of Jesus, we have to think of a special attestation of the presence of God. In all the middle stretch between these two points, there is no mention of angels in the narratives. Even the angel at the pool of Bethesda in Jn. 5⁴ is only a marginal figure which most likely does not belong to the original text at all. And it is only a conjecture of the people that an angel talks with Jesus in Jn. 12²⁹. In this connexion we may also recall the saying of Jesus to Peter at His arrest (Mt. 26⁵³) : " Thinkest thou that I cannot now pray to my Father, and he shall presently give me more than twelve legions of angels ? But how then shall the scriptures be fulfilled, that thus it must be ? " If this verse is compared with others (Mk. 8³⁸ ; Mt. 16²⁷, 25³¹ ; Lk. 9²⁶) which speak of the appearance of angels with the Son of Man at His *parousia,* it is obvious that the great silence in the middle of the records cannot be accidental. The narrators do not intend to give us any stories about angels in this section. We may even say that the marginal references in Mk. 1¹²ᶠ· and Lk. 22⁴³ have more the character of indications than genuine stories. It is true that in Jn. 1⁵¹, in a saying which is clearly reminiscent of the story of Jacob in Gen. 28¹², we are told that the disciples are to see heaven opened, and the angels ascending and descending upon the Son of Man. But none of the Evangelists ever records anything of this nature. Why not ? The idea that they are not present and do not take part in earthly happenings is too much at variance with the general biblical view of angels, and especially with what we are told concerning their specific relationship to Jesus Christ, to serve as an explanation. Here, if anywhere, they are surely present and have a part. But there is no particular mention of them in this section. They are not distinguished as particular figures as in the Old Testament, or Acts, or the beginning and end of the Gospels. The reason for this is that we have to do here in the strictest sense with the final doing of the will of God on earth in itself and as such. When " the Word was made flesh, and dwelt among us (and we beheld his glory) " (Jn. 1¹⁴), it was true on the one side that for a time " he was made a little lower than the angels " (Heb. 2⁹), because as opposed to them He became an earthly creature and in relationship to their heavenly being He partook of a lesser and lowlier. But was not this self-humiliation of God in His Son the meaning and goal of the will of His mercy ? Could or can the majesty of the God who was in Christ to reconcile the world to Himself (2 Cor. 5¹⁸) be more lofty and glorious than in its revelation and expression in the fact that for a time " he was made a little lower than the angels " ? Was He ever more genuinely their Head and Lord than in this self-abasement beneath them ? Are there not good reasons, then, to forget their manifestations and acts at this point where their ministry, too, was completed with the action of God ? This does not mean that we deny them. How could we deny them ? But at this point where for a time they stand above Jesus Christ we must think of them as pushed back into purely passive witness, into the function of privileged spectators. Here if anywhere they had simply to look on and watch and learn. Here we have an obvious anticipation of what Paul says concerning them in 1 Cor. 15²⁴, namely, that in the perfect kingdom of God which commences with the general and definitive revelation of Jesus Christ, and in which even the work of Christ will be consummated and have no further future, they will not be destroyed, but they will certainly lose their power in the sense that their active function will have attained its goal and will therefore be dismissed as superfluous ; although it is to be noted in this connexion that, according to Mk. 8[38] and par., they themselves will first be revealed again in and with the *parousia* of Jesus Christ, and this time in their full relevance for the earthly occurrence which is concluded. Something of this suppression of the angels is to be seen already in the first *parousia* of Jesus Christ. It is to be noted that even in the stories at the beginning and end of the Gospels they never appear with Jesus Himself, but are introduced only as messengers and witnesses announcing Him as it were from a distance. The holy dependence of angelic existence, which is both their greatness and their limitation, is thus expressed in the fact that there is this eloquent silence concerning them in the middle section of the Gospels. Place is found for them in the Bible where the consummating action of God Himself is not yet or no longer visible to man directly. Where this is visible, they are not destroyed and therefore they are not denied—how could they be when their whole existence aims at this consummating action of God ?— but their particular light is outshone like that of a candle in the noonday sun, and the biblical text honours them by no longer thinking of them, or not yet doing so again. The time and occasion, not of their existence, but of reference to them, are given their limit by the entry of the Lord Himself to whom they witness. This law of the central section of the Gospels might well be described as a law of the whole biblical doctrine of angels. The saying of John the Baptist in Jn. 3[30] : " He must increase, but I must decrease," is no less true of them. And it is true of them in a far more radical sense than it is of any human witness, because for all the humility in which alone it can succeed when God is present, human witness forms in contrast to theirs the final goal of the action of God on earth. According to the witness of the Bible God came among men and His Word became flesh in order to evoke in earthly creatures praise like the decreasing witness of the Baptist. We cannot say this of the witness of angels. This is not a final goal of the will and work of God. Angels really come only to go again. Hence it is the case in the whole Bible that whereas man thinks he must perish when God causes Himself to be seen and heard by him (cf. Is. 6), but is really constituted a witness by this experience, angels (including the mighty seraphim of Is. 6) help man to see and hear, but when they have discharged this commission they really do withdraw (never recurring, for example, in the biblical account of the activity and prophecy of Isaiah). It is of the very essence of the matter that this should be the case. In the light of this lacuna in the Gospel records we can also understand why it is that although angels are often mentioned they have no constitutive role in the New Testament Epistles. To the extent that the apostolic community has to do with the reality, presence and efficacy of the Spirit in whom the Lord Himself is present in the midst of His community, angels cannot have in the *kerygma*, *didache*, or ethical instruction of the apostles even the relatively independent role and significance undoubtedly ascribed to them in New Testament thinking as such and plainly enjoyed by them according to the witness of Acts. They fade away like the stars before the dawn. It is hard to see how Paul could have explained this phenomenon otherwise than by saying that we honour angels by thinking of their Lord, because in so doing we recognise that their service has not been rendered in vain. On the other hand, we dishonour them if we try to ascribe to them independent special functions where the Lord is present in the fulness of His Spirit. In the light of a true understanding of this lacuna, the basic answer to the question why there are not many more references to them in both Old and New Testaments is to the effect that although both Old and New Testaments are the preceding and following annunciation of God's own action they are also the attestation of His present action, of eschatological reality in the relationship between God and man. The more expressly the latter theme is treated in the Bible, the less we can reasonably expect to hear of angels. The ministry of angels is that of the annunciation which precedes and follows. For the most part, then, we meet them in the Bible where there is still or again a certain distance in the reference to God's own action.

It is in this sense that they appear in their relationship to Jesus Christ at the beginning and end of the Gospels. At the beginning, or before the beginning of the true Gospel account of the life and suffering and death of Jesus, the angel of God under the name of Gabriel plays an emphatic role with his twofold message, first to Zacharias (Lk. 1⁵ᶠ·), and then to Mary (Lk. 1²⁶ᶠ·). The general nature of the ministry of angels may be seen very clearly in the angelic figure of this chapter. Yet he comes with a highly specific function, as the herald of what will be decisively accomplished by God. We know from the conclusion of the chapter, and from what follows, the nature of this work. In the first place, there will be born a final and supreme prophet personifying the whole of the Old Testament and its message of a holy God, its call for conversion to Him, its hope and its threat. But this prophet will be only the precursor preparing the way for Another who is very different and far greater, the Son of God Himself born as man, Israel's Comforter and King, Judge and Redeemer. Thus the promise and the Law will both emerge again in living strength. But this time they will not be present *in abstracto*, or in their own historical form. They will stand in direct relationship to the fulfilment which comes down from God in heaven, to the presence of God Himself, not to give further promises or to make further demands, but to make the cause of man His own, taking it personally into His own hands. The ministry of the ἄγγελος κυρίου of Lk. 1 is to announce this coming event, which is twofold and yet one, since the first is only the preparation for the second. The angel himself is only the preceding shadow or sound of this event. He is only the herald of the God who will come in person in this event. As in the early accounts of the history of the covenant, there again appears the heaven which comes to earth with God Himself, epitomised in the form of the one angel of the one God. That he is really a heavenly creature may be seen from the first effect of his appearance on both those to whom he comes. Zacharias and Mary are both said to be " troubled " (Lk. 1¹², ²⁹). And they are both told not to fear (1¹³, ³⁰). It is not the fact that he is a heavenly creature, and therefore strange to earthly beings, which makes the angel an angel. It is his message, the Word of God which he has to deliver in all his strangeness as a heavenly creature. And for both the persons concerned, and therefore in relation both to the coming precursor and the coming Christ Himself, this message obviously has the character of an annunciation of the covenant of grace which is not merely promised again but is now fulfilled. It is, therefore, a glad message. This is seen in the case of Mary : " Hail, thou that art highly favoured, the Lord is with thee " (v. 28, cf. the salutation in Jud. 6¹² : " The Lord is with thee, thou mighty man of valour "), and then again : " Thou hast found favour with God " (v. 30). But it is also seen in the saying to Zacharias in v. 14 : " Thou shalt have joy and gladness ; and many shall rejoice at his birth," and then later when there is given to him, as a punishment for his unbelief, the confirmatory sign which he has requested : " I am sent . . . to show thee these glad tidings " (v. 19). And to this there corresponds equally clearly, when the announced event begins to come to pass, and has already done so in part, the unequivocally positive, grateful and joyful tenor of the songs of praise both of Mary (v. 46 f.) and Zacharias (v. 68 f.). These two canticles form the climax of the chapter, and if we are rightly to understand the advent-angel of the chapter we do well to begin by considering them. What the ministry of the angel accomplishes according to this story, and what is obviously therefore the meaning and purpose of his mission, is that the human creation to which he announces the coming of the kingdom, its King and its last and first witness, is thereby caused to break out in praise of the One who has willed this and begun to accomplish it ; into praise of His mercy (note that the word occurs in both songs) as it is revealed and operative in this action. But what does it mean to praise God's mercy ? The hymns as such are only an expression of the praise, not merely verbal and mental, but existential and actual, to which the earthly creation is stirred by the heavenly. It consists in the fact that men look and move willingly and readily to the One who comes, as earthly creatures who have appropriated what is said to them even though they know that they are in no position for what is said to come to them and actually to happen, it being highly improbable in the case of Zacharias and quite impossible in that of Mary, so that a miracle is involved in both cases. They have appropriated it because it is a matter of the helping and saving presence of God, of the mystery of His grace. The advent-angel announces that the mystery of God's grace will take place in all its im-probability and impossibility, and this is what the two concerned, Zacharias the priest in the temple and the Virgin Mary in Nazareth, have both actually appropriated in their different ways. They coincide in the fact that they are obedient. The difference is that, although Mary first raises a question (v. 34), she is content with the word of the angel : " Behold the handmaid of the Lord ; be it unto me according to thy word " (v. 38), whereas Zacharias asks for a sign, and becomes obedient only when he is given what seems to be a punitive sign. Here then, as in the story of Manoah in Jud. 13²ᶠ·, the man seems to be the less gifted partner of the angel. But the difference is not decisive. The fulfilment of what is announced by the angel is neither retarded by the more sluggish obedience of Zacharias nor initiated by the more spontaneous obedience of Mary. We cannot, therefore, regard Mary as *corredemptrix* in virtue of her *Fiat voluntas tua*. The angel has actually indicated to both their calling to the service of the One who comes. God Himself has actually brought home His Word to both. They are both obedient to their heavenly calling in accordance with the incite-ment of the angel. And their two songs confirm the fact that there has taken place, and not in vain, a visitation of the earthly creation not only by God but also by the heavenly creation. What the angel was in relation to both, i.e., the servant of God, one who stands before God and is sent by Him, he is archetypally for what they themselves will be at the end of the story, or rather—for they stand at the head of a great host—for what all those will be after them whom the coming One Himself will call and gather to His community. The ministry of the angel will find its correspondence in their earthly ministry, his heavenly mission in their earthly mission. He cannot be more than the One who announces their calling. It is God Himself who calls Zacharias, Mary and all who will be called after them. But the angel of Lk. 1 is the one who mightily announces this and all divine calling. In relationship and analogy to Lk. 1 we must also understand the appearance of the angel to Joseph in Mt. 1²⁰⁻²⁵, by which he too is in his own way called to the service of the One who comes from God.

There follows in Lk. 2⁹⁻¹⁵ the appearance of the angel in the nativity story itself. It takes place immediately after the event which was announced in Lk. 1 has now taken place. The oneness of the event for all its duplication in Christ and His forerunner, and the true order in the duplication, are confirmed by the fact that the coming of the kingdom announced by the angel is the birth of Jesus Christ which that of John can only precede. Now, when Christ the Lord is born in the city of David, the time is fulfilled, the last time has come, the will of God has begun to be done on earth as it is in heaven, the calling of Zacharias and Mary has found its meaning and content, and these two are shown to be the head of the people of God of the last day. Now—the angelic appearance and message of the nativity story are a retrospective announcement of this Now. It is to be noted that those who are already called and placed in the service of God neither need nor receive it. Hence it does not take place in the vicinity of the cradle at Bethlehem where artists love to depict it. There what has taken place speaks for itself. Where the Son of God Himself is, the presence of heaven is attested in His presence without any particular need to be visible and audible. The angelic appearance and message are to those who are outside, to the shepherds in the fields who are the first to join those who are called and who with them become the first human witnesses of what has taken place. The ἄγγελος κυρίου comes no less unexpectedly to the shepherds than to Zacharias, Mary and Joseph. When we are told that the δόξα κυρίου, the radiance of God, the revelation of His glory, majesty and power, shone round about them, this does not merely indicate the cosmic reality and perceptibility of the announcement made to them, nor does it merely denote that they have to do with a heavenly experience and therefore one which is new and strange to them as earthly creatures. It does show this, as appears from the fact that they too are afraid, and that the " Fear not " has to be said above all to them. For if with the coming of the angel of the Lord heaven is manifested above the earth, and therefore something strange happens on earth, this is no reason for amazement or terror. For in truth it is the light of God which in this form breaks into the darkness of earth and illumines them. And it is not to blind but to enlighten, not to crush and destroy but to liberate, that the glory, majesty and power of God are revealed to them. Hence the continuation in the message of the angel is again : " Behold, I bring you good tidings of great joy, which shall be to all people " (παντὶ τῷ λαῷ, to the whole host of those who shall come to know of this happening, to the whole people of the last time already called and sanctified by this happening). Once again, therefore, the angel is clearly and unequivocally an evangelical angel. His word is exclusively of the covenant of grace. But it is of the fulfilled covenant, of what God has now done and accomplished in His mercy : " For unto you is born this day in the city of David the σωτήρ, which is Christ the Lord." At the end of Israel's history there has now come its meaning and goal ; at the end of the promise of the Old Testament the promised reality. The radiance of God streams over the dark earth because a child is born. The presence of heaven on earth has the sole purpose of attesting the birth and existence of this child, the redemption accomplished and the lordship of God established in Him. And it is the clear intention of this heavenly witness that men as represented first by the shepherds should not be transfixed by amazement or terror at the revelation imparted to them, as later legends have usually depicted the matter, but that they should be moved to seek and find the child for themselves. The direction with which the angel sends the shepherds away from himself to the child in the manger is the decisive service which he can and must render as an angel. The radiance of God has shone round about them, and the great announcement of the event has been made, only in order that they may run—as they actually do— and see for themselves, thus becoming witnesses on their own account of what has taken place. The ministry of the angel draws their attention, too, to the community, to their own ministry, to the fact that they are also to be witnesses.

And now the text shows in an extraordinary way that it is the ministry of all heaven which is rendered to man with this purpose of pointing them to the event as such, to the child in the manger. For here alone in the Bible we are told that there was with the angel the multitude of the heavenly host, the full complement of the host of Yahweh. All heaven bears witness to θεὸς ἐν ὑψίστοις, to His majesty, and to the glory proper to Him in this majesty, but to His majesty and glory in view of the fact that He has so inconceivably condescended and humbled Himself. And in view of this true majesty of God, of the secret of the grace of His majestic being, it bears witness to the peace on earth created by Him among the men of His good-pleasure, in the midst of the people of those elected and called by Him, which as such are already taken from the earthly conflict which they still endure and for whom the last time and the reign of peace have already dawned. All heaven, heaven as such, becomes presence, appearance and word, and proclaims God—God in His highest throne, in His majesty—as the One who has taken earth to Himself. And all heaven, heaven as such, summons man to join the people of His good-pleasure, the community which knows and values and confesses His grace. This is the action or ministry of angels in retrospect of the beginning of the doing of the will of God on earth as this has taken place in the birth of Jesus Christ.

The third Evangelist especially has thus surrounded his account of this event with this account of the angels. It is to be noted again that they have no part in the event as such. They cannot anticipate it. They can only announce that it will take place. They neither see nor hear it taking place. When it has taken place, they can only point to God Himself and His completed act. When they have done this, they return to heaven, and for a long time we hear no more about them. Both before and after the event their function is merely to declare it. They do not issue any summons of their own. It is not they who awaken Mary and Zacharias to obedience. It is not they who set the shepherds on the way to Bethlehem. Indeed, it is particularly emphasised that the shepherds decided to go of themselves. But the angels drew attention to the fact that Christ would come and that He had come, and that it was necessary to be ready for the coming One and to seek in His lowliness the One who had come. Their activity acquires and has its substance in the fact that Christ actually will come and has come, and that the calling of His people—not by their power, but by the shining of that of God—will actually take place. Their ministry consists in making visible and audible on earth this whole happening whose subject and author is God Himself. As the heavenly creation, they are the medium in which this is possible. The third Evangelist regards it as right and necessary, in his account of the beginning of the things fulfilled among us (Lk. 1^1), to lay on this medium the particular stress which he does actually lay on it in chapters 1 and 2. We must consider the impression which this makes on the reader. On the one hand, it increases the surprise and strangeness without which we cannot appraise or understand the event announced by the angels. Unless we see it at an appropriate distance, we cannot see this event as the Saviour and His prophet. We are set at this distance when we read that it was announced by angels. But this is only one side of the matter. For the announcement by the angels also introduces a certain softening. Seen in the mirror of the angelic message, the event is recognisable as one which for all its strangeness is a real event in our cosmic sphere, so that it is possible and meaningful not only to keep our distance but to take up an attitude and enter into a relationship to it. By his visible and audible introduction of heaven, Luke achieves the twofold effect of enabling the reader to see the event at a distance, but at a possible and meaningful distance which includes a relationship, or conversely to see it in a relationship, but in a relationship which entails a suitable distance. It is the ministry of angels on earth which corresponds exactly to this twofold impression. Apart from some traces in Matthew, Luke is the only Evangelist to make this impression. It is a subject for enquiry how far this is of a piece with his distinctive theology. But it may be noted that Matthew really attains the same effect by calling the kingdom of God the kingdom of heaven. At all events, Luke's distinction of the beginning of the history of Jesus by the ministry of angels was intentional and is certainly instructive. Here at least in the New Testament we are made conscious by it of the distinctive atmosphere in which it became true and recognisable that ὁ λόγος σὰρξ ἐγένετο. But there are also good reasons why Luke should stand alone to the extent that this reference is not to be found in the Gospel tradition as a whole and does not seem to correspond to any principle. The angels demand our attention, but they refuse to be set systematically in the foreground of interest.

We pass over the references in the stories of the temptation and the passion, to which allusion has already been made, and turn at once to the opposite pole of the records, the history of the forty days. It is to be noted that in exact correspondence to their appearances before and after the birth of Jesus, and also to the position and function in the whole context of the record, they again appear at the beginning and the end in this part of the tradition. Whenever the Resurrected Himself appears—and His appearances form the heart of the presentation—there is no mention of angels. They are visible and audible as witnesses before and after He Himself is seen and heard and touched by His own. Primarily and decisively they are present before. Only once, at the beginning of Acts, do they make a last appearance in retrospect of the forty days.

As concerns their appearance at or before the beginning of the Easter appearances, all four Evangelists agree that something takes place in the early morning on the first day of the week after the death and burial of Jesus. In respect of the external facts and circumstances, there are from the very first differences which temporarily seem to disappear but then become even more acute. As concerns the participants, for example, John speaks only of Mary Magdalene (20[1]), Matthew of Mary and the other Mary (28[1]), Mark of these two and a Salome (Mk. 16[1]), and Luke of these two and a Joanna (24[10]). In Matt. 28[4] and Lk. 24[4] the scene was outside the sepulchre, whereas in Mk. 16[5] and Jn. 20[11f.] it was inside. In Matt. 28[2] they met the ἄγγελος κυρίου, in Mk. 16[5] a νεανίσκος, in Lk. 24[4] ἄνδρες δύο (obviously angels), and in Jn. 20[12] δύο ἄγγελοι. All four accounts refer to their white robes or radiant appearance. In Matt. 28[2f.] we are told that the angel of the Lord has come down from heaven, rolled away the stone and seated himself upon it. But the meaning of the Evangelist can hardly be that this took place in the presence of the women. The other three all say that the women found the grave open and empty, and were then addressed by the angel or angels. From this point there is almost complete unity in relation to the angelic message. It is true that in Jn. 20[13] it simply consists in the question to Mary : " Woman, why weepest thou ? ", but we can recognise the question in what the angel or angels say to the women according to the Synoptists. The question implies that there is no reason to weep, nor to complain : " They have taken away my Lord, and I know not where they have laid him." Why not ? In Lk. 24[5] the decisive saying of the angel again has the form of a question, although this time the answer is explicit within the question : " Why seek ye the living among the dead ? " The explicit answer as such, which is the whole point of the Johannine account too, is to the following effect : " He is not here : for he is risen, as he said. Come, see the place (but only the place) where he lay " (Mt. 28[6], Mk. 16[6]). The final reference is missing in Lk. 24[6f.], and we are given instead an explanation of the ἠγέρθη : " Remember how he spake unto you when he was yet in Galilee, saying, The Son of man must be delivered into the hands of sinful men, and be crucified, and the third day rise again."

The first point, then, is that it is by angels whose radiant appearance and heavenly character is generally emphasised that the fact of the resurrection of the Lord is declared to the first men, to these women. It is to be noted that in none of the accounts is the empty grave as such the theme of their message. Even the rather difficult account which we are given in Jn. 20[2-9] of Peter and the other disciple running to the sepulchre is obviously not meant to be understood in this way. The open and empty grave is as such a sign which needs explanation (like the unexpected pregnancy of Mary in Mt. 1[18f.]). Again, in none of the Evangelists is it the case that the Resurrected appears directly to His own before the appearance and announcement of the angels. Their appearance to the women, their declaration to them, their communication : ἠγέρθη (even in the Johannine form of the question : " Why weepest thou ? "), seems to be the inescapable medium for an initial knowledge of this event. The appearance and announcement of the angels cannot, of course, be more than this medium. They have no part at all in the occurrence of the resurrection itself. Even the angel of Matthew who rolls away the stone is not to be thought of as co-operating in the actual resurrection of the Lord.

But as the medium of the knowledge of this happening the angels must immediately withdraw. The second purpose of their appearance and content of their message is to tell the women to go to the disciples and let them know that they will see the risen Jesus Himself. This is expressly stated in Mt. 28⁷ and Mk. 16⁷, and it is implicit in the recollection of the prediction of the passion and resurrection in Lk. 24⁷, and everywhere Galilee is explicitly mentioned as the place where this direct encounter between the Resurrected and His disciples will take place. From this point, the accounts are again confused. According to Mk. 16⁸ the women do not seem to have carried out this commission : " They went out quickly, and fled from the sepulchre ; for τρόμος καὶ ἔκστασις seized them : neither said they anything to any man ; for they were afraid." According to Lk. 24⁹ᶠ· they faithfully discharged their commission but were not believed by the disciples. What they told them seemed to them ὡσεὶ λῆρος until confirmed by direct appearances of the risen One to the disciples on the way to Emmaus in 24¹³⁻³², to Simon alone in 24³³ and to all of them (in Jerusalem) in 24³⁶⁻⁴⁹. According to Mt. 28⁹ᶠ· Jesus Himself appeared to the women and repeated the commission, again referring expressly to a direct meeting which the disciples were to expect with Him in Galilee. This commission was undoubtedly fulfilled by the women according to Mt. 28¹⁶, and did not meet with disbelief on the part of the disciples. According to Jn. 20¹³ᶠ·, immediately after the angel had put that question to Mary and received from her that complaint by way of answer, Mary turned and was faced by Jesus Himself. It is He who now gives the order : " Go to my brethren, and say unto them, I ascend unto my Father, and your Father." She carries out the order, and according to this account there is an appearance of the Resurrected to all the disciples (except in the first instance Thomas) on the evening of the same day in Jerusalem. Our present concern is, of course, with the part played by the angels in these happenings. And the remarkable thing is that for all the contradictions there can be no doubt not only that it is they who first announce the fact of the resurrection but also that it is they who initiate the repetition of the announcement. With what success ? In John there is no mention of any commission given to the women, and they are immediately crowded out by Jesus Himself. In Mark they do not seem to execute the commission at all, and in Luke they do so to no effect. Possibly the meaning in Matthew is that it was only respected and successful when it had been repeated by Jesus Himself. In all cases the commission given by the angels does not seem to be adequate in itself. In all cases Jesus Himself, His appearance and Word, is the agent who gives power to the commission and its execution, and who finally compels the disciples to recognise His presence as the Resurrected. Without Him there could not have taken place the movement initiated at His empty tomb, just as without Him it would not have been true that He was not in the tomb but risen. And yet angels stand at the beginning as the first witnesses of the fact and therefore as those who set in train the ensuing movement. They do not create anything. They do not accomplish anything. They are simply there. But they cannot fail to be there, not as a condition of what happens or of the knowledge of what happens, but for the characterisation, illumination, emphasising and distinction of what happens and of its knowledge by men. Here, too, they show that where God is present and active on earth heaven is also present and active, thus characterising the absolute uniqueness and mystery of the presence and activity of God. We might well repeat what we said concerning their introduction into the Lucan accounts of the beginning of the history of Jesus. Their introduction into the close of the history intentionally awakens in the reader the twofold impression that, by the appearance and announcement of the angels and the presence of heaven with God Himself, he is both set at an appropriate distance and also placed in a meaningful relationship to the event recorded. If we consider this impression, we are given a characteristic view of what is meant by the ministry of angels both in its greatness and in its limitation. In this connexion it might be worth further enquiry why at the conclusion, as opposed to the beginning, the four Evangelists agree in making express reference to the ministry of angels.

But in this case, too, we have a particular concluding narrative as well, namely, that at the end of the forty days. At the heart of this period the angels are as little visible as during the birth of Jesus proper or in the central tract of the Gospel record as a whole. Jesus is not accompanied by an angel when He appears. The angels appear again only when His appearances as the Resurrected are over. The account of this post-ascension appearance is to be found in Ac. 1[10-11]: " And while they looked stedfastly toward heaven as he went up, behold, two men stood by them in white apparel." The assertion of the heavenly and therefore the divine character of the event of the forty days is thus an express conclusion from its end as well as its beginning. Nor is it any accident that we owe this account to the author to whom we are also indebted for Lk. 1–2. The framework of mystery closes around this last item in the tradition and therefore around the Gospel record as a whole. The two angels mark this conclusion. Yet it is remarkable that their saying does not as it were seal the conclusion but makes it a new beginning : " Ye men of Galilee, why stand ye gazing up into heaven ? This same Jesus, which is taken up from you into heaven, shall so come in like manner as ye have seen him go into heaven."

This is best understood, perhaps, from the consequent action of the disciples. It is strikingly modest. It consists simply in the fact (v. 12 f.) that the eleven returned to Jerusalem and there assembled with the women and Mary the mother of Jesus and His brethren in an upper room obviously well-known to them all. Why ? " These all continued with one accord in prayer and supplication." That is all. They are not yet the community of Pentecost. But they are this community *in spe*, the little flock to whom, according to Lk. 12[32], there will be given the kingdom, i.e., the presence and grace and power of their Lord, i.e., the Spirit. The two angels have not given them the Spirit. No angels will give them the Spirit. As the angels only marked the conclusion of the Easter account and the whole Gospel record, so their appearance and message only marks that which now begins, the history of the apostles, i.e., Church history in the presence and under the guidance of the Holy Ghost. God Himself has accomplished and revealed what is now accomplished and revealed behind them. And God Himself will establish the results and control the ensuing events. But this new thing from God has not yet commenced. What we are told concerning the disciples and the women, that they continued in prayer, corresponds exactly to the strait in which they found themselves between what God has already done and what He will do but has not yet done. But what we are told concerning the disciples and the women takes place under the sign of, and in correspondence with, that which is said to them by the angels. The saying is retrospective, but also prospective. It refers to the past, but also to the future. It is a saying between the times, reminding us of the sayings to Zacharias and Mary. It is a plain deduction from the actual wording, as well as from the consequent action of the disciples, that it claims those who are addressed for waiting upon God and for willingness and readiness for His future. But the waiting and the willingness and readiness are different from those of Lk. 1. Between them there lies the history of the fulfilment of the Christmas message right up to its revelation in the story of Easter. This history of fulfilment and revelation is now concluded and therefore present in all its fulness to those who are now claimed for waiting upon God and willingness and readiness for His future. " This same Jesus . . . is taken up from you into heaven." They know for whom they must wait, for whose future they must be willing and ready. They know in whom they are at one. They know to whom they pray, and for whose sake they continue in prayer. It is a matter of the Lord of this history. He has now concluded it. He has brought them (the disciples and the women) into the strait between yesterday and to-morrow. But is it really a strait ? Do they not exist already in illimitable freedom ? For the concluded yesterday was this Jesus, the Lord of this history. What cannot take place in the history which is just commencing when that which has concluded is this history ? What will not be its end and goal when its beginning is the conclusion of this history ? Where will it not lead when it begins with the fact that this Jesus is taken up into heaven ? Who and what is not to be expected from heaven ? The saying of the angels under the sign of which the disciples and the women continue with one accord in prayer must obviously run as it does : " This same Jesus . . . shall so come in like manner as ye have seen him go into heaven." It would not be this Jesus, nor would the concluded history be this history, nor would the beginning made with this conclusion, the beginning of the history of the apostles or Church history, be this beginning, if the end and goal to which it moves did not correspond, and the One who had come and gone were not to come again. Who else should come but the One who had come already ? He *was*, and therefore who else can be the One who is to be ? He was the Alpha, and therefore who else can be the Omega ? Where else can those who come from Him go except to Him ? How can this One who has come fail to come again ? For He did not come in vain. By His coming the doing of the will of God on earth was begun. Indeed, it was achieved once and for all, and perfectly revealed in His person. He Himself became man, and united humanity in Himself. How can He be untrue to Himself ? How can He fail to confess His work, His people, the earth on which He has so greatly magnified the mercy of God and therefore the glory of God ? But again, how can He come again otherwise than He has gone ? How else can all earthly occurrence terminate but in the glory with which the events of the forty days and therefore of His whole epiphany and *parousia* conclude ? He is the One who has appeared to His own as the Victor over death and therefore as the Lord. As this Victor and Lord He has gone up into heaven. But as the Victor and Lord He will also come again in the fulness whose ἀπαρχή or ἀρραβών is His resurrection, the conclusion of His history and the beginning of that of His community.

This, then, is the purport of the saying of the angels in Ac. 1¹¹. With its indication that the frontier of the Gospel story forms the announcement of the final horizon of all earthly occurrence it is perhaps the most powerful and comprehensive of all the sayings attributed to angels in the Bible. For what other saying embraces so fully the mystery of the incarnate Word and therefore the mystery of God ? At any rate, it is the most important in practice. Indicating that the frontier of this particular history is the horizon of all history, it is an authoritative direction to the Christian community in every age. It tells it that it belongs to the place where this One who has come is expected as the One who comes. More than angelic appearances and sayings are needed, of course, to awaken and gather the community, to rule it by judgment and grace, continually to conduct it to knowledge and service, continually to quicken and sustain it—the community which will occupy this place, existing in the world in retrospect of this frontier and in prospect of this horizon. Men will also be needed for this purpose, apostles, prophets, evangelists, the bearers of the manifold gifts of the Spirit, all proclaiming with their many voices that it belongs to this place, warning it against any aberration, and calling it back when it is guilty of aberration. But angels are needed to say this first, to tell it that the frontier may and must also be its horizon. Angels are needed to set up the sign under which we may live patiently, cheerfully and confidently *post Christum*. And therefore we can say that Luke has introduced these angels at the right place, at the end of the incomparable history of Jesus which is the beginning of that of the apostles and therefore of the Church.

So much, then, for the ministry and therefore the being of angels in relationship to Jesus Christ. We have not exhausted the theme. For instance, it would be significant and instructive to consider why it is that in so many passages (e.g., Mt. 13[41], 24[31], 25[31] and par. ; 1 Thess. 4[16] ; 2 Thess. 1[7]) we are told that at His second coming, unlike His first, Jesus Christ will manifest Himself with His angels and obviously to some extent with their active participation, after which, if our interpretation of 1 Cor. 15[24] is correct, there will be that complete suspension of their function. This clearly means that the ministry of angels, the whole participation of heaven in earthly occurrence, although it is necessarily concealed here and now in its distinctive invisibility, will finally be revealed and declared with the lordship of Jesus Christ which is also hidden here and now.

Again, beyond the christological field in the narrower sense we might consider much that is said about the ministry of angels away from the centre but within its radius in the history of Israel and that of the New Testament community. There are many interesting and pregnant passages upon which we have only touched in passing if at all. But I know of none which would really lead us any further in the subject. Our present purpose is not a complete biblical angelology. We have simply taken the most important examples to illustrate the decisive matters which claim our attention in dogmatics.

And now we have reached a point where we can answer the question of the right name or term for the distinctive reality with which we are concerned. Does it best correspond to the matter itself if we continue to use the word which is current in all modern languages, i.e., " angels," and, if we are to content with the term, how are we to understand it ? We must begin by stating that it is not only legitimate but advisable to accept the common title.

From the essay of W. Baumgartner already quoted, I take the following conclusions. The Hebrew has no specific word for the concept. *Maleak* simply means a messenger. In Hebrew, therefore, the general term is used in a particular sense to denote an angel. And in these cases it is usually distinguished either by a genitival connexion with the name of God or by the use of the possessive pronoun. Thus according to Baumgartner the *maleak Yahweh* is not a particular angel in distinction from others, but the messenger of Yahweh in distinction from ordinary messengers, i.e., an angel. The facts concerning the introduction of the latter term are as follows. In itself the Greek ἄγγελος is not a particular designation. But in the New Testament the secular usage of the word is so strongly pushed into the background that the distinction of the word becomes a *fait accompli*. On this basis, perhaps, the Vulgate is fairly consistent in using *nuntius* for an ordinary messenger and *angelus* for a heavenly, and in this it has been followed not only by English but also by German, Dutch, Swedish, French, Italian, Spanish etc.

There are good material reasons for this procedure. The distinctive matter requires a distinctive term. We evade the problem, or deny the intended reality, if we refuse to accept a distinctive word. And the term " angel " commends itself on three counts.

First, it describes the reality which calls for description, irrespective of the question of its being, in the light of its function and activity.

Second, it describes this activity as the conveyance of a message, the making of an announcement, the giving of a witness.

Third, it explains this activity (according to the sense which it has acquired in its history) as one which in an emphatic way, unique of its kind, and distinguished by its immediacy from the corresponding activities of other beings, is exercised in the service of God.

According to our previous deliberations this is an outline of the reality which it is our task to describe and name. No other word corresponds so exactly to this outline as the word " angel." If we decide for this word, we do so (in the sense of the statements which we have just made) with the following more precise definitions of our understanding of the term.

What angels are is to be understood wholly and exclusively from their function and activity. They are wholly and utterly angels, messengers. They are beings which are as they are engaged in the action thereby denoted. We grope in the void if we speak of a being of angels presupposed in this action and distinguishable from it. They are heavenly beings. But heaven is the upper cosmos inconceivable to us. We know of it only that it is the intracosmic Whence of the divine speech and action in the conceivable cosmos, and that to this extent it is the upper cosmos in relation to the latter. But we know nothing of its being as such, nor therefore of that of heavenly creatures. We know them only in their action and service as God's messengers. There is thus no place for any questions concerning their person or form or qualities or nature in abstraction from their action as God's messengers. There is no place, as we have seen, for any question of their numbers. We say exactly the same when we speak of one angel as when we speak of an infinite host. For one angel acts and speaks as all and for all, and all can and do only confirm what is spoken and done by one. ˉ There is also no place, as we have seen, for any question of the mutual relationship, of an internal order and hierarchy of heaven. Naturally, we cannot deny or suppress the fact that angels exist. But we deny that they exist otherwise than in the execution of their office. Thus the use of the term " angel " excludes the error of so much angelology both ancient and modern, both positive and negative. The basic meaning of the term must be taken in all seriousness when we use it.

Again, the description in the term " angel " of their action as messengers, as bringers of news, as heralds and witnesses, must not be taken in any weak sense, but with all strictness. When as heavenly beings, coming with God Himself from above, they act and speak in the service of God, their speech and action is that of very special messengers, supremely competent, authorised and powerful, and quite incomparable. In the title I have called them " The Ambassadors of God," and in so doing I have had in mind the implications of the word as it is used in diplomacy.

An ambassador does not belong to the government which he represents. He merely represents it. He does not pursue any policy of his own, but only that of his government. He has no independent ideas or initiative. His activity consists wholly in representing as exactly and fully as possible the intentions of the government, with which he has always to identify his own. But while this is the sum of his activity, he represents his government with full authority. He is no mere emissary or official or commissar. Within the limits of his appointment as an ambassador he may and must speak and act in the place and name of his government. Its honour and dignity are his. In his person we have to do with it, and his government will unhesitatingly acknowledge the decisions and steps which he takes. We respect his government by respecting him, and an insult to him is an insult to his government. It is in this way, but in a supreme sense, that the angels are the ambassadors of God.

They have specific messages to give and tasks to perform. They are not God or secondary gods. They are creatures, and as such they are wholly under God. As heavenly creatures they are this in an even stricter sense than is true of earthly, for unlike the latter, as we have seen, they have no autonomy (just as a private citizen pursuings his private concerns enjoys a very different independence of speech and action from the accredited ambassador of his country, although naturally without the privileges of the latter). But while angels as heavenly beings are only under God, and are what they are only in His service, they have behind them and for them the whole authority and glory and power of God in the performance of this service and the execution of this office. Where the angel is, there God Himself is present. Thus an angel never speaks half-truths or does things by halves. We can rely on what an angel says. There can be no contesting what he says, or appeal against his decisions, or opposition to his actions. This is not because he himself is high and infallible and powerful. It is because he represents God in His speech and actions. He is the divine plenipotentiary whom God Himself acknowledges and in whose words and decisions we are dealing directly with the intentions of God Himself. In this way then, in this strong sense of the term, he is the messenger of God. The same cannot be said of any prophet or apostle. If in certain situations a man is the messenger of God with this supreme authority, we can only say that it is an angel who speaks and acts through this man.

There are passages in the Bible which seem to take account of this possibility. For example, we are told in Ac. 6[15] that when the council looked on Stephen " they saw his face as it had been the face of an angel." Again, in Gal. 4[14] Paul reminds his readers that they had received him " as an angel of God, even as Jesus Christ." Again, in Heb. 13[2] we read of some who, exercising Christian hospitality, entertained angels unawares. In the Old Testament we are told in 2 Sam. 14[17] that the wise woman of Tekoah said to David : " For as an angel of God, so is my lord the king to discern good and bad." Again, we read in Zech. 12[8] that in that day the house of David shall be as heavenly beings, " as the angel of the Lord before them." Again, in Hag. 1[13] the prophet is explicitly called " the Lord's messenger." The same is said of the priest in Mal. 2[7], where we read that " his lips keep knowledge, and they seek the law at his mouth." And in Mt. 11[10] John the Baptist is expressly equated with the messenger of Ex. 23[20] who goes before the face of the Lord and prepares the way for His people. Along the same lines we are probably to seek the solution to the riddle of Rev. 2–3, where the human leaders of the communities of Asia Minor are openly called ἄγγελοι.

But this only brings out the more clearly the distinction of angelic speech and action. The fact that it has this distinction is the further point which we have to keep in mind and to maintain in our use of the word " angel " in the sense of " messenger."

But a third point is that, if we use the word " angel," we must keep clearly in view the specific meaning of the term " God " with which it stands in such close relationship. The decisive thing about their activity, and therefore about their being as extraordinary ambassadors, is that they are the messengers of God. They are not the manifestations of an idea, or the expressions of a power, or the bearers of any news or announcement or witness. They are not a mere postal service for their message. In the sense stated, they are the messengers of the God attested in Holy Scripture, who in Jesus Christ has made Himself the Lord and Ally and Deliverer of man. Apart from this they are nothing. They either exist in connexion with the history which this involves, or they do not exist at all. They act only according to that which God wills and accomplishes in this history. As heaven is determined by this, so are heavenly beings. As God Himself is not an imaginary or supposedly or genuinely experienced being of supreme perfection, power or dignity, but the One who has acted and revealed Himself in Jesus Christ, so the angels are not hypostases and mediators subordinated to and co-ordinated with this supreme being, and superior to man, but in the sense described messengers of the one true God living, active and revealed as Father, Son and Holy Ghost. If we keep to this fact, it is easy and self-evident to avoid the basic error concerning their being, as though it were to be sought somewhere behind their activity. It is easy and self-evident to cling to the root-meaning of the word " angel " (i.e., messenger). And it is natural to see and maintain the extraordinary force which the word carries in their case. But whatever lies to the right hand or to the left of this concept of a messenger of God—and of this one God—cannot possibly be described by the term " angel," no matter what it may be or however real it may be in itself.

Our reference is, of course, to the Christian use of the term " angel." What has been meant and thought and written and maintained and taught in both ancient and more modern times concerning the being and existence and activity of the possible hypostases and mediators of others gods, we commit into the hands of the inventors and adherents of the relevant systems and messages and writings in which these figures occur. We are obviously unable to prevent them using the term " angel " for what they think they may know and accept and believe in this respect. We insist, however, that whatever lies to the right hand or to the left of the reality whose concept is decisively given by its relationship to the living, active and revealed God of Holy Scripture, does not correspond to the Christian idea of an angel and does not deserve to be called an angel according to the Christian use. In the nature and significance decisively ascribed to them, the angels of Thomas Aquinas are not angels in the Christian sense. Nor are the angels of R. M. Rilke in the various stages of his poetry, including the last.

Nor are the angels of so many mythical, spiritualistic, occult, theosophical and anthroposophical systems, nor those of the popularly phantastic imagination of so many individual dreamers or whole circles of such. Nor are the beings which under this name have met with so much ridicule and scepticism and denial. Whether or not these beings exist is a matter which need not be decided in the present context. The decision which has to be made here is that, whether they are real or unreal, maintained or denied, feared, loved or even scorned, they belong to a different sphere from that in respect of which Holy Scripture speaks of angels. The decision which has to be made is that as Christians and theologians we must refrain from speaking of such beings as angels, and that we must certainly not be so foolish as to try to learn from an acquaintance with such beings what is to be understood by angels in the Christian sense of the term.

By way of appendix to this final explanation of the name and concept of angels a last question may be explicitly raised and answered which has probably been quietly present in all our previous discussions. I formulate it intentionally in the false form in which it is usually put. Do the reality and ministry of angels belong only to the history which took place then and there according to the witness of Holy Scripture, to the history of the establishment of the divine covenant with the fathers of the Israel, the appearance of Jesus Christ and the institution of His community ? Or do angels belong to cosmic occurrence generally, and therefore to the history of all ages, and therefore to our own history too, including the life-history of each individual ?

The question is wrongly put because there is no such alternative. The history which begins with the patriarchs, has its centre in Jesus Christ and concludes with the apostles, is not enclosed as the history of the covenant of grace—we must remember what took place at its centre—in a " then and there " in which it is alien and remote in relation to what did and does and will take place before and afterwards in other places and on other occasions. If angels belong to the history of the covenant, they cannot be remote and alien in relation to other events before and after. Again, world occurrence generally, including that in which we ourselves participate or will participate, is not autonomous in relation to the history of the covenant, to the divine speech and action in Jesus Christ. In this history all history, and therefore our own, has its meaning and centre. By it the existence of all earthly creatures, of all humanity and of each individual man past, present and future, is illuminated, determined and controlled. All existence has its root there, hastening towards and proceeding from it. The history of the Christian community especially, as the movement of the inner circle around this centre, proceeds from and hastens towards it to the extent that it recognises the goal of all occurrence in the revelation of the validity of what took place then and there. Because it lives in this hope and expectation, it lives— in virtue of the Holy Spirit poured out thence—in and with what took place there. But all creation unwittingly does the same in a wider circle around the Christian community. Hence if what took place there did not take place without the angels, the same is necessarily true of the life of the community in every age, of world occurrence generally, and of all individual and personal occurrence. Where, known or unknown, Jesus Christ is present, living and powerful by His Spirit, there, known or unknown, the ministry of angels is also executed.

It is clear that this cannot be grasped and expressed as a generally known or recognisable truth. But the same is true of the existence and kingdom of God and His presence, life and power in Jesus Christ. This, too, is a particular truth—*kerygma*, confession, Spirit, revelation—where it is really grasped and expressed. Similarly the ministry of angels in the narrower and wider circle of occurrence distinct from that of the history of the covenant is *kerygma*, confession, Spirit and revelation, and therefore not an element in a general outlook or philosophy of life or history. But the Christian message and therefore Church dogmatics has to do with this particular truth and its universal significance. It is self-evident that the reality of the ministry of angels cannot be restricted to the history attested in the Bible, but that by reason of the central and universal significance of this particular occurrence we must (or may) count on it that this ministry is also rendered, and is genuine and effective, in the narrower and wider circle as well.

Where and when is the problem not raised which we have now seen to be the problem of angelology, i.e., the problem of the mystery of the presence and speech and action of God in our sphere and therefore in the lower cosmos, the problem of heaven on earth, and therefore the problem of the purposeful proximity and distance, distance and proximity, without which God would not encounter earthly creation either in majesty or intimacy, in holiness or grace, and therefore genuinely as God ? Where He does this, He always does it through the ministry of angels. For He does it through His Holy Spirit. And the work of His Holy Spirit is to make us participants in the history of the covenant of grace, as fellow-citizens, house-fellows and contemporaries with the patriarchs and prophets, the apostles and evangelists. Life in the Spirit, and under His guidance, consists quite simply in participation in this history. But to have a part in this history is to have a part in the ministry of angels which took place within it. Where the kingdom of God is, there the strict and saving mystery of God is at work, and therefore the kingdom of heaven, and therefore, in all their imperceptibility and humility, in the unreserved selflessness and objectivity which distinguishes them from all earthly creatures, the angels.

In conclusion we must insist with some stringency that where this is the case the real angels attested in the Bible are at their own work in their own way. There is thus no place for speculation. If it were a matter of something else, angelic beings might well be occupied with marvellous works either proper or ascribed to them. On the other hand, they might not. But either way, our own concern is with what is. For real angels the only thing which matters is the glory of God on earth. They serve earthly creatures by showing them the proximity and distance, the distance and proximity, in short the mystery of God, and therefore God Himself. They attest Him to earthly creatures as these require according to the wisdom of God, and it is therefore most unlikely that they should do so as they themselves think desirable, interesting or remarkable according to their own wisdom. In doing this, they do, of course, enlighten and guide, help and keep, protect and save. But this simply means that God does all these things, and they are His witnesses proclaiming His praise and summoning to His praise in great events and small, cosmic and personal, thus ministering not only to Him but to earthly creatures as well. That they are present as His servants in what God does means that they show earthly creatures that it is He who does it, that He is so faithful and gracious and patient. And in so doing they render to earthly creatures, to us, their proper service, the only benefit that we can expect at their hands.

Regard should be had to the context in which Ps. 34[6f.] speaks of this ministry of angels. First we read : " This poor man cried, and the Lord heard him, and saved him out of all his troubles " ; then : " The angel of the Lord encampeth round about them that fear him, and delivereth them " ; and finally : " O taste and see that the Lord is good : blessed is the man that trusteth in him." The same is true of Ps. 91[9f.] : " Thou hast made the Lord, which is my refuge, even the most High, thy habitation." It is to the man who does this, to his confirmation in this action, that the continuation applies : " There shall no evil befall thee, neither shall any plague come nigh thy dwelling. For he shall give his angels charge over thee, to keep thee in all thy ways. They shall bear thee up in their hands, lest thou dash thy foot against a stone." In this connexion we recall the misuse which the devil made of this passage in Mt. 4[6]. The passage is misused when it is thought that the angels are present to give man sensational help in his own plans by sending things which are pleasant and warding off those which are not. They are indeed present, but in such a way as to make known to him the help of God. They serve him, but in such a way that they set his history in relationship to the history of the covenant of grace as this applies to him and embraces him. They are there for him personally and directly, but in such a way that in the very greatest and the very smallest things they place him before the mystery of God. *In hoc sunt constituti, ut praesentiorem eius opem nobis testentur . . ., mediatore Christo nos retinent, ut ab eo prorsus pendeamus, in eo recumbamus, ad eum feramur et ipso acquiescamus* (Calvin, *Instit.* I, 14, 12). If we do not see or try to evade the high objectivity of this service, we do better to confess that we know nothing about angels, and therefore not to call upon them or to think that we can expect anything from or have anything to do with them.

At this point we may say a few words about the so-called national angels. In the days of the Third Reich they figured prominently in the philosophy of history of certain German theologians. But the idea cannot really be proved from Dan. 10[13], for in this passage the prince of Persia who opposes Michael and the other angels is clearly depicted as a demonic figure and not as an angel of God. Yet within the divine overruling of the world why should there not be particular angelic relationships to the existence and way and role of historical collectives ? In this connexion, however, we are not really to think of nations but of states as the forces of order established by man. The concepts of order and power so often applied to angels in the New Testament Epistles seem to point in this direction. The only thing is that if we look in this direction we should not forget the high objectivity of the angels or plunge into the theology of the Iliad, ascribing to angels the character of protective deities for the representation in heaven of national and political interests. If the angels represent any interests of order and power in history, they are those of God. We have thus to understand the service which they render to the different historical groupings and their development in the following sense—that, always in the context of the history of the covenant as the guiding thread of the whole, they are witnesses to His mystery in the course of political history and its various combinations. There can be no doubt that we do have to reckon with their ministry in this respect.

And finally we may again refer to the question of what are called guardian angels in relation to individuals. There are passages in the Bible which seem to support this view. The strongest is Job 33²⁸ᶠ·, which unmistakeably refers to the effective advocacy of an angel on behalf of a man before the throne of God. Yet even there we are not told that this one in a thousand is specifically or permanently the angel of this particular man. Again, in Ac. 12¹⁵ we are told that when the Christians assembled in the house of Mary heard the imprisoned Peter knocking at the door, but did not realise that it was he in person, they expressed the view : ὁ ἄγγελός ἐστιν αὐτοῦ. But in this case it is an open question, as Calvin rightly observed (*Instit.* I, 14, 7), whether they are not merely toying with a popular notion. At all events the expression does not force us to conclude that " his " angel is his guardian angel. On the other hand, the angel who in this passage actually frees Peter and might therefore be described as his guardian angel is not described as " his angel " but simply as " the angel of the Lord." The saying in Mt. 18¹⁰, however, is the one which is most commonly adduced in favour of this view : " Take heed that ye despise not one of these little ones ; for I say unto you ὅτι οἱ ἄγγελοι αὐτῶν (ἐν οὐρανοῖς is missing in some manuscripts) διὰ παντὸς βλέπουσι τὸ πρόσωπον τοῦ πατρός μου ἐν οὐρανοῖς." It is certainly stated here that the heavenly Father of Jesus stands in a particular relationship to these little ones which is mediated by angels. But it does not say, as even Calvin maintained, that each of them has his own angel charged to be a guardian angel. The popularity of this concept in the Early Church and ever since is suspicious. Does it not owe more to the heathen notion of the " genius," usually accompanied even more capriciously by the " daemon," than to the biblical passages quoted in its favour ? Most of the older Reformed dogmaticians, in contrast to the more easy-going Lutherans, refused to take up the matter. Quite apart from any questions of disposition, it might be asked why there should not be a particular relationship between angelic reality and each individual. Is not this necessarily the case ? Does not the relationship between God and man (by the Word and Spirit of God) always have an individual character ? But does this necessarily imply a permanent private angel for each private person ? The most forceful, because positive, objection to this view was again brought by Calvin, who maintained that the divine care for an individual is not committed only to one angel, *sed omnes uno consensu vigilantur pro salute nostra.* If we do not think it sufficient that all the hosts of heaven keep watch over us, what will be the value of thinking that one angel in particular is our guardian ? This is sound angelology. In Ps. 91¹¹ᶠ·, which emphasises most plainly the protective function of angels, the reference is not to one angel but to many. And here, too, we must remember that the protection of angels consists in the fact that by their witness to God they keep those committed to them in fellowship with God, and therefore genuinely keep and secure them. In the life of each man they prosecute the cause of the kingdom of God, and therefore they are the best possible representatives of the cause of this man himself.

And now to conclude our consideration of the kingdom of heaven and the ambassadors of God we must take a brief look at a very different sphere.

We are forced to do this because a primitive and fatal association has always brought together these two spheres of angels and demons from the days of the Fathers to those of Neo-Protestantism. We shall not bring them into the same close relationship as formerly. But there is good reason to cast a momentary glance at demons immediately after our discussion of the angels, for demons are best considered in contrast to the theme of this discussion.

Why must our glance be brief ? Because we have to do at this point with a sinister matter about which the Christian and the theologian must know but in which he must not linger or become too deeply engrossed, devoting too much attention to it in an exposition like our own. In its own way it is very real. " The prospect was neither instructive nor pleasing," was the experience and judgment of Goethe when he stood on the top of Vesuvius and looked for a while into its open crater. And if we do not share this experience and judgment on the edge of the crater where we now find ourselves, we surely cannot see what is to be seen there. Sinister matters may be very real, but they must not be contemplated too long or studied too precisely or adopted too intensively. It has never been good for anyone—including (and particularly) Martin Luther— to look too frequently or lengthily or seriously or systematically at demons (who for Luther were usually compressed into the single figure of the devil). It does not make the slightest impression on the demons if we do so, and there is the imminent danger that in so doing we ourselves might become just a little or more than a little demonic. The very thing which the demons are waiting for, especially in theology, is that we should find them dreadfully interesting and give them our serious and perhaps systematic attention. In this way they can finally catch out, not bad theologians, but good. For this reason, having consciously and intentionally devoted a full discussion to the angels, we shall take only a brief look at this matter. It is not a question of treating them lightly, but of handling them as best befits their nature. A quick, sharp glance is not only all that is necessary but all that is legitimate in their case.

I have called this sphere a very different one from that of angels. This brings us right up against a materially decisive point. Indeed, it brings us right up against *the* decisive point, against the whole problem and its legitimate solution. The two spheres do not belong together either by origin or nature. The demons are not as it were the poor relations, or the vicious, disreputable and troublesome relations of angels. Between heaven and hell, between that which comes from above and its opposite which meets and resists it from below and would like to be above, there is nothing in common. It is thus quite inappropriate to speak of God and the devil or angels and demons in the same breath. They have no common denominator. They do not grow from a common root. If we maintain that they do, or portray them as if this were the case, we obviously do not know what we are talking about when we speak either about angels or demons.

The older theology was responsible for very serious confusion when it spoke about angels and demons under the title *De bonis et malis angelis*, or simply *De angelis*, as though they could both be brought under the one concept " angels," like the white and black pieces at chess which are both brought out of the same box and can both be put back in it at the end of the game. To be sure, Mt. 25⁴¹ speaks of the devil and his angels, Rev. 12⁷ of the dragon and his angels, and 2 Cor. 12⁷ of the angel of Satan. Again ἄγγελοι are obviously to be regarded as hostile powers in the list in Rom. 8³⁸. But when these beings are brought into the same connexion with the διάβολος or δράκων or σατανάς, as elsewhere ἄγγελος is with κύριος or θεός, it is obvious that this is simply a manner of speech from which we cannot legitimately conclude that there is a genus " angel " and that within this genus there are the two species, the angels of God and the angels of the devil. The genitive of origin and nature obviously divides the two classes of ἄγγελος in such a way that there can be no question of any correlation between them but only that of absolute and exclusive antithesis. Just as the word " nonsense " does not denote a particular species of sense, but that which is negated and excluded by sense, so *angeli mali* are not a particular species of angels, but the reality which is condemned, negated and excluded by the opposing angels which as such are *angeli boni*. In the few biblical passages in which angels and demons are seen together at all (as in the " war in heaven " of Rev. 12⁷ᶠ· or the brief encounter at the temptation in Mk. 1¹²), they are always understood to be in radical conflict. This radical conflict ought to have been regarded as a radical and essential determination on both sides. The devil and demons ought never to have been seen or understood otherwise than in this essential conflict.

The demons are the opponents of the heavenly ambassadors of God, as the latter are the champions of the kingdom of heaven and therefore of the kingdom of God on earth. Angels and demons are related as creation and chaos, as the free grace of God and nothingness, as good and evil, as life and death, as the light of revelation and the darkness which will not receive it, as redemption and perdition, as *kerygma* and myth. Perhaps the last analysis is best adapted to bring out the matter most sharply. At any rate, we cannot exaggerate the sharpness of the antithesis. No concern lest we fall into dualism and the consequent intolerance, no need for synthesis, must prevent us from insisting on the unconditional antithesis of the two spheres. God is the Lord of the demonic sphere, and it derives from Him, just as in a wholly different way He is the Lord of the angelic sphere and it too derives from Him. But we cannot see or say too clearly that it is in a wholly different way. There can be no question of God Himself and therefore the angelic sphere ceasing to oppose the demonic. There can be no question of the sovereignty of God and therefore the superiority of the angelic sphere over the demonic coming to a kind of agreement with the latter or concluding a kind of armistice, which entails a certain measure of recognition. To be sure, the latter is brought into subjection and service. But it is not recognised. Its overthrow is a genuine overthrow. In its final manifestation it will even mean its destruction. According to Matthew 25[41] there is an eternal fire which the Father of Jesus has prepared for the devil and his angels. And the demonic sphere for its part, even though it stands under the sovereignty of God, and in its own way derives from Him, and is subjected to Him and brought into His service, does not cease to be the demonic sphere and therefore a sphere of contradiction and opposition which as such can only be overthrown and hasten to destruction. Thus the glance which we have to cast at this sphere can only be a sharp glance, a glance of aversion and not in any sense of secret respect or reverence or admiration. We cannot believe in the devil and demons as we may believe in angels when we believe in God. We have a positive relationship to that in which we believe. But there is no positive relationship to the devil and demons. We cannot ignore them. We must know about them, but only as the limit of that to which a positive relationship is possible and legitimate and obligatory. We can know about them only in such a way that—as and because we believe in God and His angels—we oppose to them the most radical unbelief. They are *the* myth, the myth of all mythologies. Faith in God and His angels involves demythologisation in respect of the devil and demons ; but not in the superficial phenomenological sense current to-day, in which they are grouped with the angels and even with God's own Word and work as the figures of a world-outlook which has now been superseded. It would no doubt suit them very well to be grouped with the angels, with the wonders of the reconciling act and re-surrection of Jesus Christ, and finally with God Himself, and in this exalted company to be " demythologised," to have their reality denied, to be interpreted away. Demons are only the more magnified if they are placed in the framework of the conflict between a modern and an ancient system, and called in question in this exalted company. The demythologisation which will really hurt them as required cannot consist in questioning their existence. Theological exorcism must be an act of the unbelief which is grounded in faith. It must consist in a resolute denial that they belong to this exalted company. It must consist in the fact that in the light, not of a world-outlook but of Christian truth, they are seen to be a myth, the myth which lurks in all myths, the lie which is the basis all other lies, so that a positive relationship to them, an attitude of respect and reverence and obedience, is quite impossible.

There has always flourished in Christianity and its theology a supposedly very realistic demonology which has suffered from the lack of this safeguard. It begins with respect instead of aversion, with reverence instead of anger and scorn. It gazes at the poisonous serpent instead of striking it. It moves from the very outset in the secret respect and admiration, or at least in an atmosphere of curiosity, where distaste is the only possible attitude. It derives from a kind of awe that there should be anything of this kind. It attests and demands *a priori* a kind of faith, or seriously and explicitly real faith, in the matter, at the same time and in the same sense as it attests and demands faith in the angels and Christ and God. It proceeds from the fact that there can and must be a positive relationship to the matter. It had already misunderstood the biblical references to this whole sphere by overlooking their consistently critical and even negative character, not noticing that the Bible only touches on this sphere at all as it shows God and His angels to be in conflict with it, that it is concerned with the rejection and ultimate destruction of the devil and demons, that it does not in the least require us to consider or take this sphere seriously in and for itself, that the realism of the Bible in this respect consists exclusively in the clarity and vigour with which we are comforted and warned and set on our guard against this sphere, but called away from it rather than to it, being commanded merely to give it a passing glance and then to turn our backs upon it. The trouble is that this was not perceived when so strong and as it was supposed so scriptural a demonology was set alongside angelology, and then Christology, and then the doctrine of creation and reconciliation, and then eschatology. So great was the honour which it was thought must be paid to this sphere that the doctrine of the devil and demons became an integral part of the Christian message, and in many cases the part in which Christian preachers and theologians believed they should display their zeal and realism. The result was that all Christianity, even when there were no witch-hunts and the like, acquired a more or less pervasive odour of demonism, becoming something which from this dark chamber seemed to spread abroad, and did actually spread abroad, menace, anxiety, melancholy, oppression, or tragic excitement. And this had the consequence that when in the light of witch-hunts a protest was made against this chamber by the Jesuit Friedrich von Spee and the Dutch Reformed Balthasar Bekker (*Die bezauberte Welt*, 1680), it necessarily led to the Enlightenment and thus to a protest against the whole Christian message. And the further consequence has been that in all subsequent discussion the view has had to be taken into account that angelology, Christology and Christian theology generally form a whole with a particular demonology, and that this whole has either to be accepted, rejected, or, in the process of a general demythologisation in the name of the modern outlook, reduced to a definite anthropology. It was fatal that at the time of the Enlightenment the way was entered which led from a criticism of demonology to a contesting of theology generally. But it was even more fatal that orthodoxy gave good cause for following this path. And it is even more fatal still that to this very day attempts are made to champion a demonology which will only give cause to take this path again and again. How remarkable it is that in what Scripture says and does not say about the demonic sphere it could be overlooked that the fear of God and fear of the devil do not belong together but are mutually exclusive, the sole task of theology in this matter being to show and say that it is the fear of God which overcomes and excludes fear of the devil ! How remarkable it is that even to-day this is not self-evident !

What is the origin and nature of the devil and demons ? The only possible answer is that their origin and nature lie in nothingness.

As we have seen in the preceding section, this is the element of contradiction and opposition which exists on the left hand of God and is thus subject to His world-dominion, but which constitutes a threat to His creation. In biblical terms we can also describe it as chaos, or darkness, or evil, or (to the extent that this signifies a power rather than a place) Hades. Or we might call it the being which exists only as it denies all true being, and is denied by it. Everything which had to be said about this element is also to be said of demons as the opponents of God's heavenly ambassadors. They are. As we cannot deny the peculiar existence of nothingness, we cannot deny their existence. They are null and void, but they are not nothing. They are, but only in their own way ; they are, but improperly. Their being is neither that of God nor that of the creature, neither that of heavenly creatures nor that of earthly, for they are neither the one nor the other. They are not divine but non-divine and anti-divine. On the other hand, God has not created them, and therefore they are not creaturely. They are only as God affirms Himself and the creature and thus pronounces a necessary No. They exist in virtue of the fact that His turning to involves a turning from, His election a rejection, His grace a judgment. They are as they are judged, repudiated and excluded by God, and as always and everywhere and in every way, with all the expressions of their being, they can only prove that they are not condemned accidentally or capriciously, but legitimately. They can only hate God and His creation. They can only exist in the attempt to rage against God and to spoil His creation. They can only be disruptive in relation to Himself and His creation, His history with it and His work upon it. For this very reason they are improperly. This disruptive being is what God never willed, and never does nor will. It is that which, because its being is improper being, can only stand to all eternity under His non-willing, on His left hand, condemned by Him and hastening to destruction.

This is all to be said of demons as of nothingness. They are not different from the latter. They do not stand apart. They derive from it. They themselves are always nothingness. They are nothingness in its dynamic, to the extent that it has form and power and movement and activity. This is how Holy Scripture understands this alien element. Hence it does not understand it as a being which is somewhere and somehow at repose in its improper nature, which in greater or lesser proximity can be considered and assessed with corresponding calm, which can be integrated into a total picture of God and the world, and which can be theoretically mastered and held at a distance. Holy Scripture regards nothingness as a kingdom, based upon a claim to power and a seizure of power, yet not consisting anywhere, but always on the march, always invading and attacking. Its decisive insight is that God Himself is the superior and victorious Opponent of nothingness, the One who has taken up this problem and made it His own, and whose kingdom confronts nothingness and contains it within its frontiers. Hence it does not render it innocuous by viewing it in the theoretical way in which man would like to see it, nor does it adopt the defeatist attitude of absolutising it as man feels impelled to do when for some reason or other he finds it impossible to rob it of its sting by treating it theoretically. It sees it as God Himself sees it, and especially as God Himself treats it, as He deals with it. It thus sees it as a kingdom. And because it starts from the view that God sees and therefore treats all things, including nothingness, with justice, i.e., according to their true being, it is for the Bible no mere figure of speech or poetic fancy or expression of human concern but the simple truth that nothingness has this dynamic, that it is a kingdom on the march and engaged in invasion and assault : not a kingdom which has to be feared ; a kingdom of that which is improper ; a kingdom which by the very fact that God confronts it is characterised from the very outset as weak and futile ; a kingdom which is usurped and not legitimate, transitory and not eternal ; yet a real kingdom, a nexus of form and power and movement and activity, of real menace and danger within its appointed limits. This is how Holy Scripture sees nothingness. And this is how it also sees demons. In this sense it reckons with their actuality.

We can see at once the similarity of this sphere with that of angels, with the kingdom of God, the kingdom of heaven. We can see the reason for the misunderstanding in which it could be thought necessary not merely to contrast but to co-ordinate the two kingdoms, regarding demons not merely as opponents but as relatives and colleagues of the angels. For do we not have to do here with accredited ambassadors, with principalities and powers ? Is not our earthly sphere visited in this case, too, by an alien and mysterious dominion ? Is not man placed in both cases under a real mystery ? Is there not, then, a final relationship of being, a final similarity ? Yet this is the very thing which we must never say, but resolutely oppose, in relation to these two kingdoms, the kingdom of heaven and that of demons. In relation to these two kingdoms means in relation to the attitude of God, and therefore of His creature, to these two kingdoms. Where God says Yes and No, where He is affirmed and denied, where He is praised and blasphemed, where He is served and hampered, where His will is done and sabotaged, for all the similarity there is no relationship or homogeneity. And the same is true with reference to the creature. Where its Creator and therefore its own being are proclaimed and where they are both denied and plunged in darkness, where it is a matter of its salvation and of its corruption, where it is affirmed and denied, where it is helped and hampered and even destroyed, for all the similarity there is no relationship or homogeneity. God Himself, and the creature bound to Him and blessed and enlightened by Him, comes between the two kingdoms, separating and distinguishing them, so that there can be no real question of any conspectus or confusion. This is possible only where God is forgotten (or where it is forgotten who and what God is) and it is thought necessary to see and compare an abstract kingdom of good and an equally abstract kingdom of evil, and angels and demons no less abstractly as the champions of these two spheres. This misfortune ought to be quite impossible in a Christian theology. The similarity of the two spheres ought not to prevent a radical prohibition of their co-ordination.

What is the basis of this similarity? It rests on the fact that *in se* nothingness is falsehood. As such it fashions and gives itself similarity with the kingdom of God. It ascribes and arrogates to itself a being which, because it is neither God nor an earthly nor heavenly creature, cannot belong to it. In so doing, it is falsehood in its very being. It lies against God by desiring to rule and reveal itself alongside Him, to be as great and important as He is. And it lies against the creature by desiring to play in relation to it the role of a fellow-ruler. It lies by pretending, in all its nothingness, that it is for God and the creature a relevant and serious factor which has to be taken into significant account. It lies by proclaiming that it can intervene between the grace of God and the salvation of the creature, rendering the grace of God weak and ineffective and hampering and retarding the salvation of the creature. It lies by attempting to ingratiate itself with God and to impose upon the creature. It lies by pretending to be glorious and attractive on the one side or terrifying on the other. It lies by assuming form and power for a particular purpose. It lies in its whole movement and activity, in its whole march, in its whole invasion and assault. It lies in its representation of itself as a kingdom with a leader and subjects, as a system of government with legislative, executive and judicial organs. It lies by opposing itself as such to the kingdom of God. And in so doing—and this is our present concern—it lies by opposing its own messengers, the demons, to the angels of God, attempting to give them the same names and appearance and activity. It lies when it does this, when it pretends that it, too, comes down from heaven to earth as a superior power or a whole host of superior powers, that it, too, has something to institute on earth, that its will is to be done on earth in opposition to the will of God.

We must not deceive ourselves and say that it does not really do all these things, or is not real in all these things. One form of the triumph which nothingness can achieve is to represent itself as a mere appearance with no genuine reality. Let us only be proud and enlightened and unafraid and unconcerned in face of it! Let us only persuade ourselves that there is nothing in it, that there is no devil and no kingdom of evil and demons as his plenipotentiaries, as effective powers and forces in the life of nations and societies, in the psychical and physical life of men and their relationships, that we can control our being without having to take into account this alien lordship or considering that where it is not broken all being and enterprise and achievement on earth is fundamentally corrupt and worthless ! Nothingness lies also and supremely by trivialising and concealing itself, spreading abroad a carefree optimism, being content simply to be present, to be in fact a powerful kingdom subtly controlled, and thus to declare, express and maintain its power. Nothingness rejoices when it notices that it is not noticed, that it is boldly de-mythologised, that humanity thinks it can tackle its lesser and greater problems with a little morality and medicine and psychology and aesthetics, with progressive politics or occasionally a philosophy of unprecedented novelty—if only its own reality as nothingness remains beautifully undisclosed and intact.

But there is another side to the matter. We must not dream and say that in all that it does and is nothingness can be anything but falsehood. The other form of its triumph is to present itself as though it were no lie, as though it really had something to proclaim, as though it could really found and organise a kingdom, as though it could really come down from heaven to earth, as though its powers and forces were really agents which could contradict and withstand the grace of God and the salvation of the creature, as though it had rights over against God and the creature which entitled it to fear and respect. Let us only admire it for its independent truth ! Let us only integrate the devil and the kingdom of demons and evil into the same system in which elsewhere and according to their different character we also treat of God and Christ and true man and the angels ! Let us only do this kingdom the honour of taking it seriously in this sense ! If nothingness can only succeed in making itself noticeable in this way as the truth, it is jubilant on the other side. Nothing could suit it better than to find a sure place in the philosophical outlook of man or the world of human thought, securing recognition as a serious co-worker and opponent of God and man. But it may be that as such it again falls under suspicion, that its truth becomes a matter of doubt, that man grows tired of treating it with too great trepidation and respect. In these circumstances, there is always scope for a new cycle of enlightenment and demy-thologisation, for morality, medicine, psychology, aesthetics, politics, philosophy or even piety and religion to take the stage as the true liberators, and for a reassertion of the undisclosed and intact dominion of negated nothingness. There is alternation in this matter. If we ignore demons, they deceive us by concealing their power until we are again constrained to respect and fear them as powers. If we absolutise them, respecting and fearing them as true powers, they have deceived us by concealing their character as falsehood, and it will be only a little while before we try to ignore and are thus deceived by them again. Nothingness is falsehood. It exists as such, having a kind of substance and person, vitality and spontaneity, form and power and movement. As such it founds and organises its kingdom. And demons are its exponents, the powers of falsehood in a thousand different forms. Its kingdom is indeed very similar to the kingdom of heaven with its angels. And this imitation of the kingdom of heaven and its angels, the uncanny resemblance to this very different sphere in which it dares to present itself, is the crown of its existence as falsehood. It, too, is an invisible and incomprehensible kingdom. It, too, is undoubtedly superior to man and the whole earthly creation. It, too, has in its midst a kind of throne and ruler. It, too, has an enterprise and movement aimed at earth and man. It, too, has powerful messengers who attest and proclaim a kind of mystery, who do this with a kind of humility and objectivity, and who obviously stand in its service. The word " too " is the real mark of this kingdom as the kingdom of falsehood. Nothingness wants to do everything *too*, and not only what creatures are and can do and accomplish, but also and supremely what God is and wills and does. Nor does it merely want to do, but it actually does, or tries to do, what God does. It plays at creation and redemption, providence and dominion. It plays at Law and Gospel, grace and judgment. All falsehood! It constructs a false heaven with a false God, a false throne from which false messengers are despatched, to proclaim a false mystery with all the humility and objectivity of falsehood. There is no other word for it—it is all a mimicry.

But we must not overlook or deny the fact that the performance is real and constantly successful. We cannot deny the power and powers of falsehood in a thousand different forms. We cannot deny that in their infamous way they are real and brisk and vital, often serious and solemn, but always sly and strong, and always present in different combinations of these qualities, forming a dreadful fifth or sixth dimension of existence. Where? But surely the real question is : Where not ? They are there in the depths of the soul which we regard as most properly our own. They are there in the relationships between man and man, and especially between man and woman. They are there in the developments of individuals and their mutal relationships. They are there in the concern and struggle for daily bread, and especially for that which each thinks is also necessary in his case. They are there in that in which man seeks his satisfaction or which he would rather avoid as undesirable, in his care and carelessness, in the flaming up and extinguishing of his passions, in his sloth and zeal, in his inexplicable stupidity and astonishing cleverness, in his systematisation and anarchism, in his progress, equilibrium and retrogression, in the great common ventures of what is called culture, science, art, technics and politics, in the conflict and concord of classes, peoples and nations, in the savage dissensions but also the beautiful agreements and tolerances in the life of the Church, and not least in the *rabies* and even more so the *inertia theologorum*. We cannot really deny but must see and recognise and know that in, with and under all these things there is constantly played out the mimicry of nothingness—the play of that which is absolutely useless and worthless, yet which is not prepared to allow that this is the case, but pretends to be vitally necessary and of supreme worth. We cannot deny but must soberly recognise that in all these things the demons are constantly present and active like the tentacles of an octopus. Fortunately the angels are also present and active. But there can be no doubt that the demons are there too, beings which betray their nature by this fatal " too."

Yet it is as well not to consider this without recognising that they are only the powers of falsehood. As falsehood they are really powerful. Indeed, because they are so thorough, because they imitate no less than God and His kingdom and angels, because nothingness always masquerades as the highest and deepest, the first and the last, they are always much more powerful than we expect or concede, and can always turn our defences or cut off our escape, seizing us at the very point from which we try to resist them or where we try to find refuge from them. They are powers indeed, and yet they are only the powers of falsehood. Hence we must not regard them as real powers, or the mimicry with which they make fools of us as reality. They work so long and extensively and deeply as they can work as lies, and are not shown to be such, or set over against the truth, and thus dispelled as lies. Anything other or less than the truth is no match for them, whether it takes the form of mental purification, zealous good will, knowledge or technics. Because they are the powers of falsehood, of the great and comprehensive falsehood which imitates even God and His angels, it is child's play for them to surround and imprison the man who encounters them armed only with these weapons. Only the truth is strong enough to meet them. This is so immediately, basically and conclusively. Yet it must be the whole truth, the real truth, the truth of God and His kingdom and angels, the truth which they have attempted to imitate and in the imitation of which they are so powerful. Other truths may be most profound and excellent, but they are of no value because they cannot touch, let alone destroy, their power, the power of imitation and falsehood which makes them so great and dangerous.

The truth of God dispels them as and because in confrontation with it they are disclosed, unmasked and stripped as the powers of falsehood. This is the insight which is even more important in relation to demons than the fact that they exist, and exist always and everywhere as forces. The fact is that they exist always and everywhere where the truth of God is not present and proclaimed and believed and grasped, and therefore does not speak and shine and rule. This is the limit and destruction of demons. This extinguishes them as lies and therefore as forces. This negates, condemns and rejects nothingness and all its representatives. This contradicts the contradiction and opposes the opposition ; and it does so radically and definitively. It does so simply by speaking for itself as the truth, and thus separating from itself the lie as such and showing it to be a lie. It reveals the devil and all devils for what they are. It shows that they are tempters falsely suggesting that there is something better than the obedience to which we are summoned and for which we are empowered by the Word and work of God. It shows that they are accusers who falsely charge us when, in spite of all that speaks against us, we see ourselves set with quiet consciences on the right way by the Word and work of God. It shows that they are tyrants who falsely pretend to have the right and power to make us their prisoners and slaves, puppets who must dance on their wires, when we are really placed in the freedom of the children of God by His Word and work. It shows that they are spirits of complaint which falsely depress us and rob us of our humour by persuading us that the natural limits of our physical and psychical existence are a constriction, curse and misfortune, when we are really borne, sustained and even uplifted by God within these limits. It shows that they are poltergeists which falsely alarm us when we may really have a total and radical peace on the basis of the Word and work of God. As the truth of God shows nothingness and its representatives the demons in their true nature, and thus shows the falsity of their claim and enterprise, it disarms them and makes them impotent. That the lie should be exposed is what is most appropriate to the lie itself and most helpful to those who are threatened, oppressed and tormented by its power. This is what is done by the truth of God. And as it is done the lie loses the vital breath which enables it to threaten, oppress and torment. It is vanquished and driven from the field.

This, then, is what Holy Scripture has to tell us concerning demons. It certainly does not say that they do not exist or have no power or do not constitute this threat. It is quite evident that their existence and nature are very definitely taken into account, and it is surprising that this is more expressly the case in the New Testament than the Old. But this is inevitable, for in the light of the fulfilled and completed covenant of grace, of the kingdom of God coming from heaven to earth, that which contradicts and resists it, as it is driven from the field, is seen much more clearly than where there is only a movement towards the fulfilment and the kingdom is only announced. But the contradiction and resistance are now seen to be nothingness, and its representatives the powers of falsehood, unreal beings unmasked as falsehood and thus robbed of their powers. What might be called biblical demonology is in fact only a negative reflection of biblical Christology and soteriology. What is revealed is the kingdom of Satan and his angels as this is already assaulted and mortally threatened, and indeed radically destroyed ; demonic being, not in its concealment and therefore powerful, but unmasked and therefore disarmed ; not its march and attack and even victory, but its defeat and withdrawal and flight ; not an earth and humanity controlled, visited and plagued by demons, but liberated from them ; not a world bewitched but exorcised ; not a community and Christendom believing in demons but opposing to them in faith that resolute disbelief ; in short, the triumph of truth over falsehood. But it is the truth of God which triumphs ; it is really His Word and work. It is Jesus Christ, God in His person, who as the Lord and Victor overthrows nothingness and its lying powers. It is in the history of His conflict, of the kingdom of God dawning in Him, and therefore in the history of His humiliation to the death of the cross and His resurrection and exaltation to the right hand of the Father, that it is not merely true, but at the cost of the sacrifice of the Son of God and therefore in glory it becomes true, that nothingness and the demons have nothing to declare. The reference is thus to faith in Him, to obedience to Him as Lord and Saviour, to life in His community, to the proclamation and hearing of the message of the salvation which has appeared in Him, when we are summoned in the New Testament to follow His triumph over demonic being. In Jesus Christ Himself this triumph is won only in the history of that conflict. And our celebration of it, our liberation from demons, can take place only as we participate in this history. And as the angels were witnesses of this history, encountering demons as witnesses of the victory, they are always present as described when it is a matter of summoning men, and making them able and willing, to participate in this history, in this conflict and triumph. They witness for the truth which has fought and conquered and will continually be revealed and known in the light of that conflict and victory. And in the genuine power of this truth they are for us continually the counter-witnesses to the lying messengers of the kingdom of falsehood.

We may conclude with a short observation on the doctrine of the Early Church concerning the relationship between angels and demons. We refer to the view constantly held in ancient and modern times that the demons are "fallen angels." At an earlier date this was linked with the saying in Is. 14[12] which describes the king of Babylon as the radiant star of the morning (*lucifer*) cast down from heaven. The remarkable passage in Gen. 6[1-14] was related to this verse. Most strongly of all Jude 6 seemed and seems to point in this direction, with its mention of angels which did not keep their ἀρχή and lost their ἴδιον οἰκητήριον. We might also refer to 2 Pet. 2[4] with its reference to angels who sinned. But these texts are so uncertain and obscure that it is inadvisable to allow them to push us in this direction. However they may have to be expounded, against their exposition along these lines there has to be set the intolerable artificiality with which attempts have been made to use them as a basis for the development of the doctrine of a fall of angels and therefore of an explanation of the existence of the devil and demons. And literally all the insights which we have gained concerning the being and ministry of angels, and developed at least concerning the character and activity of demons, are necessarily false if this doctrine is correct. It is, in fact, one of the bad dreams of the older dogmatics. It arises from the superfluous need to ground our knowledge of the fall of man upon the notion of a metaphysical prelude which it was quite inappropriately thought should be located in heaven. It derives from the definitely illegitimate attempt not to allow nothingness to be what it is but to bring it into systematic connexion with God and the creature, to understand, explain and deduce its possibility (the possibility of the impossible) and essence (the essence of non-essence). And it stems from a frightful misunderstanding of the kingdom of heaven and angels, as though the freedom of these creatures were not a real freedom if it were not for them too, or had not been once in some primal epoch, the so-called *liberum arbitrium*, i.e., the freedom to become fools. Along these lines we do not rightly understand the freedom of the earthly creature, of man, let alone of the heavenly. To bring angels and demons under the common denominator of this fatal concept of freedom is to confuse and obscure everything that is to be said of both. A true and orderly angel does not do what is ascribed to some angels in this doctrine (in obscure speculation concerning this derivation). And on the other hand it cannot be said that a real demon has ever been in heaven. The demons merely act as if they came from heaven. But the devil was never an angel. He was a murderer ἀπ' ἀρχῆς. He never stood in the truth. No truth was ever in him. He speaks falsehood, and he does so ἐκ τῶν ἰδίων, because he is a liar and the father of lies. This is how he is described in Jn. 8⁴⁴, and it agrees with everything else that we are told in the New Testament concerning him and demons. But of angels we must say with Jas. 1¹⁷ : " Every good gift and every perfect gift is from above, and cometh down from the Father of lights, with whom is no variableness, neither shadow of turning." And reference may also be made to the preceding verse (v. 16) : " Do not err, my beloved brethren."

INDEXES

I. SCRIPTURE REFERENCES

II. NAMES

III. SUBJECTS

God—
condescension, 357, 431.
faithfulness, 12, 41, 53, 56, 217, 356, 428.
Father, 28, 142, 172, 433, 440.
freedom, 10, 79 f., 93 f., 109.
glory, 431.
grace, *q.v.*
hiddenness, 198, 256.
holiness, 332, 353, 361.
honour, 517.
judgment, *q.v.*
lordship, 12, 16 f., 19, 26, 31 f., 59, 93, 130, 154 ff., 233, 245 f., 255 f., 285 f., 371, 447, 496, 520 f.
ordering, 165 ff.
love, 8, 89, 94, 116 f., 118, 138, 188.
mercy, 120, 186 f., 323 f., 452.
modes of being, 246, 440.
movement, 428 ff.
mystery, 144, 468.
  v. Angel/mystery of God.
name, 271, 277, 448.
omnipotence, 71, 120, 150, 187, 204.
rest, 7, 47, 70.
righteousness, 322 f., 325 f.
simplicity, 138.
throne, *v.* Heaven/throne.
triunity, 246, 430, 440.
uniqueness, 231 f.
will, 189, 237, 286, 308, 430, 444, 477.
work, 42 f., 119.
  opus ad extra, 42 f., 119.
  opus alienum—opus proprium, 353.
world-rule, *v.* lordship.
wrath, 77 f., 309.
God, Doctrine of, 3 f., 144, 178.
Good, The, 359.
Grace, 52, 67, 73, 80, 108, 118, 149, 181, 224, 255, 282, 285, 308, 353, 356.
Grace, Election of, 4 f., 8, 36, 45 f., 52, 67 ff., 78 f., 98 f., 218, 225, 351, 523.
eternal decree, 4, 10, 119, 497.
Gubernatio, 154 ff.
  v. Providence/rule.

Heathenism, 124.
Heaven, 236 ff., 389, 422 ff., 432, 443.
benefits, 434 f.
cosmos, upper, 236 f., 421, 432, 442, 512.
  v. Creation/hierarchy.
earth, 418 ff.
cf. Creation/hierarchy.
incomprehensibility, 424, 437.
invisibility, 424.
kingdom of, 237, 369 ff., 418 ff., 433 ff., 442 f.

knowledge, 442 f.
likeness, 427.
mystery, 442.
nature, 424 ff.
occurrence, 444 ff., 477.
place of God, 437 f., 442 f.
reality, 443, 459.
revelation, 426, 433, *q.v.*
Scripture, Holy, 426, *q.v.*
superiority, 426, 433, 480.
throne of God, 237, 438, 441, 464.
witness, 444.
Hell, 305, 521.
Hermeneutics, 374 f., 402 f.
History, *v.* Covenant History, World History.
historicism, 374 f.
legend, saga, 352, 374 ff.
Hymn, 291.

Islam, 28, 30, 98, 113.
Israel, 50, 59, 84, 177 ff., 190, 216, 491.
new, 181.

Jesus Christ, 25 ff., 35 ff., 58 f., 82, 84 f., 89, 105, 119, 130, 132, 141 f., 148, 157, 175 ff., 184, 196, 225, 236, 241, 247, 255 ff., 268, 271 f., 275, 287, 301, 311, 328, 355, 363 f., 419, 428, 435 ff., 473, 475, 487, 530.
cf. Grace, Word of God.
ascension, 439, 509.
birth, 504 f.
cross, 305, 312, 360, 471.
Head, 271.
humiliation, 501 f.
incarnation, 435.
resurrection, 440, 470, 507 f.
return, 366.
session, 438 f., 444.
Judaism, 28, 30, 210 ff., 219.
culture, 213 f.
enigma, 219.
existence, 213 ff.
history, 214.
people, 215.
race, 213.
religion, 214.
speech, 213.
state of Israel, 212 ff.
Synagogue, 214.
Judgment, 79, 89, 217, 355, 361, 523.

Kingdom of God, 41 ff., 155 ff., 367 f., 418 ff., 428 ff., 433, 450, 477, 516.
cf. Heaven.

Law, 309 f., 314.
Liberalism, 32 f., 66.
Life, Christian, 262 ff.